Visual Basic and Algorithmic Thinking for the Complete Beginner

Copyright © 2015 by Aristides S. Bouras and Loukia V. Ainarozidou

http://www.bouraspage.com

ISBN-13: 978-1511798969

ISBN-10: 1511798963

Printed in the U.S.A.

The following are either registered trademarks or trademarks of Microsoft Corporation in the United States and/or other countries: Microsoft, Windows, IntelliSense, SQL Server, .NET Framework, Visual Studio, and Visual Basic.

Oracle and Java are registered trademarks of Oracle and/or its affiliates.

Other names may be trademarks of their respective owners.

Warning and Disclaimer

This book is designed to provide information about learning "Algorithmic Thinking," mainly through the use of Visual Basic programming language. Every effort has been taken to make this book compatible with all previous releases of Visual Basic, and it is almost certain to be compatible with any future releases of Visual Basic.

The information is provided on an "as is" basis. The authors shall have neither liability nor responsibility to any person or entity with respect to any loss or damages arising from the information contained in this book or from the use of the files that may accompany it.

This book is dedicated to
to all our teachers,
especially the great ones.

Contents at a Glance

Table of Contents

Preface

About the Authors

Aristides S. Bouras

Aristides[1] S. Bouras was born in 1973. During his early childhood, he discovered a love of computer programming. He got his first computer at the age of 12, a Commodore 64, which incorporated a ROM-based version of the BASIC programming language and 64 kilobytes of RAM!!!

He holds a degree in Computer Engineering from the Technological Educational Institute of Piraeus, and a degree in Electrical and Computer Engineering from the Democritus Polytechnic University of Thrace.

He worked as a software developer at a company that specialized in industrial data flow and labelling of products. His main job was to develop software applications for data terminals (originally in TALL and later in VB.NET language), as well as PC software applications for collecting and storing data on a Microsoft SQL Server®.

He has developed many applications such as warehouse managing systems and websites for companies and other organizations. Nowadays, he works as a high school teacher. He mainly teaches courses in computer networks, programming tools for the Internet/intranets, and databases.

He is married to Loukia V. Ainarozidou and they have two children.

Loukia V. Ainarozidou

Loukia V. Ainarozidou was born in 1975. She got her first computer at the age of 13, an Amstrad CPC6128 with 128 kilobytes of RAM and an internal 3-inch floppy disk drive!!!

She holds a degree in Computer Engineering from the Technological Educational Institute of Piraeus, and a degree in Electrical and Computer Engineering from the Democritus Polytechnic University of Thrace.

She worked as a supervisor in the data logistics department of a company involved in the packaging of fruit and vegetables. Nowadays, she works as a high school teacher. She mainly teaches courses in computer networks, computer programming, and digital design.

She is married to Aristides S. Bouras and they have two children.

---

[1] Aristides (530 BC–468 BC) was an ancient Athenian statesman and general. The ancient historian Herodotus cited him as "the best and most honorable man in Athens." He was so fair in all that he did that he was often referred to as "Aristides the Just." He flourished in the early quarter of Athens's Classical period and helped Athenians defeat the Persians at the battles of Salamis and Plataea.

Acknowledgments

If it weren't for Dr. Yannis T. Kappos, we may never have written this book. As a renowned author of technical books on AutoCAD, he inspired us to take a seat and start writing. We wish to express our enormous appreciation to him for generously spending his time answering all of our questions—even the foolish ones.

We would also like to extend our thanks, with particular gratefulness, to our friend and senior editor Victoria (Vicki) Austin for her assistance in copy editing. Without her, this book might not have reached its full potential. With her patient guidance and valuable and constructive suggestions, she helped us bring this book up to a higher level!

How This Book is Organized

The book you hold in your hands follows the spiral curriculum teaching approach, a method proposed in 1960 by Jerome Bruner, an American psychologist. According to this method, as a subject is being taught, basic ideas are revisited at intervals—at a more sophisticated level each time—until the reader achieves a complete understanding of the subject. First, the reader learns the basic elements without worrying about the details. Later, more details are taught and basic elements are mentioned again and again, eventually being stored in the brain's long term memory.

According to Jerome Bruner, learning requires the student's active participation, experimentation, exploration, and discovery. This book contains many examples, most of which can be practically performed. This gives the reader the opportunity to get his or her hands on Visual Basic® and become capable of creating his or her own programs.

Who Should Buy This Book?

This book is for anyone who wants to learn computer programming and knows absolutely nothing about it. Of course, if you are wondering whether this book is going to teach you how to create amazing applets or incredible desktop or mobile applications, the answer is "no"—that is a job for other books. So many books out there can teach you those skills in Visual Basic, C#, or Java. Many of them even claim that they can teach you in 24 hours! Don't laugh! They probably can do that, but all of them take one thing for granted—that the reader knows some basics about computer programming. None of those books, unfortunately, bothers to teach you the first thing that a novice programmer needs to learn, which is "Algorithmic Thinking."

Algorithmic Thinking involves more than just learning code. It is a problem solving process that involves learning *how to* code. With 800 pages, and containing more than 300 solved and 400 unsolved exercises, over 450 true/false, 150 multiple choice, and 180 review questions (the solutions and the answers to which can be found on the Internet), this book is ideal for students, teachers, professors, novices or average programmers, or for anyone who wants to start learning or teaching computer programming using the proper conventions and techniques.

Where to Find Answers to Review Questions and Exercises

Answers to all of the review questions, as well as the solutions to all review exercises, are available free of charge on the Internet. You can download them from the following address:

http://www.bouraspage.com

How to Report Errata

Although we have taken great care to ensure the accuracy of our content, mistakes do occur. If you find a mistake in this book, either in the text or the code, we encourage you to report it to us. By doing so, you can save other readers from frustration and, of course, help us to improve the next version of this book. If you find any errata, please feel free to report them by visiting the following address:

http://www.bouraspage.com

Once your errata are verified, your submission will be accepted and the errata will be uploaded to our website, and added to any existing list of errata.

Conventions Used in This Book

Following are some explanations on the conventions used in this book. "Conventions" refer to the standard ways in which certain parts of the text are displayed.

Visual Basic Statements

This book uses plenty of examples written in Visual Basic language. Visual Basic statements are shown in a typeface that looks like this.

```
This is a Visual Basic statement
```

Keywords, Variables, Procedures, and Arguments Within the Text of a Paragraph

Keywords, variables, procedures, and arguments are sometimes shown within the text of a paragraph. When they are, the special text is shown in a typeface different from that of the rest of the paragraph. For instance, `first_name = 5` is an example of a Visual Basic statement within the paragraph text.

Words in Italics

You may notice that some of the special text is also displayed in italics. In this book, italicized words are general types that must be replaced with the specific name appropriate for your data. For example, the general form of a Visual Basic statement may be presented as

```
Sub name ( arg1 As type1, arg2 As type2 )
```

In order to complete the statement, the keywords *name*, *type1*, *arg1*, *type2*, and *arg2* must be replaced with something meaningful. When you use this statement in your program, you might use it in the following form.

```
Sub display_rectangle (width As Integer, height As Integer)
```

Three dots (…): an Ellipsis

In the general form of a statement you may also notice three dots (…), also known as an "ellipsis," following a list in an example. They are not part of the statement. An ellipsis indicates that you can have as many items in the list as you want. For example, the ellipsis in the general form of the statement

```
display_messages ( arg1, arg2, … )
```

indicates that the list may contain more than two arguments. When you use this statement in your program, your statement might be something like this.

```
display_messages ( message1, "Hello", message2, "Hi!" )
```

Square Brackets

The general form of some statements or procedures may contain "square brackets" [ ], which indicate that the enclosed section is optional. For example, the general form of the statement

```
str.Substring ( startIndex [, length ] )
```

indicates that the section [, *length*] can be omitted.

The following two statements produce different results but they are both syntactically correct.

```
a = str.Substring (3)
b = str.Substring (3, 9)
```

The Dark Header

Most of this book's examples are shown in a typeface that looks like this.

```
project_31_2_3
Sub Main()
  Dim a, b As Integer

  a = 1
  b = 2
  Console.Write(a + b)

  Console.ReadKey()
End Sub
```

The dark header `project_31_2_3` on top indicates the filename that you must open to test the program. All the examples that contain this header can be found free of charge on the Internet. You can download them from the following address

http://www.bouraspage.com

Notices

Very often this book uses notices to help you better understand the meaning of a concept. Notices look like this.

> *Notice: This typeface designates a note.*

Something Already Known or Something to Remember

Very often this book can help you recall something you have already learned (probably in a previous chapter). Other times, it will draw your attention to something you should memorize. Reminders look like this.

> *Remember! This typeface designates something to recall or something that you should memorize.*

Section 1

Introductory Knowledge

Chapter 1

How a Computer Works

1.1   Introduction

In today's society, almost every task requires the use of a computer. In schools, students use computers to search the Internet and to send emails. At work, people use them to make presentations, to analyze data, and to communicate with customers. At home, people use them to play games and to chat with other people all over the world. Of course, don't forget smartphones such as iPhones. They are computers as well!

Computers can perform so many different tasks because of their ability to be programmed. In other words, a computer can perform any job that a program tells it to. A program is a set of statements (often called instructions or "commands") that a computer follows in order to perform a specific task.

Programs (usually referred as "application software") are essential to a computer, because without them a computer is a dummy machine that can do nothing at all. The program actually tells the computer what to do and when to do it. The programmer or the software developer is the person who designs, creates, and tests computer programs.

This book introduces you to the basic concepts of computer programming using the Visual Basic language.

1.2   What is Hardware?

The term "hardware" refers to all devices or components that make up a computer. If you have ever opened the case of a computer or a laptop you have probably seen many of its components, such as the microprocessor (CPU), the memory, and the hard disk. A computer is not a device but a system of devices that all work together. The basic components of a typical computer system are discussed here.

- ➢ **The Central Processing Unit (CPU)**

    This is the part of a computer that actually performs all the tasks defined in a program.

- ➢ **Main Memory (RAM – Random Access Memory)**

    This is the area where the computer holds the program (while it is being executed/run) as well as the data that the program is working with. All programs and data stored in this type of memory are lost when you shut down your computer or you unplug it from the wall outlet.

- ➢ **Secondary Storage Devices**

    This is usually the hard disk, and sometimes (but more rarely) the CD/DVD drive. In contrast to main memory, this type of memory can hold data for a longer period of time, even if there is no power to the computer. However, programs stored in this memory cannot be directly executed. They must be transferred to a much faster memory; that is, the main memory.

- ➢ **Input Devices**

    Input devices are all those devices that collect data from the outside world and enter them into the computer for further processing. Keyboards, mice, and microphones are all input devices.

> **Output Devices**
>
> Output devices are all those devices that output data to the outside world. Monitors (screens) and printers are output devices.

1.3   What is Software?

Everything that a computer does is under the control of software. There are two categories of software: system software and application software.

System software is the program that controls and manages the basic operations. For example, it controls the internal operations of a computer, manages all devices connected to it, saves data, loads data, and allows other programs to be executed. Windows, Linux, Mac OS X, Android, and iOS are all examples of system software. Another term for this category of programs is "operating systems."

Application software refers to all the other programs that you use for your everyday tasks, such as browsers, word processors, notepads, games, and many more.

1.4   How a Computer Executes (Runs) a Program

When you turn on your computer, the main memory (RAM) is completely empty. The first thing the computer needs to do is to transfer the operating system from the hard disk to the main memory.

After the operating system is loaded to main memory, you can execute (run) any program (application software) you like. This is usually done by clicking, double clicking, or tapping the program's corresponding icon. For example, let's say you click on the icon of your favorite word processor. This action orders your computer to load (or copy) the word processing program from your hard disk to the main memory so the CPU can execute it.

> **Remember**! Programs are stored on secondary storage devices such as hard disks. When you install a program on your computer, the program is actually copied to your hard disk. But when you execute a program, the program is copied (loaded) from your hard disk to the main memory, and that copy of the program is executed.
>
> **Notice**: The terms "run" and "execute" are synonymous.

1.5   Compilers and Interpreters

Computers can execute programs that are written in a strictly defined computer language. You cannot write a program using a natural language such as English or Greek, because your computer won't understand you!

But what does a computer actually understand? A computer can understand a specific low-level language called the "machine language." In a machine language all statements (or commands) are made up of zeros and ones. The following is an example of a program written in a machine language, that calculates the sum of two numbers.

```
0010 0001 0000 0100
0001 0001 0000 0101
0011 0001 0000 0110
0111 0000 0000 0001
```

Shocked? Don't worry, you are not going to write programs this way. Hopefully, no one writes computer programs this way anymore. Nowadays, all programmers write their programs in a high-level language and then they use a special program to translate them into a machine language. There are two types of programs that programmers use to perform translation: compilers and interpreters.

A compiler is a program that translates statements written in a high-level language into a separate machine language program. The machine language program can then be executed any time you wish. After the translation, the compiler is no longer required.

An interpreter is a program that simultaneously translates and executes the statements written in a high-level language. As the interpreter reads each individual statement in the program, it translates it into a machine language code and then directly executes it. This process is repeated for every statement in the program.

1.6   What is Source Code?

The statements (often called instructions or commands) that the programmer writes in a high-level language are called "source code" or simply "code." The programmer first types the source code into a program known as a code editor, and then uses either a compiler to translate it into a machine language program, or an interpreter to translate and execute it at the same time. Visual Studio® is an example of an Integrated Development Environment (IDE) that enables programmers to both write and execute their source code. You will learn more about Visual Studio in Chapter 3.

1.7   Review Questions: True/False

Choose **true** or **false** for each of the following statements.

1. Modern computers can perform so many different tasks because they have many gigabytes of RAM.
2. A computer can operate without a program.
3. A hard disk is an example of hardware.
4. Data can be stored in main memory (RAM) for a long period of time, even if there is no power to the computer.
5. Data is stored in main memory (RAM), but programs are not.
6. Speakers are an example of an output device.
7. Windows and Linux are examples of software.
8. A media player is an example of system software.
9. When you turn on your computer, the main memory (RAM) already contains the operating system.
10. When you open your word processing application, it is actually copied from a secondary storage device to the main memory (RAM).
11. In a machine language, all statements (commands) are a sequence of zeros and ones.
12. Nowadays, a computer cannot understand zeros and ones.
13. Nowadays, software is written in a language composed of ones and zeros.
14. Software refers to the physical components of a computer.
15. In a high-level computer programming language, the computer does not understand zeros and ones.
16. The compiler and the interpreter are software.
17. The compiler translates source code to an executable file.
18. The interpreter creates a machine language program.

19. After the translation, the interpreter is not required anymore.

20. Source code can be written using a simple text editor.

21. Source code can be executed by a computer without compilation or interpretation.

22. A program written in machine language requires compilation (translation).

23. A compiler translates a program written in a high-level language.

1.8   Review Questions: Multiple Choice

Select the correct answer for each of the following statements.

1. Which of the following is **not** computer hardware?
   a. a hard disk
   b. a DVD disc
   c. a sound card
   d. the main memory (RAM)

2. Which of the following is **not** a secondary storage device?
   a. a DVD reader/writer device
   b. a hard disk
   c. a USB flash drive
   d. RAM

3. Which one of the following operations can**not** be performed by the CPU?
   a. Transfer data to the main memory (RAM).
   b. Display data to the user.
   c. Transfer data from the main memory (RAM).
   d. Perform arithmetic operations.

4. A touch screen is
   a. an input device.
   b. an output device.
   c. both of the above

5. Which of the following is **not** software?
   a. Windows
   b. Linux
   c. iOS
   d. a video game
   e. a web browser
   f. All of the above are software.

6. Which of the following statements is correct?
   a. Programs are stored on the hard disk.
   b. Programs are stored on DVD discs.
   c. Programs are stored in main memory (RAM).
   d. All of the above are correct.

7. Which of the following statements is correct?

    a. Programs can be executed directly from the hard disk.

    b. Programs can be executed directly from a DVD disc.

    c. Programs can be executed directly from the main memory (RAM).

    d. All of the above are correct.

    e. None of the above is correct.

8. Programmers can**not** write computer programs in

    a. machine language.

    b. natural language such as English, Greek, and so on.

    c. Visual Basic.

9. A compiler translates

    a. a program written in machine language into a high-level language program.

    b. a program written in a natural language (English, Greek, etc.) into a machine language program.

    c. a program written in high-level language into a machine language program.

    d. none of the above

    e. all of the above

10. Machine language is

    a. a language that machines use to communicate with each other.

    b. a language made up of numerical instructions that is used directly by a computer.

    c. a language that uses English words for operations.

11. If two identical statements are one after the other, the interpreter

    a. translates the first one and executes it, then it translates the second one and executes it.

    b. translates the first one, then translates the second one, and then executes them both.

    c. translates only the first one (since they are identical) and then executes it two times.

Chapter 2
Visual Basic

2.1   What is Visual Basic?

Visual Basic is a widely used general-purpose computer programming language that allows programmers to create desktop or mobile applications, large-scale applications, embedded systems, client-server applications, web pages, applets, and many other types of software.

Although it is implemented primarily on Windows, Visual Basic is designed to be a platform-independent language. It is intended to let programmers "write once, run anywhere," meaning that code is written once but can run on any combination of hardware and operating system without being recompiled.

2.2   What is the Difference Between a Script and a Program?

Technically speaking, a script is *interpreted* whereas a program is *compiled*, but this is actually not their main difference. There is another small yet more important difference between them!

The main purpose of a script written in a scripting language such as JavaScript, or VBA (Visual Basic for Applications) is to control another application. So you can say that, in some ways JavaScript controls the web browser, and VBA controls a Microsoft® Office application such as MS Word or MS Excel.

On the other hand, a program written in a programming language such as Visual Basic, C++, or C# executes independently of any other application. A program is compiled into a separate set of machine language instructions that can then be executed as stand-alone any time the user wishes.

> **Notice**: *Macros of Microsoft Office are scripts written in VBA. Their purpose is to automate certain functions within Microsoft Office.*
>
> **Remember**! *A script requires a hosting application in order to execute. A script cannot be executed as stand-alone.*

2.3   Why You Should Learn Visual Basic

Visual Basic is what is known as a "high-level" computer language. The Visual Basic coding style is very easy to understand and very efficient. Visual Basic is a very flexible yet powerful language, making it most suitable for developing medium-scale applications, embedded systems, client-server applications, art applications, music players, or even video games.

Visual Basic is everywhere! It is used on desktop computers, on laptops, and even in data centers costing millions of dollars. With a huge community of developers worldwide, Visual Basic enables efficient development of exciting applications and services. There are millions—probably even billions—of lines of code already written in Visual Basic and your possibilities for code reuse are huge! This is why many companies and organizations prefer using Visual Basic to any other programming language. This is also a very good reason why you should actually learn Visual Basic!

2.4   How Visual Basic Works

Computers do not understand natural languages such as English or Greek, so you need a computer language such as Visual Basic to communicate with them. Visual Basic is a very powerful high-level computer language. The Visual Basic compiler converts Visual Basic language to a language" that computers can actually understand, and that is known as the "machine language."

Actually, Visual Basic is a special case of a computer programming language that uses two compilers. The first one translates Visual Basic statements into an intermediate language called Common Intermediate Language (CIL), which is a language similar to Java's bytecode. The CIL code is stored on disk in an executable file called an *assembly*, typically with an extension of .exe. Later, when a user wants to execute the file, the .NET Framework performs a Just In Time (JIT) compilation to convert the CIL code into low-level machine language code for direct execution on the hardware.

Now come some reasonable questions: *Why all this trouble? Why does Visual Basic translate twice? Why are Visual Basic statements not directly translated into machine language code?* The answer lies in the fact that Visual Basic is designed to be a platform-independent programming language. This means that a program is written once but it can be executed on any device, regardless of its operating system or its architecture, as long as the .NET Framework is installed on it. In the past, programs had to be recompiled, or even rewritten, for each computer platform. One of the biggest advantages of Visual Basic is that you only have to write and compile a program once! In **Figure 2–1** you can see how statements written in Visual Basic are compiled into CIL code and how CIL code can then be executed on any platform that has the corresponding .NET Framework installed on it.

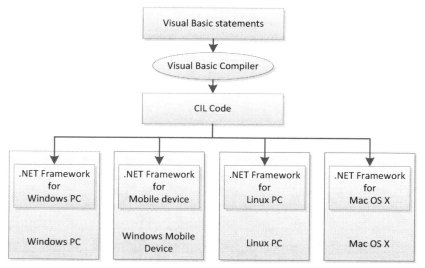

Figure 2–1 Executing Visual Basic statements on different platforms

Notice: Please note that, at the time you read this book, .NET Framework for Linux and Mac OS X may still not be available. Be patient though! On 12 November 2014, Microsoft announced that .NET will be open source, letting developers build .NET applications on multiple platforms. Obviously this is a very promising future of the .NET Framework for Linux and Mac!

Chapter 3
Software Packages to Install

3.1 Visual Studio

Visual Studio is an Integrated Development Environment (IDE) that provides a great set of tools for many programming languages such as Visual Basic, C++, C#, and F#, and lets you easily create applications for Microsoft Windows, as well as websites, web applications and web services. Via extensions installed separately, Visual Studio can support even more languages such as Python, M, and Ruby.

Visual Studio is much more than a text editor. It can indent lines, match words and brackets, and highlight source code that is written incorrectly. It also provides automatic code (IntelliSense®), which means that as you type, it displays a list of possible completions.

The IDE also provides hints to help you analyze your code and find any potential problems. It even suggests some simple solutions to fix those problems.

You can use the Visual Studio not only to write but also to execute your programs directly from the IDE.

Visual Studio has a large community of users all around the world and this is why it comes in so many different flavors. There is Visual Studio Ultimate, Visual Studio Premium, Visual Studio Professional, Team Foundation Server, Visual Studio Express, Team Foundation Server Express, and Visual Studio Community. All of them can be installed on Windows operating systems. The most amazing thing, however, is that the last three of them are free of charge and can be used by individual developers to create their own free or paid apps!

3.2 How to Set Up Visual Studio Community

To install Visual Studio Community, you can download it free of charge from the following address:

https://www.visualstudio.com/en-us/downloads/download-visual-studio-vs

From the Visual Studio Downloads page on visualstudio.com, scroll down to the heading for Visual Studio Community & Express, and select and download the latest version of the one called "Community." When the download is complete, run the corresponding installer.

The first screen of the Visual Studio installer (as shown in **Figure 3–1)** prompts you to select the installation folder for Setup. You can leave the proposed folder that appears there. Then, you must read and agree to the License Terms and Privacy Policy. You are also given the option to join the Visual Studio Experience Improvement Program to help Microsoft improve the quality, reliability, and performance of Visual Studio.

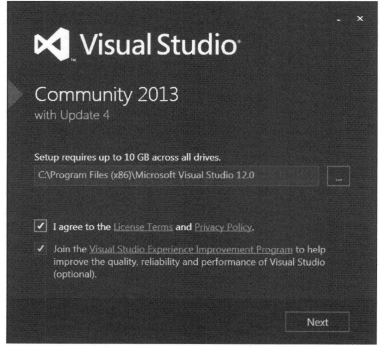

Figure 3–1 Selecting the installation folder in the Visual Studio installer

> **Notice**: *The installation folder proposed on your computer may differ from that in* **Figure 3–1** *depending on the versions of the Visual Studio or Windows that you have.*

On the next screen of the Visual Studio installer, you can keep and install all the proposed features or you can uncheck them all (as shown in **Figure 3–2)**, as they are not required by this book.

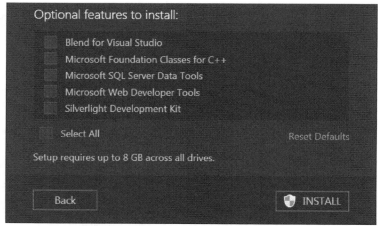

Figure 3–2 Optional features to install in the Visual Studio installer

Next, click on the "Install" button in the bottom right-hand corner of the installation window.

When the installation process is complete, you can launch Visual Studio. You will see a Welcome screen as shown in **Figure 3-3**. You can sign in or you can just click on the "Not now, maybe later" link.

Figure 3-3 The Visual Studio welcome page

On the next screen, set the "Development Settings" to "General" and choose a color theme of your choice, as shown in **Figure 3-4**. This book uses the blue color theme.

Figure 3-4 Selecting the Development Settings and color theme

Click on the "Start Visual Studio" button in the bottom right-hand corner of the Visual Studio window. The Visual Studio Community environment opens and should look like the one shown in **Figure 3–5**.

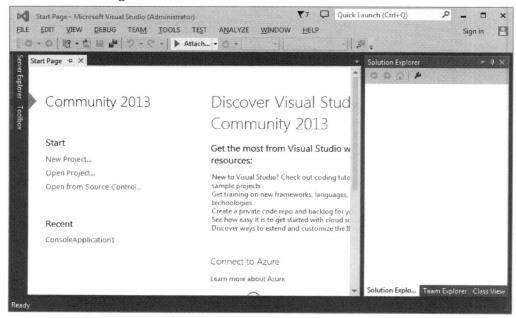

Figure 3–5 The Visual Studio IDE

One thing that this book does in order to save paper is to decrease the number of spaces per indent to two. From the main menu in the Visual Studio window, select TOOLS→Options. In the popup window that appears, click on the dropdown arrow to expand the Text Editor→Visual Basic→Tabs. This will open the "Tabs" Options for Visual Basic, as shown in **Figure 3–6**. Make sure that the Indenting option is selected as "Smart."

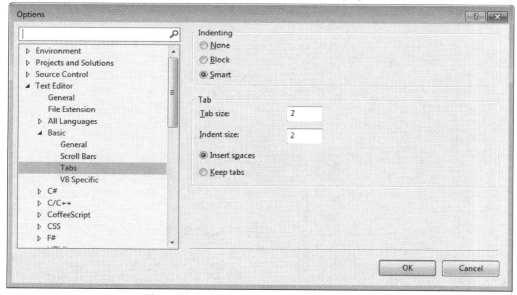

Figure 3–6 The Editor's "Options" dialog box

Set the fields "Tab size" and "Indent size" to 2. Then, make sure that "Insert spaces" is selected (instead of "Keep tabs.")

Click on the "OK" button at the bottom of the Options screen.

Visual Studio has been configured properly! Now it's time to conquer the world of Visual Basic! In the upcoming chapters you will learn all about how to create Visual Basic projects, how to write Visual Basic programs, and so many tips and tricks useful in your first steps as a budding programmer!

Review Questions in "Introductory Knowledge"

Answer the following questions.

1. What is hardware?
2. List the five basic components of a typical computer system.
3. Which part of the computer actually executes the programs?
4. Which part of the computer holds the program and its data while the program is running?
5. Which part of the computer holds data for a long period of time, even when there is no power to the computer?
6. How do you call the device that collects data from the outside world and enters them into the computer?
7. List some examples of input devices.
8. How do you call the device that outputs data from the computer to the outside world?
9. List some examples of output devices.
10. What is software?
11. How many software categories are there, and what are their names?
12. A word processing program belongs to what category of software?
13. What is a compiler?
14. What is an interpreter?
15. What is meant by the term "machine language"?
16. What is source code?
17. What is Visual Basic?
18. What is the difference between a script and a program?
19. What are some of the possible uses of Visual Basic?
20. What is Visual Studio?

Section 2
Getting Started with Visual Basic

Chapter 4
Introduction to Basic Algorithmic Concepts

4.1   What is an Algorithm?

An algorithm is a strictly defined finite sequence of well-defined statements (often called instructions or commands) that provides the solution to a problem or to a specific class of problems for any acceptable set of input values (if there are any inputs). In other words, an algorithm is a step-by-step procedure to solve a given problem. The term "finite" means that the algorithm should reach an end point and cannot run forever.

You can find algorithms everywhere in your real life, not just in computer science. For example, the process for preparing toast or a cup of tea can be expressed as an algorithm. Certain steps, in a certain order, must be followed in order to achieve your goal.

4.2   The Algorithm for Making a Cup of Tea

The following is an algorithm for making a cup of tea.

1. Put the teabag in a cup.
2. Fill the kettle with water.
3. Boil the water in the kettle.
4. Pour some of the boiled water into the cup.
5. Add milk to the cup.
6. Add sugar to the cup.
7. Stir the tea.
8. Drink the tea.

As you can see, there are certain steps that must be followed. These steps are in a specific order, even though some of the steps could be rearranged. For example, steps 5 and 6 can be reversed. You could add the sugar first, and the milk afterwards.

Please keep in mind that the order of some steps can probably be changed but you can't move them far away from where they should be. For example, you can't move step 3 ("Boil the water in the kettle.") to the end of the algorithm, because you will end up drinking a cup of iced tea (and not a warm one) which is totally different from your initial goal!

4.3   Properties of an Algorithm

An algorithm must satisfy the following properties:

➢ **Input**: The algorithm must have input values from a specified set.

➢ **Output**: The algorithm must produce the output values from a specified set of input values. The output values are the solution to a problem.

➢ **Finiteness**: For any input, the algorithm must terminate after a finite number of steps.

➢ **Definiteness**: All steps of the algorithm must be precisely defined.

➢ **Effectiveness**: It must be possible to perform each step of the algorithm correctly and in a finite amount of time. That is, its steps must be basic enough so that, for example, someone using a pencil and a paper could carry them out exactly, and in a finite amount of time. It is not enough that each step is definite (or precisely defined), but it must also be feasible.

4.4   Okay About Algorithms. But What is a Computer Program Anyway?

A computer program is nothing more than an algorithm that is written in a language that computers can understand, like Visual Basic, Java, C++, or C#.

A computer program cannot actually *make* you a cup of tea or cook your dinner, although an algorithm can guide you through the steps to do it yourself. However, programs can (for example) be used to calculate the average value of a set of numbers, or to find the maximum value among them. Artificial intelligence programs can even play chess or solve logic puzzles.

4.5   The Party of Three!

There are always three parties involved in an algorithm—the one that writes the algorithm, the one that executes it, and the one that uses or enjoys it.

Let's take an algorithm for preparing a meal, for example. Someone writes the algorithm (the author of the recipe book), someone executes it (probably your mother, who prepared the meal following the steps from the recipe book), and someone uses it (probably you, who enjoys the meal).

Now consider a real computer program. Let's take a video game, for example. Someone writes the algorithm in a computer language (the programmer), someone or something executes it (usually a laptop or a computer), and someone else uses it or plays with it (the user).

Be careful, because sometimes the terms "programmer" and "user" can be confusing. When you *write* a computer program, for that period of time you are "the programmer." However, when you *use* your own program, you are "the user."

4.6   The Three Main Stages Involved in Creating an Algorithm

Three main stages are involved in creating an algorithm: data input, data processing, and results output. The order is specific and cannot be changed.

Consider a computer program that finds the average value of three numbers. First, the program must prompt the user to enter the numbers (data input). Next, the program calculates the average value of the numbers (data processing). Finally, the program displays the result on the computer's screen (results output).

Let's take a look at these stages in more detail.

1. Prompt the user to enter a number.
2. Prompt the user to enter a second number.   } **Input**
3. Prompt the user to enter a third number.
4. Calculate the sum of the three numbers.
5. Divide the sum by 3.   } **Processing**
6. Display the result on the screen.   } **Output**

In some rare situations, the input stage may be absent and the computer program may be composed of only two stages. For example, consider a computer program that is written to calculate the following sum.

$$1 + 2 + 3 + 4 + 5 + 6 + 7 + 8 + 9 + 10$$

In this example, the user enters no values at all because the computer knows exactly what to do. It must calculate the sum of the numbers 1 to 10.

Now let's take a look at the same example, slightly altered. Consider a computer program that is written to calculate the following sum.

$$1 + 2 + 3 + \cdots + N$$

Of course, this sum is not the same as the previous one. In this example, the user needs to input some data. The computer cannot decide by itself about the exact value of number N. This value must be entered by the user. Once the user enters a value for N, the computer can proceed to calculate the result. For example, if the user enters the number 5, the computer can then find the result of 1 + 2 + 3 + 4 + 5.

4.7   Flowcharts

A flowchart is a graphical method of presenting an algorithm, usually on paper. It is the visual representation of the algorithm's flow of execution. In other words, it visually represents how the flow of execution proceeds from one statement to the next until the end of the algorithm is reached. A flowchart cannot be entered directly into a computer as is. It must first be converted into a programming language such as Visual Basic.

The basic symbols that flowcharts use are shown in **Table 4–1**.

Table 4-1 Flowchart Symbols and Their Functions

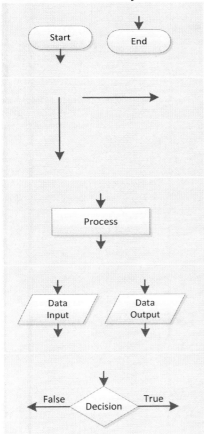

Start/End: Represents the beginning or the end of an algorithm. The Start symbol has one exit and the End symbol has one entrance.

Arrow: Shows the flow of execution. An arrow coming from one symbol and ending at another symbol shows that control passes to the symbol that the arrow is pointing to. Arrows are always drawn as straight lines going up and down or sideways (never at an angle).

Process: Represents a process or mathematical (formula) calculation. The Process symbol has one entrance and one exit.

Data Input/Output: Represents the data input or the results output. In most cases, data comes from a keyboard and results are displayed on a screen. The Data input/output symbol has one entrance and one exit.

Decision: Indicates the point at which a decision is made. Based on a given condition (which can be true or false), the algorithm will follow either the right or the left path. The Decision symbol has one entrance and two (and always only two) exits.

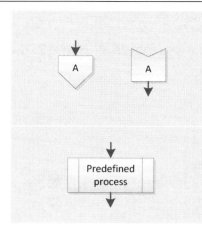

Off-page connectors: Show continuation of a flowchart onto another page. They are used to connect segments on multiple pages when a flowchart gets too big to fit onto one sheet of paper. The outgoing off-page connector symbol has one entrance and the incoming off-page connector symbol has one exit.

Subprogram (predefined process): Depicts subprograms that are formally defined elsewhere, such as in a separate flowchart. The Predefined process symbol has one entrance and one exit.

An example of a flowchart is shown in **Figure 4–1.** The algorithm prompts the user to enter three numbers and then calculates their average value and displays it on the computer screen.

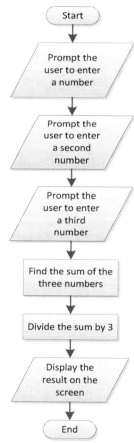

Figure 4–1 Flowchart for an algorithm that calculates and displays the average of three numbers

Remember! *A flowchart always begins and ends with a Start/End symbol!*

Exercise 4.7-1   *Finding the Average Value of Three Numbers*

Design an algorithm that calculates the average value of three numbers. Whenever the average value is below 10, a message "Fail!" should be displayed. Otherwise, if the average value is 10 or above, a message "Pass!" should be displayed.

Solution

In this problem, two different messages must be displayed, but only one can appear each time the algorithm is executed; the wording of the message depends on the average value. The flowchart for the algorithm is presented next.

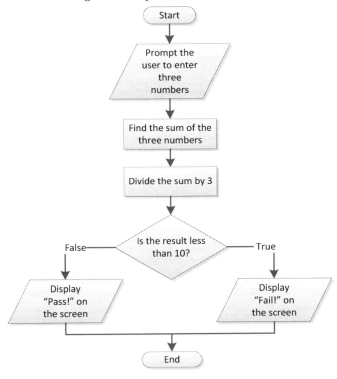

Notice: *To save paper, you can prompt the user to enter all three numbers using one single oblique parallelogram.*

Remember! *A Decision symbol always has one entrance and two exit paths!*

Of course it is very soon for you to start creating your own algorithms. This particular exercise is quite simple and is presented in this chapter as an exception, just for demonstration purposes. You need to learn more before you start creating your own algorithms or even Visual Basic programs. Just be patient! In a few chapters the big moment will come!

4.8   What are "Reserved Words"?

In a computer language, "reserved words" are all those words that have a strictly predefined meaning—they are reserved for special use and cannot be used for any other purpose. For example, the words Start, End, Read, and Write in flowcharts have a predefined meaning. They are used to represent the beginning, the end, the data input, and the results output, respectively.

Reserved words exist in all high-level computer languages as well. In Visual Basic, there are many reserved words such as If, While, Else, and For. Their meanings are predefined, so these words cannot be used for any other purposes.

> **Notice**: *Reserved words in a computer language are often called keywords.*

4.9 What is the Difference Between a Statement and a Command?

There is a big discussion on the Internet about whether there is, or is not, any difference between a statement and a command. Some people prefer to use the term "statement," and some others the term "command." For a novice programmer, there is no difference; both are instructions to the computer!

4.10 What is Structured Programming?

Structured programming is a software development method that uses modularization and structured design. This means that large programs are broken down into smaller modules and each individual module uses structured code, which means that the statements are organized in a specific manner that minimizes errors and misinterpretation. As its name suggests, structured programming is done in a structured programming language and Visual Basic is one such language.

The structured programming concept was formalized in 1966 by Corrado Böhm[1] and Giuseppe Jacopini[2]. They demonstrated theoretical computer program design using sequences, decisions, and iterations.

4.11 The Three Fundamental Control Structures

There are three fundamental control structures in structured programming.

> ➢ **Sequence Control Structure**: This refers to the line-by-line execution, in which statements are executed sequentially, in the same order in which they appear in the program. They might, for example, carry out a series of read or write operations, arithmetic operations, or assignments to variables.

> ➢ **Decision Control Structure**: Depending on whether a condition is true or false, the decision control structure may skip the execution of an entire block of statements or even execute one block of statements instead of another.

> ➢ **Loop Control Structure**: This is a control structure that allows the execution of a block of statements multiple times until a specified condition is met.

If you didn't quite understand the deeper meaning of these three control structures, don't worry, because upcoming chapters will analyze them very thoroughly. Patience is a virtue. All you have to do for now is wait!

---

[1] Corrado Böhm (1923–) is a computer scientist known especially for his contribution to the theory of structured programming, and for the implementation of functional programming languages.

[2] Giuseppe Jacopini (1936–2001) was a computer scientist. His most influential contribution is the theorem about structured programming, published along with Corrado Böhm in 1966, under the title "Flow Diagrams, Turing Machines, and Languages with Only Two Formation Rules."

(Bohm, C., and Jacopini, G., "Flow Diagrams, Turing Machines, and Languages with Only Two Formation Rules," *Communications of the ACM* 9(5), (May, 1966), 366–371.)

Exercise 4.11-1   *Understanding Control Structures Using Flowcharts*

Using flowcharts, give an example for each type of control structure.

Solution

Example of a Sequence Control Structure

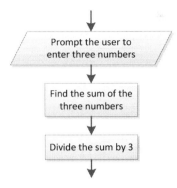

Example of a Decision Control Structure

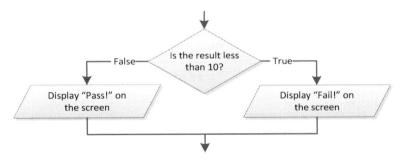

Example of a Loop Control Structure

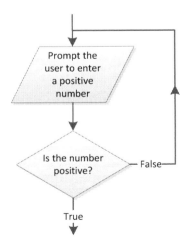

4.12   Your First Visual Basic Program

Converting a flowchart to a computer language such as Visual Basic results in a Visual Basic program. A Visual Basic program is nothing more than a text file including Visual Basic statements. Visual Basic programs can even be written in your text editor application! Keep in mind, though, that using Visual Studio to write Visual Basic programs is a much better solution due to all of its included features that can make your life easier.

A Visual Basic program must always contain a `Main` subprocedure, as shown here.

```
Sub Main()

    'Visual Basic code goes here

    Console.ReadKey()
End Sub
```

A Visual Basic source code is saved on your hard disk with the default .vb file extension.

Here is a very simple Visual Basic program that displays just three messages on the screen.

```
Sub Main()

    Console.WriteLine("Hello World!")
    Console.WriteLine("Hallo Welt!")
    Console.Write("The End")

    Console.ReadKey()
End Sub
```

> **Notice**: The `Console.ReadKey()` statement at the end of each program ensures that the output window stays open and waits for the user to press any key to close it.

4.13   What is the Difference Between Syntax Errors and Logic Errors?

When programmers write code in a high-level language there are two types of errors that they might make: syntax errors and logic errors.

Syntax errors are mistakes such as misspelled keywords, a missing punctuation character, a missing bracket, or a missing closing parenthesis. Fortunately, Visual Studio detects these errors as you type and underlines the erroneous statements with a wavy blue line. If you try to execute a Visual Basic program that includes syntax errors, you will get error messages on your screen and the program won't be executed. You must correct all the errors and then try to execute the program again.

Logic errors are those errors that prevent your program from doing what you expected it to do. With logic errors you get no warning at all. Your code may compile and run but the result is not the expected one. Logic errors are the most difficult errors to detect. You must revisit your program thoroughly to determine where your error is. For example, consider a Visual Basic program that prompts the user to enter three numbers, and then calculates and displays their average value. The programmer, however, made a typographical error; one of his or her statements divides the sum of the three numbers by 5, and not by 3 as it should. Of course the Visual Basic program is executed as usual, without any error messages, prompting the user to enter three numbers and displaying a result, but obviously not the correct one! It is the programmer who has to find and correct the erroneously written Visual Basic statement, not the computer or the compiler!

4.14   Commenting Your Code

When you write a small and easy program, anyone can understand how it works just by reading it line-by-line. However, long programs are difficult to understand, sometimes even by the same person who wrote them. Comments are extra information that can be included in a program to make it easier to read and understand. You can add explanations and other pieces of information, including:

> ➢ who wrote the program
> ➢ when the program was created or last modified
> ➢ what the program does
> ➢ how the program works

However, you should not over-comment. There is no need to explain every line of your program. Add comments only when a specific portion of your program is hard to follow.

In Visual Basic, you can add comments using the apostrophe character (') as shown here.

```
'Created By Bouras Aristides
'Date created: 12/25/2003
'Date modified: 04/03/2008
'Description: This program displays some messages on the screen

Sub Main()
  Console.WriteLine("Hello Zeus!")   'display a message on the screen

  'display a second message on the screen
  Console.WriteLine("Hello Hera!")

  'This is a comment        Console.Write("The End")

  Console.ReadKey()
End Sub
```

As you can see in the preceding program, you can add comments above a statement or at the end of it, but not in front of it. Look at the last statement, which is supposed to display the message "The End." This statement is never executed because it is considered part of the comment.

4.15   User-Friendly Programs

What is a "user-friendly" program? It's the one that the user considers a friend instead of an enemy, the one that can be used easily by a novice user.

If you want to write user-friendly programs you have to put yourself in the shoes of the user. Users want the computer to do their job their way, with a minimum of effort. Hidden menus, imprecise labels and directions, and misleading error messages are all things that can make a program user-unfriendly!

The law that best defines user-friendly designs is the Law of Least Astonishment: "*The program should act in a way that least astonishes the user.*" This law is also commonly referred to as the Principle of Least Astonishment (POLA).

4.16   Review Questions: True/False

Choose **true** or **false** for each of the following statements.

1. The process for preparing a meal is actually an algorithm.
2. Algorithms are used only in computer science.
3. An algorithm can run forever.
4. In an algorithm, you can relocate a step in any position you wish.
5. An algorithm should produce the correct output values for just one set of input values.
6. Computers can play chess.
7. An algorithm can always become a computer program.
8. Programming is the process of creating a computer program.
9. There are always three parties involved in a computer program: the programmer, the computer, and the user.
10. The programmer and the user can sometimes be the same person.
11. It is possible for a computer program to output no results.
12. A flowchart is a computer program.
13. A flowchart is composed of a set of geometric shapes.
14. A flowchart is a method used to represent an algorithm.
15. You can design a flowchart without using any Start/End symbols.
16. You can design a flowchart without using any Process symbols.
17. You can design a flowchart without using any Data input/output symbols.
18. A flowchart should always include at least one Decision symbol.
19. In a flowchart, a Decision symbol can have one, two, or three exit paths, depending on the given problem.
20. Reserved words are all those words that have a strictly predefined meaning.
21. Structured programming includes structured design.
22. Visual Basic is a structured computer language.
23. The basic principle of structured programming is that it includes only four fundamental control structures.
24. One statement, written ten times, is considered a loop control structure.
25. Decision control structure refers to the line-by-line execution.
26. A misspelled keyword is considered a logic error.
27. A Visual Basic program can be executed even though it contains logic errors.
28. A semicolon at the end of a statement is considered a syntax error.
29. An exclamation mark at the end of a statement cannot prevent the whole Visual Basic program from being executed.
30. One of the advantages of structured programming is that no errors are made while writing a computer program.
31. Logic errors are caught during compilation.
32. Syntax errors are the most difficult errors to detect.
33. A program that calculates the area of a triangle but outputs the wrong results contains logic errors.

34. When a program includes no output statements, it contains syntax errors.

35. A program should always contain comments.

36. If you add comments to a program, the computer can more easily understand it.

37. You can add comments anywhere in a program.

38. Comments are not visible to the users of a program.

39. A program is called user-friendly if it can be used easily by a novice user.

40. The acronym POLA stands for "Principle of Least Amusement."

4.17   Review Questions: Multiple Choice

Select the correct answer for each of the following statements.

1. An algorithm is a strictly defined finite sequence of well-defined statements that provides the solution to
    a. a problem.
    b. a specific class of problems.
    c. both of the above

2. Which of the following is **not** a property that an algorithm should satisfy?
    a. effectiveness
    b. fittingness
    c. definiteness
    d. input

3. A computer program is
    a. an algorithm.
    b. a sequence of instructions.
    c. both of the above
    d. none of the above

4. When someone prepares a meal, he or she is the
    a. "programmer."
    b. "user."
    c. none of the above

5. Which of the following does **not** belong in the three main stages involved in creating an algorithm?
    a. data production
    b. data input
    c. data output
    d. data processing

6. A flowchart can be
    a. presented on a piece of paper.
    b. entered directly into a computer as is.
    c. both of the above

7. A rectangle in a flowchart represents
    a. input/output.

    b.   a processing operation.

    c.   a decision.

    d.   none of the above

8.   Which of the following is/are control structures?

    a.   a decision

    b.   a sequence

    c.   a loop

    d.   All of the above are control structures.

9.   Which of the following Visual Basic statements contains a syntax error?

    a.   `Console.Write(Hello Poseidon)`

    b.   `Console.WriteLine("It's me! I contain a syntax error!!!")`

    c.   `Console.WriteLine("Hello Athena")`

    d.   none of the above

10. Which of the following `Console.WriteLine` statements is actually executed?

    a.   `'Console.WriteLine("Hello Apollo")`

    b.   `'Console.WriteLine("Hello Artemis")`

    c.   `'This will be executed' Console.WriteLine("Hello Ares")`

    d.   `Console.WriteLine("Hello Aphrodite") 'This will be executed`

    e.   none of the above

Chapter 5
Variables and Constants

5.1　What is a Variable?

In computer science, a variable is a location in the computer's main memory (RAM) where you can store a value and change it as the program executes.

Picture a variable as a transparent box in which you can insert and hold one thing at a time. Because the box is transparent, you can also examine what it contains. Moreover, if you have two or more boxes you can give each box a unique name. For example, you could have three boxes, each containing a different number, and you could name the boxes numberA, numberB, and numberC.

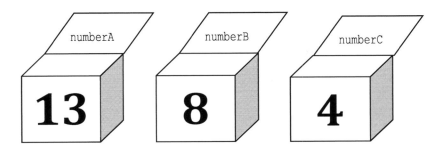

The boxes named numberA, numberB and numberC in the example contain the numbers 13, 8, and 4, respectively. Of course, you can examine or even alter the contained value of each one of these boxes at any time.

Now, let's say that someone asks you to find the sum of the values of the first two boxes and then store the result in the last box. The steps you must follow are:

1. Take a look at the first two boxes and examine the contained values.
2. Use your CPU (this is your brain) to calculate the sum (the result).
3. Insert the result in the last box. However, since each box can contain only one single value at a time, the value 4 is actually replaced by the number 21.

The boxes now look like this.

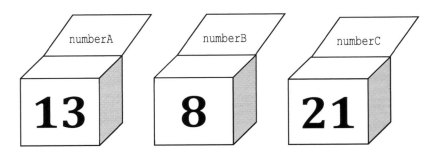

In a flowchart, the action of storing a value in a variable is represented by a left arrow

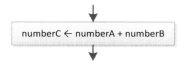

This action is usually expressed as "Assign a value, or the result of an expression, to a variable." The left arrow is called the "value assignment operator."

> **Notice**: *Please note that this arrow always points to the left. You are not allowed to use right arrows. Also, on the left side of the arrow only one single variable should exist.*

In real computer science, the three boxes are actually three individual regions in main memory (RAM), named numberA, numberB and numberC.

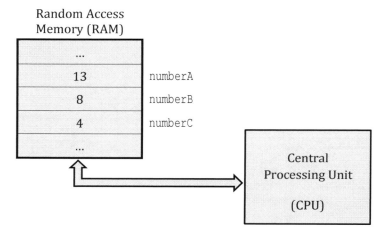

When a program instructs the CPU to execute the statement

numberC ← numberA + numberB

it follows the same three-step process as in the previous example.

1. The number 13 is transferred from the RAM's region named numberA to the CPU.

   The number 8 is transferred from the RAM's region named numberB to the CPU.

   (This is the first step, in which you examined the values contained in the first two boxes.)

2. The CPU calculates the sum of 13 + 8.

   (This is the second step, in which you used your brain to calculate the sum, or result.)

3. The result, 21, is transferred from the CPU to the RAM's region named numberC, replacing the existing number 4.

   (This is the third step, in which you inserted the result in the last box.)

After execution, the RAM looks like this.

RAM

...	
13	numberA
8	numberB
21	numberC
...	

> **Remember!** *While a Visual Basic program is running, a variable can hold various values, but only one value at a time. When you assign a value to a variable, this value remains stored until you assign a new value. The old value is lost.*

A variable is one of the most important elements in computer science because it helps you interact with data stored in the main memory (RAM). Soon, you will learn all about how to declare and use variables in Visual Basic.

5.2   What is a Constant?

Sometimes you may need to use a value that cannot change while the program is running. Such a value is called a "constant." In simple terms, you could say that a constant is a locked variable. This means that when a program begins to run and a value is assigned to the constant, nothing can change the value of the constant while the program is running. For example, in a financial program an interest rate can be declared as a constant.

A descriptive name for a constant can also improve the readability of your program and help you avoid errors. For example, let's say that you are using the value 3.14159265 (but not as a constant) at many points throughout your program. If you make an error when typing the number, this will produce the wrong results. But, if this value is given a name, any typographical error in the name is detected by Visual Basic, and you are notified with an error message.

In a flowchart, you can represent the action of setting a constant equal to a value with the equals sign, (=).

Const VAT = 0.2

> **Notice:** *This book uses the reserved word* Const *to distinguish a constant from a variable.*

Consider an algorithm that lets the user enter the prices of three different products and then calculates and displays the 20% Value Added Tax (known as VAT) for each product. The flowchart in **Figure 5-1** shows this process when no constant is used.

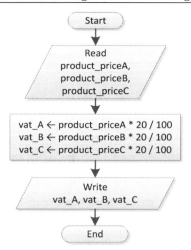

Figure 5–1 Calculating the 20% VAT for three products without the use of a constant

Even though this algorithm is absolutely correct, the problem is that the author used the 20% VAT (20/100) three times. If this were an actual computer program, the CPU would be forced to calculate the result of the division (20/100) three individual times.

> **Notice**: *Generally speaking, division and multiplication are time consuming operations that must be avoided when possible.*

A much better solution would be to use a variable, as shown in **Figure 5–2**. This reduces the number of division and multiplication operations and also decreases the potential for typographical errors.

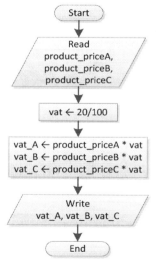

Figure 5–2 Calculating the 20% VAT for three products using a variable, vat

This time the division (20/100) is calculated only once, and then its result is used to calculate the VAT of each product.

But even now, the algorithm (which might later become a computer program) isn't perfect; vat is a variable and any programmer could accidentally change its value.

The ideal solution would be to change the variable vat to a constant VAT, as shown in **Figure 5-3**.

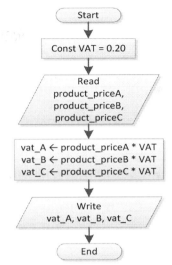

Figure 5-3 Calculating the 20% VAT for three products using a constant, VAT

Notice: *Please note that when a constant is declared, the equals symbol (=) is used instead of the left arrow.*

This last solution is the best choice for many reasons.

➢ No one, including the programmer, can change the value of VAT just by accidentally writing a statement such as VAT ← 0.60 in any position of the program.

➢ The potential for typographical errors is minimized.

➢ The number of multiplication and division operations is kept as low as possible.

➢ If one day the finance minister decides to increase the Value Added Tax from 20% to 22%, the programmer needs to change just one line of code!

5.3   How Many Types of Variables and Constants Exist in Visual Basic?

Many different types of variables and constants exist in all computer languages. The reason for this diversity is the different types of data each variable or constant can hold. Most of the time, variables and constants hold the following types of data.

➢ **Integers**: Integer values are positive or negative numbers without any fractional part, such as 5, 100, 135, -25, and -5123.

➢ **Reals**: Real values are positive or negative numbers that include a fractional part, such as 5.14, 7.23, 5.0, 3.14, and -23.78976. Real values are also known as "floats."

➢ **Booleans**[1]: Boolean variables or constants can hold only one of two values: True or False.

---

[1] George Boole (1815–1864) was an English mathematician, philosopher, and logician. He is best known as the architect of what is now called Boolean logic (Boolean algebra), the basis of the modern digital computer.

> ➤ **Characters**: Characters are alphanumeric values (always enclosed in double quotes) such as "a", "c", "Hello Zeus", "I am 25 years old", or "Peter Loves Jane For Ever". A sequence of characters is also known as a "string"!!! (Probably the word "string" makes you visualize something wearable, but unfortunately it's not. Please keep your dirty precious mind focused on computer science!)

5.4   Rules for Naming Variables in Visual Basic

Certain rules must be followed when assigning names to your variables.

> ➤ The name of a variable can contain only Latin characters (English uppercase or lowercase characters), numbers, and the underscore character (_). Examples of variable names are firstName, last_name1, and age.

> ➤ Variable names are not case sensitive, which means there is no difference between uppercase and lowercase characters. For example, the myVAR, myvar, MYVAR, and MyVar names are actually referring to the same variable.

> ➤ No space characters are allowed. If a variable is described by more than one word, you can use the underscore character (_) between the words. For example, the variable name student age is wrong. Instead, you might use student_age, or even studentAge.

> ➤ A valid variable name can start with a letter, or an underscore. Numbers are allowed, but they cannot be used at the beginning of the variable name. For example the variable name 1student_name is not properly written. Instead, you might use something like student_name1 or student1_name.

> ➤ A variable name is usually chosen in a way that describes the meaning and the role of its contained data. For example, a variable that holds a temperature value might be named temperature, temp, or even t.

5.5   Rules for Naming Constants in Visual Basic

Certain rules must be followed when assigning names to your constants.

> ➤ The name of a constant can contain only Latin characters (English uppercase or lowercase characters), numbers, and the underscore character (_). Moreover, even though lowercase letters are permitted, it is advisable to use only uppercase letters. This helps you to visually distinguish constants from variables. Examples of constant names are VAT and COMPUTER_NAME.

> ➤ Constant names are not case sensitive, which means there is no difference between uppercase and lowercase characters. For example, the myCONST, myconts, MYCONST, and MyConst names are actually referring to the same constant.

> ➤ No space characters are allowed. If a constant is described by more than one word, you can use the underscore character (_) between the words. For example, the constant name COMPUTER NAME is wrong. Instead, you might use COMPUTER_NAME, or even COMPUTERNAME.

> ➤ A valid constant name can start with a letter, or an underscore. Numbers are allowed, but they cannot be used at the beginning of the constant name. For example, the constant name 1COMPUTER_NAME is not properly written. Instead, you might use something like COMPUTER_NAME1 or COMPUTER1_NAME.

> ➤ A constant name is usually chosen in a way that describes the meaning and the role of its contained data. For example, a constant that holds the Value Added Tax might be named VAT, or VALUE_ADDED_TAX.

5.6   What Does the Phrase "Declare a Variable" Mean?

Declaration is the process of reserving a portion in main memory (RAM) for storing the contents of a variable. In many high-level computer languages (including Visual Basic), the programmer must write a specific statement to reserve that portion in the RAM. In most cases, they even need to specify the variable type so that the compiler or the interpreter knows exactly how much space to reserve.

Here are some examples showing how variables are declared in different high-level computer languages.

Declaration Statement	High-level Computer Language
Dim sum As Integer	Visual Basic
int sum;	C#, C++, Java, and many more
sum: Integer;	Pascal, Delphi
var sum;	Javascript

5.7   How to Declare Variables in Visual Basic

Visual Basic is a strongly typed programming language. This means that each variable must have a specific data type associated with it. For example, a variable can hold an integer, a real, or a character. In Visual Basic some of the primitive data types are: Boolean, Integer, Float, Double, Decimal, and Char. Which one to use depends on the given problem! To be more specific:

> type **Boolean** can hold only two possible values: that is, True or False
> type **Byte** can hold an unsigned integer between 0 and 255
> type **SByte** can hold a signed integer between -128 and +127.
> type **UShort** can hold an unsigned integer between 0 and +65535.
> type **Short** can hold a signed integer between -32768 and +32767
> type **UInteger** can hold an unsigned integer between 0 and $+2^{32} - 1$.
> type **Integer** can hold a signed integer between -2^{31} and $+2^{31} - 1$
> type **ULong** can hold an unsigned integer between 0 and $+2^{64} - 1$.
> type **Long** can hold a signed integer between -2^{63} and $+2^{63} - 1$
> type **Single** can hold a signed real of single precision
> type **Double** can hold a signed real of double precision
> type **Decimal** can hold a signed real of high precision (with 28-29 significant digits)
> type **Char** can hold a single character.

In many computer languages, there is one more variable type called "String", which can hold a sequence of characters. These sequences of characters, or "strings" are usually enclosed in double quotes, such as "Hello Zeus", "I am 25 years old", and so on. Visual Basic also supports strings, but keep in mind that a string in Visual Basic is not a primitive data type. Without going into detail, a string in Visual Basic is declared the same way as you declare a primitive data type such as Integer, Byte, or Double, but internally Visual Basic stores and handles them in a quite different way.

To declare a variable, the general form of the Visual Basic statement is

```
Dim name As type [ = value ]
```

where

> ➤ *type* can be Boolean, Byte, Short, Integer, String and so on
> ➤ *name* is a valid variable name
> ➤ *value* can be any valid initial value

Below are some examples of how to declare variables.

```
Dim number1 As Integer
Dim found As Boolean
Dim first_name As String
Dim student_name As String
```

In Visual Basic you can declare and directly assign an initial value to a variable. The next code fragment

```
Dim num As Integer = 5
Dim name As String = "Hera"
Dim favorite_character As Char = "w"
```

is equivalent to

```
Dim num As Integer
Dim name As String
Dim favorite_character As Char

num = 5
name = "Hera"
favorite_character = "w"
```

> **Notice:** *In Visual Basic, you can represent the action of assigning a value to a variable by using the equals (=) sign. This is equivalent to the left arrow in flowcharts.*
>
> **Notice:** *Please note that in Visual Basic you assign a value to a variable of type String or Char using double quotes (" ").*

Last but not least, you can declare many variables of the same type on one line by separating them with commas.

```
Dim a, b As Integer
Dim x, y, z As Double
```

5.8   How to Declare Constants in Visual Basic

You can declare constants in Visual Basic using the keyword Const.

```
Const name = value
```

The following examples show how to declare constants in Visual Basic.

```
Const VAT = 0.22
Const NUMBER_OF_PLAYERS = 25
Const FAVORITE_SONG = "We are the world"
Const FAVORITE_CHARACTER = "w"
```

Once a constant is defined, its value cannot be changed while the program is running.

5.9   Review Questions: True/False

Choose **true** or **false** for each of the following statements.

1. A variable is a location in the computer's secondary storage device.
2. For a value assignment operator in a flowchart, you can use either a left or a right arrow.
3. A variable can change its content while the program executes.
4. A constant can change its content while the program executes.
5. The value 10.0 is an integer.
6. A Boolean variable can hold only one of two values.
7. The value "10.0" enclosed in double quotes is a real value.
8. In computer science, a string is something that you can wear.
9. The name of a variable can contain numbers.
10. A variable can change its name while the program executes.
11. The name of a variable cannot be a number.
12. The name of a constant must always be a descriptive one.
13. The name `student name` is not a valid variable name.
14. The name `student_name` is a valid constant name.
15. The name of a constant can contain uppercase and lowercase letters.
16. In Visual Basic, there is no need to declare a variable.
17. In Visual Basic, you must always declare at least one constant.

5.10   Review Questions: Multiple Choice

Select the correct answer for each of the following statements.

1. A variable is a place in
    a. a hard disk.
    b. a DVD disc.
    c. a USB flash drive.
    d. all of the above
    e. none of the above
2. A variable can hold
    a. one value at a time.
    b. many values at a time.
    c. all of the above
    d. none of the above
3. Using constants in a Visual Basic program
    a. helps programmers to completely avoid typographical errors.
    b. helps programmers to avoid using division and multiplication.
    c. all of the above
    d. none of the above
4. Which of the following is an integer?
    a. 5.0

        b.   -5

        c.   "5"

        d.   none of the above is an integer.

5.   A Boolean variable can hold the value

        a.   one.

        b.   "True".

        c.   `True`.

        d.   none of the above

6.   In Visual Basic, strings are

        a.   enclosed in single quotes.

        b.   enclosed in double quotes.

        c.   both of the above

7.   Which of the following is **not** a valid Visual Basic variable?

        a.   `city_name`

        b.   `cityName`

        c.   `cityname`

        d.   `city-name`

8.   You can define a constant by using the keyword `Const`. Once a constant is defined,

        a.   it can never be changed.

        b.   it can be changed using the keyword `Const` again.

        c.   Both of the above are correct.

5.11   Review Exercises

Complete the following exercises.

1.   Match each element from the first column with one element from the second column.

Value		Data Type	
1.	"True"	a.	Boolean
2.	123	b.	Real
3.	False	c.	String
4.	10.0	d.	Integer

2.   Match each element from the first column with one element from the second column.

Value		Data Type	
1.	The name of a person	e.	Boolean
2.	The age of a person	f.	Real
3.	The result of the division 5/2	g.	Integer
4.	Is it black or is it white?	h.	String

Chapter 6
Handling Input and Output

6.1 Which Statement Outputs Messages and Results on a User's Screen?

A flowchart uses the oblique parallelogram and the reserved word "Write" to display a message or the final results to the user's screen.

where *arg1*, *arg2*, and *arg3* can be variables, expressions, or even strings enclosed in double quotes.

The oblique parallelogram that you have just seen is equivalent to

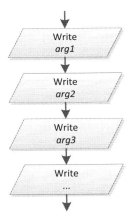

In Visual Basic, you can achieve the same result by using the statement

```
Console.Write(arg1 & arg2 & arg3 & … )
```

or the equivalent sequence of statements.

```
Console.Write(arg1)
Console.Write(arg2)
Console.Write(arg3)
…
```

> **Remember!** *If you want to display a string on the screen, the string must be enclosed in double quotes.*

The following Visual Basic program:

```
Sub Main()
  Dim a As Integer

  a = 5 + 6
  Console.Write("The sum of 5 and 6 is " & a)

  Console.ReadKey()
End Sub
```

displays the message shown in **Figure 6–1**.

The sum of 5 and 6 is 11

Figure 6–1 A string displayed on the screen

> ***Notice****: Please note the space inserted at the end of the first string in Visual Basic, just after the word "is." If you remove it, the number 11 will get too close to the last word and the output on the screen will be*
>
> *The sum of 5 and 6 is11*

You can also calculate the result of a mathematical expression directly in a Console.Write statement. The following statement:

```
Sub Main()
  Console.Write("The sum of 5 and 6 is " & (5 + 6))

  Console.ReadKey()
End Sub
```

displays exactly the same message as the statements in **Figure 6–1**.

6.2   How to Output Special Characters

Look carefully at the following example:

```
Sub Main()
  Console.Write("Morning")
  Console.Write("Evening")
  Console.Write("Night")

  Console.ReadKey()
End Sub
```

Although you may believe that these three messages are displayed one under the other, the actual output result is shown in **Figure 6–2**.

Figure 6-2 The output result displays on one line

In order to output a "line break" you must put the built-in constant `vbCrLf` after every string.

```
Sub Main()
   Console.Write("Morning" & vbCrLf)
   Console.Write("Evening" & vbCrLf)
   Console.Write("Night" & vbCrLf)

   Console.ReadKey()
End Sub
```

or use the `Console.WriteLine()` statement as follows

```
Sub Main()
   Console.WriteLine("Morning")
   Console.WriteLine("Evening")
   Console.WriteLine("Night")

   Console.ReadKey()
End Sub
```

The output result now appears in **Figure 6-3**.

Figure 6-3 The output result now displays line breaks

Keep in mind that the same result can also be accomplished with one single statement.

```
Console.Write("Morning" & vbCrLf & "Evening" & vbCrLf & "Night")
```

Another interesting built-in constant is the `vbTab` which can be used to output a "tab stop." The tab character is useful for aligning output.

```
Sub Main()
   Console.Write("John" & vbTab)
   Console.Write("George" & vbCrLf)
```

```
    Console.Write("Sofia" & vbTab)
    Console.Write("Mary")

    Console.ReadKey()
End Sub
```

The output result now appears in **Figure 6-4**.

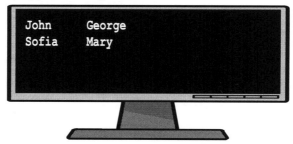

Figure 6-4 The output result now displays tabs

Of course, the same result can be accomplished with one single statement.

```
Console.Write("John" & vbTab & "George" & vbCrLf & "Sofia" & vbTab & "Mary")
```

6.3   Which Statement Lets the User Enter Data?

Do you recall the three main stages involved in creating an algorithm or a computer program? The first stage was the "data input" stage, in which the computer lets the user enter data such as numbers, their name, their address, or their year of birth.

A flowchart uses the oblique parallelogram and the reserved word "Read" to let a user enter his or her data.

where *var_name1*, *var_name2*, and *var_name3* must be variables only.

The oblique parallelogram that you have just seen is equivalent to

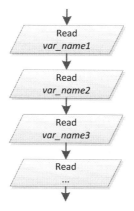

> **Notice:** When a Read statement is executed, the flow of execution is interrupted until the user has entered all the data. When data entry is complete, the flow of execution continues to the next statement. Usually data are entered from a keyboard.

In Visual Basic, data input is accomplished using the following Visual Basic statements

```
Dim var_name_str As String
Dim var_name_short As Short
Dim var_name_int As Integer
Dim var_name_long As Long
Dim var_name_dbl As Double

'Read a string from the keyboard
var_name_str = Console.ReadLine()

'Read a short integer from the keyboard
var_name_short = Console.ReadLine()

'Read an integer from the keyboard
var_name_int = Console.ReadLine()

'Read a long integer from the keyboard
var_name_long = Console.ReadLine()

'Read a real from the keyboard
var_name_dbl = Console.ReadLine()
```

where

➤ var_name_str can be any variable of type String.

➤ var_name_short can be any variable of type Short.

➤ var_name_int can be any variable of type Integer.

➤ var_name_long can be any variable of type Long.

➤ var_name_dbl can be any variable of type Double.

The following code fragment lets the user enter his or her name and age.

```
Dim name As String
Dim age As Byte

name = Console.ReadLine()
age = Console.ReadLine()
Console.Write("Wow, you are already" & age & "years old," & name & "!")
```

However, it could be even better if, before each data input, a "prompt" message is displayed. This makes the program more user-friendly. For example, look at the following program.

```
Dim name As String
Dim age As Byte

Console.Write("What is your name? ")
name = Console.ReadLine()
```

```
Console.Write("What is your age? ")
age = Console.ReadLine()

Console.Write("Wow, you are already" & age & "years old," & name & "!")
```

The corresponding flowchart fragment looks like this.

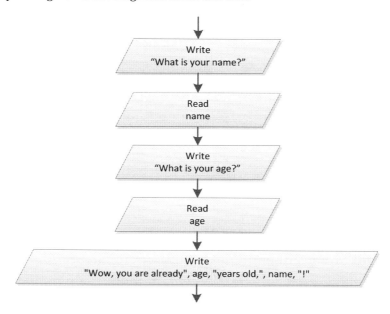

Now when a user executes your program he or she knows exactly what to enter.

> **Notice**: *In this book there is a subtle difference between the words "prompts" and "lets." When the wording of an exercise says "Write a Visual Basic program that **prompts** the user to enter..." this means that you must include a prompt message before every data input. On the other hand, when the wording of an exercise says "Write a Visual Basic program that **lets** the user enter..." this means that you are not actually required to include a prompt message; that is, it is not wrong to include one but you don't have to!*

6.4   Review Questions: True/False

Choose **true** or **false** for each of the following statements.

1. In Visual Basic, the word `Console` is a reserved word.

2. The `Console.WriteLine` statement can be used to display a message or the content of a variable.

3. When the `Console.ReadLine()` statement is executed, the flow of execution is interrupted until the user has entered a value.

4. One single statement, `Console.ReadLine()`, can be used to enter multiple data values.

5. Before data input, a prompt message must always be displayed.

6.5   Review Questions: Multiple Choice

Select the correct answer for each of the following statements.

1.   The statement `Console.Write("Hello")` displays

    a.   the word `Hello` (without the double quotes).

    b.   the word `"Hello"` (including the double quotes).

    c.   the content of the variable `Hello`.

    d.   none of the above

2.   The statement `Console.Write("Hello" & vbCrLf & "Hermes")` displays

    a.   the message `Hello Hermes`.

    b.   the word `Hello` in one line and the word `Hermes` in the next one.

    c.   the message `HelloHermes`.

    d.   the message `HellovbCrLfHermes`.

    e.   none of the above

3.   The statement `data1_data2 = Console.ReadLine()`

    a.   lets the user enter a value and assigns it to variable `data1`. Variable `data2` remains empty.

    b.   lets the user enter a value and assigns it to variable `data1_data2`.

    c.   lets the user enter two values and assigns them to variables `data1` and `data2`.

    d.   none of the above

Chapter 7
Operators

7.1 The Value Assignment Operator

The most commonly used operator in Visual Basic is the value assignment operator (=). For example, the Visual Basic statement

```
x = 5
```

assigns a value of 5 to variable x.

As you read in Chapter 5, this is equivalent to the left arrow used in flowcharts.

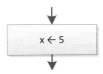

Probably the left arrow used in a flowchart is more convenient and clearer than the value assignment operator (=) sign because it shows in a more graphical way that the value or the result of an expression on the right is assigned to a variable on the left.

Be careful! The (=) sign is not equivalent to the one used in mathematics. In mathematics, the expression x = 5 is read as "x is equal to 5." However, in Visual Basic the expression x = 5 is read as "assign the value 5 to x" or "set x equal to 5." They look the same but they act differently!

In mathematics, the following two lines are equivalent:

```
x = y + z
y + z = x
```

The first one can be read as "x is equal to the sum of y and z" and the second one as "the sum of y and z is equal to x."

On the other hand, in Visual Basic, the following two statements are definitely **not** equivalent. In fact, the second one is considered wrong!

```
x = y + z
y + z = x
```

The first statement seems quite correct. It can be read as "*Set x equal to the sum of y and z*" or "*Assign the sum of y and z to x.*"

But what about the second one? Think! Is it possible to assign the value of x to y + z? The answer is obviously a big "NO!"

> **Remember!** *In Visual Basic, the variable on the left side of the (=) sign represents a region in main memory (RAM) where a value can be stored. Thus, on the left side only one single variable must exist! However, on the right side there can be a number, a variable, a string, or even a complex mathematical expression.*

In **Table 7–1** you can find some examples of value assignments.

Table 7-1 Examples of Value Assignments

`a = 9`	Assign a value of 9 to variable a.
`b = c`	Assign the content of variable c to variable b.
`d = "Hello Zeus"`	Assign the string *Hello Zeus* to variable d.
`d = a + b`	Calculate the sum of the contents of variables a and b and assign the result to variable d.
`b = a + 1`	Calculate the sum of the content of variable a and 1 and assign the result to variable b. Please note that the content of variable a is not altered.
`a = a + 1`	Calculate the sum of the content of variable a and 1 and assign the result back to variable a. In other words, increase variable a by one.

Confused about the last one? Are you thinking about your math teacher right now? What would he/she say if you had written a = a + 1 on the blackboard? Can you personally think of a number that is equal to the number itself plus one? Are you nuts? This means that 5 is equal to 6 and 10 is equal to 11!

Obviously, things are different in computer science. The statement a = a + 1 is absolutely acceptable! It instructs the CPU to retrieve the value of variable a from main memory (RAM), to increase the value by one, and to assign the result back to variable a. The old value of variable a is replaced by the new one.

Still don't get it? Let's take a look at how the CPU and main memory (RAM) cooperate with each other in order to execute the statement A ← A + 1 (this is the same as the statement a = a + 1 in Visual Basic).

Let's say that there is a region in memory, named A and it contains the number 13

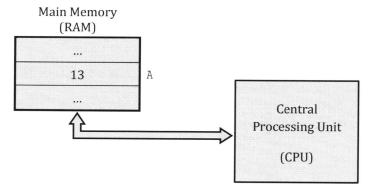

When a program instructs the CPU to execute the statement

$$A \leftarrow A + 1$$

the following procedure is executed:

 ➢ the number 13 is transferred from the RAM's region named A to the CPU;

 ➢ the CPU calculates the sum of 13 and 1; and

 ➢ the result, 14, is transferred from the CPU to the RAM's region named A replacing the existing number, 13.

After execution, the RAM looks like this.

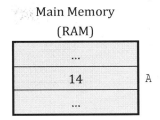

Main Memory
(RAM)

7.2 Arithmetic Operators

Just like every high-level programming language, Visual Basic supports almost all types of arithmetic operators.

Arithmetic Operator	Description
+	Addition
-	Subtraction
*	Multiplication
/	Division
\	Quotient after integer division
Mod	Remainder after integer division (Modulus)
^	Exponentiation

The first four operators are straightforward and need no further explanation.

The integer division operator (\ ) returns the quotient of an integer division, which means that

```
a = 13 \ 3
```

assigns a value of 4 to variable a.

The (\ ) operator can be used with floating-point numbers as well. For example, the operation

```
b = 14.4 \ 3
```

assigns a value of 4 to variable b.

Correspondingly, the modulus operator (Mod) returns the remainder of an integer division, which means that

```
c = 13 Mod 3
```

assigns a value of 1 to variable c.

The modulus operator (Mod) can be used with floating-point numbers as well, but the result is a real. For example, the operation

```
d = 14.4 Mod 3
```

assigns a value of 2.4 (and not 2, as you may mistakenly expect) to variable d.

The exponentiation operator (^) raises the number on the left of the operator to the power of the number on the right. For example, the operation

```
f = 2 ^ 3
```

assigns a value of 8 to variable f.

> **Notice:** *The exponentiation operator (^) can be used to calculate the square root of a number as well. It is known from mathematics that $\sqrt[z]{X}=X^{\frac{1}{z}}$. So, you can write* y = x ^ (1/2) *to calculate the square root of* x *or you can even write* y = x ^ (1/3) *to calculate the cube root of* x, *and so on!*

In mathematics, as you already know, you are allowed to use parentheses as well as braces and brackets.

$$y = \frac{5}{2}\left\{3 + 2\left[4 + 7\left(7 - \frac{4}{3}\right)\right]\right\}$$

However, in Visual Basic there is no such thing as braces and brackets. Parentheses are all you have; therefore, the same expression should be written using parentheses instead of braces or brackets.

```
y = 5 / 2 * (3 + 2 * (4 + 7 * (7 - 4 / 3)))
```

One other thing that is legal in mathematics but not in Visual Basic is that you can skip the multiplication operator and write 3x, meaning *"3 times x."* In Visual Basic, however, you must always use an asterisk anywhere a multiplication operation exists. This is one of the most common mistakes novice programmers make when they write mathematical expressions in Visual Basic.

7.3   What is the Precedence of Arithmetic Operators?

Arithmetic operators follow the same precedence rules as in mathematics, and these are: exponentiation is performed first, multiplication and division are performed next, and addition and subtraction are performed last.

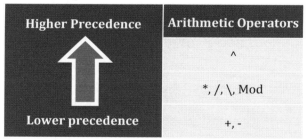

Higher Precedence	Arithmetic Operators
⬆	^
	*, /, \, Mod
Lower precedence	+, -

When multiplication and division exist in the same expression, and since both are of the same precedence, they are performed left to right (the same way as you read), which means that the expression

```
y = 6 / 3 * 2
```

is equivalent to $y = \frac{6}{3} \cdot 2$, and assigns a value of 4 to variable y, (division is performed before multiplication).

If you want, however, the multiplication to be performed before the division, you can use parentheses to change the precedence, that is:

```
y = 6 / (3 * 2)
```

which is equivalent to $y = \frac{6}{3 \cdot 2}$

> **Notice:** *Visual Basic programs can be written using your computer's text editor application, but keep in mind that it is not possible to write fractions in the form of $\frac{6}{3}$ or $\frac{4x+5}{6}$. Forget it! There is no equation editor in a text editor! All fractions must be written on one single line. For example, $\frac{6}{3}$ should be written as 6 / 3, and $\frac{4x+5}{6}$ should be written as (4 * x + 5) / 6.*

The order of operations can be summarized as follows:

1. Any operations enclosed in parentheses are performed first.
2. Any exponentiations are performed next.
3. Then, any multiplication and division operations are performed from left to right.
4. In the end, any addition and subtraction operations are performed from left to right.

So, in statement `y = (20 + 3) + 12 + 2 ^ 3 / 4 * 3`

the operations are performed as follows:

1. 20 is added to 3, yielding a result of 23.
2. 2 is raised to the power of 3, yielding a result of 8.
3. 8 is divided by 4, yielding a result of 2. This result is then multiplied by 3, yielding a result of 6.
4. 23 is added to 12, yielding a result of 35. This result is then added to 6, yielding a final result of 41.

Next is the same sequence of operations presented in a more graphical way.

```
(20 + 3) + 12 + 2 ^ 3 / 4 * 3
    |
    v
(20 + 3) + 12 + 2 ^ 3 / 4 * 3
                  |
                  v
      23  +  12 + 8 / 4 * 3
                    |
                    v
      23  +  12  +  2  *  3
                       |
                       v
      23  +  12   +    6
          |
          v
         35     +     6
          |
          v
         41
```

7.4 Compound Assignment Operators

Visual Basic offers a special set of operators known as compound assignment operators, which can help you write code faster.

Operator	Description	Example	Equivalent to
+=	Addition assignment	a += b	a = a + b
-=	Subtraction assignment	a -= b	a = a - b
*=	Multiplication assignment	a *= b	a = a * b
/=	Division assignment	a /= b	a = a / b
\=	Integer division assignment	a \= b	a = a \ b
^=	Exponentiation assignment	a ^= b	a = a ^ b

Looking at the *"Equivalent to"* column, it becomes clear that same result can be achieved by just using the classic assignment (=) operator. So the question that arises here is *why do these operators exist?*

The answer is simple: It's a matter of convenience. Once you start using them, your life finds a different meaning!

Notice: Please keep in mind that flowcharts are a loose method to represent an algorithm. Although the use of compound assignment operators is allowed in flowcharts, this book uses only the commonly accepted operators shown in the "Equivalent to" column. For example, the Visual Basic statement a += b *is represented in a flowchart as*

Exercise 7.4-1 *Which Visual Basic Statements are Syntactically Correct?*

Which of the following Visual Basic assignment statements are syntactically correct?

i.	a = -10	*v.*	a = COWS	*ix.*	a = True
ii.	10 = b	*vi.*	a + b = 40	*x.*	a \= 2
iii.	a_b = a_b + 1	*vii.*	a = 3 b	*xi.*	a += 1
iv.	a = "COWS"	*viii.*	a = "True"	*xii.*	a =* 2

Solution

i.   **Correct.** It assigns the integer value -10 to variable a.

ii. **Wrong.** On the left side of the assignment operator, only variables can exist.

iii. **Correct.** It increases variable a_b by one.

iv. **Correct.** It assigns the string (the text) COWS to variable a.

v.   **Correct.** It assigns the content of constant COWS to variable a.

vi. **Wrong.** On the left side of the assignment operator, only one variable can exist.

vii. **Wrong.** It should have been written as a = 3 * b.

viii. **Correct.** It assigns the string True to variable a.

ix. **Correct.** It assigns the value True to variable a.

x. **Correct**. This is equivalent to a = a \ 2.

xi. **Correct**. This is equivalent to a = a + 1

xii. **Wrong**. It should have been written as a *= 2 (which is equivalent to a = a * 2)

Exercise 7.4-2   *Finding Variable Types*

What is the type of each of the following variables?

i. a = 15	iii. b = "15"	v. b = True
ii. width = "10 meters"	iv. temp = 13.5	vi. b = "True"

Solution

i. The value 15 belongs to the set of integers, thus the variable a is an integer.

ii. The "*10 meters*" is text, thus the width variable is a string.

iii. The "15" is text string, thus the b variable is a string.

iv. The value 13.5 belongs to the set of real numbers, thus the variable temp is real.

v. The value True is Boolean, thus variable b is a Boolean.

vi. The value True is a text, thus variable b is a string.

7.5   String Operators

There are two operators that can be used to concatenate (join) strings.

Operator	Description	Example	Equivalent to
&	Concatenation	a = "Hi" & " there"	
&=	Concatenation assignment	a &= "Hello"	a = a & "Hello"

> **Notice**: *Joining two separate strings into a single one is called "concatenation."*

The following example displays "What's up, dude?"

```
Sub Main()
  Dim a, b, c As String

  a = "What's "
  b = "up, "
  c = a + b
  c &= "dude?"

  Console.Write(c)

  Console.ReadKey()
End Sub
```

Exercise 7.5-1   *Concatenating Names*

Write a Visual Basic program that prompts the user to enter his or her first and last name (assigned to two different variables) and then joins them together in a single string (concatenation).

Solution

The Visual Basic program is shown here.

```
Sub Main()
  Dim first_name, last_name, full_name As String

  Console.Write("Enter first name: ")
  first_name = Console.ReadLine()
  Console.Write("Enter last name: ")
  last_name = Console.ReadLine()

  full_name = first_name + " " + last_name
  Console.Write(full_name)

  Console.ReadKey()
End Sub
```

Notice: *Please note the extra space character added between the first and last name*

7.6 Review Questions: True/False

Choose **true** or **false** for each of the following statements.

1. The statement x = 5 can be read as *"Variable x is equal to 5."*
2. The value assignment operator assigns the result of an expression to a variable.
3. A string can be assigned to a variable only by using the Console.ReadLine() statement.
4. The statement 5 = y assigns value 5 to variable y.
5. On the right side of a value assignment operator an arithmetic operator must always exist.
6. On the left side of a value assignment operator more than one variable can exist.
7. You cannot use the same variable on both sides of a value assignment operator.
8. The statement a = a + 1 decrements variable a by one.
9. In Visual Basic, the word Modulus is a reserved word.
10. The statement x = 0 Mod 5 assigns a value of 5 to variable x.
11. The operation 5 Mod 0 is not possible.
12. Division and multiplication have the higher precedence among the arithmetic operators.
13. When division and multiplication operators co-exist in an expression, multiplication operations are performed before division.
14. The expression 8 / 4 * 2 is equal to 1.
15. The expression 4 + 6 / 6 + 4 is equal to 9.
16. The expression a + b + c / 3 calculates the average value of three numbers.
17. The statement a += 1 is equivalent to a = a + 1.
18. The statement a = "True" assigns a Boolean value to variable a.
19. The statement a = 2·a doubles the content of variable a.

20. The statements a += 2 and a = a - (-2) are not equivalent.

21. The statement a -= a + 1 always assigns a value of -1 to variable a.

22. The statement a = "George" & " Malkovich" assigns value GeorgeMalkovich to variable a.

23. The following code fragment satisfies the property of definiteness.

```
Dim a, b As Integer
Dim x As Double
a = Console.ReadLine()
b = Console.ReadLine()
x = a / (b - 7)
Console.WriteLine(x)
```

7.7   Review Questions: Multiple Choice

Select the correct answer for each of the following statements.

1. Which of the following Visual Basic statements assigns a value of 10 to variable a?

     a.   10 = a

     b.   a ← 10

     c.   a = 100 / 10

     d.   none of the above

2. The statement a = b can be read as

     a.   assign the content of variable a to variable b.

     b.   variable b is equal to variable a.

     c.   assign the content of variable b to variable a.

     d.   none of the above

3. The expression 0 Mod 10 + 2 is equal to

     a.   7.

     b.   2.

     c.   12.

     d.   none of the above

4. Which of the following Visual Basic statements is syntactically correct?

     a.   a = 4 * 2 y - 8 / (4 * q)

     b.   a = 4 * 2 * y - 8 / 4 * q)

     c.   a = 4 * 2 * y - 8 / (4 */ q)

     d.   none of the above

5. Which of the following Visual Basic statements is syntactically correct?

     a.   a ^ 5 = b

     b.   b = a ^ 5

     c.   a =^ 5

6. Which of the following Visual Basic statements assigns value `George Malkovich` to variable `a`?

    a. `a = "George" & " " & "Malkovich"`

    b. `a = "George" & " Malkovich"`

    c. `a = "George " & "Malkovich"`

    d. all of the above

7. The following code fragment

```
x = 2
x += 1
```

does **not** satisfy the property of

    a. finiteness.

    b. definiteness.

    c. effectiveness.

    d. none of the above

8. The following code fragment

```
Dim a As Integer
Dim x As Double

a = Console.ReadLine()
x = 1 / a
```

does **not** satisfy the property of

    a. finiteness.

    b. input.

    c. effectiveness.

    d. none of the above

7.8 Review Exercises

Complete the following exercises.

1. Which of the following Visual Basic assignment statements are syntactically correct?

i.	`a ← a + 1`	vi.	`a = 40"`
ii.	`a += b`	vii.	`a = b · 5`
iii.	`a b = a b + 1`	viii.	`a =& "True"`
iv.	`a = a + 1`	ix.	`fdadstwsdgfgw = 1`
v.	`a = hello`	x.	`a = a**5`

2. What is the type of each of the following variables?

i.	`a = "False"`	iii.	`b = "15 meters"`	v.	`b = 13.0`
ii.	`w = False`	iv.	`weight = "40"`	vi.	`b = 13`

3. Match each element from the first column with one element from the second column.

Operation		Result	
i.	1 / 2	a.	100
ii.	1 / 2 * 2	b.	0.25
iii.	0 Mod 10 * 10	c.	0
iv.	10 Mod 2 + 7	d.	0.5
		e.	7
		f.	1

4. What displays on the screen after executing each of the following code fragments?

i.
```
a = 5
b = a * a + 1
Console.WriteLine(b + 1)
```

ii.
```
a = 9
b = a / 3 * a
Console.WriteLine(b + 1)
```

5. What displays on the screen after executing each of the following code fragments?

i.
```
a = 5
a += a - 5
Console.WriteLine(a)
```

ii.
```
a = 5
a = a + 1
Console.WriteLine(a)
```

6. What is the result of each of the following operations?

i. 21 Mod 5

ii. 10 Mod 2

iii. 11 Mod 2

iv. 10 Mod 6 Mod 3

v. 0 Mod 3

vi. 100 / 10 Mod 3

7. What displays on screen after executing each of the following code fragments?

i.
```
a = 5
b = 2
c = a Mod (b + 1)
d = (b + 1) Mod (a + b)
Console.WriteLine(c & "*" & d)
```

ii.
```
a = 0.4
b = 8
a += 0.1
c = a * b Mod b
Console.WriteLine(c)
```

8. Calculate the result of the expression a Mod b for the following cases.

i. a = 20, b = 3

ii. a = 15, b = 3

iii. a = 22, b = 3

iv. a = 0, b = 3

v. a = 3, b = 0

vi. a = 2, b = 2

9. Calculate the result of the expression

$$b * (a \ Mod \ b) + a / b$$

for each of the following cases.

i. a = 10, b = 5

ii. a = 10, b = 4

10. What displays on the screen after executing the following code fragment?

```
a = "My name is"
a &= " "
```

```
a = a & "George Malkovich"
Console.WriteLine(a)
```

11. Fill in the gaps in each of the following code fragments so that they display a value of 5.

i.
```
a = 2
a = a - ......
Console.WriteLine(a)
```

ii.
```
a = 4
b = a * 0.5
b += a
a = b - ......
Console.WriteLine(a)
```

12. What displays on the screen after executing the following code fragment?

```
city = "California"
California = city
Console.WriteLine(city & ", " & California)
```

Chapter 8
Trace Tables

8.1   What is a Trace Table?

A trace table is a technique used to test algorithms or computer programs for logic errors that occur while the algorithm or program executes.

The trace table simulates the flow of execution. Statements are executed step by step, and the values of variables change as an assignment statement is executed.

Trace tables are typically used by novice programmers to help them visualize how a particular algorithm or program works. Trace tables can also help advanced programmers detect logic errors.

A typical trace table is shown here.

Step	Statement	Notes	variable1	variable2	variable3
1					
2					
...					

Let's see a trace table in action! For the following Visual Basic program, a trace table is created to determine the values of the variables in each step.

```vb
Sub Main()
  Dim x, y, z As Integer

  x = 10
  y = 15
  z = x * y
  z += 1
  Console.Write(z)

  Console.ReadKey()
End Sub
```

The trace table for this program is shown below. Notes are optional, but they help the reader to better understand what is really happening.

Step	Statement	Notes	x	y	z
1	x = 10	The value 10 is assigned to variable x.	10	?	?
2	y = 15	The value 15 is assigned to variable y.	10	15	?
3	z = x * y	The result of the product x * y is assigned to z.	10	15	150
4	z += 1	Variable z is incremented by one.	10	15	151
5	Console.Write(z)	The value 151 is displayed.			

Exercise 8.1-1　　*Creating a Trace Table*

What result is displayed when the following program is executed?

```vb
Sub Main()
    Dim Ugly, Beautiful, Handsome As String

    Ugly = "Beautiful"
    Beautiful = "Ugly"
    Handsome = Ugly

    Console.Write("Beautiful")
    Console.Write(Ugly)
    Console.Write(Handsome)

    Console.ReadKey()
End Sub
```

Solution

Let's create a trace table to find the output result.

Step	Statement	Notes	Ugly	Beautiful	Handsome
1	Ugly = "Beautiful"	The string "Beautiful" is assigned to the variable Ugly.	**Beautiful**	?	?
2	Beautiful = "Ugly"	The string "Ugly" is assigned to the variable Beautiful.	Beautiful	**Ugly**	?
3	Handsome = Ugly	The value of variable Ugly is assigned to the variable Handsome.	Beautiful	Ugly	**Beautiful**
4	Console.Write("Beautiful")	The string "Beautiful" is displayed.			
5	Console.Write(Ugly)	The string "Beautiful" is displayed.			
6	Console.Write(Handsome)	The string "Beautiful" is displayed.			

Exercise 8.1-2　　*Swapping Values of Variables*

Write a Visual Basic program that lets the user enter two values, in variables a and b. At the end of the program, the two variables should swap their values. For example, if variables a and b contain the values 5 and 7 respectively, after swapping their values, variable a should contain the value 7 and variable b should contain the value 5!

Solution

The following program, even though it may seem correct, is erroneous and doesn't really swap the values of variables a and b!

```
Sub Main()
  Dim a, b As Integer

  a = Console.ReadLine()
  b = Console.ReadLine()

  a = b
  b = a

  Console.WriteLine(a)
  Console.WriteLine(b)

  Console.ReadKey()
End Sub
```

Let's see why! Suppose the user enters two values, 5 and 7. The trace table is shown here.

Step	Statement	Notes	a	b
1	a = Console.ReadLine()	User enters the value 5	5	?
2	b = Console.ReadLine()	User enters the value 7	5	7
3	a = b	The value of variable b is assigned to variable a. Value 5 is lost!	7	7
4	b = a	The value of variable a is assigned to variable b	7	7
5	Console.WriteLine(a)	The value 7 is displayed		
6	Console.WriteLine(b)	The value 7 is displayed		

Oops! Where is the value 5?

The solution wasn't so obvious after all! So, how do you really swap values anyway?

Consider two glasses: a glass of orange juice (called glass A), and a glass of lemon juice (called glass B). If you want to swap their content, all you must do is find and use one extra empty glass (called glass C).

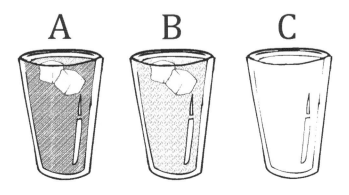

The steps that must be followed are:

  1.   Empty the contents of glass A (orange juice) into glass C.

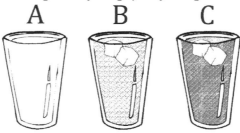

  2.   Empty the contents of glass B (lemon juice) into glass A.

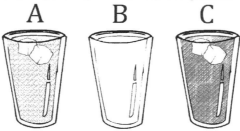

  3.   Empty the contents of glass C (orange juice) into glass B.

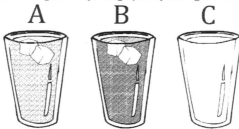

Swapping completed successfully!

You can follow the same steps to swap the contents of two variables in Visual Basic.

```
Sub Main()
  Dim a, b, c As Integer

  a = Console.ReadLine()
  b = Console.ReadLine()

  c = a    'Empty the contents of glass A (orange juice) into glass C
  a = b    'Empty the contents of glass B (lemon juice) into glass A
  b = c    'Empty the contents of glass C (orange juice) into glass B

  Console.WriteLine(a)
  Console.WriteLine(b)

  Console.ReadKey()
End Sub
```

> **Notice:** Please note the apostrophe characters (') after each of the three assignment statements. The text after apostrophe character is considered a comment and is never executed.

Exercise 8.1-3   *Swapping Values of Variables – A Second Approach*

Write a Visual Basic program that lets the user enter two numeric values, in variables a and b. In the end, the two variables should swap their values.

Solution

Since the variables contain only numeric values, you can use the following Visual Basic program.

```
Sub Main()
    Dim a, b As Integer

    a = Console.ReadLine()
    b = Console.ReadLine()

    a = a + b
    b = a - b
    a = a - b

    Console.WriteLine(a)
    Console.WriteLine(b)

    Console.ReadKey()
End Sub
```

> **Notice:** Compared to previous exercise, the only major disadvantage of this method is that it cannot swap the contents of alphanumeric variables (strings).

Exercise 8.1-4   *Creating a Trace Table*

Create a trace table to determine the values of the variables in each step of the Visual Basic program for three different executions.

The input values for the three executions are: (i) 0.3, (ii) 4.5, and (iii) 10.

```
Sub Main()
    Dim a, b, c As Double

    b = Console.ReadLine()
    c = 3
    c = c * b
    a = 10 * c Mod 10

    Console.Write(a)

    Console.ReadKey()
End SubSolution
```

i. For the input value of 0.3, the trace table looks like this.

Step	Statement	Notes	a	b	c
1	b = Console.ReadLine()	User enters value 0.3	?	0.3	?
2	c = 3		?	0.3	3
3	c = c * b		?	0.3	0.9
4	a = 10 * c Mod 10		9	0.3	0.9
5	Console.Write(a)	The value 9 is displayed			

ii. For the input value of 4.5, the trace table looks like this.

Step	Statement	Notes	a	b	c
1	b = Console.ReadLine()	User enters value 4.5	?	4.5	?
2	c = 3		?	4.5	3
3	c = c * b		?	4.5	13.5
4	a = 10 * c Mod 10		5	4.5	13.5
5	Console.Write(a)	The value 5 is displayed			

iii. For the input value of 10, the trace table looks like this.

Step	Statement	Notes	a	b	c
1	b = Console.ReadLine()	User enters value 10	?	10	?
2	c = 3		?	10	3
3	c = c * b		?	10	30
4	a = 10 * c Mod 10		0	10	30
5	Console.Write(a)	The value 0 is displayed			

Exercise 8.1-5   *Creating a Trace Table*

Create a trace table to determine the values of the variables in each step when a value of 3 is entered.

```
Sub Main()
    Dim a, b, c, d As Double

    a = Console.ReadLine()

    b = a + 10
    a = b * (a - 3)
    c = 3 * b / 6
    d = c * c
    d -= 1
```

```
    Console.Write(d)

    Console.ReadKey()
End Sub
```

Solution

For the input value of 3, the trace table looks like this.

Step	Statement	Notes	a	b	c	d
1	a = Console.ReadLine()	User enters value 3	3	?	?	?
2	b = a + 10		3	13	?	?
3	a = b * (a - 3)		0	13	?	?
4	c = 3 * b / 6		0	13	6.5	?
5	d = c * c		0	13	6.5	42.25
6	d -= 1		0	13	6.5	41.25
7	Console.Write(d)	The value 41.25 is displayed				

8.2   Review Questions: True/False

Choose **true** or **false** for each of the following statements.

1. A trace table is a technique for testing a computer.
2. Trace tables help a programmer find errors in a computer program.
3. You cannot write a computer program without first creating its corresponding trace table.
4. In order to swap the values of two integer variables, you always need an extra variable.

8.3   Review Exercises

Complete the following exercises.

1. Create a trace table to determine the values of the variables in each step of the Visual Basic program for three different executions.

   The input values for the three executions are: (i) 3, (ii) 4, and (iii) 1.

```
Sub Main()
    Dim a, b, c, d As Integer

    a = Console.ReadLine()

    a = (a + 1) * (a + 1) + 6 / 3 * 2 + 20
    b = a Mod 13
    c = b Mod 7
    d = a * b * c
    Console.Write(a & ", " & b & ", " & c & ", " & d)

    Console.ReadKey()
End Sub
```

2. Create a trace table to determine the values of the variables in each step of the Visual Basic program for two different executions.

The input values for the two executions are: (i) 3, 4; and (ii) 4, 4

```
Sub Main()
  Dim a, b, c, d, e As Double

  a = Console.ReadLine()
  b = Console.ReadLine()

  c = a + b
  d = 1 + a / b * c + 2
  e = c + d
  c += d + e
  e -= 1
  d -= c + d Mod c
  Console.Write(c & ", " & d & ", " & e)

  Console.ReadKey()
End Sub
```

Chapter 9
Using Visual Studio

9.1   Creating a New Visual Basic Project

So far you have learned some really good basics about Visual Basic programs. Now it's time to learn how to enter programs into the computer, execute them, see how they perform, and see how they display the results.

The first thing you must do is create a new Visual Basic project. Visual Studio provides a wizard to help you do that. Start Visual Studio, and from its main menu select "FILE→New→ Project" as shown in **Figure 9–1**.

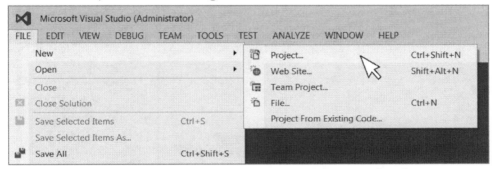

Figure 9–1 Starting a new Visual Basic project from Visual Studio

The "New Project" dialog box appears. In the left pane, select "Installed", and then click on the dropdown arrow to expand the "Visual Basic→Windows Desktop". From the middle pane, select "Console Application" as shown in **Figure 9–2**. In the "Name" field, type "testingProject" and click on the "OK" button.

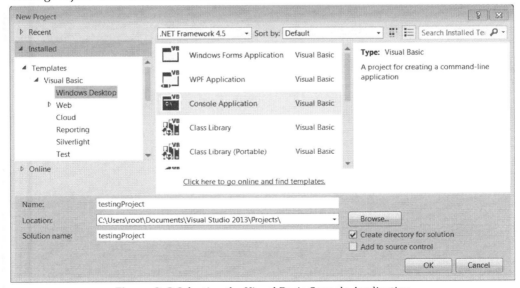

Figure 9–2 Selecting the Visual Basic Console Application

The project is created and opened in your Visual Studio environment. You should see the following components (see **Figure 9–3**):

- ➢ the "Solution Explorer" window, which contains a tree view of the components of the projects, including source files, libraries that your code may depend on, and so on.

- ➢ the "Source Editor" window with the file called "Module1.vb" open. In this file you can write your Visual Basic code. Of course, one single project can contain many such files.

- ➢ the "Output" window in which Visual Studio displays messages useful for the programmer.

- ➢ other windows such as the "Properties" window which are, however, not necessary for this book's purposes.

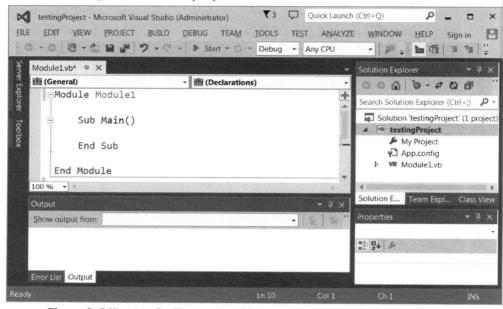

Figure 9–3 Viewing the "Projects" and "Source Editor" windows in Visual Studio

9.2   Writing and Executing a Visual Basic Program

You have just seen how to create a new Visual Basic project. Let's now write the following (terrifying, and quite horrifying!) Visual Basic program and try to execute it.

```
Module Module1

  Sub Main()
    Console.Write("Hello World")
    Console.ReadKey()
  End Sub

End Module
```

In the window "Module1.vb", place the cursor between the lines "Sub Main()" and "End Sub". Type only the first character, "C," from the Console statement by tapping the "C" key on your keyboard. A popup window appears, as shown in **Figure 9–4**. This window contains all available Visual Basic statements, and other items that begin with the character "C."

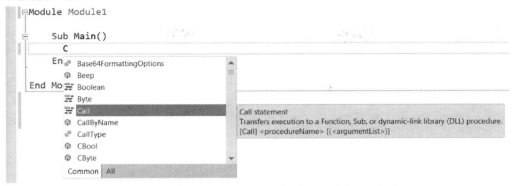

Figure 9–4 The popup screen in the Source Editor window

> **Notice**: *You can highlight a selection by using the up and down arrow keys on your keyboard.*

Type the second character, "o," from the Console statement. Now the options have become fewer, as shown here.

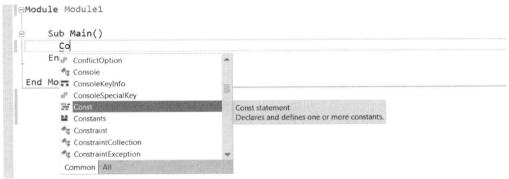

Select the option Console and hit the period "." key. The statement is automatically entered into your program, as shown next!

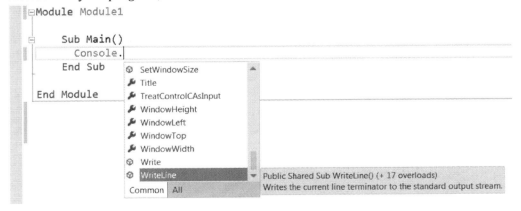

Complete the statement by writing `Console.Write("Hello  World")`. Then, continue typing the rest of the Visual Basic program (as shown in **Figure 9–5**). Your Visual Studio environment should look like this.

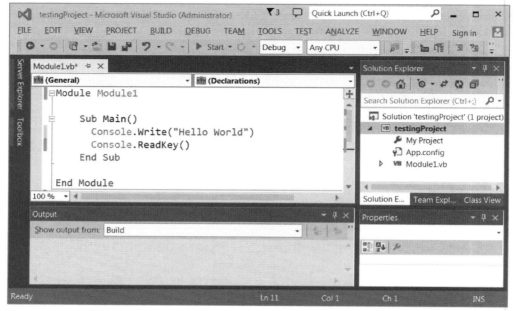

Figure 9–5 Entering a Visual Basic program in the "Program.cs" file

Now let's try to execute the program! From the toolbar, click on the "Start" ▶ toolbar icon. Alternatively, from the main menu, you can select "DEBUG→Start Debugging" or even hit the F5 key. The Visual Basic program executes and the output is displayed in the "Output" window as shown in **Figure 9–6**.

Figure 9–6 Viewing the results of the executed program in the Output window

Congratulations! You have just written and executed your first Visual Basic program!

Now let's write another Visual Basic program, one that prompts the user to enter his or her name. Type the following Visual Basic statements into Visual Studio and hit F5 to execute the project.

```
                              project_9_2
Module Module1
  Sub Main()
    Dim name As String

    Console.Write("Enter your name: ")
    name = Console.ReadLine()
    Console.WriteLine("Hello " & name)
```

```
    Console.ReadKey()
  End Sub
End Module
```

> **Remember**! You can execute a program by clicking on the "Start" ▶ button, or by selecting "DEBUG→Start Debugging" from the main menu, or even by hitting the F5 key.

Once you execute the program, the message "Enter your name" is displayed in the "Output" window. The program waits for you to enter your name, as shown in **Figure 9-7**.

Figure 9-7 Viewing a prompt in the Output window

Type your name and hit the "Enter ↵" key. Once you do that, your computer continues executing the rest of the statements. When execution finishes, the final output is as shown in **Figure 9-8**.

Figure 9-8 Responding to the prompt in the Output window

9.3   What "Debugging" Means

Debugging is the process of finding and reducing the number of defects (bugs) in a computer program, in order to make it perform as expected.

There is a myth about the origin of the term "debugging." In 1940, while Grace Hopper[1] was working on a Mark II Computer at Harvard University, her associates discovered a bug (a moth) stuck in a relay (an electrically operated switch). This bug was blocking the proper operation of the Mark II computer. So, while her associates where trying to remove the bug, Grace Hopper remarked that they were "debugging" the system!

9.4   Debugging Visual Basic Programs with Visual Studio

As you already know, when someone writes code in a high-level language there are two types of errors that he or she might make—syntax errors and logic errors. Visual Studio provides all the necessary tools to help you debug your programs and find the errors.

---

[1] Grace Murray Hopper (1906–1992) was an American computer scientist and US Navy admiral. She was one of the first programmers of the Harvard Mark I computer, and developed the first compiler for a computer programming language known as A–0 and later a second one, known as B–0 or FLOW-MATIC.

Debugging syntax errors

Fortunately, Visual Studio detects syntax errors while you are typing (or when you are trying to run the project) and underlines them with a wavy blue line as shown in **Figure 9-9.**

```
Sub Main()
    Dim a, b As Intager
    a = 5
    b = a + 10

    Console.ReadKey()
End Sub
```

Figure 9-9 In the Visual Studio, syntax errors are underlined with a wavy blue line

All you have to do is correct the corresponding error and the blue line will disappear at once. However, if you are not certain about what is wrong with your code, you can just place your mouse cursor on the erroneous line. Visual Studio will try to help you by showing a popup window with a brief explanation of the error, as shown in **Figure 9-10.**

```
Module Module1

    Sub Main()
        Dim a, b As Intager
        a = 5              Type 'Intager' is not defined.
        b = a + 10

        Console.ReadKey()
    End Sub

End Module
```

Figure 9-10 The Visual Studio shows an explanation of a syntax error

Moreover, if you click on the error icon ⊗, Visual Studio will try to help you by showing a list of possible solutions, as shown in **Figure 9-11.**

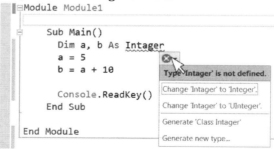

Figure 9-11 The Visual Studio shows a list of possible solutions

Debugging logic errors by executing programs step by step

Compared to syntax errors, logic errors are more difficult to find. Since the Visual Studio cannot spot and underline logic errors, you are all alone! Let's look at the following Visual Basic program, for example. It prompts the user to enter two numbers and calculates and displays their sum. However, it contains a logic error!

```
                           project_9_4a
Sub Main()
```

```
  Dim SI, a, b, Sl As Double

  SI = 0
  Console.Write("Enter 1st value: ")
  a = Console.ReadLine()
  Console.Write("Enter 2nd value: ")
  b = Console.ReadLine()
  Sl = a + b
  Console.Write("The sum is: " & SI)
  Console.ReadKey()
End Sub
```

If you type this program into Visual Studio, you will notice that there is not even one wavy blue line indicating any error. If you run the program, however, and enter two values, 5 and 3, you can see for yourself that even though the sum of 5 and 3 is 8, Visual Studio insists that it is zero, as shown in **Figure 9–12**.

Figure 9–12 Viewing the result of a logic error in the Output window

What the heck is going on? Of course for an expert programmer, correcting this error would be a piece of cake. But for you, a novice one, even though you are trying hard you find nothing wrong. So, where is the error?

Sometimes human eyes get so tired that they cannot see the obvious. So, let's try to use some magic! Let's try to execute the program step by step using the debugger. This gives you the opportunity to observe the flow of execution and take a closer look at the current values of variables in each step.

Start the debugger by selecting "DEBUG→Step Over" from the main menu or by hitting the F10 key. By doing this, you enable the debugger and more icons are displayed on the toolbar.

The program counter (the yellow arrow ⇨ icon in the gray margin) stops at the first line of the program as shown in **Figure 9–13**.

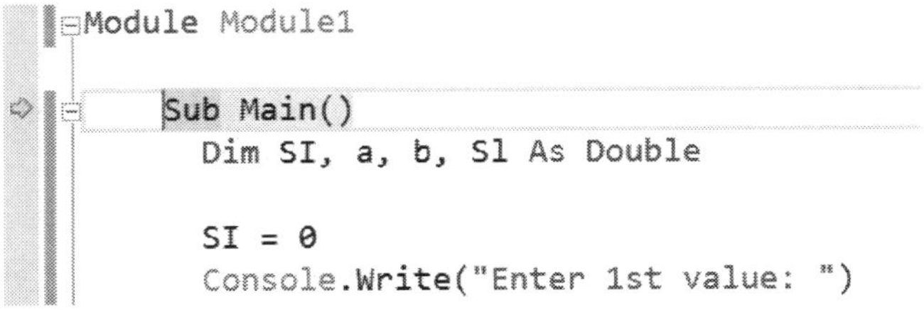

```
⊟Module Module1

⇨  ⊟   Sub Main()
          Dim SI, a, b, Sl As Double

          SI = 0
          Console.Write("Enter 1st value: ")
```

Figure 9–13 Using the debugger in the Visual Studio

Notice: *The program counter shows you, at any time, which statement is the next to be executed.*

Click on the "Step Over" ⬒ icon on the toolbar or hit the F10 key again. This action moves and places the program counter on the SI = 0 statement. In this step, the statement SI = 0 is not yet executed. Hit the F10 key again. Now the statement SI = 0 is executed, and the program counter moves to the subsequent Visual Basic statement, which is the next to be executed.

In the "Locals" window, you can watch all the variables declared in main memory (RAM) and the value they contain during each step of execution as shown in **Figure 9–14**.

Locals		▾ ♯ ×
Name	Value	Type
✷ a	0.0	Double
● b	0.0	Double
● SI	0.0	Double
● SI	0.0	Double
Autos Locals Watch 1		

Figure 9–14 Variables and their values are displayed in the Variables window of the debugger

Click on the "Step Over" ⬒ toolbar icon again. The second statement is executed. You can go back to the "Output" window and see the output result (see **Figure 9–15**).

Figure 9–15 Viewing a prompt in the Output window

Click on the "Step Over" ⬒ toolbar icon again. The third Visual Basic statement is executed and the program waits for you to enter a value. Place the cursor inside the "Output" window, type the value 5, and hit the "Enter ↵" key.

The program counter moves to the fourth Visual Basic statement. Click on the "Step Over" ⬒ toolbar icon twice. This action executes the fourth and fifth Visual Basic statements. Place the cursor inside the "Output" window, type the value 3, and hit the "Enter ↵" key.

The program counter moves to the sixth Visual Basic statement. Click on the "Step Over" ⬒ toolbar icon once again. The statement S1 = a + b is executed. What you expected here was the sum of 5.0 and 3.0, which is 8.0, to be assigned to variable SI. Instead of this, the value 8.0 is assigned to the variable S1, as shown in **Figure 9–16.**

Locals		▾ ♯ ×
Name	Value	Type
● a	5.0	Double
● b	3.0	Double
● SI	0.0	Double
● SI	8.0	Double
Autos Locals Watch 1		

Figure 9–16 All declared variables are displayed in the Locals window of the debugger

Now it becomes more obvious to you! You mistakenly declared two variables in the main memory (RAM), the variable SI and the variable S1. So, when the flow of execution goes to the last statement, Console.Write("The sum is: " + SI) the value 0 instead of the value 8 is displayed.

Congratulations! You have just found the error! Click on the "Stop Debugging" ■ toolbar icon to cancel execution, correct the error by changing variable S to s, and you are ready! You just performed your first debugging! Re-execute the program and you will now see that it calculates and displays the sum correctly.

Debugging logic errors by adding breakpoints

Debugging step by step has a big disadvantage. You have to click on the "Step Over" ↳ toolbar icon again and again until you reach the position where the error might be. Can you imagine yourself doing this in a large program?

For large programs there is another approach. If you suspect that the error is somewhere at the end of the program there is no need to debug all of it right from the beginning. You can add a marker (called a "breakpoint") where you think that the error might be, execute the program and when flow of execution reaches that breakpoint, the flow of execution will pause automatically. You can then take a closer look at the current values of the variables at the position where the program was paused.

> *Notice: When the program pauses, you have two options for resuming the execution: you can add a second breakpoint somewhere below in the program, click on the "Continue" ▶ toolbar icon, and allow the program to continue execution until that new breakpoint; or, you can just use the "Step Over" ↳ toolbar icon and execute the program step by step thereafter.*

The next Visual Basic program prompts the user to enter two values and calculates their average value.

However, the program contains a logic error. When the user enters the values 10 and 12, the value 16, instead of 11, is displayed.

```
                          project_9_4b
Sub Main()
   Dim a, b, average As Double

   Console.Write("Enter 1st value: ")
   a = Console.ReadLine()
   Console.Write("Enter 2nd value: ")
   b = Console.ReadLine()
   average = a + b / 2
   Console.Write("The average value is: " & average)
   Console.ReadKey()
End Sub
```

You suspect that the problem is somewhere at the end of the program. However, you do not want to debug the entire program, but just the portion in which the error might be. So, let's try to add a breakpoint at the average = a + b / 2 statement (see **Figure 9–17**). There are two ways to do this: you can click in the left gray margin on the corresponding line, or you can place the cursor at the line of interest and hit the F9 key.

```
Module Module1

    Sub Main()
        Dim a, b, average As Double

        Console.Write("Enter 1st value: ")
        a = Console.ReadLine()
        Console.Write("Enter 2nd value: ")
        b = Console.ReadLine()
        average = a + b / 2
        Console.Write("The average value is: " & average)
        Console.ReadKey()
    End Sub

End Module
```

Figure 9–17 Adding a breakpoint to a program

> *Notice: You know that a breakpoint has been set when the red circle* ● *appears in the gray margin and the corresponding line has purple background highlighting it.*

Hit F5 to start the program. Enter the values 10 and 12 when requested in the output window. You will notice that just after you enter the second number and hit the "Enter ↵" key, the flow of execution pauses at the breakpoint. (You will see that the purple breakpoint highlighting is replaced by the yellow highlighting of the program counter.)

> *Remember! You can run a project by selecting "DEBUG→Start Debugging" from the main menu or by hitting the F5 key.*

Now you can take a closer look at the current values of the variables. Variables a and b contain the values 10.0 and 12.0 respectively, as they should, so there is nothing wrong with the data input, as shown in **Figure 9–18**.

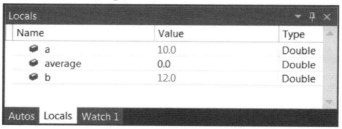

Figure 9–18 Viewing the current values of the variables in the Variables window

Click on the "Step Over" ⤵ toolbar icon once. The statement average = a + b / 2 executes and the main memory (RAM) now contains the following values (see **Figure 9–19**).

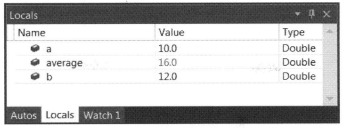

Figure 9–19 Viewing the current values of the variables in the Variables window

There it is! You just found the statement that erroneously assigns a value of 16.0, instead of 11.0, to the variable average! And now comes the difficult part; you should consider why this happens!

After two days of thinking, it becomes obvious! You had just forgotten to enclose a + b inside parentheses; thus, only the variable b was divided by 2. Click on the "Stop Debugging" ■ toolbar icon, remove all breakpoints, correct the error by enclosing a + b inside parentheses and you are ready! Re-execute the program and see now that it calculates and displays the average value correctly.

> *Notice: You can remove a breakpoint the same way you added it: click in the left gray margin on the corresponding line number, or place the cursor at the line that contains a breakpoint and hit the F9 key.*

9.5   Review Exercises

Complete the following exercises.

1. Type the following Visual Basic program into Visual Studio and execute it step by step. Determine why it doesn't calculate correctly the sum of 1 + 3 + 5.

```
Sub Main()
    Dim SS, S1, S3, S5, S As Integer

    SS = 0
    S1 = 1
    S3 = 3
    S5 = 5


    S = S1 + S3 + SS

    Console.Write(S)

    Console.ReadKey()
End Sub
```

2. Create a trace table to determine the values of the variables in each step of the Visual Basic program for two different executions. Then, type the program in the Visual Studio, execute it step by step, and confirm the results.

    The input values for the two executions are: (i) 5, 5; and (ii) 4, 8.

```
Sub Main()
    Dim a, b, c, d, e As Double

    a = Console.ReadLine()
```

```
    b = Console.ReadLine()

    c = a + b
    d = 5 + a / b * c + 2
    e = c - d
    c -= d + c
    e -= 1
    d -= c + a Mod c

    Console.Write(c & ", " & d & ", " & e)

    Console.ReadKey()
End Sub
```

3. Create a trace table to determine the values of the variables in each step of the Visual Basic program for three different executions. Then, type the program in the Visual Studio, execute it step by step, and confirm the results.

   The input values for the three executions are: (i) 0.50, (ii) 3, and (iii) 15.

```
Sub Main()
    Dim a As Integer
    Dim b, c As Double

    b = Console.ReadLine()

    c = 5
    c = c * b
    a = 10 * c Mod 10

    Console.Write(a)

    Console.ReadKey()
End Sub
```

Review Questions in "Getting Started with Visual Basic"

Answer the following questions.
1. What is an algorithm?
2. Give the algorithm for making a cup of coffee.
3. What are the five properties of algorithms?
4. Can an algorithm execute forever?
5. What is a computer program?
6. What are the three parties involved in an algorithm?
7. What are the three stages that make up a computer program?
8. Can a computer program be made up of two stages?
9. What is a flowchart?
10. Can a flowchart be entered into a computer as is?
11. What are the basic symbols that flowcharts use?
12. What is meant by the term "reserved words"?
13. What is structured programming?
14. What are the three fundamental control structures of structured programming?
15. Give an example of each control structure using flowcharts.
16. Can a programmer write Visual Basic programs in a text editor?
17. What is a syntax error? Give one example.
18. What is a logic error? Give one example.
19. What type of error is caused by a misspelled keyword, a missing punctuation character, or the incorrect use of an operator?
20. Why should a programmer add comments in his or her code?
21. Why should a programmer write user-friendly programs?
22. What does the acronym POLA stand for?
23. What is a variable?
24. How many variables can exist on the left side of the left arrow in flowcharts?
25. In which part of a computer are the values of the variables stored?
26. What is a constant?
27. How can constants be used to help programmers?
28. Why should a computer program avoid division and multiplication operations whenever possible?
29. What are the four fundamental types of variables and constants in Visual Basic?
30. What does the phrase "declare a variable" mean?
31. How do you declare a variable in Visual Basic? Give an example.
32. How do you declare a constant in Visual Basic? Give an example.
33. What symbol is used in flowcharts to display a message?
34. What special Visual Basic constant is used to output a "line break"?
35. What symbol is used in flowcharts to let the user enter data?

36. Which symbol is used in Visual Basic as a value assignment operator, and how is it represented in a flowchart?
37. Which arithmetic operators does Visual Basic support?
38. What is a modulus operator?
39. Summarize the rules for the precedence of arithmetic operators.
40. What compound assignment operators does Visual Basic support?
41. What string operators does Visual Basic support?
42. What is a trace table?
43. What are the benefits of using a trace table?
44. Describe the steps involved in swapping the contents (either numeric or alphanumeric) of two variables.
45. Two methods for swapping the values of two variables have been proposed in this book. Which one is better, and why?
46. What does the term "debugging" mean?
47. Describe the way in which Visual Studio helps you find syntax errors.
48. Describe the ways in which Visual Studio helps you find logic errors.

Section 3

Sequence Control Structures

Chapter 10
Introduction to Sequence Control Structures

10.1 What is the Sequence Control Structure?

"Sequence control structure" refers to the line-by-line execution by which statements are executed sequentially, in the same order in which they appear in the program. They might, for example, carry out a series of read or write operations, arithmetic operations, or assignments to variables.

The sequence control structure is the simplest of the three fundamental control structures that you learned about in Chapter 4. The following program shows an example of Visual Basic statements that are executed sequentially.

```
                        project_10_1
Sub Main()
  Dim a, b As Double

  Console.Write("Enter a number: ")
  a = Console.ReadLine()

  b = a ^ 2

  Console.Write("The square of " & a & " is " & b)

  Console.ReadKey()
End Sub
```

Exercise 10.1-1   Calculating the Area of a Parallelogram

Write a Visual Basic program that calculates and displays the area of a parallelogram.

Solution

The area of a parallelogram can be calculated using the following formula:

$$Area = Base \times Height$$

In this exercise, the user enters values for *Base* and *Height* and the program calculates and displays the area of the parallelogram. The solution to this problem is shown here.

```
                        project_10_1_1
Sub Main()
  Dim area, base_parallelogram, height_parallelogram As Double

  Console.Write("Enter the length of Base: ")
  base_parallelogram = Console.ReadLine()
  Console.Write("Enter the length of Height: ")
  height_parallelogram = Console.ReadLine()

  area = base_parallelogram * height_parallelogram
```

```
Console.Write("The area of the parallelogram is " & area)

  Console.ReadKey()
End Sub
```

Exercise 10.1-2   *Calculating the Area of a Circle*

Write a Visual Basic program that calculates and displays the area of a circle.

Solution

The area of a circle can be calculated using the following formula:

$$Area = \pi \cdot Radius^2$$

The value of π is a known quantity, which is 3.14159. Therefore, the only value the user has to enter is a value for *Radius*. The solution to this problem is shown here.

```
                        project_10_1_2a
Sub Main()
  Dim area, radius As Double

  Console.Write("Enter the length of Radius: ")
  radius = Console.ReadLine()

  area = 3.14159 * radius ^ 2

  Console.Write("The area of the circle is " & area)

  Console.ReadKey()
End Sub
```

A much better approach would be with to use a constant, PI.

```
                        project_10_1_2b
Const PI = 3.14159

Sub Main()
  Dim area, radius As Double

  Console.Write("Enter the length of Radius: ")
  radius = Console.ReadLine()

  area = PI * radius ^ 2

  Console.Write("The area of the circle is " & area)

  Console.ReadKey()
End Sub
```

Notice: Please note that the constant PI is declared outside of the subprocedure Main.

Remember! *The exponentiation operation has a higher precedence and is performed before the multiplication operation.*

Exercise 10.1-3   *Calculating Fuel Economy*

In the United States, a car's fuel economy is measured in miles per gallon, or MPG. A car's MPG can be calculated using the following formula:

$$MPG = \frac{miles\ driven}{gallons\ of\ gas\ used}$$

Write a Visual Basic program that prompts the user to enter the total number of miles he or she has driven and the gallons of gas used. Then the program should calculate and display the car's MPG.

Solution

This is quite a simple case. The user enters the total number of miles he or she has driven and the gallons of gas used, and then the program should calculate and display the car's MPG.

```
                          project_10_1_3
Sub Main()
  Dim gallons, miles_driven, mpg As Double

  Console.Write("Enter miles driven: ")
  miles_driven = Console.ReadLine()
  Console.Write("Enter gallons of gas used: ")
  gallons = Console.ReadLine()

  mpg = miles_driven / gallons

  Console.Write("Your car's MPG is: " & mpg)

  Console.ReadKey()
End Sub
```

Exercise 10.1-4   *Where is the Car? Calculating Distance Traveled*

A car starts from rest and moves with a constant acceleration along a straight horizontal road for a given time. Write a Visual Basic program that prompts the user to enter the acceleration and the time the car traveled, and then calculates and displays the distance traveled. The required formula is

$$S = u_o + \frac{1}{2}at^2$$

where

> ➢   **S** is the distance the car traveled, in meters (m)
> ➢   **u$_o$** is the initial velocity (speed) of the car, in meters per second (m/sec)
> ➢   **t** is the time the car traveled, in seconds (sec)
> ➢   **a** is the acceleration, in meters per second^2 (m/sec^2)

Solution

Since the car starts from rest, the initial velocity (speed) u_0 is zero. Thus, the formula becomes

$$S = \frac{1}{2}at^2$$

and the Visual Basic program is

```
                            project_10_1_4
Sub Main()
  Dim S, a, t As Double

  Console.Write("Enter acceleration: ")
  a = Console.ReadLine()
  Console.Write("Enter time traveled: ")
  t = Console.ReadLine()

  S = 0.5 * a * t ^ 2

  Console.Write("Your car traveled " & S & " meters")

  Console.ReadKey()
End Sub
```

Remember! *The exponentiation operation has a higher precedence and is performed before the multiplication operations.*

Exercise 10.1-5   *Kelvin to Fahrenheit*

Write a Visual Basic program that converts a temperature value from degrees Fahrenheit[1] to its degrees Kelvin[2] equivalent. The required formula is

$$1.8 \times Kelvin = Fahrenheit + 459.67$$

Solution

The formula given cannot be used in your program as is. In a computer language such as Visual Basic, it is not permitted to write

```
1.8 * kelvin = fahrenheit + 459.67
```

Remember! *In the position on the left side of the (=) sign, only one single variable may exist. This variable is actually a region in RAM where a value can be stored.*

---

[1] Daniel Gabriel Fahrenheit (1686–1736) was a German physicist, engineer, and glass blower who is best known for inventing both the alcohol and the mercury thermometers, and for developing the temperature scale now named after him.
[2] William Thomson, 1st Baron Kelvin (1824–1907), was an Irish-born British mathematical physicist and engineer. He is widely known for developing the basis of absolute zero (the Kelvin temperature scale), and for this reason a unit of temperature measure is named after him. He discovered the Thomson effect in thermoelectricity and helped develop the second law of thermodynamics.

The program converts degrees Fahrenheit to degrees Kelvin. The value for degrees Fahrenheit is a known value and it is given by the user, whereas the value for degrees Kelvin is what the Visual Basic program should calculate. So, you need to solve for Kelvin. After a bit of work, the formula becomes

$$Kelvin = \frac{Fahrenheit + 459.67}{1.8}$$

and the Visual Basic program is shown here.

```
                          project_10_1_5
Sub Main()
  Dim fahrenheit, kelvin As Double

  Console.Write("Enter a temperature in Fahrenheit: ")
  fahrenheit = Console.ReadLine()

  kelvin = (fahrenheit + 459.67) / 1.8

  Console.Write("The temperature in Kelvin is " & kelvin)

  Console.ReadKey()
End Sub
```

Exercise 10.1-6   *Calculating Sales Tax*

An employee needs a program to enter the before-tax price of a product and calculate its final price. Assume a value added tax (VAT) of 19%.

Solution

The sales tax can be easily calculated. You must multiply the before-tax price of the product by the sales tax rate. Be careful—the sales tax is not the final price, but only the tax amount.

The after-tax price can be calculated by adding the initial before-tax price and the sales tax that you calculated beforehand.

In this program you can use a constant named VAT for the sales tax rate.

```
                          project_10_1_6
Const VAT = 0.19

Sub Main()
  Dim price_after_tax, price_before_tax, sales_tax As Double

  Console.Write("Enter the before-tax price of a product: ")
  price_before_tax = Console.ReadLine()

  sales_tax = price_before_tax * VAT
  price_after_tax = price_before_tax + sales_tax

  Console.Write("The after-tax price is: " & price_after_tax)

  Console.ReadKey()
```

```
End Sub
```

> **Notice**: Please note that the constant VAT is declared outside of the subprocedure Main.

Exercise 10.1-7   *Calculating a Sales Discount*

Write a Visual Basic program that prompts the user to enter the price of an item and the discount offered as a percentage (on a scale of 0 to 100). The program should then calculate and display the new price.

Solution

The discount amount can be easily calculated. You must multiply the before-discount price of the product by the discount value and then divide it by 100. The division is necessary since the user enters a value for the discount on a scale of 0 to 100. Be careful—the result is not the final price but only the discount amount.

The final after-discount price can be calculated by subtracting the discount amount that you calculated beforehand from the initial before-discount price.

```
                            project_10_1_7
Sub Main()
    Dim discount As Integer
    Dim discount_amount, price_after_discount, price_before_discount As Double

    Console.Write("Enter the price of a product: ")
    price_before_discount = Console.ReadLine()

    Console.Write("Enter the discount offered (0 - 100): ")
    discount = Console.ReadLine()

    discount_amount = price_before_discount * discount / 100
    price_after_discount = price_before_discount - discount_amount

    Console.Write("The price after discount is: " & price_after_discount)

    Console.ReadKey()
End Sub
```

Exercise 10.1-8   *Calculating the Sales Tax Rate and Discount*

Write a Visual Basic program that prompts the user to enter the before-tax price of an item and the discount offered as a percentage (on a scale of 0 to 100). The program should then calculate and display the new price. Assume a sales tax rate of 19%.

Solution

This exercise is just a combination of the previous two exercises!

```
                            project_10_1_8
Const VAT = 0.19

Sub Main()
```

```
Dim discount As Integer
Dim discount_amount, price_after_discount, price_after_tax As Double
Dim price_before_discount, sales_tax As Double

Console.Write("Enter the price of a product: ")
price_before_discount = Console.ReadLine()

Console.Write("Enter the discount offered (0 - 100): ")
discount = Console.ReadLine()

discount_amount = price_before_discount * discount / 100
price_after_discount = price_before_discount - discount_amount

sales_tax = price_after_discount * VAT
price_after_tax = price_after_discount + sales_tax

Console.Write("The discounted after-tax price is: " & price_after_tax)

Console.ReadKey()
End Sub
```

10.2   Review Exercises

Complete the following exercises.

1. Write a Visual Basic program that prompts the user to enter values for base and height, and then calculates and displays the area of a triangle.

2. Write a Visual Basic program that prompts the user to enter two angles of a triangle, and then calculates and displays the third angle.

   Hint: The sum of the measures of the interior angles of any triangle is 180 degrees

3. Write a Visual Basic program that lets a student enter his or her grades from four tests, and then calculates and displays the average grade.

4. Write a Visual Basic program that prompts the user to enter a value for radius, and then calculates and displays the perimeter of a circle.

5. Write a Visual Basic program that prompts the user to enter the charge for a meal in a restaurant, and then calculates and displays the amount of a 10% tip, 7% sales tax, and the total of all three amounts.

6. A car starts from rest and moves with a constant acceleration along a straight horizontal road for a given time in seconds. Write a Visual Basic program that prompts the user to enter the acceleration (in m/sec²) and the time traveled (in sec) and then calculates the distance traveled. The required formula is

$$S = u_o + \frac{1}{2}at^2$$

7. Write a Visual Basic program that prompts the user to enter a temperature in degrees Fahrenheit, and then converts it into its degrees Celsius[3] equivalent. The required formula is

$$\frac{C}{5} = \frac{F - 32}{9}$$

8. The Body Mass Index (BMI) is often used to determine whether a person is overweight or underweight for his or her height. The formula used to calculate the BMI is

$$BMI = \frac{weight \cdot 703}{height^2}$$

    Write a Visual Basic program that prompts the user to enter his or her weight (in pounds) and height (in inches), and then calculates and displays the user's BMI.

9. Write a Visual Basic program that prompts the user to enter the subtotal and gratuity rate (on a scale of 0 to 100) and then calculates the tip and total. For example if the user enters 30 and 10, the Visual Basic program should display "Tip is $3.00 and Total is $33.00".

10. An employee needs a program to enter the before-tax price of three products and then calculate the final after-tax price of each product, as well as their average value. Assume a value added tax (VAT) of 20%.

11. An employee needs a program to enter the after-tax price of a product, and then calculate its before-tax price. Assume a value added tax (VAT) of 20%.

12. Write a Visual Basic program that prompts the user to enter the initial price of an item and the discount offered as a percentage (on a scale of 0 to 100), and then calculates and displays the final price and the amount of money saved.

13. Write a Visual Basic program that prompts the user to enter the electric meter reading in kilowatt-hours (kWh) at the beginning and end of a month. The program should calculate and display the amount of kWh consumed and the amount of money that must be paid given a cost of each kWh of $0.06 and a value added tax (VAT) of 20%.

14. Write a Visual Basic program that prompts the user to enter two numbers, which correspond to current month and current day of the month, and then calculates the number of days until the end of the year. Assume that each month has 30 days.

---

[3] Anders Celsius (1701–1744) was a Swedish astronomer, physicist, and mathematician. He founded the Uppsala Astronomical Observatory in Sweden and proposed the Celsius temperature scale, which takes his name.

Chapter 11
Manipulating Numbers

11.1 Introduction

Just like every high-level programming language, Visual Basic provides many procedures that can be used whenever and wherever you wish. Procedures are nothing more than a block of statements packaged as a unit that has a name and performs a specific task.

To better understand procedures, let's take Heron's[1] iterative formula that calculates the square root of a positive number.

$$x_{n+1} = \frac{1}{2}\left(x_n + \frac{y}{x_n}\right)$$

where

> ➢ y is the number for which you want to find the square root
>
> ➢ x_n is the n-th iteration value of the square root of y

Please don't be disappointed! No one at the present time calculates the square root of a number this way. Fortunately, Visual Basic includes a procedure for that purpose! This procedure, which is actually a small subprogram, has been given the name `Math.Sqrt` and the only thing you have to do is call it by its name and it will do the job for you. Procedure `Math.Sqrt` probably uses Heron's iterative formula, or perhaps a formula of another ancient or modern mathematician. The truth is that you don't really care! What really matters is that `Math.Sqrt` gives you the right result! An example is shown here.

```
Sub Main()
   Dim x, y As Double

   x = Console.ReadLine()
   y = Math.Sqrt(x)
   Console.Write(y)

   Console.ReadKey()
End Sub
```

Even though Visual Basic supports many mathematical functions, this chapter covers only those absolutely necessary for this book's purpose. However, if you need even more information you can visit

https://msdn.microsoft.com/en-us/library/system.math

> **Notice**: *Mathematical functions are used whenever you need to calculate a square root, the sine, the cosine, an absolute value, and so on.*

---

[1] Heron of Alexandria (c. 10–c. 70 AD) was an ancient Greek mathematician, physicist, astronomer, and engineer. He is considered the greatest experimenter of ancient times. He described the first recorded steam turbine engine, called an "aeolipile" (sometimes called a "Hero engine"). Heron also described a method of iteratively calculating the square root of a positive number. Today, though, he is known best for the proof of "Heron's Formula" which finds the area of a triangle from its side lengths.

11.2   Useful Mathematical Procedures

Absolute value

```
Math.Abs( number )
```

This returns the absolute value of *number*.

Example

project_11_2a

```
Sub Main()
  Dim a, b As Integer

  a = -5
  b = Math.Abs(a)

  Console.WriteLine(Math.Abs(a))        'outputs: 5
  Console.WriteLine(b)                  'outputs: 5
  Console.WriteLine(Math.Abs(-5.2))     'outputs: 5.2
  Console.WriteLine(Math.Abs(5.2))      'outputs: 5.2


  Console.ReadKey()
End Sub
```

Cosine

```
Math.Cos( number )
```

This returns the cosine of *number*. The value of *number* must be expressed in radians.

Example

project_11_2b

```
Sub Main()
  Dim a, p As Double

  p = 3.14159265
  a = Math.Cos(2 * p)
  Console.WriteLine(a)                  'outputs: 1

  Console.ReadKey()
End Sub
```

Integer value

```
Fix( number )
```

This returns the integer portion of *number*.

Example

project_11_2c

```
Sub Main()
  Dim a As Double = 5.4

  Console.WriteLine(Fix(a))             'outputs: 5
  Console.WriteLine(Fix(34))            'outputs: 34
  Console.WriteLine(Fix(34.9))          'outputs: 34
```

```
Console.WriteLine(Fix(-34.999))          'outputs: -34

Console.ReadKey()
End Sub
```

Pi

```
Math.PI
```

This returns the value of π.

Example

```
                         project_11_2e
Sub Main()
  Console.WriteLine(Math.PI)          'outputs: 3.14159265358979
  Console.ReadKey()
End Sub
```

> **Notice**: *Please note that* PI *is a constant, not a procedure. This is why no parentheses are used.*

Random

```
Next(minimum_value, maximum_value)
```

This returns a pseudo-random integer between *minimum_value* and *maximum_value - 1*. Procedure Next() is defined in the Random class.

Example

```
                         project_11_2g
Sub Main()
  Dim rnd As New Random()

  'output a random integer between 0 and 65535
  Console.WriteLine(rnd.Next(0, 65536))

  'output a random integer between 0 and 10
  Console.WriteLine(rnd.Next(0, 11))

  'output a random integer between -20 and 20
  Console.WriteLine(rnd.Next(-20, 21))

  Console.ReadKey()
End Sub
```

> **Notice**: *Random numbers are widely used in computer games. For example, an "enemy" may show up at a random time or move in random directions. Moreover, random numbers are used in simulation programs, in statistical programs, in computer security to encrypt data, and so on.*

Round

```
Math.Round( number )
```

This returns the closest integer.

If you want the rounded value of *number* to a specified *precision*, you can use the following formula:

$$Math.Round(number * 10 \char94 precision) / 10 \char94 precision$$

Example

```
                          project_11_2j
Sub Main()
  Dim a, y As Double

  a = 5.9
  Console.WriteLine(Math.Round(a))          'outputs: 6
  Console.WriteLine(Math.Round(5.4))        'outputs: 5

  a = 5.312
  y = Math.Round(a * 10 ^ 2) / 10 ^ 2
  Console.WriteLine(y)                       'outputs: 5.31

  a = 5.315
  y = Math.Round(a * 10 ^ 2) / 10 ^ 2
  Console.WriteLine(y)                       'outputs: 5.32

  Console.Write(Math.Round(2.3447 * 1000) / 1000)        'outputs: 2.345
  Console.ReadKey()
End Sub
```

Sine

```
Math.Sin( number )
```

This returns the sine of *number*. The value of *number* must be expressed in radians.

Example

```
                          project_11_2k
Sub Main()
  Dim a As Double

  a = Math.Sin(3 * Math.PI / 2)
  Console.WriteLine(a)                       'outputs: -1.0
  Console.ReadKey()
End Sub
```

Square root

```
Math.Sqrt( number )
```

This returns the square root of *number*.

Example

```
                          project_11_2l
Sub Main()
  Console.WriteLine(Math.Sqrt(9))           'outputs: 3
  Console.WriteLine(Math.Sqrt(2))           'outputs: 1.4142135623731
  Console.ReadKey()
End Sub
```

Tangent

```
Math.Tan( number )
```

This returns the tangent of *number*. The value of *number* must be expressed in radians.

Example

```
                          project_11_2m
Sub Main()
  Dim a As Double

  a = Math.Tan(10)
  Console.WriteLine(a)              'outputs: 0.648360827459087
  Console.ReadKey()
End Sub
```

Exercise 11.2-1   *Calculating the Distance Between Two Points*

Write a Visual Basic program that prompts the user to enter the coordinates (x, y) of two points and then calculates the straight line distance between them. The required formula is

$$d = \sqrt{(x_1 - x_2)^2 + (y_1 - y_2)^2}$$

Solution

In this exercise, you need to use the procedure Math.Sqrt(), which returns the square root of a number.

To simplify things, the terms $(x_1 - x_2)^2$ and $(y_1 - y_2)^2$ are calculated individually and the results are assigned to two temporary variables.

The Visual Basic program is shown here.

```
                          project_11_2_1a
Sub Main()
  Dim d, x1, x2, x_temp, y1, y2, y_temp As Double

  Console.Write("Enter coordinates for point A: ")
  x1 = Console.ReadLine()
  y1 = Console.ReadLine()

  Console.Write("Enter coordinates for point B: ")
  x2 = Console.ReadLine()
  y2 = Console.ReadLine()

  x_temp = (x1 - x2) ^ 2
  y_temp = (y1 - y2) ^ 2

  d = Math.Sqrt(x_temp + y_temp)

  Console.Write("Distance between points: " & d)
  Console.ReadKey()
End Sub
```

Now let's see another approach.

You should realize that it is actually possible to perform an operation within a procedure call. Doing that, the result of the operation is used as an argument for the procedure. This is a writing style that most programmers prefer to follow because it can save a lot of code lines.

The Visual Basic program is shown here.

```
                            project_11_2_1b
Sub Main()
    Dim d, x1, x2, y1, y2 As Double

    Console.Write("Enter coordinates for point A: ")
    x1 = Console.ReadLine()
    y1 = Console.ReadLine()

    Console.Write("Enter coordinates for point B: ")
    x2 = Console.ReadLine()
    y2 = Console.ReadLine()

    d = Math.Sqrt((x1 - x2) ^ 2 + (y1 - y2) ^ 2)

    Console.Write("Distance between points: " & d)
    Console.ReadKey()
End Sub
```

Exercise 11.2-2   How Far Did the Car Travel?

A car starts from rest and moves with a constant acceleration along a straight horizontal road for a given distance. Write a Visual Basic program that prompts the user to enter the acceleration and the distance the car traveled and then calculates the time traveled. The required formula is

$$S = u_o + \frac{1}{2}at^2$$

where

➢   *S is the distance the car traveled, in meters (m)*
➢   *u_o is the initial velocity (speed) of the car, in meters per second (m/sec)*
➢   *t is the time the car traveled, in seconds (sec)*
➢   *a is the acceleration, in meters per second^2 (m/sec^2)*

Solution

Since the car starts from rest, the initial velocity (speed) u_0 is zero. Thus, the formula becomes

$$S = \frac{1}{2}at^2$$

Now, if you solve for time, the final formula becomes

$$t = \sqrt{\frac{2S}{a}}$$

In Visual Basic, you can use the `Math.Sqrt()` procedure, which returns the square root of a number.

```
project_11_2_2
Sub Main()
  Dim S, a, t As Double

  Console.Write("Enter acceleration: ")
  a = Console.ReadLine()
  Console.Write("Enter distance traveled: ")
  S = Console.ReadLine()

  t = Math.Sqrt(2 * S / a)

  Console.Write("Your car traveled for " & t & " seconds")
  Console.ReadKey()
End Sub
```

11.3   Review Questions: True/False

Choose **true** or **false** for each of the following statements.

1.   In general, procedures are small subprograms that solve small problems.

2.   Every programmer must use Heron's iterative formula to calculate the square root of a positive number.

3.   The `Math.Abs()` procedure returns the absolute position of an item.

4.   The statement `Fix(3.59)` returns a result of 3.6.

5.   The `Math.PI` constant is equal to 3.14.

6.   The statement `2 ^ 3` returns a result of 9.

7.   The `Next()` procedure can also return negative random numbers.

8.   There is a 50% possibility that the statement `y = rnd.Next(0, 2)` will assign a value of 1 to variable `y`.

9.   The statement `Math.Round(3.59)` returns a result of 4.

10. To calculate the sinus of 90 degrees, you have to write `y = Math.Sin(Math.PI / 2)`.

11. The statement `y = Math.Sqrt(-2)` is valid.

12. The following code fragment satisfies the property of definiteness.

```
Dim a, b, x As Double
a = Console.ReadLine()
b = Console.ReadLine()
x = a * Math.Sqrt(b)
Console.WriteLine(x)
```

11.4   Review Questions: Multiple Choice

Select the correct answer for each of the following statements.

1.   Which of the following calculates the result of the variable `a` raised to the power of 2?

     a.   `y = a * a`

    b. `y = a ^ 2`

    c. `y = a * a / a * a`

    d. all of the above

2. What is the value of the variable `y` when the statement `y = Math.Abs(+5.2)` is executed?

    a. -5.2

    b. -5

    c. 0.2

    d. 5.2

    e. none of the above

3. Which of the following calculates the sinus of 180 degrees?

    a. `Math.Sin(180)`

    b. `Math.Sin(Math.PI)`

    c. all of the above

    d. none of the above

4. What is the value of the variable `y` when the statement `y = Fix(5/2)` is executed?

    a. 2.5

    b. 3

    c. 2

    d. 0.5

5. What is the value of the variable `y` when the statement `y = Math.Sqrt(4) ^ 2` is executed?

    a. 4

    b. 2

    c. 8

    d. 16

6. What is the value of the variable `y` when the statement `y = Math.Round(5.2) / 2` is executed?

    a. 2

    b. 2.5

    c. 2.6

    d. none of the above

11.5 Review Exercises

Complete the following exercises.

1. Create a trace table to determine the values of the variables in each step of the Visual Basic program for two different executions.

    The input values for the two executions are: (i) 9, and (ii) 4.

```
Sub Main()
  Dim a As Double
  Dim b, c As Integer
```

```
    a = Console.ReadLine()

    a += 6 / Math.Sqrt(a) * 2 + 20
    b = Math.Round(a) Mod 4
    c = b Mod 3

    Console.Write(a & ", " & b & ", " & c)

    Console.ReadKey()
End Sub
```

2. Create a trace table to determine the values of the variables in each step of the Visual Basic program for two different executions.

The input values for the two executions are: (i) -2, and (ii) -3

```
Sub Main()
    Dim a, b, c As Integer

    a = Console.ReadLine()

    b = Math.Abs(a) Mod 4 + a ^ 4
    c = b Mod 5

    Console.Write(b & ", " & c)

    Console.ReadKey()
End Sub
```

3. Write a Visual Basic that prompts the user to enter an angle θ in radians and then calculates and displays the angle in degrees. It is given that $2\pi = 360°$.

4. Write a Visual Basic program that calculates the hypotenuse of a right-angled triangle, given its two right angle sides A and B. It is known from the Pythagorean[2] theorem that

$$hypotenuse = \sqrt{A^2 + B^2}$$

5. Write a Visual Basic program that prompts the user to enter the angle θ (in degrees) of a right-angled triangle and the length of its adjacent side, and then calculates the length of the opposite side. It is known that $2\pi = 360°$, and

$$\tan(\theta) = \frac{Opposite}{Adjacent}$$

---

[2] Pythagoras of Samos (c. 571–c. 497 BC) was a famous Greek mathematician, philosopher, and astronomer. He is best known for the proof of the important Pythagorean theorem. He was an influence for Plato. His theories are still used in mathematics today.

Chapter 12

Complex Mathematical Expressions

12.1 Writing Complex Mathematical Expressions

In Chapter 7 you learned all about arithmetic operators but little about how to use them and how to write your own complex mathematical expressions. In this chapter, you are going to learn how easy is to convert mathematical expressions to Visual Basic statements.

> **Remember!** *Arithmetic operators follow the same precedence rules as in mathematics, which means that multiplication and division are performed before addition and subtraction. Moreover, when multiplication and division co-exist in the same expression, and since both are of the same precedence, these operations are performed left to right.*

Exercise 12.1-1 *Representing Mathematical Expressions in Visual Basic*

Which of the following Visual Basic statements correctly represent the following mathematical expression?

$$x = \frac{1}{10 + z}27$$

i. `x = 1 * 27 / 10 + z`	*v.* `x = (1 / 10 + z) * 27`
ii. `x = 1 · 27 / (10 + z)`	*vi.* `x = 1 / ((10 + z) * 27)`
iii. `x = 27 / 10 + z`	*vii.* `x = 1 / ( 10 + z) * 27`
iv. `x = 27 / (10 + z)`	*viii.* `x = 1 / ( 10 + z) / 27`

Solution

i. **Wrong.** Since the multiplication and the division are performed before the addition, this is equivalent to $x = \frac{1}{10}27 + z$.

ii. **Wrong.** An asterisk should have been used for multiplication.

iii. **Wrong.** Since the division is performed before the addition, this is equivalent to $x = \frac{27}{10} + z$.

iv. **Correct.** This is equivalent to $x = \frac{27}{10 + z}$.

v. **Wrong.** Inside parentheses, the division is performed before the addition. This is equivalent to $x = \left(\frac{1}{10} + z\right)27$.

vi. **Wrong.** Parentheses are executed first and this is equivalent to $x = \frac{1}{(10+z)27}$.

vii. **Correct.** Division is performed before multiplication (left to right). The term $\frac{1}{10+z}$ is calculated first and then, the result is multiplied by 27.

viii.   **Wrong**. This is equivalent to $= \dfrac{\frac{1}{10+z}}{27}$

Exercise 12.1-2   *Writing a Mathematical Expression in Visual Basic*

Write a Visual Basic program that calculates the mathematical expression

$$y = 10\,x - \frac{10 - z}{4}$$

Solution

First, you must distinguish between the data input and the output result. Obviously, the output result is assigned to y and the user must enter values for x and z. The solution for this exercise is shown here.

```
                           project_12_1_2
Sub Main()
    Dim x, y, z As Double

    Console.Write("Enter value for x: ")
    x = Console.ReadLine()
    Console.Write("Enter value for z: ")
    z = Console.ReadLine()

    y = 10 * x - (10 - z) / 4

    Console.Write("The result is: " & y)

    Console.ReadKey()
End Sub
```

Exercise 12.1-3   *Writing a Complex Mathematical Expression in Visual Basic*

Write a Visual Basic program that calculates the mathematical expression

$$y = \frac{5\dfrac{3x^2 + 5x + 2}{7w - \dfrac{1}{z}} - z}{4\dfrac{3 + x}{7}}$$

Solution

Oops! Now the expression is more complex! In fact, it is much more complex! So, let's take a look at a quite different approach.

The main idea is to break the complex expression into smaller, simpler expressions and assign each sub-result to temporary variables. In the end, you can build the original expression out of all these temporary variables! This approach is presented here.

```
                           project_12_1_3a
Sub Main()
    Dim denominator, nominator, temp1, temp2, temp3, w, x, y, z As Double
```

```
Console.Write("Enter value for x: ")
x = Console.ReadLine()
Console.Write("Enter value for w: ")
w = Console.ReadLine()
Console.Write("Enter value for z: ")
z = Console.ReadLine()

temp1 = 3 * x ^ 2 + 5 * x + 2
temp2 = 7 * w - 1 / z
temp3 = (3 + x) / 7
nominator = 5 * temp1 / temp2 - z
denominator = 4 * temp3

y = nominator / denominator

Console.Write("The result is: " & y)

Console.ReadKey()
End Sub
```

You may say, "*Okay, but I wasted so many variables and as everybody knows, each variable is a portion of main memory. How can I write the original expression in one single line and waste less memory?*"

This job may be a piece of cake for an advanced programmer, but what about you? What about a novice programmer?

The next method will help you write even the most complex mathematical expressions without any syntax or logic errors! The rule is very simple. "*After breaking the complex expression into smaller, simpler expressions and assigning each sub-result to temporary variables, start backwards and replace each variable with its assigned expression. Be careful though! When you replace a variable with an expression, you must always enclose the expression in parentheses!*"

Confused? Don't be! It's easier in action. Let's try to rewrite the previous Visual Basic program. Starting backwards, replace variables nominator and denominator with their assigned expressions. The result is

```
y = (5 * temp1 / temp2 - z) / (4 * temp3)
```
          nominator   denominator

Notice: *Please note the extra parentheses added.*

Now you must replace variables temp1, temp2, and temp3 with their assigned expressions, and the one-line expression is complete!

```
y = (5 * (3 * x ^ 2 + 5 * x + 2)/(7 * w - 1 / z) - z)/(4 * ((3 + x) / 7))
```
              temp1   temp2   temp3

It may look scary at the end but it wasn't that difficult, was it?

The Visual Basic program can now be rewritten

```
                          project_12_1_3b
Sub Main()
  Dim w, x, y, z As Double

  Console.Write("Enter value for x: ")
  x = Console.ReadLine()
  Console.Write("Enter value for w: ")
  w = Console.ReadLine()
  Console.Write("Enter value for z: ")
  z = Console.ReadLine()

  y = (5 * (3 * x ^ 2 + 5 * x + 2)/(7 * w - 1 / z) - z)/(4 * ((3 + x) / 7))

  Console.Write("The result is: " & y)

  Console.ReadKey()
End Sub
```

12.2 Review Exercises

Complete the following exercises.

1. Match each element from the first table with one **or more** elements from the second table.

Expression
i.   5 / x ^ 2 * y + x ^ 3
ii.   5 / (x ^ 3 * y) + x ^ 2

Expression
a.   5 * y / x ^ 2 + x ^ 3
b.   5 * y / x * x + x ^ 3
c.   5 / (x * x * x * y) + x * x
d.   5 / (x * x * x) * y + x * x
e.   5 * y / (x * x) + x * x * x
f.   1 / (x * x * x * y) * 5 + x * x
g.   y / (x * x) * 5 + x ^ 3
h.   1 / (x * x) * 5 * y + x / x * x * x

2. Write the following mathematical expressions in Visual Basic using one line of code for each.

     i. $y = \dfrac{(x+3)^{5w}}{7(x-4)}$

ii.　$y = \sqrt[5]{\left(3x^2 - \dfrac{1}{4}x^3\right)}$

iii.　$y = \dfrac{\sqrt{x^4 - 2x^3 - 7x^2 + x}}{\sqrt[3]{4\left(7x^4 - \frac{3}{4}x^3\right)(7x^2 + x)}}$

iv.　$y = \dfrac{x}{x - 3(x-1)} + \left(x\sqrt[5]{x} - 1\right)\dfrac{1}{(x^3 - 2)(x-1)^3}$

v.　$y = \left(\sin\left(\dfrac{\pi}{3}\right) - \cos\left(\dfrac{\pi}{2}w\right)\right)^2$

vi.　$y = \dfrac{\left(\sin\left(\frac{\pi}{2}x\right) + \cos\left(\frac{3\pi}{2}w\right)\right)^3}{\left(\tan\left(\frac{2\pi}{3}w\right) - \sin\left(\frac{\pi}{2}x\right)\right)^{\frac{1}{2}}} + 6$

3.　Write a Visual Basic program that prompts the user to enter a value for x and then calculates and displays the result of the following mathematical expression.

$$y = \sqrt{x}(x^3 + x^2)$$

4.　Write a Visual Basic program that prompts the user to enter a value for x and then calculates and displays the result of the following mathematical expression.

$$y = \dfrac{7x}{2x + 4(x^2 + 4)}$$

Suggestion: Try to write the expression in one line of code.

5.　Write a Visual Basic program that prompts the user to enter a value for x and w and then calculates and displays the result of the following mathematical expression.

$$y = \dfrac{x^{x+1}}{\left(\tan\left(\frac{2w}{3} + 5\right) - \tan\left(\frac{x}{2} + 1\right)\right)^3}$$

Suggestion: Try to write the expression in one line of code

6.　Write a Visual Basic program that prompts the user to enter a value for x and w and then calculates and displays the result of the following mathematical expression.

$$y = \dfrac{3 + w}{6x - 7(x + 4)} + \left(x\sqrt[5]{3w} + 1\right)\dfrac{5x + 4}{(x^3 + 3)(x - 1)^7}$$

Suggestion: Try to write the expression in one line of code.

7.　Write a Visual Basic program that prompts the user to enter a value for x and w and then calculates and displays the result of the following mathematical expression.

$$y = \dfrac{x^x}{\left(\sin\left(\frac{2w}{3} + 5\right) - x\right)^2} + \dfrac{(\sin(3x) + w)^{x+1}}{\left(\sqrt{7w}\right)^{\frac{3}{2}}}$$

Suggestion: Try to write the expression in one line of code

8. Write a Visual Basic program that prompts the user to enter the lengths of all three sides A, B, and C, of a triangle and then calculates and displays the area of the triangle. You can use Heron's formula, which has been known for nearly 2,000 years!

$$Area = \sqrt{S(S - A)(S - B)(S - C)}$$

where S is the semi-perimeter

$$S = \frac{A + B + C}{2}$$

Chapter 13
Exercises With a Quotient and a Remainder

13.1 Introduction

What types of problems might require the use of the quotient and the remainder of an integer division? There is no simple answer to that question! However, quotients and remainders can be used to:

➢ split a number into individual digits

➢ examine if a number is odd or even

➢ convert an elapsed time (in seconds) to hours, minutes, and seconds

➢ convert an amount of money (in USD) to a number of $100 notes, $50 notes, $20 notes, and such

➢ calculate the greatest common divisor

➢ determine if a number is a palindrome

➢ count the number of digits within a number

➢ determine how many times a specific digit occurs within a number

Of course, these are some of the uses and certainly you can find so many others. Next you will see some exercises that make use of the quotient and the remainder of integer division.

Exercise 13.1-1 *Calculating the Quotient and Remainder of Integer Division*

Write a Visual Basic program that prompts the user to enter two integers and then calculates the quotient and the remainder of the integer division.

Solution

You can use the (\ ) and the (Mod) operators of Visual Basic. The former performs an integer division and returns the integer quotient whereas the latter performs an integer division and returns the integer remainder. The solution is presented here.

```
                          project_13_1_1
Sub Main()
  Dim number1, number2, q, r As Integer

  Console.Write("Enter first number: ")
  number1 = Console.ReadLine()

  Console.Write("Enter second number: ")
  number2 = Console.ReadLine()

  q = number1 \ number2
  r = number1 Mod number2

  Console.Write("Integer Quotient: " & q & vbCrLf & "Integer Remainder: " & r)
```

```
    Console.ReadKey()
End Sub
```

> **Notice**: In flowcharts, in order to calculate the quotient of an integer division, you can use the popular DIV operator. An example is shown here.
>
>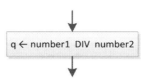

Exercise 13.1-2   *Finding the Sum of Digits*

Write a Visual Basic program that prompts the user to enter a four-digit integer and then calculates the sum of its digits.

Solution

What you should keep in mind here is that the statement

```
number = Console.ReadLine()
```

in the beginning of the program assigns the given four-digit integer to one single variable, number, and not to four individual variables.

So, first you must split the integer into its four digits and assign each digit to a separate variable. Then you can calculate the sum of these four variables and get the required result. There are two approaches available.

First Approach

Let's try to understand the first approach using an arithmetic example. Take the number 6753, for example.

First digit = 6	The first digit can be isolated if you divide the given number by 1000 to get the integer quotient digit1 = 6753 \ 1000
Remaining digits = 753	The remaining digits can be isolated if you divide the given number by 1000 to get the integer remainder r = 6753 Mod 1000
Second digit = 7	The second digit can be isolated if you divide the remaining digits by 100 to get the integer quotient digit2 = 753 \ 100
Remaining digits = 53	The remaining digits are now r = 753 Mod 100
Third digit = 5	The third digit can be isolated if you divide the remaining digits by 10 to get the integer quotient digit3 = 53 \ 10

Fourth digit = 3	The last remaining digit, which happens to be the fourth digit, is `digit4 = 53 Mod 10`

The Visual Basic program that solves this algorithm is shown here.

```
project_13_1_2a
Sub Main()
  Dim digit1, digit2, digit3, digit4, number, r, sum As Integer

  Console.Write("Enter a four-digit integer: ")
  number = Console.ReadLine()

  digit1 = number \ 1000
  r = number Mod 1000

  digit2 = r \ 100
  r = r Mod 100

  digit3 = r \ 10
  digit4 = r Mod 10

  sum = digit1 + digit2 + digit3 + digit4
  Console.Write(sum)

  Console.ReadKey()
End Sub
```

The trace table for the program that you have just seen is shown here.

Step	Statement	Notes	number	digit1	digit2	digit3	digit4	r	sum
1	`Console.Write("Enter a …`	The message "Enter a …" is displayed							
2	`number = Console.ReadLine()`	User enters 6753	6753	?	?	?	?	?	?
3	`digit1 = number \ 1000`		6753	6	?	?	?	?	?
4	`r = number Mod 1000`		6753	6	?	?	?	753	?
5	`digit2 = r \ 100`		6753	6	7	?	?	753	?
6	`r = r Mod 100`		6753	6	7	?	?	53	?
7	`digit3 = r \ 10`		6753	6	7	5	?	53	?
8	`digit4 = r Mod 10`		6753	6	7	5	3	53	?
9	`sum = digit1+digit2+digit3+digit4`		6753	6	7	5	3	53	18

| 10 | `Console.Write(sum)` | Value 18 is displayed |

To further help you, there is also a general purpose Visual Basic program that can be used to split any given integer. Since the length of your program depends on the number of digits, N, all you have to do is write N-1 pairs of statements.

```
Console.Write("Enter an N-digit integer: ")
number = Console.ReadLine()

digit1 = number \ 10^(N-1)
r = number Mod 10^(N-1)

digit2 = r \ 10^(N-2)
r = r Mod 10^(N-2)

.

.

.

digit(N-2) = r \ 100
r = r Mod 100

digit(N-1) = r \ 10
digitN = r Mod 10
```

For example, if you want to split a six-digit integer, you need to write five pairs of statements.

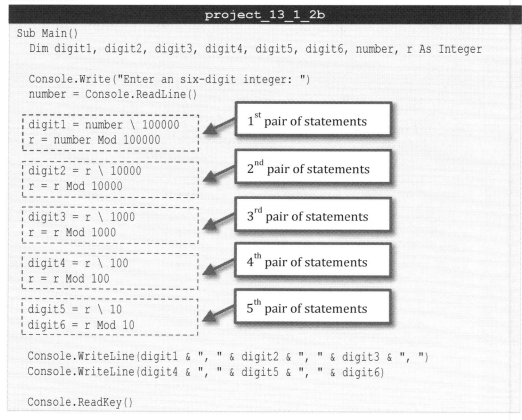

```
                        project_13_1_2b
Sub Main()
    Dim digit1, digit2, digit3, digit4, digit5, digit6, number, r As Integer

    Console.Write("Enter an six-digit integer: ")
    number = Console.ReadLine()

    digit1 = number \ 100000        1st pair of statements
    r = number Mod 100000

    digit2 = r \ 10000              2nd pair of statements
    r = r Mod 10000

    digit3 = r \ 1000              3rd pair of statements
    r = r Mod 1000

    digit4 = r \ 100              4th pair of statements
    r = r Mod 100

    digit5 = r \ 10              5th pair of statements
    digit6 = r Mod 10

    Console.WriteLine(digit1 & ", " & digit2 & ", " & digit3 & ", ")
    Console.WriteLine(digit4 & ", " & digit5 & ", " & digit6)

    Console.ReadKey()
```

```
End Sub
```

Second Approach

Once more, let's try to understand the second approach using an arithmetic example. Take the same number, 6753, for example.

Fourth digit = 3	The fourth digit can be isolated if you divide the given number by 10 to get the integer remainder `digit1 = 6753 Mod 10`
Remaining digits = 675	The remaining digits can be isolated if you divide the given number by 10 to get the integer quotient `r = 6753 \ 10`
Third digit = 5	The third digit can be isolated if you divide the remaining digits by 10 to get the integer remainder `digit3 = 675 Mod 10`
Remaining digits = 67	The remaining digits are now `r = 675 \ 10`
Second digit = 7	The second digit can be isolated if you divide the remaining digits by 10 to get the integer remainder `digit3 = 67 Mod 10`
First digit = 6	The last remaining digit, which happens to be the first digit, is `digit1 = 67 \ 10`

The Visual Basic program for this algorithm is shown here.

```
project_13_1_2c
Sub Main()
  Dim digit1, digit2, digit3, digit4, number, r, sum As Integer

  Console.Write("Enter a four-digit integer: ")
  number = Console.ReadLine()

  digit4 = number Mod 10
  r = number \ 10

  digit3 = r Mod 10
  r = r \ 10

  digit2 = r Mod 10
  digit1 = r \ 10

  sum = digit1 + digit2 + digit3 + digit4
  Console.Write(sum)

  Console.ReadKey()
End Sub
```

To further help you, there is also a general purpose Visual Basic program that can be used to split any given integer. This program uses the second approach. Once again, since the length of your program depends on the number of the digits, N, all you have to do is write N-1 pairs of statements.

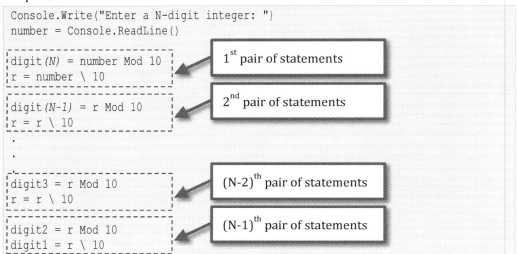

```
Console.Write("Enter a N-digit integer: ")
number = Console.ReadLine()

digit(N) = number Mod 10        1st pair of statements
r = number \ 10

digit(N-1) = r Mod 10           2nd pair of statements
r = r \ 10
        .
        .
digit3 = r Mod 10               (N-2)th pair of statements
r = r \ 10

digit2 = r Mod 10               (N-1)th pair of statements
digit1 = r \ 10
```

For example, if you want to split a five-digit integer, you must use four pairs of statements.

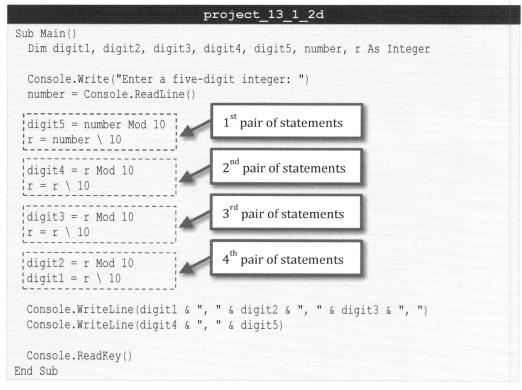

```
project_13_1_2d
Sub Main()
    Dim digit1, digit2, digit3, digit4, digit5, number, r As Integer

    Console.Write("Enter a five-digit integer: ")
    number = Console.ReadLine()

    digit5 = number Mod 10      1st pair of statements
    r = number \ 10

    digit4 = r Mod 10           2nd pair of statements
    r = r \ 10

    digit3 = r Mod 10           3rd pair of statements
    r = r \ 10

    digit2 = r Mod 10           4th pair of statements
    digit1 = r \ 10

    Console.WriteLine(digit1 & ", " & digit2 & ", " & digit3 & ", ")
    Console.WriteLine(digit4 & ", " & digit5)

    Console.ReadKey()
End Sub
```

Exercise 13.1-3   *Displaying an Elapsed Time*

Write a Visual Basic program that prompts the user to enter an integer that represents an elapsed time in seconds and then displays it in the format "DD days HH hours MM minutes and SS seconds". For example if the user enters the number 700005, the message "8 days 2 hours 26 minutes and 45 seconds" must be displayed.

Solution

As you may already know, there are 60 seconds in a minute, 3600 seconds in an hour, and 86400 seconds in a day.

Let's try to analyze number 700005 using the first approach.

Days = 8	The number of days can be isolated if you divide the given integer by 86400 to get the integer quotient `days = 700005 \ 86400`
Remaining seconds = 8805	The remaining seconds can be isolated if you divide the given integer by 86400 to get the integer remainder `r = 700005 Mod 86400`
Hours = 2	The number of hours can be isolated if you divide the remaining seconds by 3600 to get the integer quotient `hours = 8805 \ 3600`
Remaining seconds = 1605	The remaining seconds are now `r = 8805 Mod 3600`
Minutes = 26	The number of minutes can be isolated if you divide the remaining seconds by 60 to get the integer quotient `minutes = 1605 \ 60`
Seconds = 45	The last remainder, which happens to be the number of seconds left, is `seconds = 1605 Mod 60`

The Visual Basic program for this algorithm is as follows.

```
                          project_13_1_3
Sub Main()
    Dim days, hours, minutes, number, r, seconds As Integer

    Console.Write("Enter a period of time in seconds: ")
    number = Console.ReadLine()

    days = number \ 86400    ' 60 * 60 * 24 = 86400
    r = number Mod 86400

    hours = r \ 3600         ' 60 * 60 = 3600
```

```
    r = r Mod 3600

    minutes = r \ 60
    seconds = r Mod 60

    Console.WriteLine(days & " days " & hours & " hours ")
    Console.Write(minutes & " minutes and " & seconds & " seconds")

    Console.ReadKey()
End Sub
```

Exercise 13.1-4   *Reversing a Number*

Write a Visual Basic program that prompts the user to enter a three-digit integer and then reverses it. For example, if the user enters the number 375, the number 573 should be displayed.

Solution

To isolate the three digits of the given number, you can use either first or second approach. Afterward, the only difficulty in this exercise is to build the reversed number. Take the number 375, for example. The three digits, after isolation, are

```
digit1 = 3
digit2 = 7
digit3 = 5
```

You can build the reversed number by simply calculating the sum of the products:

$$\text{digit3} \times 100 + \text{digit2} \times 10 + \text{digit1} \times 1$$

For a change, you can split the given number using the second approach. The Visual Basic program will look like this.

```
                        project_13_1_4
Sub Main()
    Dim digit1, digit2, digit3, number, r, reversed As Integer

    Console.WriteLine("Enter a three-digit integer: ")
    number = Console.ReadLine()

    digit3 = number Mod 10        'This is the rightmost digit
    r = number \ 10

    digit2 = r Mod 10             'This is the digit in the middle
    digit1 = r \ 10              'This is the leftmost digit

    reversed = digit3 * 100 + digit2 * 10 + digit1
    Console.Write(reversed)

    Console.ReadKey()
End Sub
```

13.2   Review Exercises

Complete the following exercises.

1. Write a Visual Basic program that prompts the user to enter any integer and then multiplies its last digit by 8 and displays the result.

    Hint: You can isolate the last digit of any integer using a modulus 10 operation.

2. Write a Visual Basic program that prompts the user to enter a five-digit integer and then reverses it. For example, if the user enters the number 32675, the number 57623 must be displayed.

3. Write a Visual Basic program that prompts the user to enter an integer and then it displays 1 when the number is odd; otherwise, it displays 0. Try not to use any decision control structures since you haven't learned anything about them yet!

4. Write a Visual Basic program that prompts the user to enter an integer and then it displays 1 when the number is even; otherwise, it displays 0. Try not to use any decision control structures since you haven't learned anything about them yet!

5. Write a Visual Basic program that prompts the user to enter an integer representing an elapsed time in seconds and then displays it in the format "WW weeks DD days HH hours MM minutes and SS seconds." For example, if the user enters the number 2000000, the message "3 weeks 23 days 3 hours 33 minutes and 20 seconds" should be displayed.

6. Inside an ATM bank machine there are notes of $20, $10, $5, and $1. Write a Visual Basic program that prompts the user to enter the amount of money he or she wants to withdraw (using an integer value) and then displays the least number of notes the ATM should give. For example, if the user enters an amount of $76, the program should display the message "3 notes of $20, 1 note of $10, 1 note of $5, and 1 note of $1".

7. A robot arrives on the moon in order to perform some experiments. Each of the robot's steps is 25 inches long. Write a Visual Basic program that prompts the user to enter the number of steps the robot made and then calculates and displays the distance traveled in miles, feet, yards, and inches. For example, if the distance traveled is 100000 inches, the program should display the message "1 mile, 1017 yards, 2 feet, and 4 inches".

    It is given that
    - ➢ 1 mile = 63360 inches
    - ➢ 1 yard = 36 inches
    - ➢ 1 foot = 12 inches

Chapter 14
Manipulating Strings

14.1 Introduction

Generally speaking, a string is anything that you can type using the keyboard, including letters, symbols (such as &, *, and @), and digits. Sometimes a program deals with data that comes in the form of strings (text). In Visual Basic, a string is always enclosed in double quotes like this: " ".

Each statement in the next example outputs a string.

```
Sub Main()
  Console.Write("Everything enclosed in double quotes is a ")
  Console.WriteLine("string, even the numbers below:")
  Console.WriteLine("3, 4, 7")
  Console.Write("You can even mix letters, symbols and ")
  Console.WriteLine("numbers like this:")
  Console.Write("The result of 3 + 4 equals to 4")

  Console.ReadKey()
End Sub
```

Strings are everywhere—from word processors, to web browsers, to text messaging programs. Many exercises in this book actually make extensive use of strings. Even though Visual Basic supports many useful procedures for manipulating strings, this chapter covers only those procedures that are absolutely necessary for this book's purpose. However, if you need even more information you can visit

https://msdn.microsoft.com/en-us/library/system.string_methods

> **Notice**: *Visual Basic string procedures can be used when there is a need, for example, to isolate a number of characters from a string, to remove spaces that might exist at the beginning of it, or to convert all of its characters to uppercase.*
>
> **Remember**! *Procedures are nothing more than small subprograms that solve small problems. A subprogram can be defined as a block of statements packaged as a unit that has a name and performs a specific task.*

14.2 The Position of a Character in a String

Let's use the text «Hello World» for the following example. The string consists of 11 characters (including the space character between the two words). The position of each character is shown here.

0	1	2	3	4	5	6	7	8	9	10
H	e	l	l	o		W	o	r	l	d

Visual Basic numerates characters assuming that the first one is at position 0, the second one is at position 1, and so on. Please note that the space between the two words is considered a character as well.

> **Remember!** *A space is a character just like any other character. Just because nobody can see it, it doesn't mean it doesn't exist!*

14.3 Retrieving an Individual Character From a String

Visual Basic allows you to retrieve the individual characters of a string using substring notation. You can use index 0 to access the first character, index 1 to access the second character, and so on. The index of the last character is 1 less than the length of the string. The following Visual Basic program shows an example.

```
                            project_14_3
Sub Main()
  Dim a As String

  a = "Hello World"

  Console.WriteLine(a(0))       'it displays the first letter
  Console.WriteLine(a(6))       'it displays the letter W
  Console.WriteLine(a(10))      'it displays the last letter

  Console.ReadKey()
End Sub
```

> **Notice**: *Please note that the space between the words "Hello" and "World" is considered a character as well. So, the letter W exists in position 6 and not in position 5.*

If you attempt to use an invalid index such as a negative one or an index greater than the length of the string, Visual Basic displays an error message as shown in **Figure 14–1**.

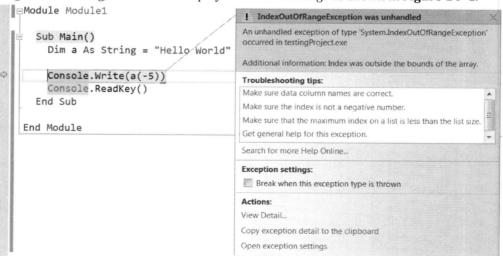

Figure 14–1 An error message indicating an invalid index

> **Remember!** *String indexes must be in a range from 0 to one less than the length of the string.*

Exercise 14.3-1   *Displaying a String Backwards*

Write a Visual Basic program that prompts the user to enter any string with four letters and then displays its contents backwards. For example, if the string entered is "Zeus", the program should display "sueZ".

Solution

Let's say that user's input is assigned to variable `str`. You can access the fourth letter using `str(3)`, the third letter using `str(2)`, and so on.

The Visual Basic program is shown here.

```
                        project_14_3_1
Sub Main()
  Dim str As String

  Console.Write("Enter a word with four letters: ")
  str = Console.ReadLine()

  Console.Write(str(3))
  Console.Write(str(2))
  Console.Write(str(1))
  Console.Write(str(0))

  Console.ReadKey()
End Sub
```

14.4   Useful String Procedures

Trimming

Trimming is the process of removing whitespace characters from the beginning or the end of a string.

Some of the whitespace characters that are removed with the trimming process are:

  ➢   an ordinary space
  ➢   a tab
  ➢   a new line (line feed)
  ➢   a carriage return

For example, you can trim any spaces that the user mistakenly entered at the end or at the beginning of a string.

The procedure that you can use to trim a string is

```
subject.Trim()
```

This removes any whitespace characters from both the beginning and the end of *subject*.

Example

```
                        project_14_4a
Sub Main()
  Dim a, b As String

  a = "         Hello            "
```

```
    b = a.Trim()

    Console.WriteLine(b & " Poseidon!")       'Outputs: Hello Poseidon!

    Console.ReadKey()
End Sub
```

String replacement

```
subject.Replace( search, replace )
```

This searches in *subject* and replaces all occurrences of the *search* string with the *replace* string.

Example

```
                         project_14_4b
Sub Main()
    Dim a, b As String

    a = "I am newbie in Java. Java rocks!"
    b = a.Replace("Java", "VB")

    Console.WriteLine(b)                  'Outputs: I am newbie in VB. VB rocks

    Console.ReadKey()
End Sub
```

Counting the number of characters

```
subject.Length
```

This returns the length of *subject* or, in other words, the number of characters *subject* consists of (including space characters, symbols, numbers, and so on).

Example

```
                         project_14_4c
Sub Main()
    Dim a, b As String
    Dim k As Integer

    a = "Hello Olympians!"
    Console.WriteLine(a.Length)           'Outputs: 16

    b = "I am newbie in Visual Basic"
    k = b.Length
    Console.WriteLine(k)                  'Outputs: 27

    Console.ReadKey()
End Sub
```

Notice: Please note that Length *is not a procedure. This is why there are no parentheses.*

Finding string position

```
subject.IndexOf( search )
```

This finds the numeric position of the first occurrence of *search* in *subject*.

Example

```
                          project_14_4d
Sub Main()
  Dim i As Integer
  Dim a As String

  a = "I am newbie in Visual Basic. Visual Basic rocks!"
  i = a.IndexOf("newbie")

  Console.WriteLine(i)                      'Outputs: 5

  Console.ReadKey()
End Sub
```

Remember! *The first character is at position 0.*

Converting to lowercase or uppercase

There are two procedures that let you convert all letters in a string to lowercase or uppercase.

To lowercase

```
subject.ToLower()
```

This returns the *subject*, converted to lowercase.

Example

```
                          project_14_4e
Sub Main()
  Dim a, b As String

  a = "My NaMe is JohN"
  b = a.ToLower()

  Console.WriteLine(b)                      'Outputs: my name is john

  Console.ReadKey()
End Sub
```

To uppercase

```
subject.ToUpper()
```

This returns the *subject*, converted to uppercase.

Example

```
                          project_14_4f
Sub Main()
  Dim a, b As String
```

```
    a = "My NaMe is JohN"
    b = a.ToUpper()

    Console.WriteLine(b)                    'Outputs: MY NAME IS JOHN

    Console.ReadKey()
End Sub
```

Getting part of a string

```
subject.Substring( beginIndex [, length ] )
```

This returns a portion of *subject*. Specifically, it starts from position *beginIndex* and returns a substring of *length* characters. The argument *length* is optional. If it is omitted, the substring starting from position *beginIndex* until the end of *subject* is returned.

Example

project_14_4g

```
Sub Main()
    Dim a As String

    a = "Hello Athena"

    Console.WriteLine(a.Substring(6, 3))    'Outputs: Ath
    Console.WriteLine(a.Substring(6, 6))    'Outputs: Athena
    Console.WriteLine(a.Substring(7))       'Outputs: thena

    Console.ReadKey()
End Sub
```

Retrieving an individual character

```
subject( index )
```

This returns the character located at *subject*'s specified *index*. As already mentioned, the string indexes start from zero. The index of the last character is 1 less than the length of the string.

Example

project_14_4h

```
Sub Main()
    Dim a As String = "Hello Hermes"

    Console.WriteLine(a(0))                 'outputs: H
    Console.WriteLine(a(11))                'outputs: s
    Console.WriteLine(a(5))                 'outputs a space character

    Console.ReadKey()
End Sub
```

Comparing strings

```
subject.CompareTo( string )
```

This returns a value less than 0 if *subject* is lexicographically less than *string*; and a value greater than 0 if *subject* is lexicographically greater than *string*.

The term "lexicographically" means that the letter "A" is considered "less than" the letter "B", the letter "B" is considered "less than" the letter "C," and so on. Of course, if two strings contain words in which the first letter is identical, Visual Basic moves on and compares their second letters and perhaps their third letters (if necessary). For example, the word "backspace" is considered "less than" the word "backwards" because the fifth letter, "s", is "less than" the fifth letter, "w."

Example

```
                              project_14_4k
Sub Main()
   Dim a As String = "backspace"
   Dim b As String = "backwards"
   Dim c As String = "Backspace"
   Dim d As String = "winter"


   Console.WriteLine(a.CompareTo(b))        'outputs: -1
   Console.WriteLine(a.CompareTo(c))        'outputs: -1
   Console.WriteLine(c.CompareTo(a))        'outputs: 1
   Console.WriteLine(d.CompareTo(c))        'outputs: 1


   Console.ReadKey()
End Sub
```

Notice: *Please note that the letters "b" and "B" are considered two different letters.*

Converting a string to a number

```
Int32.TryParse( x_str, x )
Int64.TryParse( x_str, x )
Double.TryParse( x_str, x )
```

These procedures convert the string representation of a number contained in a string variable x_str to its numeric equivalent, and then assign the result to the numeric variable x. The procedures return True if the conversion is successful, and False otherwise.

Example

```
                              project_14_4i
Sub Main()
   Dim a As Integer
   Dim b As Double
   Dim s As String
   Dim result As Boolean

   s = "15"
   'The next statement assigns value 15 to integer variable a
   'and value True to variable result
   result = Int32.TryParse(s, a)

   Console.WriteLine(result)                'This displays True
   Console.WriteLine(a)                     'This displays 15
```

```
s = "3.14"
'The next statement assigns value 3.14 to double variable b
'and value True to variable result
result = Double.TryParse(s, b)

Console.WriteLine(result)          'This displays True
Console.WriteLine(b)               'This displays 3.14

s = "Hello"
'The next statement assigns value False to variable result
result = Int32.TryParse(s, a)

Console.WriteLine(result)          'This displays False

Console.ReadKey()
End Sub
```

Exercise 14.4-1   *Switching the Order of Names*

Write a Visual Basic program that prompts the user to enter in one single string both first and last name. In the end, the program should change the order of the two names.

Solution

This exercise is not the same as the one that you learned in Chapter 8, which swapped the numeric values of two variables. In this exercise, you must split the string and assign each name to a different variable. If you manage to do so, then you can just rejoin them in a different order.

Let's try to understand this exercise using an example. The string that you must split and the position of its individual character is shown here.

0	1	2	3	4	5	6	7	8
T	o	m		S	m	i	t	h

The character that visually separates the first name from the last name is the space character between them. The problem is that this character is not always at position 3. Someone can have a short first name like "Tom" and someone else can have a longer one like "Robert". Thus, you need something that actually finds the position of the space character regardless of the content of the string.

Procedure IndexOf() is what you are looking for! If you use it to find the position of the space character in the string "Tom Smith", it returns the value 3. But if you use it to find the space character in another string, such as "Angelina Brown", it returns the value 8 instead.

> *Notice: The value 3 is not just the position where the space character exists. It also represents the number of characters that the word "Tom" contains! The same applies to the value 8 that is returned for the string "Angelina Brown". It represents both the position where the space character exists and the number of characters that the word "Angelina" contains!*

The Visual Basic program for this algorithm is shown here.

```
                            project_14_4_1
Sub Main()
  Dim full_name, name1, name2 As String
  Dim space_pos As Integer

  Console.Write("Enter your full name: ")
  full_name = Console.ReadLine()

  'find the position of space character. This is also the number
  'of characters first name contains
  space_pos = full_name.IndexOf(" ")

  'get space_pos number of characters starting from position 0
  name1 = full_name.Substring(0, space_pos)

  'get the rest of the characters starting from position space_pos + 1
  name2 = full_name.Substring(space_pos + 1)

  full_name = name2 + " " + name1
  Console.Write(full_name)

  Console.ReadKey()
End Sub
```

Notice: *Please note that this program cannot be applied to a Spanish name such as "Maria Teresa García Ramírez de Arroyo." The reason is obvious!*

Exercise 14.4-2   *Creating a Login ID*

Write a Visual Basic program that prompts the user to enter his or her last name and then creates a login ID from the first four letters of the name (in lowercase) and a three-digit random integer.

Solution

To create a random integer you can use the Next() procedure. Since you need a random integer of three digits, the range must be between 100 and 999.

The Visual Basic program for this algorithm is shown here.

```
                            project_14_4_2
Sub Main()
  Dim random_int As Integer
  Dim last_name As String
  Dim rnd As New Random()

  Console.Write("Enter last name: ")
  last_name = Console.ReadLine()

  'Get Random integer between 100 and 999
  random_int = rnd.Next(100, 1000)
```

```
   Console.Write(last_name.Substring(0, 4).ToLower() & random_int)

   Console.ReadKey()
End Sub
```

> **Notice**: Please note how the procedure Substring() is chained to the procedure ToLower(). The result of the first procedure is used as a subject for the second procedure. This is a writing style that most programmers prefer to follow because it helps to save a lot of code lines. Of course you can chain as many procedures as you wish, but if you chain too many of them, no one will be able to understand your code.

Exercise 14.4-3   *Creating a Random Word*

Write a Visual Basic program that displays a random word consisting of five letters.

Solution

To create a random word you need a string that contains all 26 letters of the English alphabet. Then you can use the Next() procedure to choose a random letter between position 0 and 25.

The Visual Basic program for this algorithm is shown here.

```
                        project_14_4_3
Sub Main()
  Dim alphabet As String
  Dim rnd As New Random()

  alphabet = "abcdefghijklmnopqrstuvwxyz"

  Console.Write(alphabet(rnd.Next(0, 26)))
  Console.Write(alphabet(rnd.Next(0, 26)))
  Console.Write(alphabet(rnd.Next(0, 26)))
  Console.Write(alphabet(rnd.Next(0, 26)))
  Console.Write(alphabet(rnd.Next(0, 26)))

  Console.ReadKey()
End Sub
```

14.5   Review Questions: True/False

Choose **true** or **false** for each of the following statements.

1.   A string is anything that you can type using the keyboard.
2.   Strings must be enclosed in parentheses.
3.   The phrase "Hi there!" contains 8 characters.
4.   In the phrase "Hi there!" the letter "t" is at position 3.
5.   The statement y = a(1) assigns the second letter of the string contained in variable a to variable y.

6. The statement

```
y = a(-1)
```

is a valid statement.

7. Trimming is the process of removing whitespace characters from the beginning or the end of a string.

8. The statement `y = "Hello          Aphrodite".Trim()` assigns the value "HelloAphrodite" to variable y.

9. The statement `Console.Write("Hi there!".Replace("Hi", "Hello"))` displays the message "Hello there!".

10. The following code fragment

```
a = "Hi there"
index = a.IndexOf("the")
```

assigns the value 4 to the variable index.

11. The statement `Console.Write("hello there!".ToUpper())` displays the message "Hello There".

12. The following code fragment

```
a = "Hello there!"
Console.Write(a.Substring(0))
```

displays the message "Hello there!".

13. The statement `Console.Write(a.Substring(0, a.Length))` displays some letters of the variable a.

14. The statement `Console.Write(a.Substring(a.Length - 1, 1))` is equivalent to the statement `Console.Write(a(a.Length - 1))`.

15. The following code fragment

```
y = "hello there!"
Console.Write(y.ToUpper().Substring(0, 5))
```

displays the word "HELLO".

16. The following code fragment

```
y = "HELLO THERE!"
Console.Write(y.ToLower())
```

displays the message "Hello there!".

17. The statement `Console.Write(a.Substring(0, 1))` is equivalent to the statement `Console.Write(a(0))`.

14.6 Review Questions: Multiple Choice

Select the correct answer for each of the following statements.

1. Which of the following is **not** a string?
   a. "Hello there!"
   b. "13"
   c. "13.5"
   d. All of the above are strings.

2. In which position does the space character in the string "Hello Zeus!", exist?

   a. 6

   b. 5

   c. Space is not a character.

   d. none of the above

3. The statement `Console.Write(a.Substring(a.Length - 1, 1))` displays

   a. the last character of variable `a`.

   b. the second to last character of variable `a`.

   c. The statement is not valid.

4. The statement

```
a.Trim().Replace("a", "b").Replace("w", "y")
```

   is equivalent to the statement

   a. `a.Replace("a", "b").Replace("w", "y").Trim()`

   b. `a.Replace("a", "b").Trim().Replace("w", "y")`

   c. `a.Trim().Replace("w", "y").Replace("a", "b")`

   d. all of the above

5. The statement `a.Replace(" ", "")`

   a. adds a space between each letter in the variable `a`.

   b. removes all space characters from the variable `a`.

   c. empties the variable `a`.

6. The statement `"  Hello  ".Replace(" ", "")` is equivalent to the statement

   a. `"  Hello  ".Replace("", " ")`.

   b. `"  Hello  ".Trim()`.

   c. all of the above

   d. none of the above

7. The following code fragment

```
a = ""
Console.Write(a.Length)
```

   displays

   a. nothing.

   b. 1.

   c. 0.

   d. The statement is invalid.

   e. none of the above

8. Which value assigns the following code fragment

```
to_be_or_not_to_be = "2b Or Not 2b"
Shakespeare = to_be_or_not_to_be.IndexOf("b")
```

   to the variable `Shakespeare`?

   a. 1

   b. 2

    c.   6

    d.   none of the above

9.   What does the following code fragment?

```
a = "Hi there"
b = a.Substring(a.IndexOf(" ") + 1)
```

    a.   It assigns the word "Hi" to the variable b.

    b.   It assigns a space character to the variable b.

    c.   It assigns the word "there" to the variable b.

    d.   none of the above

10. What does the following code fragment?

```
a = "Hi there"
b = a.Replace("Hi", "Hello")
```

    a.   It assigns the string "Hello there" to the variable a.

    b.   It displays the message "Hello there".

    c.   all of the above

    d.   none of the above

14.7 Review Exercises

Complete the following exercises.

1.   Write a Visual Basic program that prompts the user to enter his or her first name, middle name, last name, and his or her preferred title (Mr., Mrs., Ms., Dr., and so on) and displays them formatted in all the following ways.

    Title FirstName MiddleName LastName

    FirstName MiddleName LastName

    LastName, FirstName

    LastName, FirstName MiddleName

    LastName, FirstName MiddleName, Title

    FirstName LastName

For example, assume that the user enters the following:

    First name: Aphrodite

    Middle name: Maria

    Last name: Boura

    Title: Ms.

The program should display the user's name formatted in all the following ways:

    Ms. Aphrodite Maria Boura

    Aphrodite Maria Boura

    Boura, Aphrodite

    Boura, Aphrodite Maria

    Boura, Aphrodite Maria, Ms.

    Aphrodite Boura

2.   Write a Visual Basic program that creates and displays a random word consisting of five letters. The first letter must be a capital letter.

3. Write a Visual Basic program that prompts the user to enter his or her name and then creates a secret password consisting of three letters (in lowercase) randomly picked up from his or her name, and a random four-digit number. For example, if the user enters "Vassilis Bouras" a secret password can probably be one of "sar1359" or "vbs7281" or "bor1459".

Review Questions in "Sequence Control Structures"

Answer the following questions.

1. What is a sequence control structure?
2. What operations can a sequence control structure perform?
3. Give some examples of how you can use the quotient and the remainder of an integer division.
4. What is a procedure?
5. What does the term "chain a procedure" mean?

Section 4

Decision Control Structures

Chapter 15
Introduction to Decision Control Structures

15.1   What is a Decision Control Structure?

All you have learned so far is just the sequence control structure, where statements are executed sequentially, in the same order in which they appear in the program. However, in serious Visual Basic programming, rarely do you want the statements to be executed sequentially. Many times you want a block of statements to be executed in one situation and an entirely different block of statements to be executed in another situation. This is where a decision control structure can take action!

A decision control structure evaluates a Boolean expression or a set of Boolean expressions and then decides which block of statements to execute.

15.2   What is a Boolean Expression?

A Boolean expression is an expression that results in a Boolean value, that is, either True or False.

15.3   How to Write Boolean Expressions

A simple Boolean expression is written as

Operand1   Comparison Operator   Operand2

where

> ➤ *Operand1* and *Operand2* can be values, variables or mathematical expressions
> ➤ *Comparison Operator* can be one of those shown in **Table 15-1**

Table 15–1 Comparison Operators in Visual Basic

Comparison Operator	Description
=	Equal (not assignment)
<>	Not equal
>	Greater than
<	Less than
>=	Greater than or equal to
<=	Less than or equal to

Remember: *In Visual Basic, in order to test if one string is lexicographically "greater" or "less" than another string, you need to use the* CompareTo() *procedure. For example, the statement* a.CompareTo(b) *compares the content of the string variable* a *to the content of string variable* b *and returns a value greater than 0 if variable* a *is lexicographically greater than variable* b, *or a value less than 0 if variable* a *is lexicographically less than variable* b.

Here are some examples of Boolean expressions:

> x = 5. This can be read as "*test if* x *is equal to 5*"

> x > y. This can be read as "*test if* x *is greater than* y"

> x <= y. This can be read as "*test if* x *is less than or equal to* y"

> x <> 3 * y + 4. This can be read as "*test if* x *is not equal to the result of the expression* 3 * y + 4"

> s = "Hello" This can be read as "test if s is equal to the word 'Hello'"

> **Notice**: *For humans, Boolean expressions should be interpreted as questions. They should be read as "Is something equal to/greater than/less than something else?" and the answer is just a "Yes" or a "No"* (True *or* False).

Moreover, given that a Boolean expression actually returns a value (True or False), this value can be directly assigned to a variable. For example, the expression

```
a = x > y
```

assigns a value of True or False to Boolean variable a. It can be read as "*If the content of variable* x *is greater than the content of variable* y, *assign the value* True *to variable* a; *otherwise, assign the value* False." This next example displays the value True on the screen.

```
Sub Main()
    Dim x, y As Integer
    Dim a As Boolean

    x = 8
    y = 5
    a = x > y

    Console.Write(a)

    Console.ReadKey()
End Sub
```

Exercise 15.3-1   *Filling in the Table*

Fill in the following table with the words "True" or "False" according to the values of the variables a, b, and c.

a	b	c	a = 10	b <= a	c > 3 * a - b
3	-5	7			
10	10	21			
-4	-2	-9			

Solution

Some notes about the table:

> The Boolean expression a = 10 is True when the content of the variable a is 10.

> The Boolean expression b <= a is True when b is less than or equal to a.

> ➤ The Boolean expression c > 3 * a - b is True when c is greater than the result of the expression 3 * a - b. Please be careful with the cases where b is negative. For example, in the first line, a is equal to 3 and b is equal to -5. The result of the expression 3 * a - b is 3 * 3 - (-5) = 3 * 3 + 5 = 14.

So, the table becomes

a	b	c	a = 10	b <= a	c > 3 * a - b
3	-5	7	False	True	False
10	10	21	True	True	True
-4	-2	-9	False	False	True

15.4   Logical Operators and Complex Boolean Expressions

A more complex Boolean expression can be built of simpler Boolean expressions and can be written as

> Boolean_Expression1   **Logical Operator**   Boolean_Expression2

where

> ➤ Boolean_Expression1 and Boolean_Expression2 can be any Boolean expression
> ➤ Logical Operator can be one of those shown in **Table 15-2**

Table 15–2 Logical Operators in Visual Basic

Logical Operator	Description
And	Also known as logical conjunction
Or	Also known as logical disjunction
Not	Also known as negation or logical complement

The truth table for all three operators is shown here.

Boolean Expression1 (BE1)	Boolean Expression2 (BE2)	BE1 And BE2	BE1 Or BE2	Not(BE1)
False	False	False	False	True
False	True	False	True	True
True	False	False	True	False
True	True	True	True	False

Are you still confused? You shouldn't be! It is quite simple!

> ➤ The result of the logical operator And is True when both BE1 **and** BE2 are True.
> ➤ The result of the logical operator Or is True when either BE1 **or** BE2 is True (at least one).
> ➤ The logical operator Not just reverses the result of a Boolean expression. In this table, when BE1 is True the result is False and vice versa.

Next are some examples of complex Boolean expressions. The parentheses are not really necessary. They are used just for increased readability.

- ➤ `(x = 5) And (x > y)`. This can be read as *"test if x is equal to 5 and greater than y"*
- ➤ `(x > y) Or (x = 3)`. This can be read as "test if *x is greater than y or equal to 3*"
- ➤ `Not(x < y)`. This can be read as "test if *x is **not** less than y*" or, in other words, "*test if x is greater than or equal to y*"

15.5 What is the Order of Precedence of Logical Operators?

A very complex Boolean expression may use several logical operators like the one shown here

$$x > y \ \textbf{Or} \ \ x = 5 \ \ \textbf{And} \ \ x <= z \ \ \textbf{Or Not}(z = 1)$$

So, a reasonable question is "which logical operation is performed first?"

Logical operators follow the same precedence rules that apply to the majority of programming languages. The order of precedence is: logical complements (`Not`) are performed first, logical conjunctions (`And`) are performed next, and logical disjunctions (`Or`) are performed at the end.

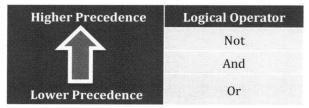

Higher Precedence	Logical Operator
	Not
	And
Lower Precedence	Or

> **Notice**: *You can always use parentheses to change the default precedence.*

15.6 What is the Order of Precedence of Arithmetic, Comparison, and Logical Operators?

In many cases, an expression may contain different type of operators, such as the one shown here.

$$a \ * \ b \ + \ 2 \ > \ 21 \ Or \ Not(c = b \ / \ 2) \ And \ c > 13$$

In such cases, arithmetic operations are performed first, comparison operations are performed next, and logical operations are performed at the end, as shown in the following table.

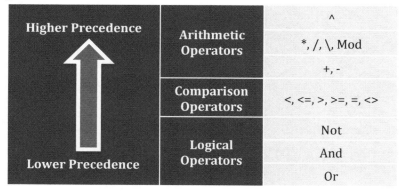

Higher Precedence	Arithmetic Operators	^
		*, /, \, Mod
		+, -
	Comparison Operators	<, <=, >, >=, =, <>
	Logical Operators	Not
		And
Lower Precedence		Or

Exercise 15.6-1 *Filling in the Truth Table*

Fill in the following table with the words "True" or "False" according to the values of the variables a, b and c.

a	b	c	a > 2 Or c > b And c > 2	Not(a > 2 Or c > b And c > 2)
1	-5	7		
10	10	3		
-4	-2	-9		

Solution

To calculate the result of complex Boolean expressions you can use the following graphical method.

For a = 1, b = -5, c = 7,

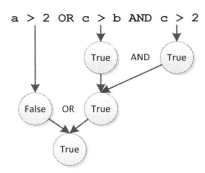

the final result is True.

> **Remember!** *The AND operation has a higher precedence and is performed before the OR operation.*

For a = 10, b = 10, c = 3,

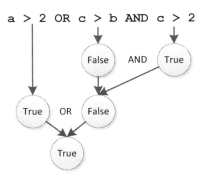

the final result is True.

For a = -4, b = -2, c = -9,

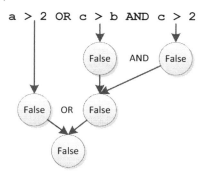

the final result is False.

The values in the table's fifth column can be calculated very easily because the Boolean expression in its column heading is almost identical to the one in the fourth column. The only difference is the Not operator in front of the expression. So, the values in the fifth column can be calculated by simply negating the results in the fourth column!

The final truth table is shown here.

a	b	c	a > 2 Or c > b And c > 2	Not(a > 2 Or c > b And c > 2)
1	-5	7	True	False
10	10	3	True	False
-4	-2	-9	False	True

Exercise 15.6-2   *Calculating the Results of Complex Boolean Expressions*

Calculate the results of the following complex Boolean expressions when variables a, b, c, *and* d *contain the values 5, 2, 7, and -3 respectively.*

    i.   (3 * a + b / 47 - c * b / a > 23) And (b <> 2)

    ii.   (a * b - c / 2 + 21 * c / 3) Or (a >= 5)

Solution

Don't be scared! The results can be found very easily. All you need is to recall what applies to And and Or operators.

    i.   The result of an And operator is True when both Boolean expressions are True. If you take a closer look, the result of the Boolean expression on the right (b <> 2) is False. So, you don't have to waste your time calculating the result of the Boolean expression on the left. The final result is definitely False.

    ii.   The result of an Or operator is True when at least one Boolean expression is True. If you take a closer look, the result of the Boolean expression on the right (a >= 5) is actually True. So, don't bother calculating the result of the Boolean expression on the left. The final result is definitely True.

Exercise 15.6-3 *Converting English Sentences to Boolean Expressions*

A head teacher asks the students to raise their hands according to their age. He wants to find the students who are

   i.   *between the ages of 9 and 12.*

   ii.   *under the age of 8 and over the age of 11.*

   iii.   *8, 10, and 12 years old.*

   iv.   *between the ages of 6 and 8, and between the ages of 10 and 12.*

   v.   *neither 10 nor 12 years old.*

Solution

To compose the required Boolean expressions, a variable `age` is used.

   i.   The first sentence can be graphically represented as shown here.

Be careful though! It is valid to write $9 \le age \le 12$ in mathematics, but in a computer language this is not possible. You must split the expression into two parts.

<code>age >= 9 And age <= 12</code>

For your confirmation, you can test this Boolean expression for several values inside and outside of the region of interest. For example, the result of the expression is `False` for the age values 7, 8, 13, and 17. On the contrary, for the age values 9, 10, 11, and 12, the result is `True`.

   ii.   The second sentence can be graphically represented as shown here.

> **Notice**: *Please note the absence of the two circles. This means that the values 8 and 11 are not included within the two regions of interest.*

Be careful with the sentence "Under the age of 8 and over the age of 11". It's a trap! Don't make the mistake of writing

<code>age < 8 And age > 11</code>

There is no person on the planet Earth that can be under the age of 8 **and** over the age of 11 concurrently!

The trap is in the word "**and**". Try to rephrase the sentence and make it *"Children! Please raise your hand if you are under the age of 8 **or** over the age of 11."* Now it's better and the correct Boolean expression becomes

<code>age < 8 Or age > 11</code>

For your confirmation, you can test this expression for several values inside and outside of the regions of interest. For example, the result of the expression is `False` for the age values 8, 9, 10 and 11. On the contrary, for the age values 6, 7, 12, and 15, the result is `True`.

iii.   Oops! Another trap with the **"and"** word again! Obviously, the next Boolean expression is wrong.

<code>age = 8 And age = 10 And age = 12</code>

As before, there isn't any student who is 8 **and** 10 **and** 12 years old concurrently! Once again, the correct Boolean expression must use the Or operator.

<code>age = 8 Or age = 10 Or age = 12</code>

For your confirmation, you can test this expression for several values inside and outside of the regions of interest. For example, the result of the expression is False for the age values 7, 9, 11, and 13. For the age values 8, 10, and 12, the result is True.

iv.   This sentence can be graphically represented as shown here.

and the Boolean expression is

<code>age >= 6 And age <= 8 Or age >= 10 And age <= 12</code>

For your confirmation, the result of the expression is False for the age values 5, 9, 13, and 16. For the age values 6, 7, 8, 10, 11, and 12, the result is True.

v.   The Boolean expression for last sentence can be written as

<code>age <> 10 And age <> 12</code>

> **Remember!** *When the arrows of the region of interest are pointing toward each other, a logical operator* And *must be used; otherwise, a logical operator* Or *must be used.*
>
>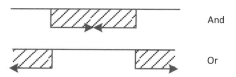

15.7   How to Negate Boolean Expressions

Negation is the process of reversing the meaning of a Boolean expression. There are two approaches used to negate a Boolean expression.

First Approach

The first approach is the easiest one. Just use a Not operator in front of the original Boolean expression and your negated Boolean expression is ready! For example,

if the original Boolean expression is x > 5 And y = 3,

the negated Boolean expression becomes Not(x > 5 And y = 3).

> *Notice: Please note that the entire expression must be enclosed in parentheses. It would be completely incorrect if you had written the expression without parentheses, as* Not x > 5 And y = 3. *In this case the* Not *operator would negate only the first Boolean expression,* x > 5.

Second Approach

The second approach is a little bit more complex but not difficult to learn. All you must do is negate every operator according to the following table.

Original Operator	Negated Operator
=	<>
<>	=
>	<=
<	>=
<=	>
>=	<
And	Or
Or	And
Not	Not

> **Notice**: Please note that the Not operator remains intact.

For example,

if the original Boolean expression is x > 5 And y = 3,

the negated Boolean expression becomes x <= 5 Or y <> 3.

Exercise 15.7-1   Negating Boolean Expressions

Negate the following Boolean expressions using both approaches.

   i.   b <> 4

  ii.   a * 3 + 2 > 0

 iii.   Not(a = 5 And b >= 7)

  iv.   a = True

   v.   b > 7 And Not(x > 4)

  vi.   a = 4 Or b <> 2

Solution

First Approach

   i.   Not(b <> 4)

  ii.   Not(a * 3 + 2 > 0)

 iii.   Not(Not(a = 5 And b >= 7)), or the equivalent a = 5 And b >= 7

> **Notice**: Two negations result in an affirmative. That is, two Not operators in a row negate each other.

  iv.   Not(a = True)

   v.   Not(b > 7 And Not(x > 4))

  vi.   Not(a = 4 Or b <> 2)

Second Approach

   i.   b = 4

ii.   `a * 3 + 2 <= 0`

> **Notice:** *Please note that arithmetic operators are **not** negated. Don't you ever dare replace the plus (+) with a minus (-) operator!*

iii.   `Not(a <> 5 Or b < 7)`

> **Notice:** *Please note that* `Not` *operator remains intact.*

iv.   `a <> True`

v.   `b <= 7 Or Not(x <= 4)`

vi.   `a <> 4 And b = 2`

15.8   Review Questions: True/False

Choose **true** or **false** for each of the following statements.

1.   A Boolean expression is an expression that always results in one of two values.
2.   A Boolean expression includes at least one logical operator.
3.   In Visual Basic, the expression `x == 5` tests if the variable `x` is equal to 5.
4.   The statement

```
a = b > c
```

is not a valid Visual Basic statement.

5.   The Boolean expression `b < 5` tests if the variable `b` is 5 or less.
6.   The `And` operator is also known as a logical disjunction operator.
7.   The `Not` operator is also known as a logical complement operator.
8.   The result of a logical conjunction of two Boolean expressions equals the result of the logical disjunction of them, given that both Boolean expressions are `True`.
9.   The result of a logical disjunction of two Boolean expressions is definitely `True`, given that the Boolean expressions have different values.
10. The expression `c = 3 And d > 7` is considered a complex Boolean expression.
11. The result of the logical operator `Or` is `True` when both operands (Boolean expressions) are `True`.
12. The result of the Boolean expression `Not(x = 5)` is `True` when the variable `x` contains any value except 5.
13. The `Not` operator has the highest precedence among logical operators.
14. The `Or` operator has the lowest precedence among logical operators.
15. In the Boolean expression `x > y Or x = 5 And x <= z`, the `And` operation is performed before the `Or` operation.
16. In the Boolean expression `a * b + c > 21 Or c = b / 2`, the program first tests if `c` is greater than 21.
17. When a teacher wants to find the students who are under the age of 8 and over the age of 11, the corresponding Boolean expression is `age < 8 And a > 11`.
18. The Boolean expression `x < 0 And x > 100` is, for any value of `x`, always `False`.
19. The Boolean expression `x > 0 Or x < 100` is, for any value of `x`, always `True`.

20. The Boolean expression x > 5 is equivalent to Not (x < 5).

21. The Boolean expression Not(x > 5 And y = 5) is not equivalent to Not(x > 5) And y = 5.

22. In William Shakespeare[1]'s *Hamlet* (Act 3, Scene 1), the main character says "To be, or not to be: that is the question:.... " If you write this down as a Boolean expression To_Be Or Not(To_Be), the result of the "Shakespearean" expression is always True for the following code fragment.

```
B = That_is_the_question Mod 2 / 2
To_Be = 2 * B = 1
result = To_Be Or Not(To_Be)
```

where variable That_is_the_question contains numeric values.

23. The Boolean expression Not(Not(x > 5)) is equivalent to x > 5.

15.9   Review Questions: Multiple Choice

Select the correct answer for each of the following statements.

1. Which of the following is **not** a comparison operator?

    a. >=

    b. =

    c. <

    d. All of the above are comparison operators.

2. Which of the following is not a Visual Basic logical operator?

    a. Nor

    b. Not

    c. All of the above are logical operators.

    d. None of the above is a logical operator.

3. If variable x contains a value of 5, what value does the statement y = x Mod 2 = 1 assign to variable y?

    a. True

    b. False

    c. none of the above

4. If variable x contains a value of 5, what value does the statement y = x Mod 2 = 0 Or Fix(x / 2) = 2 assign to variable y?

    a. True

    b. False

    c. none of the above

5. The temperature in a laboratory room should be between 50 and 80 degrees Fahrenheit. Which of the following Boolean expressions tests for this condition?

    a. t >= 50 Or t <= 80

[1] William Shakespeare (1564–1616) was an English poet, playwright, and actor. He is often referred to as England's national poet. He wrote about 40 plays and several long narrative poems. His works are counted among the best representations of world literature. His plays have been translated into every major living language and are still performed today.

    b. `t > 50 And t < 80`

    c. `t >= 50 And t <= 80`

    d. `t > 50 Or t < 80`

6. Which of the following is equivalent to the Boolean expression `t = 3 Or t > 30` ?

    a. `t = 3 And Not(t <= 30)`

    b. `t = 3 And Not(t < 30)`

    c. `Not(t <> 3) Or Not(t < 30)`

    d. `Not(t <> 3 And t <= 30)`

15.10 Review Exercises

Complete the following exercises.

1. Match each element from the first column with one or more elements from the second column.

Operator		Sign	
i.	Logical operator	a.	Mod
ii.	Arithmetic operator	b.	+=
iii.	Comparison operator	c.	And
iv.	Assignment operator (in general)	d.	<
		e.	Or
		f.	>=
		g.	Not
		h.	=
		i.	*=
		j.	/

2. Fill in the following table with the words "True" or "False" according to the values of variables a, b, and c.

a	b	c	a <> 1	b > a	c / 2 > 2 * a
3	-5	8			
1	10	20			
-4	-2	-9			

3. Fill in the following table with the words "True" or "False" according to the values of the Boolean expressions BE1 and BE2.

Boolean Expression1 (BE1)	Boolean Expression2 (BE2)	BE1 Or BE2	BE1 And BE2	Not(BE2)
False	False			
False	True			

True	False
True	True

4. Fill in the following table with the words "True" or "False" according to the values of variables a, b, and c.

a	b	c	a > 3 Or c > b And c > 1	a > 3 And c > b Or c > 1
4	-6	2		
-3	2	-4		
2	5	5		

5. For x = 4, y = -2 and flag = True, fill in the following table with the corresponding values.

Expression	Value
(x + y) ^ 3	
(x + y) / (x ^ 2 - 14)	
(x - 1) = y + 5	
x > 2 And y = 1	
x = 1 Or y = -2 And Not(flag = False)	
Not(x >= 3) And (x Mod 2 > 1)	

6. Calculate the result of each the following complex Boolean expressions when variables a, b, c, and d contain the values 6, -3, 4, and 7 respectively.

    i.   (3 * a + b / 5 - c * b / a > 4) And (b <> -3)

    ii.   (a * b - c / 2 + 21 * c / 3 <> 8) Or (a >= 5)

7. A head teacher asks the students to raise their hands according to their age. He wants to find the students who are:

    i.   under the age of 12, but not those who are 8 years old.

    ii.   between the ages of 6 and 9, and also those who are 11 years old.

    iii. over the age of 7, but not those who are 10 or 12 years old.

    iv. 6, 9, and 11 years old.

    v.   between the ages of 6 and 12, but not those who are 8 years old.

    vi. neither 7 nor 10 years old.

To compose the required Boolean expressions, use a variable age.

8. Negate the following Boolean expressions without using the Not operator.

    i.   x = 4 And y <> 3   iv. x <> False

    ii.   x + 4 <= 0   v.   Not(x >= 4 Or z > 4)

    iii. Not(x > 5) Or y = 4   vi. x <> 2 And x >= -5

9. As you already know, two negations result in an affirmative. Write the equivalent of the following Boolean expressions by negating them twice (applying both methods).

i.   `x >= 4 And y <> 10`

ii.   `x - 2 >= 9`

iii. `Not(x >= 2) Or y <> 4`

iv. `x <> False Or y = 3`

v.   `Not(x >= 2 And y >= 2)`

vi. `x <> -2 And x <= 2`

Chapter 16
The Single-Alternative Decision Structure

16.1 The Single-Alternative Decision Structure

This is the simplest decision control structure. It includes a statement or block of statements on the "true" path only.

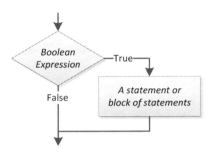

If the Boolean expression evaluates to True, the statement, or block of statements, of the structure is executed; otherwise, the statements are skipped.

The general form of the Visual Basic statement is

```
If Boolean_Expression Then
    A statement or block of statements
End If
```

When only one single statement is used in the If statement, you can write it on one single line, like this:

```
If Boolean_Expression Then One Single Statement
```

Exercise 16.1-1   *Trace Tables and Single-Alternative Decision Structures*

Design the corresponding flowchart and create a trace table to determine the values of the variables in each step of the next Visual Basic program for two different executions.

The input values for the two executions are (i) 10, and (ii) 51.

```
                        project_16_1_1
Sub Main()
    Dim a, y As Integer

    a = Console.ReadLine()

    y = 5
    If a * 2 > 100 Then
        a = a * 3
        y = a * 4
    End If

    Console.Write(a & " " & y)
```

```
    Console.ReadKey()
End Sub
```

Solution

The flowchart is shown here.

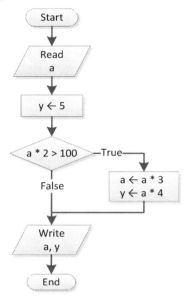

The trace tables for each input are shown here.

i.   For the input value of 10, the trace table looks like this.

Step	Statement	Notes	a	y
1	`a = Console.ReadLine()`	User enters the value 10	**10**	?
2	`y = 5`		10	5
3	`If a * 2 > 100 Then`	This evaluates to False		
4	`Console.Write(a & " " & y)`	The values 10, 5 are displayed		

ii. For the input value of 51, the trace table looks like this.

Step	Statement	Notes	a	y
1	`a = Console.ReadLine()`	User enters the value 51	**51**	?
2	`y = 5`		51	**5**
3	`If a * 2 > 100 Then`	This evaluates to True		
4	`a = a * 3`		**153**	5
5	`y = a * 4`		153	**612**

| 6 | `Console.Write(a & " " & y)` | The values 153, 612 are displayed |

Exercise 16.1-2   *The Absolute Value of a Number*

Design a flowchart and write the corresponding Visual Basic program that lets the user enter a number and then displays its absolute value.

Solution

Actually, there are two approaches. The first approach uses a single-alternative decision structure, whereas the second one uses the built-in `Math.Abs()` procedure.

First Approach – Using a single-alternative decision structure

The approach is simple. If the user enters a negative value, for example -5, this value is changed and displayed as +5. A positive number or zero, however, should remain as is. The solution is shown in the flowchart that follows.

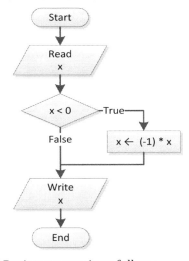

The corresponding Visual Basic program is as follows.

```
                      project_16_1_2a
Sub Main()
  Dim x As Double

  x = Console.ReadLine()

  If x < 0 Then
    x = (-1) * x
  End If

  Console.Write(x)

  Console.ReadKey()
End Sub
```

Second Approach – Using the `Math.Abs()` procedure

In this case, you need just a few lines of code without any decision control structure!

```
                         project_16_1_2b
Sub Main()
   Dim x As Double

   x = Console.ReadLine()
   Console.Write(Math.Abs(x))

   Console.ReadKey()
End Sub
```

16.2   Review Questions: True/False

Choose **true** or **false** for each of the following statements.

1. The single-alternative decision structure is used when a sequence of statements must be executed.

2. You use a single-alternative decision structure to allow other programmers to more easily understand your program.

3. It is a possible that none of the statements enclosed in a single-alternative decision structure will be executed.

4. In a flowchart, the Decision symbol represents the beginning and the end of an algorithm.

5. The following code

    ```
    Const If = 5
    Sub Main()
       Dim x As Integer

       x = If + 5
       Console.Write(x)

       Console.ReadKey()
    End Sub
    ```

    is syntactically correct.

6. The single-alternative decision structure uses the reserved keyword `Else`.

7. The following code fragment satisfies the property of definiteness.

    ```
    If b <> 3 Then
       x = a / (b - 3)
    End If
    ```

8. The following Visual Basic program satisfies the property of definiteness.

    ```
    Sub Main()
       Dim a, b, x As Double

       a = Console.ReadLine()
       b = Console.ReadLine()

       If b <> 3 Then
    ```

```
        x = a / (b - 3)
    End If
    Console.Write(x)

    Console.ReadKey()
End Sub
```

16.3 Review Questions: Multiple Choice

Select the correct answer for each of the following statements.

1. The single-alternative decision structure is used when

    a. statements are executed one after another.

    b. a decision must be made before executing some statements.

    c. none of the above

    d. all of the above

2. The single-alternative decision structure includes a statement or block of statements on

    a. the false path only.

    b. both paths.

    c. the true path only.

3. In the following code fragment,

```
If x = 3 Then x = 5
    y += 1
```

    the statement y += 1 is executed

    a. only when variable x contains a value of 3.

    b. only when variable x contains a value of 5.

    c. only when variable x contains a value other than 3.

    d. either way.

4. In the following code fragment,

```
If x Mod 2 = 0 Then y += 1
```

    the statement y += 1 is executed when

    a. variable x is exactly divisible by 2.

    b. variable x contains an even number.

    c. variable x does not contain an odd number.

    d. all of the above

    e. none of the above

5. In the following code fragment,

```
x = 3 * y
If x > y Then y += 1
```

    the statement y += 1 is

    a. always executed.

    b. never executed.

    c. executed either way.

    d.   executed only when variable y contains positive values.

    e.   none of the above

16.4   Review Exercises

Complete the following exercises.

1.   Identify the syntax errors in the following Visual Basic program:

```
Sub Main()
    Dim x, y As Double

    x = Console.ReadLine()

    y ← - 5
    If x * y / 2 > 20
      y =- 1
      x += 4 * x²
    End if

    Console.Write(x, y)

    Console.ReadKey()
End Sub
```

2.   Create a trace table to determine the values of the variables in each step of the following Visual Basic program for two different executions. Then, design the corresponding flowchart.

The input values for the two executions are (i) 10, and (ii) -10.

```
Sub Main()
    Dim x, y As Double

    x = Console.ReadLine()

    y = - 5
    If x * y / 2 > 20 Then
      y -= 1
      x -= 4
    End If
    If x > 0 Then
      y += 30
      x = x ^ 2
    End If

    Console.Write(x & ", " & y)

    Console.ReadKey()
End Sub
```

3.   Create a trace table to determine the values of the variables in each step of the following Visual Basic program for two different executions. Then, design the corresponding flowchart.

The input values for the two executions are (i) -11, and (ii) 11.

```
Sub Main()
    Dim x, y As Integer

    x = Console.ReadLine()

    y = 8
    If Math.Abs(x) > 10 Then
        y += x
        x -= 1
    End If
    If Math.Abs(x) > 10 Then
        y *= 3
    End If

    Console.Write(x & ", " & y)

    Console.ReadKey()
End Sub
```

4. Create a trace table to determine the values of the variables in each step of the following Visual Basic program for two different executions. Then, design the corresponding flowchart.

    The input values for the two executions are (i) 1, 2, 3; and (ii) 4, 2, 1.

```
Sub Main()
    Dim x, y, z As Integer

    x = Console.ReadLine()
    y = Console.ReadLine()
    z = Console.ReadLine()

    If x + y > z Then x = y + z
    If x > y + z Then y = x + z
    If x > y - z Then z = x - z Mod 2

    Console.Write(x & ", " & y & ", " & z)

    Console.ReadKey()
End Sub
```

5. Write a Visual Basic program that prompts the user to enter a number, and then displays the message "Positive" when the given number is positive.

6. Write a Visual Basic program that prompts the user to enter two numbers, and then displays the message "Positive" when both given numbers are positives.

7. Write a Visual Basic program that prompts the user to enter a value and then displays the message "Numeric" when the given value is a numeric value.

    Hint: Use the TryParse() procedure.

8. Write a Visual Basic program that prompts the user to enter a string, and then displays the message "Uppercase" when the given string contains only uppercase characters.

    Hint: Use the ToUpper() procedure.

9. Write a Visual Basic program that prompts the user to enter a string, and then displays the message "Many characters" when the given string contains more than 20 characters.

   Hint: Use the .Length property.

10. Write a Visual Basic program that prompts the user to enter four numbers and, if one of them is negative, it displays the message "Among the given numbers, there is a negative one!"

11. Write a Visual Basic program that prompts the user to enter two numbers. If the first number given is greater than the second one, the program should swap their values. In the end, the program should display the numbers, always in ascending order.

12. Write a Visual Basic program that prompts the user to enter three temperature values measured at three different points in New York, and then displays the message "Heat Wave" if the average value is greater than 60 degrees Fahrenheit.

Chapter 17
The Dual-Alternative Decision Structure

17.1 The Dual-Alternative Decision Structure

This type of decision control structure includes a statement or block of statements on both paths.

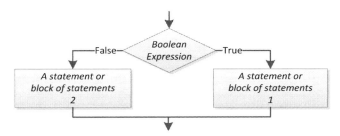

If the Boolean expression evaluates to True, the statement or block of statements 1 is executed; otherwise, the statement or block of statements 2 is executed.

The general form of the Visual Basic statement is

```
If Boolean_Expression Then
    A statement or block of statements 1
Else
    A statement or block of statements 2
End If
```

Exercise 17.1-1   *Finding the Output Message*

For the following flowchart, determine the output message for three different executions.

The input values for the three executions are (i) 3, (ii) -3, and (iii) 0.

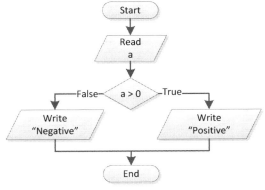

Solution

i.   When the user enters the value 3, the Boolean expression evaluates to True. The flow of execution follows the right path and the message "Positive" is displayed.

ii.   When the user enters the value -3, the Boolean expression evaluates to `False`. The flow of execution follows the left path and the message "Negative" is displayed.

iii. When the user enters the value 0, the Boolean expression evaluates to `False`. Inevitably, the flow of execution follows the left path again and the message "Negative" is displayed!

> **Notice**: Obviously, something is not quite right with this flowchart! As you already know, zero is not a negative value! In fact, it is not a positive value either. Later in this book, when you learn all about nested decision control structures, you will learn how to display a third message that will say "The number entered is zero".
>
> **Remember!** A Decision symbol has one entrance and two exit paths! You cannot have a third exit!

Exercise 17.1-2   Trace Tables and Dual-Alternative Decision Structures

Create a trace table to determine the values of the variables in each step of the next Visual Basic program for two different executions.

The input values for the two executions are (i) 5, and (ii) 10.

```
                          project_17_1_2
Sub Main()
  Dim a, z, w, y As Double

  a = Console.ReadLine()

  z = a * 10
  w = (z - 4) * (a - 3) / 7 + 36

  If z >= w And a < z Then
    y = 2 * a
  Else
    y = 4 * a
  End If

  Console.Write(y)

  Console.ReadKey()
End Sub
```

Solution

i.   For the input value of 5, the trace table looks like this.

Step	Statement	Notes	a	z	w	y
1	a = Console.ReadLine()	User enters the value 5	5	?	?	?
2	z = a * 10		5	50	?	?
3	w = (z - 4) * (a - 3) / 7 + 36		5	50	**49.142**	?

4	If z >= w And a < z Then	This evaluates to True				
5	y = 2 * a		5	50	49.142	**10**
6	Console.Write(y)	The value 10 is displayed				

ii. For the input value of 10, the trace table looks like this.

Step	Statement	Notes	a	z	w	y
1	a = Console.ReadLine()	User enters the value 10	**10**	?	?	?
2	z = a * 10		10	**100**	?	?
3	w = (z - 4) * (a - 3) / 7 + 36		10	100	**132**	?
4	If z >= w And a < z Then	This evaluates to False				
5	y = 4 * a		10	100	132	**40**
6	Console.Write(y)	The value 40 is displayed				

Exercise 17.1-3 *Who is the Greatest?*

Design a flowchart and write the corresponding Visual Basic program that lets the user enter two numbers A and B and then determines and displays the greater of the two numbers.

Solution

This exercise can be solved using either the single- or dual-alternative decision structure. So, let's use them both!

First Approach – Using a dual-alternative decision structure

This approach tests if the value of number B is greater than that of number A. If so, number B is the greatest; otherwise, number A is the greatest.

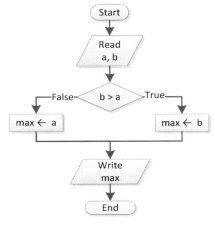

and the Visual Basic program is as follows.

```
                    project_17_1_3a
Sub Main()
  Dim a, b, max As Double
```

```
a = Console.ReadLine()
b = Console.ReadLine()

If b > a Then
    max = b
Else
    max = a
End If

Console.Write("Greatest value: " & max)

Console.ReadKey()
End Sub
```

Second Approach – Using a single-alternative decision structure

This approach initially assumes that number A is probably the greatest value (this is why it assigns the value of variable a to variable max). However, if it turns out that number B is actually greater than number A, then the greatest value is updated, that is, variable max is assigned a new value, the value of variable b. Thus, whatever happens, in the end, variable max always contains the greatest value!

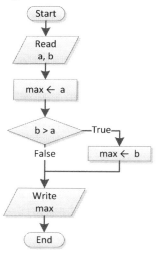

Notice: *Please note that this exercise is trying to determine the greatest value and not which variable this value is actually assigned to (to variable A or to variable B).*

The Visual Basic program is shown here.

project_17_1_3b

```
Sub Main()
    Dim a, b, max As Double

    a = Console.ReadLine()
    b = Console.ReadLine()

    max = a
```

```
    If b > a Then
        max = b
    End If

    Console.Write("Greatest value: " & max)

    Console.ReadKey()
End Sub
```

Exercise 17.1-4   *Finding Odd and Even Numbers*

Design a flowchart and write the corresponding Visual Basic program that prompts the user to enter an integer, and then displays a message indicating whether this number is odd or even.

Solution

In this exercise, you need to find a way to determine whether a number is odd or even. You need to find a common attribute between all even numbers, or between all odd numbers. And actually there is one! All even numbers are exactly divisible by 2. So, when the result of the operation x Mod 2 equals 0, x is even; otherwise, x is odd.

Next you can find various odd and even numbers:

> ➤   Odd numbers: 1, 3, 5, 7, 9, 11, …
> ➤   Even numbers: 0, 2, 4, 6, 8, 10, 12, ….

Notice: *Please note that zero is considered an even number.*

The flowchart is shown here.

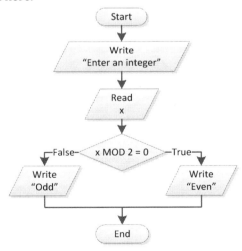

and the Visual Basic program is as follows.

```
                            project_17_1_4
Sub Main()
    Dim x As Integer

    Console.Write("Enter an integer: ")
```

```
  x = Console.ReadLine()

  If x Mod 2 = 0 Then
    Console.WriteLine("Even")
  Else
    Console.WriteLine("Odd")
  End If

  Console.ReadKey()
End Sub
```

Exercise 17.1-5   *Weekly Wages*

Gross pay depends on the pay rate and the total number of hours worked per week. However, if someone works more than 40 hours, he or she gets paid time-and-a-half for all hours worked over 40. Design a flowchart and write the corresponding Visual Basic program that lets the user enter a pay rate and the hours worked and then calculates and displays the gross pay.

Solution

This exercise can be solved using the dual-alternative decision structure. When the hours worked are over 40, the gross pay is calculated as follows:

gross pay = (pay rate) × 40 + 1.5 × (pay rate) × (all hours worked over 40)

The flowchart that solves this problem is shown here.

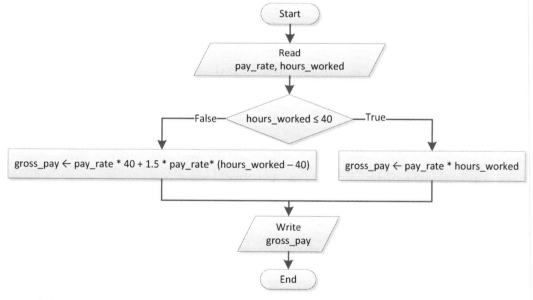

and the Visual Basic program is shown here.

```
                          project_17_1_5
Sub Main()
  Dim hours_worked As Integer
  Dim pay_rate, gross_pay As Double
```

```
pay_rate = Console.ReadLine()
hours_worked = Console.ReadLine()

If hours_worked <= 40 Then
  gross_pay = pay_rate * hours_worked
Else
  gross_pay = pay_rate * 40 + 1.5 * pay_rate * (hours_worked - 40)
End If

Console.Write("Gross Pay: " & gross_pay)

Console.ReadKey()
End Sub
```

17.2 Review Questions: True/False

Choose **true** or **false** for each of the following statements.

1. It is a possible that none of the statements enclosed in a dual-alternative decision structure will be executed.

2. The dual-alternative decision structure must include at least two statements.

3. The dual-alternative decision structure uses the reserved keyword Else.

4. The statement

    ```
    Const Else = 5
    ```

    is syntactically correct.

5. In a dual-alternative decision structure, the evaluated Boolean expression can return more than two values.

6. The following code fragment satisfies the property of effectiveness.

    ```
    Dim x, y, z As Integer

    x = Console.ReadLine()
    y = Console.ReadLine()
    z = Console.ReadLine()

    If x > y And x > z Then
      Console.WriteLine("Value " & x & " is the greatest one")
    Else
      Console.WriteLine("Value " & y & " is the greatest one")
    End If
    ```

17.3 Review Questions: Multiple Choice

Select the correct answer for each of the following statements.

1. The dual-alternative decision structure includes a statement or block of statements on

    a. the false path only.

    b. both paths.

    c. the true path only.

2. In the following code fragment,

```
If x Mod 2 = 0 Then
   x = 0
Else
   y += 1
End If
```

the statement y += 1 is executed when

    a.   variable x is exactly divisible by 2.

    b.   variable x contains an even number.

    c.   variable x contains an odd number.

    d.   none of the above

3.   In the following code fragment,

```
If x = 3 Then
   x = 5
Else
   x = 7
End If
   y += 1
```

the statement y += 1 is executed

    a.   when variable x contains a value of 3.

    b.   when variable x contains a value other than 3.

    c.   both of the above

17.4   Review Exercises

Complete the following exercises.

1.   Create a trace table to determine the values of the variables in each step of the next Visual Basic program for two different executions. Then, design the corresponding flowchart.

The input values for the two executions are (i) 3, and (ii) 0.5.

```
Sub Main()
   Dim a, z, y As Double

   a = Console.ReadLine()
   z = a * 3 - 2
   If z >= 1 Then
      y = 6 * a
   Else
      z += 1
      y = 6 * a + z
   End If
   Console.Write(z & ", " & y)

   Console.ReadKey()
End Sub
```

2.   Create a trace table to determine the values of the variables in each step of the next Visual Basic program. Then, design the corresponding flowchart.

```
Sub Main()
```

```
Dim x, y, z As Double

x = 3
y = x ^ 3 + 9
z = 2 * x + y - 4
If x > y Then
    y = z Mod x
    z = Math.Sqrt(x)
Else
    x = z Mod y
    z = Math.Sqrt(y)
End If
Console.Write(x & ", " & y & ", " & z)
Console.ReadKey()
End Sub
```

3. Write the Visual Basic program that corresponds to the following flowchart and
    then create a trace table to determine the values of the variables in each step for
    two different executions.

    The input values for the two executions are (i) 10, and (ii) 2,

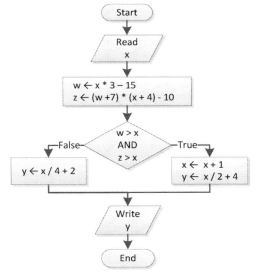

4. Write a Visual Basic program that lets the user enter an integer, and then
    displays a message indicating whether or not the given number is a multiple of 6.

5. Write a Visual Basic program that lets the user enter an integer, and then
    displays one of two possible messages. One message indicates if the given
    number is a multiple of 6 or a multiple of 7; the other message indicates if the
    given number is neither a multiple of 6 nor a multiple of 7.

6. Write a Visual Basic program that lets the user enter an integer, and then
    displays a message indicating whether or not the given number is a multiple of 4.
    Moreover, the Visual Basic program should display the structure of the given
    integer, including the given integer, the quotient, and any remainder. For
    example, if the given integer is 14, the message "14 = 3 x 4 + 2" should be
    displayed.

7. Write a Visual Basic program that lets the user enter an integer, and then displays a message indicating whether or not the given integer is a four-digit integer.

   Hint: Four-digit integers are between 1000 and 9999.

8. Design a flowchart and write the corresponding Visual Basic program that lets the user enter two values, and then determines and displays the smaller of the two values. Assume that the user enters two different values.

9. Write a Visual Basic program that lets the user enter three numbers, and then displays a message indicating whether or not the given numbers can be lengths of the three sides of a triangle.

   Hint: In any triangle, the length of each side is less than the sum of the lengths of the other two sides.

10. Write a Visual Basic program that lets the user enter three numbers, and then displays a message indicating whether or not the given numbers can be lengths of the three sides of a right triangle (or right-angled triangle). You can use lengths of 3, 4 and 5 to test your program.

    Hint: Use the Pythagorean theorem.

11. Athletes in the long jump at the Olympic Games in Athens in 2004 participated in three different qualifying jumps. Assume that in order to qualify, an athlete had to achieve an average jump distance of 8 meters. Write a Visual Basic program that prompts the user to enter the three performances, and then displays the messages "Qualified" or "Disqualified" depending on whether the average value is greater or less than 8 meters.

12. Gross pay depends on the pay rate and the total number of hours worked per week. However, if someone works more than 40 hours, he or she gets paid double for all hours worked over 40. Design a flowchart and write the corresponding Visual Basic program that lets the user enter the pay rate and hours worked and then calculates and displays net pay. Net pay is the amount of pay that is actually paid to the employee after any deductions. Deductions include taxes, health insurance, retirement plans, on so on. Assume a total deduction of 30%.

13. Regular servicing will keep your vehicle more reliable, reducing the chance of breakdowns, inconvenience and unnecessary expenses. In general, there are two types of service you need to perform:

    a. a minor service every 6000 miles

    b. a major service every 12000 miles

    Write a Visual Basic program that prompts the user to enter the miles traveled, and then calculates and displays how many miles are left until the next service, as well as the type of the next service.

14. Two cars start from rest and move with a constant acceleration along a straight horizontal road for a given time. Write a Visual Basic program that prompts the user to enter the time the two cars traveled (same for both cars) and the acceleration for each one of them, and then calculates and displays the distance between them as well as a message "Car A is first" or "Car B is first" depending on which car is leading the race. The required formula is

$$S = u_o + \frac{1}{2}at^2$$

Chapter 18
The Multiple-Alternative Decision Structure

18.1 The Multiple-Alternative Decision Structure

The multiple-alternative decision structure is used to expand the number of alternatives, as shown in the following flowchart fragment.

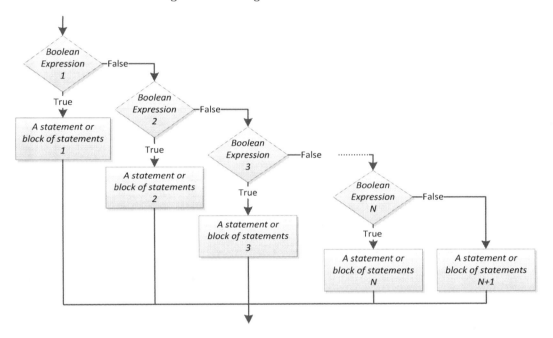

When a multiple-alternative decision structure is executed, *Boolean Expression 1* is evaluated. If *Boolean Expression 1* evaluates to True, the corresponding statement or block of statements that immediately follows it is executed and the rest of the structure is skipped. In other words, the flow of execution continues to any remaining statements that may exist **after** the multiple-alternative decision structure. However, if *Boolean Expression 1* evaluates to False, the flow of execution evaluates *Boolean Expression 2*. If it evaluates to True, the corresponding statement or block of statements that immediately follows it is executed and the rest of the structure is skipped. This process continues until one Boolean expression evaluates to True or until no more Boolean expressions are left.

The last statement or block of statements N+1 is executed when none of the previous Boolean expressions has evaluated to True. Moreover, this last statement or block of statements N+1 is optional and can be omitted. It depends on the algorithm you are trying to solve.

The general form of the Visual Basic statement is

```
If Boolean_Expression 1 Then
    A statement or block of statements 1
ElseIf Boolean_Expression 2 Then
```

```
    A statement or block of statements 2
ElseIf Boolean_Expression 3 Then
    A statement or block of statements 3
  .

  .

  .

ElseIf Boolean_Expression N Then
    A statement or block of statements N
Else
    A statement or block of statements N+1
End Sub
```

Exercise 18.1-1   *Trace Tables and Multiple-Alternative Decision Structures*

Create a trace table to determine the values of the variables in each step for three different executions of the next Visual Basic program.

The input values for the three executions are (i) 5, 8; (ii) -13, 0; and (iii) 1, -1.

project_18_1_1

```
Sub Main()
  Dim a, b As Integer

  a = Console.ReadLine()
  b = Console.ReadLine()

  If a > 3 Then
    Console.WriteLine("Variable A greater than 3")
  ElseIf a > 4 And b <= 10 Then
    Console.Write("Variable A greater than 4 ")
    Console.WriteLine("and B less than or equal to 10")
  ElseIf a * 2 = -26 Then
    Console.WriteLine("Variable A times 2 is equal to -26")
    b += 1
  ElseIf b = 1 Then
    Console.WriteLine("Variable B is equal to 1")
  Else
    Console.Write("Display this when none of the ")
    Console.WriteLine("above evaluates to True")
  End If

  Console.Write("The end!")

  Console.ReadKey()
End Sub
```

Solution

i.   For the input values of 5 and 8, the trace table looks like this.

Step	Statement	Notes	a	b
1	a = Console.ReadLine()	User enters the value 5	5	?

Step	Statement	Notes	a	b
2	b = Console.ReadLine()	User enters the value 8	5	**8**
3	If a > 3 Then	This evaluates to True		
4	Console.WriteLine("Variable A greater than 3")	The message "Variable A greater than 3" is displayed		
5	Console.Write("The end!")	The message "The end!" is displayed		

Notice: *Please note that even though the second Boolean expression* (a > 4 And b <= 10) *could also have evaluated to* True, *it was not checked.*

ii. For the input values of -13 and 0, the trace table looks like this.

Step	Statement	Notes	a	b
1	a = Console.ReadLine()	User enters the value -13	**-13**	?
2	b = Console.ReadLine()	User enters the value 0	-13	**0**
3	If a > 3 Then	This evaluates to False		
4	ElseIf a > 4 And b <= 10 Then	This evaluates to False		
5	ElseIf a * 2 = -26 Then	This evaluates to True		
6	Console.WriteLine("Variable A times 2 is equal to -26")	The message "Variable A times 2 is equal to -26" is displayed		
7	b += 1		-13	**1**
8	Console.Write("The end!")	Message "The end!" is displayed		

Notice: *Please note that after step 7 the fourth Boolean expression* (b = 1) *could also have evaluated to* True, *but it was not checked.*

iii. For the input values of 1 and -1, the trace table looks like this.

Step	Statement	Notes	a	b
1	a = Console.ReadLine()	User enters the value 1	**1**	?
2	b = Console.ReadLine()	User enters the value -1	1	**-1**
3	If a > 3 Then	This evaluates to False		
4	ElseIf a > 4 And b <= 10 Then	This evaluates to False		
5	ElseIf a * 2 = -26 Then	This evaluates to False		
6	ElseIf b = 1 Then	This evaluates to False		
7	Console.Write("Display this …	The message "Display this when none of the above evaluates to True" is displayed		
8	Console.Write("The end!")	The message "The end!" is displayed		

Exercise 18.1-2   *Counting the Digits*

Write a Visual Basic program that prompts the user to enter an integer between 0 and 999 and then counts its total number of digits. In the end, a message "You entered a N-digit number" is displayed, where N is the total number of digits.

Solution

The following Visual Basic program assumes that the user enters a valid number between 0 and 999, and therefore does not include checking the validity of data input.

```
                          project_18_1_2
Sub Main()
  Dim x, count As Integer

  Console.Write("Enter an integer (0 - 999): ")
  x = Console.ReadLine()

  If x <= 9 Then
    count = 1
  ElseIf x <= 99 Then
    count = 2
  Else
    count = 3
  End If

  Console.Write("You entered a " & count & "-digit number")

  Console.ReadKey()
End Sub
```

18.2   Review Questions: True/False

Choose **true** or **false** for each of the following statements.

1. The multiple-alternative decision structure is used to expand the number of alternatives.

2. The multiple-alternative decision structure can have at most three alternatives.

3. In a multiple-alternative decision structure, once a Boolean expression evaluates to True, the next Boolean expression is evaluated.

4. In a multiple-alternative decision structure, the last statement or block of statements N+1 (appearing below the Else Visual Basic keyword) is always executed.

5. In a multiple-alternative decision structure, the last statement or block of statements N+1 (appearing below the Else Visual Basic keyword) is executed when at least one of the previous Boolean expressions has evaluated to True.

6. In a multiple-alternative decision structure, the last statement or block of statements N+1, and by extension the Else Visual Basic keyword, can be omitted.

7. In the following code fragment,

```
If a = 1 Then
    x = x + 5
ElseIf a = 2 Then
    x = x - 2
ElseIf a = 3 Then
    x = x - 9
Else
    x = x + 3
End If
y += 1
```

the statement `y += 1` is executed only when variable `a` contains a value other than 1, 2, or 3.

18.3   Review Exercises

Complete the following exercises.

1. Create a trace table to determine the values of the variables in each step for four different executions of the next Visual Basic program.

The input values for the four executions are (i) 5, (ii) 150, (iii) 250, and (iv) -1.

```
Sub Main()
    Dim q, b As Integer

    q = Console.ReadLine()

    If q > 0 And q <= 50 Then
        b = 1
    ElseIf q > 50 And q <= 100 Then
        b = 2
    ElseIf q > 100 And q <= 200 Then
        b = 3
    Else
        b = 4
    End If
    Console.Write(b)

    Console.ReadKey()
End Sub
```

2. Create a trace table to determine the values of the variables in each step for three different executions of the next Visual Basic program.

The input values for the three executions are (i) 5, (ii) 150, and (iii) -1.

```
Sub Main()
    Dim amount, discount, payment As Double

    amount = Console.ReadLine()
    discount = 0

    If amount < 20 Then
        discount = 0
```

```
    ElseIf amount >=20 And amount < 60 Then
      discount = 5
    ElseIf amount >= 60 And amount < 100 Then
      discount = 10
    ElseIf amount >= 100 Then
      discount = 15
    End If
    payment = amount - amount * discount / 100

    Console.Write(discount & ", " & payment)

    Console.ReadKey()
  End Sub
```

3. Design a flowchart and write the corresponding Visual Basic program that lets the user enter an integer between -9999 and 9999, and then counts its total number of digits. In the end, a message "You entered a N-digit number" is displayed, where N is the total number of digits.

4. Write a Visual Basic program that displays the following menu:

    1. Convert USD to Euro (EUR)
    2. Convert USD to British Pound Sterling (GBP)
    3. Convert USD to Japanese Yen (JPY)
    4. Convert USD to Canadian Dollar (CAD)

    It then prompts the user to enter a choice (of 1, 2, 3, or 4) and an amount in US dollars and calculates and displays the required value. It is given that

    ➤ $1 = 0.72 EUR (€)
    ➤ $1 = 0.60 GBP (£)
    ➤ $1 = ¥ 102.15 JPY
    ➤ $1 = 1.10 CAD ($)

5. Write a Visual Basic program that prompts the user to enter the number of a month between 1 and 12, and then displays the corresponding season. It is given that

    ➤ Winter includes months 12, 1, and 2
    ➤ Spring includes months 3, 4, and 5
    ➤ Summer includes months 6, 7, and 8
    ➤ Fall (Autumn) includes months 9, 10, and 11

6. Write a Visual Basic program that prompts the user to enter a number between 1.0 and 4.9, and then displays the number as English text. For example, for the number 2.3, it should display "Two point three".

7. The most popular and commonly used grading system in the United States uses discrete evaluation in the form of letter grades. Design a flowchart and write the corresponding Visual Basic program that prompts the user to enter a letter between A and F, and then displays the corresponding percentage according to the following table.

Grade	Percentage
A	90 – 100
B	80 – 89
C	70 – 79
D	60 – 69
E / F	0 – 59

Chapter 19
The Case Decision Structure

19.1　The Case Decision Structure

The case decision structure is a simplified version of the multiple-alternative decision structure. It helps you write code faster and increases readability, especially for algorithms that require complex combinations of decision structures.

The case decision structure is used to expand the number of alternatives in the same way as the multiple-alternative decision structure does. The big difference between them is that the evaluated variable or expression in a case decision structure must be the same in all cases.

The case decision structure and the multiple-alternative decision structure even share the same flowchart.

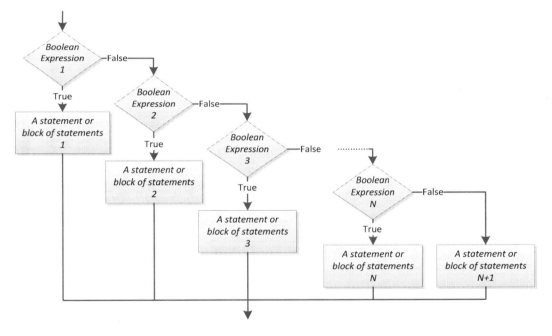

As in the multiple-alternative decision structure, when a case decision structure is executed, *Boolean Expression 1* is evaluated. If *Boolean Expression 1* evaluates to True, the corresponding statement or block of statements that immediately follows it is executed and the rest of the structure is skipped. In other words, the flow of execution continues to any remaining statements that may exist **after** the multiple-alternative decision structure. However, if *Boolean Expression 1* evaluates to False, the flow of execution evaluates *Boolean Expression 2*. If it evaluates to True, the corresponding statement or block of statements that immediately follows it is executed and the rest of the structure is skipped. This process continues until one Boolean expression evaluates to True or until no more Boolean expressions are left.

The last statement or block of statements N+1 is executed when none of the previous Boolean expressions has evaluated to `True`. Moreover, this last statement or block of statements N+1 is optional and can be omitted. It depends on the algorithm that you are trying to solve.

The general form of the Visual Basic statement is

```
Select Case a variable or an expression to evaluate
  Case expression_list-1
    A statement or block of statements 1
  Case expression_list-2
    A statement or block of statements 2
  Case expression_list-3
    A statement or block of statements 3
    .
    .
    .
  Case expression_list-N
    A statement or block of statements N
  Case Else
    A statement or block of statements N+1
End Select
```

where *expression_list* can be one of the following

➢ expression. For example, you can write

  ➢ `x + y`
  ➢ `a + 1`
  ➢ `x^2 + y^2`

➢ *expression-1, expression-2, expression-3, … expression-N*. For example, you can write

  ➢ `1, 4, 7, 9`
  ➢ `x, y + 1, z / 2`

➢ *expression-1* To *expression-2*. For example, you can write

  ➢ `x To y`
  ➢ `1 To 10`
  ➢ `x + 1 To a +b`

➢ `Is` *ComparisonOperator expression*. For example, you can write

  ➢ `Is > 10`
  ➢ `Is <= x + 35`
  ➢ `Is >=10, Is <= 20`

An example that uses the case decision structure is shown here.

project_19_1a

```
Sub Main()
  Dim x, y As Integer

  x = Console.ReadLine()
  y = Console.ReadLine()
```

```
Select Case x
  Case 10                        'If x = 10
    Console.Write("A")
  Case 11, 15, 19                'If x = 11 Or x = 15 Or x = 19
    Console.Write("B")
  Case 17 To 25                  'If x >= 17 And x <= 25
    Console.Write("C")
  Case Is >= 100                 'If x >= 100
    Console.Write("D")
  Case Is >= 0, Is <= -50        'If x >= 0 Or x <= -50
    Console.Write("E")
  Case y                         'If x = y
    Console.Write("F")
  Case y + 1                     'If x = y + 1
    Console.Write("G")
  Case y + 10, y / 2, y ^ 2      'If x = y + 10 Or x = y / 2 Or x = y ^ 2
    Console.Write("H")
  Case Else
    Console.Write("No Match!")
End Select

Console.ReadKey()
End Sub
```

A simpler example that uses the case decision structure is shown here.

```
                          project_19_1b
Sub Main()
  Dim name As String

  Console.Write("What is your name? ")
  name = Console.ReadLine()

  Select Case name
    Case "John"
      Console.WriteLine("You are my cousin!")
    Case "Aphrodite"
      Console.WriteLine("You are my sister!")
    Case "Loukia"
      Console.WriteLine("You are my mom!")
    Case "George"
      Console.WriteLine("Sorry, I don't know you.")
  End Select

  Console.ReadKey()
End Sub
```

Notice: *The last statement or last block of statements N+1 is optional and can be omitted (you need to omit the keywords* Case Else *as well).*

Exercise 19.1-1 *The Days of the Week*

Design a flowchart and write the corresponding Visual Basic program that prompts the user to enter a number between 1 and 7, and then displays the corresponding day (Sunday, Monday, and so on). If the value entered is invalid, an error message should be displayed.

Solution

The flowchart is shown here.

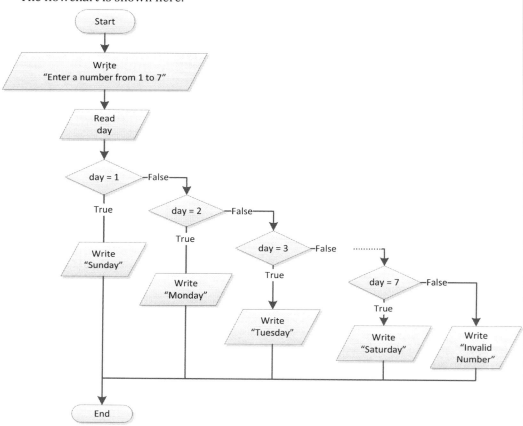

This Visual Basic program can be written using either a case decision structure or a multiple-alternative decision structure. Let's try them both!

First Approach – Using a case decision structure

```
                        project_19_1_1a
Sub Main()
  Dim day As Integer

  Console.Write("Enter a number between 1 and 7: ")
  day = Console.ReadLine()

  Select Case day
    Case 1
```

```
         Console.WriteLine("Sunday")
    Case 2
         Console.WriteLine("Monday")
    Case 3
         Console.WriteLine("Tuesday")
    Case 4
         Console.WriteLine("Wednesday")
    Case 5
         Console.WriteLine("Thursday")
    Case 6
         Console.WriteLine("Friday")
    Case 7
         Console.WriteLine("Saturday")
    Case Else
         Console.WriteLine("Invalid Number")
   End Select

   Console.ReadKey()
End Sub
```

Second Approach – Using a multiple-alternative decision structure

```
                          project_19_1_1b
Sub Main()
  Dim day As Integer

  Console.Write("Enter a number between 1 and 7: ")
  day = Console.ReadLine()

  If day = 1 Then
     Console.WriteLine("Sunday")
  ElseIf day = 2 Then
     Console.WriteLine("Monday")
  ElseIf day = 3 Then
     Console.WriteLine("Tuesday")
  ElseIf day = 4 Then
     Console.WriteLine("Wednesday")
  ElseIf day = 5 Then
     Console.WriteLine("Thursday")
  ElseIf day = 6 Then
     Console.WriteLine("Friday")
  ElseIf day = 7 Then
     Console.WriteLine("Saturday")
  Else
     Console.WriteLine("Invalid Number")
  End If

  Console.ReadKey()
End Sub
```

19.2   Review Questions: True/False

Choose **true** or **false** for each of the following statements.

1. The case decision structure is used to expand the number of alternatives.

2. The case decision structure can always be used instead of a multiple-alternative decision structure.

3. The case decision structure can have as many alternatives as the programmer wishes.

4. In a case decision structure, the last statement or block of statements N+1 (appearing below the `Case Else` Visual Basic keywords) is always executed.

5. In a case decision structure, the last statement or block of statements N+1 (appearing below the `Case Else` Visual Basic keywords) is executed when none of the previous cases has evaluated to `True`.

6. The last statement or block of statements N+1, as well as the `Case Else` Visual Basic keywords, cannot be omitted.

7. In the following Visual Basic program,

```
Select Case a
  Case 1, 2
    x = x - 2
  Case 3
    x = x - 9
  Case Else
    x = x + 3
    y += 1
End Select
```

the statement `y += 1` is executed only when variable `a` contains a value other than 1, 2, or 3.

19.3   Review Exercises

Complete the following exercises.

1. Create a trace table to determine the values of the variables in each step of the next Visual Basic program for three different executions. Then, design the corresponding flowchart.

The input values for the three executions are (i) 1, (ii) 3, and (iii) 250.

```
Sub Main()
  Dim a, x, y As Integer

  a = Console.ReadLine()
  x = 0
  y = 0

  Select Case a
    Case 1
      x = x + 5
      y = y + 5
    Case 2
      x = x - 2
      y -= 1
```

```
      Case 3
          x = x - 9
          y = y + 3
      Case Else
          x = x + 3
          y += 1
      End Select
      Console.Write(x & ", " & y)


      Console.ReadKey()
  End Sub
```

2. Create a trace table to determine the values of the variables in each step of the next Visual Basic program for three different executions. Then, design the corresponding flowchart.

The input values for the three executions are (i) 10, 2, 5; (ii) 5, 2, 3; and (iii) 4, 6, 2.

```
Sub Main()
    Dim a, x As Integer
    Dim y As Double

    a = Console.ReadLine()
    x = Console.ReadLine()
    y = Console.ReadLine()

    Select Case a
        Case 10
            x = x Mod 2
            y = y ^ 2
        Case 3
            x = x * 2
            y -= 1
        Case 5
            x = x + 4
            y += 7
        Case Else
            x -= 3
            y += 1
    End Select

    Console.Write(x & ", " & y)

    Console.ReadKey()
End Sub
```

3. Write a Visual Basic program that prompts the user to enter the number of a month, and then displays the corresponding name (January for 1, February for 2, and so on). If the value entered is invalid, an error message should be displayed.

4. Design a flowchart and write the corresponding Visual Basic program that displays the following menu:

    1. Convert Miles to Yards

2. Convert Miles to Feet

3. Convert Miles to Inches

It then prompts the user to enter a choice (of 1, 2, or 3) and a distance in miles. Then, it calculates and displays the required value. However, if the choice entered is invalid, an error message should be displayed. It is given that

➢ 1 mile = 1760 yards

➢ 1 mile = 5280 feet

➢ 1 mile = 63360 inches

5. Roman numerals are shown in the following table.

Number	Roman Numeral
1	I
2	II
3	III
4	IV
5	V
6	VI
7	VII
8	VIII
9	IX
10	X

Write a Visual Basic program that prompts the user to enter a Roman numeral between I and X, and then displays the corresponding number. However, if the choice entered is invalid, an error message should be displayed.

6. An online CD shop awards points to its customers based on the total number of audio CDs purchased each month. The points are awarded as follows:

➢ If the customer purchases 1 CD, he or she is awarded 3 points.

➢ If the customer purchases 2 CDs, he or she is awarded 10 points.

➢ If the customer purchases 3 CDs, he or she is awarded 20 points.

➢ If the customer purchases 4 CDs or more, he or she is awarded 45 points.

Write a Visual Basic program that prompts the user to enter the total number of CDs that he or she has purchased in a month, and then displays the number of points awarded. Assume that the user enters values greater than 0.

7. Write a Visual Basic program that prompts the user to enter his or her name, and then displays "Good morning NN" or "Good evening NN" or "Good night NN", where NN is the name of the user. The message to be displayed must be chosen randomly.

8. Write a Visual Basic program that lets the user enter a word such as "zero", "one" or "two", and then converts it into the corresponding digit, such as 0, 1, or 2. This should be done for the numbers 0 to 9. Display "I don't know this number!" when the user enters an unknown.

9. The Beaufort[1] scale is an empirical measure that relates wind speed to observed conditions on land or at sea. Write a Visual Basic program that prompts the user to enter the Beaufort number, and then displays the corresponding description from the following table. However, if the number entered is invalid, an error message should be displayed.

Beaufort Number	Description
0	Calm
1	Light air
2	Light breeze
3	Gentle breeze
4	Moderate breeze
5	Fresh breeze
6	Strong breeze
7	Moderate gale
8	Gale
9	Strong gale
10	Storm
11	Violent storm
12	Hurricane force

[1] Francis Beaufort (1774 –1857) was an Irish hydrographer and officer in Britain's Royal Navy. He is the inventor of the Beaufort wind force scale.

Chapter 20
Nested Decision Control Structures

20.1   What are Nested Decision Control Structures?

Nested decision control structures are decision control structures that are "nested" (enclosed) within a path of another decision control structure. This means that one If statement can nest (enclose) another If statement, and the nested If statement can nest (enclose) another If statement, and so on. There are no practical limitations to how deep this nesting can go. As long as the syntax rules are not violated, you can nest as many decision control structures as you wish. For practical reasons however, as you move to three or four levels of nesting, the entire decision structure becomes very complex and difficult to understand. So, try to keep your code as simple as possible by breaking large nested decision control structures into multiple smaller ones, or by using other types of decision control structures.

An example of a nested decision control structure is shown here.

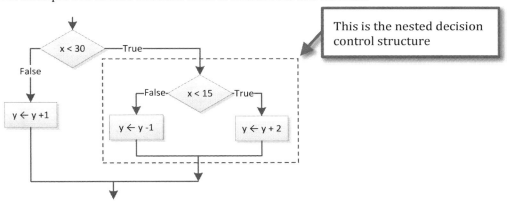

This can be rearranged to become

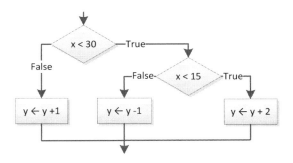

and the Visual Basic program is shown here.

```
If x < 30 Then
  If x < 15 Then
    y = y + 2
  Else
```

```
      y -= 1
   End If
Else
   y += 1
End If
```

You can even nest case decision structures inside dual-alternative decision structures.

project_20_1

```
Sub Main()
   Dim x As Integer

   Console.Write("Enter a number: ")
   x = Console.ReadLine()

   If x < 1 Or x > 3 Then
      Console.WriteLine("Invalid Number")
   Else
      Select Case x
         Case 1
            Console.WriteLine("1st choice selected")
         Case 2
            Console.WriteLine("2nd choice selected")
         Case 3
            Console.WriteLine("3rd choice selected")
      End Select
   End If

   Console.ReadKey()
End Sub
```

> This is a nested
> case decision structure

Notice: *Please note that keywords* Case Else *are missing from the* Select *statement.*

In general, you can nest any control structure inside any other control structure as long as you keep them syntactically and logically correct. However, you should always try to keep your program as simple as possible because complex code may lead to invalid results.

Exercise 20.1-1   *Trace Tables and Nested Decision Control Structures*

Create a trace table to determine the values of the variables in each step of the next Visual Basic program for three different executions.

The input values for the three executions are (i) 13, (ii) 18, and (iii) 30.

project_20_1_1

```
Sub Main()
   Dim x, y As Integer

   x = Console.ReadLine()
   y = 10

   If x < 30 Then
```

```
    If x < 15 Then
        y = y + 2
    Else
        y -= 1
    End If
Else
    y += 1
End If

Console.Write(y)

Console.ReadKey()
End Sub
```

Solution

i. For the input value of 13, the trace table looks like this.

Step	Statement	Notes	x	y
1	x = Console.ReadLine()	User enters the value 13	13	?
2	y = 10		13	10
3	If x < 30 Then	This evaluates to True		
4	If x < 15 Then	This evaluates to True		
5	y = y + 2		13	12
6	Console.Write(y)	The value 12 is displayed		

ii. For the input value of 18, the trace table looks like this.

Step	Statement	Notes	x	y
1	x = Console.ReadLine()	User enters the value 18	18	?
2	y = 10		18	10
3	If x < 30 Then	This evaluates to True		
4	If x < 15 Then	This evaluates to False		
5	y -= 1		18	9
6	Console.Write(y)	The value 9 is displayed		

iii. For the input value of 30, the trace table looks like this.

Step	Statement	Notes	x	y
1	x = Console.ReadLine()	User enters the value 30	30	?
2	y = 10		30	10
3	If x < 30 Then	This evaluates to False		
4	y += 1		30	11
5	Console.Write(y)	The value 11 is displayed		

Exercise 20.1-2   *Positive, Negative or Zero?*

Design a flowchart and write the corresponding Visual Basic program that lets the user enter a number from the keyboard and then displays the messages "Positive", "Negative", or "Zero" depending on whether the given value is greater than, less than, or equal to zero.

Solution

The flowchart is shown here.

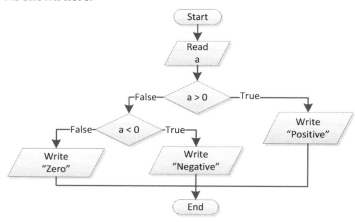

This Visual Basic program can be written using either a nested decision control structure or a multiple-alternative decision structure. Let's try them both!

First approach – Using a nested decision control structure

```
                          project_20_1_2a
Sub Main()
  Dim a As Double

  a = Console.ReadLine()

  If a > 0 Then
    Console.WriteLine("Positive")
  Else
    If a < 0 Then
      Console.WriteLine("Negative")
    Else
      Console.WriteLine("Zero")
    End If
  End If

  Console.ReadKey()
End Sub
```

Second approach – Using a multiple-alternative decision structure

```
                          project_20_1_2b
Sub Main()
  Dim a As Double
```

```
a = Console.ReadLine()

If a > 0 Then
   Console.WriteLine("Positive")
ElseIf a < 0 Then
   Console.WriteLine("Negative")
Else
   Console.WriteLine("Zero")
End If

   Console.ReadKey()
End Sub
```

20.2 A Mistake That You Will Probably Make!

In flowcharts, a very common mistake that novice programmers make is to leave some paths unconnected, as shown here.

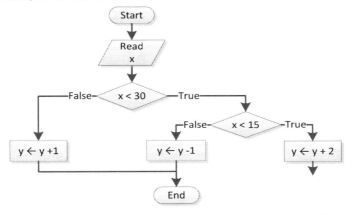

Please keep in mind that every path tries to reach the end of the algorithm, thus you cannot leave any of them unconnected.

On the other hand, try to avoid flowcharts that use many End symbols, as shown below, since these algorithms are difficult to read and understand.

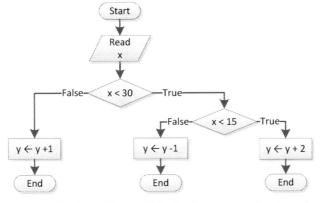

So, let's say that you are in the middle of designing a flowchart, and you want to start closing all of its decision control structures.

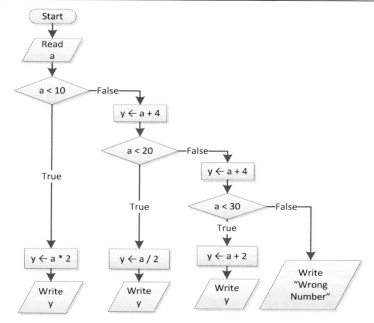

Just remember that the decision control structure that opens last should be the first one to close! In this example, the last decision control structure is the one that evaluates the expression a < 30. This is the first one that you need to close, as shown here.

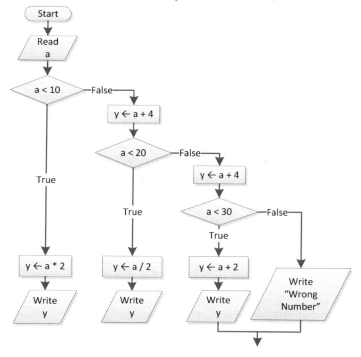

Next, you need to close the second to last decision control structure as shown here.

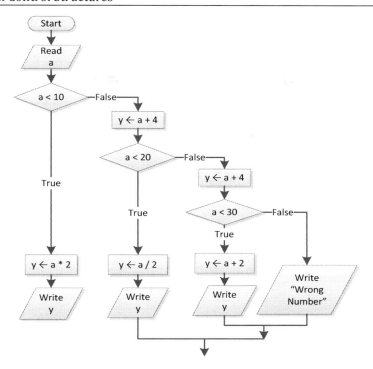

And finally, you need to close the third to last decision control structure as shown here.

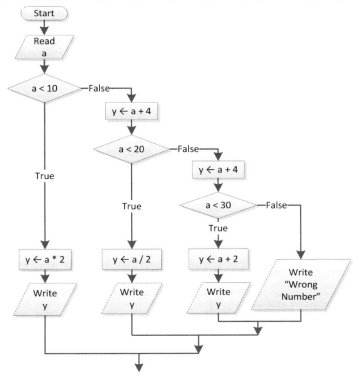

The last flowchart can be rearranged to become like the one shown here.

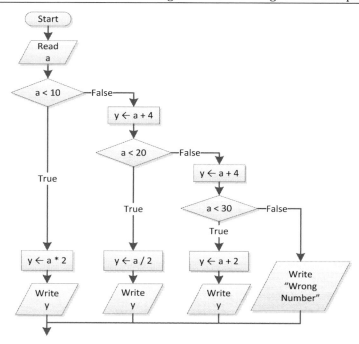

20.3   Review Questions: True/False

Choose **true** or **false** for each of the following statements.

1. Nesting of decision control structures describes a situation in which one or more than one paths of a decision control structure enclose other decision control structures.

2. Nesting level can go as deep as the programmer wishes.

3. When a problem can be solved using either a case decision structure or nested decision control structures, the second option is better because the program becomes more readable.

4. It is possible to nest a multiple-alternative decision structure within a case decision structure, but not the opposite.

5. When designing flowcharts with nested decision control structures, the decision control structure that opens last should be the first one to close.

20.4   Review Exercises

Complete the following exercises.

1. Create a trace table to determine the values of the variables in each step of the next Visual Basic program for four different executions.

    The input values for the four executions are (i) 20, 1; (ii) 20, 3; (iii) 12, 8; and (iv) 50, 0.

    ```
    Sub Main()
        Dim x, y As Integer

        x = Console.ReadLine()
        y = Console.ReadLine()
    ```

```
            If x < 30 Then
               Select Case y
                  Case 1
                     x = x Mod 3
                     y = 5
                  Case 2
                     x = x * 2
                     y = 2
                  Case 3
                     x = x + 5
                     y += 3
                  Case Else
                     x -= 2
                     y += 1
               End Select
            Else
               y += 1
            End If
            Console.WriteLine(x & ", " & y)

            Console.ReadKey()
         End Sub
```

2.   Create a trace table to determine the values of the variables in each step of the
     next Visual Basic program for four different executions.

     The input values for the four executions are (i) 60, 25; (ii) 50, 8; (iii) 20, 15; and
     (iv) 10, 30.

```
Sub Main()
   Dim x, y As Integer

   x = Console.ReadLine()
   y = Console.ReadLine()

   If (x + y) / 2 <= 20 Then
      If y < 10 Then
         x = x Mod 3
         y += 2
      ElseIf y < 20 Then
         x = x * 5
         y += 2
      Else
         x = x - 2
         y += 3
      End If
   Else
      If y < 15 Then
         x = x Mod 4
         y = 2
      ElseIf y < 23 Then
         x = x Mod 2
         y -= 2
```

```
    Else
        x = 2 * x + 5
        y += 1
      End If
    End If


    Console.Write(x & ", " & y)


    Console.ReadKey()
  End Sub
```

3. Write a Visual Basic program that prompts the user to enter the lengths of three sides of a triangle, and then determines whether or not the given numbers can be lengths of the three sides of a triangle. If the lengths are not valid, a corresponding message should be displayed; otherwise the program should further determine whether the triangle is

    a. equilateral

        Hint: In an equilateral triangle, all sides are equal.

    b. right (or right-angled)

        Hint: Use the Pythagorean Theorem.

    c. not special

    Hint: In any triangle, the length of each side is less than the sum of the lengths of the other two sides.

4. Inside an automated teller machine (ATM) there are notes of $10, $5, and $1. Write a Visual Basic program to emulate the way this ATM works. At the beginning, the machine prompts the user to enter the four-digit PIN and then checks for PIN validity (assume "1234" as the valid PIN). If given PIN is correct, the program should prompt the user to enter the amount of money (an integer value) that he or she wants to withdraw and finally it displays the least number of notes the ATM should dispense. For example, if the user enters an amount of $36, the program should display "3 notes of $10, 1 note of $5, and 1 note of $1". Moreover, if the user enters a wrong PIN, the machine will allow him or her two retries. If the user enters an incorrect PIN all three times, the message "PIN locked" should be displayed and the program should end.

5. Write a Visual Basic program that prompts the user to enter two values, one for temperature and one for wind speed. If the temperature is above 75 degrees Fahrenheit, the day is considered hot, otherwise it is cold. If the wind speed is above 12 miles per hour, the day is considered windy, otherwise it is not windy. The program should display one single message, depending on values given. For example, if a user enters 60 for temperature and 10 for wind speed, the program should display "The day is cold and not windy".

Chapter 21
Tips and Tricks with Decision Control Structures

21.1   Introduction

This chapter is dedicated to teaching you some useful tips and tricks that can help you write "better" code. You should always keep them in mind when you design your own algorithms, or even your own Visual Basic programs.

These tips and tricks can help you increase your code's readability and help make the code shorter or even faster. Of course there is no single perfect methodology because on one occasion the use of a specific tip or trick may help, but on another occasion the same tip or trick may have exactly the opposite result. Most of the time, code optimization is a matter of programming experience.

> **Remember**! Smaller algorithms are not always the best solution to a given problem. In order to solve a specific problem, you might write a very short algorithm that unfortunately proves to consume a lot of CPU time. On the other hand, you may solve the same problem with another algorithm which, even though it seems longer, calculates the result much faster.

21.2   Choosing a Decision Control Structure

The following diagram can help you decide which decision control structure is a better choice for a given problem depending on the number of variables checked.

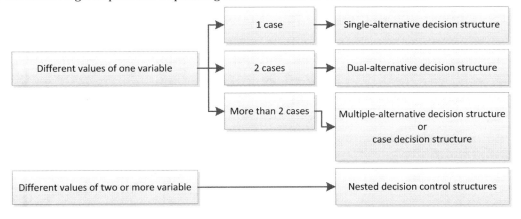

21.3   Streamlining the Decision Control Structure

Look carefully at the following flowchart fragment given in general form.

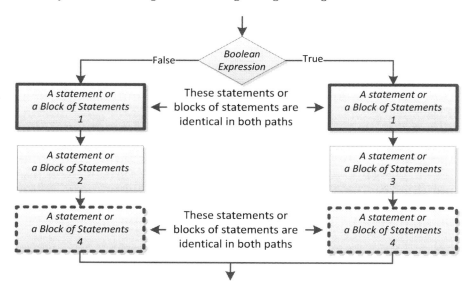

As you can see, two identical statements or blocks of statements exist at the beginning and two other identical statements or blocks of statements exist at the end of both paths of the dual-alternative decision structure. This means that, regardless of the result of the Boolean expression, these statements are executed either way. Thus, you can simply move them outside and (respectively) right before and right after the dual-alternative decision structure, as shown in this equivalent structure.

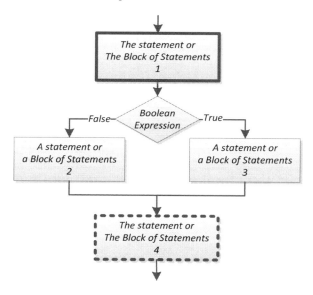

The same tip can be applied to any decision control structure, as long as an identical statement or block of statements exists in all paths. Of course, there are also cases where this tip cannot be applied.

Are you still confused? Next, you will find some exercises that can help you to understand better.

Exercise 21.3-1 *"Shrinking" the Algorithm*

Redesign the following flowchart using fewer statements.

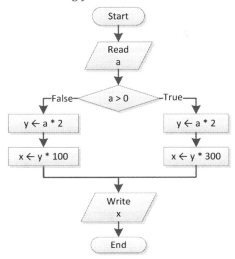

Solution

As you can see, the statement y ← a * 2 exists in both paths of the dual-alternative decision structure. This means that, regardless of the result of the Boolean expression, this statement is executed either way. Therefore, you can simply move the statement outside and right before the dual-alternative decision structure, as shown here.

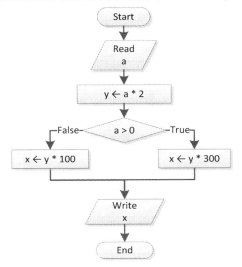

Exercise 21.3-2 *"Shrinking" the Visual Basic Program*

Rewrite the following Visual Basic program using fewer statements.

```
Sub Main()
```

```
    Dim a, y As Integer

    a = Console.ReadLine()

    If a > 0 Then
        y = a * 4
        Console.Write(y)
    Else
        y = a * 3
        Console.Write(y)
    End If

    Console.ReadKey()
End Sub
```

Solution

As you can see, the statement Console.Write(y) exists in both paths of the dual-alternative decision structure. This means that, regardless of the result of the Boolean expression, this statement is executed either way. Therefore, you can simply move the statement outside and right after the dual-alternative decision structure, as shown here.

```
Sub Main()
    Dim a, y As Integer

    a = Console.ReadLine()

    If a > 0 Then
        y = a * 4
    Else
        y = a * 3
    End If

    Console.Write(y)

    Console.ReadKey()
End Sub
```

Exercise 21.3-3   *"Shrinking" the Algorithm*

Redesign the following flowchart using fewer statements.

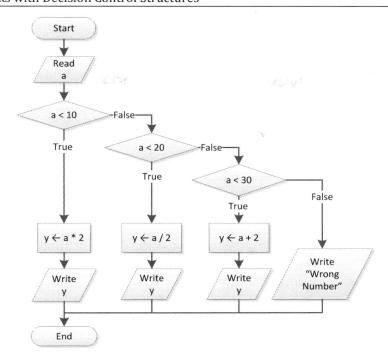

Solution

In this case, nothing special can be done. If you try to move the `Write y` statement outside of the multiple-alternative decision structure, the resulting flowchart that follows is definitely **not** equivalent to the initial one.

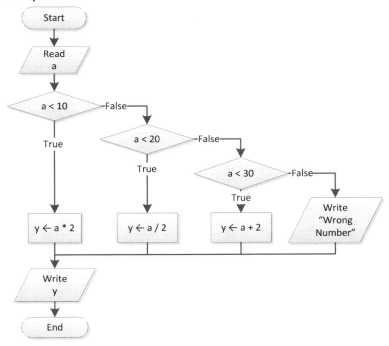

This is because of the last path on the right side which, in the initial flowchart, didn't include the `Write y` statement.

Examine both flowcharts to see whether they produce the same result. For example, suppose a user enters a wrong number. In both flowcharts, the flow of execution goes to the `Write "Wrong Number"` statement. After that, the initial flowchart executes no other statements but on the contrary, the second flowchart executes an extra `Write y` statement.

> **Remember!** *You cannot move a statement or block of statements outside of a decision control structure if it does not exist in all paths.*

You may now wonder whether there is any other way to move the `Write y` statement outside of the multiple-alternative decision structure. The answer is "yes," but you need to slightly rearrange the flowchart. You need to completely remove the last path on the right and use a brand new decision control structure in the beginning to check whether or not the given number is wrong. One possible solution is shown here.

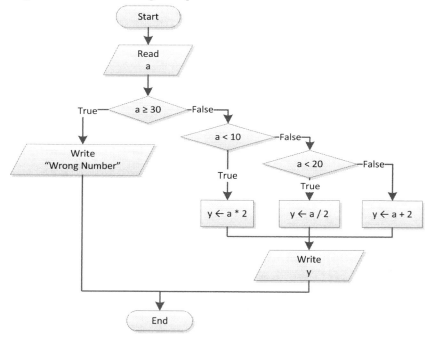

and the Visual Basic program is

```
Sub Main()
  Dim a, y As Double

  a = Console.ReadLine()

  If a >= 30 Then
    Console.WriteLine("Wrong Number")
  Else
    If a < 10 Then
      y = a * 2
    ElseIf a < 20 Then
```

```
        y = a / 2
     Else
        y = a + 2
     End If


     Console.WriteLine(y)
   End If


   Console.ReadKey()
 End Sub
```

21.4 Logical Operators – to Use, or not to Use: That is the Question!

There are some cases in which you can use a logical operator instead of nested decision control structures, and this can lead to increased readability. Take a look at the following flowchart fragment given in general form.

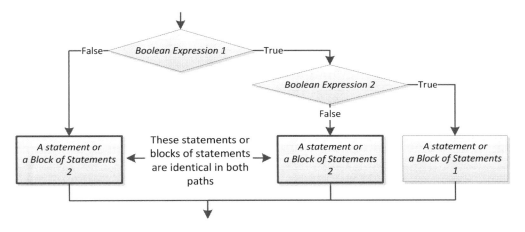

As you can see, the statement or block of statements 1 is executed only when **both** Boolean expressions evaluate to True. The statement or block of statements 2 is executed in all other cases. Therefore, this flowchart fragment can be redesigned using the AND logical operator.

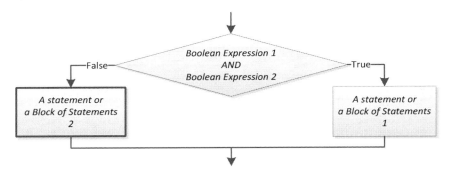

Now, let's take a look at another flowchart fragment given in general form.

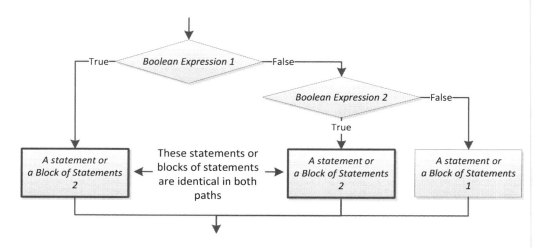

In this flowchart fragment, the statement or block of statements 2 is executed when **either** Boolean expression 1 evaluates to True **or** Boolean expression 2 evaluates to True. Therefore, you can redesign this flowchart fragment using the OR logical operator as shown here.

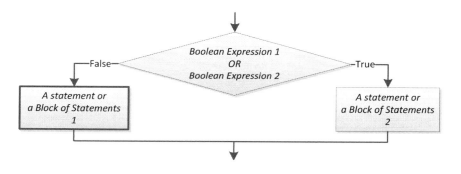

Notice: *Obviously, these methodologies can be adapted to be used on nested decision control structures as well.*

Exercise 21.4-1   *Rewriting the Code*

Rewrite the following Visual Basic program using logical operators.

```
Sub Main()
  Dim today, name As String

  today = Console.ReadLine()
  name = Console.ReadLine()

  If today = "February 16" Then
    If name = "Loukia" Then
      Console.WriteLine("Happy Birthday!!!")
    Else
      Console.WriteLine("No match!")
    End If
```

```
    Else
        Console.WriteLine("No match!")
    End If

    Console.ReadKey()
End Sub
```

Solution

The `Console.WriteLine("Happy Birthday!!!")` statement is executed only when **both** Boolean expressions evaluate to `True`. The statement `Console.WriteLine("No match!")` is executed in all other cases. Therefore, you can rewrite the Visual Basic program using the `And` logical operator.

```
Sub Main()
    Dim today, name As String

    today = Console.ReadLine()
    name = Console.ReadLine()

    If today = "February 16" And name = "Loukia" Then
        Console.WriteLine("Happy Birthday!!!")
    Else
        Console.WriteLine("No match!")
    End If

    Console.ReadKey()
End Sub
```

Exercise 21.4-2   *Rewriting the Code*

Rewrite the following Visual Basic program using logical operators.

```
Sub Main()
    Dim a, b, y As Integer

    a = Console.ReadLine()
    b = Console.ReadLine()

    y = 0
    If a > 10 Then
        y += 1
    ElseIf b > 20 Then
        y += 1
    Else
        y -= 1
    End If

    Console.Write(y)

    Console.ReadKey()
End Sub
```

Solution

The y += 1 statement is executed when **either** variable a is greater than 10 **or** variable b is greater than 20. Therefore, you can rewrite the Visual Basic program using the Or logical operator.

```vb
Sub Main()
    Dim a, b, y As Integer

    a = Console.ReadLine()
    b = Console.ReadLine()

    y = 0
    If a > 10 Or b > 20 Then
        y += 1
    Else
        y -= 1
    End If

    Console.Write(y)

    Console.ReadKey()
End Sub
```

21.5   Merging Two or More Single-Alternative Decision Structures

Many times, an algorithm contains two or more single-alternative decision structures in a row which actually evaluate the same Boolean expression. An example is shown here.

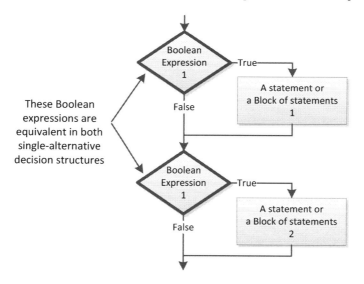

When a situation like this occurs, you can just merge all single-alternative decision structures to a single one as shown here.

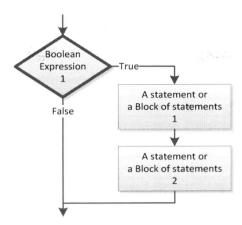

> **Remember!** *The single-alternative decision structures need to be adjacent to each other. If any statement exists between them, you can't merge them unless you are able to move this statement to somewhere else in your code.*

Exercise 21.5-1   *Merging the Decision Control Structures*

In the following Visual Basic program, merge the single-alternative decision structures.

```vbnet
Sub Main()
  Dim a As Integer

  a = Console.ReadLine()

  If a > 0 Then
    Console.WriteLine("Hello")
  End If

  If a > 0 Then
    Console.WriteLine("Hermes")
  End If

  Console.ReadKey()
End Sub
```

Solution

The first and second decision control structures are evaluating exactly the same Boolean expressions, so they can simply be merged into a single one.

The Visual Basic program becomes

```vbnet
Sub Main()
  Dim a As Integer

  a = Console.ReadLine()

  If a > 0 Then
    Console.WriteLine("Hello")
```

```
        Console.WriteLine("Hermes")
    End If

    Console.ReadKey()
End Sub
```

Exercise 21.5-2   *Merging the Decision Control Structures*

In the following Visual Basic program, merge as many single-alternative decision structures as possible.

```
Sub Main()
    Dim a, y, b As Integer

    a = Console.ReadLine()

    y = 0

    If a > 0 Then
        y += 1
    End If

    b = Console.ReadLine()              'This statement is not affected by
                                        'the previous decision control
                                        'structure and does not affect the
                                        'next one
    If Not(a <= 0) Then
        Console.WriteLine("Hello Hera")
    End If

    a += 1                              'The previous and next decision control
                                        'structures are dependent upon this
                                        'statement
    If a > 0 Then
        Console.WriteLine("Hallo Welt")
    End If

    Console.Write(b)

    Console.ReadKey()
End Sub
```

Solution

If you take a closer look at the Visual Basic program, it becomes clear that the first and second decision control structures are actually evaluating exactly the same Boolean expression. Negation of a > 0 results in a <= 0, and a second negation of a <= 0 (using the Not operator this time) results in Not(a <= 0). Thus, a > 0 is in fact equivalent to Not(a <= 0).

Remember! *Two negations result in an affirmative.*

However, between the first and second decision control structures there is the statement b = Console.ReadLine(), which prevents you from merging them into a single one. Fortunately, this statement can be moved to the beginning of the program since it doesn't really affect the rest flow of execution.

On the other hand, between the second and third decision control structures there is the statement a += 1, which also prevents you from merging; however, this statement cannot be moved anywhere else because it does affect the rest of the flow of execution (the second and third decision control structures are dependent upon this statement). Thus, the third decision control structure cannot be merged with the first and second ones!

The final Visual Basic program looks like this.

```vb
Sub Main()
  Dim a, b, y As Integer

  a = Console.ReadLine()
  b = Console.ReadLine()

  y = 0

  If a > 0 Then
    y += 1
    Console.WriteLine("Hello Hera")
  End If

  a += 1

  If a > 0 Then
    Console.WriteLine("Hallo Welt")
  End If

  Console.Write(b)

  Console.ReadKey()
End Sub
```

21.6 Replacing Two Single-Alternative Decision Structures with a Dual-Alternative One

Take a look at the next example.

```vb
If a > 40 Then
  'Do something
End If

If a <= 40 Then
  'Do something else
End If
```

The first decision control structure evaluates variable a to test if it is bigger than 40, and right after that, a second decision control structure evaluates the same variable again to test if it is less than or equal to 40!

This is a very common "mistake" that novice programmers make. They use two single-alternative decision structures even though one dual-alternative decision structure can accomplish the same thing.

The previous example can be rewritten using only one dual-alternative decision structure, as shown here.

```
If a > 40 Then
  'Do something
Else
  'Do something else
End If
```

Even though both examples are absolutely correct and work perfectly well, the second alternative is better. The CPU needs to evaluate only one Boolean expression, which results in faster execution time.

> *Notice: The two single-alternative decision structures must be adjacent to each other. If any statement exists between them, you can't "merge" them (that is, replace them with a dual-alternative decision structure) unless you are able to move this statement to somewhere else in your code.*

Exercise 21.6-1   *"Merging" the Decision Control Structures*

In the following Visual Basic program, "merge" as many single-alternative decision structures as possible.

```
Sub Main()
  Dim a, y, b As Integer

  a = Console.ReadLine()

  y = 0

  If a > 0 Then
    y += 1
  End If

  b = Console.ReadLine()          'This statement is not affected by
                                  'the previous decision control
                                  'structure and does affect the next
                                  'one. Thus, it can be moved to the
                                  'beginning of the program

  If Not(a > 0) Then
    Console.WriteLine("Hello Zeus")
  End If

  If y > 0 Then                   'Unfortunately this decision control
    Console.WriteLine(y + 5)      'structure can't be merged with
  End If                          'the next one…

  y += 1                          '… because of this statement

  If y <= 0 Then
```

```
        Console.WriteLine(y + 12)
    End If

    Console.ReadKey()
End Sub
```

Solution

The first decision control structure evaluates variable a to test if it is greater than zero, and just right after that the second decision control structure evaluates variable a again to test if it is not greater than zero. Even though there is the statement b = Console.ReadLine() between them, this statement can be moved somewhere else because it doesn't really affect the rest of the flow of execution.

On the other hand, between the third and fourth decision control structures there is the statement y += 1 which also prevents you from merging. However, this statement cannot be moved anywhere else because it does affect the rest of the flow of execution (the third and fourth decision control structures are dependent upon this statement). Therefore, the third and fourth decision control structures cannot be merged!

The final Visual Basic program becomes

```
Sub Main()
    Dim a, b, y As Integer

    a = Console.ReadLine()
    b = Console.ReadLine()

    y = 0

    If a > 0 Then
        y += 1
    Else
        Console.WriteLine("Hello Zeus")
    End If

    If y > 0 Then
        Console.WriteLine(y + 5)
    End If

    y += 1

    If y <= 0 Then
        Console.WriteLine(y + 12)
    End If

    Console.ReadKey()
End Sub
```

21.7   Put the Boolean Expressions Most Likely to be True First

Both the multiple-alternative and the case decision structure often need to check several Boolean expressions before deciding which statement or block of statements to execute. In the next decision control structure,

```
If Boolean_Expression 1 Then
  A statement or block of statements 1
ElseIf Boolean_Expression 2 Then
  A statement or block of statements 2
End If
```

the program first tests if *Boolean_Expression 1* is True and if not, it tests if *Boolean_Expression 2* is True.

However, what if *Boolean_Expression 1* is False most of the time and *Boolean_Expression 2* is True most of the time? This means that time is wasted testing *Boolean_Expression 1*, which is usually False, before testing *Boolean_Expression 2*, which is usually True.

To make your programs more efficient, you can put the Boolean expressions that are most likely to be True at the beginning, and the Boolean expressions that are most likely to be False at the end, using either a multiple-alternative or a case decision structure as shown here.

```
If Boolean_Expression 2 Then
  A statement or block of statements 2
ElseIf Boolean_Expression 1 Then
  A statement or block of statements 1
End If
```

> **Remember!** *Although this method may seem nonessential, every little bit of time that you save can add up to make your programs run faster and more efficiently.*

Exercise 21.7-1   *Rearranging the Boolean Expressions*

According to an ultra-high top secret report, America's favorite pets are dogs, with cats at second place, guinea pigs next, and parrots coming in last. In the following Visual Basic program, rearrange the Boolean expressions to make the program run faster and more efficiently.

```
Sub Main()
  Dim kind As String

  Console.Write("What is your favorite pet? ")
  kind = Console.ReadLine()

  Select Case kind
    Case "Parrots"
      Console.WriteLine("It screeches!")
    Case "Guinea pig"
      Console.WriteLine("It squeaks")
    Case "Dog"
      Console.WriteLine("It barks")
    Case "Cat"
      Console.WriteLine("It meows")
  End Select
  Console.ReadKey()
End Sub
```

Solution

For this top secret report, you can rearrange the Visual Basic program to make it run a little bit faster for most of the cases.

```vbnet
Sub Main()
  Dim kind As String

  Console.Write("What is your favorite pet? ")
  kind = Console.ReadLine()

  Select Case kind
    Case "Dog"
      Console.WriteLine("It barks")
    Case "Cat"
      Console.WriteLine("It meows")
    Case "Guinea pig"
      Console.WriteLine("It squeaks")
    Case "Parrots"
      Console.WriteLine("It screeches!")
  End Select

  Console.ReadKey()
End Sub
```

21.8 Converting a Case Decision Structure to a Multiple-Alternative Decision Structure, and Vice Versa

Converting a case decision structure to a multiple-alternative decision structure is quite easy. All you need to do is get the variable or the expression that the switch statement evaluates and use it in the multiple-alternative decision structure for all cases.

Case Decision Structure

Multiple-Alternative Decision Structure

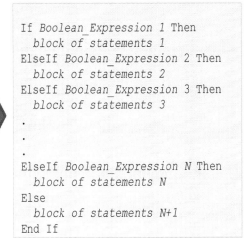

```
Select Case var_expr
  Case expression_list-1
    block of statements 1
  Case expression_list-2
    block of statements 2
  Case value-3
    block of statements 3
    .
    .

    .
  Case expression_list-N
    block of statements N
  Case Else
    block of statements N+1
End Select
```

```
If Boolean_Expression 1 Then
  block of statements 1
ElseIf Boolean_Expression 2 Then
  block of statements 2
ElseIf Boolean_Expression 3 Then
  block of statements 3
  .
  .

  .
ElseIf Boolean_Expression N Then
  block of statements N
Else
  block of statements N+1
End If
```

Notice: *The opposite conversion (from multiple-alternative decision structure to case decision structure) is possible as long as the same variable or expression is evaluated for all paths.*

Exercise 21.8-1   *Converting the Visual Basic Program*

Rewrite the following Visual Basic program using the multiple-alternative decision structure.

```
Sub Main()
  Dim option As Integer

  Console.WriteLine("What is your name? ")
  Console.WriteLine("1) John")
  Console.WriteLine("2) Aphrodite")
  Console.WriteLine("3) Loukia")
  Console.Write("Select an option: ")
  option = Console.ReadLine()

  Select Case option
    Case 1
      Console.WriteLine("You are my cousin!")
    Case 2
      Console.WriteLine("You are my sister!")
    Case 3
      Console.WriteLine("You are my mom!")
    Case Else
      Console.WriteLine("Sorry, I don't know you.")
  End Select

  Console.ReadKey()
End Sub
```

Solution

The multiple-alternative decision structure should evaluate variable `option` for all paths.

```
Sub Main()
  Dim option As Integer

  Console.WriteLine("What is your name? ")
  Console.WriteLine("1) John")
  Console.WriteLine("2) Aphrodite")
  Console.WriteLine("3) Loukia")
  Console.Write("Select an option: ")
  option = Console.ReadLine()

  If option = 1 Then
    Console.WriteLine("You are my cousin!")
  ElseIf option = 2 Then
    Console.WriteLine("You are my sister!")
  ElseIf option = 3 Then
    Console.WriteLine("You are my mom!")
  Else
    Console.WriteLine("Sorry, I don't know you.")
  End If
```

```
    Console.ReadKey()
End Sub
```

Exercise 21.8-2   *Converting the Visual Basic Program*

Rewrite the following Visual Basic program using the case decision structure.

```
Sub Main()
  Dim x As Integer

  Console.Write("Enter an integer: ")
  x = Console.ReadLine()

  If x = 1 Or x = 2 Or x = 3 Then
    Console.WriteLine("You entered 1, 2, or 3")
  ElseIf x >= 4 And x <= 10 Then
    Console.WriteLine("You entered an integer between 3 and 10")
  ElseIf x = 11 Then
    Console.WriteLine("You entered 11")
  ElseIf x > 11 Then
    Console.WriteLine("You entered an integer greater than 11")
  ElseIf x < -10 Or x > -5 Then
    Console.WriteLine("You entered a negative integer")
  Else
    Console.WriteLine("You entered -10, -9, -8, -7, -6, -5")
  End If

  Console.ReadKey()
End Sub
```

Solution

In this program, the same variable is evaluated for all paths, thus the conversion is possible and is shown here.

```
Sub Main()
  Dim x As Integer

  Console.Write("Enter an integer: ")
  x = Console.ReadLine()

  Select Case x
    Case 1, 2, 3
      Console.WriteLine("You entered 1, 2, or 3")
    Case 4 To 10
      Console.WriteLine("You entered an integer between 3 and 10")
    Case 11
      Console.WriteLine("You entered 11")
    Case Is > 11
      Console.WriteLine("You entered an integer greater than 11")
    Case Is < -10, Is > -5
```

```
        Console.WriteLine("You entered a negative integer")
      Case Else
        Console.WriteLine("You entered -10, -9, -8, -7, -6, -5")
   End Select

   Console.ReadKey()
End Sub
```

Exercise 21.8-3   *Converting the Visual Basic Program*

Rewrite the following Visual Basic program using the case decision structure.

```
Sub Main()
   Dim x, y As Double

   Console.Write("Enter a number: ")
   x = Console.ReadLine()
   Console.Write("Enter a second number: ")
   y = Console.ReadLine()

   If x < 5 Then
      Console.WriteLine("Variable x is less than 5")
   ElseIf y = 3 Then
      Console.WriteLine("Variable y equals to 3")
   ElseIf x + y = 24 Then
      Console.WriteLine("The sum of x + y equals to 24")
   ElseIf Math.Sqrt(x) = 4 Then
      Console.WriteLine("The square root of x equals to 4")
   Else
      Console.WriteLine("None of the above")
   End If

   Console.ReadKey()
End Sub
```

Solution

As you already know, the conversion from a multiple-alternative decision structure to a case decision structure is possible as long as the same variable or expression is evaluated for all paths. In this exercise, however, each path evaluates a different variable or expression. For that reason, the conversion to the Select statement is not possible.

21.9   Converting a Multiple-Alternative Decision Structure to Nested Decision Control Structures, and Vice Versa

The next Visual Basic statements, given in general form, can help you easily convert from a multiple-alternative decision structure to nested decision control structures, and vice versa.

Multiple-Alternative
Decision Structure

```
If Boolean Expr 1 Then
   block of statements 1
ElseIf Boolean Expr 2 Then
   block of statements 2
ElseIf Boolean Expr 3 Then
   block of statements 3
   .
   .
   .

ElseIf Boolean Expr N Then
   block of statements N
Else
   block of statements N+1
End If
```

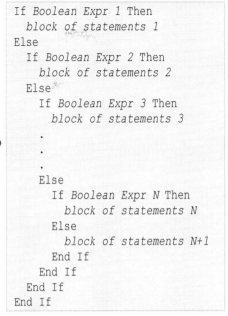

Nested
Decision Control Structures

```
If Boolean Expr 1 Then
   block of statements 1
Else
   If Boolean Expr 2 Then
      block of statements 2
   Else
      If Boolean Expr 3 Then
         block of statements 3
      .
      .
      .
      Else
         If Boolean Expr N Then
            block of statements N
         Else
            block of statements N+1
         End If
      End If
   End If
End If
```

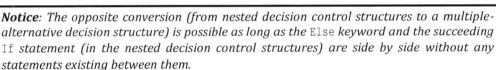

Notice: *The opposite conversion (from nested decision control structures to a multiple-alternative decision structure) is possible as long as the* `Else` *keyword and the succeeding* `If` *statement (in the nested decision control structures) are side by side without any statements existing between them.*

Exercise 21.9-1 *Converting the Visual Basic Program*

Rewrite the Visual Basic program using nested decision control structures.

```
Sub Main()
  Dim x, y, result As Double

  Console.Write("Enter a number: ")
  x = Console.ReadLine()
  Console.Write("Enter a second number: ")
  y = Console.ReadLine()

  result = x * y

  If x < 0 And y < 0 Then
    Console.WriteLine("The result of the multiplication of")
    Console.WriteLine("two negative numbers is positive. For example")
    Console.WriteLine(x & " * (" & y & ") equals to +" & result)
  ElseIf x < 0 Then
    Console.WriteLine("The result of the multiplication of a negative")
    Console.WriteLine("with a positive number is negative. For example")
    Console.WriteLine(x & " * " & y & " equals to " & result)
  ElseIf y < 0 Then
```

```
      Console.WriteLine("The result of the multiplication of a positive")
      Console.WriteLine("with a negative number is negative. For example")
      Console.WriteLine(x & " * (" & y & ") equals to " & result)
    Else
      Console.WriteLine("The result of the multiplication of")
      Console.WriteLine("two positive numbers is positive. For example")
      Console.WriteLine(x & " * " & y & " equals to +" & result)
    End If

    Console.ReadKey()
  End Sub
```

Solution

Using what you learned so far, the Visual Basic program becomes

```
Sub Main()
  Dim x, y, result As Double

  Console.Write("Enter a number: ")
  x = Console.ReadLine()
  Console.Write("Enter a second number: ")
  y = Console.ReadLine()

  result = x * y

  If x < 0 And y < 0 Then
    Console.WriteLine("The result of the multiplication of")
    Console.WriteLine("two negative numbers is positive. For example")
    Console.WriteLine(x & " * (" & y & ") equals to +" & result)
  Else
    If x < 0 Then
      Console.WriteLine("The result of the multiplication of a negative")
      Console.WriteLine("with a positive number is negative. For example")
      Console.WriteLine(x & " * " & y & " equals to " & result)
    Else
      If y < 0 Then
        Console.WriteLine("The result of the multiplication of a positive")
        Console.WriteLine("with a negative number is negative. For example")
        Console.WriteLine(x & " * (" & y & ") equals to " & result)
      Else
        Console.WriteLine("The result of the multiplication of")
        Console.WriteLine("two positive numbers is positive. For example")
        Console.WriteLine(x & " * " & y & " equals to +" & result)
      End If
    End If
  End If

  Console.ReadKey()
End Sub
```

Exercise 21.9-2   *Converting the Visual Basic Program*

Rewrite the Visual Basic program using a multiple-alternative decision structure.

```
Sub Main()
  Dim x, y As Double

  Console.WriteLine("Enter a number: ")
  x = Console.ReadLine()
  Console.WriteLine("Enter a second number: ")
  y = Console.ReadLine()

  If x > 5 Then
    Console.WriteLine("Variable x is greater than 5")
  Else
    x = x + y
    Console.WriteLine("Hello Zeus!")
    If x = 3 Then
      Console.WriteLine("Variable x equals to 3")
    Else
      x = x - y
      Console.WriteLine("Hello Olympians!")
      If x + y = 24 Then
        Console.WriteLine("The sum of x + y equals to 24")
      Else
        Console.WriteLine("Nothing of the above")
      End If
    End If
  End If

  Console.ReadKey()
End Sub
```

Solution

This is the case in which you can't proceed with the conversion because there are some statements (in bold) existing between the `Else` and `If` keywords.

21.10 Converting a Case Decision Structure to Nested Decision Control Structures, and Vice Versa

Converting a case decision structure to nested decision control structures is quite easy. All you need to do is get the variable or the expression that the switch statement evaluates and use it in all nested decision control structures.

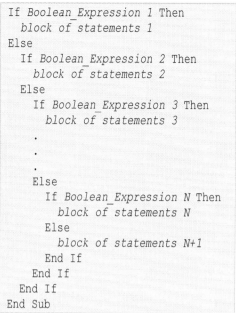

Case Decision Structure	**Nested Decision Control Structures**

```
Select Case var_expr
  Case expression_list-1
    block of statements 1
  Case expression_list-2
    block of statements 2
  Case expression_list-3
    block of statements 3
      .
      .
      .
  Case expression_list-N
    block of statements N
  Case Else
    block of statements N+1
End Select
```

```
If Boolean_Expression 1 Then
  block of statements 1
Else
  If Boolean_Expression 2 Then
    block of statements 2
  Else
    If Boolean_Expression 3 Then
      block of statements 3
      .
      .
      .
    Else
      If Boolean_Expression N Then
        block of statements N
      Else
        block of statements N+1
      End If
    End If
  End If
End Sub
```

> **Notice**: The opposite conversion (from nested decision control structures to a case decision structure) is possible as long as the `Else` keyword and the succeeding `If` statement (in the nested decision control structures) are side by side without any statements existing between them, and as long as the same variable or expression is evaluated for all paths.

Exercise 21.10-1   *Converting the Visual Basic Program*

Rewrite the Visual Basic program using nested decision control structures.

```
Sub Main()
  Dim name As String

  Console.WriteLine("What is your name?")
  name = Console.ReadLine()

  Select Case name
    Case "John", "Stelios"
      Console.WriteLine("You are my cousin!")
    Case "Aphrodite"
      Console.WriteLine("You are my sister!")
    Case "Loukia"
      Console.WriteLine("You are my mom!")
    Case Else
      Console.WriteLine("Sorry, I don't know you.")
  End Select

  Console.ReadKey()
End Sub
```

Solution

All nested decision control structures should evaluate the same variable name.

```
Sub Main()
  Dim name As String

  Console.WriteLine("What is your name?")
  name = Console.ReadLine()

  If name = "John" Or name = "Stelios" Then
    Console.WriteLine("You are my cousin!")
  Else
    If name = "Aphrodite" Then
      Console.WriteLine("You are my sister!")
    Else
      If name = "Loukia" Then
        Console.WriteLine("You are my mom!")
      Else
        Console.WriteLine("Sorry, I don't know you.")
      End If
    End If
  End If

  Console.ReadKey()
End Sub
```

Exercise 21.10-2 *Converting the Visual Basic Program*

Rewrite the Visual Basic program using the case decision structure.

```
Sub Main()
  Dim x, y As Integer

  Console.WriteLine("Enter a integer: ")
  x = Console.ReadLine()
  Console.WriteLine("Enter a second integer: ")
  y = Console.ReadLine()

  If x = 1 Then
    Console.WriteLine("Hello Zeus!")
  Else
    x = x + y
    Console.WriteLine("Hello Olympians!")
    If x = 2 Then
      Console.WriteLine("Hello to everyone!")
    Else
      x = x - y
      Console.WriteLine("Hello again!")
      If x = 3 Then
        Console.WriteLine("Hello and goodbye!")
      Else
```

```
            Console.WriteLine("Gooooooood morning NY!")
        End If
      End If
    End If

    Console.ReadKey()
End Sub
```

Solution

Once again, this is a case in which you can't proceed with the conversion because there are some statements (in bold) existing between Else and If keywords.

21.11 What is Code Indentation and Why is it so Important?

As you've been reading through this book, you may wonder why space characters appear in front of the Visual Basic statements and why these statements are not written at the leftmost edge of the paragraph, as in the following example.

```
Sub Main()
Dim x, y As Integer

Console.Write("Enter a number: ")
x = Console.ReadLine()
Console.Write("Enter a second number: ")
y = Console.ReadLine()
If x > 5 Then
Console.WriteLine("Variable x is greater than 5")
Else
x = x + y
Console.WriteLine("Hello Zeus!")
If x = 3 Then
Console.WriteLine("Variable x equals to 3")
Else
x = x - y
Console.WriteLine("Hello Olympians!")
If x + y = 24 Then
Console.WriteLine("The sum of x + y equals to 24")
Else
Console.WriteLine("Nothing of the above")
End If
End If
End If
Console.ReadKey()
End Sub
```

The answer is obvious! A code without indentation is difficult to read and understand. Anyone who reads a code written this way gets confused about the If - Else pairing (that is, to which If an Else belongs). Moreover, if a long Visual Basic program is written this way, it is almost impossible to find, for example, the location of a forgotten End If.

Code indentation can be defined as a way to organize your source code. Indentation formats the code using spaces or tabs in order to improve readability. Well indented code is very helpful, even if it takes some extra effort, because in the long run it saves you a lot of time when you revisit your code. Unfortunately, it is sometimes overlooked and the trouble occurs at a later time. Following a particular programming style helps you to avoid syntax and logic errors. It also helps programmers to more easily study and understand code written by others.

> **Notice**: *Code indentation is similar to the way authors visually arrange the text of a book. Instead of writing long series of sentences, they break the text into chapters and paragraphs. This action doesn't change the meaning of the text but it makes it easier to read.*

All statements that appear inside an If statement must always be indented. For example, by indenting the statements inside a dual-alternative decision structure, you visually set them apart. As a result, anyone can tell at a glance which statements are executed when the Boolean expression evaluates to True, and which are executed when the Boolean expression evaluates to False.

> **Notice**: *Only humans have difficulty reading and understanding a program without indentation. A computer can execute any code, written with or without indentation, as long as it contains no syntax errors.*

21.12 Using the "From Inner to Outer" Method in Decision Control Structures

"From inner to outer" is a method proposed by this book to help you learn "Algorithmic Thinking" from the inside out. This method first manipulates and designs the inner (nested) control structures. Then, as the algorithm is developed, more and more control structures are added, nesting the previous ones.

Let's try the following example.

Design a flowchart that lets the user enter a number and, if its last digit is equal to 5, a message "Last digit equal to 5" is displayed; otherwise, a message "Nothing special" is displayed. Moreover, if the user enters a non-numeric character, an error message should be displayed.

First, you can design the inner decision structure that displays the messages "Last digit equal to 5" or "Nothing special" (depending on the last digit). The flowchart fragment is shown here.

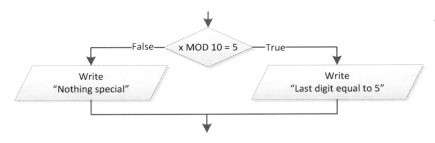

> **Remember!** *You can isolate the last digit of any number using the modulus 10 operation. It is not necessary to know the exact number of digits.*

Now let's deal with the data validation problem. In this exercise, you need to test whether or not the user has entered a valid numeric value. If not, an error message should be displayed; otherwise, you can proceed to check the last digit. The outer decision structure is shown in the flowchart that follows.

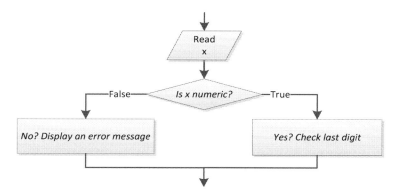

Now, you can combine both flowchart fragments, nesting the first into the second one and the final flowchart becomes

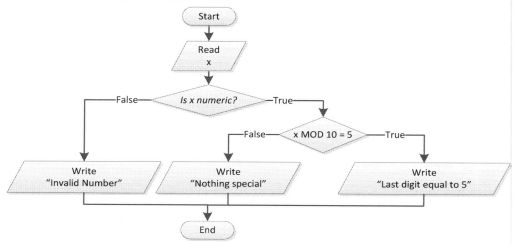

Now you may wonder why we go to all this trouble. It was too easy and it could have been designed as usual without the use of the "from inner to outer" method. Yes, you are probably right. But imagine this method used in very large and complicated control structures. It can help you design error-free flowcharts or even Visual Basic programs and save you a lot of effort! This book uses this method wherever and whenever it seems necessary.

21.13 Review Questions: True/False

Choose **true** or **false** for each of the following statements.

1. Smaller algorithms are always the best solution to a given problem.
2. You can move a statement outside, and right before, a dual-alternative decision structure as long as it exists at the beginning of both paths of the decision structure.
3. You can always use a logical operator instead of nested decision control structures to increase readability.

4. Two single-alternative decision structures can be merged into one single-alternative decision only when they are in a row and when they evaluate the same Boolean expression.

5. Conversion from a dual-alternative decision structure to two single-alternative decision structures is always possible.

6. Two single-alternative decision structures can be "merged" into (actually, replaced by) one dual-alternative decision only when they are in a row and only when they evaluate the same Boolean expression.

7. Conversion from a case decision structure to a multiple-alternative decision structure is always possible.

8. Conversion from a multiple-alternative decision structure to a case decision structure is always possible.

9. Conversion from a multiple-alternative decision structure to nested decision control structures is always possible.

10. Conversion from nested decision control structures to a multiple-alternative decision structure is always possible.

11. Conversion from a case decision structure to nested decision control structures is always possible.

12. Conversion from nested decision control structures to a case decision structure is always possible.

13. Visual Basic programs written without code indentation cannot be executed by a computer.

21.14 Review Questions: Multiple Choice

Select the correct answer for each of the following statements.

1. The following two programs

```
Sub Main()
    Dim a As Integer

    a = Console.ReadLine()
    If a > 40 Then
        a += 1
        Console.WriteLine(a * 2)
    Else
        a += 1
        Console.WriteLine(a * 3)
    End If

    Console.ReadKey()
End Sub
```

```
Sub Main()
    Dim a As Integer

    a = Console.ReadLine()
    a += 1
    If a > 40 Then
        Console.WriteLine(a * 2)
    Else
        Console.WriteLine(a * 3)
    End If

    Console.ReadKey()
End Sub
```

    a. produce the same result.

    b. produce the same result, but the right program is faster.

    c. do not produce the same result.

    d. none of the above

2. The following two programs

```
Sub Main()
  Dim a As Integer

  a = Console.ReadLine()
  If a > 40 Then
    Console.WriteLine(a * 2)
  End If
  If a > 40 Then
    Console.WriteLine(a * 3)
  End If

  Console.ReadKey()
End Sub
```

```
Sub Main()
  Dim a As Integer

  a = Console.ReadLine()
  If a > 40 Then
    Console.WriteLine(a * 2)
    Console.WriteLine(a * 3)
  End If

  Console.ReadKey()
End Sub
```

a. produce the same results, but the left program is faster.

b. produce the same results, but the right program is faster.

c. do not produce the same results.

d. none of the above

3. The following two programs

```
Sub Main()
  Dim a, b, y As Integer

  a = Console.ReadLine()
  b = Console.ReadLine()

  y = 5

  If a > 15 Or b < 25 Then
    y -= 1
  Else
    y += 1
  End If
  Console.Write(y)

  Console.ReadKey()
End Sub
```

```
Sub Main()
  Dim a, b, y As Integer

  a = Console.ReadLine()
  b = Console.ReadLine()

  y = 5

  If a > 15 Then
    y -= 1
  ElseIf b < 25 Then
    y -= 1
  Else
    y += 1
  End If
  Console.Write(y)

  Console.ReadKey()
End Sub
```

a. produce the same result.

b. do not produce the same result.

c. neither of the above

4. The following two programs

```
Sub Main()
    Dim a As Integer


    a = Console.ReadLine()


    If a > 40 Then
        Console.WriteLine(a * 2)
    Else
        Console.WriteLine(a * 3)
    End If


    Console.ReadKey()
End Sub
```

```
Sub Main()
    Dim a As Integer


    a = Console.ReadLine()


    If a > 40 Then
        Console.WriteLine(a * 2)
    End If
    If a <= 40 Then
        Console.WriteLine(a * 3)
    End If


    Console.ReadKey()
End Sub
```

    a.   produce the same result, but the left program is faster.

    b.   produce the same result, but the right program is faster.

    c.   do not produce the same result.

    d.   none of the above

5. The following code fragment

```
If a = 5 Then
    Console.WriteLine("Hello Zeus!")
ElseIf b = 6 Then
    Console.WriteLine("Hello Hermes!")
ElseIf c = 7 Then
    Console.WriteLine("It's all Greek to me!")
End If
```

    a.   cannot be converted to a case decision structure because it does not contain the `Else` keyword.

    b.   cannot be converted to a case decision structure because it does not evaluate the same variable for all paths.

    c.   neither of the above

6. The following code fragment

```
If a = 1 Then
    Console.WriteLine("Hello Dionysus!")
Else
    a = a * x
    If a = 5 Then
        Console.WriteLine("Hello Hera!")
    Else
        Console.WriteLine("It's all Greek to me!")
    End If
End If
```

    a.   cannot be converted to a multiple-alternative decision structure because it evaluates the same variable for all paths.

    b.   can be converted to a multiple-alternative decision structure.

    c. cannot be converted to a multiple-alternative decision structure because of the `a = a * x` statement.

    d. none of the above

7. The following code fragment

```
If a = 1 Then
   Console.WriteLine("Hello Poseidon!")
Else
   x = a * x
   If x = 5 Then
      Console.WriteLine("Hello Hephaestus!")
   Else
      Console.WriteLine("It's all Greek to me!")
   End If
End If
```

    a. cannot be converted to a case decision structure because of the `x = a * x` statement.

    b. cannot be converted to a case decision structure because it does not evaluate the same variable for all paths.

    c. both of the above

8. The following program

```
Sub Main()
Dim x As Integer
x = Console.ReadLine()
If x < 0 Then
x = (-1) * x
Console.WriteLine(x)
End If
Console.ReadKey()
End Sub
```

cannot be executed by a computer because

    a. it does not use code indentation.

    b. it includes syntax errors.

    c. it includes logic errors.

    d. none of the above

21.15 Review Exercises

Complete the following exercises.

1. Rewrite the following Visual Basic program using fewer statements.

```
Sub Main()
   Dim a, x, y As Integer

   y = Console.ReadLine()

   If a > 0 Then
      x = Console.ReadLine()
      a = x * 4 * y
```

```
      Console.WriteLine(y)
      a += 1
    Else
      x = Console.ReadLine()
      a = x * 2 * y + 7
      Console.WriteLine(y)
      a -= 1
    End If
    Console.Write(a)

    Console.ReadKey()
  End Sub
```

2. Redesign the following flowchart using fewer statements.

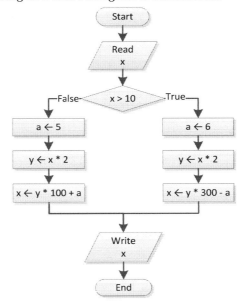

3. Rewrite the following Visual Basic program using fewer statements.

```
Sub Main()
  Dim a, y As Double

  a = Console.ReadLine()

  If a < 1 Then
    y = 5 + a
    Console.WriteLine(y)
  ElseIf a < 5 Then
    y = 23 / a
    Console.WriteLine(y)
  ElseIf a < 10 Then
    y = 5 * a
    Console.WriteLine(y)
  Else
    Console.WriteLine("Error!")
```

```
      End If

   Console.ReadKey()
End Sub
```

4. Rewrite the following Visual Basic program using logical operators.

```
Sub Main()
   Dim day, month As Integer
   Dim name As String

   day = Console.ReadLine()
   month = Console.ReadLine()
   name = Console.ReadLine()

   If day = 16 Then
      If month = 2 Then
         If name = "Loukia" Then
            Console.WriteLine("Happy Birthday!!!")
         Else
            Console.WriteLine("No match!")
         End If
      Else
         Console.WriteLine("No match!")
      End If
   Else
      Console.WriteLine("No match!")
   End If

   Console.ReadKey()
End Sub
```

5. A teacher asks her students to rewrite the following Visual Basic program without using logical operators.

```
Sub Main()
   Dim a, b, c, d As Double

   a = Console.ReadLine()
   b = Console.ReadLine()
   c = Console.ReadLine()

   If a > 10 And c < 2000 Then
      d = (a + b + c) / 12
      Console.WriteLine("The result is: " & d)
   Else
      Console.WriteLine("Error!")
   End If

   Console.ReadKey()
End Sub
```

One student wrote the following Visual Basic program:

```
Sub Main()
```

```
   Dim a, b, c, d As Double

   a = Console.ReadLine()
   b = Console.ReadLine()
   c = Console.ReadLine()

   If a > 10 Then
      If c < 2000 Then
         d = (a + b + c) / 12
         Console.WriteLine("The result is: " & d)
      Else
         Console.WriteLine("Error!")
      End If
   End If

   Console.ReadKey()
End Sub
```

Determine if the program produces the same results for all possible paths as the one given by his teacher. If not, try to modify it and make it work the same way.

6. Rewrite the following Visual Basic program using only single-alternative decision structures.

```
Sub Main()
   Dim a, b, c, d As Double

   a = Console.ReadLine()
   b = Console.ReadLine()
   c = Console.ReadLine()

   If a > 10 Then
      If b < 2000 Then
         If c <> 10 Then
            d = (a + b + c) / 12
            Console.WriteLine("The result is: " & d)
         End If
      End If
   Else
      Console.WriteLine("Error!")
   End If

   Console.ReadKey()
End Sub
```

7. In the following Visual Basic program, "merge" the single-alternative decision structures.

```
Sub Main()
   Dim a, b, y As Integer

   a = Console.ReadLine()

   y = 3
```

```
    If a > 0 Then
       y = y * a
    End If
    b = Console.ReadLine()
    If Not(a <= 0) Then
       Console.WriteLine("Hello Zeus")
    End If

    Console.Write(y & ", " & b)

    Console.ReadKey()
End Sub
```

8. In the following Visual Basic program, "merge" the single-alternative decision structures.

```
Sub Main()
    Dim a, b, y As Double

    a = Console.ReadLine()

    y = 0
    If a > 0 Then
       y = y + 7
    End If
    b = Console.ReadLine()
    If Not(a > 0) Then
       Console.WriteLine("Hello Zeus")
    End If
    If a <= 0 Then
       Console.WriteLine(Math.Abs(a))
    End If
    Console.Write(y)

    Console.ReadKey()
End Sub
```

9. According to research from 2013, the most popular operating system on tablet computers was iOS, with Android being in second place and Microsoft Windows in last place. In the following Visual Basic program, rearrange the Boolean expressions to make the program run more efficiently for most of the cases.

```
Sub Main()
    Dim os As String

    Console.Write("What is your tablet's OS? ")
    os = Console.ReadLine()

    If os = "Windows" Then
       Console.WriteLine("Microsoft")
    ElseIf os = "iOS" Then
       Console.WriteLine("Apple")
    ElseIf os = "Android" Then
```

```
        Console.WriteLine("Google")
    End If

    Console.ReadKey()
End Sub
```

10. Rewrite the following Visual Basic program using the multiple-alternative decision structure.

```
Sub Main()
    Dim a As Integer
    Dim x, y As Double

    a = Console.ReadLine()
    x = Console.ReadLine()
    y = Console.ReadLine()

    Select Case a
        Case 3, 15, 25
            x = x / 4
            y = y ^ 5
        Case 7 To 12
            x = x * 3
            y += 1
        Case Is > 52
            x = x Mod 4
            y += 9
        Case Else
            x -= 9
            y += 1
    End Select

    Console.Write(x & ", " & y)

    Console.ReadKey()
End Sub
```

11. Rewrite the Visual Basic program of the previous exercise using nested decision control structures.

12. Rewrite the following Visual Basic program using the case decision structure.

```
Sub Main()
    Dim color As Integer

    Console.WriteLine("1. Red")
    Console.WriteLine("2. Green")
    Console.WriteLine("3. Blue")
    Console.WriteLine("4. White")
    Console.WriteLine("5. Black")
    Console.WriteLine("6. Gray")
    Console.Write("Select a color: ")
    color = Console.ReadLine()
```

```
    Console.Write("Your color in hexadecimal is: ")

    If color = 1 Then
       Console.WriteLine("FF0000")
    ElseIf color = 2 Then
       Console.WriteLine("00FF00")
    ElseIf color = 3 Then
       Console.WriteLine("0000FF")
    ElseIf color = 4 Then
       Console.WriteLine("FFFFFF")
    ElseIf color = 5 Then
       Console.WriteLine("000000")
    ElseIf color = 6 Then
       Console.WriteLine("7F7F7F")
    Else
       Console.WriteLine("Unknown color!")
    End If

    Console.ReadKey()
End Sub
```

13. Rewrite the Visual Basic program of the previous exercise using nested decision control structures.

14. Write the following Visual Basic program using correct indentation and then rewrite it using a multiple-alternative decision structure.

```
Sub Main()
Dim a As Integer
a = Console.ReadLine()
If a > 1000 Then
Console.WriteLine("Big Positive")
Else
If a > 0 Then
Console.WriteLine("Positive")
Else
If a < -1000 Then
Console.WriteLine("Big Negative")
Else
If a < 0 Then
Console.WriteLine("Negative")
Else
Console.WriteLine("Zero")
End If
End If
End If
Console.ReadKey()
End If
End Sub
```

15. Write the following Visual Basic program using correct indentation and then rewrite it using nested decision control structures.

```
Sub Main()
```

```
Dim a, y As Double
a = Console.ReadLine()
If a < 1 Then
y = 5 + a
Console.WriteLine(y)
ElseIf a < 5 Then
y = 23 / a
Console.WriteLine(y)
ElseIf a < 10 Then
y = 5 * a
Console.WriteLine(y)
Else
Console.WriteLine("Error!")
End If
Console.ReadKey()
End Sub
```

Chapter 22
Flowcharts with Decision Control Structures

22.1 Introduction

By working through the previous chapters, you've become familiar with all the decision control structures. Since flowcharts are an ideal way to learn "Algorithmic Thinking" and to help you better understand specific control structures, this chapter is dedicated to teaching you how to convert a Visual Basic program to a flowchart, or a flowchart to a Visual Basic program.

22.2 Converting Visual Basic Programs to Flowcharts

To convert a Visual Basic program to its corresponding flowchart, you need to recall all the decision control structures and their corresponding flowcharts. They are all summarized here.

The single-alternative decision structure

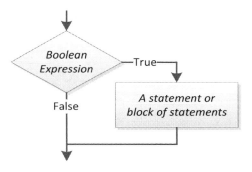

The dual-alternative decision structure

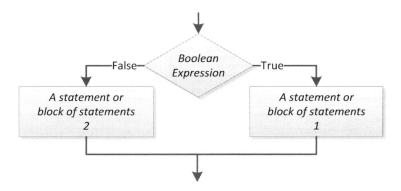

The multiple-alternative decision structure and the case decision structure

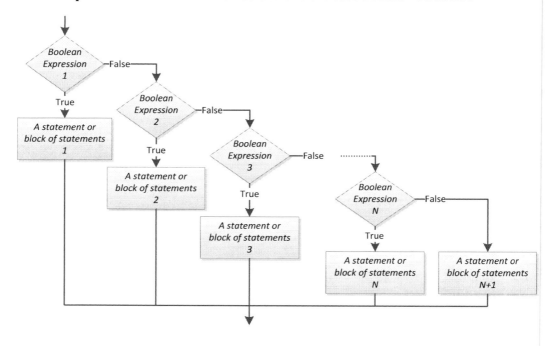

Exercise 22.2-1   *Designing the Flowchart*

Design the flowchart that corresponds to the following code fragment.

```
Dim a As Integer

a = Console.ReadLine()
If a Mod 10 = 0 Then
    a += 1
    Console.WriteLine(a)
End If
```

Solution

This is quite easy! It uses a single decision control structure. The corresponding flowchart is shown here.

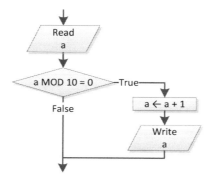

Exercise 22.2-2   *Designing the Flowchart*

Design the flowchart that corresponds to the following Visual Basic program.

```
Sub Main()
  Dim x, z, w, y, a As Double

  x = Console.ReadLine()

  z = x ^ 3
  w = (z - 4) * (x - 3 ) / 7 + 36
  If z >= w And x < z Then
    y = 2 * x
  Else
    y = 4 * x
    a += 1
  End If

  Console.Write(y)

  Console.ReadKey()
End Sub
```

Solution

This Visual Basic program uses a dual-alternative decision structure. Its corresponding flowchart is shown here.

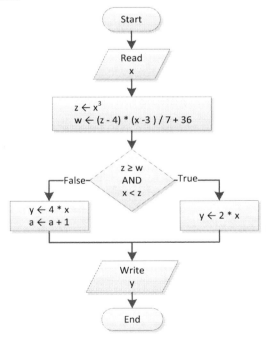

> **Remember!** A flowchart is a very loose method of representing an algorithm. Thus, it is quite permissible to write x^3 or even to use the Visual Basic operator (^). Do whatever you wish; everything is permitted, on condition that anyone familiar with flowcharts can clearly understand what you are trying to say!

Exercise 22.2-3   *Designing the Flowchart*

Design the flowchart that corresponds to the following code fragment given in general form.

```
If Boolean_Expression A Then
   Block of statements A1
   If Boolean_Expression B Then
      Block of statements B1
   End If
   Block of statements A2
Else
   Block of statements A3
   If Boolean_Expression C Then
      Block of statements C1
   Else
      Block of statements C2
   End If
End If
```

Solution

For better observation, the initial code fragment is presented again with all the nested decision control structures enclosed in rectangles.

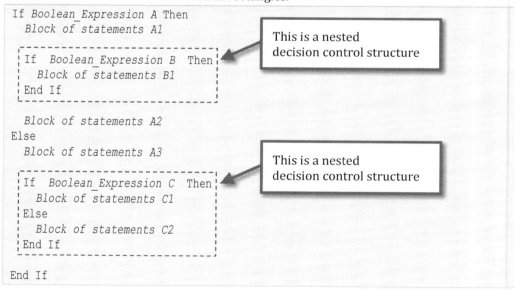

and the flowchart fragment in general form is shown here.

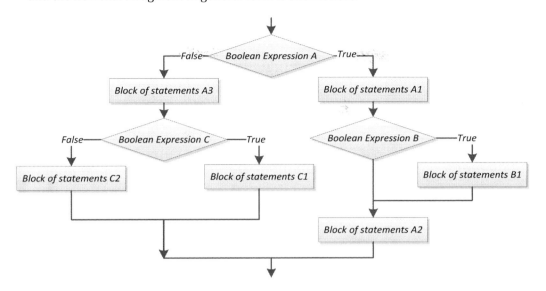

Exercise 22.2-4   Designing the Flowchart

Design the flowchart that corresponds to the following Visual Basic program.

```
Sub Main()
  Dim a, y, b As Double

  a = Console.ReadLine()

  If a < 0 Then
    y = a * 2
  ElseIf a < 10 Then
    y = a / 2
  ElseIf a < 100 Then
    y = a + 2
  Else
    b = Console.ReadLine()
    y = a * b
    If y > 0 Then
      y -= 1
    Else
      y += 1
    End If
  End If

  Console.Write(y)

  Console.ReadKey()
End Sub
```

Solution

In this Visual Basic program, a dual-alternative decision structure (`If y > 0`) is nested within a multiple-alternative decision structure.

The flowchart is shown here.

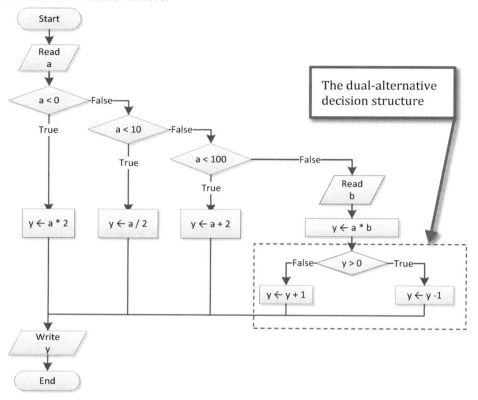

22.3 Converting Flowcharts to Visual Basic Programs

This conversion is not always an easy one. There are cases in which the flowchart designers follow no particular rules, so the initial flowchart may need some modifications before it can become a Visual Basic program. An example of one such case is shown here.

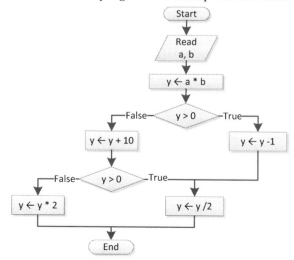

As you can see, the decision control structures included in this flowchart fragment match none of the structures that you have already learned, such as the single-alternative, the dual-alternative, and the multiple-alternative. Thus, you have only one choice and this is to modify the flowchart by adding extra statements or removing existing ones until known decision control structures start to appear. Following are some exercises in which the initial flowchart does need modification.

Exercise 22.3-1   *Writing the Visual Basic Program*

Write the Visual Basic program that corresponds to the following flowchart.

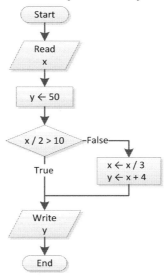

Solution

This is quite easy. The only obstacle you must overcome is that the true and false paths are not quite in the right positions. You need to use the true path, and not the false path, to actually include the statements in the decision control structure.

It is possible to switch the two paths, but you also need to negate the corresponding Boolean expression. The following two flowchart fragments are equivalent.

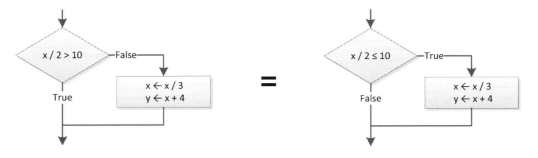

Thus, the flowchart now looks like this.

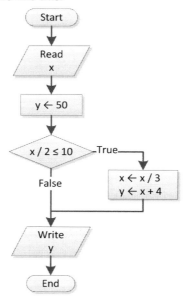

and the corresponding Visual Basic program is shown here.

```
Sub Main()
  Dim x, y As Double

  x = Console.ReadLine()

  y = 50
  If x / 2 <= 10 Then
    x = x /3
    y = x + 4
  End If
  Console.Write(y)

  Console.ReadKey()
End Sub
```

Exercise 22.3-2   *Writing the Visual Basic Program*

Write the Visual Basic program that corresponds to the following flowchart.

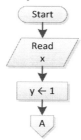

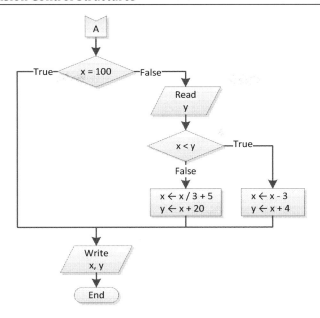

Solution

Once again, you need to negate the Boolean expression $x = 100$ and switch the true/false paths. The Visual Basic program is shown here.

```
Sub Main()
  Dim x, y As Double

  x = Console.ReadLine()

  y = 1

  If x <> 100 Then
    y = Console.ReadLine()
    If x < y Then
      x = x - 3
      y = x + 4
    Else
      x = x / 3 + 5
      y = x + 20
    End If
  End If

  Console.Write(x & ", " & y)

  Console.ReadKey()
End Sub
```

Exercise 22.3-3   *Writing the Visual Basic Program*

Write the Visual Basic program that corresponds to the following flowchart.

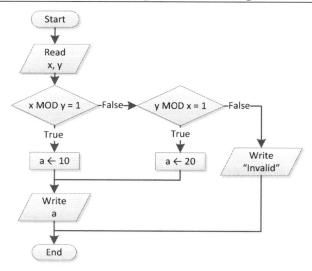

Solution

In this flowchart, the decision control structures match none of the decision control structures that you have already learned, such as the single-alternative, the dual-alternative, and the multiple-alternative. Thus, you must modify the flowchart by adding extra statements or removing existing ones until known decision control structures start to appear!

The obstacle you must overcome in this exercise is the decision control structure that evaluates the y MOD x = 1 Boolean expression. Note that when flow of execution follows the false path it executes the statement a ← 20 and then the statement Write a. Thus, if you simply add a new statement, Write a, inside its true path you can keep the flow of execution intact. The following flowchart is equivalent to the initial one.

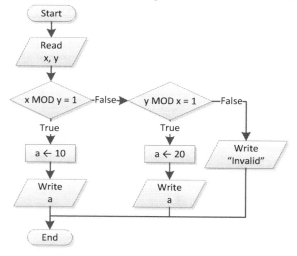

and the Visual Basic program is

```
Sub Main()
  Dim x, y, a As Integer
```

```
x = Console.ReadLine()
y = Console.ReadLine()

If x Mod y = 1 Then
    a = 10
    Console.WriteLine(a)
ElseIf y Mod x = 1 Then
    a = 20
    Console.WriteLine(a)
Else
    Console.Write("Invalid")
End If

Console.ReadKey()
End If
```

Exercise 22.3-4   *Writing the Visual Basic Program*

Write the Visual Basic program that corresponds to the following flowchart.

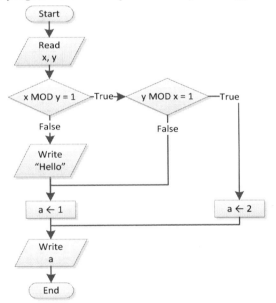

Solution

In this flowchart, the decision control structures match none of the already known decision control structures, so you must modify the flowchart!

The obstacle that you must overcome is the decision control structure that evaluates the y MOD x = 1 Boolean expression. Note that when the flow of execution follows its false path, it executes the statement a ← 1. Thus, if you simply add an extra statement a ← 1 inside its false path, you can keep the flow of execution intact. The following flowchart is equivalent to the initial one.

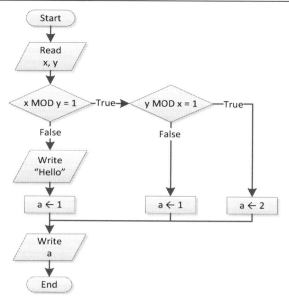

Now the flowchart contains known decision control structures and it can become a Visual Basic program. But don't be in a hurry! This flowchart, as is, can be written in Visual Basic only by using nested If statements. However, there is something better that you can do! If you negate all Boolean expressions and also switch their true/false paths, you can have a multiple-alternative decision structure, which is more convenient in Visual Basic than nested control structures. The modified flowchart is shown here.

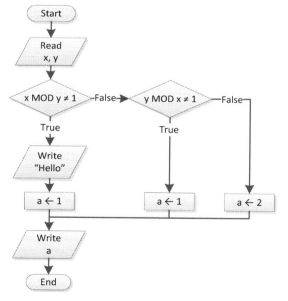

and the Visual Basic program is

```
Sub Main()
   Dim x, y, a As Integer

   x = Console.ReadLine()
   y = Console.ReadLine()
```

```
If x Mod y <> 1 Then
  Console.WriteLine("Hello")
  a = 1
ElseIf y Mod x <> 1 Then
  a = 1
Else
  a = 2
End If

Console.Write(a)

Console.ReadKey()
End Sub
```

Exercise 22.3-5   *Writing the Visual Basic Program*

Write the Visual Basic program that corresponds to the following flowchart.

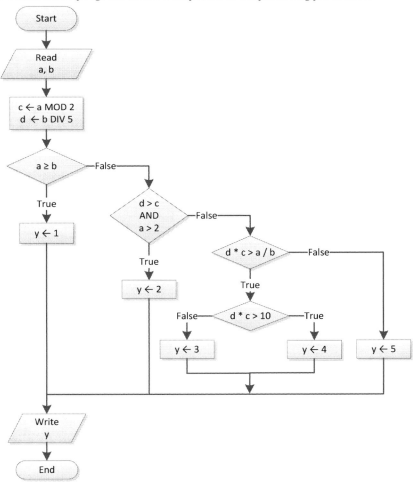

Solution

Please take a closer look at the statement d ← b DIV 5. The operator DIV is widely used in flowcharts to calculate the quotient of an integer division. In Visual Basic you can use the corresponding (\ ) operator.

This exercise uses a multiple-alternative decision structure and a dual-alternative decision structure nested inside the first one.

The Visual Basic program is shown here.

```vb
Sub Main()
    Dim a, b, c, d, y As Integer

    a = Console.ReadLine()
    b = Console.ReadLine()

    c = a Mod 2
    d = b \ 5

    If a >= b Then
        y = 1
    ElseIf d > c And a > 2 Then
        y = 2
    ElseIf d * c > a / b Then
        If d * c > 10 Then
            y = 4
        Else
            y = 3
        End If
    Else
        y = 5
    End If

    Console.Write(y)

    Console.ReadKey()
End Sub
```

This is the dual-alternative decision structure

22.4   Review Exercises

Complete the following exercises.

1.   Design the flowchart that corresponds to the following Visual Basic program.

```vb
Sub Main()
    Dim a As Integer

    a = Console.ReadLine()

    If a Mod 10 = 0 Then
        a += 1
        Console.WriteLine("Message #1")
    End If
    If a Mod 3 = 1 Then
```

```
    a += 5
    Console.WriteLine ("Message #2")
  End If
  If a Mod 3 = 2 Then
    a += 10
    Console.WriteLine ("Message #3")
  End If

  Console.Write (a)

  Console.ReadKey ()
End Sub
```

2. Design the flowchart that corresponds to the following Visual Basic program.

```
Sub Main ()
  Dim a As Integer

  a = Console.ReadLine ()

  If a Mod 10 = 0 Then
    a += 1
    Console.WriteLine ("Message #1")
  End If

  If a Mod 3 = 1 Then
    a += 5
    Console.WriteLine ("Message #2")
  Else
    a += 7
  End If
  Console.Write (a)

  Console.ReadKey ()
End Sub
```

3. Design the flowchart that corresponds to the following Visual Basic program.

```
Sub Main ()
  Dim a, y, b As Double

  a = Console.ReadLine ()

  If a < 0 Then
    y = a * 2
    If y > 0 Then
      y +=2
    ElseIf y = 0 Then
      y *= 6
    Else
      y /= 7
    End If
  ElseIf a < 22 Then
```

```
    y = a / 3
  ElseIf a < 32 Then
    y = a - 7
  Else
    b = Console.ReadLine()
    y = a - b
  End If
  Console.Write(y)

  Console.ReadKey()
End Sub
```

4. Design the flowchart that corresponds to the following code fragment given in general form.

```
If Boolean_Expression A Then
  If Boolean_Expression B Then
    Block of statements B1
  Else
    Block of statements B2
  End If
  Block of statements A1
Else
  Block of statements A2
  If Boolean_Expression C Then
    Block of statements C1
  ElseIf Boolean_Expression D Then
    Block of statements D1
  Else
    Block of statements E1
  End If
  Block of statements A3
End If
```

5. Design the flowchart that corresponds to the following Visual Basic program.

```
Sub Main()
  Dim a As Integer
  Dim y, b As Double

  a = Console.ReadLine()
  y = 0

  Select Case a
    Case 1
      y = a * 2
    Case 2
      y = a - 3
    Case 3
      y = a + 3
      If y Mod 2 = 1 Then
        y += 2
      ElseIf y = 0 Then
```

```
        y *= 6
      Else
        y /= 7
      End If
    Case 4
      b = Console.ReadLine()
      y = a + b + 2
  End Select
  Console.Write(y)

  Console.ReadKey()
End Sub
```

6. Write the Visual Basic program that corresponds to the following flowchart.

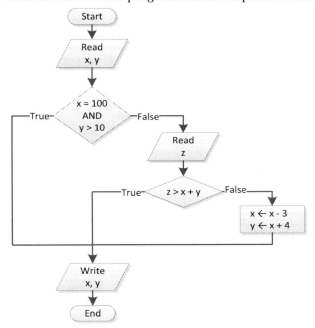

7. Write the Visual Basic program that corresponds to the following flowchart.

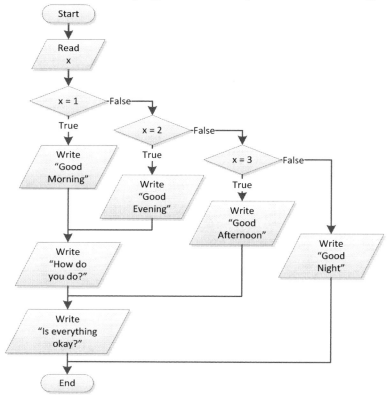

8. Write the Visual Basic program that corresponds to the following flowchart.

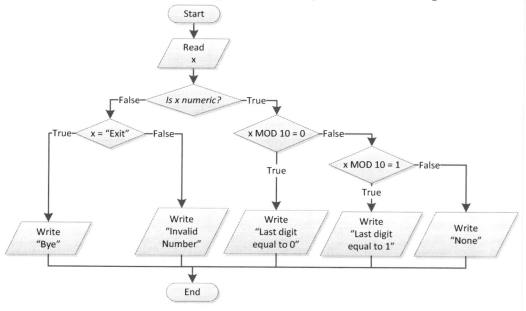

9. Write the Visual Basic program that corresponds to the following flowchart.

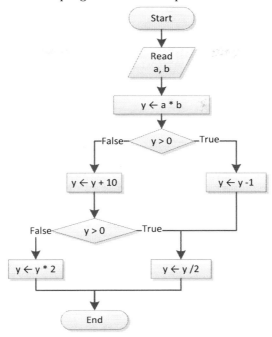

10. Write the Visual Basic program that corresponds to the following flowchart.

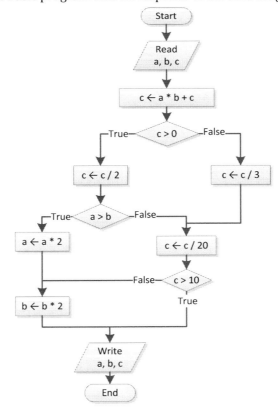

Chapter 23
More Exercises with Decision Control Structures

23.1 Simple Exercises with Decision Control Structures

Exercise 23.1-1 *Both Odds or Both Evens?*

Write a Visual Basic program that prompts the user to enter two integers and then displays a message indicating whether both numbers are odd or both are even; otherwise a message "Nothing special" is displayed.

Solution

The Visual Basic program is shown here.

```
                         project_23_1_1
Sub Main()
  Dim n1, n2 As Integer

  Console.Write("Enter an integer: ")
  n1 = Console.ReadLine()
  Console.Write("Enter a second integer: ")
  n2 = Console.ReadLine()

  If n1 Mod 2 = 0 And n2 Mod 2 = 0 Then
    Console.WriteLine("Both numbers are evens")
  ElseIf n1 Mod 2 <> 0 And n2 Mod 2 <> 0 Then
    Console.WriteLine("Both numbers are odds")
  Else
    Console.WriteLine("Nothing special!")
  End If

  Console.ReadKey()
End Sub
```

Exercise 23.1-2 *Validating Data Input and Finding if a Number is Exactly Divisible by both 5 and 8.*

Design a flowchart and write the corresponding Visual Basic program that prompts the user to enter an integer and then displays a message indicating whether this number is exactly divisible by 5 and by 8. For example, 40 is such a number. Moreover, if the user enters non-numeric characters, an error message should be displayed.

(This exercise gives you some practice in working with data validation.)

Solution

Let's design the flowchart using the "from inner to outer" method.

First, you need to design the inner (nested) decision control structure without taking data validation into consideration. Suppose variable x contains the value entered by the user. The inner decision control structure is shown in the flowchart that follows.

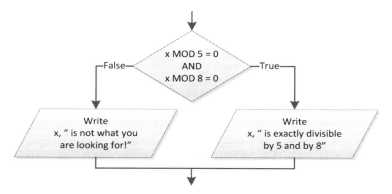

Now it's time to handle data validation. You need to test whether the user enters numeric or non-numeric characters. The flowchart fragment given in general form is shown here.

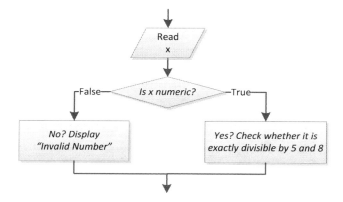

Combining both flowcharts, the final flowchart looks like this.

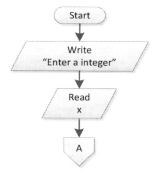

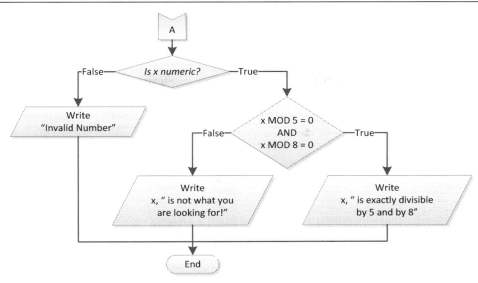

The Visual Basic program is shown here.

```
project_23_1_2
Sub Main()
  Dim x As Integer
  Dim input As String

  Console.Write("Enter an integer: ")
  input = Console.ReadLine()

  If Int32.TryParse(input, x) = True Then
    If x Mod 5 = 0 And x Mod 8 = 0 Then
      Console.WriteLine(x & " is exactly divisible by 5 and by 8")
    Else
      Console.WriteLine(x & " is not what you are looking for!")
    End If
  Else
    Console.WriteLine("Invalid Number")
  End If

  Console.ReadKey()
End Sub
```

Remember! *Procedure* `Int32.TryParse()` *converts the string representation of an integer contained in string variable* input *to its integer equivalent and then assigns the result to the integer variable* x. *It returns* `True` *if the conversion is successful, and* `False` *otherwise.*

Notice: *If the user enters non-numeric characters and you wish to display an error message you need two variables in Visual Basic: one string variable* input *to read from the keyboard, and one numeric variable* x *that is assigned the numeric representation of* input.

Exercise 23.1-3   *Is it an Integer?*

Write a Visual Basic program that prompts the user to enter a number and then displays a message indicating whether the data type of this number is integer or real. Moreover, if the user enters a non-numeric character, an error message should be displayed.

(This exercise gives you some more practice in working with data validation.)

Solution

It is well known that a number is considered an integer when it contains no fractional part. In Visual Basic, you can use the `Fix()` procedure to get the integer portion of any real number. If the number given is equal to its integer portion, then the number is considered an integer.

For example, if the user enters the integer 7, this number and its integer portion, `Fix(7)`, are equal.

On the other hand, if the user enters the real number 7.3, this number and its integer portion, `Fix(7.3)`, are not equal.

Now, suppose that variable x contains a number entered by the user. The code fragment, without data validation, would look like this.

```
If x = Fix(x) Then
    Console.WriteLine(x & " is integer")
Else
    Console.WriteLine(x & " is real")
End If
```

And now it's time to handle data validation. All you must do is combine the previous Visual Basic program with the following one.

```
Sub Main()
    Dim x As Double
    Dim input As String

    Console.Write("Enter a number: ")
    input = Console.ReadLine()

    If Double.TryParse(input, x) = True Then
        'Here goes the previous code fragment
    Else
        Console.WriteLine("Invalid number")
    End If

    Console.ReadKey()
End Sub
```

Thus, the final program looks like this.

project_23_1_3

```
Sub Main()
    Dim x As Double
    Dim input As String

    Console.Write("Enter a number: ")
```

```
input = Console.ReadLine()

If Double.TryParse(input, x) = True Then
  If x = Fix(x) Then
    Console.WriteLine(x & " is integer")
  Else
    Console.WriteLine(x & " is real")
  End If
Else
  Console.WriteLine("Invalid number")
End If

Console.ReadKey()
End Sub
```

Exercise 23.1-4   *Converting Gallons to Liters, and Vice Versa*

Write a Visual Basic program that displays the following menu:

  1. *Convert gallons to liters*

  2. *Convert liters to gallons*

The program prompts the user to enter a choice (1 or 2) and a quantity. Then, it calculates and displays the required value. It is given that

$$1\ gallon = 3.785\ liters$$

Solution

The Visual Basic program is shown here.

```
                        project_23_1_4
Const COEFFICIENT = 3.785

Sub Main()
  Dim choice As Integer
  Dim quantity, result As Double

  Console.WriteLine("1: Gallons to liters")
  Console.WriteLine("2: Liters to gallons")
  Console.Write("Enter choice: ")
  choice = Console.ReadLine()

  Console.Write("Enter quantity: ")
  quantity = Console.ReadLine()

  If choice = 1 Then
    result = quantity * COEFFICIENT
    Console.WriteLine(quantity & " gallons = " & result & " liters")
  Else
    result = quantity / COEFFICIENT
    Console.WriteLine(quantity & " liters = " & result & " gallons")
  End If
```

```
      Console.ReadKey()
    End Sub
```

Exercise 23.1-5 *Converting Gallons to Liters, and Vice Versa (with Data Validation)*

Rewrite the Visual Basic program of the previous exercise to validate the data input. Individual error messages should be displayed when the user enters a choice other than 1 or 2, or a non-numeric gas quantity.

Solution

Let's use the "from inner to outer" method. The inner code fragment has already been discussed in the previous exercise, whereas the outer Visual Basic program to validate data input is shown here.

```
Const COEFFICIENT = 3.785

Sub Main()
  Dim choice As Integer
  Dim quantity As Double
  Dim input As String

  Console.WriteLine("1: Gallons to liters")
  Console.WriteLine("2: Liters to gallons")
  Console.Write("Enter choice: ")
  choice = Console.ReadLine()

  If choice < 1 Or choice > 2 Then
    Console.WriteLine("Wrong choice!")
  Else
    Console.Write("Enter quantity: ")
    input = Console.ReadLine()
    If Double.TryParse(input, quantity) = True Then
      'Here goes the code that converts
      'gallons to liters and vice versa
    Else
      Console.WriteLine("Invalid quantity!")
    End If
  End If

  Console.ReadKey()
End Sub
```

Combining this program with the one from the previous exercise, the final Visual Basic program becomes

```
                          project_23_1_5
Const COEFFICIENT = 3.785

Sub Main()
  Dim choice As Integer
  Dim quantity, result As Double
```

```
Dim input As String

Console.WriteLine("1: Gallons to liters")
Console.WriteLine("2: Liters to gallons")
Console.Write("Enter choice: ")
choice = Console.ReadLine()

If choice < 1 Or choice > 2 Then
  Console.WriteLine("Wrong choice!")
Else
  Console.Write("Enter quantity: ")
  input = Console.ReadLine()
  If Double.TryParse(input, quantity) = True Then
    If choice = 1 Then
      result = quantity * COEFFICIENT
      Console.WriteLine(quantity & " gallons = " & result & " liters")
    Else
      result = quantity / COEFFICIENT
      Console.WriteLine(quantity & " liters = " & result & " gallons")
    End If
  Else
    Console.WriteLine("Invalid quantity!")
  End If
End If

Console.ReadKey()
End Sub
```

From previous exercise

Exercise 23.1-6   *Where is the Tollkeeper?*

In a toll gate, there is an automatic system that recognizes whether the passing vehicle is a motorcycle, a car, or a truck. Write a Visual Basic program that lets the user enter the type of the vehicle (M for motorcycle, C for car, and T for truck) and then displays the corresponding amount of money the driver must pay according to the following table.

Vehicle Type	Amount to Pay
Motorcycle	$1
Car	$2
Track	$4

If the user enters a character other than M, C, or T, a corresponding error message should be displayed.

(Some more practice with data validation!)

Solution

The solution to this problem is quite simple. The only catch is that the user may enter the uppercase letters M, C, or T, or even the lowercase letters m, c, or t. The program needs to accept both. To handle this, you can convert the user's input to uppercase using the

ToUpper() procedure. Then you need to test only for the M, C, or T characters in uppercase.

The Visual Basic program is shown here.

```
                       project_23_1_6
Sub Main()
  Dim v As String

  v = Console.ReadLine().ToUpper()

  If v = "M" Then                        'You need to test only for capital M
    Console.WriteLine("You need to pay $1")
  ElseIf v = "C" Then                    'You need to test only for capital C
    Console.WriteLine("You need to pay $2")
  ElseIf v = "T" Then                    'You need to test only for capital T
    Console.WriteLine("You need to pay $4")
  Else
    Console.WriteLine("Invalid vehicle")
  End If

  Console.ReadKey()
End Sub
```

> **Notice:** Please note how Visual Basic converts the user's input to uppercase. Procedure chaining is a programming style that most programmers prefer to follow in Visual Basic.

Exercise 23.1-7   *The Most Scientific Calculator Ever!*

Write a Visual Basic program that prompts the user to enter a number, the type of operation (+, -, *, /), and a second number. The program should execute the required operation and display the result.

Solution

The only thing that you need to take care of in this exercise is the possibility that the user could enter zero for the divisor (the second number), and as you know from mathematics, division by zero is undefined.

The following Visual Basic program uses the case decision structure to check the type of operation.

```
                       project_23_1_7
Sub Main()
  Dim a, b As Double
  Dim op As String

  Console.Write("Enter 1st number: ")
  a = Console.ReadLine()
  Console.Write("Enter type of operation: ")
  op = Console.ReadLine()
  Console.Write("Enter 2nd number: ")
  b = Console.ReadLine()
```

```
Select Case op
  Case "+"
    Console.WriteLine(a + b)
  Case "-"
    Console.WriteLine(a - b)
  Case "*"
    Console.WriteLine(a * b)
  Case "/"
    If b = 0 Then
      Console.WriteLine("Error: Division by zero")
    Else
      Console.WriteLine(a / b)
    End If
End Select

Console.ReadKey()
End Sub
```

23.2 Decision Control Structures in Solving Mathematical Problems

Exercise 23.2-1   *Finding the Value of y*

Design a flowchart and write the corresponding Visual Basic program that finds and displays the value of y (if possible) in the following formula.

$$Y = \frac{5 + x}{x} + \frac{x + 9}{x - 4}$$

Solution

In this exercise the user should not be allowed to enter values 0 or 4 because they make the denominator equal to zero. Therefore, the program needs to take these restrictions into consideration. The flowchart is shown here.

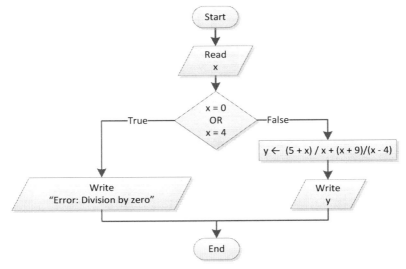

and the Visual Basic program is shown here.

```
project_23_2_1
Sub Main()
  Dim x, y As Double

  x = Console.ReadLine()

  If x = 0 Or x = 4 Then
    Console.WriteLine("Error: Division by zero!")
  Else
    y = (5 + x) / x + (x + 9) / (x - 4)
    Console.WriteLine(y)
  End If

  Console.ReadKey()
End Sub
```

Exercise 23.2-2   Finding the Values of y

Design a flowchart and write the corresponding Visual Basic program that finds and displays the values of y (if possible) in the following formula.

$$y = \begin{cases} \dfrac{7+x}{x-3} + \dfrac{3-x}{x}, & x \geq 0 \\[3mm] \dfrac{40x}{x-5} + 3, & x < 0 \end{cases}$$

Solution

The formula has two different results.

1. When x is greater than or equal to zero, the value of y in $\dfrac{7+x}{x-3} + \dfrac{3x}{x}$ can be found following the method shown in the previous exercise.

2. However, for an x less than zero, a small detail can save you some lines of Visual Basic code. If you look carefully, you can see that there are no restrictions on the fraction $\dfrac{40x}{x-5}$ because x can never be +5.

The flowchart is shown here.

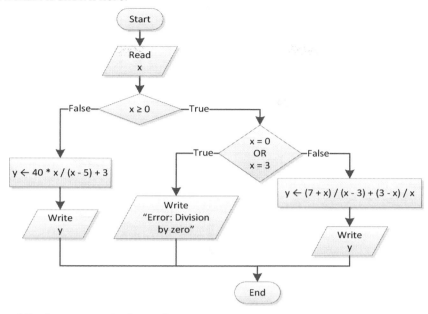

The Visual Basic program is shown here.

```
                          project_23_2_2
Sub Main()
  Dim x, y As Double

  x = Console.ReadLine()

  If x >= 0  Then
    If x = 0 Or x = 3 Then
      Console.WriteLine("Error: Division by zero!")
    Else
      y = (7 + x) / (x - 3) + (3 - x) / x
      Console.WriteLine(y)
    End If
  Else
    y = 40 * x / (x - 5) + 3
    Console.WriteLine(y)
  End If

  Console.ReadKey()
End Sub
```

Exercise 23.2-3   Validating Data Input and Finding the Values of y

Rewrite the Visual Basic program of the previous exercise to validate the data input. An error message should be displayed when the user enters non-numeric characters.

(Again, you will get more practice with data validation!)

Solution

All you need to do is combine the previous exercise with the following Visual Basic program.

```
Sub Main()
  Dim x As Double
  Dim input As String

  input = Console.ReadLine()

  If Double.TryParse(input, x) = True Then
    'Here goes the code of the previous exercise
  Else
    Console.WriteLine("Invalid number")
  End If

  Console.ReadKey()
End Sub
```

Combining this with the program of the previous exercise, the final program becomes

```
                    project_23_2_3
```

```
Sub Main()
  Dim x, y As Double
  Dim input As String

  input = Console.ReadLine()

  If Double.TryParse(input, x) = True Then
    If x >= 0  Then
      If x = 0 Or x = 3 Then
        Console.WriteLine("Error: Division by zero!")
      Else
        y = (7 + x) / (x - 3) + (3 - x) / x
        Console.WriteLine(y)
      End If
    Else
      y = 40 * x / (x - 5) + 3
      Console.WriteLine(y)
    End If
  Else
    Console.WriteLine("Invalid number")
  End If

  Console.ReadKey()
End Sub
```

From previous exercise

Exercise 23.2-4   *Solving the Linear Equation ax + b = 0*

Design a flowchart and write the corresponding Visual Basic program that finds and displays the root of the linear equation

$$ax + b = 0$$

Solution

The equation $ax + b = 0$, when solved for x, becomes $x = -b / a$. The user must enter values for coefficients a and b, and the program should find the value for x.

Yet, you need to realize that, depending on user's entered data, three possible situations can arise:

i.   The user might enter the value 0 for coefficient a and a non-zero value for coefficient b. The division by zero, as you already know from mathematics, is undefined.

ii.   The user might enter the value 0 for coefficient a and the value 0 for coefficient b. The result has no defined value, and it is called indeterminate form.

iii. The user might enter any other pair of values.

Therefore, these three situations result in three paths, respectively.

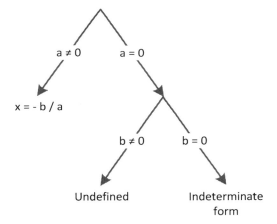

The next flowchart is designed with the use of a multiple-alternative decision structure.

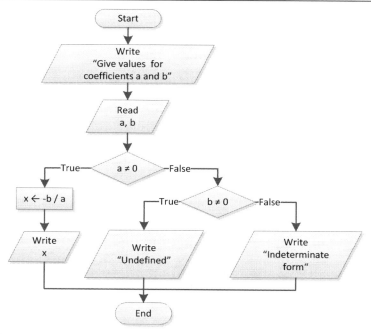

The Visual Basic program is shown here.

```
                              project_23_2_4
Sub Main()
  Dim a, b, x As Double

  Console.Write("Enter a value for coefficient a: ")
  a = Console.ReadLine()
  Console.Write("Enter a value for coefficient b: ")
  b = Console.ReadLine()

  If a <> 0 Then
    x = -b / a
    Console.WriteLine(x)
  ElseIf b <> 0 Then
    Console.WriteLine("Undefined")
  Else
    Console.WriteLine("Indeterminate form")
  End If

  Console.ReadKey()
End Sub
```

Exercise 23.2-5   *Solving the Quadratic Equation $ax^2 + bx + c = 0$*

Design a flowchart and write the corresponding Visual Basic program that finds and displays the roots of the quadratic equation

$$ax^2 + bx + c = 0$$

Solution

This problem can be divided into two individual subproblems depending on the value of coefficient a. If coefficient a is equal to zero, the equation becomes a linear equation, $bx + c = 0$, for which the solution was given in the previous exercise. If coefficient a is not equal to zero, the roots of the equation can be found using the discriminant D. Please note that this solution finds no complex roots when $D < 0$; this is beyond the scope of this book.

All necessary paths are shown here.

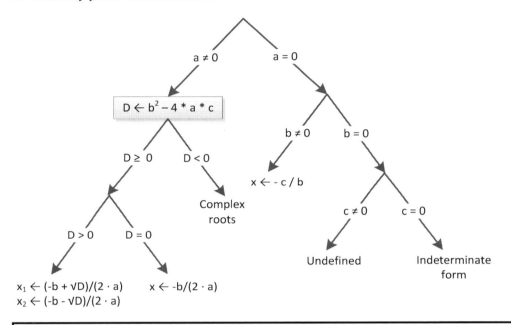

Notice: *The path on the right* ($a = 0$) *is the solution to the linear equation* $bx + c = 0$, *which was shown in the previous exercise.*

Using this diagram you can design the following flowchart.

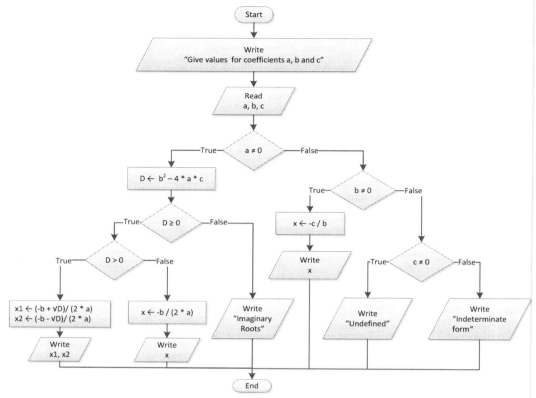

The Visual Basic program is shown here.

```
project_23_2_5
```

```
Sub Main()
  Dim a, b, c, D, x1, x2, x As Double

  Console.Write("Enter values for coefficients a, b and c: ")
  a = Console.ReadLine()
  b = Console.ReadLine()
  c = Console.ReadLine()

  If a <> 0 Then
    D = b ^ 2 - 4 * a * c
    If D >= 0 Then
      If D > 0 Then
        x1 = (-b + Math.Sqrt(D)) / (2 * a)
        x2 = (-b - Math.Sqrt(D)) / (2 * a)
        Console.WriteLine("Roots: " & x1 & ", " & x2)
      Else
        x = -b / (2 * a)
        Console.WriteLine("One double root: " & x)
      End If
    Else
      Console.WriteLine("Complex Roots")
    End If
  Else
```

```
    If b <> 0 Then
      x = -c / b
      Console.WriteLine("Root: " & x)
    ElseIf c <> 0 Then
      Console.WriteLine("Undefined")
    Else
      Console.WriteLine("Indeterminate form")
    End If
  End If

  Console.ReadKey()
End Sub
```

23.3 Finding Minimum and Maximum Values with Decision Control Structures

Suppose there are some men and you want to find the lightest one. Let's say that each one of them comes by and tells you his weight. What you must do is, memorize the weight of the first person that has come by and for each new person, you have to compare his weight with the one that you keep memorized. If he is heavier, you ignore his weight. However, if he is lighter, you need to forget the previous weight and memorize the new one. The same procedure continues until all the people have come by.

Let's ask four men to come by at a random order. Assume that their weights, in order of appearance, are 165, 170, 160, and 180 pounds.

Procedure	Value of Variable min in Your Mind!
The first person comes by. He weighs 165 pounds. Keep his weight in your mind (imagine a variable in your mind named min.)	min = 165
The second person comes by. He weighs 170 pounds. He does not weigh less than the weight you are keeping in variable min, so you must ignore his weight. Variable min in your mind still contains the value 165.	min = 165
The third person comes by. He weighs 160 pounds, which is less than the weight you are keeping in variable min, so you must forget the previous value and keep the value 160 in variable min.	min = 160
The fourth person comes by. He weighs 180 pounds. He does not weigh less than the weight you are keeping in variable min, so you must ignore his weight. Variable min still contains the value 160.	min = 160

When the procedure finishes, the variable min in your mind contains the weight of the lightest man!

Following are the flowchart and the corresponding Visual Basic program that prompts the user to enter the weight of four people and then finds and displays the lightest weight.

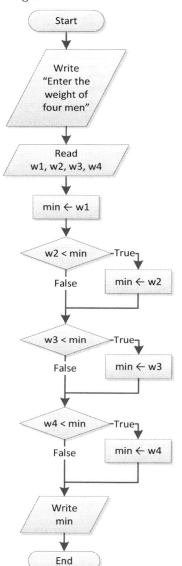

```
project_23_3
Sub Main()
    Dim w1, w2, w3, w4, min As Double

    Console.Write("Enter the weight ")
    Console.WriteLine("of four men:")

    w1 = Console.ReadLine()
    w2 = Console.ReadLine()
    w3 = Console.ReadLine()
    w4 = Console.ReadLine()

    'memorize the weight of the first person
    min = w1

    'If second one is lighter, forget
    'everything and memorize this weight
    If w2 < min Then
        min = w2
    End If

    'If third one is lighter, forget
    'everything and memorize this weight
    If w3 < min Then
        min = w3
    End If

    'If fourth one is lighter, forget
    'everything and memorize this weight
    If w4 < min Then
        min = w4
    End If

    Console.Write(min)

    Console.ReadKey()
End Sub
```

Notice: *You can find the maximum instead of the minimum value by simply replacing the "less than" with a "greater than" operator in all Boolean expressions.*

Exercise 23.3-1   *Finding the Name of the Heaviest Person*

Write a Visual Basic program that prompts the user to enter the weights and the names of three people and then displays the name and the weight of the heaviest person.

Solution

In this exercise, along with the maximum weight, you need to store in another variable the name of the person who actually has that weight. The Visual Basic program is shown here.

```
                           project_23_3_1
Sub Main()
  Dim w1, w2, w3, max As Integer
  Dim n1, n2, n3, m_name As String

  Console.Write("Enter the weight of the first person: ")
  w1 = Console.ReadLine()

  Console.Write("Enter the name of the first person: ")
  n1 = Console.ReadLine()

  Console.Write("Enter the weight of the second person: ")
  w2 = Console.ReadLine()

  Console.Write("Enter the name of the second person: ")
  n2 = Console.ReadLine()

  Console.Write("Enter the weight of the third person: ")
  w3 = Console.ReadLine()

  Console.Write("Enter the name of the third person: ")
  n3 = Console.ReadLine()

  max = w1
  m_name = n1          'This variable holds the name of the heaviest person

  If w2 > max Then
    max = w2
    m_name = n2        'Someone Else is heavier. Keep his or her name.
  End If

  If w3 > max Then
    max = w3
    m_name = n3        'Someone Else is heavier. Keep his or her name.
  End If

  Console.WriteLine("The heaviest person is " & m_name)
  Console.Write("His or her weight is " & max)

  Console.ReadKey()
End Sub
```

> **Notice:** In case the two heaviest people happen to have the same weight, the name of the first one in order is found and displayed.

23.4   Exercises with Series of Consecutive Ranges of Values

As you have already seen, in many problems the value of a variable or the result of an expression can define which statement or block of statements should be executed. In the exercises that follow, you will learn how to test if a value or the result of an expression belongs within a specific range of values (from a series of consecutive ranges of values).

Suppose that you want to display a message indicating the types of clothes a woman might wear at different temperatures.

Outdoor Temperature (in degrees Fahrenheit)	Types of Clothes a Woman Might Wear
Temperature < 45	Sweater, coat, jeans, shirt, shoes
45 ≤ Temperature < 65	Sweater, jeans, jacket, shoes
65 ≤ Temperature < 75	Capris, shorts, t-shirt, tank top, flip flops, athletic shoes
75 ≤ Temperature	Shorts, t-shirt, tank top, skort, skirt, flip flops

At first glance you might be tempted to use single-alternative decision structures. It is not wrong actually but if you take a closer look, it becomes clear that each condition is interdependent, which means that when one of these evaluates to True, none of the others should be evaluated. You need to select just one alternative from a set of possibilities.

There are actually two decision control structures that can be used for this purpose, and these are the multiple-alternative decision structure and nested decision control structures. However, the multiple-alternative decision structure is the best choice. It is more convenient and increases readability.

Exercise 23.4-1   *Calculating the Discount*

Write a Visual Basic program that calculates the discount that customers receive based on the dollar amount of their order. If the total amount ordered is less than $30, no discount is given. If the total amount is equal to or greater than $30 and less than $70, a discount of 5% is given. If the total amount is equal to or greater than $70 and less than $150, a discount of 10% is given. If the total amount is $150 or more, the customer receives a discount of 20%.

Solution

The following table summarizes the various discounts that are offered.

Range	Discount
amount < $30	0%
$30 ≤ amount < $70	5%
$70 ≤ amount < $150	10%
$150 ≤ amount	20%

The Visual Basic program is as follows.

```
project_23_4_1a
Sub Main()
  Dim amount, discount, payment As Double

  Console.Write("Enter total amount: ")
  amount = Console.ReadLine()

  If amount < 30 Then
    discount = 0
  ElseIf amount >= 30 And amount < 70 Then
    discount = 5
  ElseIf amount >= 70 And amount < 150 Then
    discount = 10
  ElseIf amount >= 150 Then
    discount = 20
  End If

  payment = amount - amount * discount / 100

  Console.WriteLine("You got a discount of " & discount & "%")
  Console.Write("You must pay $" & payment)

  Console.ReadKey()
End Sub
```

A closer examination, however, reveals that the Boolean expressions written in bold are not actually required. For example, when the first Boolean expression evaluates to False, the flow of execution continues to evaluate the second Boolean expression, in which, variable amount is definitely greater than or equal to 30. Therefore, the Boolean expression amount >= 30, when evaluated, is certainly True and thus can be omitted. The same logic applies to all cases; you can omit all Boolean expressions written in bold. The final Visual Basic program is shown here, with all unnecessary evaluations removed.

```
project_23_4_1b
Sub Main()
  Dim amount, discount, payment As Double

  Console.Write("Enter total amount: ")
  amount = Console.ReadLine()

  If amount < 30 Then
    discount = 0
  ElseIf amount < 70 Then
    discount = 5
  ElseIf amount < 150 Then
    discount = 10
  Else
    discount = 20
  End If
```

```
   payment = amount - amount * discount / 100

   Console.WriteLine("You got a discount of " & discount & "%")
   Console.Write("You must pay $" & payment)

   Console.ReadKey()
End Sub
```

Exercise 23.4-2   *Validating Data Input and Calculating the Discount*

*Rewrite the Visual Basic program of the previous exercise to validate the data input.
Individual error messages should be displayed when the user enters any non-numeric or
negative values.*

Solution

Let's try once again the "from inner to outer" method. The inner code fragment has
already been discussed in the previous exercise, whereas the outer Visual Basic program
that validates data input is shown here.

```
Sub Main()
   Dim amount, discount, payment As Double
   Dim input As String

   Console.Write("Enter total amount: ")
   input = Console.ReadLine()

   If Double.TryParse(input, amount) = False Then
     Console.WriteLine("Entered value contains non-numeric characters")
   ElseIf amount < 0 Then
     Console.WriteLine("Entered value is negative")
   Else
     'Here goes the code that calculates
     'and displays the discount offered
   End If

   Console.ReadKey()
End Sub
```

Combining this with the program of the previous exercise, the final program becomes

```
                          project_23_4_2
Sub Main()
   Dim amount, discount, payment As Double
   Dim input As String

   Console.Write("Enter total amount: ")
   input = Console.ReadLine()

   If Double.TryParse(input, amount) = False Then
     Console.WriteLine("Entered value contains non-numeric characters")
   ElseIf amount < 0 Then
     Console.WriteLine("Entered value is negative")
```

```
Else
   If amount < 30 Then
      discount = 0
   ElseIf amount < 70 Then
      discount = 5
   ElseIf amount < 150 Then
      discount = 10
   Else
      discount = 20
   End If
   payment = amount - amount * discount / 100

   Console.WriteLine("You got a discount of " & discount & "%")
   Console.WriteLine("You must pay $" & payment)
End If

Console.ReadKey()
End Sub
```

From previous
exercise

Exercise 23.4-3   *Sending a Parcel*

In a post office, the shipping cost for sending a medium parcel depends on its weight and whether its destination is inside or outside the country. Shipping costs are calculated according to the following table.

Parcel's Weight (in lb)	Destination Inside the Country (in USD per lb)	Destination Outside the Country (in USD)
weight < 1	$0.010	$10
1 ≤ weight < 2	$0.013	$20
2 ≤ weight < 4	$0.015	$50
4 ≤ weight	$0.020	$60

Design a flowchart and write the corresponding Visual Basic program that prompts the user to enter the weight of a parcel and its destination (I: inside the country, O: outside the country) and then calculates and displays the shipping cost.

Solution

Here is the flowchart.

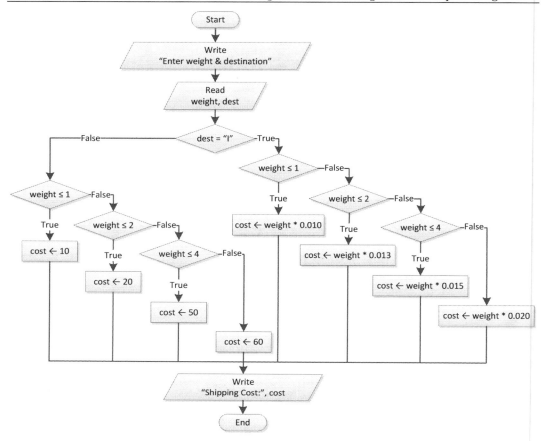

The Visual Basic program is shown here.

```
project_23_4_3
Sub Main()
  Dim weight, cost As Double
  Dim dest As String

  Console.Write("Enter weight and destination: ")
  weight = Console.ReadLine()
  dest = Console.ReadLine()

  If dest.ToUpper() = "I" Then
    If weight <= 1 Then
      cost = weight * 0.010
    ElseIf weight <= 2 Then
      cost = weight * 0.013
    ElseIf weight <= 4 Then
      cost = weight * 0.015
    Else
      cost = weight * 0.020
    End If
  Else
```

```
      If weight <= 1 Then
         cost = 10
      ElseIf weight <= 2 Then
         cost = 20
      ElseIf weight <= 4 Then
         cost = 50
      Else
         cost = 60
      End If
   End If

   Console.Write("Shipping cost: " & cost)
   Console.ReadKey()
End Sub
```

Notice: *A user may enter the letter I (for destination) in lowercase or uppercase. The procedure* `ToUpper()` *ensures that the program executes properly for both cases.*

Exercise 23.4-4   *Finding the Values of y*

Design a flowchart and write the corresponding Visual Basic program that finds and displays the values of y (if possible) in the following formula

$$y = \begin{cases} \dfrac{x}{x-3} + \dfrac{8+x}{x+1}, & -5 < x \le 0 \\[2mm] \dfrac{40x}{x-8}, & 0 < x \le 6 \\[2mm] \dfrac{3x}{x-9}, & 6 < x \le 20 \\[2mm] |x|, & for\ all\ other\ values\ of\ x \end{cases}$$

Solution

In this exercise, there are two restrictions on the fractions:

1. In fraction $\dfrac{8+x}{x+1}$, the value of x cannot be -1.

2. In fraction $\dfrac{3x}{x-9}$, the value of x cannot be +9.

For all other fractions, it's impossible for the denominators to be set to zero because of the range in which x belongs.

The Visual Basic program is shown here.

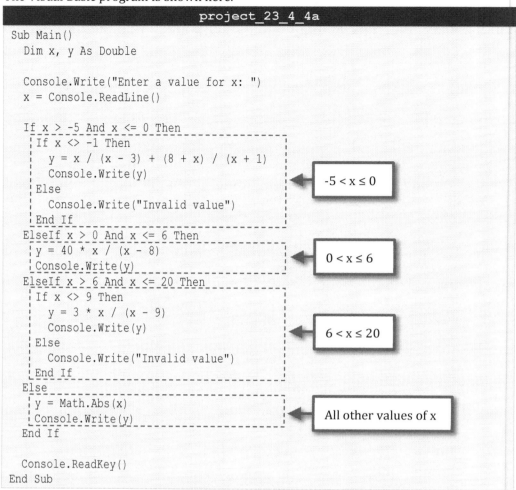

```
                          project_23_4_4a
Sub Main()
  Dim x, y As Double

  Console.Write("Enter a value for x: ")
  x = Console.ReadLine()

  If x > -5 And x <= 0 Then
    If x <> -1 Then
      y = x / (x - 3) + (8 + x) / (x + 1)
      Console.Write(y)                          -5 < x ≤ 0
    Else
      Console.Write("Invalid value")
    End If
  ElseIf x > 0 And x <= 6 Then
    y = 40 * x / (x - 8)
    Console.Write(y)                            0 < x ≤ 6
  ElseIf x > 6 And x <= 20 Then
    If x <> 9 Then
      y = 3 * x / (x - 9)
      Console.Write(y)                          6 < x ≤ 20
    Else
      Console.Write("Invalid value")
    End If
  Else
    y = Math.Abs(x)
    Console.Write(y)                            All other values of x
  End If

  Console.ReadKey()
End Sub
```

If you are wondering whether you can remove all Console.Write(y) statements and write them as a single statement at the end of the program, the answer is "no." Since there is even one path that does not include the Console.Write(y) statement, you must write the same statement, again and again, in every path required.

One thing you should learn in computer programming, however, is that you should never give up! By modifying your code a little, checking for invalid values in the beginning, gives you the opportunity to remove the statement Console.Write(y) outside of all paths and move it at the end of them. The modified Visual Basic program is shown here.

```
                          project_23_4_4b
Sub Main()
  Dim x, y As Double

  Console.Write("Enter a value for x: ")
  x = Console.ReadLine()

  If x = -1 Or x = 9 Then
    Console.Write("Invalid value")
```

```
Else
    If x > -5 And x <= 0 Then
        y = x / (x - 3) + (8 + x) / (x + 1)
    ElseIf x > 0 And x <= 6 Then
        y = 40 * x / (x - 8)
    ElseIf x > 6 And x <= 20 Then
        y = 3 * x / (x - 9)
    Else
        y = Math.Abs(x)
    End If
    Console.Write(y)
End If

Console.ReadKey()
End Sub
```

Now, if you are speculating about whether the Boolean expressions in bold are redundant, the answer is "no" again. Suppose you do remove them and the user enters a value of -20 for x. The flow of execution then reaches the Boolean expression x <= 0, which evaluates to True. Then the fraction $\frac{x}{x-3} + \frac{8+x}{x+1}$, instead of the absolute value of x, is calculated.

Yet still there is hope! Next, you can find a proposed solution in which unnecessary Boolean expressions are actually removed. The trick here is that the case of the absolute value of x is examined first.

```
                        project_23_4_4c
Sub Main()
    Dim x, y As Double

    Console.WriteLine("Enter a value for x: ")
    x = Console.ReadLine()

    If x = -1 Or x = 9 Then
        Console.Write("Invalid value")
    Else
        If x <= -5 Or x > 20 Then
            y = Math.Abs(x)
        ElseIf x <= 0 Then
            y = x / (x - 3) + (8 + x) / (x + 1)
        ElseIf x <= 6 Then
            y = 40 * x / (x - 8)
        Else
            y = 3 * x / (x - 9)
        End If
        Console.Write(y)
    End If

    Console.ReadKey()
End Sub
```

> **Notice**: *It is obvious that one problem can have many solutions. It is up to you to find the optimal one!*

Exercise 23.4-5   *Progressive Rates and Electricity Consumption*

The LAV Electricity Company charges subscribers for their electricity consumption according to the following table (monthly rates for domestic accounts). Assume that all extra charges such as transmission service charges and distribution charges are all included.

Kilowatt-hours (kWh)	USD per kWh
kWh ≤ 500	$0.10
501 ≤ kWh ≤ 2000	$0.25
2001 ≤ kWh ≤ 4000	$0.40
4001 < kWh	$0.60

Write a Visual Basic program that prompts the user to enter the total number of kWh consumed and then calculates and displays the total amount to pay.

Please note that the rates are progressive.

Solution

The term "progressive rates" means that when a customer consumes, for example, 2200 kWh, not all of the kilowatt-hours are charged at $0.40. The first 500 kWh are charged at $0.10, the next 1500 kWh are charged at $0.25 and only the last 200 kWh are charged at $0.40. Thus, the customer must pay

$$500 \times \$0.10 + 1500 \times \$0.25 + 200 \times \$0.40 = \$505$$

The same logic can be used to calculate the total amount to pay when the customer consumes, for example, 4300 kWh. The first 500 kWh are charged at $0.10, the next 1500 kWh are charged at $0.25, the next 2000 kWh are charged at 0.40, and only the last 300 kWh are charged at $0.60. Thus, the customer must pay

$$500 \times \$0.10 + 1500 \times \$0.25 + 2000 \times \$0.40 + 300 \times \$0.60 = \$1405$$

The Visual Basic program is shown here.

```
project_23_4_5
Sub Main()
  Dim kwh As Integer
  Dim t As Double

  Console.Write("Enter number of Kilowatt-hours consumed: ")
  kwh = Console.ReadLine()

  If kwh <= 500 Then
    t = kwh * 0.10
  ElseIf kwh <= 2000 Then
    t = 500 * 0.10 + (kwh - 500) * 0.25
  ElseIf kwh <= 4000 Then
    t = 500 * 0.10 + 1500 * 0.25 + (kwh - 2000) * 0.40
  Else
```

```
        t = 500 * 0.10 + 1500 * 0.25 + 2000 * 0.4 + (kwh - 4000) * 0.60
    End If
    Console.Write("Total amount to pay: " & t)

    Console.ReadKey()
End Sub
```

Exercise 23.4-6   *Progressive Rates, Electricity Consumption, Taxes, Data Validation and Code Optimization, All in One!*

Rewrite the Visual Basic program of the previous exercise, to validate the data input. Individual error messages should be displayed when the user enters any non-numeric or negative values. Moreover, you need to optimize the program to calculate the results as quickly as possible.

Federal, state, and local taxes add a total of 10% to each bill.

Solution

To optimize the code, you need to decrease the total number of multiplication, addition, and subtraction operations that the previous program had. For example, the statement

```
t = 500 * 0.10 + (kwh - 500) * 0.25
```

can also be written as

```
t = 50 + (kwh - 500) * 0.25
```

or even better as

```
t = 0.25 * kwh - 75
```

Similarly, the statement

```
t = 500 * 0.10 + 1500 * 0.25 + (kwh - 2000) * 0.40
```

can also be written as

```
t = 50 + 375 + (kwh - 2000) * 0.40
```

or even better as

```
t = 425 + (kwh - 2000) * 0.40
```

and finally as

```
t = 0.4 * kwh - 375
```

Now that everything about the inner code fragment has been clarified, data validation can be achieved by following the "from inner to outer" method. The outer Visual Basic program given in general form that validates data input is

```
Sub Main()
    Dim kwh As Integer
    Dim input As String

    Console.Write("Enter number of Kilowatt-hours consumed: ")
    input = Console.ReadLine()

    If Int32.TryParse(input, kwh) = False Then
        Console.WriteLine("Entered value contains non-numeric characters")
```

```
    ElseIf kwh < 0 Then
      Console.WriteLine("Entered value is negative")
    Else
      'Here goes the code that calculates
      'and displays the total amount to pay
    End If

    Console.ReadKey()
  End Sub
```

Combining this program with the last program from the previous exercise and applying code optimization, the Visual Basic program becomes

project_23_4_6

```
Sub Main()
  Dim kwh As Integer
  Dim t As Double
  Dim input As String

  Console.Write("Enter number of Kilowatt-hours consumed: ")
  input = Console.ReadLine()

  If Int32.TryParse(input, kwh) = False Then
    Console.WriteLine("Entered value contains non-numeric characters")
  ElseIf kwh < 0 Then
    Console.WriteLine("Entered value is negative")
  Else
    If kwh <= 500 Then
      t = kwh * 0.10
    ElseIf kwh <= 2000 Then
      t = 0.25 * kwh - 75
    ElseIf kwh <= 4000 Then
      t = 0.4 * kwh - 375
    Else
      t = 0.6 * kwh - 1175
    End If
```

From previous exercise after applying code optimization

```
    t = 1.10 * t   'This is equivalent to t = t + t * 10 / 100
                   'but more efficient

    Console.WriteLine("Total amount to pay (taxes included): " & t)
  End If

  Console.ReadKey()
End Sub
```

> **Notice**: It becomes clear now that, even though this program is more efficient than the one of the previous exercise, it is very difficult to read. No one who reads this program can understand that t = 0.6 * kWh - 1175 is actually t = 500 * 0.10 + 1500 * 0.25 + 2000 * 0.4 + (kWh - 4000) * 0.60. Many times, when efficiency is not important, programmers do sacrifice efficiency for readability. This program is shown to demonstrate how a program can be made more efficient. But you don't have to follow this kind of writing, at least not for now anyway. After all, today's computers are so fast that you don't have to worry about efficiency. Until the time at which you become the next Mark Zuckerberg of Facebook or the next Bill Gates of Microsoft, please write readable programs! This book as well, since it addresses novice programmers, mostly prefers readability to efficiency.

Exercise 23.4-7   *Progressive Rates and Text Messaging Services*

The LAV Cell Phone Company charges customers a basic rate of $8 per month to send text messages. Additional rates are charged based on the total number of text messages sent, as shown in the following table.

Number of Text Messages Sent	Additional Rates (in USD per text message)
Up to 50	Free of charge
51 – 150	$0.05
151 and above	$0.10

Federal, state, and local taxes add a total of 10% to each bill.

Write a Visual Basic program that prompts the user to enter the number of text messages sent and then calculates and displays the total amount to pay.

Please note that the rates are progressive.

Solution

The Visual Basic program is presented here.

```
project_23_4_7
Sub Main()
  Dim count As Integer
  Dim extra, total_without_tax, tax, total As Double

  Console.Write("Enter number of text messages sent: ")
  count = Console.ReadLine()

  If count <= 50 Then
    extra = 0
  ElseIf count <= 150 Then
    extra = (count - 50) * 0.05
  Else
    extra = 100 * 0.05 + (count - 150) * 0.10
  End If
```

```
    total_without_tax = 8 + extra
    tax = total_without_tax * 10 / 100
    total = total_without_tax + tax
    Console.Write("Total amount to pay: " & total)

    Console.ReadKey()
End Sub
```

23.5   Exercises of a General Nature with Decision Control Structures

Exercise 23.5-1   *Finding a Leap Year*

Write a Visual Basic program that prompts the user to enter a year and then displays a message indicating whether or not it is a leap year. Moreover, if the user enters non-numeric characters, an error message should be displayed.

(Note that this involves data validation!)

Solution

A year is a leap year when at least one of the following conditions is met:

1.   **1st Condition**: The year is exactly divisible by 4, and not by 100.
2.   **2nd Condition**: The year is exactly divisible by 400.

In the following table, some years are not leap years because none of the conditions evaluates to True.

Year	Conditions		Leap Year
1600	1st Condition:	False, because it is exactly divisible by 4, and also by 100	Yes
	2nd Condition:	**True**, because it is exactly divisible by 400	
1900	1st Condition:	False, because it is exactly divisible by 4, and also by 100	No
	2nd Condition:	False, because it is not exactly divisible by 400	
1918	1st Condition:	False, because it is not exactly divisible by 4	No
	2nd Condition:	False, because it is not exactly divisible by 400	
2000	1st Condition:	False, because it is exactly divisible by 4, and also by 100	Yes
	2nd Condition:	**True**, because it is exactly divisible by 400	
2002	1st Condition:	False, because it is not exactly divisible by 4	No
	2nd Condition:	False, because it is not exactly divisible by 400	
2004	1st Condition:	**True**, because it is exactly divisible by 4, and not by 100	Yes
	2nd Condition:	False, because it is not exactly divisible by 400	
2016	1st Condition:	**True**, because it is exactly divisible by 4, and not by 100	Yes
	2nd Condition:	False, because it is not exactly divisible by 400	

The Visual Basic program is shown here.

```
                        project_23_5_1
Sub Main()
  Dim y As Integer
  Dim input As String

  Console.Write("Enter a year: ")
  input = Console.ReadLine()

  If Int32.TryParse(input, y) = False Then
    Console.WriteLine("Invalid Number")
  Else
    If y Mod 4 = 0 And y Mod 100 <> 0 Or y Mod 400 = 0 Then
      Console.WriteLine("Leap year!")
    Else
      Console.WriteLine("Not a leap year")
    End If
  End If

  Console.ReadKey()
End Sub
```

Remember! *The* And *operator has a higher precedence than the* Or *operator.*

Exercise 23.5-2 *Displaying the Days of the Month*

Write a Visual Basic program that prompts the user to enter a month and a year and then displays how many days are in that month. The program needs to take into consideration the leap years. In case of a leap year, February has 29 instead of 28 days.

Solution

The Visual Basic program is shown here.

```
                        project_23_5_2a
Sub Main()
  Dim m, y As Integer

  Console.Write("Enter month 1 - 12: ")
  m = Console.ReadLine()
  Console.Write("Enter year: ")
  y = Console.ReadLine()

  If m = 2 Then
    If y Mod 4 = 0 And y Mod 100 <> 0 Or y Mod 400 = 0 Then
      Console.WriteLine("This month has 29 days")
    Else
      Console.WriteLine("This month has 28 days")
    End If
  ElseIf m = 4 Or m = 6 Or m = 9 Or m = 11 Then
    Console.WriteLine("This month has 30 days")
```

```
   Else
      Console.WriteLine("This month has 31 days")
   End If

   Console.ReadKey()
End Sub
```

Below, the same problem is solved again, using, however, the case decision structure.

project_23_5_2b

```
Sub Main()
   Dim m, y As Integer

   Console.Write("Enter month 1-12: ")
   m = Console.ReadLine()
   Console.Write("Enter year: ")
   y = Console.ReadLine()

   Select Case m
      Case 2
         If y Mod 4 = 0 And y Mod 100 <> 0 Or y Mod 400 = 0 Then
            Console.WriteLine("This month has 29 days")
         Else
            Console.WriteLine("This month has 28 days")
         End If
      Case 4, 6, 9, 11
         Console.WriteLine("This month has 30 days")
      Case Else
         Console.WriteLine("This month has 31 days")
   End Select

   Console.ReadKey()
End Sub
```

Exercise 23.5-3　　Is the Number a Palindrome?

A palindrome is a number that remains the same after reversing its digits. For example, the number 13631 is a palindrome. Write a Visual Basic program that lets the user enter a five-digit integer and tests whether or not this number is a palindrome. Moreover, individual error messages should be displayed when the user enters any non-numeric characters or any integer with either less than or more than five digits.

(Note that this involves data validation!)

Solution

To test if the user enters a palindrome number, you need to split its digits into five different variables as you learned in Chapter 13. Then, you can check whether the 1st digit is equal to the 5th digit and the 2nd digit is equal to the 4th digit. If this evaluates to True, the number is a palindrome.

To validate data input, you need to check whether the user has entered a five-digit number. Keep in mind that all five-digit numbers are in the range of 10000 to 99999. Therefore, you can just restrict the data input to within this range.

In order to display many different error messages, the best practice is to use a multiple-alternative decision structure which first checks data input validity for all cases, and then tries to solve the required problem. For example, if you need to check for various errors, you can do something like the following.

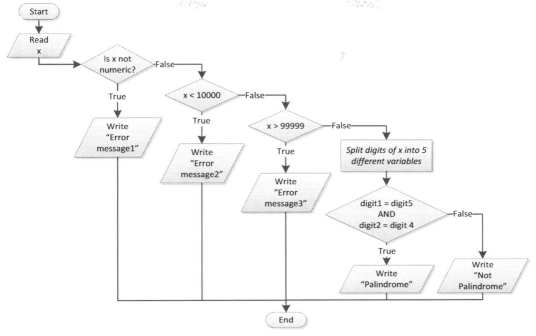

The final Visual Basic program is shown here.

```
                        project_23_5_3
Sub Main()
  Dim x, digit1, r, digit2, digit3, digit4, digit5 As Integer
  Dim input As String

  input = Console.ReadLine()

  If Int32.TryParse(input, x) = False Then
    Console.WriteLine("You entered non-numeric characters")
  ElseIf x < 10000 Then
    Console.WriteLine("You entered less than five digits")
  ElseIf x > 99999 Then
    Console.WriteLine("You entered more than five digits")
  Else
    digit1 = x \ 10000
    r = x Mod 10000

    digit2 = r \ 1000
    r = r Mod 1000

    digit3 = r \ 100
    r = r Mod 100
```

```
      digit4 = r \ 10
      digit5 = r Mod 10

      If digit1 = digit5 And digit2 = digit4 Then
        Console.WriteLine("Palindrome")
      Else
        Console.WriteLine("Not Palindrome")
      End If
    End If

    Console.ReadKey()
  End Sub
```

Exercise 23.5-4   *Checking for Proper Capitalization and Punctuation*

Write a Visual Basic program that prompts the user to enter a sentence and then checks it for proper capitalization and punctuation. The program should determine if the string begins with an uppercase letter and ends with a punctuation mark (check only for periods, question marks, and exclamation marks).

Solution

In this exercise you need to isolate the first and the last character of the string. As you already know, you can access any individual character of a string using substring notation. You can use index 0 to access the first character, index 1 to access the second character, and so on.

Thus, you can isolate the first character of a string using the following Visual Basic statement.

```
first_char = sentence(0)
```

On the other hand, the index of the last character is 1 less than the length of the string. But, how long is that string?

You can find the length of any string using the .Length property. The following code fragment isolates the last character of a string.

```
length = sentence.Length
last_char = sentence(length - 1)
```

or you can even write it with one single statement.

```
last_char = sentence(sentence.Length - 1)
```

The Visual Basic program is shown here.

```
                        project_23_5_4
Sub Main()
  Dim sentence, first_char, last_char As String
  Dim sentence_is_okay As Boolean

  Console.Write("Enter a sentence: ")
  sentence = Console.ReadLine()

  'Get first character
  first_char = sentence(0)
```

```
'Get last character
last_char = sentence(sentence.Length - 1)

sentence_is_okay = True

If first_char <> first_char.ToUpper() Then
  sentence_is_okay = False
ElseIf last_char <> "." And last_char <> "?" And last_char <> "!" Then
  sentence_is_okay = False
End If

If sentence_is_okay = True Then
  Console.WriteLine("Sentence is okay!")
End If

Console.ReadKey()
End Sub
```

In the beginning, the program assumes that the sentence is okay (sentence_is_okay = True). Then, it checks for proper capitalization and proper punctuation and if something goes wrong, it assigns the value False to the variable sentence_is_okay.

23.6   Review Exercises

Complete the following exercises.

1. Design a flowchart and write the corresponding Visual Basic program that lets the user enter two integers and then displays a message indicating whether at least one integer is odd; otherwise, a message "Nothing special" is displayed. Moreover, if the user enters non-numeric values, an error message should be displayed.

2. Design a flowchart and write the corresponding Visual Basic program that lets the user enter two integers and then displays a message indicating whether or not they are both divisible exactly by 3 and by 4. For example, 12 is such a number. Moreover, individual error messages should be displayed when the user enters any non-numeric values or any floats.

3. Write a Visual Basic program that displays the following menu:

    1.   Convert Kelvin to Fahrenheit

    2.   Convert Fahrenheit to Kelvin

    3.   Convert Fahrenheit to Celsius

    4.   Convert Celsius to Fahrenheit

    It then prompts the user to enter a choice (of 1 to 4) and a temperature value. It then calculates and displays the required value. Moreover, individual error messages should be displayed when the user enters a choice other than 1, 2, 3, or 4, or a non-numeric temperature value.

    It is given that

    $$1.8 \times Kelvin = Fahrenheit + 459.67$$

    and

$$\frac{Celsius}{5} = \frac{Fahrenheit - 32}{9}$$

4. Write a Visual Basic program that prompts the user to enter an integer, the type of operation (+, -, *, /, DIV, MOD, POWER), and a second integer. The program should execute the required operation and display the result.

5. Design a flowchart and write the corresponding Visual Basic program that finds and displays the value of y (if possible) in the following formula.

$$y = \frac{5x + 3}{x - 5} + \frac{3x^2 + 2x + 2}{x + 1}$$

6. Design a flowchart and write the corresponding Visual Basic program that finds and displays the values of y (if possible) in the following formula.

$$y = \begin{cases} \dfrac{x^2}{x + 1} + \dfrac{3 - \sqrt{x}}{x + 2}, & x \geq 10 \\ \dfrac{40x}{x - 9} + 3x, & x < 10 \end{cases}$$

Moreover, an error message should be displayed when the user enters any non-numeric characters.

7. Write a Visual Basic program that finds and displays the values of y (if possible) in the following formula.

$$y = \begin{cases} \dfrac{x}{\sqrt{x + 30}} + \dfrac{(8 + x)^2}{x + 1}, & -15 < x \leq -10 \\ \dfrac{|40x|}{x - 8}, & -10 < x \leq 0 \\ \dfrac{3x}{\sqrt{x - 9}}, & 0 < x \leq 25 \\ x - 1, & \text{for all other values of x} \end{cases}$$

8. Write a Visual Basic program that prompts the user to enter the ages of three people and then finds and displays the age in the middle.

9. Write a Visual Basic program that prompts the user to enter the name and the ages of three people and then displays the name of the youngest person or the oldest person, depending on which one is closer to the third age in the middle.

10. A three-digit integer is called an Armstrong number when the sum of the cubes of its digits is equal to the number itself. The number 371 is such a number, since $3^3 + 7^3 + 1^3 = 371$. Write a Visual Basic program that lets the user enter a three-digit integer and then displays a message indicating whether or not the given number is an Armstrong one. Moreover, individual error messages should be displayed when the user enters any non-numeric characters or any numbers other than three-digit ones.

11. Write a Visual Basic program that prompts the user to enter a day (1 – 31), a month (1 – 12), and a year and then finds and displays how many days are left until the end of that month. The program should take into consideration the leap years. In the case of a leap year, February has 29 instead of 28 days.

12. Write a Visual Basic program that lets the user enter a word of six letters and then displays a message indicating whether or not every second letter is

capitalized. The word "AtHeNa" is such a word, but it can be also given as "aThEnA".

13. A book store sells e-books for $10 each. Quantity discounts are given according to the following table.

Quantity	Discount
3 – 5	10%
6 – 9	15%
10 – 13	20%
14 – 19	27%
20 or more	30%

Write a Visual Basic program that prompts the user to enter the total number of e-books purchased and then displays the amount of discount (if any), and the total amount of the purchase after the discount.

14. In a supermarket, the discount that customers receive based on the before-tax amount of their order is presented in next table.

Range	Discount
amount < 50	0%
50 ≤ amount < 100	1%
100 ≤ amount < 200	2%
250 ≤ amount	3%

Write a Visual Basic program that calculates the discount that customers receive (if any) based on the amount of their order after adding a VAT (Value Added Tax) of 19%. Moreover, individual error messages should be displayed when the user enters any non-numeric or negative values.

15. The Body Mass Index (BMI) is often used to determine whether an adult person is overweight or underweight for his or her height. The formula used to calculate the BMI of an adult person is

$$BMI = \frac{weight \cdot 703}{height^2}$$

Write a Visual Basic program that prompts the user to enter his or her age, weight (in pounds) and height (in inches) and then displays a description according to the following table.

Body Mass Index	Description
BMI < 15	Very severely underweight
15.0 ≤ BMI < 16.0	Severely underweight
16.0 ≤ BMI < 18.5	Underweight
18.5 ≤ BMI < 25	Normal
25.0 ≤ BMI < 30.0	Overweight
30.0 ≤ BMI < 35.0	Severely overweight

35.0 ≤ BMI	Very severely overweight

The message "Invalid age" should be displayed when the user enters an age less than 18.

16. The LAV Water Company charges for subscribers' water consumption according to the following table (monthly rates for domestic accounts).

Water Consumption (cubic feet)	USD per cubic foot
consumption ≤ 10	$3
11 ≤ consumption ≤ 20	$5
21 ≤ consumption ≤ 35	$7
36 ≤ consumption	$9

Write a Visual Basic program that prompts the user to enter the total amount of water consumed (in cubic feet) and then calculates and displays the total amount to pay. Please note that the rates are progressive. Federal, state, and local taxes add a total of 10% to each bill. Moreover, individual error messages should be displayed when the user enters any non-numeric or negative values.

17. Write a Visual Basic program that prompts the user to enter his or her taxable income and the number of his or her children and then calculates the total tax to pay according to the following table. However, total tax is reduced by 2% when the user has at least one child. Please note that the rates are progressive.

Taxable Income (USD)	Tax Rate
income ≤ 8000	10%
8000 < income ≤ 30000	15%
30000 < income ≤ 70000	25%
70000 < income	30%

18. The Beaufort scale is an empirical measure that relates wind speed to observed conditions on land or at sea. Write a Visual Basic program that prompts the user to enter the wind speed and then displays the corresponding Beaufort number and description according to the following table. Moreover, individual error messages should be displayed when the user enters any non-numeric or negative values. Also, if wind speed is 3 Beaufort or less, an additional message "It's Fishing Day!!!" should be displayed.

Wind Speed (miles per hour)	Beaufort Number	Description
wind speed < 1	0	Calm
1 ≤ wind speed < 4	1	Light air
4 ≤ wind speed < 8	2	Light breeze
8 ≤ wind speed < 13	3	Gentle breeze
13 ≤ wind speed < 18	4	Moderate breeze
18 ≤ wind speed < 25	5	Fresh breeze

25 ≤ wind speed < 31	6	Strong breeze
31 ≤ wind speed < 39	7	Moderate gale
39 ≤ wind speed < 47	8	Gale
47 ≤ wind speed < 55	9	Strong gale
55 ≤ wind speed < 64	10	Storm
64 ≤ wind speed < 74	11	Violent storm
74 ≤ wind speed	12	Hurricane force

Review Questions in "Decision Control Structures"

Answer the following questions.

1. What is a Boolean expression?
2. Which comparison operators does Visual Basic support?
3. Which logical operator performs a logical conjunction?
4. Which logical operator performs a logical disjunction?
5. When the result of a logical operator And is True?
6. When the result of a logical operator Or is True?
7. State the order of precedence of logical operators.
8. State the order of precedence of arithmetic, comparison, and logical operators.
9. Design the flowchart and write the corresponding Visual Basic statement (in general form) of a single-alternative decision structure. Describe how this decision structure operates.
10. Design the flowchart and write the corresponding Visual Basic statement (in general form) of a dual-alternative decision structure. Describe how this decision structure operates.
11. Design the flowchart and write the corresponding Visual Basic statement (in general form) of a multiple-alternative decision structure. Describe how this decision structure operates.
12. Design the flowchart and write the corresponding Visual Basic statement (in general form) of a case decision structure. Describe how this decision structure operates.
13. What does the term "nesting a decision structure" mean?
14. How deep can the nesting of decision control structures go? Is there any practical limit?
15. When is the conversion from a multiple-alternative decision structure to a case decision structure possible?
16. When is the conversion from a nested decision control structure to a multiple-alternative decision structure possible?
17. When is the conversion from a nested decision control structure to a case decision structure possible?
18. What is code indentation?
19. Create a diagram that shows all possible paths for solving a linear equation.
20. Create a diagram that shows all possible paths for solving a quadratic equation.
21. When is a year considered a leap year?
22. What is a palindrome number?

Section 5

Loop Control Structures

Chapter 24
Introduction to Loop Control Structures

24.1 What is a Loop Control Structure?

A loop control structure is a control structure that allows the execution of a statement or block of statements multiple times until a specified condition is met.

24.2 From Sequence Control to Loop Control Structures

The next example lets the user enter four numbers and it then calculates and displays their sum. As you can see, there is no loop control structure yet, just the familiar sequence control structure.

```
Sub Main()
    Dim a, b, c, d, sum As Double

    a = Console.ReadLine()
    b = Console.ReadLine()
    c = Console.ReadLine()
    d = Console.ReadLine()

    sum = a + b + c + d

    Console.WriteLine(sum)

    Console.ReadKey()
End Sub
```

This program is quite short—very short actually! However, think of an analogous program that lets the user enter 1000 numbers instead of four! Can you imagine writing the statement `Console.ReadLine()` 1000 times? Wouldn't it be much easier if you could write this statement only once but "tell" the computer to execute it 1000 times? Of course it would be! But for this you need a loop control structure!

However, if you want to use a loop control structure in this example, you need to modify this program a little. To do so, you have a riddle to solve: you are allowed to use only two variables, a and sum. Yes, you heard it! This program should prompt the user to enter four numbers and then it will calculate and display their sum, <u>but</u> it must do it with only two variables! Can you find a way? Hmmm... it's obvious what you are thinking right now: *"The only thing that I can do with two variables is to read one single value in* a *and then assign that value to* sum.*"* Your thinking is quite correct, and it is presented here.

```
a = Console.ReadLine()
sum = a
```

which can equivalently be written as

```
sum = 0

a = Console.ReadLine()
sum = sum + a
```

And now what? Now, there are three things that you can actually do, and these are: think, think, and of course, think!

The first number has been stored in variable sum, so variable a is now free for further use! Thus, you can reuse variable a to read a second value which will also be accumulated in variable sum, as follows.

```
sum = 0

a = Console.ReadLine()
sum = sum + a

a = Console.ReadLine()
sum = sum + a
```

> **Notice:** Statement sum = sum + a accumulates the value of a to sum. For example, if variable sum contains the value 5 and variable a contains the value 3, the statement sum = sum + a assigns the value 8 to variable sum.

Since the second number has been accumulated in variable sum, variable a can be re-used! Of course, this process can go on again and again until all four numbers are read and accumulated in variable sum. The final Visual Basic program is as follows. Please note that this program does not use any loop control structure yet!

```
sum = 0

a = Console.ReadLine()
sum = sum + a

a = Console.ReadLine()
sum = sum + a

a = Console.ReadLine()
sum = sum + a

a = Console.ReadLine()
sum = sum + a

Console.WriteLine(sum)
```

Since user must enter 4 numbers, this pair of statements should be written 4 times.

> **Notice:** The main difference between this program and the initial one is that this one has four identical pairs of statements.

Of course, this example can be expanded to read and find the sum of more than four numbers. However, as it becomes clear, you can't write that pair of statements over and over again because soon you will realize how painful this is. Moreover, if you forget to write at least one pair of statements, it will ultimately lead to incorrect results.

What you really need here is to keep only one pair of those statements but use a loop control structure that executes it four times (or even 1000 times, if you wish). You can use something like the following code fragment.

```
sum = 0
```

```
execute_these_statements_4_times (
  a = Console.ReadLine()
  sum = sum + a
)

Console.WriteLine(sum)
```

Obviously there isn't any *execute_these_statements_4_times* statement in Visual Basic. This is for demonstration purposes only but soon enough you will learn everything about all the loop control structures that Visual Basic supports!

24.3 Review Questions: True/False

Choose **true** or **false** for each of the following statements.

1. A loop control structure is a structure that allows the execution of a statement or block of statements multiple times until a specified condition is met.

2. It is possible to use a sequence control structure that prompts the user to enter 1000 numbers and then calculates their sum.

3. The following code fragment

   ```
   sum = 10
   a = 0
   sum = sum + a
   ```

   accumulates the value 10 in variable sum.

4. The following Visual Basic program

   ```
   Sub Main()
       Dim a, sum As Integer
       a = 5
       sum = sum + a
       Console.WriteLine(sum)

       Console.ReadKey()
   End Sub
   ```

   satisfies the property of definiteness.

5. The following two code fragments

   ```
   a = 5
   sum = a
   ```

   and

   ```
   sum = 0
   a = 5
   sum = sum + a
   ```

   are considered equivalent.

Chapter 25
The Pre-Test Loop Structure

25.1 The Pre-Test Loop Structure

The pre-test loop structure is shown in the following flowchart.

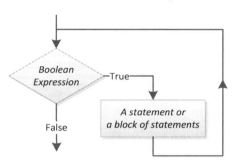

> **Notice**: The Decision symbol (the diamond, or rhombus) is used both in decision control structures and in loop control structures. However, in loop control structures, one of the diamond's exits always has an upward direction.

Let's see what happens when the flow of execution reaches a pre-test loop structure. If the Boolean expression evaluates to `True`, the statement or block of statements of the structure is executed and the flow of execution goes back to the point just above the Decision symbol. If the Boolean expression evaluates to `True` again, the process repeats. When the Boolean expression evaluates to `False`, the flow of execution exits the loop.

> **Notice**: A "pre-test loop structure" is named this way because first the Boolean expression is evaluated, and afterwards the statement or block of statements of the structure is executed.
>
> **Notice**: Because the Boolean expression is evaluated before entering the loop, a pre-test loop may perform from zero to many iterations.
>
> **Notice**: Each time the statement or block of statements of the structure is executed, the term used in computer science is "the loop is iterating" or "the loop performs an iteration."

The general form of the Visual Basic statement is

```
Do While Boolean_Expression
  A statement or block of statements
Loop
```

The following example displays the numbers 1 to 10.

```
                        project_25_1
Sub Main()
  Dim i As Integer
```

```
  i = 1
  Do While i <= 10
    Console.WriteLine(i)
    i += 1
  Loop

  Console.ReadKey()
End Sub
```

> **Notice**: Please note that the statements inside the structure are indented. Just as in decision control structures, this indentation makes programs easier to read and understand. By using indentation, you visually set those statements apart from the rest of the structure.

Exercise 25.1-1   Designing the Flowchart and Counting the Total Number of Iterations

Design the corresponding flowchart for the following Visual Basic program. How many iterations does this Visual Basic program perform?

```
Sub Main()
  Dim i As Integer

  i = 4
  Do While i > 0
    i -= 1
  Loop

  Console.Write("The end")

  Console.ReadKey()
End Sub
```

Solution

The corresponding flowchart is as follows.

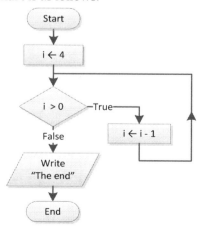

Next, a trace table can help you observe the flow of execution.

Step	Statement	Notes	i
1	i = 4		4
2	Do While i > 0	This evaluates to True	
3	i = i - 1		3
4	Do While i > 0	This evaluates to True	
5	i = i - 1		2
6	Do While i > 0	This evaluates to True	
7	i = i - 1		1
8	Do While i > 0	This evaluates to True	
9	i = i - 1		0
10	Do While i > 0	This evaluates to False	
11	Console.Write("The end")	The message "The end" is displayed	

Steps 2–3: 1st Iteration
Steps 4–5: 2nd Iteration
Steps 6–7: 3rd Iteration
Steps 8–9: 4th Iteration

As you can see from the trace table, the total number of iterations is four.

Now, let's draw some conclusions!

➢ If you want to find the total number of iterations, you need to count the number of times the statement or block of statements of the structure is executed and not the number of times the Boolean expression is evaluated.

➢ In a pre-test loop structure, when the statement or block of statements of the structure is executed N times, the Boolean expression is evaluated N+1 times.

Exercise 25.1-2   *Counting the Total Number of Iterations*

How many iterations does this Visual Basic program perform?

```
Sub Main()
  Dim i As Integer

  i = 4
  Do While i >= 0
    i -= 1
  Loop

  Console.Write("The end")

  Console.ReadKey()
End Sub
```

Solution

This exercise is almost identical to the previous one. The only difference is that the Boolean expression here remains True, even for i = 0. Therefore, it performs an additional iteration, that is, five iterations.

Exercise 25.1-3   *Designing the Flowchart and Counting the Total Number of Iterations*

Design the corresponding flowchart for the following Visual Basic program. How many iterations does this Visual Basic program perform?

```vb
Sub Main()
  Dim i As Integer

  i = 1
  Do While i <> 6
    i += 2
  Loop

  Console.Write("The end")

  Console.ReadKey()
End Sub
```

Solution

The corresponding flowchart is as follows.

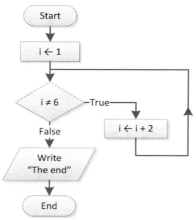

Now, let's create a trace table to observe the flow of execution.

Step	Statement	Notes	i	
1	i = 1		1	
2	Do While i <> 4	This evaluates to True		1st Iteration
3	i += 2		3	
4	Do While i <> 4	This evaluates to True		2nd Iteration
5	i += 2		5	
6	Do While i <> 4	This evaluates to True		3rd Iteration
7	i += 2		7	
8	Do While i <> 4	This evaluates to True		

9	...	...
10	...	...

As you can see from the trace table, since the value 6 is never assigned to variable i, this program will iterate for an infinite number of times! Obviously, this program does not satisfy the property of finiteness.

Exercise 25.1-4   Counting the Total Number of Iterations

How many iterations does this Visual Basic program perform?

```
Sub Main()
  Dim i As Integer

  i = -10
  Do While i > 0
    i -= 1
  Loop

  Console.Write("The end")

  Console.ReadKey()
End Sub
```

Solution

Initially, the value -10 is assigned to variable i. The Boolean expression directly evaluates to False and the flow of execution goes right to the Console.Write("The end") statement. Thus, this program performs zero iterations.

Exercise 25.1-5   Finding the Sum of 10 Numbers

Using a pre-test loop structure, write a Visual Basic program that lets the user enter 10 numbers and then calculates and displays their sum.

Solution

Do you remember the example in Chapter 24 for calculating the sum of four numbers? At the end, after a little work, the proposed Visual Basic program became

```
Sub Main()
  Dim sum, a As Double

  sum = 0

  execute_these_statements_4_times (
    a = Console.ReadLine()
    sum = sum + a
  )

  Console.Write(sum)

  Console.ReadKey()
```

```
End Sub
```

Now, you need a way to "present" the statement *execute_these_statements_4_times* with real Visual Basic statements. The Do While-Loop statement is actually able to do this, but you need one extra variable to count the total number of iterations. Then, when the desired number of iterations has been performed, the flow of execution should exit the loop.

Following is a general purpose Visual Basic fragment that iterates for the number of times specified by *total_number_of_iterations*,

```
i = 1
Do While  i <= total_number_of_iterations
  A statement or block of statements
  i += 1
Loop
```

where *total_number_of_iterations* can be a constant value or even a variable or an expression.

> **Notice**: The name of the variable i is not binding. You can use any variable name you wish such as counter, count, k, and more.

After combining this program with the previous one, the final program becomes

project_25_1_5

```
Sub Main()
  Dim sum, a As Double
  Dim i As Integer

  sum = 0

  i = 1
  Do While i <= 4
    a = Console.ReadLine()
    sum = sum + a

    i += 1
  Loop

  Console.Write(sum)

  Console.ReadKey()
End Sub
```

This pair of statements is executed 4 times forcing the user to enter 4 numbers.

Exercise 25.1-6　Finding the Product of 20 Numbers

Write a Visual Basic program that lets the user enter 20 numbers and then calculates and displays their product.

Solution

If you were to use a sequence control structure, it would be something like the next code fragment.

```
p = 1

a = Console.ReadLine()
p = p * a

a = Console.ReadLine()
p = p * a

...

...

a = Console.ReadLine()
p = p * a
```

This should be written 20 times

> **Notice**: *Please note that variable* p *is initialized to 1 instead of 0. This is necessary for the statement* p = p * a *to operate properly; the final product would be zero otherwise.*

Using knowledge from the previous exercise, the final program becomes

```
                        project_25_1_6
Sub Main()
  Dim p, a As Double
  Dim i As Integer

  p = 1

  i = 1
  Do While i <= 20
    a = Console.ReadLine()
    p = p * a

    i += 1
  Loop

  Console.Write(p)

  Console.ReadKey()
End Sub
```

Exercise 25.1-7   *Finding the Product of N Numbers*

Write a Visual Basic program that lets the user enter N numbers and then calculates and displays their product. The value of N should be given by the user at the beginning of the program.

Solution

In this exercise, the total number of iterations depends on a value that the user must enter. Following is a general purpose Visual Basic fragment that iterates for N times, where N is given by the user.

```
n = Console.ReadLine()

i = 1
```

```
Do While i <= n
  A statement or block of statements
  i += 1
Loop
```

According to what you have learned so far, the final program becomes

project_25_1_7

```
Sub Main()
  Dim i, n As Integer
  Dim p, a As Double

  n = Console.ReadLine()

  p = 1

  i = 1
  Do While i <= n
    a = Console.ReadLine()
    p = p * a

    i += 1
  Loop

  Console.Write(p)

  Console.ReadKey()
End Sub
```

Exercise 25.1-8   *Finding the Sum of Odd Numbers*

Design a flowchart and write the corresponding Visual Basic program that lets the user enter 20 integers, and then calculates and displays the sum of the odd numbers.

Solution

This is quite easy. What the program must do inside the loop is check whether or not a given number is odd and, if it is, that number should accumulate to variable sum; even numbers should be ignored. The flowchart is as follows.

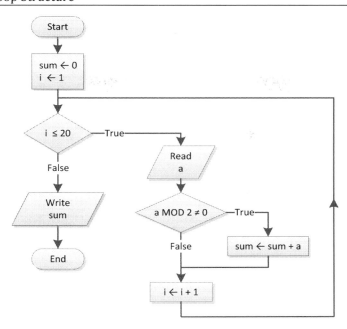

The corresponding Visual Basic program is as follows.

```
                              project_25_1_8
Sub Main()
  Dim sum, i, a As Integer

  sum = 0

  i = 1
  Do While i <= 20
    a = Console.ReadLine()
    If a Mod 2 <> 0 Then
      sum = sum + a
    End If
    i += 1
  Loop

  Console.Write(sum)

  Console.ReadKey()
End Sub
```

Exercise 25.1-9   *Finding the Sum of an Unknown Quantity of Numbers*

Write a Visual Basic program that lets the user enter numeric values repeatedly until the value -1 is entered. When data input is completed, the sum of the numbers entered should be displayed. (The value of -1 should not be included in the final sum.) Next, create a trace table to check if your program operates properly using 10, 20, 5, and -1 as input values.

Solution

In this exercise, the total number of iterations is unknown. If you were to use decision control structures, your program would look something like the code fragment that follows.

```
Sub Main()
    Dim sum, a As Double

    sum = 0

    a = Console.ReadLine()
    If a <> -1 Then
        sum = sum + a
        a = Console.ReadLine()
        If a <> -1 Then
            sum = sum + a
            a = Console.ReadLine()
            If a <> -1 Then
                sum = sum + a
                a = Console.ReadLine()
                ...
                ...
            End If
        End If
    End If

    Console.Write(sum)

    Console.ReadKey()
End Sub
```

This is the part of the program that actually repeats

Now let's rewrite this program using a loop control structure instead. The final program is presented next. If you try to follow the flow of execution, you will find that it operates equivalently to the previous one.

```
project_25_1_9
Sub Main()
    Dim sum, a As Double

    sum = 0

    a = Console.ReadLine()
    Do While a <> -1
        sum = sum + a
        a = Console.ReadLine()
    Loop

    Console.Write(sum)

    Console.ReadKey()
End Sub
```

Now let's create a trace table to determine if this program operates properly using 10, 20, 5, and -1 as input values.

Step	Statement	Notes	a	sum
1	sum = 0		?	0
2	a = Console.ReadLine()		10	0
3	Do While a <> -1	This evaluates to True		
4	sum = sum + a		10	10
5	a = Console.ReadLine()		20	10
6	Do While a <> -1	This evaluates to True		
7	sum = sum + a		20	30
8	a = Console.ReadLine()		5	30
9	Do While a <> -1	This evaluates to True		
10	sum = sum + a		5	35
11	a = Console.ReadLine()		-1	35
12	Do While a <> -1	This evaluates to False		
13	Console.Write(sum)	The value 35 is displayed		

As you can see, in the end, variable sum contains the value 35, which is, indeed, the sum of the values 10 + 20 + 5. Moreover, the final given value of -1 does not participate in the final sum.

25.2 Review Questions: True/False

Choose **true** or **false** for each of the following statements.

1. A pre-test loop may perform zero iterations.

2. In flowcharts, both exits of the diamond symbol in a pre-test loop structure, have an upwards direction.

3. The statement or block of statements of a pre-test loop structure is executed at least one time.

4. A pre-test loop stops iterating when its Boolean expression evaluates to True

5. In a pre-test loop structure, when the statement or block of statements of the structure is executed N times, the Boolean expression is evaluated N - 1 times.

6. In the following code fragment

```
i = 1
Do While i <= 10
   Console.WriteLine("Hello")
Loop
i += 1
```

the word "Hello" is displayed 10 times

7. The following Visual Basic program

```
Sub Main()
   Dim i As Integer = 1

   Do While i <> 10
```

```
    Console.WriteLine("Hello")
    i += 2
  Loop

  Console.ReadKey()
End Sub
```

does **not** satisfy the property of finiteness

25.3   Review Questions: Multiple Choice

Select the correct answer for each of the following statements.

1.   In flowcharts, the diamond symbol is being used
   a.   in decision control structures.
   b.   in loop control structures.
   c.   all of the above

2.   In the following code fragment

```
i = 1
Do While i < 10
    Console.WriteLine("Hello Hermes")
    i += 1
Loop
```

the message "Hello Hermes" is displayed
   a.   10 times.
   b.   9 times.
   c.   1 time.
   d.   0 times.
   e.   none of the above

3.   In the following code fragment

```
i = 1
Do While i < 10
    Console.WriteLine("Hi!")
Loop
Console.WriteLine("Hello Ares")
i += 1
```

the message "Hello Ares" is displayed
   a.   10 times.
   b.   1 time.
   c.   0 times.
   d.   none of the above

4.   In the following code fragment

```
i = 1
Do While i < 10
    i += 1
Loop
Console.WriteLine("Hi!")
```

```
Console.WriteLine("Hello Aphrodite")
```

the message "Hello Aphrodite" is displayed

    a.   10 times.

    b.   1 time.

    c.   0 times.

    d.   none of the above

5.   In the following code fragment

```
i = 1
Do While i >= 10
    Console.WriteLine("Hi!")
    Console.WriteLine("Hello Apollo")
    i += 1
Loop
```

the message "Hello Apollo" is displayed

    a.   10 times.

    b.   1 time.

    c.   0 times.

    d.   none of the above

6.   The following Visual Basic program calculates and displays the sum of

```
Sub Main()
    Dim n, i As Integer
    Dim s, a As Double

    n = Console.ReadLine()
    s = 0
    i = 1
    Do While i < n
        a = Console.ReadLine()
        s = s + a
        i += 1
    Loop
    Console.Write(s)

    Console.ReadKey()
End Sub
```

    a.   as many numbers as the value of variable n denotes.

    b.   as many numbers as the result of the expression n - 1 denotes.

    c.   as many numbers as the value of variable i denotes.

    d.   none of the above

25.4 Review Exercises

Complete the following exercises.

1.   Create a trace table to determine the values of the variables in each step of the next Visual Basic program. How many iterations does this Visual Basic program perform?

```
Sub Main()
  Dim i, x As Integer

  i = 3
  x = 0
  Do While i >= 0
    i -= 1
    x += i
  Loop
  Console.Write(x)

  Console.ReadKey()
End Sub
```

2. Design the corresponding flowchart and create a trace table to determine the values of the variables in each step of the next Visual Basic program. How many iterations does this Visual Basic program perform?

```
Sub Main()
  Dim i As Integer

  i = -5
  Do While i > 10
    i -= 1
  Loop
  Console.Write(i)

  Console.ReadKey()
End Sub
```

3. Create a trace table to determine the values of the variables in each step of the next Visual Basic program. How many iterations does this Visual Basic program perform?

```
Sub Main()
  Dim a, b, c, d As Integer

  a = 2
  Do While a <= 10
    b = a + 1
    c = b * 2
    d = c - b + 1
    Select Case d
      Case 4
        Console.WriteLine(b & ", " & c)
      Case 5
        Console.WriteLine(c)
      Case 8
        Console.WriteLine(a & ", " & b)
      Case Else
        Console.WriteLine(a & ", " & b & ", " & d)
    End Select
    a += 4
```

```
Loop

    Console.ReadKey()
End Sub
```

4. Create a trace table to determine the values of the variables in each step of the next Visual Basic program. How many iterations does this Visual Basic program perform?

```
Sub Main()
    Dim a, b, c, d, x As Integer

    a = 1
    b = 1
    c = 0
    d = 0
    Do While b < 2
        x = a + b
        If x Mod 2 <> 0 Then
            c = c + 1
        Else
            d = d + 1
        End If
        a = b
        b = c
        c = d
    Loop

    Console.ReadKey()
Loop
```

5. Fill in the gaps in the following code fragments so that all loops perform exactly four iterations.

i.
```
a = 3
Do While a > ......
    a -= 1
Loop
```

ii.
```
a = 5
Do While a < ......
    a += 1
Loop
```

iii.
```
a = 9
Do While a <> 10
    a = a + ......
Loop
```

iv.
```
a = 1
Do While a <> ......
    a -= 2
Loop
```

v.
```
a = 2
Do While a < ......
    a = 2 * a
Loop
```

vi.
```
a = 1
Do While a < ......
    a = a + 0.1
Loop
```

6. Write a Visual Basic program that lets the user enter N numbers and then calculates and displays their sum and their average. The value of N should be given by the user at the beginning of the program.

7. Write a Visual Basic program that lets the user enter N integers and then calculates and displays the product of those that are even. The value of N should be given by the user at the beginning of the program.

8. Write a Visual Basic program that lets the user enter 100 integers and then calculates and displays the sum of those with a last digit of 0. For example, the values 10, 2130, and 500 are such numbers.

    Hint: You can isolate the last digit of any integer using a modulus 10 operation.

9. Write a Visual Basic program that lets the user enter 20 integers and then calculates and displays the sum of those that consist of three digits.

    Hint: All three-digit integers are between 100 and 999.

10. Write a Visual Basic program that lets the user enter numeric values repeatedly until the value 0 is entered. When data input is completed, the product of the numbers entered should be displayed. (The last 0 entered should not be included in the final product.) Next, create a trace table to check if your program operates properly using 3, 2, 9, and 0 as input values.

11. The population of a town is now at 30000 and is expanding at a rate of 3% per year. Write a Visual Basic program to determine how many years it will take for the population to exceed 100000.

Chapter 26
The Post-Test Loop Structure

26.1 The Post-Test Loop Structure

The post-test loop structure is shown in the following flowchart.

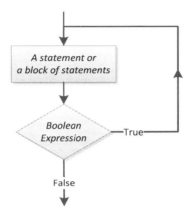

> **Remember!** In loop control structures, one of the diamond's exits always has an upward direction.

Let's see what happens when the flow of execution reaches a post-test loop structure. The statement or block of statements of the structure is directly executed and if the Boolean expression evaluates to `True`, the flow of execution goes back to the point just above the statement or block of statements of the structure. The statement or block of statements is executed once more and if the Boolean expression evaluates to `True` again, the process repeats. When the Boolean expression evaluates to `False`, the flow of execution exits the loop.

> **Notice:** The post-test loop differs from the pre-test loop in that first the statement or block of statements of the structure is executed and afterwards the Boolean expression is evaluated. Consequently, the post-test loop performs at least one iteration!

> **Notice:** Each time the statement or block of statements of the structure is executed, the term used in computer science is "the loop is iterating" or "the loop performs an iteration."

The general form of the Visual Basic statement is

```
Do
    A statement or block of statements
Loop While Boolean_Expression
```

The following example displays the numbers 1 to 10.

```
                          project_26_1
Sub Main()
```

```
    Dim i As Integer

    i = 1
    Do
       Console.WriteLine(i)
       i += 1
    Loop While i <= 10

    Console.ReadKey()
End Sub
```

Exercise 26.1-1   *Designing the Flowchart and Counting the Total Number of Iterations*

Design the corresponding flowchart for the following Visual Basic program. How many iterations does this Visual Basic program perform?

```
Sub Main()
    Dim i As Integer

    i = 3
    Do
       i -= 1
    Loop While i > 0
    Console.Write("The end")

    Console.ReadKey()
End Sub
```

Solution

The corresponding flowchart is as follows.

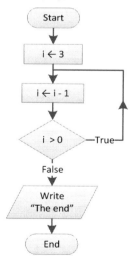

Now, let's create a trace table to observe the flow of execution.

Step	Statement	Notes	i
1	i = 3		3
2	i = i - 1		2
3	Loop While i > 0	This evaluates to True	
4	i = i - 1		1
5	Loop While i > 0	This evaluates to True	
6	i = i - 1		0
7	Loop While i > 0	This evaluates to False	
8	Console.Write("The end")	The message "The end" is displayed	

Steps 2 and 3: 1st Iteration
Steps 4 and 5: 2nd Iteration
Steps 6 and 7: 3rd Iteration

As you can see from the trace table, the total number of iterations is three.

Now, let's draw some conclusions!

➢ If you have to find the total number of iterations, you can count the number of times the statement or block of statements of the structure is executed but also the number of times the Boolean expression is evaluated, since both numbers are equal.

➢ In a post-test loop structure, when the statement or block of statements of the structure is executed N times, the Boolean expression is evaluated N times as well.

Exercise 26.1-2 *Counting the Total Number of Iterations*

How many iterations does this Visual Basic program perform?

```vb
Sub Main()
    Dim i As Integer

    i = 3
    Do
        i -= 1
    Loop While i >= 0
    Console.Write("The end")

    Console.ReadKey()
End Sub
```

Solution

This exercise is almost identical to the previous one. The only difference is that the Boolean expression here remains True even for i = 0. Therefore, it performs an additional iteration, that is, four iterations.

Exercise 26.1-3   *Designing the Flowchart and Counting the Total Number of Iterations*

Design the corresponding flowchart for the following Visual Basic program. How many iterations does this Visual Basic program perform? What happens if you switch the post-test loop structure with a pre-test loop structure?

```
Sub Main()
  Dim i As Integer

  i = -1
  Do
    i -= 1
    Console.WriteLine("Hello there!")
  Loop While i > 0
  Console.Write("The end")

  Console.ReadKey()
End Sub
```

Solution

The corresponding flowchart is as follows.

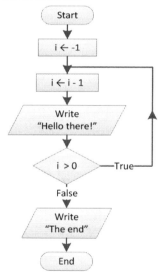

Initially the value -1 is assigned to variable i. Inside the loop, variable i is decremented by one (value -2 is assigned) and the message "Hello there!" is displayed. Finally, the Boolean expression evaluates to False and the flow of execution goes right to the Console.Write("The end") statement. Thus, this program performs one iteration!

Now, let's see what happens when a pre-test loop structure is used instead.

```
Sub Main()
  Dim i As Integer

  i = -1
  Do While i > 0
```

```
    i -= 1
    Console.WriteLine("Hello there!")
  Loop
  Console.Write("The end")

  Console.ReadKey()
End Sub
```

The value -1 is assigned to variable i. The Boolean expression evaluates to False and the flow of execution goes directly to the Console.Write("The end") statement. Thus, this program performs zero iterations!

> **Remember!** A pre-test loop structure may perform zero iterations in contrast to the post-test loop structure which performs **at least** one iteration!

Exercise 26.1-4   *Counting the Total Number of Iterations*

How many iterations does this Visual Basic program perform?

```
Sub Main()
  Dim i As Integer

  i = 1
  Do
    i = i + 2
  Loop While i <> 4
  Console.Write("The end")

  Console.ReadKey()
End Sub
```

Solution

Let's create a trace table to observe the flow of execution.

Step	Statement	Notes	i	
1	i = 1		1	
2	i = i + 2		3	1st Iteration
3	Loop While i <> 4	This evaluates to True		
4	i = i + 2		5	2nd Iteration
5	Loop While i <> 4	This evaluates to True		
6	i = i + 2		7	3rd Iteration
7	Loop While i <> 4	This evaluates to True		
8	...	...		
9	...	...		

As you can see from the trace table, since the value 4 is never assigned to variable i, this program will iterate for an infinite number of times! Obviously, this program does not satisfy the property of finiteness.

Exercise 26.1-5 *Finding the Product of N Numbers*

Write a Visual Basic program that lets the user enter N numbers and then calculates and displays their product. The value of N should be given by the user at the beginning of the program. What happens if you switch the post-test loop structure with a pre-test loop structure?

Solution

The program that finds and displays the product of N numbers using a pre-test loop structure has already been analyzed in Chapter 25, so, there is no need to explain any details again. For your convenience however, the following solution uses both a pre-test and a post-test loop structure.

project_26_1_5a	project_26_1_5b
| ```
Sub Main()
  Dim n, i As Integer
  Dim p, a As Double

  n = Console.ReadLine()

  p = 1

  i = 1
  Do While i <= n
    a = Console.ReadLine()
    p = p * a

    i += 1
  Loop

  Console.Write(p)

  Console.ReadKey()
End Sub
``` | ```
Sub Main()
  Dim n, i As Integer
  Dim p, a As Double

  n = Console.ReadLine()

  p = 1

  i = 1
  Do
    a = Console.ReadLine()
    p = p * a

    i += 1
  Loop While i <= n

  Console.Write(p)

  Console.ReadKey()
End Sub
``` |

Now watch carefully! If the user enters any value greater than zero, both programs operate exactly the same way.

The two Visual Basic programs, however, operate in different ways when the user enters a non-positive[1] value. For example, if the value 0 is entered, the left program performs **zero** iterations whereas the right program performs **one** iteration!

> **Remember**! A pre-test loop structure may perform zero iterations in contrast to the post-test loop structure, which performs **at least** one iteration!

---

[1] A quantity that is either zero or negative.

If you want to make both programs equivalent, you need to add to the right program an If statement (just before the Do keyword) in order to check if variable n contains a positive value. But it's not the right time for this conversation yet. In Chapter 29, you will learn all about converting a pre-test loop structure to its post-test loop structure equivalent and vice versa and unquestionably, after conversion, both programs (the initial and the resulting one) will be totally equivalent, which means that they will perform an equal number of iterations for any given input values.

Exercise 26.1-6 *Finding the Product of an Unknown Quantity of Numbers*

Write a Visual Basic program that lets the user enter numeric values repeatedly until the value –1 is entered. When data input is completed, the product of the numbers entered should be displayed. (The value of –1 should not be included in final product.) Next, create a trace table to check if your program operates properly using 2, 4, 5, and –1 as input values.

Solution

The Visual Basic program is as follows.

```
                          project_26_1_6
Sub Main()
  Dim p, a As Double

  p = 1

  a = Console.ReadLine()
  Do
    p = p * a
    a = Console.ReadLine()
  Loop While a <> -1

  Console.Write(p)

  Console.ReadKey()
End Sub
```

Now let's create a trace table to determine if the program operates properly.

Step	Statement	Notes	a	p
1	p = 1		?	1
2	a = Console.ReadLine()		2	1
3	p = p * a		2	2
4	a = Console.ReadLine()		4	2
5	Loop While a <> -1	This evaluates to True		
6	p = p * a		4	8
7	a = Console.ReadLine()		5	8
8	Loop While a <> -1	This evaluates to True		
9	p = p * a		5	40

10	`a = Console.ReadLine()`	**-1** 40
11	`Loop While a <> -1`	This evaluates to `False`
12	`Console.Write(p)`	The value 40 is displayed

As you can see, in the end, variable p contains the value 40, which is, indeed, the product of the values 2 × 4 × 5. Moreover, the final given value -1 does not participate in the final sum.

26.2   Review Questions: True/False

Choose **true** or **false** for each of the following statements.

1.   A post-test loop may perform zero iterations.

2.   A post-test loop stops iterating when its Boolean expression evaluates to `False`.

3.   In a post-test loop structure, when the statement or block of statements of the structure is executed N times, its Boolean expression is evaluated N times as well.

4.   You cannot nest a decision control structure inside a post-test loop structure.

5.   In the following code fragment

```
i = 1
Do
    Console.WriteLine("Hello")
Loop While i >= 10
```

the word "Hello" is displayed an infinite number of times.

8.   The following Visual Basic program

```
Sub Main()
    Dim i As Integer

    Do
        Console.WriteLine("Hello")
        i += 1
    Loop While i <= 10

    Console.ReadKey()
End Sub
```

satisfies the property of definiteness.

9.   The following Visual Basic program

```
Sub Main()
    Dim b As Integer
    Dim a As Double

    b = Console.ReadLine()
    Do
        a = 1 / (b - 1)
        b += 1
    Loop While b <= 10

    Console.ReadKey()
```

```
End Sub
```

does **not** satisfy the property of definiteness.

26.3 Review Questions: Multiple Choice

Select the correct answer for each of the following statements.

1. A post-test loop structure
    a. performs one iteration more than the pre-test loop structure does.
    b. always performs the same number of iterations as the pre-test loop structure does.
    c. none of the above

2. In a post-test loop structure, the statement or block of statements of the structure
    a. are executed before the loop's Boolean expression is evaluated.
    b. are executed after the loop's Boolean expression is evaluated.
    c. none of the above

3. In the following code fragment

```
i = 1
Do
   Console.WriteLine("Hello Poseidon")
   i += 1
Loop While i > 5
```

    the message "Hello Poseidon" is displayed
    a. 5 times.
    b. 1 time.
    c. 0 times.
    d. none of the above

4. In the following code fragment

```
i = 1
Do
   Console.WriteLine("Hello Athena")
   i += 5
Loop While i <> 50
```

    the message "Hello Athena" is displayed
    a. at least one time.
    b. at least 10 times.
    c. an infinite number of times.
    d. all of the above

5. In the following code fragment

```
i = 0
Do
   Console.WriteLine("Hello Apollo")
Loop While i > 10
```

    the message "Hello Apollo" is displayed

   a.   at least one time.

   b.   an infinite number of times.

   c.   none of the above

26.4   Review Exercises

Complete the following exercises.

1.   Identify the syntax error(s) in the following Visual Basic program.

```
Sub Main()
    Dim i As Integer = 3

    Loop
        i =- 1
    While i > 0
    Console.Write("The end")

    Console.ReadKey()
End Sub
```

2.   Create a trace table to determine the values of the variables in each step of the next Visual Basic program. How many iterations does this Visual Basic program perform?

```
Sub Main()
    Dim y, x As Integer

    y = 5
    x = 38
    Do
        y *= 2
        x += 1
        Console.WriteLine(y)
    Loop While y < x

    Console.ReadKey()
End Sub
```

3.   Create a trace table to determine the values of the variables in each step of the next Visual Basic program. How many iterations does this Visual Basic program perform?

```
Sub Main()
    Dim x As Integer

    x = 1
    Do
        If x Mod 2 = 0 Then
            x += 1
        Else
            x += 3
        End If
        Console.WriteLine(x)
    Loop While x < 12
```

```
        Console.ReadKey()
    End Sub
```

4. Create a trace table to determine the values of the variables in each step of the next Visual Basic program. How many iterations does this Visual Basic program perform?

```
Sub Main()
    Dim x, y As Double

    y = 2
    x = 0
    Do
        y = y ^ 2
        If x < 256 Then
            x = x + y
        End If
        Console.WriteLine(x & ", " & y)
    Loop While y < 65535

    Console.ReadKey()
End Sub
```

5. Create a trace table to determine the values of the variables in each step of the next Visual Basic program. How many iterations does this Visual Basic program perform?

```
Sub Main()
    Dim a, b, c, d, x As Integer

    a = 2
    b = 4
    c = 0
    d = 0
    Do
        x = a + b
        If x Mod 2 <> 0 Then
            c = c + 5
        ElseIf d Mod 2 = 0 Then
            d = d + 5
        Else
            c = c + 3
        End If
        a = b
        b = d
    Loop While c < 11

    Console.ReadKey()
End Sub
```

6. Fill in the gaps in the following code fragments so that all loops perform exactly six iterations.

i.
```
a = 5
Do
    a -= 1
Loop While a > ......
```

ii.
```
a = 12
Do
    a += 1
Loop While a < ......
```

iii.
```
a = 20
Do
    a = a + ......
Loop While a <> 23
```

iv.
```
a = 100
Do
    a -= 20
Loop While a <> ......
```

v.
```
a = 2
Do
    a = 2 * a
Loop While a <> ......
```

vi.
```
a = 10
Do
    a = a + 0.25
Loop While a <= ......
```

7. Fill in the gaps in the following code fragments so that all display the value 10 at the end.

i.
```
x = 0
y = 0
Do
    x += 1
    y += 2
Loop While x <= ......
Console.Write(y)
```

ii.
```
x = 1
y = 20
Do
    x -= 1
    y -= 2.5
Loop While x >= ......
Console.Write(y)
```

iii.
```
x = 3
y = 2.5
Do
    x -= 1
    y *= 2
Loop While x >= ......
Console.Write(y)
```

iv.
```
x = 30
y = 101532
Do
    x -= ......
    y = y \ 10
Loop While x >= 0
Console.Write(y)
```

8. Design a flowchart and write the corresponding Visual Basic program that lets the user enter 50 integers and then calculates and displays the sum of those that are odd and the sum of those that are even.

9. Write a Visual Basic program that lets the user enter N integers and then calculates and displays the product of those that are negative. The value of N should be given by the user at the beginning of the program, and the final product should always be displayed as a positive value. Assume that the user enters a value greater than 0 for N.

10. Write a Visual Basic program that prompts the user to enter five integers and then calculates and displays the product of all three-digit integers with a first digit of 5. For example, the values 512, 555, and 593 are all such numbers

    Hint: All three-digit integers with a first digit of 5 are between 500 and 599.

11. Write a Visual Basic program that prompts the user to enter positive numbers repeatedly until a non-positive one is entered. When data input is completed, the sum of the numbers entered should be displayed. (The last non-positive number

entered should not be included in the final sum.) Next, create a trace table to check if your program operates properly using 5, 2, 3, and 0 as input values.

12. The population of a beehive is now at 50000, but due to environmental reasons it is contracting at a rate of 10% per year. Write a Visual Basic program to determine how many years it will take for the population to be less than 20000.

Chapter 27
Counted Loop Structures

27.1 Counted Loop Structures

In Chapters 25 and 26, as you certainly noticed, both pre-test and post-test loop structures were used to iterate for a known but also for an unknown number of times. For example, both pre-test and post-test loop structures were used to

- ➢ find the sum of 10 given numbers. In this case, the total number of iterations was specific and known even before the loop started iterating.
- ➢ find the sum of some given numbers until the user entered the value -1. In this case, the total number of iterations was actually unknown before the loop started iterating.

A counted loop structure, though, can be used only when the number of iterations is known before the loop starts iterating.

The following flowchart is used when iteration for a specific number of times is required. A variable *counter* is used to control the total number of times the loop iterates.

The following flowchart fragment is given in general form.

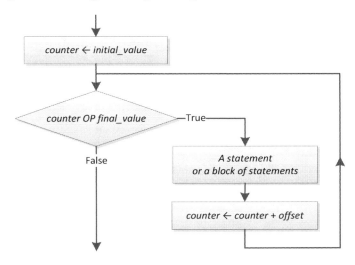

where

- ➢ *counter* must always be a variable
- ➢ *initial_value*, *final_value* and *offset* can be a constant value or even a variable or an expression. In case of a variable or an expression, however, the content or the result correspondingly must be invariable inside the loop.
- ➢ *OP* must be <= when *offset* is positive (or zero) and >= when *offset* is negative.

Let's see what happens when the flow of execution reaches a counted loop structure. An initial value is assigned to variable *counter* and if the Boolean expression evaluates to True, the statement or block of statements of the structure is executed. The variable *counter* is incremented (or decremented) by *offset* and the flow of execution goes back to the point just above the diamond symbol. If the Boolean expression evaluates to True again, the process repeats. When the Boolean expression evaluates to False, the flow of execution exits the loop.

> **Notice**: *A counted loop structure is actually a pre-test loop structure. Because of this, it may perform from zero to many iterations.*

Now let's see an example in which variable i increments from 1 to 11, allowing the loop to perform 10 iterations.

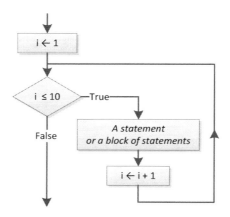

When the flow of execution reaches the counted loop structure, the initial value 1 is assigned to variable i, the Boolean expression evaluates to True, and the statement or block of statements of the structure is executed. The variable i increments by one and the flow of execution goes back to the point just above the diamond symbol. The Boolean expression evaluates to True again and the process repeats. When, after 10 iterations, the value of variable i becomes 11, the Boolean expression evaluates to False and the flow of execution exits the loop.

> **Notice**: *Please note that the flow of execution exits the loop when the value of* counter *(variable* i*) actually exceeds* final_value*. In this example, when the flow of execution does finally exit the loop, counter* i *does not contain the final value 10 but the next one in order, which is the value 11.*

Of course, you can create counted loop structures using the Do While-Loop or even the Do-Loop While statement. However, since counted loop structures are so frequently used in computer programming, almost every computer language, including Visual Basic, incorporates a special statement that is much more readable and convenient than the Do While-Loop and Do Loop-While statements—and this is the For statement.

In accordance with previous flowchart fragment, the general form of the For statement, is

```
For counter = initial_value To final_value [ Step offset ]
    A statement or block of statements
Next
```

> **Notice**: *Please note that* offset *is optional. When offset is +1, you can omit the* Step *offset part.*

> **Notice**: *You don't have to increment or decrement the* counter *variable inside the loop because it is automatically done at the end of each loop iteration.*
>
> **Notice:** *Don't ever dare alter the value of* counter *inside the loop! The same applies to* initial_value, final_value, *and* offset *(in case they are variables and not constant values). This makes your code unreadable and could lead to incorrect results. If you insist, though, please use a* Do While-Loop *or a* Do-Loop While *statement instead.*

The following example displays the numbers 1 to 10.

```
project_27_1a
Sub Main()
  Dim i As Integer

  For i = 1 To 10 Step 1
    Console.WriteLine(i)
  Next

  Console.ReadKey()
End Sub
```

Of course, when variable *counter* increments by 1 (*offset* = 1), you can omit the Step 1 part. The previous example can also be written as

```
project_27_1b
Sub Main()
  Dim i As Integer

  For i = 1 To 10
    Console.WriteLine(i)
  Next

  Console.ReadKey()
End Sub
```

The following example displays even numbers from 10 to 2.

```
project_27_1c
Sub Main()
  Dim i As Integer

  For i = 10 To 2 Step -2
    Console.WriteLine(i)
  Next

  Console.ReadKey()
End Sub
```

Exercise 27.1-1   *Designing the Flowchart and Creating the Trace Table*

Design the corresponding flowchart and create a trace table to determine the values of the variables in each step of the next Visual Basic program when the input value 1 is entered.

```
Sub Main()
```

```
    Dim a, i As Integer

    a = Console.ReadLine()

    For i = -3 To 3 Step 2
      a = a * 3
    Next
    Console.Write(i & ", " & a)

    Console.ReadKey()
  End Sub
```

Solution

The corresponding flowchart is as follows.

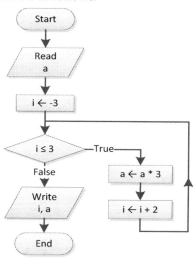

> **Notice:** You should keep in mind that a counted loop structure is actually a pre-test loop structure!

If you rewrite the program using the Do While-Loop statement the result is as follows.

```
Sub Main()
  Dim a, i As Integer

  a = Console.ReadLine()

  i = -3
  Do While i <= 3
    a = a * 3
    i += 2
  Loop

  Console.Write(i & ", " & a)

  Console.ReadKey()
```

```
End Sub
```

Now, in order to create a trace table for a `For` statement you have two choices: you can use either the corresponding flowchart or the equivalent program written with the `Do While-Loop` statement.

Step	Statement	Notes	a	i	
1	a = Console.ReadLine()		1	?	
2	i = -3		1	-3	
3	i <= 3	This evaluates to True			
4	a = a * 3		3	-3	1st Iteration
5	i += 2		3	-1	
6	i <= 3	This evaluates to True			
7	a = a * 3		9	-1	2nd Iteration
8	i += 2		9	1	
9	i <= 3	This evaluates to True			
10	a = a * 3		27	1	3rd Iteration
11	i += 2		27	3	
12	i <= 3	This evaluates to True			
13	a = a * 3		81	3	4th Iteration
14	i += 2		81	5	
15	i <= 3	This evaluates to False			
16	Console.Write(i & ", " & a)	The values 5, 81 are displayed			

> *Notice: Please note that the flow of execution exits the loop when the value of counter* `i` *exceeds* `final_value`. *In this example, when the flow of execution does finally exit the loop, counter* `i` *does not contain the final value 3 but the next one in order, which is the value 5.*

Exercise 27.1-2   *Creating the Trace Table*

Create a trace table to determine the values of the variables in each step of the next Visual Basic program when the input value 4 is entered.

```
Sub Main()
  Dim a, i As Integer

  a = Console.ReadLine()

  For i = 6 To a Step -1
    Console.WriteLine(i)
  Next
```

```
      Console.ReadKey()
    End Sub
```

Solution

Once again the program can be rewritten using the Do While-Loop statement.

```
Sub Main()
  Dim a, i As Integer

  a = Console.ReadLine()

  i = 6
  Do While i >= a
    Console.WriteLine(i)
    i -= 1
  Loop

  Console.ReadKey()
End Sub
```

Following is the trace table used to determine the values of the variables in each step.

Step	Statement	Notes	a	i
1	a = Console.ReadLine()		4	?
2	i = 6		4	6
3	i >= a	This evaluates to True		
4	Console.WriteLine(i)	The value 6 is displayed		
5	i -= 1		4	5
6	i >= a	This evaluates to True		
7	Console.WriteLine(i)	The value 5 is displayed		
8	i -= 1		4	4
9	i >= a	This evaluates to True		
10	Console.WriteLine(i)	The value 4 is displayed		
11	i -= 1		4	3
12	i >= a	This evaluates to False		

Exercise 27.1-3   Counting the Total Number of Iterations

Count the total number of iterations performed by the following code fragment for two different executions.

The input values for the two executions are: (i) 5, and (ii) 6.

```
n = Console.ReadLine()
For i = 5 To n
  Console.WriteLine(i)
```

```
Next
```

Solution

In order to better understand what really goes on, instead of creating a trace table, you can just design its corresponding flowchart fragment.

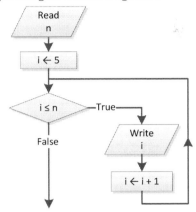

From this flowchart fragment you can see that

i. for the input value 5, the Boolean expression evaluates to True and the flow of execution enters the loop. Variable i increases to 6, the Boolean expression evaluates to False, and the flow of execution exits the loop. Thus, the loop performs one iteration.

ii. for the input value 6 the loop obviously performs two iterations.

Exercise 27.1-4   *Finding the Sum of 10 Numbers*

Write a Visual Basic program that prompts the user enter 10 numbers and then calculates and displays their sum.

Solution

In Chapter 25, the solution proposed with a Do While-Loop statement was the following:

```
Sub Main()
  Dim i As Integer
  Dim sum, a As Double

  sum = 0

  i = 1
  Do While i <= 10
    a = Console.ReadLine()
    sum = sum + a

    i += 1
  Loop

  Console.Write(sum)
```

```
    Console.ReadKey()
End Sub
```

It's now very easy to rewrite it using a `For` statement and have it display a prompt message before every data input.

```
                         project_27_1_4
Sub Main()
    Dim i As Integer
    Dim sum, a As Double

    sum = 0

    For i = 1 To 10
        Console.Write("Enter a number: ")
        a = Console.ReadLine()
        sum = sum + a
    Next

    Console.Write(sum)

    Console.ReadKey()
End Sub
```

> **Notice:** Please note the absence of the `i = i + 1` statement inside the loop control structure. In a `For` statement, `counter` (variable `i`) automatically increases, either way, at the end of each loop iteration.

Exercise 27.1-5   *Finding the Square Roots from 0 to N*

Write a Visual Basic program that prompts the user to enter an integer and then calculates and displays the square root of all integers from 0 to that given integer.

Solution

In this exercise the counted loop structure should increase the value of variable `counter`, starting from 0, until it reaches the given value. The Visual Basic program is as follows.

```
                         project_27_1_5
Sub Main()
    Dim num, i As Integer

    Console.Write("Enter an integer: ")
    num = Console.ReadLine()

    For i = 0 To num
        Console.WriteLine(Math.Sqrt(i))
    Next

    Console.ReadKey()
End Sub
```

27.2 Rules that Apply to Counted Loop Structures

There are certain rules you should always follow when writing programs with counted loop structures, since they can save you from undesirable side effects.

> **Rule 1**: The `counter` variable can appear in a statement inside the loop but its value should never be altered. The same applies to `initial_value`, `final_value`, and `offset` in case they are variables and not constant values.

> **Rule 2**: The `offset` should never be zero. If it is set to zero, the loop performs an infinite number of iterations!

> **Rule 3**: If `initial_value` is smaller than `final_value` and the `offset` is negative, the loop performs zero iterations. Breaking this rule on purpose, however, can be useful in certain situations.

> **Rule 4**: If `initial_value` is greater than `final_value` and the `offset` is positive, the loop performs zero iterations. Breaking this rule on purpose, however, can be useful in certain situations.

Exercise 27.2-1   *Counting the Total Number of Iterations*

How many iterations does the following code fragment perform?

```
For i = 5 To 10
  Console.WriteLine(i)
  i -= 1
Next
```

Solution

This program breaks the first rule of counted loop structures, which states, *The counter variable can appear in a statement inside the loop but its value should never be altered.*

The corresponding flowchart fragment that follows can help you better understand what really goes on.

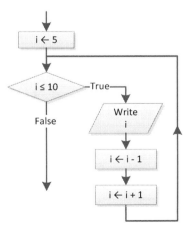

As you can see, since the initial value 5 of variable i is less than 10, the flow of execution enters the loop. Inside the loop, however, the statement i ← i - 1 eliminates the statement i ← i + 1 and this results in a non-incrementing variable i, which can never reach *final_value* 10. Thus, the loop performs an infinite number of iterations.

> **Remember!** *You should never alter the value of* counter *variable inside the loop. The same applies to* initial_value, final_value, *and* offset *(in case they are variables and not constant values).*

Exercise 27.2-2   *Counting the Total Number of Iterations*

How many iterations does the following code fragment perform?

```
For i = 5 To 10 Step 0
  Console.WriteLine(i)
Next
```

Solution

This program breaks the second rule of counted loop structures, which states, *The* offset *should never be zero.*

The corresponding flowchart fragment that follows can help you better understand what really goes on.

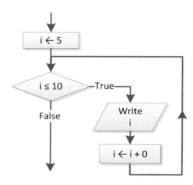

As you can see, since the initial value 5 of variable i is less than 10, the flow of execution enters the loop. However, the statement i ← i + 0 never increments variable i and this results in a non-incrementing variable i, which can never reach final_value 10. Thus, the loop performs an infinite number of iterations.

> **Remember!** *The* offset *should never be zero.*

Exercise 27.2-3   *Counting the Total Number of Iterations*

How many iterations does the following code fragment perform?

```
For i = 5 To 10 Step -1
  Console.WriteLine(i)
Next
```

Solution

This program breaks the third rule of counted loop structures, which states, *If* initial_value *is smaller than* final_value *and the* offset *is negative, the loop performs zero iterations.*

The corresponding flowchart fragment that follows can help you better understand what really goes on.

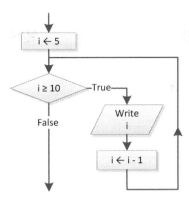

When the flow of execution reaches the loop control structure, the value 5 is assigned to variable i. However, the Boolean expression evaluates to False and the flow of execution never enters the loop! Thus, the loop performs zero iterations.

> **Remember!** Breaking the third rule of counted loop structures on purpose can be useful in certain situations.

Exercise 27.2-4   *Counting the Total Number of Iterations*

How many iterations does the following code fragment perform?

```
For i = 10 To 5
  Console.WriteLine(i)
Next
```

Solution

This program breaks the fourth rule of counted loop structures, which states, *If* initial_value *is greater than* final_value *and the* offset *is positive, the loop performs zero iterations.*

The corresponding flowchart fragment that follows can help you better understand what really goes on.

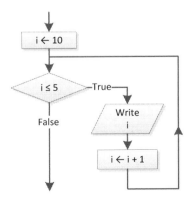

> **Remember!** If you omit the keyword Step, the offset is set to +1 by default.

When the flow of execution reaches the loop control structure, the value 10 is assigned to variable i. However, the Boolean expression evaluates to False and the flow of execution never enters the loop! Thus, the loop performs zero iterations.

> **Notice:** Breaking the fourth rule of counted loop structures on purpose can be useful in certain situations.

Exercise 27.2-5   *Finding the Average Value of N Numbers*

Write a Visual Basic program that prompts the user to enter N numbers and then calculates and displays their average value. The value of N should be given by the user at the beginning of the program. Add all necessary checks to make the program satisfy the property of definiteness.

Solution

The solution is presented next.

```
project_27_2_5
Sub Main()
  Dim n, i As Integer
  Dim a, sum, average As Double

  Console.Write("Enter quantity of numbers to enter: ")
  n = Console.ReadLine()

  sum = 0
  For i = 1 To n
    Console.WriteLine("Enter number No " & i & ": ")
    a = Console.ReadLine()
    sum = sum + a
  Next

  If n > 0 Then
    average = sum / n
    Console.WriteLine("The average value is: " & average)
  Else
    Console.WriteLine("You didn't enter any number!")
  End If

  Console.ReadKey()
End Sub
```

> **Notice:** Please note that if the user enters a non-positive value for variable n, the For statement performs zero iterations. Even though it breaks the fourth rule of counted loop structures, in this particular exercise, this situation is very useful.

> **Notice:** *The* If n > 0 *statement, next to the loop control structure, is necessary because if the user enters the value 0 for variable* n, *the program avoids any division-by-zero errors, thereby satisfying the property of definiteness.*

27.3   Review Questions: True/False

Choose **true** or **false** for each of the following statements.

1. In a counted loop structure, the value of `counter` increments or decrements automatically at the end of each loop.

2. A counted loop structure can be used when the number of iterations is known.

3. In a counted loop structure, the statement or block of statements of the loop is executed at least one time.

4. In a counted loop structure, the `initial_value` cannot be greater than the `final_value`.

5. When flow of execution exits a counted loop structure, the value of `counter` is equal to `final_value`.

6. In a counted loop structure, the value of `initial_value`, `final_value` and `offset` can be either an integer or a float.

7. The only case in which a counted loop structure does not satisfy the property of finiteness is when `offset` is set to zero.

8. In a counted loop structure, the `counter` variable can appear in a statement inside the loop but its value should never be altered.

9. In a counted loop structure, the `offset` can be zero for certain situations.

10. In the following code fragment

    ```
    For i = 0 To 10
       Console.WriteLine("Hello")
    Next
    ```

    the word "Hello" is displayed 10 times.

11. The following code fragment

    ```
    b = Console.ReadLine()
    For i = 0 To 10 Step b
       Console.WriteLine("Hello")
    Next
    ```

    satisfies the property of finiteness.

12. The following code fragment

    ```
    Dim b, i As Integer
    Dim a As Double

    b = Console.ReadLine()
    For i = 0 To 10
       a = Math.Sqrt(b) + i
       b *= 2
    Next
    ```

    satisfies the property of definiteness.

27.4   Review Questions: Multiple Choice

Select the correct answer for each of the following statements.

1. A counted loop structure
    a. executes one iteration more than the equivalent post-test loop structure does.
    b. executes one iteration less than the equivalent post-test loop structure does.
    c. none of the above

2. A counted loop structure can be used in a problem in which
    a. the user enters numbers repeatedly until the value −1 is entered.
    b. the user enters numbers repeatedly until the value entered is greater than *final_value*.
    c. all of the above
    d. none of the above

3. In a counted loop structure *initial_value*, *final_value*, and *offset* can be
    a. a constant value.
    b. a variable.
    c. an expression.
    d. all of the above

4. In a counted loop structure, when *initial_value*, *final_value*, and *offset* are variables, their values
    a. cannot change inside the loop.
    b. should not change inside the loop.
    c. none of the above

5. In a counted loop structure, when *counter* increments, the *offset* should be
    a. greater than zero.
    b. equal to zero.
    c. less than zero.
    d. none of the above

6. In a counted loop structure, the initial value of *counter*
    a. must be 1.
    b. can be 1.
    c. cannot be a negative one.
    d. none of the above

7. In a counted loop structure, the variable *counter* increments or decrements automatically
    a. at the end of each iteration.
    b. at the beginning of each iteration.
    c. It does not increment automatically.
    d. none of the above

8. In the following code fragment

```
i = 1
For i = 5 To 5
  Console.WriteLine("Hello Hera")
Next
```

the message "Hello Hera" is displayed

    a. 5 times.

    b. 1 time.

    c. 0 times.

    d. none of the above

9. In the following code fragment

```
For i = 5 To 4
  i = 1
  Console.WriteLine("Hello Artemis")
Next
```

the message "Hello Artemis" is displayed

    a. 1 time.

    b. an infinite number of times.

    c. 0 times.

    d. none of the above

10. In the following code fragment

```
For i = 5 To 5
  i = 1
  Console.WriteLine("Hello Ares")
Next
```

the message "Hello Ares" is displayed

    a. 1 time.

    b. an infinite number of times.

    c. 0 times.

    d. none of the above

11. In the following code fragment

```
For i = 2 To 8
  If i Mod 2 = 0 Then
    Console.WriteLine("Hello Demeter")
  End If
Next
```

the message "Hello Demeter" is displayed

    a. 8 times.

    b. 7 times.

    c. 5 times.

    d. none of the above

12. In the following code fragment

```
For i = 4 To 5 Step 0.1
```

```
    Console.WriteLine("Hello Dionysus")
Next
```

the message "Hello Dionysus" is displayed

  a. 1 time.

  b. 2 times.

  c. 10 times.

  d. 11 times.

13. In the following code fragment

```
k = 0
For i = 1 To 5 Step 2
  k = k + i
Next
Console.WriteLine(i)
```

the value displayed is

  a. 3.

  b. 6.

  c. 9.

  d. none of the above

14. In the following code fragment

```
k = 0
For i = 100 To -100 Step -5
  k = k + i
Next
Console.WriteLine(i)
```

the value displayed is

  a. -95.

  b. -100.

  c. -105.

  d. none of the above

27.5 Review Exercises

Complete the following exercises.

  1. Create a trace table to determine the values of the variables in each step of the next Visual Basic program. How many iterations does this Visual Basic program perform?

```
Sub Main()
    Dim a, b, j As Integer

    a = 0
    b = 0
    For j = 0 To 8 Step 2
        If j < 5 Then
            b += 1
        Else
            a += j - 1
```

```
        End If
    Next
    Console.Write(a & ", " & b)

    Console.ReadKey()
End Sub
```

2. Create a trace table to determine the values of the variables in each step of the next Visual Basic program for two different executions.

    The input values for the two executions are: (i) 10, and (ii) 21.

```
Sub Main()
    Dim a, b, j As Integer

    a = Console.ReadLine()
    b = a
    For j = a - 5 To a Step 2
        If j Mod 2 <> 0 Then
            b = a + j + 5
        Else
            b = a - j
        End If
    Next
    Console.Write(b)

    Console.ReadKey()
End Sub
```

3. Create a trace table to determine the values of the variables in each step of the next Visual Basic program for the input value 12.

```
Sub Main()
    Dim a, j, x, y As Integer

    a = Console.ReadLine()
    For j = 2 To a - 1 Step 3
        x = j * 3 + 3
        y = j * 2 + 10
        If y - x > 0 Or x > 30 Then
            y *= 2
        End If
        x += 4
        Console.WriteLine(x & ", " & y)
    Next

    Console.ReadKey()
End Sub
```

4. Fill in the gaps in the following code fragments so that all loops perform exactly five iterations.

    i.
```
For a = 5 To ......
    b += 1
Next
```

ii.
```
For a = 0 To ...... Step 0.5
    b += 1
Next
```

iii.
```
For a = ...... To -15 Step -2
    b += 1
Next
```

iv.
```
For a = -11 To -15 Step ......
    b += 1
Next
```

5. Design a flowchart and write the corresponding Visual Basic program that prompts the user to enter 20 numbers and then calculates and displays their product and their average value.

6. Write a Visual Basic program that prompts the user to enter a number in degrees and then calculates and displays the sinus of all numbers from 0 to that given number, using an offset of 0.5. It is given that $2\pi = 360°$.

7. Design a flowchart and write the corresponding Visual Basic program that prompts the user to enter 30 four-digit integers and then calculates and displays the sum of those with a first digit of 5 and a last digit of 3. For example, values 5003, 5923, and 5553 are all such integers.

8. Design a flowchart and write the corresponding Visual Basic program that prompts the user to enter N integers and then displays the total number of those that are even. The value of N should be given by the user at the beginning of the program. Moreover, if all integers given are odd, the message "You entered no even integers" should be displayed.

9. Design a flowchart and write the corresponding Visual Basic program that prompts the user to enter 50 integers and then calculates and displays the average value of those that are odd and the average value of those that are even.

10. Design a flowchart and write the corresponding Visual Basic program that prompts the user to enter two integers into variables start and finish and then displays all integers from start to finish. However, at the beginning the program should check if variable start is bigger than variable finish. If this happens, the program should swap their values so that they are always in the proper order.

11. Design a flowchart and write the corresponding Visual Basic program that prompts the user to enter two integers into variables start and finish and then displays all integers from start to finish that are multiples of five. However, at the beginning the program should check if variable start is bigger than variable finish. If this happens, the program should swap their values so that they are always in the proper order.

12. Write a Visual Basic program that prompts the user to enter a real and an integer and then displays the result of the first number raised to the power of the second number, without using the exponentiation operator (^).

13. Write a Visual Basic program that prompts the user to enter a message and then displays the number of words it contains. For example, if the string entered is "My name is Bill Bouras", the program should display "The message entered

contains 5 words". Assume that the words are separated by a single space character.

Hint: Use the .Length property to get the number of characters that the given message contains.

14. Write a Visual Basic program that prompts the user to enter any string and then displays the average number of letters in each word. For example, if the string entered is "My name is Aphrodite Boura", the program should display "The average number of letters in each word is 4.4". Space characters should not be counted.

Chapter 28
Nested Loop Control Structures

28.1   What is a Nested Loop?

A nested loop is a loop within another loop or, in other words, an inner loop within an outer one.

The outer loop controls the number of complete iterations of the inner loop, which means that the first iteration of the outer loop triggers the inner loop to start iterating until completion. Then the second iteration of the outer loop triggers the inner loop to start iterating until completion again. This process repeats until the outer loop has performed all of its iterations.

Take the following Visual Basic program, for example.

```
                          project_28_1
For i = 1 To 2
  For j = 1 To 3
    Console.WriteLine(i & " " & j)          Nested loop
  Next
Next
```

The outer loop, the one that is controlled by variable i, controls the number of complete iterations that the inner loop performs. That is, when variable i contains the value 1, the inner loop performs three iterations (for j = 1, j = 2, and j = 3). The inner loop finishes but the outer loop needs to perform one more iteration (for i = 2), so the inner loop starts over and performs three new iterations again (for j = 1, j = 2 and j = 3).

The previous example can be likened to the following one.

```
Dim j, i As Integer

i = 1                          'outer loop assigns value 1 to variable i
For j = 1 To 3                 'and inner loop performs three iterations
   Console.WriteLine(i & " " & j)
Next

i = 2                          'outer loop assigns value 2 to variable i
For j = 1 To 3                 'and inner loop starts over and
   Console.WriteLine(i & " " & j)   'performs three new iterations
Next
```

The output result is as follows.

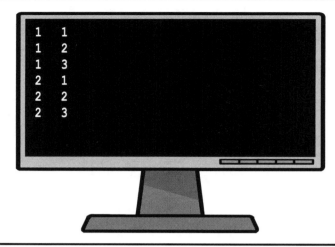

Remember! *As long as the syntax rules are not violated, you can nest as many loop control structures as you wish. For practical reasons however, as you move to four or five levels of nesting, the entire loop structure becomes very complex and difficult to understand. However, experience shows that the maximum levels of nesting that you will do in your entire life as a programmer is probably three or four.*

Notice: *There is no need for the inner and outer loops to be of the same type. For example, a* For *statement may nest (enclose) a* Do While-Loop *statement, or vice versa.*

Exercise 28.1-1   *Say "Hello Zeus". Designing the Flowchart and Counting the Total Number of Iterations*

Design the corresponding flowchart for the next code fragment, and find the number of times message "Hello Zeus" is displayed.

project_28_1_1

```
For i = 1 To 4
  For j = 1 To 3
    Console.WriteLine("Hello Zeus")
  Next
Next
```

Solution

The corresponding flowchart is as follows. The inner loop is marked with a dashed rectangle.

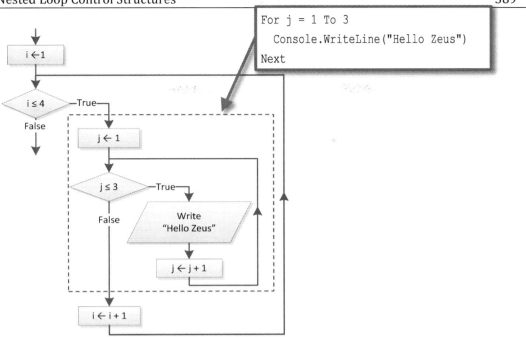

```
For j = 1 To 3
    Console.WriteLine("Hello Zeus")
Next
```

Now, let's try to count the number of times message "Hello Zeus" is displayed. By studying the corresponding flowchart you can see that the values of variables i and j (in order of appearance) are as follows:

> For i = 1, the inner loop performs 3 iterations (for j = 1, j = 2, and j = 3) and the message "Hello Zeus" is displayed 3 times.

> For i = 2, the inner loop performs 3 iterations (for j = 1, j = 2, and j = 3) and the message "Hello Zeus" is displayed 3 times.

> For i = 3, the inner loop performs 3 iterations (for j = 1, j = 2, and j = 3) and the message "Hello Zeus" is displayed 3 times.

> For i = 4, the inner loop performs 3 iterations (for j = 1, j = 2, and j = 3) and the message "Hello Zeus" is displayed 3 times.

Therefore, the message "Hello Zeus" is displayed a total of 4 × 3 = 12 times.

Remember! The outer loop controls the number of complete iterations of the inner one!

Exercise 28.1-2   *Creating the Trace Table*

Design the corresponding flowchart for the next code fragment, and determine the value that variable a *contains at the end.*

```
a = 1
i = 5
Do While i < 7
    For j = 1 To 3 Step 2
        a = a * j + i
    Next
    i += 1
Loop
```

```
Console.Write(a)
```

Solution

Following is the corresponding flowchart. The inner loop is marked with a dashed rectangle.

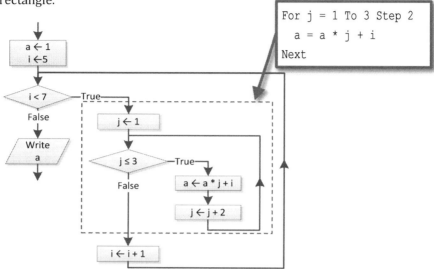

With the help of the flowchart you can now create the following trace table.

Step	Statement	Notes	a	i	j
1	a = 1		1	?	?
2	i = 5		1	5	?
3	i < 7	This evaluates to True			
4	j = 1		1	5	1
5	j <= 3	This evaluates to True			
6	a = a * j + i		6	5	1
7	j = j + 2		6	5	3
8	j <= 3	This evaluates to True			
9	a = a * j + i		23	5	3
10	j = j + 2		23	5	5
11	j <= 3	This evaluates to False			
12	i = i + 1		23	6	5
13	i < 7	This evaluates to True			
14	j = 1		23	6	1
15	j <= 3	This evaluates to True			
16	a = a * j + i		29	6	1

17	j = j + 2		29	6	3
18	j <= 3	This evaluates to True			
19	a = a * j + i		93	6	3
20	j = j + 2		93	6	5
21	j <= 3	This evaluates to False			
22	i = i + 1		93	7	5
23	i < 7	This evaluates to False			
24	Console.Write(a)	The value 93 is displayed			

At the end of the program, variable a contains the value 93.

28.2 Rules that Apply to Nested Loops

Beyond the four rules that apply to counted loop structures, there are two extra rules that you should always follow when writing programs with nested loops, since they can save you from undesirable side effects.

➢ **Rule 1**: The inner loop must begin and end entirely within the outer loop, which means that the loops must not overlap.

➢ **Rule 2**: An outer loop and the inner (nested) loop must not use the same *counter* variable.

Exercise 28.2-1 *Breaking the First Rule*

Design a flowchart fragment that breaks the first rule of nested loops, which states, "The inner loop must begin and end entirely within the outer loop."

Solution

The following flowchart fragment breaks the first rule of nested loops.

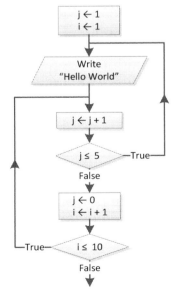

If you try to follow the flow of execution, you can see how smoothly it performs 5 × 10 = 50 iterations. No one can tell that this flowchart is wrong; on the contrary, it is absolutely correct. The problem, however, is that this flowchart is completely unreadable. No one can tell, at first glance, what this flowchart really does. Moreover, this structure matches none of the already known loop control structures that you have been taught, so it cannot become a Visual Basic program as is. Try to avoid this kind of nested loop!

Exercise 28.2-2   *Counting the Total Number of Iterations*

Find the number of times message "Hello" is displayed.

```
For i = 1 To 3
  For i = 5 To 1 Step -1
    Console.WriteLine("Hello")
  Next
Next
```

Solution

This program breaks the second rule of nested loops, which states, "*An outer loop and the inner (nested) loop must not use the same* counter *variable.*"

At first glance, one would think that the word "Hello" is displayed 3 × 5 = 15 times. However, a closer second look reveals that things are not always as they seem. Let's design the corresponding flowchart.

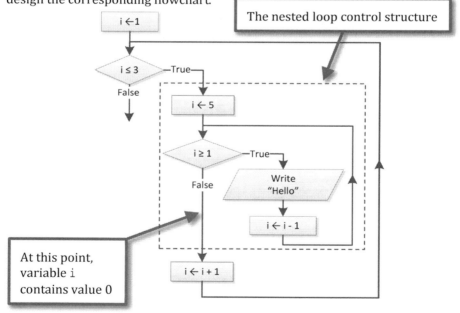

If you try to follow the flow of execution in this flowchart fragment, you can see that when the inner loop completes all of its four iterations, variable i contains the value 0. Then, variable i increments by 1 and the outer loop repeats again. This process can continue forever since variable i can never exceed the value 3 that the Boolean expression of the outer loop requires. Therefore, the message "Hello" is displayed an infinite number of times.

28.3 Review Questions: True/False

Choose **true** or **false** for each of the following statements.

1. A nested loop is an inner loop within an outer one.

2. The maximum number of levels of nesting in a loop control structure is four.

3. When two loop control structures are nested one within the other, the loop that starts last should complete first.

4. When two loop control structures are nested one within the other, they must not use the same variable as *counter*.

5. In the following code fragment

```
For i = 1 To 3
  For j = 1 To 3
    Console.WriteLine("Hello")
  Next
Next
```

the word "Hello" is displayed six times.

6. In the following code fragment

```
For i = 1 To 2
  For j = 1 To 3
    For k = 1 To 4 Step 2
      Console.WriteLine("Hello")
    Next
  Next
Next
```

the word "Hello" is displayed 12 times.

7. In the following code fragment

```
For i = 1 To 3
  For i = 3 To 1 Step -1
    Console.WriteLine("Hello")
  Next
Next
```

the word "Hello" is displayed an infinite number of times.

8. In the following code fragment

```
For i = 1 To 3
  j = 1
  Do
    Console.WriteLine("Hello")
    j += 1
  Loop While j < 4
Next
```

the word "Hello" is displayed nine times.

28.4 Review Questions: Multiple Choice

Select the correct answer for each of the following statements.

1. In the following code fragment

```
For i = 1 To 2
```

```
   For j = 1 To 2
      Console.WriteLine("Hello")
   Next
Next
```

the values of variables i and j (in order of appearance) are

    a.   j = 1, i = 1, j = 1, i = 2, j = 2, i = 1, j = 2, i = 2

    b.   i = 1, j = 1, i = 1, j = 2, i = 2, j = 1, i = 2, j = 2

    c.   i = 1, j = 1, i = 2, j = 2

    d.   j = 1, i = 1, j = 2, i = 2

2.   In the following code fragment

```
x = 2
Do While x > -2
   Do
      x -= 1
      Console.WriteLine("Hello Hestia")
   Loop While x < -2
Loop
```

the message "Hello Hestia" is displayed

    a.   4 times.

    b.   an infinite number of times.

    c.   0 times.

    d.   none of the above

3.   In the following code fragment

```
x = 1
Do While x <> 500
   For i = x To 3
      Console.WriteLine("Hello Artemis")
   Next
   x += 1
Loop
```

the message "Hello Artemis" is displayed

    a.   an infinite number of times.

    b.   1500 times.

    c.   6 times.

    d.   none of the above

4.   The following code fragment

```
For i = 1 To 3
   For j = 1 To i
      Console.Write(i * j & ", ")
   Next
Next
Console.Write("The End!")
```

displays

    a.   1, 2, 4, 3, 6, 9, The End!

       b.   1, 2, 3, 4, 6, 9, The End!

       c.   1, 2, The End!, 4, 3, The End!, 6, 9, The End!

       d.   none of the above

5.   The following code fragment

```
For i = 1 To 10
  For i = 10 To 1 Step -1
    Console.WriteLine("Hello Dionysus")
  Next
Next
```

does **not** satisfy the property of

       a.   definiteness.

       b.   finiteness.

       c.   effectiveness.

       d.   none of the above

28.5 Review Exercises

Complete the following exercises.

1.   Fill in the gaps in the following code fragments so that all code fragments display the message "Hello Hephaestus" exactly 100 times.

    i.
```
For a = 7 To ......
  For b = 1 To 25
    Console.WriteLine("Hello Hephaestus")
  Next
Next
```

    ii.
```
For a = 0 To ...... Step 0.5
  For b = 10 To 19
    Console.WriteLine("Hello Hephaestus")
  Next
Next
```

    iii.
```
For a = ...... To -15 Step -2
  For b = 10 To 0.5 Step -0.5
    Console.WriteLine("Hello Hephaestus")
  Next
Next
```

    iv.
```
For a = -11 To -15 Step -1
  For b = 100 To ...... Step 2
    Console.WriteLine("Hello Hephaestus")
  Next
Next
```

2.   Design the corresponding flowchart and create a trace table to determine the values of the variables in each step of the next code fragment.

```
a = 1
For j = 1 To 2 Step 0.5
  i = 10
  Do While i < 30
```

```
    a = a + j + i
    i += 10
  Loop
Next
Console.Write(a)
```

3. Create a trace table to determine the values of the variables in each step of the next code fragment. How many times is the statement s = s + i * j executed?

```
s = 0
For i = 1 To 4
  For j = 3 To i Step -1
    s = s + i * j
  Next
Next
Console.Write(s)
```

4. Create a trace table to determine the values of the variables in each step of the next Visual Basic program for three different executions. How many iterations does this Visual Basic program perform?

The input values for the three executions are: (i) NO, (ii) YES, NO; and (iii) YES, YES, NO.

```
Sub Main()
    Dim s, y, i As Integer
    Dim ans As String

    s = 1
    y = 25
    Do
        For i = 1 To 3
            s = s + y
            y -= 5
        Next
        ans = Console.ReadLine()
    Loop While ans = "YES"
    Console.Write(s)

    Console.ReadKey()
End Sub
```

5. Write a Visual Basic program that displays an hours and minutes table in the following form.

0	0
0	1
0	2
0	3
...	
0	59
1	0
1	1

1	2
1	3
...	
23	59

Please note that the output is aligned with tabs.

6. Using nested loop control structures, write a Visual Basic program that displays the following output.

5 5 5 5 5

4 4 4 4

3 3 3

2 2

1

7. Using nested loop control structures, write a Visual Basic program that displays the following output.

0

0 1

0 1 2

0 1 2 3

0 1 2 3 4

0 1 2 3 4 5

8. Using nested loop control structures, write a Visual Basic program that displays the following rectangle.

```
*   *   *   *   *   *   *   *   *   *

*   *   *   *   *   *   *   *   *   *

*   *   *   *   *   *   *   *   *   *

*   *   *   *   *   *   *   *   *   *
```

9. Write a Visual Basic program that prompts the user to enter an integer N between 3 and 20 and then displays a square of size N on each side. For example, if the user enters 4 for N, the program should display as shown here.

```
*   *   *   *

*   *   *   *

*   *   *   *

*   *   *   *
```

10. Write a Visual Basic program that prompts the user to enter an integer N between 3 and 20 and then displays a hollow square of size N on each side. For example, if the user enters 4 for N, the program should display as shown here.

```
*   *   *   *

*           *

*           *

*   *   *   *
```

11. Using nested loop control structures, write a Visual Basic program that displays the following triangle.

```
*
*   *
*   *   *
*   *   *   *
*   *   *   *   *
*   *   *   *
*   *   *
*   *
*
```

Chapter 29
Tips and Tricks with Loop Control Structures

29.1 Introduction

This chapter is dedicated to teaching you some useful tips and tricks that can help you write "better" code. You should always keep them in mind when you design your own algorithms, or even your own Visual Basic programs.

These tips and tricks can help you increase your code's readability, help you choose which loop control structure is better to use in each given problem, and help make the code shorter or even faster. Of course there is no single perfect methodology because on one occasion the use of a specific tip or trick may help, but on another occasion the same tip or trick may have exactly the opposite result. Most of the time, code optimization is a matter of programming experience.

> **Remember!** Smaller algorithms are not always the best solution to a given problem. In order to solve a specific problem, you might write a very short algorithm that unfortunately proves to consume a lot of CPU time. On the other hand, you may solve the same problem with another algorithm which, even though it seems longer, calculates the result much faster.

29.2 Choosing a Loop Control Structure

The following diagram can help you choose which loop control structure is better to use in each given problem, depending on the number of iterations.

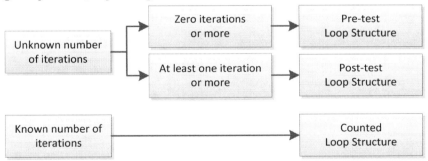

> **Notice:** This diagram recommends the best option, not the only option. For example, when the number of iterations is known, it is not wrong to use a pre-test or a post-test loop structure instead. The proposed counted loop structure, though, is better since it is more convenient.

29.3 The "Ultimate" Rule

One question that often preys on programmers' minds when using pre-test or post-test loop structures, is how to determine which statements should be written inside, and which outside, the loop control structure and in which order.

There is one simple yet powerful rule—the "Ultimate" rule! Once you follow it, the potential for making a logic error is reduced to zero!

The "Ultimate" rule states:

> ➢ The variable or variables that participate in a loop's Boolean expression should be initialized before entering the loop.

> ➢ The value of the variable or variables that participate in a loop's Boolean expression should be updated (altered) within the loop and just before the loop's Boolean expression is evaluated.

For example, if variable x is the variable that participates in a loop's Boolean expression, a pre-test loop structure should always be in the following form,

```
initialize x
Do While Boolean_Expression (x)
   A statement or block of statements
   Update/alter x
Loop
```

and a post-test loop structure should always be in the following form,

```
initialize x
Do
   A statement or block of statements
   Update/alter x
Loop While Boolean_Expression (x)
```

where

> ➢ *initialize* x is any statement that assigns an initial value to variable x. It can be either an input statement such as Console.ReadLine(), or an assignment statement using the assignment operator (=). In a post-test loop structure though, this statement may sometimes be redundant and can be omitted since initialization of x can occur directly inside the loop.

> ➢ *Boolean_Expression* (x) can be any Boolean expression from a simple to a complex one, dependent on variable x.

> ➢ *Update/alter* x is any statement that alters the value of x such as an input statement Console.ReadLine(), an assignment statement using the assignment operator (=), or even compound assignment operators. It should always be the last statement in the loop.

Following are some examples that use the "Ultimate" rule.

Example 1

```
a = Console.ReadLine()          'Initialization of a
Do While a > 0
   Console.WriteLine(a)
   a = a - 1                    'Update/alteration of a
Loop
```

Example 2

```
s = 0
y = Console.ReadLine()          'Initialization of y
Do While y <> -99
   s = s + y
   y = Console.ReadLine()       'Update/alteration of y
Loop
```

Example 3

```
s = 0                          'Initialization of s
Do
  y = Console.ReadLine()
  s = s + y                    'Update/alteration of s
Loop While s < 1000
```

Example 4

```
y = 0                          'Initialization of y
Do
  y = Console.ReadLine()       'Update/alteration of y
Loop While y < 0
```

In this example, though, initialization of variable y outside the loop is redundant and can be omitted since initialization can also be done inside the loop, as follows.

```
Do
  y = Console.ReadLine()       'Initialization and update/alteration of y
Loop While y < 0
```

Example 5

```
Sub Main()
  Dim odd, even, x As Integer

  odd = 0                      'Initialization of odd
  even = 0                     'Initialization of even
  Do While odd + even < 5
    x = Console.ReadLine()
    If x Mod 2 = 0 Then
      odd += 1                 'Update/alteration of odd
    Else
      even += 1                'Update/alteration of even
    End If
  Loop

  Console.Write("Odds: " & odd & vbCrLf & "Evens: " & even)

  Console.ReadKey()
End Sub
```

Now, you will realize why you should always follow the "Ultimate" rule!" Let's say that the wording of this fifth example was:

Write a Visual Basic program that lets the user enter five numbers and then displays the total number of odds and evens given.

This exercise was given to a class, and a student gave the following Visual Basic program as an answer.

```
Sub Main()
  Dim even, odd, x As Integer

  even = 0
  odd = 0
  x = Console.ReadLine()
```

```
    Do While even + odd < 5
        If x Mod 2 = 0 Then
            even += 1
        Else
            odd += 1
        End If
        x = Console.ReadLine()
    Loop

    Console.Write("Odds: " & odd & vbCrLf & "Evens: " & even)

    Console.ReadKey()
End Sub
```

At first sight the program looks correct, but it is also true that it contains a logic error, and unfortunately a difficult one. Can you spot it?

If you try to follow the flow of execution, you can confirm by yourself that the program runs smoothly—so smoothly that it makes you wonder if this book is reliable or if you should throw it away!

The problem becomes clear only when you try to enter all five of the expected values. The trace table that follows can help you determine where the problem lies. Assume that the user wants to enter the values 5, 10, 2, 4, and 20.

Step	Statement	Notes	even	odd	x
1	even = 0		0	?	?
2	odd = 0		0	0	?
3	x = Console.ReadLine()	User enters the value 5	0	0	5
4	Do While even + odd < 5	This evaluates to True			
5	If x Mod 2 = 0 Then	This evaluates to False			
6	odd += 1		0	1	5
7	x = Console.ReadLine()	User enters the value 10	0	1	10
8	Do While even + odd < 5	This evaluates to True			
9	If x Mod 2 = 0 Then	This evaluates to True			
10	even += 1		1	1	10
11	x = Console.ReadLine()	User enters the value 2	1	1	2
12	Do While odd + even < 5	This evaluates to True			
13	If x Mod 2 = 0 Then	This evaluates to True			
14	even += 1		2	1	2
15	x = Console.ReadLine()	User enters the value 4	2	1	4

16	Do While odd + even < 5	This evaluates to True			
17	If x Mod 2 = 0 Then	This evaluates to True			
18	even += 1		3	1	4
19	x = Console.ReadLine()	User enters the value 6	3	1	20
20	Do While odd + even < 5	This evaluates to True			
21	If x Mod 2 = 0 Then	This evaluates to True			
22	even += 1		4	1	20
23	x = Console.ReadLine()	User enters the value ??????????	4	1	????

And here is the logic error! At step 23, the computer asks the user to enter an additional sixth number!

> **Remember**! You needed a Visual Basic program that lets the user enter five numbers, not six!

One could say, "Okay, let's change the loop's Boolean expression from even + odd < 5 *to* even + odd < 4. *This can help!*" Unfortunately, this change makes things worse, because now the flow of execution exits the loop earlier, before the last given value, 20, can be counted as even.

This is why you should always go by the book! Try to write Example 5 (not the student's version) into Visual Studio and see how perfectly it operates, prompting the user to enter five and not six numbers!

29.4 Breaking Out of a Loop

Loops can consume too much CPU time so you have to be very careful when you use them. There are times when you need to break out of, or end, a loop before it completes all of its iterations, usually when a specified condition is met.

Suppose there is a counted loop structure that searches for a given letter within a string, as shown in the next Visual Basic program.

```
Sub Main()
  Dim i As Integer
  Dim s, letter As String
  Dim found As Boolean

  s = "I have a dream"

  Console.Write("Enter a letter to search: ")
  letter = Console.ReadLine()

  found = False
  For i = 0 To s.Length - 1
    If s(i) = letter Then
      found = True
    End If
```

```
    Next

    If found = True Then
       Console.WriteLine("Letter " & letter & " found!")
    End If

    Console.ReadKey()
End Sub
```

Now suppose that the user enters the letter "h". As you already know, the counted loop structure iterates a specified number of times, and it doesn't care if the letter is actually found or not. Even though the letter "h" does exist at the second position of variable s, the loop unfortunately continues to iterate until the end of the string, thus wasting CPU time.

Someone may say *"So what? Variable s contains just 14 characters. No big deal!"* But it is a big deal, actually! In large scale data processing everything counts, so you should be very careful when using loop control structure, especially those that iterate too many times.

There are two approaches that can help you make programs like the previous one run faster. The main idea, in both of them, is to break out of the loop when a specified condition is met; in this case when the given letter is found.

First Approach – Using the Exit For statement

You can break out of a loop before it actually completes all of its iterations by using the Exit For statement.

Look at the following Visual Basic program. When the given letter is found within variable s, the flow of execution immediately exits the For loop.

```
                          project_29_4a
Sub Main()
    Dim i As Integer
    Dim s, letter As String
    Dim found As Boolean

    s = "I have a dream"

    Console.Write("Enter a letter to search: ")
    letter = Console.ReadLine()

    found = False
    For i = 0 To s.Length - 1
      If s(i) = letter Then
        found = True
        Exit For
      End If
    Next

    If found = True Then
       Console.WriteLine("Letter " & letter & " found!")
    End If

    Console.ReadKey()
End Sub
```

Second Approach – Using a flag

This book tries to use the Exit For statement as little as possible, and only in certain situations in which it really helps you make your code better. That's because the Exit For statement doesn't actually exist in all computer languages; and since this book's intent is to teach you "Algorithmic Thinking" (and not just special statements that only Visual Basic supports), let's look at an alternate approach.

To break out of a loop using a flag, there is one methodology that you can always follow: the counted loop structure must be converted to a pre-test loop structure, and the Boolean expression of the loop must be modified to evaluate an extra variable. In the following Visual Basic program this extra variable is the variable found which, when the given letter is found within variable s, forces the flow of execution to immediately exit the loop.

```
                          project_29_4b
Sub Main()
    Dim i As Integer
    Dim s, letter As String
    Dim found As Boolean

    s = "I have a dream"

    letter = Console.ReadLine()

    found = False
    i = 0
    Do While i <= s.Length - 1 And found = False
        If s(i) = letter Then
            found = True
        End If
        i += 1
    Loop

    If found = True Then
        Console.WriteLine("Letter " & letter & " found!")
    End If

    Console.ReadKey()
End Sub
```

> **Notice**: *Imagine variable* found *as a flag. Initially, the flag is not "raised"* (found = False). *The flow of execution enters the loop, and the loop continues iterating as long as the flag is down* (Do While … found = False). *When something (usually a condition) raises the flag (assigns value* True *to variable* found*), the flow of execution exits the loop.*

29.5   Cleaning Out Your Loops

As you already know, loops can consume too much CPU time, so you must be very careful and use them sparingly. Although a large number of iterations is sometimes inevitable, there are always things that you can do to make your loops perform better.

The next code fragment calculates the average value of the numbers 1, 2, 3, 4, 5, … 10000.

```
s = 0
i = 1
Do
  total = 10000
  s = s + i
  i += 1
Loop While i <= total

average = s / total

Console.Write(average)
```

What you should always keep in mind when using loops, especially those that perform many iterations, is to avoid putting any statement inside a loop that serves no purposes in that loop. In the previous example, the statement total = 10000 is such a statement. Unfortunately, as long as it exists inside the loop, the computer executes it 10000 times for no reason, which of course affects the computer's performance.

To resolve this problem, you can simply move this statement outside the loop, as follows.

```
s = 0
i = 1
total = 10000
Do
  s = s + i
  i += 1
Loop While i <= total

average = s / total

Console.Write(average)
```

Exercise 29.5-1   *Cleaning Out the Loop*

The following code fragment calculates the average value of numbers 1, 2, 3, 4, … 10000. Try to move as many statements as possible outside the loop to make the program more efficient.

```
s = 0
For i = 1 To 10000
  s = s + i
  average = s / 10000
Next

Console.Write(average)
```

Solution

One very common mistake that novice programmers make when calculating average values is to put the statement that calculates the average inside the loop. Think about it! Imagine that you want to calculate your average grade in school. Your first step would be to calculate the sum of the grades for all of the courses that you're taking. Then, when all your grades have been summed up, you would divide that sum by the number of courses that you're taking.

> **Notice**: *Calculating an average is a two-step process.*

Therefore, it is pointless to calculate the average value inside the loop. You can move this statement outside and right after the loop, and leave the loop just to sum up the numbers as follows.

```
s = 0
For i = 1 To 10000
    s = s + i
Next
average = s / 10000

Console.Write(average)
```

Exercise 29.5-2   Cleaning Out the Loop

The next formula

$$S = \frac{1}{1^1 + 2^2 + 3^3 + \cdots + N^N} + \frac{2}{1^1 + 2^2 + 3^3 + \cdots + N^N} + \cdots + \frac{N}{1^1 + 2^2 + 3^3 + \cdots + N^N}$$

is solved using the following Visual Basic program, where N is given by the user.

```
Sub Main()
    Dim n, i, j, denom As Integer
    Dim s As Double

    Console.Write("Enter N: ")
    n = Console.ReadLine()
    s = 0
    For i = 1 To n
        denom = 0
        For j = 1 To n
            denom += j ^ j
        Next
        s += i / denom
    Next

    Console.Write(s)

    Console.ReadKey()
End Sub
```

Try to move as many statements as possible outside the loop to make the program more efficient.

Solution

As you can see from the formula, the denominator is common for all fractions. Thus, it is pointless to calculate it again and again for every fraction. You can calculate the denominator just once and use the result many times, as follows.

```
Sub Main()
    Dim n, i, j, denom As Integer
    Dim s As Double

    Console.Write("Enter N: ")
    n = Console.ReadLine()

    denom = 0
    For j = 1 To n
        denom += j ^ j
    Next

    s = 0
    For i = 1 To n
        s += i / denom
    Next

    Console.Write(s)

    Console.ReadKey()
End Sub
```

> This code fragment calculates the denominator.

29.6   Endless Loops and How to Avoid Them

All loop control structures must include a way to stop endless iterations from occurring within them. This means that there should be something inside the loop that eventually makes the flow of execution exit the loop.

The next example contains an endless loop (also known as an infinite loop). Unfortunately, the programmer forgot to increase variable i inside the loop; therefore, variable i can never reach the value 10.

```
i = 1
Do While i <> 10
    Console.WriteLine("Hello there!")
Loop
```

Remember! *If a loop cannot stop iterating, it is called an endless loop or an infinite loop.*

An endless loop continues to iterate forever and the only way to stop it from iterating is to use magic forces! For example, when an application in a Windows operating system "hangs" (probably because the flow of execution entered an endless loop), the user must use the key combination ALT+CTRL+DEL, which forces the application to end. In Visual Studio, on the other hand, when you accidentally write and execute an endless loop, you can just click on the "Stop Debugging" ■ toolbar icon and the Visual Basic compiler immediately stops any action.

So, always remember to include at least one such statement that makes the flow of execution exit the loop. But still, this is not always enough! Take a look at the following code fragment.

```
i = 1
Do While i <> 10
   Console.WriteLine("Hello there!")
   i += 2
Loop
```

Even though this code fragment does contain one such statement (i += 2), unfortunately the flow of execution never exits the loop because the value 10 is never assigned to variable i.

One thing that you can do to avoid this type of mistake is to never check the *counter* variable using = and <> comparison operators, especially in cases in which the *counter* variable increments or decrements by a value other than 1. You can use <, <=, >, and >= comparison operators instead; they guarantee that the flow of execution exits the loop when the variable *counter* exceeds termination value. The previous example can be fixed by replacing the <> with a <, or even a <= comparison operator.

```
i = 1
Do While i < 10
   Console.WriteLine("Hello there!")
   i += 2
Loop
```

29.7   Converting from a Counted Loop Structure to a Pre-Test Loop Structure

The conversion from a counted loop structure to a pre-test loop structure is quite easy. All you need to do is get the *counter* variable of the For statement and use it within the Do While-Loop statement, as follows.

Counted Loop Structure

```
For counter = initial_value To final_value Step offset
   A statement or block of statements
Next
```

Pre-Test Loop Structure

```
counter = initial_value
Do While counter OP final_value
   A statement or block of statements
   counter = counter + offset
Loop
```

where

➢   *counter* must always be a variable.

➢   *initial_value*, *final_value*, and *offset* can be a constant value or even a variable or an expression.

> ➤ *OP* must be <= when *offset* is positive (or zero) and >= when *offset* is negative.

> **Remember!** *Be careful not to forget to include the statement that increments or decrements the* counter *variable at the end of the pre-test loop structure, because otherwise the loop will iterate endlessly!*

Exercise 29.7-1   *Converting the Visual Basic Program*

Rewrite the following Visual Basic program using the pre-test loop structure.

```
Sub Main()
  Dim i As Integer
  Dim x As Double

  x = 2

  For i = -4 To 4
    x = x ^ 2
  Next

  Console.Write(x)

  Console.ReadKey()
End Sub
```

Solution

Following is the program of the exercise, written again, with some notes on it.

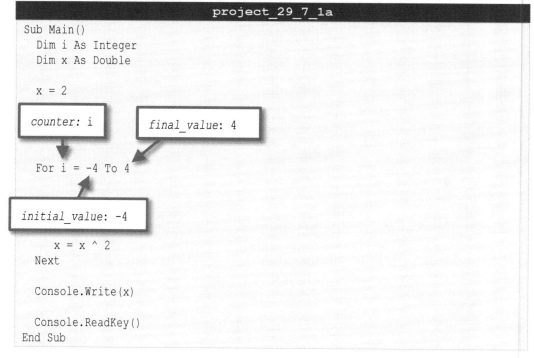

```
                          project_29_7_1a
Sub Main()
  Dim i As Integer
  Dim x As Double

  x = 2

  counter: i            final_value: 4


  For i = -4 To 4

initial_value: -4

    x = x ^ 2
  Next

  Console.Write(x)

  Console.ReadKey()
End Sub
```

Now, with everything clarified, the Visual Basic program can be rewritten using the pre-test loop structure.

```
                              project_29_7_1b
Sub Main()
  Dim i As Integer
  Dim x As Double

  x = 2        OP: <=

  i = -4
  Do While i <= 4        offset: 1
    x = x ^ 2
    i = i + 1
  Loop

  Console.Write(x)

  Console.ReadKey()
End Sub
```

If you type and execute both programs in Visual Studio, you can find out for yourself that they both display the same result.

Exercise 29.7-2   *Converting the Visual Basic Program*

Rewrite the following Visual Basic program using the pre-test loop structure.

```
Sub Main()
  Dim f, j As Integer
  Dim x As Double

  f = Console.ReadLine()
  x = 3

  For j = 20 To f Step -5
    x = x / 2
  Next

  Console.Write(x)

  Console.ReadKey()
End Sub
```

Solution

Here is the program of the exercise, written again, with some notes on it.

```
                              project_29_7_2a
Sub Main()
  Dim f, j As Integer
  Dim x As Double
```

```
   f = Console.ReadLine()
   x = 3
```

┌─────────────────┐   ┌─────────────────┐
│ counter: j   │   │ offset: -5   │
└─────────────────┘   └─────────────────┘

```
   For j = 20 To f Step -5
```

┌──────────────────────┐   ┌──────────────────────┐
│ initial value: 20   │   │ final value: f   │
└──────────────────────┘   └──────────────────────┘

```
     x = x / 2
   Next

   Console.Write(x)

   Console.ReadKey()
End Sub
```

Now, with everything clarified, the Visual Basic program can be rewritten using the pre-test loop structure.

project_29_7_2b

```
Sub Main()
   Dim f, j As Integer
   Dim x As Double

   f = Console.ReadLine()
   x = 3
                    ┌──────────┐
                    │ OP: >=   │
                    └──────────┘
   j = 20
   Do While j >= f
     x = x / 2
     j -= 5
   Loop

   Console.Write(x)

   Console.ReadKey()
End Sub
```

29.8   Converting from a Pre-Test Loop Structure to a Counted Loop Structure

In Visual Basic, the conversion from a pre-test loop structure to a counted loop structure can be done only under certain circumstances. Throughout the rest of this chapter, you will encounter situations in which conversion **cannot be carried out.**

> **Notice**: *In some computer programming languages, such as C++, C#, and Java (to name a few), you can **always** do this type of conversion.*

Following is the general form of the pre-test loop structure, in which conversion can actually be carried out in the majority of the programming languages.

Pre-Test Loop Structure

```
counter = initial_value
Do While counter OP final_value1
  A statement or block of statements 1
  counter = counter + offset
  A statement or block of statements 2
Loop
```

Counted Loop Structure

```
For counter = initial_value To final_value2 Step offset
  A statement or block of statements 1
  A statement or block of statements 2
Next
```

where

➢ *counter* must always be a variable

➢ *initial_value*, *final_value1*, *final_value2*, and *offset* can be a constant value or even a variable or an expression. In the case of a variable or an expression, however, the content or the result correspondingly must be invariable inside the loop.

➢ *OP* can be any comparison operator (<, >, <=, >=, =, <>)

➢ any existing *counter* variable inside statement or block of statements 2 must be replaced by the expression *counter + offset*

Surely you are a little bit confused right now. Don't be! The next examples will help you put things in order.

Exercise 29.8-1   *Converting the Visual Basic Program*

Rewrite the following Visual Basic program using the counted loop structure.

```
Sub Main()
  Dim i As Integer
  Dim s As Double

  s = 0
  i = 1
  Do While i <= 9
    s = s + i ^ 2
    i += 2
  Loop

  Console.Write(s)

  Console.ReadKey()
End Sub
```

Solution

Following is the program of the exercise, written again, with some notes on it.

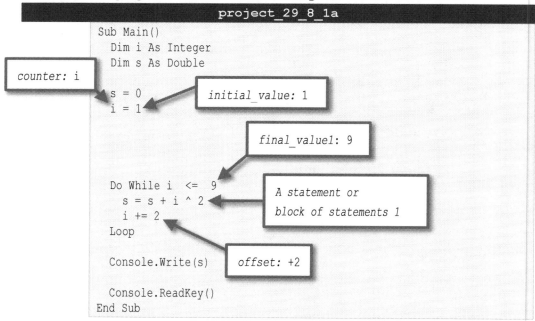

```
project_29_8_1a
Sub Main()
    Dim i As Integer
    Dim s As Double

    s = 0
    i = 1


    Do While i  <=  9
        s = s + i ^ 2
        i += 2
    Loop

    Console.Write(s)

    Console.ReadKey()
End Sub
```

counter: i

initial_value: 1

final_value1: 9

A statement or block of statements 1

offset: +2

Some extra notes:

➢ If you are wondering how to distinguish which variable is the *counter* of the pre-test loop structure, the answer is: *The* counter *is always the variable that the pre-test loop structure checks in every repetition.*

➢ Since *offset* is +2, and since the loop's Boolean expression is i <= 9, the last value of i for which the pre-test loop structure performs an iteration is the value 9. Thus, *final_value2* must be 9.

➢ Inside statement or block of statements 1, variable *counter* must remain as is.

Now, with everything clarified, the Visual Basic program can be rewritten using the counted loop structure.

```
project_29_8_1b
Sub Main()
    Dim i As Integer
    Dim s As Double

    s = 0
    For i = 1 To 9 Step 2
        s = s + i ^ 2
    Next

    Console.Write(s)

    Console.ReadKey()
End Sub
```

If you type and execute both programs in Visual Studio, you can find out for yourself that they both display the value 165.

Exercise 29.8-2   *Converting the Visual Basic Program*

Rewrite the following Visual Basic program using the counted loop structure.

```
Sub Main()
  Dim s, y As Integer

  s = 0
  y = 5
  Do While y <> -3
    s = s + 2 * y
    y = y - 2
  Loop

  Console.Write(s)

  Console.ReadKey()
End Sub
```

Solution

Following is the program of the exercise, written again, with some notes on it.

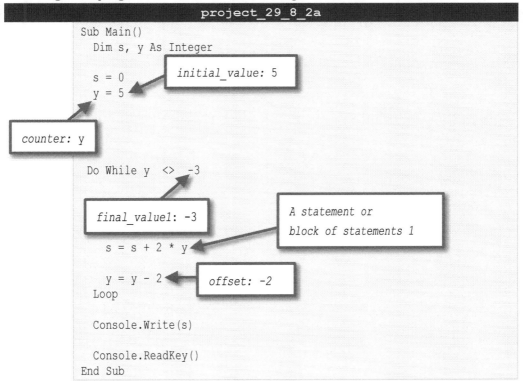

```
                          project_29_8_2a
  Sub Main()
    Dim s, y As Integer

    s = 0          initial_value: 5
    y = 5

counter: y

    Do While y  <>  -3

        final_value1: -3          A statement or
                                  block of statements 1
        s = s + 2 * y

        y = y - 2      offset: -2
    Loop

    Console.Write(s)

    Console.ReadKey()
  End Sub
```

Some extra notes:

➢ Since *offset* is -2 and since the loop's Boolean expression is y <> -3, it becomes clear that the last value of y for which the pre-test loop structure performs an iteration is the value -1. Thus, *final_value2* must be -1.

➢ Inside statement or block of statements 1, variable *counter* must remain as is.

Now, with everything clarified, the Visual Basic program can be rewritten using the counted loop structure.

project_29_8_2b

```
Sub Main()
  Dim s, y As Integer

  s = 0
  For y = 5 To -1 Step -2
    s = s + 2 * y
  Next

  Console.Write(s)

  Console.ReadKey()
End Sub
```

Exercise 29.8-3   *Converting the Visual Basic Program*

Rewrite the following Visual Basic program using the counted loop structure.

```
Sub Main()
  Dim i As Integer
  Dim s As Double

  s = 0
  i = 1
  Do While i < 6
    i += 1
    s = s + i ^ 2
  Loop

  Console.Write(s)

  Console.ReadKey()
End Sub
```

Solution

Following is the program of the exercise, written again, with some notes on it.

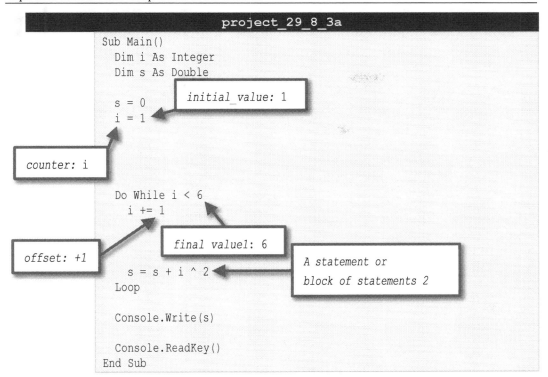

```
project_29_8_3a

Sub Main()
    Dim i As Integer
    Dim s As Double

    s = 0          initial_value: 1
    i = 1

counter: i

    Do While i < 6
        i += 1

offset: +1         final value1: 6

        s = s + i ^ 2       A statement or
    Loop                    block of statements 2

    Console.Write(s)

    Console.ReadKey()
End Sub
```

Some extra notes:

➢ The *counter* is variable i.

➢ Since *offset* is +1, and since the loop's Boolean expression is i < 6, it becomes clear that the last value of i for which the pre-test loop structure performs an iteration is the value 5. Thus *final_value2* must be 5.

➢ Inside statement or block of statements 2, variable *counter* must be replaced by the expression *counter + offset*. Thus, the statement s = s + i ^ 2 must become s = s + (i + 1) ^ 2.

Now, with everything clarified, the Visual Basic program can be rewritten using the counted loop structure.

```
project_29_8_3b

Sub Main()
    Dim i As Integer
    Dim s As Double

    s = 0
    i = 1
    For i = 1 To 5
        s = s + (i + 1) ^ 2
    Next

    Console.Write(s)

    Console.ReadKey()
End Sub
```

If you type and execute both programs in Visual Studio and execute them, you can find out for yourself that they both display the value 90.

Exercise 29.8-4   *Converting the Visual Basic Program*

Rewrite the following Visual Basic program using the counted loop structure.

```
Sub Main()
  Dim x, y As Integer

  y = 5
  x = 0
  Do While y < 1000
    x = x + 2
    y = y + x
  Loop

  Console.Write(y)

  Console.ReadKey()
End Sub
```

Solution

First of all, let's find out which of the two variables is the *counter* variable. The *counter* of the loop control structure is actually variable y, and not variable x, as you may mistakenly believe. It is easy to distinguish this because this is the variable that the pre-test loop structure checks in every repetition (y < 1000).

Now, let's see what happens inside the loop. The *counter* variable y increments by a value that is not constant because the value of variable x, unfortunately, increments in every iteration! But as you have already been taught, the counted loop structure requires a constant offset and not a variable one! Therefore, that makes this Visual Basic program unsuitable for conversion to a counted loop structure!

Notice: If you think you understood everything about converting from a pre-test loop structure to a counted loop structure, you are very much mistaken! In C#—and of course in C, C++, and Java (to name a few)—previous conversion is actually possible and is shown here!

```
static void Main() {
  int x, y;

  x = 0;
  for (y = 5; y < 1000; y += x) {
    x = x + 2;
  }

  Console.Write(y);

  Console.ReadKey();
}
```

*So, why does this book try to convince you that you cannot make this type of conversion? The answer lies in the fact that this type of conversion cannot actually be done in **every** computer language. For example, you cannot do this conversion in languages such as Visual basic, Pascal, Delphi, and many more.*

If this example were written in Visual basic, as shown next, it would be completely wrong!

```
Sub Main()
  Dim x, y As Integer

  x = 0
  For y = 5 To 1000 Step x
    x = x + 2
  Next y

  Console.WriteLine(y)

  Console.ReadKey()
End Sub
```

In Visual basic, offset is initially set to 0 and is never updated to any subsequent values of x. Thus, unfortunately, this code fragment performs infinite number of iterations.

Exercise 29.8-5   *Converting the Visual Basic Program*

Rewrite the following Visual Basic program using the counted loop structure.

```
Sub Main()
  Dim s, y As Integer

  s = 0

  y = 5
  Do While y > -9
    s = s - 2 * y
```

```
      y = y - 3
      s = s - 4 * y
   Loop

   Console.Write(s)

   Console.ReadKey()
End Sub
```

Solution

Following is the program of the exercise, written again, with some notes on it.

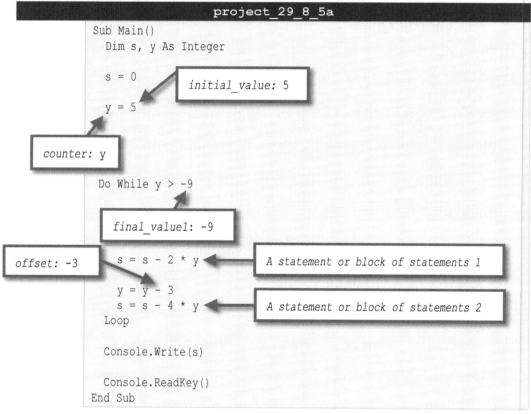

project_29_8_5a

```
Sub Main()
   Dim s, y As Integer

   s = 0                    initial_value: 5

   y = 5

   counter: y

   Do While y > -9

   final_value1: -9

   offset: -3    s = s - 2 * y    A statement or block of statements 1

      y = y - 3
      s = s - 4 * y    A statement or block of statements 2
   Loop

   Console.Write(s)

   Console.ReadKey()
End Sub
```

Some extra notes:

➤ Since *offset* is -3, and since the loop's Boolean expression is y > -9, it becomes clear that the last value of y for which the pre-test loop structure performs an iteration is the value -7. Thus, *final_value2* must be -7.

➤ Inside statement or block of statements 1, variable *counter* must remain as is.

➤ Inside statement or block of statements 2, variable *counter* must be replaced by the expression *counter + offset*. Thus, the statement s = s - 4 * y must become s = s - 4 * (y - 3).

Now, with everything clarified, the Visual Basic program can be rewritten using the counted loop structure as follows.

```
                          project_29_8_5b
Sub Main()
  Dim s, y As Integer

  s = 0

  For y = 5 To -7 Step -3
    s = s - 2 * y
    s = s - 4 * (y - 3)
  Next

  Console.Write(s)

  Console.ReadKey()
End Sub
```

If you type both programs into Visual Studio and execute them, they both display the value 90.

29.9 Converting from a Post-Test Loop Structure to a Pre-Test Loop Structure

Keep in mind that in a post-test loop structure the statement or block of statements of the structure are executed at least one time, as opposed to a pre-test loop structure, in which the statement or block of statements of the structure may never be executed.

In order to make a pre-test loop structure produce the same result(s) as a post-test loop structure, you need to write the statement or block of statements of the post-test loop structure twice, once before and once inside the pre-test structure, as follows.

Post-Test Loop Structure

```
Do
  A statement or block of statements
Loop While Boolean_Expression
```

Pre-Test Loop Structure

```
A statement or block of statements
Do While Boolean_Expression
  A statement or block of statements
Loop
```

Exercise 29.9-1   *Converting the Visual Basic Program*

Rewrite the following Visual Basic program using the pre-test loop structure.

```
                          project_29_9_1a
Sub Main()
  Dim a, b As Integer

  a = Console.ReadLine()
```

```
    b = Console.ReadLine()

    Do
      a += 2
      Console.WriteLine(a & ":" & b)
      b = b + 5
    Loop While b <= a

    Console.ReadKey()
End Sub
```

Solution

The conversion rule states that, in order to make a post-test loop structure produce the same result(s) as a pre-test loop structure, the statement or block of statements of the post-test loop structure must be written twice, once before and once inside the pre-test loop structure!

The next Visual Basic program operates exactly the same way as the initial post-test loop!

project_29_9_1b

```
Sub Main()
    Dim a, b As Integer

    a = Console.ReadLine()
    b = Console.ReadLine()

    a += 2
    Console.WriteLine(a & ":" & b)
    b = b + 5

    Do While b <= a
      a += 2
      Console.WriteLine(a & ":" & b)
      b = b + 5
    Loop

    Console.ReadKey()
End Sub
```

You need to write this block of statements twice. Once before and once inside the pre-test loop structure!

Try to type and execute this program and the initial one in Visual Studio. You will find out for yourself that they both produce the same output results for any input values.

Now, let's try **not to use** the conversion rule you just learned, and see what happens. The next Visual Basic program uses a pre-test loop structure and is supposed to produce the same results as the given post-test loop structure.

project_29_9_1c

```
Sub Main()
    Dim a, b As Integer

    a = Console.ReadLine()
    b = Console.ReadLine()
```

```
    Do While b <= a
      a += 2
      Console.WriteLine(a & ":" & b)
      b = b + 5
    Loop

    Console.ReadKey()
End Sub
```

Suppose the user enters the values 14 and 10 for variables a and b respectively. For these values, both programs perform two iterations and both display 16:10 and 18:15 on screen. They seem to produce the same results, but do they?

Let's try another pair of input values. Suppose the user enters the values 2 and 3 for variables a and b respectively. In this case, the post-test loop structure performs one iteration as opposed to the pre-test loop structure, which never enters the loop. Thus, it performs zero iterations!

So, in order to avoid this kind of problem and to be sure that your conversions are always correct, you should always go by the book. In any case, this is what rules are for!

Exercise 29.9-2   *Converting the Visual Basic Program*

Rewrite the following Visual Basic program using the pre-test loop structure.

```
                          project_29_9_2a
Sub Main()
  Dim a, b As Double

  a = 0

  Do
     b = Console.ReadLine()
     a = a + b
  Loop While a <= b ^ 2

  Console.Write(a)

  Console.ReadKey()
End Sub
```

Solution

No questions, no buts. Just follow the rule! The Visual Basic program using the pre-test loop structure becomes

```
                          project_29_9_2b
Sub Main()
  Dim a, b As Double

  a = 0

  b = Console.ReadLine()
  a = a + b
```

```
  Do While a <= b ^ 2
    b = Console.ReadLine()
    a = a + b
  Loop

  Console.Write(a)

  Console.ReadKey()
End Sub
```

Exercise 29.9-3   *Converting the Visual Basic Program*

Rewrite the following Visual Basic program using the pre-test loop structure.

```
                        project_29_9_3a
Sub Main()
  Dim a, b As Integer

  a = 0

  Do
    Console.WriteLine(a)
    b = Console.ReadLine()
    a = a + b
  Loop While a < 1000

  Console.ReadKey()
End Sub
```

Solution

Following the conversion rule, the Visual Basic program using the pre-test loop structure becomes

```
                        project_29_9_3b
Sub Main()
  Dim a, b As Integer

  a = 0

  Console.WriteLine(a)
  b = Console.ReadLine()
  a = a + b
  Do While a < 1000
    Console.WriteLine(a)
    b = Console.ReadLine()
    a = a + b
  Loop

  Console.ReadKey()
End Sub
```

This program operates perfectly well, but an alternate and even better solution is presented next. Suppose you do **not** write the statement or block of statements twice but only once inside the pre-test structure, as follows.

```
                        project_29_9_3c
Sub Main()
  Dim a, b As Integer

  a = 0

  Do While a < 1000
    Console.WriteLine(a)
    b = Console.ReadLine()
    a = a + b
  Loop

  Console.ReadKey()
End Sub
```

As you can see, variable a does not depend on user input (it is assigned the constant value 0). This means that the Boolean expression (a < 1000) definitely evaluates to True (when the program starts running) and therefore the flow of execution enters the loop. Thus, this pre-test loop performs at least one iteration (as the initial post-test loop actually does); therefore, you do not have to write the statement or block of statements twice.

In conclusion, in this particular exercise you can omit writing the block of statements outside the pre-test loop structure. This is because variable a does not depend on user input and the Boolean expression (a < 1000) definitely evaluates to True (when the program starts running). They are, without doubt, redundant since the loop can do the whole job!

29.10 Converting from a Pre-Test Loop Structure to a Post-Test Loop Structure

You already know that a post-test loop first checks its Boolean expression and then may perform from zero to many iterations. In order to make a post-test loop structure produce the same result(s) as the pre-test loop structure, you must use an additional single-decision structure that checks the Boolean expression before entering the loop.

Pre-Test Loop Structure

```
Do While Boolean_Expression
  A statement or block of statements
Loop
```

Post-Test Loop Structure

```
If Boolean_Expression Then
  Do
    A statement or block of statements
  Loop While Boolean_Expression
End If
```

Exercise 29.10-1   *Converting the Visual Basic Program*

Rewrite the following Visual Basic program using the post-test loop structure.

```
project_29_10_1a
```
```
Sub Main()
  Dim a, b As Integer

  a = Console.ReadLine()
  b = Console.ReadLine()

  Do While b <= a
    a *= 2
    b = b * 3
  Loop

  Console.Write(a & ", " & b)

  Console.ReadKey()
End Sub
```

Solution

Following the conversion rule, the Visual Basic program using the post-test loop structure becomes

```
project_29_10_1b
```
```
Sub Main()
  Dim a, b As Integer

  a = Console.ReadLine()
  b = Console.ReadLine()

  If b <= a Then
    Do
      a *= 2
      b = b * 3
    Loop While b <= a
  End If

  Console.Write(a & ", " &  b)

  Console.ReadKey()
End Sub
```

Exercise 29.10-2   *Converting the Visual Basic Program*

Rewrite the following Visual Basic program using the post-test loop structure.

```
project_29_10_2a
```
```
Sub Main()
  Dim p, a As Integer
```

```
    p = 1

    a = Console.ReadLine()
    Do While a <> -1
      p = p * a
      a = Console.ReadLine()
    Loop

    Console.Write(p)

    Console.ReadKey()
End Sub
```

Solution

Following the conversion rule, the Visual Basic program using the post-test loop structure becomes

```
                         project_29_10_2b
Sub Main()
  Dim p, a As Integer

  p = 1

  a = Console.ReadLine()
  If a <> -1 Then
    Do
      p = p * a
      a = Console.ReadLine()
    Loop While a <> -1
  End If

  Console.Write(p)

  Console.ReadKey()
End Sub
```

Exercise 29.10-3   *Converting the Visual Basic Program*

Rewrite the following Visual Basic program using the post-test loop structure.

```
                         project_29_10_3a
Sub Main()
  Dim x, y As Integer

  x = 0
  y = 1
  Do While y < 10
    x = x * 2
    y = y + 1
  Loop
```

```
    Console.Write(x)

    Console.ReadKey()
End Sub
```

Solution

Following the conversion rule, the Visual Basic program using the post-test loop structure becomes

```
                        project_29_10_3b
Sub Main()
    Dim x, y As Integer

    x = 0
    y = 1
    If y < 10 Then
      Do
        x = x * 2
        y = y + 1
      Loop While y < 10
    End If

    Console.Write(x)

    Console.ReadKey()
End Sub
```

As you can see, variable y does not depend on user input (it is assigned the constant value 1). This means that, whenever this program is executed, the Boolean expression (y < 10) definitely evaluates to True and therefore the flow of execution enters the loop. Thus, in this case, you can actually omit the decision control structure. It is not wrong to leave it there, but it is without doubt redundant.

```
                        project_29_10_3c
Sub Main()
    Dim y, x As Integer

    y = 1
    x = 0
    Do
      x = x * 2
      y = y + 1
    Loop While y < 10

    Console.Write(x)

    Console.ReadKey()
End Sub
```

29.11 Converting from a Counted Loop Structure to a Post-Test Loop Structure

This conversion doesn't have its own rules but you can use the rules you have already learned, that is, you can convert from a counted loop structure to an intermediate pre-test loop structure, and finally to a post-test loop structure, as shown in the next diagram.

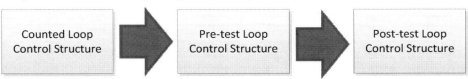

For your convenience, everything you have learned so far is presented once again.

Counted Loop Structure

```
For counter = initial_value To final_value Step offset
  A statement or block of statements
Next
```

Pre-Test Loop Structure

```
counter = initial_value
Do While counter OP final_value
  A statement or block of statements
  counter = counter + offset
Loop
```

Post-Test Loop Structure

```
counter = initial_value
If counter OP final_value
  Do
    A statement or block of statements
    counter = counter + offset
  Loop While counter OP final_value
End If
```

where

➢ *counter* must always be a variable.

➢ *initial_value*, *final_value* and *offset* can be a constant value or even a variable or an expression.

➢ *OP* must be <= when *offset* is positive and >= when *offset* is negative.

Exercise 29.11-1 *Converting the Visual Basic Program*

Rewrite the following Visual Basic program using the post-test loop structure.

```
                        project_29_11_1a
Sub Main()
  Dim start, finish, i As Integer
  Dim x As Double

  start = Console.ReadLine()
  finish = Console.ReadLine()
  x = 5

  For i = start To finish
    x = x ^ 1.5
  Next

  Console.Write(x)

  Console.ReadKey()
End Sub
```

Solution

The intermediate pre-test loop structure is as follows.

```
                        project_29_11_1b
Sub Main()
  Dim start, finish, i As Integer
  Dim x As Double

  start = Console.ReadLine()
  finish = Console.ReadLine()
  x = 5

  i = start
  Do While i <= finish
    x = x ^ 1.5
    i += 1
  Loop

  Console.Write(x)

  Console.ReadKey()
End Sub
```

and the final post-test loop structure is

```
                        project_29_11_1c
Sub Main()
  Dim start, finish, i As Integer
  Dim x As Double

  start = Console.ReadLine()
  finish = Console.ReadLine()
  x = 5
```

```
    i = start
    If i <= finish Then
      Do
        x = x ^ 1.5
        i += 1
      Loop While i <= finish
    End If

    Console.Write(x)

    Console.ReadKey()
End Sub
```

Exercise 29.11-2 *Converting the Visual Basic Program*

Rewrite the following Visual Basic program using the post-test loop structure.

```
                        project_29_11_2a
Sub Main()
  Dim i As Integer
  Dim x As Double

  x = 10

  For i = -4 To 4
    x = x ^ 2
  Next

  Console.Write(x)

  Console.ReadKey()
End Sub
```

Solution

The intermediate pre-test loop structure is as follows.

```
                        project_29_11_2b
Sub Main()
  Dim i As Integer
  Dim x As Double

  x = 10

  i = -4
  Do While i <= 4
    x = x ^ 2
    i += 1
  Loop

  Console.Write(x)
```

```
  Console.ReadKey()
End Sub
```

and the post-test loop structure is

```
                        project_29_11_2c
Sub Main()
  Dim i As Integer
  Dim x As Double

  x = 10

  i = -4
  If i <= 4 Then
    Do
      x = x ^ 2
      i += 1
    Loop While i <= 4
  End If

  Console.Write(x)

  Console.ReadKey()
End Sub
```

In this case, since variable i does not depend on user input (it is assigned the constant value -4), the decision structure is redundant and can be omitted.

```
                        project_29_11_2d
Sub Main()
  Dim i As Integer
  Dim x As Double

  x = 10

  i = -4
  Do
    x = x ^ 2
    i += 1
  Loop While i <= 4

  Console.Write(x)

  Console.ReadKey()
End Sub
```

29.12 Converting from a Post-Test Loop Structure to a Counted Loop Structure

This conversion doesn't have its own rules but you can use the rules you have already learned, that is, you can convert from a post-test loop structure to an intermediate pre-test loop structure, and finally to a counted loop structure, as shown in next diagram.

> **Remember!** In Visual Basic, the conversion from a pre-test loop structure to a counted loop structure can be done only under certain circumstances. However, in some computer programming languages, such as C++, C#, and Java (to name a few), you can **always** do this type of conversion.

The general form of the post-test loop structure, in which conversion can be carried out in the majority of the programming languages, is given next.

Post-Test Loop Structure

```
counter = initial_value
Do
  A statement or block of statements 1
  counter = counter + offset
  A statement or block of statements 2
Loop While counter OP final_value1
```

Pre-Test Loop Structure

```
counter = initial_value
A statement or block of statements 1
counter = counter + offset
A statement or block of statements 2
Do While counter OP final_value1
  A statement or block of statements 1
  counter = counter + offset
  A statement or block of statements 2
Loop
```

Counted Loop Structure

```
counter = initial_value
A statement or block of statements 1
counter = counter + offset
A statement or block of statements 2
For counter = initial_value + offset To final_value2 Step offset
  A statement or block of statements 1
  A statement or block of statements 2
Next
```

where

  ➢ *counter* must always be a variable.

> ➤ *initial_value*, *final_value1*, *final_value2* and *offset* can be a constant value or even a variable or an expression. In case of a variable or an expression, however, the content or the result correspondingly must be invariable inside the loop.

> ➤ *OP* can be any comparison operator (<, >, <=, >=, =, <>).

> ➤ inside statement or block of statements 2 (those being inside the loop), any existing *counter* variable must be replaced by the expression *counter + offset*

Exercise 29.12-1   *Converting the Visual Basic Program*

Rewrite the following Visual Basic program using the counted loop structure.

```
project_29_12_1a
```
```
Sub Main()
  Dim a, i As Integer
  Dim s As Double

  s = 0
  a = Console.ReadLine()
  i = a
  Do
    s = s + i ^ 2
    i = i + 1
  Loop While i <> 10

  Console.Write(s)

  Console.ReadKey()
End Sub
```

Solution

The intermediate pre-test loop structure is as follows.

```
project_29_12_1b
```
```
Sub Main()
  Dim a, i As Integer
  Dim s As Double

  s = 0
  a = Console.ReadLine()
  i = a
  s = s + i ^ 2
  i = i + 1
  Do While i <> 10
    s = s + i ^ 2
    i = i + 1
  Loop

  Console.Write(s)

  Console.ReadKey()
```

This is the block of statements of the post-test loop structure, here written twice; once before and once inside the pre-test loop

```
End Sub
```

and the final counted loop structure becomes

```
                         project_29_12_1c
Sub Main()
  Dim a, i As Integer
  Dim s As Double

  s = 0
  a = Console.ReadLine()
  i = a
  s = s + i ^ 2
  i = i + 1          initial_value + offset

  For i = a + 1 To 9
    s = s + i ^ 2
  Next

  Console.Write(s)

  Console.ReadKey()
End Sub
```

Exercise 29.12-2   *Converting the Visual Basic Program*

Rewrite the following Visual Basic program using the counted loop structure.

```
                         project_29_12_2a
Sub Main()
  Dim a, i As Integer
  Dim s As Double

  s = 0
  a = Console.ReadLine()
  i = a
  Do
    s = s + i
    i = i + 3
    s = s + i ^ 2
  Loop While i < 60

  Console.Write(s)

  Console.ReadKey()
End Sub
```

Solution

The intermediate pre-test loop structure is as follows.

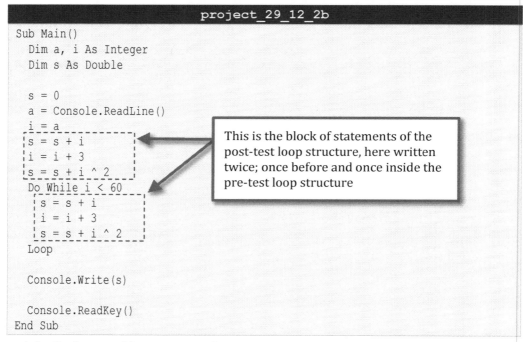

```
                          project_29_12_2b
Sub Main()
  Dim a, i As Integer
  Dim s As Double

  s = 0
  a = Console.ReadLine()
  i = a
  s = s + i
  i = i + 3
  s = s + i ^ 2
  Do While i < 60
    s = s + i
    i = i + 3
    s = s + i ^ 2
  Loop

  Console.Write(s)

  Console.ReadKey()
End Sub
```

This is the block of statements of the post-test loop structure, here written twice; once before and once inside the pre-test loop structure

and the final counted loop structure becomes

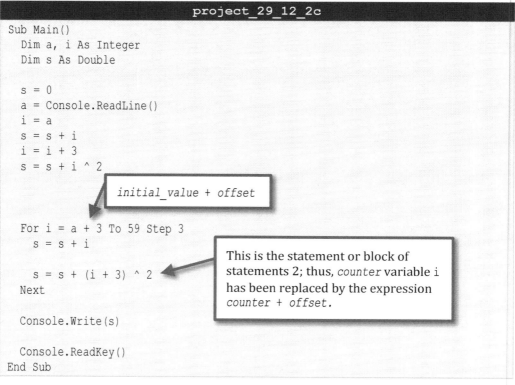

```
                          project_29_12_2c
Sub Main()
  Dim a, i As Integer
  Dim s As Double

  s = 0
  a = Console.ReadLine()
  i = a
  s = s + i
  i = i + 3
  s = s + i ^ 2


  For i = a + 3 To 59 Step 3
    s = s + i

    s = s + (i + 3) ^ 2
  Next

  Console.Write(s)

  Console.ReadKey()
End Sub
```

initial_value + offset

This is the statement or block of statements 2; thus, *counter* variable i has been replaced by the expression *counter + offset.*

29.13 Using the "From Inner to Outer" Method in Loop Control Structures

The "from inner to outer" method has already been discussed in Chapter 21. This book tries to teach you "Algorithmic Thinking" by first designing the inner (nested) control structures. Then, as the algorithm is developed, more and more control structures are added, nesting all previous ones.

Let's try the following example.

Write a Visual Basic program that displays the following multiplication table as it is shown below.

1x1=1	1x2=2	1x3=3	1x4=4	1x5=5	1x6=6	1x7=7	1x8=8	1x9=9
2x1=2	2x2=4	2x3=6	2x4=8	2x5=10	2x6=12	2x7=14	2x8=16	2x9=18
3x1=3	3x2=6	3x3=9	3x4=12	3x5=15	3x6=18	3x7=21	3x8=24	3x9=27
4x1=4	4x2=8	4x3=12	4x4=16	4x5=20	4x6=24	4x7=28	4x8=32	4x9=36
5x1=5	5x2=10	5x3=15	5x4=20	5x5=25	5x6=30	5x7=35	5x8=40	5x9=45
6x1=6	6x2=12	6x3=18	6x4=24	6x5=30	6x6=36	6x7=42	6x8=48	6x9=54
7x1=7	7x2=14	7x3=21	7x4=28	7x5=35	7x6=42	7x7=49	7x8=56	7x9=63
8x1=8	8x2=16	8x3=24	8x4=32	8x5=40	8x6=48	8x7=56	8x8=64	8x9=72
9x1=9	9x2=18	9x3=27	9x4=36	9x5=45	9x6=54	9x7=63	9x8=72	9x9=81

According to the "from inner to outer" method, you start by writing the inner control structure and then, when everything is tested and operates fine, you can add the outer control structures.

So, let's try to display only the first line of the multiplication table. Examination of this line reveals that, in each multiplication, the multiplicand is always 1. The loop control structure that displays only the first line of the multiplication table is as follows. Imagine a variable i that contains the value 1.

```
For j = 1 To 9
    Console.Write(i & "x" & j & "=" & i * j & vbTab)
Next
```

If you execute this code fragment, the result is

1x1=1   1x2=2   1x3=3   1x4=4   1x5=5   1x6=6   1x7=7   1x8=8   1x9=9

> **Remember!** *The special sequence of characters \t "displays" a tab character after each iteration. This ensures that everything is aligned properly.*

The inner (nested) loop control structure is ready. What you need now is a way to execute this control structure nine times, but each time variable i should contain a different value, from 1 to 9. This code fragment is as follows.

```
For i = 1 To 9
    'Here goes the code that displays one single line
    'of the multiplication table
    Console.WriteLine()
Next
```

> **Notice:** *The* `Console.WriteLine()` *statement is used to "display" a line break between lines.*

Now, you can combine both code fragments, nesting the first into the second one. The final Visual Basic program becomes

```
project_29_13
Sub Main()
  Dim i, j As Integer

  For i = 1 To 9
    For j = 1 To 9
      Console.Write(i & "x" & j & "=" & i * j & vbTab)
    Next
    Console.WriteLine()
  Next

  Console.ReadKey()
End Sub
```

29.14 Review Questions: True/False

Choose **true** or **false** for each of the following statements.

1. When the number of iterations is unknown, you can use the counted loop structure.

2. When the number of iterations is known, you cannot use a post-test loop structure.

3. According to the "Ultimate" rule, in a pre-test loop structure, the initialization of the variable that participates in the loop's Boolean expression should be done inside the loop.

4. According to the "Ultimate" rule, in a pre-test loop structure, the statement that updates/alters the value of the variable that participates in the loop's Boolean expression must be the last statement within the loop.

5. According to the "Ultimate" rule, in a post-test loop structure, the initialization of the variable that participates in the loop's Boolean expression can sometimes be done inside the loop.

6. According to the "Ultimate" rule, in a post-test loop structure, the update/alteration of the variable that participates in the loop's Boolean expression must be the first statement within the loop.

7. In Visual Basic, you can break out of a loop before it completes all iterations using the Exit Loop statement.

8. A statement that assigns a constant value to a variable is better placed inside a loop control structure.

9. In the following code fragment:
   ```
   For i = 1 To 30
     a = "Hello"
     Console.WriteLine(a)
   Next
   ```
   there is at least one statement that can be moved outside the counted loop structure.

10. In the following code fragment:

```
s = 0
count = 1
Do While count < 100
   a = Console.ReadLine()
   s += a
   average = s / count
   count += 1
Loop
Console.WriteLine(average)
```

there is at least one statement that can be moved outside the counted loop structure.

11. In the following code fragment:

```
s = 0
y = Console.ReadLine()
Do While y <> -99
   s = s + y
   y = Console.ReadLine()
Loop
```

there is at least one statement that can be moved outside the counted loop structure.

12. The following code fragment:

```
i = 1
Do While i <> 100
   Console.WriteLine("Hello there!")
   i += 5
Loop
```

satisfies the property of finiteness.

13. When the not equal (<>) comparison operator is used in the Boolean expression of a pre-test loop structure, the loop always iterates endlessly.

14. The following code fragment:

```
i = 0
Do
   Console.WriteLine("Hello there!")
   i += 5
Loop While i < 100
```

satisfies the property of finiteness.

15. The following code fragment:

```
For i = 0 To 10 Step 2
   x = Math.Sqrt(i, 2)
   Console.WriteLine(x)
Next
```

cannot be converted to a pre-test loop structure.

16. The following code fragment:

```
y = 0
```

```
x = 0
Do While y < 1000
  y = y + x
  x += 1
Loop
```

can be converted to a counted loop structure in all computer languages.

17. When converting from a post-test loop structure to a pre-test loop structure, there are cases in which you can omit writing the statement or block of statements of the post-test loop structure twice.

18. When converting from a pre-test loop structure to a post-test loop structure, there are cases in which you can omit the extra decision control structure.

19. The conversion from a counted loop structure to a post-test loop structure is possible but you need to convert to a pre-test loop structure first.

29.15 Review Questions: Multiple Choice

Select the correct answer for each of the following statements.

1. When the number of iterations is unknown, you can use
   a. the pre-test loop structure.
   b. the post-test loop structure.
   c. all of the above

2. When the number of iterations is known, you can use
   a. the pre-test loop structure.
   b. the post-test loop structure.
   c. the counted loop structure.
   d. all of the above

3. According to the "Ultimate" rule, in a pre-test loop structure, the initialization of the variable that participates in the loop's Boolean expression should be done
   a. inside the loop.
   b. outside the loop.
   c. all of the above

4. According to the "Ultimate" rule, in a pre-test loop structure, the update/alteration of the variable that participates in the loop's Boolean expression should be done
   a. inside the loop.
   b. outside the loop.
   c. all of the above

5. According to the "Ultimate" rule, in a post-test loop structure, the update/alteration of the variable that participates in the loop's Boolean expression should be done
   a. inside the loop.
   b. outside the loop.
   c. all of the above

6. In the following code fragment

```
s = 0
For i = 1 To 100
    s = s + i
    x = 100
    average = s / 100
Next
```

the number of statements that can be moved outside of the counted loop structure is

    a. 0.

    b. 1.

    c. 2.

    d. 3.

7.   When this comparison operator is used in the Boolean expression of a post-test loop structure, the loop iterates forever.

    a. =

    b. <=

    c. >=

    d. it depends

8.   The conversion from a counted loop structure to a pre-test loop structure

    a. cannot always be carried out.

    b. can always be carried out.

    c. can be carried out but the pre-test loop structure performs less iterations.

    d. none of the above

9.   In Visual Basic, the conversion from a pre-test loop structure to a counted loop structure

    a. cannot always be carried out.

    b. can always be carried out.

    c. can be carried out but the counted loop structure performs less iterations.

    d. none of the above

10. The conversion from a post-test loop structure to a pre-test loop structure

    a. cannot always be carried out.

    b. can always be carried out.

    c. can be carried out but the pre-test loop structure performs more iterations.

    d. none of the above

11. The conversion from a pre-test loop structure to a post-test loop structure

    a. cannot always be carried out.

    b. can always be carried out.

    c. can be carried out but the post-test loop structure performs more iterations.

    d. none of the above

12. The conversion from a counted loop structure to a post-test loop structure
    a. cannot always be carried out.
    b. can always be carried out.
    c. can be carried out but the post-test loop structure performs less iterations.
    d. none of the above

13. In Visual Basic, the conversion from a post-test loop structure to a counted loop structure
    a. cannot always be carried out.
    b. can always be carried out.
    c. can be carried out but the counted loop structure performs more iterations.
    d. none of the above

29.16 Review Exercises

Complete the following exercises.

1. The following code fragment calculates the average value of 100 numbers entered by the user. Try to move as many statements as possible outside the loop to make it more efficient.

```
s = 0
For i = 1 To 100
    number = Console.ReadLine()
    s = s + number
    average = s / 100
Next
Console.WriteLine(average)
```

2. The following formula

$$S = \frac{1}{1 \cdot 2 \cdot 3 \cdot \ldots \cdot 100} + \frac{2}{1 \cdot 2 \cdot 3 \cdot \ldots \cdot 100} + \cdots + \frac{100}{1 \cdot 2 \cdot 3 \cdot \ldots \cdot 100}$$

is solved using the following Visual Basic program.

```
Sub Main()
    Dim i, j, denom As Integer
    Dim s As Double

    s = 0
    For i = 1 To 100
        denom = 1
        For j = 1 To 100
            denom *= j
        Next
        s += i / denom
    Next
    Console.Write(s)

    Console.ReadKey()
End Sub
```

Try to move as many statements as possible outside the loop to make it more efficient.

3.   Rewrite the following code fragment using the pre-test loop structure.

```
s = 10
For i = 1 To 10
    s += Math.Sqrt(i)
Next
Console.WriteLine(s)
```

4.   Rewrite the following code fragment using the pre-test loop structure.

```
start = Console.ReadLine()
finish = Console.ReadLine()
For i = start To finish
    Console.WriteLine(i)
Next
```

5.   Rewrite the following code fragment using the counted loop structure.

```
i = 100
s = 0
Do While i > 0
    s = s + Math.Sqrt(i)
    i -= 5
Loop
Console.WriteLine(s)
```

6.   Rewrite the following code fragment using the counted loop structure.

```
s = 0
i = 1
y = 0
Do While i <= 10
    i += 1
    s = s + Math.Sqrt(y + i)
    y = y + i * 2
Loop
Console.WriteLine(s)
```

7.   Rewrite the following code fragment using the counted loop structure.

```
y = 0
i = 1
Do While i < 10
    a = Console.ReadLine()
    a += i
    i += 2
    y = y + (a + i) ^ 3
Loop
Console.WriteLine(y)
```

8.   Rewrite the following code fragment using the counted loop structure.

```
y = 1
x = 0
Do While y < 1000
    x = y ^ 2
```

```
   y = y + x
Loop
Console.WriteLine(y)
```

9. Rewrite the following code fragment using the pre-test loop structure.

```
s = 0
a = Console.ReadLine()
Do
   s += a
   a = Console.ReadLine()
Loop While a <= s
Console.WriteLine(s)
```

10. Rewrite the following code fragment using the pre-test loop structure.

```
a = 100
count = 0
Do
   Console.WriteLine(a)
   b = Console.ReadLine()
   count += 1
   a -= Math.Sqrt(b)
Loop While a >= 0
Console.WriteLine(count)
```

11. Rewrite the following code fragment using the post-test loop structure.

```
a = Console.ReadLine()
b = Console.ReadLine()
Do While b <= 1000
   a += 2
   b = b * a
   Console.WriteLine(b)
Loop
```

12. Rewrite the following code fragment using the post-test loop structure.

```
s = 0
a = Console.ReadLine()
Do While a <> -99
   s = s + a ^ 2
   a = Console.ReadLine()
Loop
Console.WriteLine(s)
```

13. Rewrite the following code fragment using the post-test loop structure.

```
x = 0
y = -10
Do While y < 10
   x = x + 2 ^ y
   y = y + 1
Loop
Console.WriteLine(x)
```

14. Rewrite the following code fragment using the post-test loop structure.

```
start = Console.ReadLine()
```

```
x = 1
For i = start To start * 2
  x = x ^ 1.1 + i
Next
Console.WriteLine(x)
```

15. Rewrite the following code fragment using the post-test loop structure.

```
x = 42
For i = 1 To 100
  x = Math.Sqrt(x) + i
  Console.WriteLine(x)
Next
```

16. Rewrite the following code fragment using the counted loop structure.

```
Sub Main()
  Dim a, i As Integer
  Dim p As Double

  p = 1
  a = Console.ReadLine()
  i = a
  Do
    p = p * i ^ 2
    i = i + 5
    p = p + i
  Loop While i < 20
  Console.Write(p)

  Console.ReadKey()
End Sub
```

17. Rewrite the following code fragment using the counted loop structure.

```
Sub Main()
  Dim start, finish, i As Integer
  Dim x As Double

  start = Console.ReadLine()
  finish = Console.ReadLine()
  x = 1000
  i = start
  If i <= finish Then
    Do
      x = Math.Sqrt(x)
      i += 2
    Loop While i <= finish
  End If
  Console.Write(x)

  Console.ReadKey()
End Sub
```

18. Write a Visual Basic program that displays every combination of two integers as well as their resulting product, for pairs of integers between 1 and 4. The output should display as follows.

```
1 x 1 = 1
1 x 2 = 2
1 x 3 = 3
1 x 4 = 4
2 x 1 = 2
2 x 2 = 4
2 x 3 = 6
2 x 4 = 8
...

...

4 x 1 = 4
4 x 2 = 8
4 x 3 = 12
4 x 4 = 16
```

19. Write a Visual Basic program that displays the multiplication table for pairs of integers between 1 and 12, as shown next. Please note that the output is aligned with tabs.

```
   |  1   2   3   4   5   6   7   8   9   10  11  12
-----------------------------------------------------
1  |  1   2   3   4   5   6   7   8   9   10  11  12
2  |  2   4   6   8   10  12  14  16  18  20  22  24
3  |  3   6   9   12  15  18  21  24  27  30  33  36
...|  ... ... ... ... ... ... ... ... ... ... ... ...
11 |  11  22  33  44  55  66  77  88  99  110 121 132
12 |  12  24  36  48  60  72  84  96  108 120 132 144
```

Chapter 30
Flowcharts with Loop Control Structures

30.1 Introduction

By working through the previous chapters, you've become familiar with all the loop control structures, how to use them, and which to use in every case. You've learned about the "Ultimate" rule, how to break out of a loop, how to convert from one loop control structure to another, and much more. Since flowcharts are an ideal way to learn "Algorithmic Thinking" and to help you better understand specific control structures, this chapter will teach you how to convert a Visual Basic program to a flowchart and vice versa, that is, a flowchart to a Visual Basic program.

30.2 Converting Visual Basic Programs to Flowcharts

To convert a Visual Basic program to a flowchart, you need to recall all loop control structures and their corresponding flowcharts. Following you will find them all summarized, plus a new one—the mid-test loop structure!

The Pre-Test Loop Structure

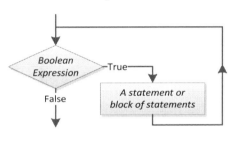

The Post-Test Loop Structure

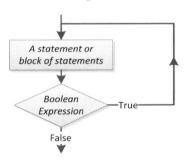

The Counted Loop Structure

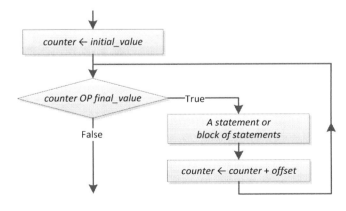

The Mid-Test Loop Structure (this is a new one!)

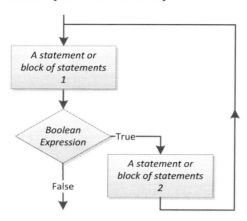

Although this loop control structure is directly supported in some computer languages such as Ada, unfortunately this is not true for the majority of the programming languages. So, in order to write the corresponding Visual Basic program, you have to convert this flowchart to something more familiar, as shown next. These two flowcharts are considered to be equivalent.

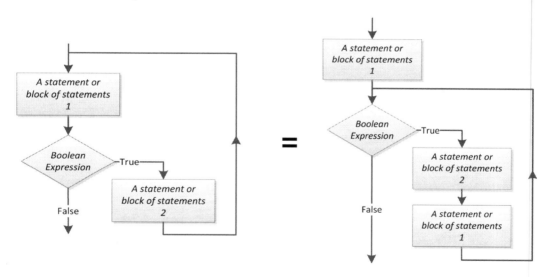

Next, you will find many exercises that can clarify things that you might still need help understanding.

Exercise 30.2-1   *Designing the Flowchart*

Design the flowchart that corresponds to the following Visual Basic program.

```
Sub Main()
    Dim i As Integer

    i = 0
    Do While i <= 100
```

```
        Console.WriteLine(i)
        i += 5
    Loop

    Console.ReadKey()
End Sub
```

Solution

This Visual Basic program contains a pre-test loop structure. The corresponding flowchart that follows includes what you have been taught so far.

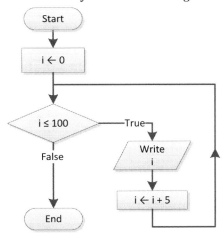

Exercise 30.2-2   *Designing the Flowchart*

Design the flowchart that corresponds to the following Visual Basic program.

```
Sub Main()
    Dim i, x As Integer

    i = 50
    Do While i > 10
        If x Mod 2 = 1 Then
            Console.WriteLine(i)
        End If
        i -= 5
    Loop

    Console.ReadKey()
End Sub
```

Solution

This Visual Basic program contains a pre-test loop structure which nests a single-alternative decision structure. The corresponding flowchart that follows includes what you have been taught so far.

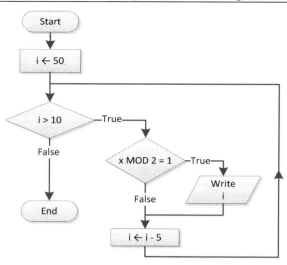

Exercise 30.2-3   *Designing the Flowchart*

Design the flowchart that corresponds to the following Visual Basic program.

```
Sub Main()
  Dim i As Integer

  i = 30
  Do
    If i Mod 8 = 0 Then
      Console.WriteLine(i & " is a multiple of 8")
    End If
    If i Mod 4 = 0 Then
      Console.WriteLine(i & " is a multiple of 4")
    End If
    If i Mod 2 = 0 Then
      Console.WriteLine(i & " is a multiple of 2")
    End If
    i -= 2
  Loop While i > 0

  Console.ReadKey()
End Sub
```

Solution

This Visual Basic program contains a post-test loop structure that nests three single-alternative decision structures. The corresponding flowchart is as follows.

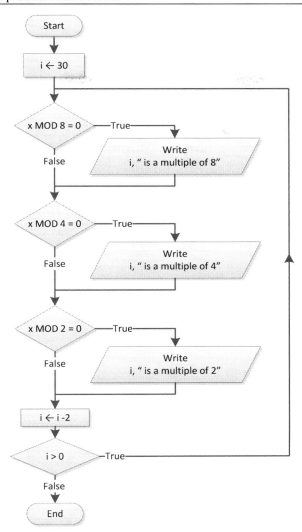

Exercise 30.2-4   *Designing the Flowchart*

Design the flowchart that corresponds to the following Visual Basic program.

```
Sub Main()
  Dim hour As Integer

  For hour = 1 To 24
    Console.WriteLine("Hour is " & hour & ":00.")
    If hour >= 4 And hour < 12 Then
      Console.WriteLine("Good Morning")
    ElseIf hour >= 12 And hour < 20 Then
      Console.WriteLine("Good Afternoon")
    ElseIf hour >= 20 And hour < 24 Then
      Console.WriteLine("Good Evening")
    ElseIf hour <= 24 Then
      Console.WriteLine("Good Night")
```

```
        End If
    Next

    Console.ReadKey()
End Sub
```

Solution

This Visual Basic program contains a counted loop structure that nests a multiple-alternative decision structure. The corresponding flowchart is as follows.

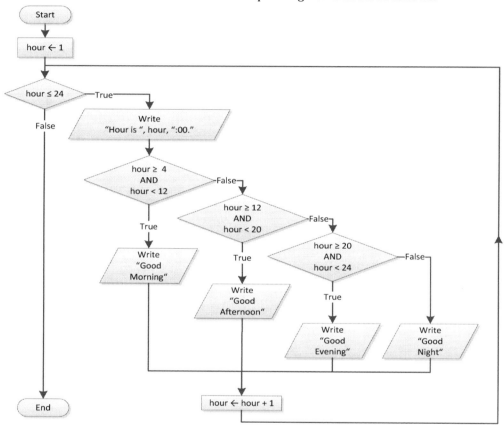

Exercise 30.2-5   Designing the Flowchart

Design the flowchart that corresponds to the following Visual Basic program.

```
Sub Main()
    Dim a, i As Integer

    a = Console.ReadLine()

    Select a
        Case 1
            For i = 1 To 9 Step 2
                Console.WriteLine(i)
```

```
      Next
    Case 2
      For i = 9 To 1 Step -2
        Console.WriteLine(i)
      Next
    Case Else
      Console.WriteLine("Nothing to do!")
  End Select
  Console.Write("The End!")

  Console.ReadKey()
End Sub
```

Solution

This Visual Basic program contains a case decision structure that nests two counted loop structures. The corresponding flowchart is as follows.

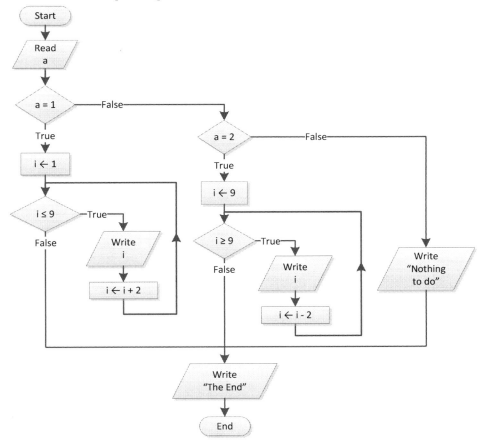

Exercise 30.2-6 *Designing the Flowchart*

Design the flowchart that corresponds to the following Visual Basic program.

```
Sub Main()
```

```
Dim n, m, sum, i, j As Integer

n = Console.ReadLine()
m = Console.ReadLine()

sum = 0
For i = 0 To n - 1
  For j = 0 To m - 1
    sum += i * j + j
  Next
Next
Console.Write(sum)

Console.ReadKey()
End Sub
```

Solution

This Visual Basic program contains nested loop control structures; a counted loop structure nested within another counted loop structure. The corresponding flowchart is as follows.

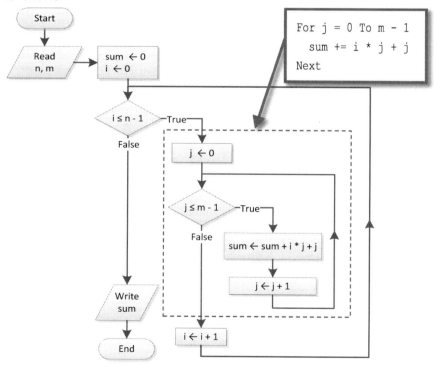

Exercise 30.2-7   *Designing the Flowchart*

Design the flowchart that corresponds to the following code fragment.

```
s = 0
For i = 0 To 99
```

```
n = Console.ReadLine()
Do While n < 0
  Console.WriteLine("Error")
  n = Console.ReadLine()
Loop
s += Math.Sqrt(n)
Next
Console.Write(s)
```

Solution

This Visual Basic program contains nested loop control structures; a pre-test loop structure nested within a counted loop structure. The corresponding flowchart is as follows.

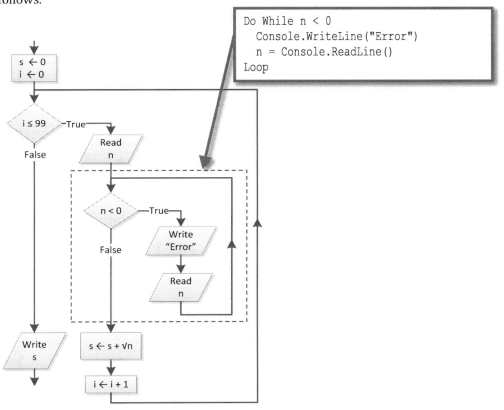

```
Do While n < 0
  Console.WriteLine("Error")
  n = Console.ReadLine()
Loop
```

30.3   Converting Flowcharts to Visual Basic Programs

This conversion is not always an easy one. There are cases in which the flowchart designers follow no particular rules, so the initial flowchart may need some modifications before it can become a Visual Basic program. The following is an example of one such case.

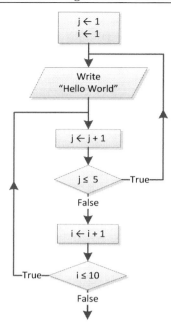

As you can see, the loop control structures included in this flowchart fragment match none of the structures that you have already learned, such the pre-test, the post-test, the counted, or even the new one, the mid-test loop structure. Thus, you have only one choice and this is to modify the flowchart by adding extra statements or removing existing ones until known loop control structures start to appear. Following are some exercises in which the initial flowchart does need modification.

Exercise 30.3-1   *Writing the Visual Basic Program*

Write the Visual Basic program that corresponds to the following flowchart fragment.

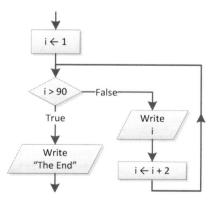

Solution

This is an easy one. The only obstacle you have to overcome is that the true and false paths are not quite in the right position. You need the true and not the false path to actually iterate. As you already know, it is possible to switch the two paths but you need to negate the Boolean expression as well. Thus, the code fragment becomes

```
i = 1
Do While i <= 90
  Console.WriteLine(i)
  i = i + 2
Loop

Console.Write("The End")
```

or you can even use a For statement

```
For i = 1 To 90 Step 2
  Console.WriteLine(i)
Next

Console.Write("The End")
```

Exercise 30.3-2   *Writing the Visual Basic Program*

Write the Visual Basic program that corresponds to the following flowchart.

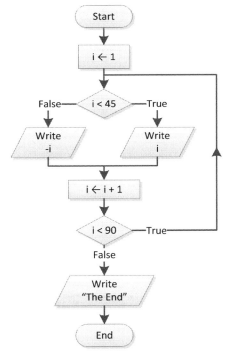

Solution

This flowchart contains a post-test loop structure that nests a dual-alternative decision structure. The Visual Basic program is as follows.

```
Sub Main()
  Dim i As Integer

  i = 1
  Do
```

```
If i < 45 Then
    Console.WriteLine(i)
Else
    Console.WriteLine(-i)
End If
    i += 1
Loop While i < 90

Console.Write("The End")

Console.ReadKey()
End Sub
```

This is the dual-alternative decision structure

Exercise 30.3-3   *Writing the Visual Basic Program*

Write the Visual Basic program that corresponds to the following flowchart.

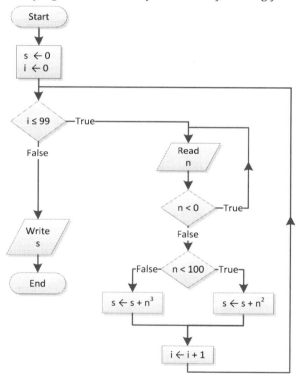

Solution

Oops! What a mess! So many diamonds here! Be careful though, because one of them is actually a decision control structure! Yes, you heard it, in this flowchart a decision control structure exists! Can you spot it?

You should be quite familiar with loop control structures so far. As you already know, in loop control structures, one of the diamond's (rhombus's) exits always has an upward direction. Thus, the following flowchart fragment, extracted from the initial one, is obviously the decision control structure that you are looking for.

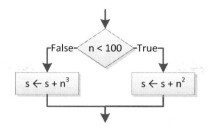

And of course, it's a dual-alternative decision structure!

Now, let's identify the rest of the structures. Right before the dual-alternative decision structure, there is a post-test loop structure. Its flowchart fragment is as follows.

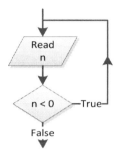

And finally, both the dual-alternative decision structure and the post-test loop structure, mentioned before, are nested within the next flowchart fragment,

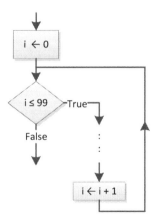

which happens to be a pre-test loop structure and can be written in Visual Basic using either a Do While-Loop or a For statement. The corresponding Visual Basic program is as follows.

```
Sub Main()
    Dim i As Integer
    Dim s, n As Double

    s = 0
    For i = 0 To 99
```

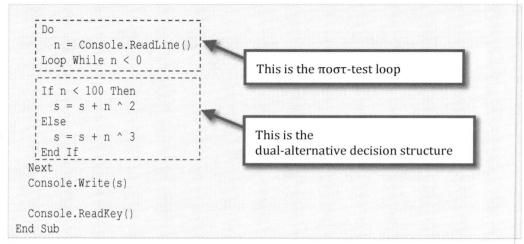

```
Do
    n = Console.ReadLine()
Loop While n < 0
```
This is the ποστ-test loop

```
If n < 100 Then
    s = s + n ^ 2
Else
    s = s + n ^ 3
End If
```
This is the
dual-alternative decision structure

```
Next
Console.Write(s)

    Console.ReadKey()
End Sub
```

Wasn't so difficult after all, was it?

Exercise 30.3-4   *Writing the Visual Basic Program*

Write the Visual Basic program that corresponds to the following flowchart.

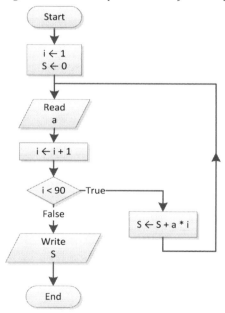

Solution

This is the mid-test loop structure mentioned previously in this chapter. Since there is no direct Visual Basic statement for this structure you must convert the flowchart to something more familiar—or you can also use the Exit Do statement as shown in the next two approaches.

First Approach – Converting the flowchart

For your convenience, the mid-test loop structure and its equivalent, using a pre-test loop structure, are as follows.

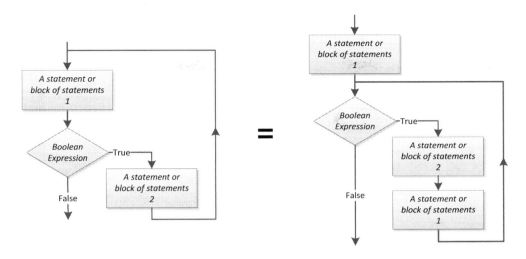

Accordingly, the initial flowchart becomes

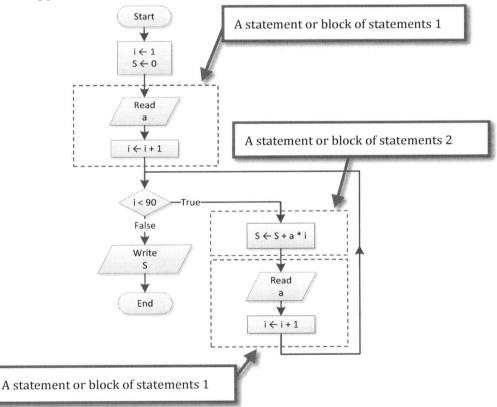

Now, it's easy to write the corresponding Visual Basic program.

```
Sub Main()
  Dim i, S, a As Integer

  i = 1
  S = 0
```

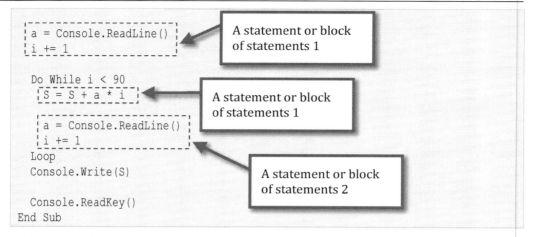

Second Approach – Using the Exit Do statement

For mid-test loops, there is actually one more approach that uses the Exit Do statement. The mid-test loop and its Visual Basic program equivalent are as follows.

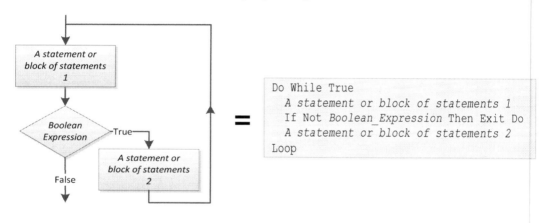

```
Do While True
    A statement or block of statements 1
    If Not Boolean_Expression Then Exit Do
    A statement or block of statements 2
Loop
```

The main idea is to create an endless loop Do While True … Loop and break out of it when the Boolean expression that exists between the two statements or blocks of statements evaluates to True.

According to this approach, the initial flowchart can be written directly in Visual Basic as follows, without actually modifying the initial flowchart.

```
Sub Main()
    Dim i, S, a As Integer

    i = 1
    S = 0
    Do While True
        a = Console.ReadLine()
        i += 1

        If i >= 90 Then Exit Do
```

A statement or block of statements 1

```
  ┌─────────────────┐
  ¦ S = S + a * i ¦
  └─────────────────┘
Loop
Console.Write(S)

Console.ReadKey()
End Sub
```

A statement or
block of statements 2

Obviously this is a much better solution! However, keep in mind that even though the
Exit Do statement can sometimes be useful, it may also lead you to write code that is
difficult to read and understand, especially when you make extensive use of it. So, please
use it cautiously and sparingly!

30.4   Review Exercises

Complete the following exercises.

1.   Design the flowchart that corresponds to the following Visual Basic program.

```
Sub Main()
    Dim i As Integer

    i = -100
    Do While i <= 100
        Console.WriteLine(i)
        i += 1
    Loop

    Console.ReadKey()
End Sub
```

2.   Design the flowchart that corresponds to the following Visual Basic program.

```
Sub Main()
    Dim i As Integer

    i = Console.ReadLine()
    Do
        Console.WriteLine(i)
        i += 1
    Loop While i <= 100

    Console.ReadKey()
End Sub
```

3.   Design the flowchart that corresponds to the following Visual Basic program.

```
Sub Main()
    Dim a, b, i As Integer

    a = Console.ReadLine()
    b = Console.ReadLine()
    For i = a To b
        Console.WriteLine(i)
    Next
    Console.ReadKey()
End Sub
```

4. Design the flowchart that corresponds to the following Visual Basic program.

```vb
Sub Main()
  Dim i, x As Integer

  i = 35
  Do While i > -35
    If x Mod 2 = 0 Then
      Console.WriteLine(2 * i)
    Else
      Console.WriteLine(3 * i)
    End If
    i -= 1
  Loop
  Console.ReadKey()

End Sub
```

5. Design the flowchart that corresponds to the following Visual Basic program.

```vb
Sub Main()
  Dim i, x As Integer

  i = -20
  Do
    x = Console.ReadLine()
    If x = 0 Then
      Console.WriteLine("Zero")
    ElseIf x Mod 2 = 0 Then
      Console.WriteLine(2 * i)
    Else
      Console.WriteLine(3 * i)
    End If
    i += 1
  Loop While i <= 20

  Console.ReadKey()
End Sub
```

6. Design the flowchart that corresponds to the following Visual Basic program.

```vb
Sub Main()
  Dim a, i As Integer

  a = Console.ReadLine()
  If a > 0 Then
    i = 0
    Do While i <= a
      Console.WriteLine(i)
      i += 5
    Loop
  Else
    Console.WriteLine("Non-Positive Entered!")
  End If
```

```
    Console.ReadKey()
End Sub
```

7. Design the flowchart that corresponds to the following Visual Basic program.

```
Sub Main()
  Dim a, i As Integer

  a = Console.ReadLine()
  If a > 0 Then
    i = 0
    Do While i <= a
      Console.WriteLine(3 * i + i / 2)
      i += 1
    Loop
  Else
    i = 10
    Do
      Console.WriteLine(2 * i - i / 3)
      i -= 3
    Loop While i >= a
  End If

  Console.ReadKey()
End Sub
```

8. Design the flowchart that corresponds to the following Visual Basic program.

```
Sub Main()
  Dim a, b, i As Integer

  a = Console.ReadLine()
  If a > 0 Then
    For i = 0 To a
      Console.WriteLine(3 * i + i / 2)
    Next
  ElseIf a = 0 Then
    b = Console.ReadLine()
    Do While b > 0
      b = Console.ReadLine()
    Loop
    Console.WriteLine(2 * a + b)
  Else
    b = Console.ReadLine()
    Do While b < 0
      b = Console.ReadLine()
    Loop
    For i = a To b
      Console.WriteLine(i)
    Next
  End If
```

```
  Console.ReadKey()
End Sub
```

9. Design the flowchart that corresponds to the following Visual Basic program.

```
Sub Main()
  Dim a, b, c, d, sum, i, j As Integer

  a = Console.ReadLine()
  b = Console.ReadLine()
  c = Console.ReadLine()
  d = Console.ReadLine()

  sum = 0
  For i = a To b - 1
    For j = c To d - 1 Step 2
      sum += i + j
    Next
  Next
  Console.Write(sum)

  Console.ReadKey()
End Sub
```

10. Design the flowchart that corresponds to the following Visual Basic program.

```
Sub Main()
  Dim i, n As Integer
  Dim s As Double

  s = 0
  For i = 1 To 50
    Do
      n = Console.ReadLine()
    Loop While n < 0
    s += Math.Sqrt(n)
  Next
  Console.Write(s)

  Console.ReadKey()
End Sub
```

11. Design the flowchart that corresponds to the following Visual Basic program.

```
Sub Main()
  Dim a, b As Integer

  Do
    Do
      a = Console.ReadLine()
    Loop While a < 0
    Do
      b = Console.ReadLine()
    Loop While b < 0
    Console.WriteLine(Math.Abs(a - b))
```

```
Loop While Math.Abs(a - b) > 100

    Console.ReadKey()
End Sub
```

12. Design the flowchart that corresponds to the following Visual Basic program.

```
Sub Main()
    Dim a, b As Integer

    Do
        Do
            a = Console.ReadLine()
            b = Console.ReadLine()
        Loop While a < 0 Or b < 0

        If a > b Then
            Console.WriteLine(a - b)
        Else
            Console.WriteLine(a * b)
        End If
    Loop While Math.Abs(a - b) > 100

    Console.ReadKey()
End Sub
```

13. Write the Visual Basic program that corresponds to the following flowchart fragment.

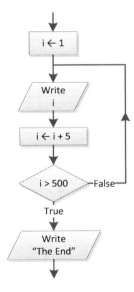

14. Write the Visual Basic program that corresponds to the following flowchart .

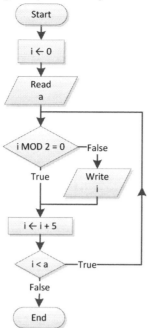

15. Write the Visual Basic program that corresponds to the following flowchart.

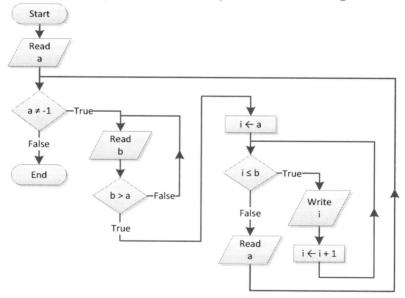

16. Write the Visual Basic program that corresponds to the following flowchart.

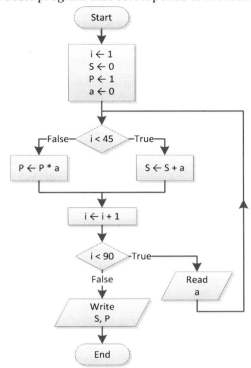

Chapter 31
More Exercises with Loop Control Structures

31.1 Simple Exercises with Loop Control Structures

Exercise 31.1-1   *Finding the Sum of 1 + 2 + 3 + ... + 100*

Write a Visual Basic program that calculates and displays the following sum:
$$S = 1 + 2 + 3 + ... + 100$$

Solution

Let's study this exercise using a sequence control structure.

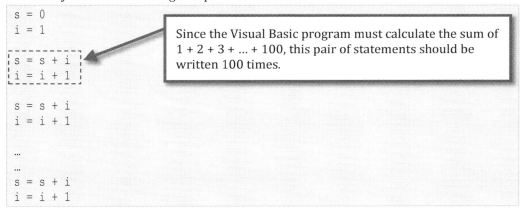

```
s = 0
i = 1

s = s + i
i = i + 1

s = s + i
i = i + 1

...

...
s = s + i
i = i + 1
```

Since the Visual Basic program must calculate the sum of 1 + 2 + 3 + ... + 100, this pair of statements should be written 100 times.

Let's use a trace table to better understand it.

Step	Statement	Notes	i	s
1	s = 0	0	?	0
2	i = 1		1	0
3	s = s + i	0 + 1 = **1**	1	1
4	i = i + 1		2	1
5	s = s + i	0 + 1 + 2 = **3**	2	3
6	i = i + 1		3	3
7	s = s + i	0 + 1 + 2 + 3 = **6**	3	6
8	i = i + 1		4	6
...	...		...	...
...	...		...	...

Last but one iteration	s = s + i		99	**4950**
	i = i + 1		**100**	4950
Last iteration	s = s + i	0 + 1 + 2 + 3 + ...+ 99 + 100 = **5050**	100	**5050**
	i = i + 1		**101**	5050

Now that everything has been cleared up, you can do the same using instead a counted loop structure that increments variable i from 1 to 100. In each iteration, its value is accumulated in variable s.

```
                          project_31_1_1
Sub Main()
  Dim s, i As Integer

  s = 0
  For i = 1 To 100
    s = s + i
  Next
  Console.Write(s)

  Console.ReadKey()
End Sub
```

Exercise 31.1-2   *Finding the Product of 2 × 4 × 6 × 8 × 10*

Write a Visual Basic program that calculates and displays the following product:
$$P = 2 × 4 × 6 × 8 × 10$$

Solution

Let's study this exercise using a sequence control structure.

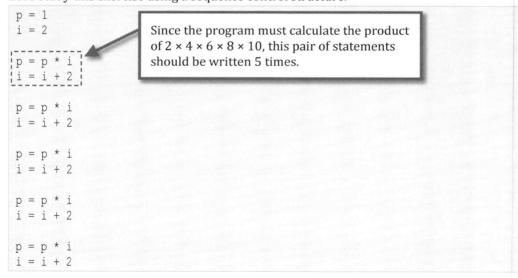

```
p = 1
i = 2

p = p * i
i = i + 2

p = p * i
i = i + 2

p = p * i
i = i + 2

p = p * i
i = i + 2

p = p * i
i = i + 2
```

Since the program must calculate the product of 2 × 4 × 6 × 8 × 10, this pair of statements should be written 5 times.

Let's use a trace table to better understand it.

Step	Statement	Notes	i	p
1	p = 1	1	?	1
2	i = 2		2	1
3	p = p * i	1 × 2 = **2**	2	2
4	i = i + 2		4	2
5	p = p * i	2 × 4 = **8**	4	8
6	i = i + 2		6	8
7	p = p * i	2 × 4 × 6 = **48**	6	48
8	i = i + 2		8	48
9	p = p * i	2 × 4 × 6 × 8 = **384**	8	384
10	i = i + 2		10	384
Last iteration	p = p * i	2 × 4 × 6 × 8 × 10 = **3840**	8	3840
	i = i + 2		12	3840

Now that everything has been cleared up, you can do the same using instead a counted loop structure that increments variable i by 2 from 2 to 10.

```
                          project_31_1_2
Sub Main()
  Dim p, i As Integer

  p = 1
  For i = 2 To 10 Step 2
    p = p * i
  Next
  Console.Write(p)

  Console.ReadKey()
End Sub
```

Exercise 31.1-3   Finding the Sum of $2^2 + 4^2 + 6^2 + ... (2N)^2$

Write a Visual Basic program that lets the user enter an integer N and then calculates and displays the following sum:

$$S = 2^2 + 4^2 + 6^2 + ... (2N)^2$$

Solution

In this exercise, variable i must increment by 2, but it must be raised to the second power before it is accumulated in variable s.

The final Visual Basic program is as follows.

```
                          project_31_1_3
Sub Main()
  Dim N, i As Integer
  Dim s As Double
```

```
N = Console.ReadLine()
s = 0
For i = 2 To 2 * N Step 2
  s = s + i ^ 2
Next

Console.Write(s)

Console.ReadKey()
End Sub
```

Exercise 31.1-4   *Finding the Sum of $3^3 + 6^6 + 9^9 + ... (3N)^{3N}$*

Write a Visual Basic program that lets the user enter an integer N and then calculates and displays the following sum:

$$S = 3^3 + 6^6 + 9^9 + ...+ (3N)^{3N}$$

Solution

This is pretty much the same as the previous exercise. The only difference is that variable i must be raised to the ith power before it is accumulated in variable s. The final Visual Basic program is as follows.

```
                          project_31_1_4
Sub Main()
  Dim N, i As Integer
  Dim s As Double

  N = Console.ReadLine()
  s = 0
  For i = 3 To 3 * N Step 3
    s = s + i ^ i
  Next

  Console.Write(s)

  Console.ReadKey()
End Sub
```

Exercise 31.1-5   *Finding the Average Value of Positive Numbers*

Write a Visual Basic program that lets the user enter 100 numbers and then calculates and displays the average value of the positive numbers. Add all necessary checks to make the program satisfy the property of definiteness.

Solution

Since the total number of iterations is known, you can use a counted loop structure. Inside the loop, however, a decision control structure must check whether or not the given number is positive; if so, it must accumulate the given number in variable s. When the flow of execution exits the loop, the average value can then be calculated. The Visual Basic program is as follows.

```
                         project_31_1_5
Sub Main()
  Dim count, i As Integer
  Dim s, x As Double

  s = 0
  count = 0
  For i = 1 To 100
    x = Console.ReadLine()
    If x > 0 Then
      s = s + x
      count += 1
    End If
  Next
  If count <> 0 Then
    Console.WriteLine(s / count)
  Else
    Console.WriteLine("No numbers entered!")
  End If

  Console.ReadKey()
End Sub
```

> **Notice:** The `If count <> 0` statement is necessary, because there is a possibility that the user may enter negative values only. By including this check, the program prevents any division-by-zero errors and thereby satisfies the property of definiteness.

Exercise 31.1-6   *Counting the Numbers According to Which is Greater*

Write a Visual Basic program that prompts the user to enter 10 pairs of numbers and then counts and displays the number of times that the first number given was greater than the second one.

Solution

Once again, a counted loop structure can be used. The Visual Basic program is as follows.

```
                         project_31_1_6
Sub Main()
  Dim count_a, count_b, i, a, b As Integer

  count_a = 0
  count_b = 0

  For i = 1 To 10
    Console.Write("Enter number A: ")
    a = Console.ReadLine()
    Console.Write("Enter number B: ")
    b = Console.ReadLine()
```

```
    If a > b Then
      count_a += 1
    ElseIf b > a Then
      count_b += 1
    End If
  Next
  Console.Write(count_a & ", " & count_b)

  Console.ReadKey()
End Sub
```

A reasonable question that someone may ask is "*Why is a multiple-decision control structure being used? Why not use a dual-alternative decision structure instead?*"

Suppose that a dual-alternative decision structure, such as the following, is used.

```
If a > b Then
  count_a += 1
Else
  count_b += 1
End If
```

In this decision control structure, the variable count_b increments when variable b is greater than variable a (this is desirable) but also when variable b is equal to variable a (this is undesirable). Using a multiple-decision control structure instead ensures that variable count_b increments only when variable b is greater than (and not when it is equal to) variable a.

Exercise 31.1-7   *Counting the Numbers According to Their Digits*

Write a Visual Basic program that prompts the user to enter 20 integers and then counts and displays the total number of one-digit, two-digit, and three-digit integers. Assume that the user enters values between 1 and 999.

Solution

Nothing new here! The Visual Basic program is as follows.

```
                           project_31_1_7
Sub Main()
  Dim count1, count2, count3, i, a As Integer

  count1 = 0
  count2 = 0
  count3 = 0

  For i = 1 To 20
    Console.Write("Enter a number: ")
    a = Console.ReadLine()

    If a <= 9 Then
      count1 += 1
    ElseIf a <= 99 Then
```

```
            count2 += 1
        Else
            count3 += 1
        End If
    Next
    Console.Write(count1 & ", " & count2 & ", " & count3)

    Console.ReadKey()
End Sub
```

Exercise 31.1-8   *How Many Numbers Fit in a Sum*

Write a Visual Basic program that lets the user enter numeric values repeatedly until the sum of them exceeds 1000. At the end, the program should display the total quantity of numbers entered.

Solution

In this case, you don't know the exact number of iterations, so you cannot use a counted loop structure. Let's use a post-test loop structure instead, but, in order to make your program free of logic errors you should follow the "Ultimate" rule discussed in Chapter 29. According to this rule, the post-test loop structure should always be as follows, given in general form.

```
initialize sum
Do
    A statement or block of statements
    Update/alter sum
Loop While Boolean_Expression(sum)
```

Following this, the Visual Basic program becomes

```
                          project_31_1_8
Sub Main()
    Dim count As Integer
    Dim sum, x As Double

    count = 0
    sum = 0                    'Initialization of sum
    Do
        x = Console.ReadLine()
        count += 1
        sum += x               'Update/alteration of sum
    Loop While sum <= 1000
    Console.Write(count)

    Console.ReadKey()
End Sub
```

Exercise 31.1-9   *Finding the Sum of Integers*

Write a Visual Basic program that prompts the user to enter integer values repeatedly until a real one is entered. At the end, the program should display the total number of positive integers entered.

Solution

Once again, you don't know the exact number of iterations, so you cannot use a counted loop structure.

According to the "Ultimate" rule, the pre-test loop structure should always be as follows, given in general form.

```
x = Console.ReadLine()      'Initialization of x
Do While Fix(x) = x
  A statement or block of statements
  x = Console.ReadLine()    'Update/alteration of x
Loop
```

> **Notice**: *In this case, using a pre-test loop structure rather than a post-test loop structure is a better option. Why? Because if the first number given is real, the pre-test loop structure ensures that the flow of execution never enters the loop!*

The final Visual Basic program is as follows.

```
                          project_31_1_9
Sub Main()
  Dim x As Double
  Dim count As Integer

  count = 0

  Console.Write("Enter a number: ")
  x = Console.ReadLine()
  Do While Fix(x) = x
    If x > 0 Then
      count += 1
    End If
    Console.Write("Enter a number: ")
    x = Console.ReadLine()
  Loop
  Console.Write(count)

  Console.ReadKey()
End Sub
```

Exercise 31.1-10   *Iterating as Many Times as the User Wishes*

Write a Visual Basic program that prompts the user to enter two numbers and then calculates and displays the first number raised to the power of the second one. The program should iterate as many times as the user wishes. At the end of each area calculation, the program should ask the user if he or she wishes to calculate the area of another rectangle. If the answer is "yes" the program should repeat; it should end otherwise. Make your program accept the answer in all possible forms such as "yes", "YES", "Yes", or even "YeS".

Solution

According to the "Ultimate" rule, the pre-test loop structure should be as follows, given in general form.

```
answer = "yes"                          'Initialization of answer
Do While answer.ToUpper() = "YES"
  //Here goes the code that
  //prompts the user to enter two numbers and then
  //calculates and displays the first number
  //raised to the power of the second one.

  Console.Write("Would you like to repeat? ")
  answer = Console.ReadLine()            'Update/alteration of answer
Loop
```

The `ToUpper()` procedure ensures that the program operates properly for any given answer: "yes", "YES", "Yes", or even "YeS" or "yEs"!

On the other hand, if you decide to use a post-test loop structure, it should be as follows, given in general form.

```
answer = "YES"                          'Redundant initialization of answer
Do
  //Here goes the code that
  //prompts the user to enter two numbers and then
  //calculates and displays the first number
  //raised to the power of the second one.

  Console.Write("Would you like to repeat? ")
  answer = Console.ReadLine()            'Update/alteration of answer
Loop While answer.ToUpper() = "YES"
```

Using a post-test loop is a better approach since the initialization of answer is actually redundant and can be omitted. Why? In contrast to the pre-test loop structure, the flow of execution enters the loop either way and initialization of answer occurs inside the loop.

Accordingly, the solution to this exercise, using a post-test loop structure becomes

```
project_31_1_10

Sub Main()
  Dim a, b As Integer
  Dim result As Double
  Dim answer As String

  Do
    Console.Write("Enter two numbers: ")
    a = Console.ReadLine()
    b = Console.ReadLine()

    result = a ^ b
    Console.WriteLine("The result is: " & result)
```

```
      Console.Write("Would you like to repeat? ")
      answer = Console.ReadLine()
   Loop While answer.ToUpper() = "YES"
End Sub
```

Exercise 31.1-11 *Finding the Sum of the Digits*

Write a Visual Basic program that lets the user enter an integer and then calculates the sum of its digits. Afterwards, use the value 4753 as an input value and create a trace table to determine the values of the variables in each step.

Solution

In Chapter 13, you learned how to split the digits of an integer when its total number of digits was known. In this exercise however, the user is allowed to enter any value, no matter how small or large; thus, the total number of the digits can be unknown.

To solve this exercise, a loop control structure could be used. The main idea is to isolate one digit at each iteration. But what you don't really know is the total number of iterations that should be performed because this number depends on the given integer. So, is this a dead end? Of course not!

Inside the loop, the given integer can be getting "smaller" and "smaller" in every iteration until eventually it becomes zero. The value of zero can serve to stop the loop control structure from iterating. For example, if the given number is 4753, it can become 475 in the first iteration, then 47, then 4, and finally 0. When it becomes 0, the iterations can stop.

Let's try to comprehend the proposed solution using the following flowchart. Some statements are written in general form.

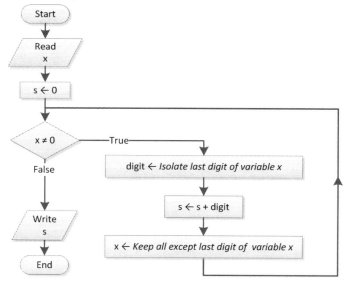

The statement

         digit ← *Isolate last digit of variable x.*

can be written using the well-known MOD 10 operation:

```
digit ← x MOD 10
```

Of course, the whole concept relies on the statement

$$x ← \textit{Keep all except last digit of variable x.}$$

This is the statement that eventually zeros the value of variable x, and the flow of execution then exits the loop. To write this statement you can use a DIV 10 operation.

```
x ← x DIV 10
```

Accordingly, the Visual Basic program becomes

project_31_1_11

```
Sub Main()
  Dim x, s, digit As Integer

  x = Console.ReadLine()
  s = 0

  Do While x <> 0
    digit = x Mod 10
    s = s + digit
    x = x \ 10           'This is the x DIV 10 operation
  Loop
  Console.Write(s)

  Console.ReadKey()
End Sub
```

Now let's create a trace table for the input value 4753.

Step	Statement	Notes	x	digit	s
1	x = Console.ReadLine()	User enters the value 4753	4753	?	?
2	s = 0		4753	?	0
3	Do While x <> 0	This validates to True			
4	digit = x Mod 10		4753	3	0
5	s = s + digit		4753	3	3
6	x = x \ 10		475	3	3
7	Do While x <> 0	This validates to True			
8	digit = x Mod 10		475	5	3
9	s = s + digit		475	5	8
10	x = x \ 10		47	5	8
11	Do While x <> 0	This validates to True			
12	digit = x Mod 10		47	7	8
13	s = s + digit		47	7	15

14	x = x \ 10		4	7	15
15	Do While x <> 0	This validates to True			
16	digit = x Mod 10		4	4	15
17	s = s + digit		4	4	19
18	x = x \ 10		0	4	19
19	Do While x <> 0	This validates to False			
20	Console.Write(s)	The value 19 is displayed			

Exercise 31.1-12 *Counting the Digits*

Write a Visual Basic program that prompts the user to enter an integer and then displays the number of its digits.

Solution

Using the method proposed in the previous exercise, the Visual Basic program is as follows.

```
                            project_31_1_12
Sub Main()
  Dim x, count As Integer

  Console.Write("Enter a number: ")
  x = Console.ReadLine()
  count = 0

  Do While x <> 0
    count += 1
    x = x \ 10
  Loop
  Console.Write(count)

  Console.ReadKey()
End Sub
```

31.2 Exercises with Nested Loop Control Structures

Exercise 31.2-1 *Displaying all Three-Digit Integers that Contain a Given Digit*

Write a Visual Basic program that prompts the user to enter a digit (0 to 9) and then displays all three-digit integers that contain that given digit at least once. For example, for the given value 7, the values 357, 771, and 700 are such integers.

Solution

There are two different approaches, actually! The first one uses just one counted loop structure while the second one uses three counted loop structures, nested one within the other. Let's analyze them both!

First Approach – Using a counted loop structure and a decision control structure

The main idea is to use a counted loop structure where the *counter* variable increments from 100 to 999. Inside the loop, the *counter* variable is split into its individual digits (digit3, digit2, digit1) and a decision control structure is used to check if at least one of its digits is equal to the given one. The Visual Basic program is as follows.

```
                         project_31_2_1a
Sub Main()
  Dim x, i, digit3, r, digit2, digit1 As Integer

  Console.Write("Enter a digit 0 - 9: ")
  x = Console.ReadLine()

  For i = 100 To 999
    digit3 = i \ 100
    r = i Mod 100

    digit2 = r \ 10
    digit1 = r Mod 10

    If digit3 = x Or digit2 = x Or digit1 = x Then
      Console.WriteLine(i)
    End If
  Next

  Console.ReadKey()
End Sub
```

Second Approach – Using nested loop control structures and a decision control structure

The main idea is to use three counted loop structures, nested one within the other. In this case, there are three *counter* variables and each one of them corresponds to one digit of the three-digit integer. The Visual Basic program is as follows.

```
                         project_31_2_1b
Sub Main()
  Dim x, digit3, digit2, digit1 As Integer

  Console.Write("Enter a digit 0 - 9: ")
  x = Console.ReadLine()

  For digit3 = 1 To 9
    For digit2 = 0 To 9
      For digit1 = 0 To 9
        If digit3 = x Or digit2 = x Or digit1 = x Then
          Console.WriteLine(digit3 * 100 + digit2 * 10 + digit1)
        End If
      Next
    Next
  Next
```

```
    Console.ReadKey()
  End Sub
```

If you follow the flow of execution, the value 100 is the first "integer" evaluated (digit1 = 1, digit2 = 0, digit3 = 0). Then, the most-nested loop control structure increments variable digit1 by one and the next value evaluated is "integer" 101. This continues until digit1 reaches the value 9; that is, until the "integer" reaches the value 109. The flow of execution then exits the most-nested loop control structure, variable digit2 increments by one, and the most-nested loop control structure starts over again, thus the values evaluated are the "integers" 110, 111, 112, ... 119. The process goes on until all integers up to the value 999 are evaluated.

> **Notice**: Please note that variable digit3 starts from 1, whereas variables digit2 and digit1 start from 0. This is necessary since the scale for three-digit numbers begins from 100 and not from 000.
>
> **Notice**: Please note how the Console.WriteLine statement composes the three-digit integer.

Exercise 31.2-2   *Displaying all Instances of a Specified Condition*

Write a Visual Basic program that displays all three-digit integers in which the first digit is smaller than the second digit and the second digit is smaller than the third digit. For example, the values 357, 456, and 159 are such integers.

Solution

There are three different approaches, actually! Let's analyze them all!

First Approach – Using a counted loop structure and a decision control structure

The Visual Basic program is as follows.

```
                           project_31_2_2a
Sub Main()
  Dim i, r, digit1, digit2, digit3 As Integer

  For i = 100 To 999
    digit3 = i \ 100
    r = i Mod 100

    digit2 = r \ 10
    digit1 = r Mod 10

    If digit3 < digit2 And digit2 < digit1 Then
      Console.WriteLine(i)
    End If
  Next

  Console.ReadKey()
End Sub
```

Second Approach – Using nested loop control structures and a decision control structure

The Visual Basic program is as follows.

```
project_31_2_2b
Sub Main()
  Dim digit3, digit2, digit1 As Integer

  For digit3 = 1 To 9
    For digit2 = 0 To 9
      For digit1 = 0 To 9
        If digit3 < digit2 And digit2 < digit1 Then
          Console.WriteLine(digit3 * 100 + digit2 * 10 + digit1)
        End If
      Next
    Next
  Next

  Console.ReadKey()
End Sub
```

Third Approach – Using nested loop control structures only

This approach is based on the previous one. The main difference between them is that in this case, variable digit1 always begins from a value greater than digit2, and variable digit2 always begins from a value greater than digit3. In that way, the first integer that will be displayed is 123.

> *Notice: There are no integers below the value 123 and above the value 789 that can validate the Boolean expression* digit3 < digit2 And digit2 < digit1 *to* True.

The Visual Basic program is as follows.

```
project_31_2_2c
Sub Main()
  Dim digit3, digit2, digit1 As Integer

  For digit3 = 1 To 7
    For digit2 = digit3 + 1 To 8
      For digit1 = digit2 + 1 To 9
        Console.WriteLine(digit3 * 100 + digit2 * 10 + digit1)
      Next
    Next
  Next

  Console.ReadKey()
End Sub
```

> *Notice: This solution is the most efficient since it doesn't use any decision control structure and, moreover, the number of iterations is kept to a minimum!*
>
> **Remember!** *As you can see, one problem can have many solutions. It is up to you to find the optimal one!*

31.3 Data Validation with Loop Control Structures

Data validation is the process of restricting data input, forcing the user to enter only valid values.

You have already encountered one method of data validation using decision control structures. Let's recall a previous example.

```
Sub Main()
  Dim x As Double
  Dim input As String

  Console.Write("Enter a number: ")
  input = Console.ReadLine()

  If Double.TryParse(input, x) = True Then
    Console.WriteLine(x & " is a number")
  Else
    Console.WriteLine("You didn't enter a number")
  End If

  Console.ReadKey()
End Sub
```

> **Remember!** *Procedure* `Double.TryParse()` *converts the string representation of a double contained in string variable* input *to its double equivalent, and then assigns the result to the double variable* x. *It returns* `True` *if the conversion is successful, and* `False` *otherwise.*

This approach, however, is not the most appropriate because if the user does enter an invalid number, the program displays the error message and the flow of execution inevitably reaches the end. The user must then execute the program again in order to re-enter a valid number.

Next, you will see three approaches given in general form that validate data input using loop control structures. If the user persistently enters an invalid value, the main idea is to prompt him or her repeatedly, until he or she gets bored and finally enters a valid one. Of course, if the user enters a valid value right from the beginning, the flow of execution simply continues to the next part of the program.

Which approach you use depends on whether or not you wish to display an error message and whether you wish to display an individual error message for each error or just a single error message for any kind of error.

First Approach – Validating data input without error messages

To validate data input without displaying any error messages, you can use the following code fragment given in general form.

```
Do
  Console.Write("Prompt message")
  input_data = Console.ReadLine()
Loop While input_data test 1 fails Or input_data test 2 fails Or …
```

Second Approach – Validating data input with one error message

To validate data input and display an error message (that is, the same error message for any type of input error), you can use the following code fragment given in general form.

```
Console.Write("Prompt message")
input_data = Console.ReadLine()
Do While input_data test 1 fails Or input_data test 2 fails Or …
  Console.WriteLine("Error message")
  Console.Write("Prompt message")
  input_data = Console.ReadLine()
Loop
```

Third Approach – Validating data input with individual error messages

To validate data input and display an error message (that is, individual error messages, one for each type of input error), you can use the following code fragment given in general form.

```
Do
  Console.Write("Prompt message")
  input_data = Console.ReadLine()
  failure = False
  If input_data test 1 fails Then
     Console.WriteLine("Error message 1")
     failure = True
  ElseIf input_data test 2 fails Then
     Console.WriteLine("Error message 2")
     failure = True
  ElseIf …

     …
  End If
Loop While failure = True
```

Exercise 31.3-1   *Finding the Square Root - Validation Without Error Messages*

Write a Visual Basic program that prompts the user to enter a numeric value and then calculates its square root. Moreover, the program should validate data input, allowing the user to enter only non-negative[1] numeric values. There is no need to display any error messages.

Solution

First, let's write the program without data validation.

```
Sub Main()
  Dim x, y As Double

  Console.Write("Enter a number: ")
  x = Console.ReadLine()

  y = Math.Sqrt(x)
  Console.WriteLine(y)
```

Data input stage without validation.

---

[1] A quantity that is either zero or positive.

```
    Console.ReadKey()
End Sub
```

To validate data input without displaying any error messages you can use the first approach. All you need to do is replace the statements marked with a dashed rectangle with the following code fragment.

```
Do
    Console.Write("Enter a non-negative number: ")
    input = Console.ReadLine()
Loop While Double.TryParse(input, x) = False Or x < 0
```

The final Visual Basic program becomes

project_31_3_1

```
Sub Main()
    Dim x, y As Double
    Dim input As String

    Do
        Console.Write("Enter a non-negative number: ")
        input = Console.ReadLine()
    Loop While Double.TryParse(input, x) = False Or x < 0

    y = Math.Sqrt(x)
    Console.Write(y)

    Console.ReadKey()
End Sub
```

Data input validation without error messages.

Exercise 31.3-2   *Finding the Square Root - Validation with One Error Message*

Write a Visual Basic program that prompts the user to enter a numeric value and then calculates its square root. Moreover, the program should validate data input and display an error message when the user enters any non-numeric or negative values.

Solution

In the previous exercise, the two statements marked with the dashed rectangle were replaced with a code fragment that validated data input without displaying any error message. The same method is followed here, except that the replacing Visual Basic fragment is based on the second approach. The Visual Basic program is as follows.

project_31_3_2

Data input validation with one single error message.

```
Sub Main()
    Dim x, y As Double
    Dim input As String

    Console.Write("Enter a non-negative number: ")
    input = Console.ReadLine()
    Do While Double.TryParse(input, x) = False Or x < 0
        Console.WriteLine("Error: Invalid number!")
        Console.Write("Enter a non-negative number: ")
        input = Console.ReadLine()
```

```
: Loop                                                               :
```

```
  y = Math.Sqrt(x)
  Console.WriteLine(y)

  Console.ReadKey()
End Sub
```

Exercise 31.3-3   *Finding the Square Root - Validation with Individual Error Messages*

Write a Visual Basic program that prompts the user to enter a numeric value and then calculates its square root Moreover, the program should validate data input and display individual error messages when the user enters any non-numeric or negative values.

Solution

To validate data input and display individual error messages for each error, you can use the third approach. The Visual Basic program is as follows.

```
                          project_31_3_3
Sub Main()
  Dim x, y As Double
  Dim failure As Boolean
  Dim input As String

  Do
    Console.Write("Enter a non-negative number: ")
    input = Console.ReadLine()

    failure = False
    If Double.TryParse(input, x) = False Then
      Console.WriteLine("Please enter numeric values!")
      failure = True
    ElseIf x < 0 Then
      Console.WriteLine("Please enter non-negative numbers!")
      failure = True
    End If
  Loop While failure = True

  y = Math.Sqrt(x)
  Console.Write(y)

  Console.ReadKey()
End Sub
```

Data input validation with an individual error message for each error.

Exercise 31.3-4   *Finding the Sum of 10 Numbers*

Write a Visual Basic program that prompts the user to enter 10 numbers and then calculates and displays their sum. Moreover, the program should validate data input and display an error message when the user enters any non-numeric or negative values.

Solution

This exercise was already discussed in Chapter 27. The only difference here is that this program should validate data input and display an error message when the user enters invalid values. For your convenience, the solution proposed in Chapter 27 is reproduced next.

```
Sub Main()
    Dim sum, a As Double
    Dim i As Integer

    sum = 0
    For i = 1 To 10
        Console.Write("Enter a number: ")
        a = Console.ReadLine()

        sum = sum + a
    Next

    Console.Write(sum)

    Console.ReadKey()
End Sub
```

Data input stage without validation

Now, replace the statements marked with a dashed rectangle with the following code fragment

```
Console.Write("Enter a number: ")
input = Console.ReadLine()
Do While Double.TryParse(input, a) = False
    Console.WriteLine("Please enter numeric values!")
    Console.WriteLine("Enter a number: ")
    input = Console.ReadLine()
Loop
```

and the final Visual Basic program becomes

project_31_3_4

```
Sub Main()
    Dim sum, a As Double
    Dim i As Integer
    Dim input As String

    sum = 0
    For i = 1 To 10
        Console.Write("Enter a number: ")
        input = Console.ReadLine()
        Do While Double.TryParse(input, a) = False
            Console.WriteLine("Please enter numeric values!")
            Console.WriteLine("Enter a number: ")
            input = Console.ReadLine()
        Loop

        sum = sum + a
```

Data input validation with one single error message

```
     Next

     Console.Write(sum)

     Console.ReadKey()
End Sub
```

> **Notice**: *The basic purpose of this exercise was to show you how to nest the loop control structure that validates data input into other already existing loop control structures.*

31.4 Using Loop Control Structures to Solve Mathematical Problems

Exercise 31.4-1 *Calculating the Area of as Many Triangles as the User Wishes*

Write a Visual Basic program that prompts the user to enter the lengths of all three sides A, B, and C of a triangle and then calculates and displays its area. You can use Heron's formula,

$$Area=\sqrt{S(S\text{-}A)(S\text{-}B)(S\text{-}C)}$$

where S is the semi-perimeter

$$S=\frac{A+B+C}{2}$$

The program should iterate as many times as the user wishes. At the end of each area calculation, the program should ask the user if he or she wishes to calculate the area of another triangle. If the answer is "yes" the program should repeat; it should end otherwise. Make your program accept the answer in all possible forms such as "yes", "YES", "Yes", or even "YeS".

Moreover, the program should validate data input and display an error message when the user enters any non-positive value.

Solution

According to the "Ultimate" rule, the post-test loop structure should be as follows, given in general form.

```
answer = "yes"                          'Redundant initialization of answer.
Do
   'Here goes the code that prompts the user to enter
   'the lengths of all three sides A, B, C of a triangle and
   'then calculates and displays its area

   Console.Write("Would you like to repeat? ")
   answer = Console.ReadLine()           'Update/alteration of answer
Loop While answer.ToUpper() = "YES"
```

> **Remember!** *The* ToUpper() *procedure ensures that the programs operates properly for any given answer "Yes", "yes", "YES" or even "YeS" or "yEs"!*

The solution to this exercise, using a post-test loop structure, is as follows.

```
                         project_31_4_1
Sub Main()
   Dim a, b, c, s, area As Double
```

```
Dim answer As String

Do
  Console.Write("Enter side A: ")
  a = Console.ReadLine()
  Do While a <= 0
    Console.Write("Invalid side. Enter side A: ")
    a = Console.ReadLine()
  Loop

  Console.Write("Enter side B: ")
  b = Console.ReadLine()
  Do While b <= 0
    Console.Write("Invalid side. Enter side B: ")
    b = Console.ReadLine()
  Loop

  Console.Write("Enter side C: ")
  c = Console.ReadLine()
  Do While c <= 0
    Console.Write("Invalid side. Enter side C: ")
    c = Console.ReadLine()
  Loop

  s = (a + b + c) / 2
  area = Math.Sqrt(s * (s - a) * (s - b) * (s - c))
  Console.WriteLine("The area is: " & area)

  Console.WriteLine("Would you like to repeat? ")
  answer = Console.ReadLine()
Loop While answer.ToUpper() = "YES"
End Sub
```

Exercise 31.4-2   *Finding x and y*

Write a Visual Basic program that displays all possible integer values of x and y within the range
-20 to +20 that validate the following formula:

$$3x^2 - 6y^2 = 6$$

Solution

If you just want to display all possible combinations of variables x and y, you can use the following Visual Basic program.

```
Sub Main()
  Dim x, y As Integer

  For x = -20 To 20
    For y = -20 To 20
      Console.WriteLine(x & ", " & y)
```

```
      Next
    Next

    Console.ReadKey()
  End Sub
```

However, from all those combinations, you need only those that validate the expression $3x^2 - 6y^2 = 6$. A decision control structure is perfect for that purpose! The final Visual Basic program is as follows.

project_31_4_2

```
Sub Main()
  Dim x, y As Integer

  For x = -20 To 20
    For y = -20 To 20
      If 3 * x ^ 2 - 6 * y ^ 2 = 6 Then
        Console.WriteLine(x & ", " & y)
      End If
    Next
  Next

  Console.ReadKey()
End Sub
```

Exercise 31.4-3   *From Russia with Love*

You can multiply two positive integers using the "Russian multiplication algorithm," which is presented in the following flowchart.

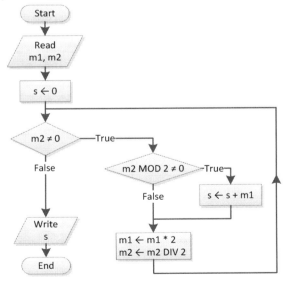

Write the corresponding Visual Basic program and create a trace table to determine the values of the variables in each step for the input values 5 and 13.

Solution

In the given flowchart, a single-alternative decision structure is nested within a pre-test loop structure. The corresponding Visual Basic program is as follows.

```
project_31_4_3a
Sub Main()
  Dim m1, m2, s As Integer

  m1 = Console.ReadLine()
  m2 = Console.ReadLine()

  s = 0
  Do While m2 <> 0
    If m2 Mod 2 <> 0 Then
      s += m1
    End If
    m1 *= 2
    m2 \= 2
  Loop
  Console.Write(s)

  Console.ReadKey()
End Sub
```

For the input values of 5 and 13, the trace table looks like this.

Step	Statement	Notes	m1	m2	s
1	m1 = Console.ReadLine()	User enters the value 5	5	?	?
2	m2 = Console.ReadLine()	User enters the value 13	5	13	?
3	s = 0		5	13	0
4	Do While m2 <> 0	This evaluates to True			
5	If m2 Mod 2 <> 0 Then	This evaluates to True			
6	s += m1		5	13	5
7	m1 *= 2		10	13	5
8	m2 \= 2		10	6	5
9	Do While m2 <> 0	This evaluates to True			
10	If m2 Mod 2 <> 0 Then	This evaluates to False			
11	m1 *= 2		20	6	5
12	m2 \= 2		20	3	5
13	Do While m2 <> 0	This evaluates to True			
14	If m2 Mod 2 <> 0 Then	This evaluates to True			
15	s += m1		20	3	25
16	m1 *= 2		40	3	25

17	m2 \= 2		40	**1**	25
18	Do While m2 <> 0	This evaluates to True			
19	If m2 Mod 2 <> 0 Then	This evaluates to True			
20	s += m1		40	1	**65**
21	m1 *= 2		**80**	1	65
22	m2 \= 2		80	**0**	65
23	Do While m2 <> 0	This evaluates to False			
24	Console.Write(s)	The value 65 is displayed which is, of course, the result of the multiplication 5 × 13			

However, one thing that you need to know about CPUs and microprocessors is that the only arithmetic operation that most of them can actually perform is addition. The majority of them perform all multiplication operations using the *Russian multiplication algorithm*.

On the other hand, in the program, there are the following two statements:

```
m1 *= 2
m2 \= 2
```

But since CPUs can't multiply or divide, how on Earth are these operations actually performed?

Things are not always as they seem! In this case, these two operations are not performed by multiplying or by dividing by 2, but by shifting binary numbers to the left or right correspondingly.

Remember! *All numbers are stored in main memory (RAM) and manipulated by the Central Processing Unit (CPU) in their binary form; that is, in a form that uses zeros and ones. For example, the value 39 is stored in main memory as 00100111.*

For example, the value 43 can be represented in binary form as 00101011 which

➤ after shifting it to the left, becomes 01010110. This is the value 86 in decimal form:
   (43 × 2 = 86).

➤ after shifting it to the right, becomes 00010101. This is the value 21 in decimal form:
   (43 DIV 2 = 21).

Remember! *Shifting a binary number to the left is equivalent to multiplying it by 2, and shifting it to the right is equivalent to dividing it by 2 (integer division).*

Notice: *After shifting a binary number to the right, the rightmost digit is lost.*

Visual Basic incorporates two special operators that have purposely not been mentioned so far. Actually, only advanced programmers use them. But since day by day you are becoming a more experienced programmer, it is worth mentioning them here. These operators are called *shifting operators* and they do the obvious: they shift an integer (the binary representation of it) to the left or to the right. The Russian multiplication algorithm is presented here once again, but without any division or multiplication operations, just simple shifts to the left and to the right!

```
                          project_31_4_3b
Sub Main()
  Dim m1, m2, s As Integer

  m1 = Console.ReadLine()
  m2 = Console.ReadLine()

  s = 0
  Do While m2 <> 0
    If m2 Mod 2 <> 0 Then
      s += m1
    End If
    m1 = m1 << 1     'This is equivalent to m1 *= 2.
                     'It shifts the bits of m1 one position to the left.

    m2 = m2 >> 1     'This is equivalent to m2 \= 2.
                     'It shifts the bits of m2 one position to the right.
  Loop
  Console.Write(s)

  Console.ReadKey()
End Sub
```

Exercise 31.4-4   *Finding the Number of Divisors*

Write a Visual Basic program that lets the user enter a positive integer and then displays the total number of its divisors.

Solution

Let's see some examples.

> ➢ The divisors of value 12 are numbers 1, 2, 3, 4, 6, 12.
> ➢ The divisors of value 15 are numbers 1, 3, 5, 15.
> ➢ The divisors of value 20 are numbers 1, 2, 4, 5, 10, 20.
> ➢ The divisors of value 50 are numbers 1, 2, 5, 10, 25, 50.

If variable x contains the given integer, all possible divisors of x are between 1 and x. Thus, all you need here is a counted loop structure that increments variable *counter* from 1 to x and checks, in each iteration, whether the value of *counter* is a divisor of x, The Visual Basic program is as follows.

```
                          project_31_4_4a
Sub Main()
  Dim x, number_of_divisors, i As Integer

  x = Console.ReadLine()

  number_of_divisors = 0
  For i = 1 To x
    If x Mod i = 0 Then
      number_of_divisors += 1
```

```
      End If
    Next
    Console.Write(number_of_divisors)

    Console.ReadKey()
End Sub
```

This program, for input value 20, performs 20 iterations. However, wouldn't it be even better if it could perform almost the half of the iterations and achieve the same result? Of course it would! So, let's make it more efficient!

As you probably know, for any integer given (in variable x)

➢ the value 1 is always a divisor.

➢ the integer given is always a divisor of itself.

➢ there are no divisors after the middle of the range 1 to x.

Accordingly, for any integer there are certainly 2 divisors, the value 1 and the given integer itself. Therefore, the program must check for other possible divisors starting from the value 2 until the middle of the range 1 to x. The improved Visual Basic program is as follows.

```
                      project_31_4_4b
Sub Main()
  Dim x, number_of_divisors, i As Integer

  x = Console.ReadLine()

  number_of_divisors = 2
  For i = 2 To x \ 2
    If x Mod i = 0 Then
      number_of_divisors += 1
    End If
  Next
  Console.Write(number_of_divisors)

  Console.ReadKey()
End Sub
```

This Visual Basic program performs less than half of the iterations that the previous program did! To be more specific, for the input value 20, this Visual Basic program performs only (20 – 2) DIV 2 = 9 iterations!

Exercise 31.4-5   Is the Number a Prime?

Write a Visual Basic program that prompts the user to enter an integer greater than 1 and then displays a message indicating if this number is a prime. A prime number is any integer greater than 1 that has no divisors other than 1 and itself. The numbers 7, 11, and 13 are all such numbers.

Solution

This exercise is based on the previous one. It is very simple! If the given integer has only two divisors, the number is a prime. The Visual Basic program is as follows.

```
                           project_31_4_5a
Sub Main()
  Dim x, number_of_divisors, i As Integer

  Console.Write("Enter an integer greater than 1: ")
  x = Console.ReadLine()

  number_of_divisors = 2
  For i = 2 To x \ 2
    If x Mod i = 0 Then
      number_of_divisors += 1
    End If
  Next

  If number_of_divisors = 2 Then
    Console.WriteLine("Number " & x & " is prime")
  End If

  Console.ReadKey()
End Sub
```

Now let's make the program more efficient. The flow of execution can break out of the loop when a third divisor is found, because this means that the given integer is definitely not a prime. There are two approaches.

First Approach – Using the Exit For statement

The first approach uses the Exit For statement, as shown in the next Visual Basic program.

```
                           project_31_4_5b
Sub Main()
  Dim x, number_of_divisors, i As Integer

  Console.Write("Enter an integer greater than 1: ")
  x = Console.ReadLine()

  number_of_divisors = 2
  For i = 2 To x \ 2
    If x Mod i = 0 Then
      number_of_divisors += 1
      Exit For
    End If
  Next

  If number_of_divisors = 2 Then
    Console.WriteLine("Number " & x & " is prime")
  End If

  Console.ReadKey()
End Sub
```

Second Approach – Using a pre-test loop structure

You can convert the counted loop structure to a pre-test loop structure and then change the Boolean expression of the loop to evaluate both variables i and number_of_divisors. As long as variable number_of_divisors is equal to 2, the loop should continue iterating. The Visual Basic program is as follows,

```
                          project_31_4_5c
Sub Main()
  Dim x, number_of_divisors, i As Integer

  Console.Write("Enter an integer greater than 1: ")
  x = Console.ReadLine()

  number_of_divisors = 2
  i = 2
  Do While i <= x \ 2 And number_of_divisors = 2
    If x Mod i = 0 Then
      number_of_divisors += 1
    End If
    i += 1
  Loop

  If number_of_divisors = 2 Then
    Console.WriteLine("Number " & x & " is prime")
  End If

  Console.ReadKey()
End Sub
```

Exercise 31.4-6   Finding all Prime Numbers from 1 to N

Write a Visual Basic program that prompts the user to enter a positive integer and then displays all prime numbers from 2 to that given integer. Moreover, the program should validate data input and display an error message when the user enters any values less than 2.

Solution

To help you, this exercise is solved using the "from inner to outer" method.

The inner code fragment that checks whether variable x contains a prime number has already been discussed in the previous exercise, so you can use it as is. On the other hand, the outer Visual Basic program follows and is shown in general form.

```
Console.Write("Enter an integer greater than 1: ")
N = Console.ReadLine()
Do While N < 2
  Console.Write("Wrong number. Enter an integer greater than 1: ")
  N = Console.ReadLine()
Loop

For x = 1 To N
  'Here goes the code that checks whether variable x contains a prime number
```

```
Next
```

Thus, combining both programs, the final Visual Basic program becomes

project_31_4_6

```
Sub Main()
  Dim N, x, number_of_divisors, i As Integer

  Console.Write("Enter an integer greater than 1: ")
  N = Console.ReadLine()
  Do While N < 2
    Console.Write("Wrong number. Enter an integer greater than 1: ")
    N = Console.ReadLine()
  Loop

  For x = 1 To N
    number_of_divisors = 2
    i = 2
    Do While i <= x / 2 And number_of_divisors = 2
      If x Mod i = 0 Then
        number_of_divisors += 1
      End If
      i += 1
    Loop
    If number_of_divisors = 2 Then
      Console.WriteLine("Number " & x & " is prime")
    End If
  Next

  Console.ReadKey()
End Sub
```

From previous exercise

Exercise 31.4-7   *Heron's Square Root*

Write a Visual Basic program that prompts the user to enter a non-negative value and then calculates its square root using Heron's formula, as follows.

$$x_{n+1} = \frac{\left(x_n + \frac{y}{x_n}\right)}{2}$$

where

> ➢   *y is the number for which you want to find the square root*
> ➢ x_n *is the n-th iteration value of the square root of y*

Moreover, the program should validate data input and display an error message when the user enters any non-numeric or negative values.

Solution

It is almost certain that you are a little bit confused and you are scratching your head right now. Don't be scared by all this math stuff! You can try to understand Heron's formula through the following flowchart instead!

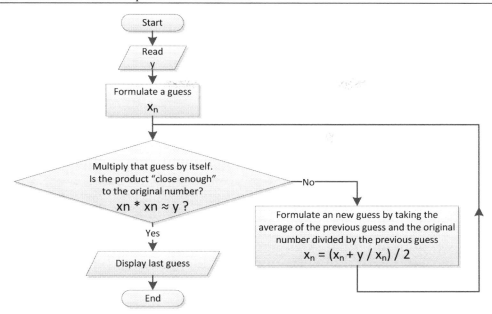

Still confused? Let's see an example. Let's find the square root of 25:

➢   Assume 8 as your first guess.

➢   The product of 8 × 8 is 64.

➢   Since 64 isn't "close enough" to 25, you can create a new guess by calculating the expression

$$\frac{\left(guess + \dfrac{number}{guess}\right)}{2} = \frac{\left(8 + \dfrac{25}{8}\right)}{2} \approx 5.56$$

➢   The product of 5.56 × 5.56 is about 30.91

➢   Since 30.91 isn't "close enough" to 25 you can create a new guess by calculating the expression

$$\frac{\left(guess + \dfrac{number}{guess}\right)}{2} = \frac{\left(5.56 + \dfrac{25}{5.56}\right)}{2} \approx 5.02$$

➢   The product of 5.02 × 5.02 is 25.2

➢   You can say that 25.2 is actually "close enough" to 25. Therefore, you can stop the whole process and say that the approximate square root of 25 is 5.02

Now, let's see the corresponding Visual Basic program.

```
                        project_31_4_7
Const ACCURACY = 0.0000000000001

Sub Main()
  Dim y, guess As Double
  Dim input As String

  Dim rnd As New Random()

  Console.Write("Enter a non-negative number: ")
  input = Console.ReadLine()
```

```
Do While Double.TryParse(input, y) = False Or y < 0
  Console.WriteLine("Invalid value. Enter a non-negative number: ")
  input = Console.ReadLine()
Loop
guess = rnd.Next(1, y)              'Make a random first guess
                                    'between 1 and given value

Do While Math.Abs(guess * guess - y) > ACCURACY    'is it "close enough"?
  guess = (guess + y / guess) / 2                  'No, create a new "guess"!
Loop
Console.Write(guess)

Console.ReadKey()
End Sub
```

> **Notice**: *Please note the way that "Is it close enough" is checked. When the absolute value of the difference | guess² − given_value | becomes less than 0.0000000000001, the flow of execution exits the loop.*

Exercise 31.4-8   *Calculating π*

Write a Visual Basic program that calculates π using the Madhava–Leibniz[2,3] series, which follows, with an accuracy of 0.0000001.

$$\frac{\pi}{4} = 1 - \frac{1}{3} + \frac{1}{5} - \frac{1}{7} + \cdots$$

Solution

The Madhava–Leibniz series can be solved for π, and becomes

$$\pi = \frac{4}{1} - \frac{4}{3} + \frac{4}{5} - \frac{4}{7} + \cdots$$

The more fractions you have, the better the accuracy! Thus, to calculate this formula the program needs to perform many iterations so as to use as many fractions as possible. But, of course, it can't iterate forever! The loop should actually stop iterating when the current value of π and the one calculated in the previous iteration are "close enough," which means that the absolute value of their difference has become very small. The constant ACCURACY defines how small this difference should be. The Visual Basic program is shown next.

---

[2] Madhava of Sangamagrama (c. 1340–c. 1425), was an Indian mathematician and astronomer from the town of Sangamagrama (present day Irinjalakuda) of India. He founded the Kerala School of Astronomy and Mathematics and was the first to use infinite series approximations for various trigonometric functions. He is often referred to as the "father of mathematical analysis."
[3] Gottfried Wilhelm von Leibniz (1646–1716) was a German mathematician and philosopher. He made important contributions to the fields of metaphysics, logic, and philosophy, as well as mathematics, physics, and history. In one of his works, *On the Art of Combination (Dissertatio de Arte Combinatoria)*, published in 1666, he formulated a model that is considered the theoretical ancestor of modern computers.

```
                         project_31_4_8
Const ACCURACY = 0.0000001
Sub Main()
  Dim sign, denom As Integer
  Dim pi, pi_previous As Double

  pi = 0

  sign = 1          'This is the sign of the first fraction
  denom = 1         'This is the denominator of the first fraction
  Do
    pi_previous = pi
    pi += sign * 4 / denom
    sign = -sign
    denom += 2
  Loop While Math.Abs(pi - pi_previous) > ACCURACY   'is it "close enough"?

  Console.Write("Pi ~= " & pi)

  Console.ReadKey()
End Sub
```

> **Notice:** *Please note the way in which variable* sign *toggles between the values -1 and +1 in each iteration.*

If you reduce the value of the constant ACCURACY, π will be calculated more and more accurately. Depending on how fast your computer is, you can calculate the first six digits of π fairly quickly. However, the time it takes to calculate each succeeding digit of π goes up exponentially. To calculate 40 digits of π on a modern computer using this method could take years!

Exercise 31.4-9 *Approximating a Real with a Fraction*

Write a Visual Basic program that prompts the user to enter a real between 1 and 100 and then tries to find the fraction $\frac{N}{M}$ that better approximates it, where N is an integer between 0 and 100 and M is an integer between 1 and 100. Moreover, the program should validate data input, allowing the user to enter only numeric values between 0 and 100. There is no need to display any error messages.

Solution

The solution is simple. All you need to do is iterate through all possible combinations of variables n and m and check which one better approximates the real given.

To iterate through all possible combinations of variables n and m, you can use a nested loop control structure, that is, two counted loop structures, one nested within the other, as follows.

```
For n = 0 To 100
  For m = 1 To 100

    …

  Next
```

```
Next
```

Notice: *The total number of iterations is 101 × 100 = 10100. Quite a big number but, for a modern computer, this is peanuts!*

The following criteria

$$minimum\ of\ \left(\left|\frac{N}{M} - real\ given\right|\right)$$

can evaluate how "good" an approximation is.

Confused? Let's try to approximate the value 0.333 with a fraction, iterating through all possible combinations of N and M.

➢　For N = 1, M = 1 the criteria equals to $\left|\frac{1}{1} - 0.333\right| = 0.6670$

➢　For N = 1, M = 2 the criteria equals to $\left|\frac{1}{2} - 0.333\right| = 0.1670$

➢　For N = 1, M = 3 the criteria equals to $\left|\frac{1}{3} - 0.333\right| = 0.0003$

➢　For N = 1, M = 4 the criteria equals to $\left|\frac{1}{4} - 0.333\right| = 0.0830$

➢　...

➢　For N = 100, M = 99 the criteria equals to $\left|\frac{100}{99} - 0.333\right| = 0.6771$

➢　For N = 100, M = 100 the criteria equals to $\left|\frac{100}{100} - 0.333\right| = 0.6670$

As you can see, the value 0.0003 is the minimum value among all possible results. Thus, the combination N = 1 and M = 3 (which corresponds to the fraction 1/3) is considered the best approximation for the value 0.333.

And now the Visual Basic program:

```
                         project_31_4_9
Sub Main()
  Dim x As Double
  Dim best_n, best_m, n, m As Integer
  Dim input As String

  Do
    Console.Write("Enter a real between 0 and 100: ")
    input = Console.ReadLine()
  Loop While Double.TryParse(input, x) = False Or x < 0 Or x > 100

  best_n = 1
  best_m = 1
  For n = 0 To 100
    For m = 1 To 100
      If Math.Abs(n / m - x) < Math.Abs(best_n / best_m - x) Then
        best_n = n
        best_m = m
      End If
    Next
  Next
  Console.Write("The fraction is: " & best_n & "/" & best_m)
```

```
        Console.ReadKey()
    End Sub
```

31.5   Finding Minimum and Maximum Values with Loop Control Structures

In Chapter 23 you learned how to find the minimum and maximum values among four values using single-alternative decision structures. Now, the following code fragment does pretty much the same but uses only one variable w to hold all of the user's given values.

```
w = Console.ReadLine()      'User enters 1st value
max = w

w = Console.ReadLine()      'User enters 2nd value
If w > max Then
  max = w
End If

w = Console.ReadLine()      'User enters 3rd value
If w > max Then
  max = w
End If

w = Console.ReadLine()      'User enters 4th value
If w > max Then
  max = w
End If
```

Except for the first pair of statements, all other blocks of statements are identical; therefore, only one of those can be enclosed within a loop control structure and be executed three times, as follows.

```
w = Console.ReadLine()              'User enters 1st value
max = w

For i = 1 To 3
  w = Console.ReadLine()            'User enters 2nd, 3rd and 4th value
  If w > max Then
    max = w
  End If
Next
```

Of course, if you want to allow the user to enter more values, you can simply increase the *final_value* of the counted loop structure.

Accordingly, if you want a program that finds and displays the heaviest person among 10 people, the solution is presented next.

project_31_5a

```
Sub Main()
  Dim w, max, i As Integer

  Console.Write("Enter a weight (in pounds): ")
```

```
    w = Console.ReadLine()
    max = w

    For i = 1 To 9
      Console.Write("Enter a weight (in pounds): ")
      w = Console.ReadLine()
      If w > max Then
        max = w
      End If
    Next
    Console.Write(max)

    Console.ReadKey()
End Sub
```

Notice: *Please note that the counted loop structure iterates one time less than the total number of values given.*

Even though this Visual Basic program operates perfectly well, let's do something different. Instead of prompting the user to enter one value before the loop and nine values inside the loop, let's prompt him or her to enter all values inside the loop.

The problem that arises here is that no matter what, before the loop starts iterating, an initial value must be assigned to variable max. You can actually assign an "almost arbitrary" initial value but this value should be chosen carefully since a wrong one may lead to incorrect results.

In this exercise, all given values have to do with people's weight. Since there is no chance of finding any person with a negative weight (at least not on planet Earth), you can safely assign the initial value -1 to variable max, as follows.

project_31_5b

```
Sub Main()
  Dim max, i, w As Integer

  max = -1

  For i = 1 To 10
    Console.Write("Enter a weight: ")
    w = Console.ReadLine()

    If w > max Then
      max = w
    End If
  Next

  Console.Write(max)

  Console.ReadKey()
End Sub
```

As soon as the flow of execution enters the loop, the user enters the first value and the decision control structure validates to True. The value -1 in variable max is overwritten by that first given value and after that, flow of execution proceeds normally.

> **Notice**: *Please note that this method cannot be used in every case. If an exercise needs to prompt the user to enter any number (not only a positive one) this method cannot be applied since the user could potentially enter only negative values. If this were to occur, the initial value -1 would never be overwritten by any of the given values. You can use this method to find the maximum value only when you know the lower limit of given values or to find the minimum value only when you know the upper limit of given values. For example, if the exercise needs to find the lightest person, you can assign the initial value +1500 to variable min, since there is no human on Earth that can be so heavy! For the record, Jon Brower Minnoch was an American who, at his peak weight, was the heaviest human being ever recorded, weighing approximately 1.400 lb!!!!!*

Exercise 31.5-1   *Validating and Finding the Minimum and the Maximum Value*

Write a Visual Basic program that prompts the user to enter the weight of 10 people and then finds the heaviest and the lightest one. Moreover, the program should validate data input and display an error message when the user enters any non-numeric, negative, zero value, or any values greater than 1500.

Solution

Using the previous exercise as a guide, you should now be able to do this with your eyes closed!

To validate data input, all you have to do is replace the following two lines of code of the previous exercise,

```
Console.Write("Enter a weight: ")
w = Console.ReadLine()
```

with the following code fragment:

```
Console.Write("Enter a weight: ")
input = Console.ReadLine()
Do While Int32.TryParse(input, w) = False Or w < 1 Or w > 1500
  Console.Write("Invalid value! Enter a weight between 1 and 1500: ")
  input = Console.ReadLine()
Loop
```

The final program is as follows.

```
                          project_31_5_1
Sub Main()
  Dim max, i, w As Integer
  Dim input As String

  max = -1

  For i = 1 To 10
    Console.Write("Enter a weight: ")
    input = Console.ReadLine()
    Do While Int32.TryParse(input, w) = False Or w < 1 Or w > 1500
```

```
        Console.Write("Invalid value! Enter a weight between 1 and 1500: ")
        input = Console.ReadLine()
    Loop

    If w > max Then
        max = w
    End If
  Next

  Console.Write(max)

  Console.ReadKey()
End Sub
```

Exercise 31.5-2   *Validating and Finding the Maximum Temperature*

Write a Visual Basic program that prompts the user to repeatedly enter the names and the average temperatures of planets from space, until the word "STOP" (used as a name) is entered. In the end, the program should display the name of the hottest planet. Moreover, since
-459.67º (on the Fahrenheit scale) is the lowest temperature possible (it is called absolute zero), the program should validate data input and display an error message when the user enters non-numeric values or values lower than absolute zero.

Solution

First, let's write the Visual Basic program without using data validation. According to the "Ultimate" rule, the pre-test loop structure should be as follows, given in general form:

```
Console.Write("Enter the name of a planet: ")
name = Console.ReadLine()                    'Initialization of name
Do While name.ToUpper() <> "STOP"
  A statement or block of statements

  Console.Write("Enter the name of a planet: ")
  name = Console.ReadLine()                  'Update/alteration of name
Loop
```

Now, let's add the rest of the statements, still without data input validation. Keep in mind that, since value -459.67º is the lower limit of the temperature scale, you can use a value lower than this as the initial value of variable max.

```
Sub Main()
  Dim max, t As Double
  Dim m_name, name As String

  max = -460
  m_name = ""

  Console.Write("Enter the name of a planet: ")
  name = Console.ReadLine()
  Do While name.ToUpper() <> "STOP"
    Console.Write("Enter its average temperature: ")
```

```
    t = Console.ReadLine()

    If t > max Then
      max = t
      m_name = name
    End If

    Console.Write("Enter the name of a planet: ")
    name = Console.ReadLine()
  Loop

  If max <> -460 Then
    Console.WriteLine("The hottest planet is: " & m_name)
  Else
    Console.WriteLine("Nothing Entered!")
  End If

  Console.ReadKey()
End Sub
```

Notice: *The* `If max <> -460 Then` *statement is required because there is a possibility that the user could enter the word "STOP" right from the beginning.*

To validate the data input, all you have to do is replace the following two lines of code:

```
Console.Write("Enter its average temperature: ")
t = Console.ReadLine()
```

with the following code fragment:

```
Console.Write("Enter its average temperature: ")
input = Console.ReadLine()
Do While Double.TryParse(input, t) = False Or t < -459.67
  Console.WriteLine("Invalid value!")
  Console.Write("Enter a value greater than -459.67 degrees: ")
  input = Console.ReadLine()
Loop
```

The final program is as follows.

```
                      project_31_5_2
Sub Main()
  Dim max, t As Double
  Dim m_name, name, input As String

  max = -460
  m_name = ""

  Console.Write("Enter the name of a planet: ")
  name = Console.ReadLine()
  Do While name.ToUpper() <> "STOP"
    Console.Write("Enter its average temperature: ")
    input = Console.ReadLine()
    Do While Double.TryParse(input, t) = False Or t < -459.67
```

```
        Console.WriteLine("Invalid value!")
        Console.Write("Enter a value greater than -459.67 degrees: ")
        input = Console.ReadLine()
    Loop

    If t > max Then
      max = t
      m_name = name
    End If

    Console.Write("Enter the name of a planet: ")
    name = Console.ReadLine()
  Loop

  If max <> -460 Then
    Console.WriteLine("The hottest planet is: " & m_name)
  Else
    Console.WriteLine("Nothing Entered!")
  End If

  Console.ReadKey()
End Sub
```

Exercise 31.5-3   *"Making the Grade"*

In a classroom, there are 20 students. Write a Visual Basic program that prompts the teacher to enter the grades (0 – 100) that students received in a math test and then displays the highest grade as well as the number of students that got an "A" (that is, 90 to 100). Moreover, the program should validate data input. Given values should be within the range 0 to 100.

Solution

Let's first write the program without data validation. Since the number of students is known, you can use the counted loop structure. For an initial value of variable max, you can use value -1 as there is no grade lower than 0.

```
Sub Main()
  Dim max, count, i, grade As Integer

  max = -1
  count = 0

  For i = 1 To 20
    Console.Write("Enter a grade for student No " & i & ": ")
    grade = Console.ReadLine()

    If grade > max Then
      max = grade
    End If

    If grade >= 90 Then
```

```
        count += 1
      End If
    Next

    Console.Write(max & " " & count)

    Console.ReadKey()
End Sub
```

Now, you can deal with data validation. As the wording of the exercise implies, there is no need to display any error messages. So, all you need to do is replace the following two lines of code:

```
Console.Write("Enter a grade for student No " & i & ": ")
grade = Console.ReadLine()
```

with the following code fragment:

```
Do
   Console.Write("Enter a grade for student No " & i & ": ")
   grade = Console.ReadLine()
Loop While grade < 0 Or grade > 100
```

and the final program becomes

project_31_5_3

```
Sub Main()
  Dim max, count, i, grade As Integer

  max = -1
  count = 0

  For i = 1 To 20
    Do
      Console.Write("Enter a grade for student No " & i & ": ")
      grade = Console.ReadLine()
    Loop While grade < 0 Or grade > 100

    If grade > max Then
      max = grade
    End If

    If grade >= 90 Then
      count += 1
    End If
  Next

  Console.Write(max & " " & count)

  Console.ReadKey()
End Sub
```

31.6   Exercises of a General Nature with Loop Control Structures

Exercise 31.6-1   *Fahrenheit to Kelvin, from 0 to 100*

Write a Visual Basic program that displays all degrees Fahrenheit from 0 to 100 and their equivalent degrees Kelvin. Use an increment value of 0.5. It is given that

$$1.8 \cdot Kelvin = Fahrenheit + 459.67$$

Solution

The formula, solved for Kelvin becomes

$$Kelvin = \frac{Fahrenheit + 459.67}{1.8}$$

All you need here is a counted loop structure that increments the value of variable fahrenheit from 0 to 100 using an *offset* of 0.5. The solution is presented next.

```
                              project_31_6_1
Sub Main()
  Dim fahrenheit, kelvin As Double

  For fahrenheit = 0 To 100 Step 0.5
    kelvin = (fahrenheit + 459.67) / 1.8
    Console.WriteLine("Fahrenheit: " & fahrenheit & " Kelvin: " & kelvin)
  Next

  Console.ReadKey()
End Sub
```

Exercise 31.6-2   *Wheat on a Chessboard*

On a chessboard you must place grains of wheat on each square, such that one grain is placed on the first square, two on the second, four on the third, and so on (doubling the number of grains on each subsequent square). How many grains of wheat will be on the chessboard in the end?

Solution

Assume a chessboard of only 2 × 2 = 4 squares and a variable grains assigned the initial value 1 (this is the number of grains of the 1st square). A counted loop structure that iterates three times can double the value of variable grains in each iteration, as shown in the next code fragment.

```
grains = 1
For i = 2 To 4
  grains = 2 * grains
Next
```

The value of variable grains at the end of each iteration is shown in the next table.

Iteration	Value of i	Value of grains
1st	2	2 × 1 = 2
2nd	3	2 × 2 = 4
3rd	4	2 × 4 = 8

At the end of the 3rd iteration, variable grains contains the value 8. This value, however, is not the total number of grains on the chessboard but only the number of grains on the 4th square. If you need to find the total number of grains on the chessboard you can sum up the grains on all squares, that is, 1 + 2 + 4 + 8 = 15.

In the real world a real chessboard contains 8 × 8 = 64 squares, thus you need to iterate for 63 times. The Visual Basic program is as follows.

```
project_31_6_2
Sub Main()
  Dim i As Integer
  Dim grains, sum As ULong

  grains = 1
  sum = 1
  For i = 2 To 64
    grains = 2 * grains
    sum = sum + grains
  Next
  Console.Write(sum)

  Console.ReadKey()
End Sub
```

In case you are wondering how big this number is, here is your answer: On the chessboard there will be 18,446,744,073,709,551,615 grains of wheat!

> **Notice**: *The reason for not declaring variables grains and sum as Integer or even Long is that both types are unable to hold such a big number. The upper limit of type Long is $+2^{63} - 1$ which, unfortunately, is not enough.*

Exercise 31.6-3   *Just a Poll*

A public opinion polling company asks 1000 citizens if they eat breakfast in the morning. Write a Visual Basic program that prompts the citizens to enter their sex (M for Male, F for Female) and their answer to the question (Y for Yes, N for No, S for Sometimes), and then calculates and displays the number of citizens that gave "Yes" as an answer, as well as the percentage of women among the citizens that gave "No" as an answer. Moreover, the program should validate data input and accept only values M or F for sex and Y, N, or S for answer.

Solution

The Visual Basic program is as follows.

```
project_31_6_3
Const CITIZENS = 1000
```

```
Sub Main()
  Dim total_yes, female_no, i As Integer
  Dim sex, answer As String

  total_yes = 0
  female_no = 0
  For i = 1 To CITIZENS
    Do
       Console.Write("Enter Sex: ")
       sex = Console.ReadLine().ToLower()
    Loop While sex <> "m" And sex <> "f"

    Do
       Console.Write("Do you eat breakfast in the morning? ")
       answer = Console.ReadLine().ToLower()
    Loop While answer <> "y" And answer <> "n" And answer <> "s"

    If answer = "y" Then
       total_yes += 1
    End If

    If sex = "f" And answer = "n" Then
       female_no += 1
    End If
  Next
  Console.Write(total_yes & " " & female_no * 100 / CITIZENS)

  Console.ReadKey()
End Sub
```

Notice: *Please note how Visual Basic converts the user's input to lowercase. Procedure chaining is a programming style that most programmers prefer to follow in Visual Basic.*

Exercise 31.6-4   *Is the Message a Palindrome?*

A palindrome is a word or sentence that reads the same both backwards and forward. (You may recall from Chapter 23 that a number can also be a palindrome!) Write a Visual Basic program that prompts the user to enter a word or sentence and then displays a message stating whether or not the given word or sentence is a palindrome. Following are some palindrome messages.

  ➢ *Anna*
  ➢ *A nut for a jar of tuna.*
  ➢ *Dennis and Edna sinned.*
  ➢ *Murder for a jar of red rum.*
  ➢ *Borrow or rob?*
  ➢ *Are we not drawn onward, we few, drawn onward to new era?*

Solution

There are some things that you should keep in mind before you start comparing the letters one by one and checking whether the first letter is the same as the last one, the second letter is the same as the last but one, and so on.

> ➤ In a given sentence or word, some letters may be in uppercase and some in lowercase. For example, in the sentence "*A nut for a jar of tuna*", even though the first and last letters are the same, unfortunately they are not considered equal. Thus, the program must first change all the letters—for example, to lowercase—and then it can start comparing them.

> ➤ There are some characters such as spaces, periods, question marks, and commas that should be removed or else the program cannot actually compare the rest of the letters one by one. For example, in the sentence "*Borrow or rob?*" the Visual Basic program may mistakenly assume that the sentence is not a palindrome because it will compare the first letter "B" with the last question mark "?"

> ➤ Assume that the sentence "*Borrow or rob?*", after changing all letters to lowercase and after removing all unwanted spaces and the question mark, becomes "borroworrob". These letters and their corresponding position in the string are as follows.

0	1	2	3	4	5	6	7	8	9	10
b	o	r	r	o	w	o	r	r	o	b

What you should keep in mind here is that the counted loop structure should iterate for only half of the letters. Can you figure out why?

The program starts the iterations and compares the letter at position 0 with the letter at position 10. Then it compares the letter at position 1 with the letter at position 9, and so on. The last iteration should be the one that compares the letters at positions 4 and 6. It is meaningless to continue checking thereafter, since all letters have already been compared.

One proposed solution is presented next. If you still have doubts about how this operates, you can use Visual Studio to execute it step by step and observe the values of the variables in each step.

```
                          project_31_6_4a
Sub Main()
  Dim last_pos, i, middle_pos, j As Integer
  Dim message, message_clean, letter, left_letter, right_letter As String
  Dim palindrome As Boolean

  Console.Write("Enter a message: ")
  message = Console.ReadLine().ToLower()

  'This is the last position of message
  last_pos = message.Length - 1

  'Create a new string which contains letters except
  'spaces, commas, periods or questionmarks
  message_clean = ""
  For i = 0 To last_pos
```

```
      letter = message(i)
      If letter <> " " And letter <> "," And
         letter <> "." And letter <> "?" Then

         message_clean += letter
      End If
   Next

   'This is the middle position of message_clean
   middle_pos = (message_clean.Length - 1) \ 2

   'This is the last position of message_clean
   j = message_clean.Length - 1
```

> This code fragment can be further improved as you can see next.

```
   'In the beginning, assume that sentence is palindrome
   palindrome = True

   'This counted loop structure compares
   'letters one by one.
   For i = 0 To middle_pos
      left_letter = message_clean(i)
      right_letter = message_clean(j)
      'If at least one pair of letters fails to validate
      'set variable palindrome to False
      If left_letter <> right_letter Then
         palindrome = False
      End If
      j -= 1
   Next

   'If variable palindrome is still True
   If palindrome = True Then
      Console.WriteLine("The message is palindrome")
   End If

   Console.ReadKey()
End Sub
```

This Visual Basic program works fine, but assume that the user enters a very large sentence that is not a palindrome. Let's say, for example, that the second letter is not the same as the last but one. Unfortunately, in this program the counted loop structure continues to iterate until the middle of the sentence despite the fact that variable palindrome has been set to False, even from the second iteration. So, let's try to make this program even better.

What you need here is a way to break out of the loop when something goes wrong. There are two approaches, actually.

First Approach – Using the Exit For statement

The first approach uses the Exit For statement. In the initial Visual Basic program, the statements marked with a dashed rectangle can be replaced with the following code fragment.

```
                           project_31_6_4b
palindrome = True
For i = 0 To middle_pos
  left_letter = message_clean(i)
  right_letter = message_clean(j)
  If left_letter <> right_letter Then
    palindrome = False
    Exit For
  End If
  j -= 1
Next
```

Second Approach – Using a flag

To break out of a loop using a flag, always follow the same methodology: The counted loop structure must be converted to a pre-test loop structure and the Boolean expression of the loop must be modified to evaluate both variables i and palindrome. As long as variable palindrome is True, the loop should continue iterating. In the initial Visual Basic program, the statements marked with a dashed rectangle can be replaced with the following code fragment.

```
                           project_31_6_4c
palindrome = True
i = 0
Do While i <= middle_pos And palindrome = True
  left_letter = message_clean(i)
  right_letter = message_clean(j)
  If left_letter <> right_letter Then
    palindrome = False
  End If
  j -= 1
  i += 1
Loop
```

> **Remember!** *Picture the variable* palindrome *as a flag. Initially, the flag is "raised"* (palindrome = True). *The flow of execution enters the loop and the loop continues iterating as long as the flag is up* (Do While … palindrome = True). *When something (usually a condition) lowers the flag (assigns value* False *to variable* palindrome*), the flow of execution exits the loop.*

31.7 Review Questions: True/False

Choose **true** or **false** for each of the following statements.

1. Data validation is the process of restricting data input, forcing the user to enter only valid values.

2. You can use a counted loop structure to validate data input.

3. You can use any loop control structure to validate data input.

4. To force a user to enter only positive numbers, without displaying any error messages, you can use the following code fragment.

```
Do
    Console.Write("Enter a positive number: ")
```

```
  input = Console.ReadLine()
Loop While Double.TryParse(input, x) = False Or x <= 0
```

5. To force a user to enter numbers between 1 and 10, you can use the following code fragment.

```
Console.Write("Enter a number between 1 and 10: ")
input = Console.ReadLine()
Do While Double.TryParse(input, x) = False Or x >= 1 Or x <= 10
  Console.WriteLine("Wrong number")
  Console.Write("Enter a number between 1 and 10: ")
  input = Console.ReadLine()
Loop
```

6. When a Visual Basic program is used to find the maximum value among 10 given values, the loop control structure that is used must always iterate 9 times.

7. In order to find the lowest number among 10 numbers given, you can use the following code fragment.

```
min = 0
For i = 1 To 10
  w = Console.ReadLine()
  If w < min Then
    min = w
  End If
Next
```

8. In order to find the highest number among 10 positive numbers given, you can use the following code fragment.

```
max = 0
For i = 1 To 10
  w = Console.ReadLine()
  If w > max Then
    max = w
  End If
Next
```

31.8 Review Exercises

Complete the following exercises.

1. Write a Visual Basic program that calculates and displays the sum of the following:

$$S = 1 + 3 + 5 + \ldots + 99$$

2. Write a Visual Basic program that lets the user enter an integer N and then calculates and displays the product of the following:

$$P = 2^1 \times 4^3 \times 6^5 \times \ldots \times 2N^{(N-1)}$$

3. Write a Visual Basic program that calculates and displays the sum of the following:

$$S = 1 + 2 + 4 + 7 + 11 + 16 + 22 + 29 + 37 + \ldots + 191$$

4. Design a flowchart and write the corresponding Visual Basic program that lets a teacher enter the total number of students as well as their grades and then calculates and displays the average value of those who got an "A", that is 90 to

100. Add all necessary checks to make the program satisfy the property of definiteness.

5. Design a flowchart and write the corresponding Visual Basic program that prompts the user to repeatedly enter numeric, non-negative values until their average value exceeds 3000. At the end, the program should display the total number of zeros entered.

6. Write a Visual Basic program that prompts the user to enter an integer between 1 and 20 and then displays all four-digit integers for which the sum of their digits is less than the integer given. For example, if the user enters 15, the value 9301 is such a number, since

$$9 + 3 + 0 + 1 < 15$$

7. Write a Visual Basic program that displays all four-digit integers that satisfy all of the following conditions:

    ➢ the number's first digit is greater than its second digit
    ➢ the number's second digit is equal to its third digit
    ➢ the number's third digit is smaller than its fourth digit

    For example, the values 7559, 3110, and 9889 are such numbers.

8. A student wrote the following code fragment which is supposed to validate data input, forcing the user to enter only values 0 and 1. Identify any error(s) in the code fragment.

```
Do While Byte.TryParse(input, x) = False And x <> 1 And x <> 0
    Console.WriteLine("Error")
    input = Console.ReadLine()
Loop
```

9. Write the code fragment that validates data input, forcing the user to enter a valid sex (M for Male, F for Female). Moreover, it should validate correctly both for lowercase and uppercase letters.

10. Write a Visual Basic program that prompts the user to enter a non-negative number and then calculates its square root. Moreover, the program should validate data input and display an error message when the user enters any non-numeric or negative values. Additionally, the user has a maximum number of two retries. If the user enters more than three non-numeric or negative values, a message "Dude, you are dumb!" should be displayed and the program execution should end.

11. The area of a circle can be calculated using the following formula:

$$\text{Area} = \pi \cdot \text{Radius}^2$$

    Write a Visual Basic program that prompts the user to enter the length of the radius of a circle and then calculates and displays its area. The program should iterate as many times as the user wishes. At the end of each area calculation, the program should ask the user if he or she wishes to calculate the area of another circle. If the answer is "yes" the program should repeat; it should end otherwise. Make your program accept the answer in all possible forms such as "yes", "YES", "Yes", or even "YeS".

    Moreover, the program should validate data input and display an error message when the user enters any non-numeric or non-positive value for Radius.

    Hint: Use the `Math.PI` constant to get the value of π.

12. Write a Visual Basic program that displays all possible integer values of x and y within the range -100 to +100 that validate (when possible) the following formula:

$$5x + 3y^2 = 0$$

13. Write a Visual Basic program that displays all possible integer values of $x, y,$ and z within the range -10 to +10 that validate the following formula:

$$\frac{x + y}{2} + \frac{3z^2}{x + 3y + 45} = \frac{x}{3}$$

14. Write a Visual Basic program that lets the user enter three positive integers and then finds their product using the Russian multiplication algorithm.

15. Write a Visual Basic program that prompts the user to enter two positive integers and then displays all prime integers between them. Moreover, the program should validate data input and display an error message when the user enters a value less than +2.

Hint: To make your Visual Basic program operate correctly, independent of which integer given is the lowest, you can swap their values (if necessary) so that they are always in the proper order.

16. Write a Visual Basic program that prompts the user to enter two positive four-digit integers and then displays all integers between them that are palindromes. Moreover, the program should validate data input and display an error message when the user enters any non-numeric characters, or any numbers other than four-digit ones.

Hint: To make your Visual Basic program operate correctly, independent of which integer given is the lowest, you can swap their values (if necessary) so that they are always in the proper order.

17. Write a Visual Basic program that displays all possible RAM sizes between 1 byte and 1GByte, such as 1, 2, 4, 8, 16, 32, 64, 128, and so on.

Hint: 1GByte equals 2^{30} bytes, or 1073741824 bytes

18. Write a Visual Basic program that displays the following sequence of numbers:

1, 11, 23, 37, 53, 71, 91, 113, 137, … 401

19. Write a Visual Basic program that displays the following sequence of numbers:

-1, 1, -2, 2, -3, 3, -4, 4, … -100, 100

20. Write a Visual Basic program that displays the following sequence of numbers:

1, 11, 111, 1111, 11111, … 11111111

21. The Fibonacci[4] sequence is a series of numbers in the following sequence:

1, 1, 2, 3, 5, 8, 13, 21, 34, 55, …

By definition, the first two numbers are 1 and 1 and each subsequent number is the sum of the previous two.

---

[4] Leonardo Pisano Bigollo (c. 1170–c. 1250), also known as Fibonacci, was an Italian mathematician. In his book *Liber Abaci* (published in 1202), Fibonacci used a special sequence of numbers to try to determine the growth of a rabbit population. Today, that sequence of numbers is known as the Fibonacci sequence. He was also one of the first people to introduce the Arabic numeral system to Europe; this is the numeral system we use today, based on ten digits with a decimal point and a symbol for zero. Before then, the Roman numeral system was being used, making numerical calculations difficult.

Write a Visual Basic program that lets the user enter a positive integer and then displays as many Fibonacci numbers as that given integer.

22. Write a Visual Basic program that lets the user enter a positive integer and then displays all Fibonacci numbers that are less than that given integer.

23. Write a Visual Basic program that prompts the user to enter a positive integer N and then finds and displays the value of y in the following formula:

$$y = \frac{2 + 4 + 6 + \; ... \; + 2N}{1 \cdot 2 \cdot 3 \cdot 4 \cdot ... \cdot N}$$

Moreover, the program should validate data input and display an error message when the user enters any non-numeric value or a value less than 1.

24. Write a Visual Basic program that prompts the user to enter an integer N and then finds and displays the value of y in the following formula

$$y = \frac{1 - 3 + 5 - 7 + \; ... \; + (2N + 1)}{N}$$

Moreover, the program should validate data input and display an error message when the user enters any non-numeric value or a value less than 1.

25. Write a Visual Basic program that prompts the user to enter an integer N and then finds and displays the value of y in the following formula:

$$y = 1 - \frac{1}{2} + \frac{1}{3} - \frac{1}{5} + ... + \frac{1}{N}$$

Moreover, the program should validate data input and display an error message when the user enters any non-numeric value or a value less than 1.

26. Write a Visual Basic program that prompts the user to enter an integer N and then finds and displays the value of y in the following formula:

$$y = \frac{1}{1^N} + \frac{1}{2^{N-1}} + \frac{1}{3^{N-2}} + ... + \frac{1}{N^1}$$

Moreover, the program should validate data input and display an error message when the user enters any non-numeric value or a value less than 1.

27. In mathematics, the factorial of a non-negative integer N is the product of all positive integers less than or equal to N, and it is denoted by N! The factorial of 0 is, by definition, equal to 1. In mathematics, you can write

$$N! = \begin{cases} 1 \cdot 2 \cdot 3 \cdot ... N, & for \; N > 0 \\ 1, & for \; N = 0 \end{cases}$$

For example, the factorial of 5 is 5! = 1 × 2 × 3 × 4 × 5 = 120.

Write a Visual Basic program that prompts the user to enter a non-negative integer N and then calculates its factorial.

28. Write a Visual Basic program that lets the user enter a value for x and then calculates and displays the exponential function e^x using the Taylor[5] series, shown next, with an accuracy of 0.00001.

$$e^x = 1 + \frac{x^1}{1!} + \frac{x^2}{2!} + \frac{x^3}{3!} + \cdots$$

Hint: Keep in mind that $\frac{x^0}{0!} = 1$.

---

[5] Brook Taylor (1685–1731) was an English mathematician who is best known for the Taylor series and his contributions to the theory of finite differences.

29. Write a Visual Basic program that lets the user enter a value for x and then calculates and displays the sine of x using the Taylor series, shown next, with an accuracy of 0.00001.

$$sinx = x - \frac{x^3}{3!} + \frac{x^5}{5!} - \frac{x^7}{7!} + \cdots$$

Hint: Keep in mind that x is in radians and $\frac{x^1}{1!} = x$.

30. Write a Visual Basic program that lets the user enter a value for x and then calculates and displays the cosine of x using the Taylor series, shown next, with an accuracy of 0.00001.

$$cosx = 1 - \frac{x^2}{2!} + \frac{x^4}{4!} - \frac{x^6}{6!} + \cdots$$

Hint: Keep in mind that x is in radians and $\frac{x^0}{0!} = 1$.

31. Write a Visual Basic program that prompts the user to enter the daily temperatures in August and then calculates and displays the average as well as the highest temperature.

Moreover, since $-459.67°$ (on the Fahrenheit scale) is the lowest temperature possible (it is called absolute zero), the program should validate data input and display individual error messages when the user enters a non-numeric or a value lower than absolute zero.

32. A scientist needs a software application to record the level of the sea based on values recorded at specific times (HH:MM), in order to extract some useful information. Write a Visual Basic program that lets the scientist enter the level of the sea, the hour, and the minutes, repeatedly until the value of 9999 (used as a sea level) is entered. Then, the program should display the highest and the lowest sea levels as well as the hour and the minutes at which these levels were recorded.

33. Suppose that the letter A corresponds to the number 1, the letter B corresponds to the number 2, and so on. Write a Visual Basic program that prompts the user to enter two integers and then displays all alphabet letters that exist between them. For example, if the user enters 3 and 6, the program should display C, D, E, F. Moreover, the program should validate data input and display individual error messages when the user enters any non-numeric, negative, or any value greater than 26.

Hint: To make your Visual Basic program operate correctly, independent of which integer given is the lowest, you can swap their values (if necessary) so that they are always in the proper order.

34. Write a Visual Basic program that assigns a random secret integer between 1 and 100 to a variable and then prompts the user to guess the number. If the integer given is less than the secret one, a message "*Your guess is smaller than my secret number. Try again.*" should be displayed. If the integer given is greater than the secret one, a message "*Your guess is bigger than my secret number. Try again.*" should be displayed. This process should repeat until the user finally finds the secret number. Then, a message "*You found it!*" should be displayed, as well as the total number of the user's attempts.

35. Expand the previous exercise/game by making it operate for two players. The player that wins is the one that finds the random secret number in fewer attempts.

36. The size of a TV screen always refers to its diagonal measurement. For example, a 40-inch TV screen is 40 inches diagonally, from one corner on top to the other corner on bottom. The old TV screens had a width-to-height aspect ratio of 4:3, which means that for every 3 inches in TV screen height, there were 4 inches in TV screen width. Today, most TV screens have a width-to-height aspect ratio of 16:9, which means that for every 9 inches in TV screen height there are 16 inches in TV screen width. Using these aspect ratios and the Pythagorean Theorem, you can easily determine that:

> **for all 4:3 TVs**

   Width = Diagonal × 0.8

   Height = Diagonal × 0.6

> **for all 16:9 TVs**

   Width = Diagonal × 0.87

   Height = Diagonal × 0.49

Write a Visual Basic program that displays the following menu:

1. 4/3 TV Screen
2. 16/9 TV Screen
3. Exit

and prompts the user to enter a choice as well as the diagonal screen size in inches. Then, the Visual Basic program should display the width and the height of the TV screen. This process will continue repeatedly, until the user selects choice 3 (Exit) from the menu.

37. Write a Visual Basic program that prompts a teacher to enter the total number of students, their grades, and their sex (M for Male, F for Female), and then calculates and displays all of the following:

   a. the average value of those who got an "A" (90 - 100)
   b. the average value of those who got a "B" (80 - 89)
   c. the average value of boys who got an "A" (90 - 100)
   d. the total number of girls that got less than "B"
   e. the highest and lowest grade
   f. the average grade of the whole class

Add all necessary checks to make the program satisfy the property of definiteness. Moreover, the program should validate data input and display an error message when the teacher enters any of the following:

> non-numeric or non-positive values for total number of students

> values other than M or F for sex

> non-numerics, negatives, or values greater than 100 for student grades

38. Write a Visual Basic program that calculates and displays the discount that a customer receives based on the amount of his or her order, according to the following table.

Amount	Discount
$0 < amount < $20	0%
$20 ≤ amount < $50	3%
$50 ≤ amount < $100	5%
$100 ≤ amount	10%

At the end of each discount calculation, the program should ask the user if he or she wishes to calculate the discount of another amount. If the answer is "yes," the program should repeat; it should end otherwise. Make your program accept the answer in all possible forms such as "yes", "YES", "Yes", or even "YeS".

Moreover, the program should validate data input and display an error message when the user enters any non-numeric or non-positive value for amount.

39. The LAV Electricity Company charges subscribers for their electricity consumption according to the following table (monthly rates for domestic accounts).

Kilowatt-hours (kWh)	USD per kWh
0 ≤ kWh ≤ 400	$0.11
401 ≤ kWh ≤ 1500	$0.22
1501 ≤ kWh ≤ 3500	$0.25
3501 ≤ kWh	$0.50

Write a Visual Basic program that prompts the user to enter the total number of kWh consumed by a subscriber and then calculates and displays the total amount to pay. This process continues until the value -1 is entered.

Moreover, the program should validate data input and display an error message when the user enters any non-numeric or negative value for kWh. An exception for the value -1 should be made.

Transmission services and distribution charges, as well as federal, state, and local taxes, add a total of 25% to each bill.

Please note that the rates are progressive.

Review Questions in "Loop Control Structures"

Answer the following questions.

1. What is a loop control structure?

2. In a flowchart, how can you distinguish a decision control structure from a loop control structure?

3. Design the flowchart and write the Visual Basic statement (in general form) of a pre-test loop structure. Explain how this loop control structure operates.

4. Why is a pre-test loop structure named this way, and what is the fewest number of iterations it may perform?

5. If the statement or block of statements of a pre-test loop structure is executed N times, how many times is the Boolean expression of the structure evaluated?

6. Design the flowchart and write the corresponding Visual Basic statement (in general form) of a post-test loop structure. Explain how this loop control structure operates.

7. Why is a post-test loop structure named this way, and what is the fewest number of iterations it may perform?

8. If the statement or block of statements of a post-test loop structure is executed N times, how many times is the Boolean expression of the structure evaluated?

9. Design the flowchart and write the corresponding Visual Basic statement (in general form) of a counted loop structure. Explain how this loop control structure operates.

10. State the rules that apply to counted loop structures.

11. What are nested loops?

12. Write an example of a program with nested loop control structures and explain how they are executed.

13. State the rules that apply to nested loops.

14. Design a diagram that could help someone decide on the best loop control structure to choose.

15. Describe the "Ultimate" rule and give an example, in general form, using both a pre-test and a post-test loop structure.

16. Suppose that a Visual Basic program uses a loop control structure to search for a given word in an electronic dictionary. Why is it critical to break out of the loop when the given word is found?

17. Why is it critical to clean out your loops?

18. What is an infinite loop?

19. Describe, using Visual Basic statements in general form, how to do a conversion from a counted loop structure to a pre-test loop structure.

20. Describe, using Visual Basic statements in general form, how to do a conversion from a pre-test loop structure to a counted loop structure.

21. Describe, using Visual Basic statements in general form, how to do a conversion from a post-test loop structure to a pre-test loop structure.

22. Describe, using Visual Basic statements in general form, how to do a conversion from a pre-test loop structure to a post-test loop structure.

23. Describe, using Visual Basic statements in general form, how to do a conversion from a counted loop structure to a post-test loop structure.

24. Describe, using Visual Basic statements in general form, how to do a conversion from a post-test loop structure to a counted loop structure.

Section 6

Arrays

Chapter 32
Introduction to Arrays

32.1 Introduction

Variables are a good way to store values in memory but they have one limitation—they can hold only one value at a time. There are many cases, however, where a program needs to process long lists of data. For example, consider the following exercise.

Write a Visual Basic program that lets the user enter the grades of 20 students (on a scale of 0–100) and then displays

   i.   *the highest grade; and*

   ii.   *the total number of students that have a grade equal to the highest grade.*

Finding the highest grade is easy and has already been discussed in Chapter 31. The code fragment is as follows.

```
max_grade = -1

For i = 1 To 20
  grade = Console.ReadLine()
  If grade > max_grade Then
    max_grade = grade
  End If
Next

Console.WriteLine(max_grade)
```

However, it becomes difficult to determine how many students have a grade equal to that highest grade because:

 ➢ while the loop iterates, the highest grade has not yet been found, and

 ➢ when the loop finally finishes iterating and the highest grade has been found, variable grade contains only that last value given. Unfortunately, all previous 19 grades have been lost, and it just doesn't seem right to have to prompt the user to enter all the grades again!

The way this program is currently written, it is impossible to compare the value of variable max_grade to all 20 values given, and to count those that are equal to that value.

What you need here is a way to keep each and every student grade in main memory (RAM) as the user inputs them so that the program can use them later; however, this is not possible for this Visual Basic program because of the way it is currently written. One possible solution would be to use 20 individual variables, as shown here.

```
a1 = Console.ReadLine()
a2 = Console.ReadLine()
a3 = Console.ReadLine()
...
a20 = Console.ReadLine()
```

Input 20 values into 20 individual variables

```
max = a1
If a2 > max Then
```

Find maximum value

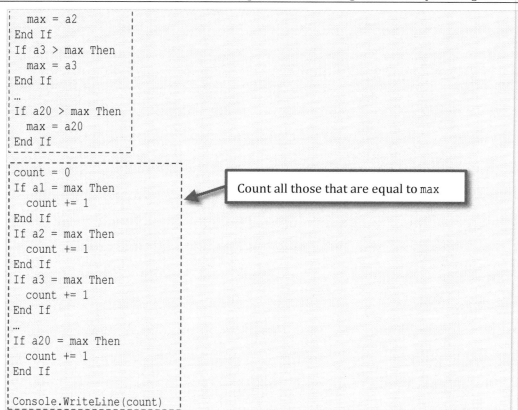

```
    max = a2
End If
If a3 > max Then
    max = a3
End If
…
If a20 > max Then
    max = a20
End If
```

```
count = 0
If a1 = max Then
    count += 1
End If
If a2 = max Then
    count += 1
End If
If a3 = max Then
    count += 1
End If
…
If a20 = max Then
    count += 1
End If

Console.WriteLine(count)
```

Count all those that are equal to max

This program appears to work fine, but what if 2000 instead of 20 grades have to be entered? Think about it—do you have the patience to write an analogous Visual Basic program for 2000 grades? Of course not! Fortunately for you, there are arrays!

32.2 What is an Array?

An array is a special type of variable that can hold multiple values at the same time under one common name. An array can be thought of as a collection of positions, each containing one value, organized in rows, columns, or a matrix. Some examples of arrays are shown here.

64	71	74	63	61	64	57

57	58	65	71	75	68	56
64	71	74	63	61	64	57
66	61	71	62	74	64	78
73	60	67	54	59	62	64

Maria
George
John
Tom
Andrew
Helen

Each item in an array is called an element. In memory, array elements are located in consecutive memory locations. Each element in an array is assigned a unique number known as its index position, or simply an index.

> **Notice**: *Arrays in computer science resemble the matrices used in mathematics. A mathematical matrix is a collection of numbers or other mathematical objects, arranged in rows and columns.*

There are one-dimensional and multidimensional arrays. A multidimensional array can be two-dimensional, three-dimensional, four-dimensional, and so on.

One-Dimensional Arrays

The following example presents a one-dimensional array that holds the grades of six students. The name of the array is Grades. For your convenience, the corresponding index is written above each element. By default, in Visual Basic, index numbering always starts at zero.

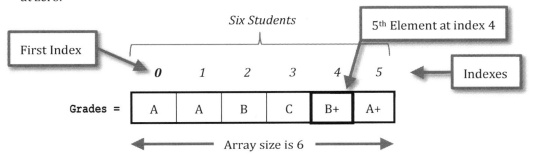

> **Remember!** *Since index numbering starts at zero, the index of the last element of an array is 1 less than the total number of elements in the array.*

You can think of an array as if it were six individual variables—Grades0, Grades1, Grades2, ... Grades5—with each variable holding the grade of one student. The advantage of the array, however, is that it can hold multiple values under one common name.

Two-Dimensional Arrays

In general, multidimensional arrays are useful for working with multiple sets of data. For example, suppose you want to hold the daily high temperatures for California for the four weeks of April. One approach would be to use four one-dimensional arrays, one for each week. Furthermore, each array would have seven elements, one for each day of the week, as follows.

Days

	0	1	2	3	4	5	6
Temperatures_week1 =	57	58	65	71	75	68	56
Temperatures_week2 =	64	71	74	63	61	64	57
Temperatures_week3 =	62	68	62	51	55	59	69
Temperatures_week4 =	73	60	67	54	59	62	64

However, this approach is a bit awkward because you would have to process each array separately. A better approach would be to use a two-dimensional array with four rows (one for each week) and seven columns (one for each day of the week), as follows.

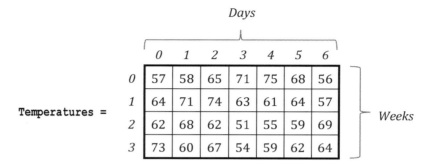

Three-Dimensional Arrays

The next example shows a three-dimensional array that holds the daily high temperatures for California for the four weeks of April for the years 2013, 2014, and 2015.

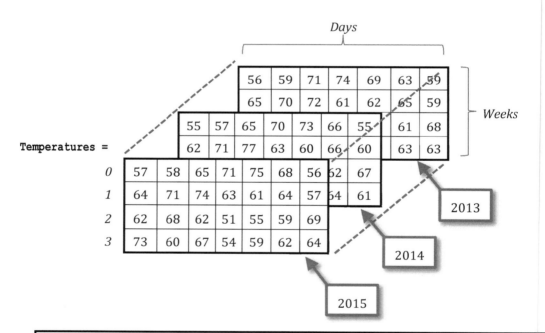

Notice: *Please note that four-dimensional, five-dimensional, or even one-hundred–dimensional arrays can exist. However, experience shows that the maximum array dimension that you will need in your life as a programmer is probably two or three.*

Exercise 32.2-1 *Designing an Array*

Design an array that can hold the ages of 14 people, and then add some typical values to the array.

Solution

This is an easy one. All you have to do is design an array with 14 positions (indexes 0 to 13). It can be an array with either one row or one column, as follows.

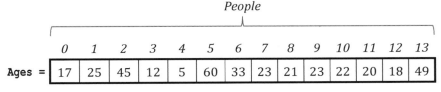

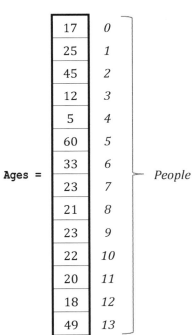

Keep in mind, however, that there are no arrays with one row or one column in Visual Basic. These concepts may exist in mathematical matrices (or in your imagination!) but not in Visual Basic. The arrays in Visual Basic are one-dimensional—end of story! If you want to visualize them having one row or one column, that is up to you.

Exercise 32.2-2 *Designing Arrays*

Design the necessary arrays to hold the names and the ages of eight people, and then add some typical values to the arrays.

Solution

This exercise can be implemented with two arrays. Let's design them with one column each.

Names =		Ages =		
John Thompson		17	0	
Ava Brown		25	1	
Ryan Miller		45	2	
Antony Harris		60	3	People
Alexander Lewis		33	4	
Samantha Clark		23	5	
Andrew Scott		21	6	
Chloe Parker		49	7	

Exercise 32.2-3   *Designing Arrays*

Design the necessary arrays to hold the names of ten people as well as the average weight (in pounds) of each person for January, February, and March. Then add some typical values to the arrays.

Solution

In this exercise, you need a one-dimensional array for names, and a two-dimensional array for people's weights.

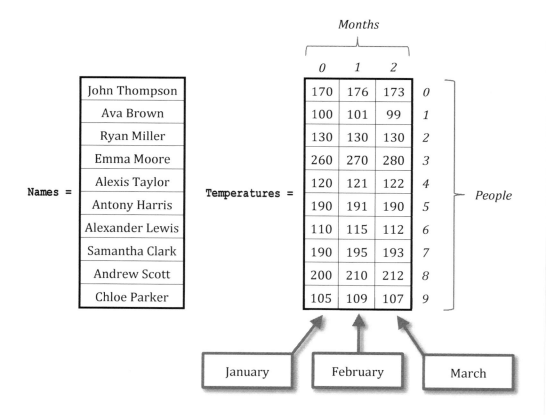

32.3   Review Questions: True/False

Choose **true** or **false** for each of the following statements.

1. Arrays are special forms of variables that can hold multiple values at the same time.

2. In memory, array elements are located in consecutive memory locations.

3. There can be only one-dimensional and two-dimensional arrays.

4. There cannot be four-dimensional arrays.

5. An array is called "multidimensional" because it can hold values of different types.

6. Each element of an array has a unique index.

7. By default, index numbering always starts at zero.

8. The index of the last element of an array is equal to the total number of elements in the array.

9. A two-hundred–dimensional array can exist.

32.4   Review Exercises

Complete the following exercises.

1. Design an array to hold the weights of five people, and then add some typical values to the array.

2. Design the necessary arrays to hold the names and the weights (in pounds) of seven people, and then add some typical values to the arrays.

3. Design the necessary arrays to hold the names of five lakes as well as the average area (in square miles) of each lake in June, July, and August. Then add some typical values to the arrays.

4. Design an array to hold the three dimensions (width, height, and depth in inches) of 10 boxes. Then add some typical values to the array.

5. Design the necessary arrays to hold the names of eight lakes as well as the average area (in square miles) and maximum depth (in feet) of each lake. Then add some typical values to the arrays.

6. Design the necessary arrays to hold the names of four lakes as well as their average areas (in square miles) for the first week of June, the first week of July, and the first week of August.

Chapter 33
One-Dimensional Arrays

33.1 Creating One-Dimensional Arrays in Visual Basic

There are two approaches that can be used to create and add values (elements) to an array in Visual Basic. Which one to use is up to you, depending on the given problem.

Let's try to create the following array, grades, using all approaches.

	0	1	2	3
grades =	B+	A+	A	C-

First Approach

You can create an array of *size* elements in Visual Basic using the following statement given in general form:

```
Dim array_name(size - 1) As type
```

where

> ➢ *size* can be any positive integer value

> ➢ *type* can be Integer, Double, String and so on

and then you can add a value (an element) to the array using the following statement, given in general form:

```
array_name(index) = value
```

where *index* is the index position of the element in the array.

The next code fragment creates the array grades and adds some values (elements) to it.

```
Dim grades(3) As String

grades(0) = "B+"
grades(1) = "A+"
grades(2) = "A"
grades(3) = "C-"
```

> **Notice:** The size of the array is 4.
>
> **Notice:** In Chapter 5 you learned about the rules that must be followed when assigning names to Visual Basic variables. Assigning names to Visual Basic arrays follows exactly the same rules!

Of course, instead of using constant values for *index*, you can also use variables or expressions, as follows.

```
Dim k As Integer
Dim grades(3) As String

k = 0

grades(k) = "B+"
```

```
grades(k + 1) = "A+"
grades(k + 2) = "A"
grades(k + 3) = "C-"
```

Second Approach

Another way to create an array and directly add values to it is shown in the next Visual Basic statement, given in general form.

```
Dim array_name() As type = {value0, value1, value2, …, valueM}
```

Using this approach, the array grades can be created using the following statement:

```
Dim grades() As String = {"B+", "A+", "A", "C-"}
```

> **Notice**: Please note that in this approach, index numbering starts at zero by default.

33.2 How to Get Values from One-Dimensional Arrays

Getting values from arrays is just a matter of pointing to a specific position. Each element of a one-dimensional array can be uniquely identified using an index. The following code fragment

```
Dim grades() As String = {"B+", "A+", "A", "C-"}
Console.Write(grades(1))
```

displays A+ on the screen.

Of course, instead of using constant values for index, you can also use variables or expressions. The following example

```
Dim grades() As String = {"B+", "A+", "A", "C-"}
k = 3
Console.Write(grades(k) & " and " & grades(k - 1))
```

displays C– and A on the screen.

Exercise 33.2-1   *Creating the Trace Table*

Create the trace table for the next code fragment.

```
Dim x As Integer
Dim a(3) As Integer

a(3) = 9
x = 0
a(x) = a(3) + 4
a(x + 1) = a(x) * 3
x += 1
a(x + 2) = a(x - 1)
a(2) = a(1) + 5
a(3) = a(3) + 1
```

Solution

Don't forget that you can manipulate each element of an array as if it were a variable. Thus, when you create a trace table for a Visual Basic program that uses an array, you can have one column for each element as follows.

Step	Statement	Notes	x	a(0)	a(1)	a(2)	a(3)
1	Dim a(3) As Integer	This creates array a with no values in it	?	?	?	?	?
2	a(3) = 9		?	?	?	?	**9**
3	x = 0		**0**	?	?	?	9
4	a(x) = a(3) + 4		0	**13**	?	?	9
5	a(x + 1) = a(x) * 3		0	13	**39**	?	9
6	x += 1		**1**	13	39	?	9
7	a(x + 2) = a(x - 1)		1	13	39	?	**13**
8	a(2) = a(1) + 5		1	13	39	**44**	13
9	a(3) = a(3) + 1		1	13	39	44	**14**

Exercise 33.2-2   *Using a Non-Existing Index*

Which properties of an algorithm are not satisfied by the following Visual Basic program?

```
Sub Main()
  Dim grades() As String = {"B+", "A+", "A", "C-"}
  Console.Write(grades(100))

  Console.ReadKey()
End Sub
```

Solution

Two properties are not satisfied by this algorithm. The first one is obvious: there is no data input. The second one is the property of definiteness. You should never refer to a non-existing element of an array and, in this exercise, there is no element at index position 100.

33.3   How to Add Values Entered by the User to a One-Dimensional Array

There is nothing new here. Instead of reading a value from the keyboard and assigning that value to a variable, you can directly assign that value to a specific position of an array. The next code fragment lets the user enter three values, and then adds these values to positions 0, 1, and 2 of the array test.

```
Dim test(2) As Integer
test(0) = Console.ReadLine()
test(1) = Console.ReadLine()
test(2) = Console.ReadLine()
```

33.4   How to Iterate Through a One-Dimensional Array

Now comes the interesting part. A program can iterate through the elements of an array using a loop control structure (usually a counted loop structure) in which the *counter* variable is used as the *index* to the array. Following is a code fragment, written in general form

```
For i = 0 To size - 1
  process array_name(i)
Next
```

in which *process* is any Visual Basic statement or block of statements that processes one element of the array at each iteration.

> **Notice:** *The name of the variable* i *is not binding. You can use any variable name you wish, such as* index, ind, j, *and many more.*

The following Visual Basic program,

```
Sub Main()
  Dim i As Integer
  Dim grades() As String = {"B+", "A+", "A", "C-"}

  For i = 0 To 3
    process grades(i)
  Next

  Console.ReadKey()
End Sub
```

"processes" all elements of the array grades, one at each iteration.

> **Notice:** *Please note that since array* grades *contains four elements, the counted loop structure should iterate from 0 to 3 and not from 1 to 4. This is because the four elements exist in positions 0, 1, 2, and 3.*

Let's see some real examples. The following code fragment lets the user enter 100 values to the array a.

```
Dim a(99) As Double
For i = 0 To 99
  a(i) = Console.ReadLine()
Next
```

The following code fragment doubles the values of all elements of the array a.

```
Dim a() As Integer = {80, 65, 60, 72, 30, 40}
For i = 0 To 5
  a(i) = a(i) * 2
Next
```

The following code fragment displays all values of the array a.

```
For i = 0 To 99
  Console.Write(a(i) & vbTab)
Next
```

Exercise 33.4-1   *Displaying Words in Reverse Order*

Write a Visual Basic program that lets the user enter ten words and then displays them in reverse order.

Solution

At first glance you might be tempted not to use an array. One possible solution would be to use ten individual variables, as follows.

```
Sub Main()
  Dim word1, word2, word3, …, word10 As String

  'Input
  word1 = Console.ReadLine()
  word2 = Console.ReadLine()
  word3 = Console.ReadLine()
  …
  word10 = Console.ReadLine()

  'Output
  Console.WriteLine(word10)
  Console.WriteLine(word9)
  Console.WriteLine(word8)
  …
  Console.WriteLine(word1)

  Console.ReadKey()
End Sub
```

If you are really satisfied with this programming style, go ahead. However, what if the wording of this exercise asked the user to enter 1000 instead of 10 words? Think about it!

Arrays are especially perfect for problems like this one. The following is an appropriate solution.

```
project_33_4_1
Sub Main()
  Dim i As Integer

  Dim words(9) As String
  For i = 0 To 9
    words(i) = Console.ReadLine()
  Next

  For i = 9 To 0 Step -1
    Console.WriteLine(words(i))
  Next

  Console.ReadKey()
End Sub
```

Remember! *Since index numbering starts at zero, the index of the last element of an array is 1 less than the total number of elements in the array.*

> **Notice**: Sometimes, the wording of an exercise may say nothing about using an array. However, this doesn't mean that you can't use one. Use arrays whenever you think they are necessary.

Exercise 33.4-2   *Displaying Positive Numbers in Reverse Order*

Write a Visual Basic program that lets the user enter 100 numbers and then displays only the positive ones in reverse order.

Solution

In this exercise, the program should accept all values from the user and store them in an array. However, within the counted loop structure that is responsible for displaying the elements of the array, a nested decision control structure should check for and display only the positive values. The solution is as follows.

```
                           project_33_4_2
Const ELEMENTS = 5

Sub Main()
  Dim i As Integer

  Dim values(ELEMENTS - 1) As Double

  For i = 0 To ELEMENTS - 1
    values(i) = Console.ReadLine()
  Next

  For i = ELEMENTS - 1 To 0 Step -1
    If values(i) > 0 Then
      Console.WriteLine(values(i))
    End If
  Next

  Console.ReadKey()
End Sub
```

> **Notice:** A very good tactic for dealing with array sizes is to use constants.
>
> **Remember!** Since index numbering starts at zero, the index of the last element of an array is 1 less than the total number of elements in the array.

Exercise 33.4-3   *Displaying Even Numbers in Odd–Numbered Index Positions*

Write a Visual Basic program that lets the user enter 100 integers into an array and then displays any even values that are stored in odd–numbered index positions.

Solution

Following is one possible solution.

```
                          project_33_4_3a
Const ELEMENTS = 100
```

```
Sub Main()
  Dim i As Integer

  Dim values(ELEMENTS - 1) As Integer
  For i = 0 To ELEMENTS - 1
    values(i) = Console.ReadLine()
  Next

  For i = 0 To ELEMENTS - 1
    If i Mod 2 <> 0 And values(i) Mod 2 = 0 Then
      Console.WriteLine(values(i))
    End If
  Next

  Console.ReadKey()
End Sub
```

However, you know that only the values in odd-numbered index positions should be examined. Therefore, in the counted loop structure that is responsible for displaying the elements of the array, instead of starting counting from 0 and using an *offset* of +1, you can start counting from 1 and use an *offset* of +2. This modification decreases the number of iterations by half. The modified Visual Basic program follows.

```
                        project_33_4_3b
Const ELEMENTS = 100

Sub Main()
  Dim i As Integer

  Dim values(ELEMENTS - 1) As Integer
  For i = 0 To ELEMENTS - 1
    values(i) = Console.ReadLine()
  Next

  For i = 1 To ELEMENTS - 1 Step 2
    If values(i) Mod 2 = 0 Then
      Console.WriteLine(values(i))
    End If
  Next

  Console.ReadKey()
End Sub
```

Exercise 33.4-4   *Finding the Sum*

Write a Visual Basic program that lets the user enter 50 numbers into an array and then calculates and displays their sum.

Solution

The solution is as follows.

project_33_4_4a

```
Const ELEMENTS = 50

Sub Main()
  Dim i As Integer
  Dim sum As Double

  Dim values(ELEMENTS - 1) As Double
  For i = 0 To ELEMENTS - 1
    values(i) = Console.ReadLine()
  Next

  sum = 0
  For i = 0 To ELEMENTS - 1
    sum = sum + values(i)
  Next

  Console.Write(sum)

  Console.ReadKey()
End Sub
```

If you are wondering if this exercise could have been solved using just one counted loop structure, the answer is "yes." An alternative solution is presented next.

project_33_4_4b

```
Const ELEMENTS = 50

Sub Main()
  Dim i As Integer
  Dim sum As Double

  Dim values(ELEMENTS - 1) As Double
  sum = 0
  For i = 0 To ELEMENTS - 1
    values(i) = Console.ReadLine()
    sum = sum + values(i)
  Next

  Console.Write(sum)

  Console.ReadKey()
End Sub
```

Let's clarify something! Even though many processes can be performed inside just one loop structure, it is simpler to carry out each individual process in a separate loop structure. This is probably not so efficient but, since you are still a novice programmer, try to adopt this programming style just for now. Later, when you have the experience and become a Visual Basic guru, you will be able to "merge" many processes in just one loop control structure.

33.5 Review Questions: True/False

Choose **true** or **false** for each of the following statements.

1. The next statement contains a syntax error.

```
Dim student names(9) As String
```

2. In a Visual Basic program, two arrays cannot have the same name.

3. In a Visual Basic program, two arrays cannot have the same number of elements.

4. You cannot use a variable as an index in an array.

5. You can use a mathematical expression as an index in an array.

6. If you use a variable as an index in an array, this variable should contain an integer value.

7. In order to calculate the sum of 20 numeric values, you must use an array.

8. You can let the user enter a value into array a using the statement `a(k) = Console.ReadLine()`

9. The following statement creates a one-dimensional array of two elements.

```
Dim names(2) As String
```

10. The following code fragment adds the value 10 to index position 7.

```
values(5) = 7
values(values(5)) = 10
```

11. The following code fragment adds the name "Sally" to index position 3.

```
Dim names(2) As String
names(2) = "John"
names(1) = "George"
names(0) = "Sally"
```

12. The following statement adds the name "Sally" to index position 2.

```
Dim names() As String = {"John", "George", "Sally"}
```

13. The following code fragment displays the name "Sally" on the screen.

```
Dim names(2) As String
k = 0
names(k) = "John"
k += 1
names(k) = "George"
k += 1
names(k) = "Sally"
k -= 1
Console.WriteLine(names(k))
```

14. The following code fragment is syntactically correct.

```
Dim names(2) As String
names(0) = "John"
names(1) = "George"
names(2) = "Sally"
Console.WriteLine(names())
```

15. The following code fragment displays the name "Maria" on the screen.

```
Dim names() As String = {"John", "George", "Sally", "Maria"}
```

```
Console.Write(names(Fix(Math.PI))
```

16. The following code fragment satisfies the property of definiteness.
```
Dim grades() As String = {"B+", "A+", "A"}
Console.Write(grades(3))
```

17. The following code fragment satisfies the property of definiteness.
```
Dim values() As Integer = {1, 3, 2, 9}
Console.Write(values(values(values(0))))
```

18. The following code fragment displays the value of 1 on the screen.
```
Dim values() As Integer = {1, 3, 2, 0}
Console.Write(values(values(values(values(0)))))
```

19. The following code fragment displays all the elements of the array.
```
Dim names() As String = {"John", "George", "Sally", "Maria"}
For i = 1 To 4
  Console.WriteLine(names(i))
Next
```

20. The following code fragment satisfies the property of definiteness.
```
Dim names() As String = {"John", "George", "Sally", "Maria"}
For i = 2 To 4
  Console.WriteLine(names(i))
Next
```

21. The following code fragment lets the user enter 100 values to array a.
```
For i = 0 To 99
  a(i) = Console.ReadLine()
Next
```

22. If array a contains 30 elements, the following code fragment doubles the values of all of its elements.
```
For i = 29 To 0 Step -1
  a(i) = a(i) * 2
Next
```

23. If array a contains 30 elements, the following code fragment displays all of them.
```
For i = 0 To 29 Step 2
  Console.WriteLine(a(i))
Next
```

33.6 Review Questions: Multiple Choice

Select the correct answer for each of the following statements.

1. The following statement
```
Dim last names(4) As String
```
   a. contains a logic error.
   b. contains a syntax error.
   c. contains two syntax errors.
   d. contains three syntax errors.

2. The following code fragment

```
Dim x As Double
x = 5
names(x / 2) = 10
```

   a. does not satisfy the property of definiteness.

   b. does not satisfy the property of finiteness.

   c. does not satisfy the property of effectiveness.

   d. none of the above

3. If variable x contains the value 4, the following statement

```
names(x + 1) = 5
```

   a. assigns the value 4 to index position 5.

   b. assigns the value 5 to index position 4.

   c. assigns the value 5 to index position 5.

   d. none of the above

4. The following code fragment

```
Dim names() As Integer = {5, 6, 9, 1, 1, 1}
```

   a. assigns the value 5 to index position 1.

   b. assigns the value 5 to index position 0.

   c. does not satisfy the property of definiteness.

   d. none of the above

5. The following code fragment

```
values(0) = 1
values(values(0)) = 2
values(values(1)) = 3
values(values(2)) = 4
```

   a. assigns the value 4 to index position 3.

   b. assigns the value 3 to index position 2.

   c. assigns the value 2 to index position 1.

   d. all of the above

   e. none of the above

6. If the array values contains numeric values, the following statement

```
Console.Write(values(values(1) - values(1 Mod 2)) - values(Fix(1/2)))
```

   a. does not satisfy the property of definiteness.

   b. always displays 0.

   c. always displays 1.

   d. none of the above

7. You can iterate through a one-dimensional array with a counted loop structure that uses

   a. variable i as a counter.

   b. variable j as a counter.

   c. variable k as a counter.

    d.   any variable as a counter.

8.   The following code fragment

```
Dim names() As String = {"George", "John", "Maria", "Sally"}
For i = 3 To 1 Step -1
  Console.WriteLine(names(i))
Next
```

    a.   displays all names in ascending order.

    b.   displays some names in ascending order.

    c.   displays all names in descending order.

    d.   displays some names in descending order.

    e.   none of the above

9.   If array a contains 30 elements, the following code fragment

```
For i = 29 To 1 Step -1
  a(i) = a(i) * 2
Next
```

    a.   doubles the values of some of its elements.

    b.   doubles the values of all of its elements.

    c.   none of the above

33.7   Review Exercises

Complete the following exercises.

1.   Create the trace table for the following code fragment.

```
Dim a(2) As Integer
a(2) = 1
x = 0
a(x + a(2)) = 4
a(x) = a(x + 1) * 4
```

2.   Create the trace table for the following code fragment.

```
Dim a(4) As Integer
a(1) = 5
x = 0
a(x) = 4
a(a(0)) = a(x + 1) Mod 3
a(a(0) / 2) = 10
x += 2
a(x + 1) = a(x) + 9
```

3.   Create the trace table for the following code fragment for three different executions.

     The input values for the three executions are: (i) 3, (ii) 4, and (iii) 1.

```
Dim a(3) As Integer
a(1) = Console.ReadLine()

x = 0
a(x) = 3
a(a(0)) = a(x + 1) Mod 2
```

```
a(a(0) Mod 2) = 10
x += 1
a(x + 1) = a(x) + 9
```

4. Create the trace table for the following code fragment for three different executions.

   The input values for the three executions are: (i) 100, (ii) 108, and (iii) 1.

```
Dim a(3) As Integer
a(1) = Console.ReadLine()
x = 0
a(x) = 3
a(a(0)) = a(x + 1) Mod 10
If a(3) > 5 Then
    a(a(0) Mod 2) = 9
    x += 1
    a(x + 1) = a(x) + 9
Else
    a(2) = 3
End If
```

5. Fill in the gaps in the following trace table. In steps 6 and 7, fill in the name of a variable; for all other cases, fill in constant values, arithmetic, or comparison operators.

Step	Statement	x	y	a(0)	a(1)	a(2)
1	Dim a(2) As Integer	?	?	?	?	?
2	x = ...	4	?	?	?	?
3	y = x -	4	3	?	?	?

4, 5	If x ...... y Then
	    a(0) = ...
	 Else
	    a(0) = y
	 End If
		4	3	1	?	?

6	a(1) = ... + 3	4	3	1	7	?
7	y = ... - 1	4	2	1	7	?
8	a(y) = (x + 5) 2	4	2	1	7	1

6. Create the trace table for the following code fragment.

```
Dim a() As Integer = {17, 12, 45, 12, 12, 49}

For i = 0 To 5
  If a(i) = 12 Then
    a(i) -= 1
  Else
    a(i) += 1
  End If
Next
```

7. Create the trace table for the following code fragment.

```
Dim a() As Integer = {10, 15, 12, 23, 22, 19}

For i = 1 To 4
  a(i) = a(i + 1) + a(i - 1)
Next
```

8. Write a Visual Basic program that lets the user enter 100 numbers in an array and then displays these values raised to the power of three.

9. Write a Visual Basic program that lets the user enter 80 numbers in an array and then displays these values in reverse order raised to the power of two.

10. Write a Visual Basic program that lets the user enter 90 integers in an array and then displays in reverse order those that are exactly divisible by 5.

11. Write a Visual Basic program that lets the user enter 50 integers in an array and then displays those that are even or greater than 10.

12. Write a Visual Basic program that lets the user enter 30 numbers in an array and then calculates and displays the sum of those that are positive.

13. Write a Visual Basic program that lets the user enter 50 integers in an array and then calculates and displays the sum of those that have two digits.

Hint: All two-digit integers are between 10 and 99.

14. Write a Visual Basic program that lets the user enter 40 numbers in an array and then calculates and displays the sum of the positive numbers and the sum of the negative ones.

15. Write a Visual Basic program that lets the user enter 20 numbers in an array and then calculates and displays their average value.

16. Write a Visual Basic program that lets the user enter 50 words and displays those that contain at least 10 characters.

Hint: Use the .Length property.

17. Write a Visual Basic program that lets the user enter 40 words and displays those that contain the letter "w" at least twice.

Hint: Use the Substring() procedure and the .Length property.

Chapter 34
Two-Dimensional Arrays

34.1 Creating Two-Dimensional Arrays in Visual Basic

An array that can hold the grades of four lessons for three students is as follows.

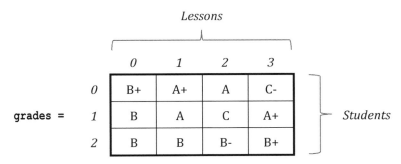

> **Notice**: A two-dimensional array has rows and columns. In this particular example, array grades *has 3 rows and 4 columns.*
>
> **Remember!** *In Chapter 5 you learned about the rules that must be followed when assigning names to Visual Basic variables. Assigning names to Visual Basic arrays follows exactly the same rules!*

As in one-dimensional arrays, there are two approaches to creating and adding values (elements) to a two-dimensional array. Let's try to create the array grades using each of these approaches.

First Approach

You can create a two-dimensional array in Visual Basic using the following statement, given in general form:

```
Dim array_name(number_of_rows - 1, number_of_columns - 1) As type
```

where

> ➤ *number_of_rows* and *number_of_columns* can be any positive integer value
> ➤ *type* can be Integer, Double, String and so on

and then you can add a value (an element) to the array using the following statement, given in general form:

```
array_name(row_index, column_index) = value
```

where *row_index* and *column_index* are the row index and the column index positions, respectively, of the element in the array.

The following code fragment creates the array grades and adds values to it.

```
Dim grades(2, 3) As String

grades(0, 0) = "B+"
```

```
grades(0, 1) = "A+"
grades(0, 2) = "A"
grades(0, 3) = "C-"
grades(1, 0) = "B"
grades(1, 1) = "A"
grades(1, 2) = "C"
grades(1, 3) = "A+"
grades(2, 0) = "B"
grades(2, 1) = "B"
grades(2, 2) = "B-"
grades(2, 3) = "B+"
```

Second Approach

Another way to create an array and directly add values to it is shown in the following Visual Basic statement, given in general form.

```
Dim array_name(,) As type = { {value0-0, value0-1, value0-2, …, value0-M},
                              {value1-0, value1-1, value1-2, …, value1-M},
                              {value2-0, value2-1, value2-2, …, value2-M},

                              …

                              {valueN-0, valueN-1, valueN-2, …, valueN-M}
                            }
```

Thus, the array grades can be created using the following statement.

```
Dim grades(,) As String = { {"B+", "A+", "A", "C-"},
                            {"B", "A", "C", "A+"},
                            {"B", "B", "B-", "B+"}
                          }
```

34.2 How to Get Values from Two-Dimensional Arrays

A two-dimensional array consists of rows and columns. The following example shows a two-dimensional array with three rows and four columns.

	Column 0	Column 1	Column 2	Column 3
Row 0				
Row 1				
Row 2				

Each element of a two-dimensional array can be uniquely identified using a pair of indexes: a row index, and a column index, as shown next.

```
array_name(row_index, column_index)
```

The following Visual Basic program creates the two-dimensional array grades having three rows and four columns, and then displays some of its elements.

```
Sub Main()
  Dim grades(,) As String = { {"B+", "A+", "A", "C-"},
                              {"B", "A", "C", "A+"},
                              {"B", "B", "B-", "B+"}
                            }

  Console.WriteLine(grades(1, 2))          'This displays C on the screen
```

```
Console.WriteLine(grades(2, 2))        'This displays B- on the screen
Console.WriteLine(grades(0, 0))        'This displays B+ on the screen

Console.ReadKey()
End Sub
```

Exercise 34.2-1   *Creating the Trace Table*

Create the trace table for the next code fragment.

```
Dim a(,) As Integer = { {0, 0},
                        {0, 0},
                        {0, 0}
                      }

a(1, 0) = 9
a(0, 1) = 1
a(0, 0) = a(0, 1) + 6
x = 2
a(x, 1) = a(0, 0) + 4
a(x - 1, 1) = a(0, 1) * 3
a(x, 0) = a(x - 1, 1) - 3
```

Solution

This code fragment uses a 3 × 2 array, that is, an array that has 3 rows and 2 columns. The trace table is as follows.

Step	Statement	Notes	x	a	
1	`Dim a(,) As Integer = { {0, 0},` `{0, 0},` `{0, 0}` `}`	This creates array a with zero values in it.	?	0 / 0 / 0	0 / 0 / 0
2	`a(1, 0) = 9`		?	0 / 9 / 0	0 / 0 / 0
3	`a(0, 1) = 1`		?	0 / 9 / 0	1 / 0 / 0
4	`a(0, 0) = a(0, 1) + 6`		?	7 / 9 / 0	1 / 0 / 0

5	x = 2	2	7	1
			9	0
			0	0

6	a(x, 1) = a(0, 0) + 4	2	7	1
			9	0
			0	11

7	a(x - 1, 1) = a(0, 1) * 3	2	7	1
			9	3
			0	11

8	a(x, 0) = a(x - 1, 1) - 3	2	7	1
			9	3
			0	11

34.3 How to Add Values Entered by the User to a Two-Dimensional Array

Just as in one-dimensional arrays, instead of reading a value entered from the keyboard and assigning that value to a variable, you can directly assign that value to a specific position of an array. The next code fragment creates a two-dimensional array test, lets the user enter four values, and adds those values to the array.

```
Dim test(1, 1) As Integer

test(0, 0) = Console.ReadLine()
test(0, 1) = Console.ReadLine()
test(1, 0) = Console.ReadLine()
test(1, 1) = Console.ReadLine()
```

34.4 How to Iterate Through a Two-Dimensional Array

Since a two-dimensional array consists of rows and columns, a program can iterate either through rows or through columns.

Iterating through rows

Iterating through rows means that row 0 is processed first, row 1 is process next, row 2 afterwards, and so on. Next there is an example of a 3 × 4 array. The arrows show the "path" that is followed when iteration through rows is performed or in other words, they show the order in which the elements are processed.

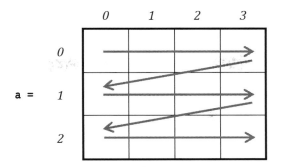

> **Remember!** *A 3 × 4 array is a two-dimensional array that has 3 rows and 4 columns. In the notation Y × X, the first number (Y) always represents the total number of rows and the second number (X) always represents the total number of columns.*

When iterating through rows, the elements of the array are processed as follows:

➤ the elements of row 0 are processed in the following order

$$a(0, 0) \rightarrow a(0, 1) \rightarrow a(0, 2) \rightarrow a(0, 3)$$

➤ the elements of row 1 are processed in the following order

$$a(1, 0) \rightarrow a(1, 1) \rightarrow a(1, 2) \rightarrow a(1, 3)$$

➤ the elements of row 2 are processed in the following order

$$a(2, 0) \rightarrow a(2, 1) \rightarrow a(2, 2) \rightarrow a(2, 3)$$

Using Visual Basic statements, let's try to process all elements of a 3 × 4 array (3 rows × 4 columns) iterating through rows.

```
i = 0                    'Variable i refers to Row 0.
For j = 0 To 3           'This loop control structure processes all
  process a(i, j)        'elements of Row 0
Next


i = 1                    'Variable i refers to Row 1.
For j = 0 To 3           'This loop control structure processes all
  process a(i, j)        'elements of Row 1
Next


i = 2                    'Variable i refers to Row 2.
For j = 0 To 3           'This loop control structure processes all
  process a(i, j)        'elements of Row 2
Next
```

Of course, the same results can be achieved using a nested loop control structure as shown next.

```
For i = 0 To 2
  For j = 0 To 3
    process a(i, j)
  Next
Next
```

Let's see some examples. The following code fragment lets the user enter 10 × 10 = 100 values to array a.

```
For i = 0 To 9
  For j = 0 To 9
    a(i, j) = Console.ReadLine()
  Next
Next
```

The following code fragment decreases all values of array a by one.

```
For i = 0 To 9
  For j = 0 To 9
    a(i, j) = a(i, j) - 1
  Next
Next
```

The following code fragment displays the values of array a.

```
For i = 0 To 9
  For j = 0 To 9
    Console.Write(a(i, j) & vbTab)
  Next
  Console.WriteLine()
Next
```

> *Notice: The* `Console.WriteLine()` *statement is used to "display" a line break between lines.*

Iterating Through Columns

Iterating through columns means that column 0 is processed first, column 1 is processed next, column 2 afterwards, and so on. Next there is an example of a 3 × 4 array. The arrows show the order in which the elements are processed.

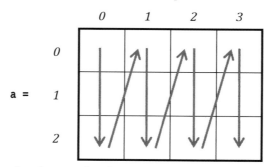

When iterating through columns, the elements of the array are processed as follows:

➢ the elements of column 0 are processed in the following order
$$a(0, 0) \rightarrow a(1, 0) \rightarrow a(2, 0)$$

➢ the elements of column 1 are processed in the following order
$$a(0, 1) \rightarrow a(1, 1) \rightarrow a(2, 1)$$

➢ the elements of column 2 are processed in the following order
$$a(0, 2) \rightarrow a(1, 2) \rightarrow a(2, 2)$$

➢ the elements of column 3 are processed in the following order
$$a(0, 3) \rightarrow a(1, 3) \rightarrow a(2, 3)$$

Using Visual Basic statements, let's try to process all elements of a 3 × 4 array (3 rows × 4 columns) by iterating through columns.

```
j = 0                           'Variable j refers to Column 0.
For i = 0 To 2                  'This loop control structure processes all
   process a(i, j)              'elements of Column 0
Next


j = 1                           'Variable j refers to Column 1.
For i = 0 To 2                  'This loop control structure processes all
   process a(i, j)              'elements of Column 1
Next


j = 2                           'Variable j refers to Column 2.
For i = 0 To 2                  'This loop control structure processes all
   process a(i, j)              'elements of Column 2
Next


j = 3                           'Variable j refers to Column 3.
For i = 0 To 2                  'This loop control structure processes all
   process a(i, j)              'elements of Column 3
Next
```

Of course, the same result can be achieved using a nested loop control structure as shown next.

```
For j = 0 To 3
   For i = 0 To 2
      process a(i, j)
   Next
Next
```

As you can see, this code fragment differs on only one single point from the one that iterates through rows: the two counted loop structures have switched places. Be careful though. Don't try switching places of the two index variables i and j in the statement process a(i, j). Take the following code fragment, for example. It tries to iterate through columns in a 3 × 4 array (3 rows × 4 columns) but it does not satisfy the property of definiteness. Can you find out why?

```
For j = 0 To 3
   For i = 0 To 2
      process a(j, i)
   Next
Next
```

The trouble arises when variable j becomes equal to 3. The statement process a(j, i) tries to process the elements at **row** index 3 (this is the fourth row) which, of course, does not exist! Still confused? Don't be! There is no row index 3 in a 3 × 4 array! Why? Since row index numbering starts at 0, only rows 0, 1, and 2 actually exist!

Exercise 34.4-1   *Displaying Reals Only*

Write a Visual Basic program that prompts the user to enter numeric values in a 5 × 7 array and then displays the indexes of the positions that contain reals.

Solution

Iterating through rows is the most popular approach, so let's use it. The solution is as follows.

```
project_34_4_1
Const ROWS = 5
Const COLUMNS = 7

Sub Main()
  Dim i, j As Integer

  Dim a(ROWS - 1, COLUMNS - 1) As Double
  For i = 0 To ROWS - 1
    For j = 0 To COLUMNS - 1
      Console.Write("Enter a value for element " & i & ", " & j & ": ")
      a(i, j) = Console.ReadLine()
    Next
  Next

  For i = 0 To ROWS - 1
    For j = 0 To COLUMNS - 1
      If a(i, j) <> Fix(a(i, j)) Then
        Console.WriteLine("A real found at position: " & i & ", " & j)
      End If
    Next
  Next

  Console.ReadKey()
End Sub
```

Exercise 34.4-2   *Displaying Odd Columns Only*

Write a Visual Basic program that prompts the user to enter numeric values in a 5 × 7 array and then displays the elements of the columns with odd-numbered indexes (that is, column indexes 1, 3, and 5).

Solution

The Visual Basic program is presented next.

```
project_34_4_2
Const ROWS = 5
Const COLUMNS = 7

Sub Main()
  Dim i, j As Integer

  Dim a(ROWS - 1, COLUMNS - 1) As Double
  For i = 0 To ROWS - 1
    For j = 0 To COLUMNS - 1
      Console.Write("Enter a value for element " & i & ", " & j & ": ")
```

```
      a(i, j) = Console.ReadLine()
   Next
 Next

 'Iterate through columns
 For j = 1 To COLUMNS - 1 Step 2        'Start from 1 and increment by 2
   For i = 0 To ROWS - 1
     Console.Write(a(i, j) & " ")
   Next
 Next

 Console.ReadKey()
End Sub
```

> **Notice:** *This book tries to use, as often as possible, variable* i *as the row index and variable* j *as the column index. Of course, you can use other variable names as well, such as* row, r *for row index, or* column, c *for column index, but variables* i *and* j *are widely used by the majority of programmers. After using them for a while, your brain will relate* i *to rows and* j *to columns. Thus, every algorithm or program that uses these variable names as indexes in two-dimensional arrays will be more readily understood.*

34.5   What's the Story on Variables i and j?

Many programmers believe that the name of variable i stands for "index" and j is used just because it is after i. Others believe that the name i stands for "integer." Probably the truth lies somewhere in the middle.

Mathematicians were using i, j, and k to designate integers in mathematics long before computers were around. Later, in FORTRAN, one of the first high-level computer languages, variables i, j, k, l, m, and n were integers by default. Thus, the first programmers picked up the habit of using variables i and j in their programs and it became a convention in most computer languages.

34.6   Square Arrays

An array that has the same number of rows and columns is called a square array. Following are some examples of square arrays.

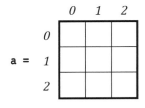

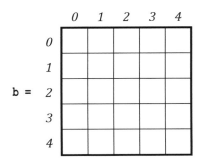

Exercise 34.6-1   *Finding the Sum of the Elements of the Main Diagonal*

Write a Visual Basic program that lets the user enter numeric values into a 10 × 10 square array and then calculates the sum of the elements of its main diagonal.

Solution

The main diagonal of a square array is the collection of those elements that runs from the top left corner to the bottom right corner. Following are some examples of square arrays with their main diagonals highlighted by a dark background.

	0	1	2
0	**10**	12	11
a = 1	23	**50**	9
2	12	11	**-3**

	0	1	2	3	4
0	**-3**	44	-12	25	22
1	10	**-1**	29	12	-9
b = 2	5	-3	**16**	22	-8
3	11	25	12	**25**	-5
4	12	22	53	44	**-15**

> *Notice: Please note that the elements of the main diagonal have their row index equal to their column index.*

You can calculate the sum of the elements of the main diagonal using two different approaches. Let's study them both.

First Approach – Iterating through all elements

In this approach, the program iterates through rows, or even through columns, and checks if the row index is equal to the column index. For square arrays, represented as N × N, the number of rows and columns is equal, so you can define just one constant, N. The solution is as follows.

```
                           project_34_6_1a
Const N = 10

Sub Main()
  Dim i, j As Integer
  Dim sum As Double

  Dim a(N - 1, N - 1) As Double
  For i = 0 To N - 1
    For j = 0 To N - 1
      a(i, j) = Console.ReadLine()
    Next
  Next

  'Calculate Sum
  sum = 0
```

```
  For i = 0 To N - 1
    For j = 0 To N - 1
      If i = j Then
          sum = sum + a(i, j)
      End If
    Next
  Next

  Console.WriteLine("Sum = " & sum)

  Console.ReadKey()
End Sub
```

> **Notice:** Please note that the program iterates through rows and checks if the row index is equal to the column index. Alternatively, the same result can be achieved by iterating through columns.
>
> **Notice:** In this approach, the nested loop control structure that is responsible for calculating the sum performs 10 × 10 = 100 iterations.

Second Approach – Iterating directly through the main diagonal

In this approach, one single loop control structure iterates directly through the main diagonal. The solution is as follows.

```
                          project_34_6_1b
Const N = 10

Sub Main()
  Dim i, j, k As Integer
  Dim sum As Double

  Dim a(N - 1, N - 1) As Double
  For i = 0 To N - 1
    For j = 0 To N - 1
      a(i, j) = Console.ReadLine()
    Next
  Next

  'Calculate Sum
  sum = 0
  For k = 0 To N - 1
    sum = sum + a(k, k)
  Next

  Console.Write("Sum = " & sum)

  Console.ReadKey()
End Sub
```

> **Notice**: *This approach is much more efficient than the first one since the total number of iterations performed by the counted loop structure that is responsible for calculating the sum is just 10.*

Exercise 34.6-2   *Finding the Sum of the Elements of the Antidiagonal*

Write a Visual Basic program that lets the user enter numeric values in a 5 × 5 square array and then calculates the sum of the elements of its antidiagonal.

Solution

The antidiagonal of a square array is the collection of those elements that runs from the top right corner to the bottom left corner of the array. Next, you can find an example of a 5 × 5 square array with its antidiagonal highlighted by a dark background.

	0	1	2	3	4
0	-3	44	-12	25	**22**
1	10	-1	29	**12**	-9
a = 2	5	-3	**16**	22	-8
3	11	**25**	12	25	-5
4	**12**	22	53	44	-15

Any element of the antidiagonal of an N × N array satisfies the following equation:

$$i + j = N - 1$$

where variables i and j correspond to the row and column indexes of the element respectively.

If you solve for j, the equation becomes

$$j = N - i - 1$$

Using this formula, you can calculate, for any value of variable i, the corresponding value of variable j. For example, in the previous 5 × 5 square array in which N equals 5, when i is 0 the value of variable j is

$$j = N - i - 1 \Leftrightarrow j = 5 - 0 - 1 = \Leftrightarrow j = 4$$

Doing this for all values of variable i, you can calculate the corresponding values of variable j as shown in the following table.

Value of Variable i	Calculated Value of Variable j
0	4
1	3
2	2
3	1
4	0

Using all this knowledge, let's now write the corresponding Visual Basic program.

```
                              project_34_6_2
Const N = 5

Sub Main()
  Dim i, j As Integer
  Dim sum As Double

  Dim a(N - 1, N - 1) As Double
  For i = 0 To N - 1
    For j = 0 To N - 1
      a(i, j) = Console.ReadLine()
    Next
  Next

  'Calculate Sum
  sum = 0
  For i = 0 To N - 1
    j = N - i - 1
    sum = sum + a(i, j)
  Next

  Console.Write("Sum = " & sum)

  Console.ReadKey()
End Sub
```

> **Notice**: Please note that the counted loop structure that is responsible for finding the sum of the elements of the antidiagonal iterates directly through the antidiagonal.

Exercise 34.6-3   *Filling in the Array*

Write a Visual Basic program that creates and displays the following array.

		0	1	2	3	4
	0	-1	20	20	20	20
	1	10	-1	20	20	20
a =	2	10	10	-1	20	20
	3	10	10	10	-1	20
	4	10	10	10	10	-1

Solution

As you can see, in the main diagonal, there is the value of -1. You already know that the main diagonal of a square array is the collection of those elements that have their row index equal to their column index. Now, what you also need is to find a common characteristic between all positions that contain the value 10, and another such common characteristic between all positions that contain the value 20.

If you look closer, you will realize that the row index of any position that contains the value 10 is always greater than its corresponding column index and, similarly, the row index of any position that contains the value 20 is always less than its corresponding column index.

Accordingly, the Visual Basic program is as follows.

```
project_34_6_3
Const N = 5

Sub Main()
  Dim i, j As Integer

  Dim a(N - 1, N - 1) As Integer
  For i = 0 To N - 1
    For j = 0 To N - 1
      If i = j Then
        a(i, j) = -1
      ElseIf i > j Then
        a(i, j) = 10
      Else
        a(i, j) = 20
      End If
    Next
  Next

  For i = 0 To N - 1
    For j = 0 To N - 1
      Console.Write(a(i, j) & vbTab)
    Next
    Console.WriteLine()
  Next

  Console.ReadKey()
End Sub
```

34.7 Review Questions: True/False

Choose **true** or **false** for each of the following statements.

1. All the positions of a two-dimensional array must contain different values.

2. In order to refer to a position of a two-dimensional array you need two indexes.

3. The two indexes of a two-dimensional array must be either both variables, or both constant values.

4. A 5 × 6 array is a two-dimensional array that has five columns and six rows.

5. To refer to an element of array a that exists at the second row and third column, you would write a(2, 3).

6. Iterating through rows means that first row of a two-dimensional array is processed first, the second row is process next, and so on.

7. You cannot use variables other than i and j to iterate through a two-dimensional array.

8. The following Visual Basic statement creates a two-dimensional array.

```
Dim names(2, 6) As Integer
```

9. The following code fragment creates a two-dimensional array of four elements.

```
Dim names(1, 1) As String
names(0, 0) = "John"
names(0, 1) = "George"
names(1, 0) = "Sally"
names(1, 1) = "Angelina"
```

10. The following code fragment adds the value 10 to the row with index 0.

```
values(0, 0) = 7
values(0, values(0, 0)) = 10
```

11. The following statement adds the name "Sally" to the row with index 1.

```
Dim names(,) As String = { {"John", "George"},
                           {"Sally", "Angelina"} }
```

12. The following code fragment displays the name "Sally" on the screen.

```
Dim names(1, 1) As String
k = 0
names(0, k) = "John"
k += 1
names(0, k) = "George"
names(1, k) = "Sally"
k -= 1
names(1, k) = "Angelina"
Console.Write(names(1, 1))
```

13. The following code fragment satisfies the property of definiteness.

```
Dim grades(,) As String = { {"B+", "A+"},
                            {"A", "C-"} }
Console.Write(grades(2, 2))
```

14. The following code fragment satisfies the property of definiteness.

```
Dim values(,) As Integer = { {1, 0},
                             {2, 0} }
Console.Write(values(values(0, 0), values(0, 1)))
```

15. The following code fragment displays the value 2 on the screen.

```
Dim values(,) As Integer = { {0, 1},
                             {2, 0} }
Console.Write(values(values(0, 1), values(0, 0)))
```

16. The following code fragment displays all the elements of a 3 × 4 array.

```
For k = 0 To 11
  i = k \ 4
  j = k Mod 4
  Console.WriteLine(names(i, j))
Next
```

17. The following code fragment lets the user enter 100 values to array a.

```
For i = 0 To 9
```

```
    For j = 0 To 9
      a(i, j) = Console.ReadLine()
    Next
  Next
```

18. If array a contains 10 × 20 elements, the following code fragment doubles the values of all of its elements.

```
For i = 9 To 0 Step -1
  For j = 19 To 0 Step -1
    a(i, j) *= 2
  Next
```

19. If array a contains 10 × 20 elements, the following code fragment displays some of them.

```
For i = 0 To 8 Step 2
  For j = 0 To 19
    Console.WriteLine(a(i, j))
  Next
Next
For i = 1 To 9 Step 2
  For j = 0 To 19
    Console.WriteLine(a(i, j))
  Next
Next
```

20. The following code fragment displays only the columns with even-numbered indexes.

```
For j = 0 To 10 Step 2
  For i = 0 To 9
    Console.WriteLine(a(i, j))
  Next
Next
```

21. A 5 × 5 array is a square array.

22. In the main diagonal of a square array, all elements have their row index equal to their column index.

23. The antidiagonal of a square array is the collection of those elements that runs from the top left corner to the bottom right corner of the array.

24. Any element of the antidiagonal of an N × N array satisfies the equation $i + j = N - 1$, where variables i and j correspond to the row and column indexes of the element respectively.

25. The following code fragment calculates the sum of the elements of the main diagonal of a N × N array.

```
sum = 0
For k = 0 To N - 1
  sum += a(k, k)
Next
```

26. The following code fragment displays all the elements of the antidiagonal of an N × N array.

```
For i = N - 1 To 0 Step -1
```

```
        Console.WriteLine(a(i, N - i - 1))
    Next
```

27. The column index of any element of a square array that is below the main diagonal is always greater than its corresponding row index.

34.8   Review Questions: Multiple Choice

Select the correct answer for each of the following statements.

1.   The following statement

```
Dim last_names(5   4) As String
```

   a.   contains a logic error.

   b.   contains a syntax error.

   c.   none of the above

2.   The following code fragment

```
Dim values(,) As Integer = { {1, 0}
                             {2, 0}}
Console.Write(values(values(0, 0) values(0, 1)))
```

   a.   contains a logic error.

   b.   contains a syntax error.

   c.   contains two syntax errors.

   d.   none of the above

3.   The following code fragment

```
x = Console.ReadLine()
y = Console.ReadLine()
names(x, y) = 10
```

   a.   does not satisfy the property of finiteness.

   b.   does not satisfy the property of effectiveness.

   c.   does not satisfy the property of definiteness.

   d.   none of the above

4.   If variable x contains the value 4, the following statement

```
names(x + 1, x) = 5
```

   a.   assigns the value 5 to the position with row index 5 and column index 4.

   b.   assigns the value 5 to the position with row index 4 and column index 5.

   c.   assigns the value 5 to the position with row index 5 and column index 5.

   d.   none of the above

5.   The following statement

```
Dim names(,) As Integer = { {3, 5, 2} }
```

   a.   assigns the value 5 to the position with row index 0 and column index 1.

   b.   assigns the value 3 to the position with row index 0 and column index 0.

   c.   assigns the value 2 to the position with row index 0 and column index 2.

   d.   all of the above

   e.   none of the above

6. The following statement

```
Dim values(0, 1) As Integer
```

    a.   creates a 1 × 2 array.

    b.   creates a 2 × 1 array.

    c.   creates a 1 × 3 array.

    d.   none of the above

7. You can iterate through a two-dimensional array with two nested loop control structures that use

    a.   variables i and j as counters.

    b.   variables k and l as counters.

    c.   variables m and n as counters.

    d.   any variables as counters.

8. The following code fragment

```
Dim names(,) As String = { {"John", "Sally"},
                           {"George", "Maria"} }

For j = 0 To 1
  For i = 1 To 0 Step -1
    Console.WriteLine(names(i, j))
  Next
Next
```

    a.   displays all names in descending order.

    b.   displays some names in descending order.

    c.   displays all names in ascending order.

    d.   displays some names in ascending order.

    e.   none of the above

9. If array a contains 30 × 40 elements, the following code fragment

```
For i = 30 To 1 Step -1
  For j = 40 To 1 Step -1
    a(i, j) *= 3
  Next
Next
```

    a.   triples the values of some of its elements.

    b.   triples the values of all of its elements.

    c.   none of the above

10. If array a contains 30 × 40 elements, the following code fragment

```
sum = 0
For i = 29 To 0 Step -1
  For j = 39 To 0 Step -1
    sum += a(i, j)
  Next
Next

average = sum / 120
```

a.   calculates the sum of all of its elements.

b.   calculates the average value of all of its elements.

c.   all of the above

11.   The following two code fragments calculate the sum of the elements of the main diagonal of an N × N array,

```
sum = 0
For i = 0 To N - 1
  For j = 0 To N - 1
    If i = j Then
      sum = sum + a(i, j)
    End If
  Next
Next
```

```
sum = 0
For k = 0 To N - 1
  sum = sum + a(k, k)
Next
```

a.   but the first one is more efficient.

b.   but the second one is more efficient.

c.   none of the above; both code fragments perform equivalently

34.9   Review Exercises

Complete the following exercises.

1.   Create the trace table for the following code fragment.

```
Dim a(1, 2) As Integer
a(0, 2) = 1
x = 0
a(0, x) = 9
a(0, x + a(0, 2)) = 4
a(a(0, 2), 2) = 19
a(a(0, 2), x + 1) = 13
a(a(0, 2), x) = 15
```

2.   Create the trace table for the following code fragment.

```
Dim a(1, 2) As Integer
For i = 0 To 1
  For j = 0 To 2
    a(i, j) = (i + 1) * 5 + j
  Next
Next
```

3.   Create the trace table for the following code fragment.

```
Dim a(2, 2) As Integer
For j = 0 To 2
  For i = 0 To 2
    a(i, j) = (i + 1) * 2 + j * 4
  Next
Next
```

4.   Try, without using a trace table, to determine the values that the array will contain when the following code fragment is executed. Do this for three different executions. The corresponding input values are: (i) 5, (ii) 9, and (iii) 3.

```
Dim a(1, 2) As Integer
x = Console.ReadLine()
For i = 0 To 1
  For j = 0 To 2
    a(i, j) = (x + i) * j
  Next
Next
```

5. Try, without using a trace table, to determine the values that the array will contain when the following code fragment is executed. Do this for three different executions. The corresponding input values are: (i) 13, (ii) 10, and (iii) 8.

```
Dim a(1, 2) As Integer
x = Console.ReadLine()
For i = 0 To 1
  For j = 0 To 2
    If j < x Mod 4 Then
      a(i, j) = (x + i) * j
    Else
      a(i, j) = (x + j) * i + 3
    End If
  Next
Next
```

6. Try, without using a trace table, to determine the values that the array will contain when the following code fragment is executed.

```
Dim a(,) As Double = { {18, 10, 35},
                       {32, 12, 19} }

For j = 0 To 2
  For i = 0 To 1
    If a(i, j) < 13 Then
      a(i, j) /= 2
    ElseIf a(i, j) < 20 Then
      a(i, j) += 1
    Else
      a(i, j) -= 4
    End If
  Next
Next
```

7. Try, without using a trace table, to determine the values that the array will contain when the following code fragment is executed.

```
Dim a(,) As Integer = { {11, 10},
                        {15, 19},
                        {22, 15} }

For j = 0 To 1
  For i = 0 To 2
    If i = 2 Then
      a(i, j) += a(i - 1, j)
    Else
      a(i, j) += a(i + 1, j)
```

```
        End If
    Next
Next
```

8. Assume that array a contains the following values.

$$
a = \begin{array}{c|c|c|c|c|} & 0 & 1 & 2 & 3 \\ \hline 0 & -1 & 15 & 22 & 3 \\ \hline 1 & 25 & 12 & 16 & 14 \\ \hline 2 & 7 & 9 & 1 & 45 \\ \hline 3 & 40 & 17 & 11 & 13 \\ \hline \end{array}
$$

What displays on the screen after executing each of the following code fragments?

i)
```
For i = 0 To 2
    For j = 0 To 2
        Console.Write(a(i, j))
        Console.Write(" ")
    Next
Next
```

ii)
```
For i = 2 To 0 Step -1
    For j = 0 To 2
        Console.Write(a(i, j))
        Console.Write(" ")
    Next
Next
```

iii)
```
For i = 0 To 2
    For j = 2 To 0 Step -1
        Console.Write(a(i, j))
        Console.Write(" ")
    Next
Next
```

iv)
```
For i = 2 To 0 Step -1
    For j = 2 To 0 Step -1
        Console.Write(a(i, j))
        Console.Write(" ")
    Next
Next
```

v)
```
For j = 0 To 2
    For i = 0 To 2
        Console.Write(a(i, j))
        Console.Write(" ")
    Next
Next
```

vi)
```
For j = 0 To 2
    For i = 2 To 0 Step -1
        Console.Write(a(i, j))
        Console.Write(" ")
    Next
Next
```

vii)
```
For j = 2 To 0 Step -1
    For i = 0 To 2
        Console.Write(a(i, j))
        Console.Write(" ")
    Next
Next
```

viii)
```
For j = 2 To 0 Step -1
    For i = 2 To 0 Step -1
        Console.Write(a(i, j))
        Console.Write(" ")
    Next
Next
```

9. Write a Visual Basic program that lets the user enter integer values in a 10 × 15 array and then displays the indexes of the positions that contain odd numbers.

10. Write a Visual Basic program that lets the user enter numeric values in a 10 × 6 array and then displays the elements of the columns with even-numbered indexes (that is, column indexes 0, 2, and 4).

11. Write a Visual Basic program that lets the user enter numeric values in a 12 × 8 array and then calculates and displays the sum of the elements that have even column indexes and odd row indexes.

12. Write a Visual Basic program that lets the user enter numeric values in an 8 × 8 square array and then calculates the average value of the elements of its main diagonal and the average value of the elements of its antidiagonal. Try to calculate both average values within the same loop control structure.

13. Write a Visual Basic program that creates and displays the following array.

	0	1	2	3	4
0	11	11	11	11	5
1	11	11	11	5	88
2	11	11	5	88	88
3	11	5	88	88	88
4	5	88	88	88	88

a =

14. Write a Visual Basic program that creates and displays the following array.

	0	1	2	3	4
0	0	11	11	11	5
1	11	0	11	5	88
2	11	11	0	88	88
3	11	5	88	0	88
4	5	88	88	88	0

a =

15. Write a Visual Basic program that lets the user enter numeric values in a 5 × 4 array and then displays the row and column indexes of the positions that contain integers.

16. Write a Visual Basic program that lets the user enter numeric values in a 10 × 4 array and then counts and displays the total number of negative elements.

17. Write a Visual Basic program that lets the user enter words in a 3 × 4 array and then displays them with a space character between them.

18. Write a Visual Basic program that lets the user enter words in a 20 × 14 array and then displays those who have less than five characters.

Hint: Use the .Length property.

19. Write a Visual Basic program that lets the user enter words in a 20 × 14 array and displays those that have less than 5 characters, then those that have less than 10 characters, and finally those that have less than 20 characters. Assume that the user enters only words with less than 20 characters.

Hint: Try to display the words using three counted loop structures nested one within the other.

Chapter 35
Tips and Tricks with Arrays

35.1   Introduction

Since arrays are handled with the same sequence, decision, and loop control structures that you learned about in previous chapters, there is no need to repeat all of that information here. However, what you will discover in this chapter is how to process each row or column of a two-dimensional array individually, how to solve problems that require the use of more than one array, and how to create a two-dimensional array from a one-dimensional array and vice versa.

35.2   Processing Each Row Individually

Processing each row individually means that every row is processed separately and the result of each row (which can be the sum, the average value, and so on) can be used individually for further processing. Suppose you have the following 4 × 5 array.

	0	1	2	3	4
0	2	3	5	2	9
1	9	8	3	14	12
2	5	2	15	20	9
3	7	8	3	5	6

Let's try to find the sum of each row individually. There are actually two approaches that you can use. Both of these approaches iterate through rows.

First Approach – Creating an auxiliary array

In this approach, the program processes each row individually and creates an auxiliary array in which each position stores the sum of one row. This approach gives you much flexibility since you can use this new array later in your program for further processing. The auxiliary array is shown on the right.

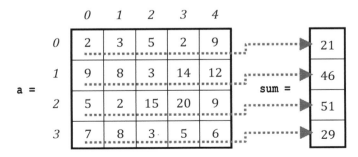

Now, let's write the corresponding code fragment. To more easily understand the process, the "from inner to outer" method is used. The following code fragment calculates the sum of the first row (row index 0) and stores the result in position 0 of the auxiliary array. Assume variable i contains the value 0.

```
s = 0
For j = 0 To COLUMNS - 1
  s += a(i, j)
Next
sum(i) = s
```

This program can equivalently be written as

```
sum(i) = 0
For j = 0 To COLUMNS - 1
  sum(i) += a(i, j)
Next
```

Now, nesting this code fragment in a counted loop structure that iterates for all rows results in the following.

```
For i = 0 To ROWS - 1
  sum(i) = 0
  For j = 0 To COLUMNS - 1
    sum(i) += a(i, j)
  Next
Next
```

Second Approach – Just find it and process it!

This approach uses no auxiliary array; it just calculates and directly processes the sum. The code fragment is as follows.

```
For i = 0 To ROWS - 1
  sum = 0
  For j = 0 To COLUMNS - 1
    sum += a(i, j)
  Next
  process sum
Next
```

What does *process sum* mean? It depends on the given problem. It may just display the sum, it may calculate the average value of each individual row and display it, or it may use the sum for calculating even more complex mathematical expressions.

For instance, the following example calculates and displays the average value of each row.

```
For i = 0 To ROWS - 1
  sum = 0
  For j = 0 To COLUMNS - 1
    sum += a(i, j)
  Next
  average = sum / COLUMNS
  Console.WriteLine(average)
Next
```

Exercise 35.2-1   *Finding the Average Value*

There are 20 students and each one of them has received his or her grades for 10 lessons. Write a Visual Basic program that prompts the user to enter the grades of each student for all lessons and then calculates and displays, for each student, all average values that are greater than 89.

Solution

Since you've learned two approaches for processing each row individually, let's use them both.

First Approach – Creating an auxiliary array

In this approach, the program processes each row individually and creates an auxiliary array in which each position stores the average value of one row. The two required arrays are shown next.

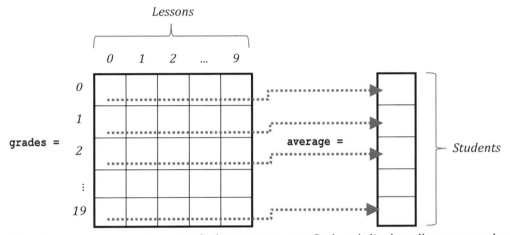

After the array `average` is created, the program can find and display all average values that are greater than 89. The Visual Basic program is as follows.

```
                          project_35_2_1a
Const STUDENTS = 20
Const LESSONS = 10

Sub Main()
  Dim i, j As Integer

  Dim grades(STUDENTS - 1, LESSONS - 1) As Integer
  For i = 0 To STUDENTS - 1
    Console.WriteLine("For student No. " & (i + 1) & "...")
    For j = 0 To LESSONS - 1
      Console.Write("enter grade for lesson No. " & (j + 1) & ": ")
      grades(i, j) = Console.ReadLine()
    Next
  Next

  'Create array average
```

```
  Dim average(STUDENTS - 1) As Double
  For i = 0 To STUDENTS - 1
    average(i) = 0
    For j = 0 To LESSONS - 1
      average(i) += grades(i, j)
    Next
    average(i) /= LESSONS
  Next

  'Display all average values that are greater than 89
  For i = 0 To STUDENTS - 1
    If average(i) > 89 Then
      Console.WriteLine(average(i))
    End If
  Next

  Console.ReadKey()
End Sub
```

Second Approach – Just find it and display it!

This approach uses no auxiliary array; it just calculates and directly displays all average values that are greater than 89. The Visual Basic program is as follows.

```
                        project_35_2_1b
Const STUDENTS = 20
Const LESSONS = 10

Sub Main()
  Dim i, j As Integer
  Dim average As Double

  Dim grades(STUDENTS - 1, LESSONS - 1) As Integer
  For i = 0 To STUDENTS - 1
    Console.WriteLine("For student No. " & (i + 1) & "...")
    For j = 0 To LESSONS - 1
      Console.Write("enter grade for lesson No. " & (j + 1) & ": ")
      grades(i, j) = Console.ReadLine()
    Next
  Next

  'Calculate the average value of each row individually
  'and directly display those who are greater than 89
  For i = 0 To STUDENTS - 1
    average = 0
    For j = 0 To LESSONS - 1
      average += grades(i, j)
    Next
    average /= LESSONS
    If average > 89 Then
      Console.WriteLine(average)
    End If
```

```
  Next

  Console.ReadKey()
End Sub
```

35.3   Processing Each Column Individually

Processing each column individually means that every column is processed separately and the result of each column (which can be the sum, the average value, and so on) can be used individually for further processing. Suppose you have the following 4 × 5 array.

	0	1	2	3	4
0	2	3	5	2	9
1	9	8	3	14	12
2	5	2	15	20	9
3	7	8	3	5	6

As before, let's try to find the sum of each column individually. Yet again, there are two approaches that you can use. Both of these approaches iterate through columns.

First Approach – Creating an auxiliary array

In this approach, the program processes each column individually and creates an auxiliary array in which each position stores the sum of one column. This approach gives you much flexibility since you can use this new array later in your program for further processing. The auxiliary array is shown at the bottom.

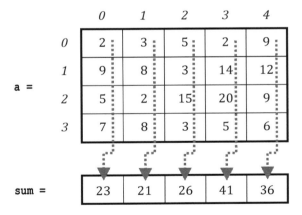

Now, let's write the corresponding code fragment. To more easily understand the process, the "from inner to outer" method is used again. The following code fragment calculates the sum of the first column (column index 0) and stores the result in position 0 of the auxiliary array. Assume variable j contains the value 0.

```
s = 0
For i = 0 To ROWS - 1
  s += a(i, j)
Next
```

```
sum(j) = s
```

This program can equivalently be written as

```
sum(j) = 0
For i = 0 To ROWS - 1
  sum(j) += a(i, j)
Next
```

Now, nesting this code fragment in a counted loop structure that iterates for all columns results in the following.

```
For j = 0 To COLUMNS - 1
  sum(j) = 0
  For i = 0 To ROWS - 1
    sum(j) += a(i, j)
  Next
Next
```

Second Approach – Just find it and process it!

This approach, as previously shown, uses no auxiliary array; it just calculates and directly processes the sum. The code fragment is as follows.

```
For j = 0 To COLUMNS - 1
  sum = 0
  For i = 0 To ROWS - 1
    sum += a(i, j)
  Next
  process sum
Next
```

Accordingly, the following code fragment calculates and displays the average value of each column.

```
For j = 0 To COLUMNS - 1
  sum = 0
  For i = 0 To ROWS - 1
    sum += a(i, j)
  Next
  Console.WriteLine(sum / ROWS)
Next
```

Exercise 35.3-1 *Finding the Average Value*

There are 10 students and each one of them has received his or her grades for five lessons. Write a Visual Basic program that prompts the user to enter the grades of each student for all lessons and then calculates and displays, for each lesson, all average values that are greater than 89.

Solution

Since you've learned two approaches for processing each column individually, let's use them both.

First Approach – Creating an auxiliary array

In this approach, the program processes each column individually and creates an auxiliary array in which each position stores the average value of one column. The two required arrays are shown next.

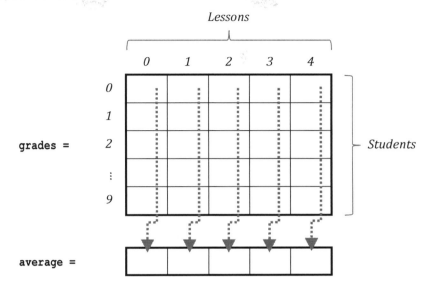

After the array average is created, the program can find and display all average values that are greater than 89. The Visual Basic program is as follows.

```
                        project_35_3_1a
Const STUDENTS = 10
Const LESSONS = 5

Sub Main()
  Dim i, j As Integer

  Dim grades(STUDENTS - 1, LESSONS - 1) As Integer
  For i = 0 To STUDENTS - 1
    Console.WriteLine("For student No. " & (i + 1) & "...")
    For j = 0 To LESSONS - 1
      Console.Write("enter grade for lesson No. " & (j + 1) & ": ")
      grades(i, j) = Console.ReadLine()
    Next
  Next

  'Create array average. Iterate through columns
  Dim average(LESSONS - 1) As Double
  For j = 0 To LESSONS - 1
    average(j) = 0
    For i = 0 To STUDENTS - 1
      average(j) += grades(i, j)
    Next
    average(j) /= STUDENTS
```

```
  Next

  'Display all average values than are greater than 89
  For j = 0 To LESSONS - 1
    If average(j) > 89 Then
      Console.WriteLine(average(j))
    End If
  Next

  Console.ReadKey()
End Sub
```

Second Approach – Just find it and display it!

This approach uses no auxiliary array; it just calculates and directly displays all average values that are greater than 89. The Visual Basic program is as follows.

project_35_3_1b

```
Const STUDENTS = 10
Const LESSONS = 5

Sub Main()
  Dim i, j As Integer
  Dim average As Double

  Dim grades(STUDENTS - 1, LESSONS - 1) As Integer
  For i = 0 To STUDENTS - 1
    Console.WriteLine("For student No. " & (i + 1) & "...")
    For j = 0 To LESSONS - 1
      Console.Write("enter grade for lesson No. " & (j + 1) & ": ")
      grades(i, j) = Console.ReadLine()
    Next
  Next

  'Calculate the average value of each column individually
  'and directly display those who are greater than 89
  For j = 0 To LESSONS - 1
    average = 0
    For i = 0 To STUDENTS - 1
      average += grades(i, j)
    Next
    average /= STUDENTS
    If average > 89 Then
      Console.WriteLine(average)
    End If
  Next

  Console.ReadKey()
End Sub
```

35.4 How to Use One-Dimensional Along with Two-Dimensional Arrays

So far, every example or exercise has used either a one-dimensional or a two-dimensional array. But what if a problem requires you to use them both? Next you will find some exercises that show you how various arrays can be used together to solve a problem.

Exercise 35.4-1 Finding the Average Value

There are 10 students and each one of them has received his or her grades for five lessons. Write a Visual Basic program that prompts the user to enter the name of each student and the grades for all lessons and then calculates and displays the names of the students who have more than one grade greater than 89.

Solution

In this exercise, you need a one-dimensional array to store the names of the students and a two-dimensional array to store the grades for each student for each lesson. There are actually two approaches. Which one to use depends clearly on you! If you decide that, in the two-dimensional array, the rows should refer to students and the columns should refer to lessons then you can use the first approach discussed below. If you decide that the rows should refer to lessons and the columns should refer to students then you can use the second approach.

First Approach – Rows for students, columns for lessons

In this approach, the two-dimensional array should have 10 rows, one for every student and 5 columns, one for every lesson. All other arrays can be placed in relation to this two-dimensional array as follows.

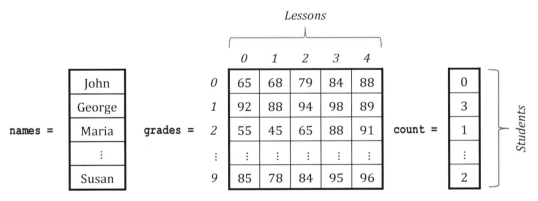

> *Notice: The auxiliary array* count *is created by the program and contains the number of grades for each student that are greater than 89.*

Now, let's see how to read values and store them in the arrays names and grades. One simple solution would be to use one loop control structure for reading names, and another, independent, loop control structure for reading grades. However, it is not very practical for the user to first enter all names and later enter all grades. A more practical way would be to prompt the user to enter one student name and then all of his or her grades, then another student name and again all of his or her grades, and so on. The solution is as follows.

```
project_35_4_1a
Const STUDENTS = 10
Const LESSONS = 5

Sub Main()
  Dim i, j As Integer

  'Read names and grades all together
  Dim names(STUDENTS - 1) As String
  Dim grades(STUDENTS - 1, LESSONS - 1) As Integer
  For i = 0 To STUDENTS - 1
    Console.Write("Enter name for student No. " & (i + 1) & ": ")
    names(i) = Console.ReadLine()
    For j = 0 To LESSONS - 1
      Console.Write("Enter grade No. " & (j + 1))
      Console.Write(" for " & names(i) & ": ")
      grades(i, j) = Console.ReadLine()
    Next
  Next

  'Create array count
  Dim count(STUDENTS - 1) As Integer
  For i = 0 To STUDENTS - 1
    count(i) = 0
    For j = 0 To LESSONS - 1
      If grades(i, j) > 89 Then
        count(i) += 1
      End If
    Next
  Next

  'Displays the names of the students who have
  'more than one grades greater than 89
  For i = 0 To STUDENTS - 1
    If count(i) > 1 Then
      Console.WriteLine(names(i))
    End If
  Next

  Console.ReadKey()
End Sub
```

Second Approach – Rows for lessons, columns for students

In this approach, the two dimensional array should have 5 rows, one for every lesson and 10 columns, one for every student. All other arrays can be placed in relation to this two-dimensional array, as shown next.

Students

names =	John	George	Maria	...	Susan
	0	1	2	...	9

	0	65	92	55	...	85
	1	68	88	45	...	78
grades =	2	79	94	65	...	84
	3	84	98	88	...	95
	4	88	89	91	...	96

Lesson

count =	0	3	1	...	2

Notice: *The auxiliary array* count *is created by the program and contains the number of grades for each lesson that are greater than 89.*

The solution is as follows.

```
                         project_35_4_1b
Const STUDENTS = 10
Const LESSONS = 5

Sub Main()
  Dim i, j As Integer

  'Read names and grades together
  Dim names(STUDENTS - 1) As String
  Dim grades(LESSONS - 1, STUDENTS - 1) As Integer
  For j = 0 To STUDENTS - 1
    Console.Write("Enter name for student No. " & (j + 1) & ": ")
    names(j) = Console.ReadLine()
    For i = 0 To LESSONS - 1
      Console.Write("Enter grade No. " & (i + 1))
      Console.Write(" for " & names(j) & ": ")
      grades(i, j) = Console.ReadLine()
    Next
  Next

  'Create array count
  Dim count(STUDENTS - 1) As Integer
  For j = 0 To STUDENTS - 1
    count(j) = 0
    For i = 0 To LESSONS - 1
      If grades(i, j) > 89 Then
        count(j) += 1
```

```
         End If
      Next
   Next

   'Displays the names of the students who have
   'more than one grades greater than 89
   For j = 0 To STUDENTS - 1
      If count(j) > 1 Then
         Console.WriteLine(names(j))
      End If
   Next

   Console.ReadKey()
End Sub
```

35.5 Creating a One-Dimensional Array from a Two-Dimensional Array

To more easily understand how to create a one-dimensional array from a two-dimensional array, let's use an example.

Write a program that creates a one-dimensional array of 12 elements from a two-dimensional array of 3 × 4 as follows: The elements of the first column of the two-dimensional array should be placed in the first three positions of the one-dimensional array, the elements of the second column should be placed in the next three positions, and so on.

An example of a 3 × 4 array is as follows.

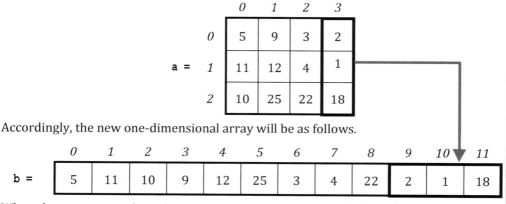

Accordingly, the new one-dimensional array will be as follows.

When the user enters data, the program can iterate, as usual, through rows but to create the new one-dimensional array, iterating through columns is more convenient. The Visual Basic program is presented next.

```
                         project_35_5
Const ROWS = 3
Const COLUMNS = 4
Const ELEMENTS = ROWS * COLUMNS

Sub Main()
   Dim i, j, k As Integer
```

```
Dim a(ROWS - 1, COLUMNS - 1) As Integer
For i = 0 To ROWS - 1
  For j = 0 To COLUMNS - 1
    Console.WriteLine("Enter a value for element " & i & ", " & j & ": ")
    a(i, j) = Console.ReadLine()
  Next
Next

Dim b(ELEMENTS - 1) As Integer

k = 0                          'This is the index of the new array.

For j = 0 To COLUMNS - 1       'Iterate through columns
  For i = 0 To ROWS - 1
    b(k) = a(i, j)
    k += 1
  Next
Next

For k = 0 To ELEMENTS - 1
  Console.Write(b(k) & vbTab)
Next

Console.ReadKey()
End Sub
```

35.6   Creating a Two-Dimensional Array from a One-Dimensional Array

To more easily understand how to create a two-dimensional array from a one-dimensional array, let's use an example.

Write a Visual Basic program that creates a two-dimensional array of 3 × 4 from a one-dimensional array of 12 elements as follow: The first three elements of the one-dimensional array should be placed in the first column of the two-dimensional array, the next three elements of the one-dimensional array should be placed in the next column of the two-dimensional array and so on.

An example of a 3 × 4 array is as follows.

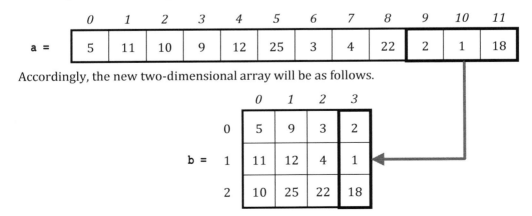

Accordingly, the new two-dimensional array will be as follows.

When the user enters data, the program can iterate, as usual, through rows but to create the new one-dimensional array, iterating through columns is more convenient. The Visual Basic program is presented next.

```
project_35_6
Const ROWS = 3
Const COLUMNS = 4
Const ELEMENTS = ROWS * COLUMNS

Sub Main()
  Dim k, j, i As Integer

  Dim a(ELEMENTS - 1) As Integer
  For k = 0 To ELEMENTS - 1
    Console.Write("Enter a value for element " & k & ": ")
    a(k) = Console.ReadLine()
  Next

  Dim b(ROWS - 1, COLUMNS - 1) As Integer

  k = 0                          'This is the index of array a.

  For j = 0 To COLUMNS - 1      'Iterate through columns
    For i = 0 To ROWS - 1
      b(i, j) = a(k)
      k += 1
    Next
  Next

  For i = 0 To ROWS - 1       'Iterate through rows
    For j = 0 To COLUMNS - 1
      Console.Write(b(i, j) & vbTab)
    Next
    Console.WriteLine()
  Next

  Console.ReadKey()
End Sub
```

35.7   Review Questions: True/False

Choose **true** or **false** for each of the following statements.

1. Processing each row individually means that every row is processed separately, and the result of each row can then be used individually for further processing.

2. The following code fragment displays the word "Okay" when the sum of the elements of each column is less than 100.

```
For i = 0 To ROWS - 1
  sum = 0
  For j = 0 To COLUMNS - 1
    sum += a(i, j)
  Next
```

```
    If sum < 100 Then Console.WriteLine("Okay")
    End If
```

3. Processing each column individually means that every column is processed separately and the result of each column can be then used individually for further processing.

4. The following code fragment displays the sum of the elements of each column.

```
sum = 0
For j = 0 To COLUMNS - 1
    For i = 0 To ROWS - 1
        sum += a(i, j)
    Next
    Console.WriteLine(sum)
Next
```

5. Suppose that there are 10 students and each one of them has received his or her grades for five lessons. Given this information, it is possible to design an array so that the rows refer to students and the columns refer to lessons, but not the other way around.

6. A one-dimensional array can be created from a two-dimensional array, but not the opposite.

7. A one-dimensional array can be created from a three-dimensional array.

35.8   Review Questions: Multiple Choice

Select the correct answer for each of the following statements.

1. The following code fragment

```
Dim sum(ROWS - 1) As Integer
For i = 0 To ROWS - 1
    sum(i) = 0
    For j = 0 To COLUMNS - 1
        sum(i) += a(i, j)
    Next
    Console.WriteLine(sum(i))
Next
```

    a.   displays the sum of the elements of each row.

    b.   displays the sum of the elements of each column.

    c.   displays the sum of all the elements of the array.

    d.   none of the above

2. The following code fragment

```
For j = 0 To COLUMNS - 1
    sum = 0
    For i = 0 To ROWS - 1
        sum += a(i, j)
    Next
    Console.WriteLine(sum)
Next
```

    a.   displays the sum of the elements of each row.

    b.   displays the sum of the elements of each column.

  c.   displays the sum of all the elements of the array.

  d.   none of the above

3.   The following code fragment

```
k = 0
For i = ROWS - 1 To 0
  For j = 0 To COLUMNS - 1 Step -1
    b(k) = a(i, j)
    k += 1
  Next
Next
```

  a.   creates a one-dimensional array from a two-dimensional array.

  b.   creates a two-dimensional array from a one-dimensional array.

  c.   none of the above

4.   The following code fragment

```
k = 0
For i = 0 To ROWS - 1
  For j = COLUMNS - 1 To 0 Step -1
    b(i, j) = a(k)
    k += 1
  Next
Next
```

  a.   creates a one-dimensional array from a two-dimensional array.

  b.   creates a two-dimensional array from a one-dimensional array.

  c.   none of the above

35.9   Review Exercises

Complete the following exercises.

1.   There are 15 students and each one of them has received his or her grades for five tests. Write a Visual Basic program that lets the user enter the grades (as a percentage) for each student for all tests. It then calculates and displays, for each student, the average grade as a letter grade according to the following table.

Grade	Percentage
A	90 – 100
B	80 – 89
C	70 – 79
D	60 – 69
E / F	0 – 59

2.   On Earth, a free-falling object has an acceleration of 9.81 m/s^2 downward. This value is denoted by g. A student wants to calculate that value using an experiment. She allows five different objects to fall downward from a known height and measures the time they need to reach the floor. She does this 10 times for each object. Then, using a formula she calculates g for each object, for each fall. But since her chronometer is not so accurate, she needs a Visual Basic

program that lets her enter all calculated values of g in a 5 × 10 array. The program should then calculate and display

    a.   for each object, the average value of g (per fall)

    b.   for each fall, the average value of g (per object)

    c.   the overall average value of g

3.   A basketball team with 15 players plays 12 matches. Write a Visual Basic program that lets the user enter, for each player, the number of points scored in each match. The program should then display

    a.   for each player, the total number of points scored

    b.   for each match, the total number of points scored

4.   Write a Visual Basic program that lets the user enter the hourly measured temperatures of 20 cities for a period of one day, and then displays the hours in which the average temperature of all the cities was below 10 degrees Fahrenheit.

5.   In a football tournament, a football team with 24 players plays 10 matches. Write a Visual Basic program that lets the user enter, for each player, a name as well as the number of goals scored in each match. The program should then display

    a.   for each player, a name and the average number of goals scored

    b.   for each match, the index number of the match (1, 2, 3, and so on) and the total number of goals scored

6.   There are 12 students and each one of them has received his or her grades for six lessons. Write a Visual Basic program that lets the user enter the name of the student as well as his or her grades in all lessons and then displays

    a.   for each student, his or her name and average grade

    b.   for each lesson, the average grade

    c.   the names of the students who have an average grade less than 60

    d.   the names of the students who have an average grade greater than 89, and the message "Bravo!" next to it

Assume that the user enters values between 0 and 100.

7.   In a song contest, each artist sings a song of his or her choice. There are five judges and 15 artists, each of whom is scored for his or her performance. Write a Visual Basic program that prompts the user to enter the names of the judges, the names of the artists, the title of the song that each artist sings, and the score they get from each judge. The program should then display

    a.   for each artist, his or her name, the title of the song, and his or her total score

    b.   for each judge, his or her name and the average value of the score he or she gave (per artist)

8.   The Body Mass Index (BMI) is often used to determine whether a person is overweight or underweight for his or her height. The formula used to calculate BMI is

$$BMI = \frac{weight \cdot 703}{height^2}$$

Write a Visual Basic program that lets the user enter into two arrays the weight (in pounds) and height (in inches) of 30 people, measured on a monthly basis, for a period of one year (January to December). The program should then calculate and display

    a.   for each person, his or her average weight, average height, and average BMI (per month)

    b.   for each person, his or her BMI in May and in August

Please not that all people are adults but some of them are between the ages of 18 and 25. This means they may still grow taller, thus their height might be different each month!

9.   Write a Visual Basic program that lets the user enter the electric meter reading in kilowatt-hours (kWh) at the beginning and at the end of a month for 1000 consumers. The program should calculate and display

    a.   for each consumer, the amount of kWh consumed and the amount of money that must be paid given a cost of each kWh of $0.07 and a value added tax (VAT) of 19%

    b.   the overall average consumption and the overall average amount of money that must be paid (per consumer)

10.   Write a Visual Basic program that prompts the user to enter an amount in US dollars and calculates and displays the corresponding currency value in Euros, British Pounds Sterling, Australian Dollars, and Canadian Dollars. The tables below contain the exchange rates for each currency for a one-week period. The program should calculate the average value of each currency and do the conversions based on that average value.

currency =

British Pound Sterling
Euro
Canadian Dollar
Australian Dollar

rate =

1.579	1.577	1.572	1.580	1.584
1.269	1.270	1.265	1.240	1.255
0.895	0.899	0.884	0.888	0.863
0.811	0.815	0.822	0.829	0.819

11.   Gross pay depends on the pay rate and the total number of hours worked per week. However, if someone works more than 40 hours, he or she gets paid time-and-a-half for all hours worked over 40. Write a Visual Basic program that lets the user enter a pay rate as well as the names of 10 employees and the number of hours that they worked each day (Monday to Friday). The program should then calculate and display

    a.   the names of the employees who worked overtime

    b.   for each employee, his or her name and the average gross pay (per day)

    c.   for each employee, his or her name, the name of the day he or she worked overtime (more than 8 hours), and the message "Overtime!"

    d.   for each day, the name of the day and the total gross pay

12. Write a Visual Basic program to create a one-dimensional array of 12 elements from the two-dimensional array shown below, as follows: the first row of the two-dimensional array should be placed in the first four positions of the one-dimensional array, the second row of the two-dimensional array should be placed in the next four positions of the one-dimensional array, and the last row of the two-dimensional array should be placed in the last four positions of the one-dimensional array.

a =

9	9	2	6
4	1	10	11
12	15	7	3

13. Write a Visual Basic program to create a 3 × 3 array from the one-dimensional array shown below, as follows: the first three elements of the one-dimensional array should be placed in the last row of the two-dimensional array, the next three elements of the one-dimensional array should be placed in the second row of the two-dimensional array, and the last three elements of the one-dimensional array should be placed in the first row of the two-dimensional array.

a =

16	12	3	5	6	9	18	19	20

Chapter 36
Flowcharts with Arrays

36.1 Introduction

In this chapter you will learn nothing new about flowcharts. Earlier, you learned that an array is actually just a special type of variable, in that an array can hold multiple values at the same time. In flowcharts, you can use arrays in the same way that you use variables.

36.2 Converting Visual Basic Programs to Flowcharts

Since there is nothing new to discuss, let's directly proceed to solve some exercises!

Exercise 36.2-1   *Designing the Flowchart*

Design the flowchart that corresponds to the following Visual Basic program.

```
Const ELEMENTS = 100

Sub Main()
  Dim i As Integer

  Dim values(ELEMENTS - 1) As Integer
  For i = 0 To ELEMENTS - 1
    values(i) = Console.ReadLine()
  Next

  For i = 0 To ELEMENTS - 1
    If values(i) < 0 Then
      Console.WriteLine(values(i))
    End If
  Next

  Console.ReadKey()
End Sub
```

Solution

In this Visual Basic program, there are two counted loop structures, the second of which nests a single-alternative decision structure. The corresponding flowchart is presented next.

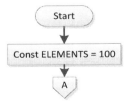

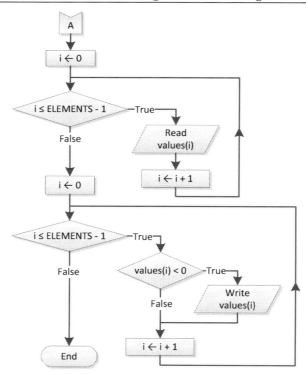

> **Notice**: Please note that since flowcharts are a loose method to represent an algorithm it would also be correct to write values[i] instead of values(i).

Exercise 36.2-2   *Designing the Flowchart*

Design the flowchart that corresponds to the following Visual Basic program.

```
Const ELEMENTS = 50

Sub Main()
  Dim i As Integer

  Dim evens(ELEMENTS - 1) As Integer
  For i = 0 To ELEMENTS - 1
    Do
      evens(i) = Console.ReadLine()
    Loop While evens(i) Mod 2 <> 0
  Next

  For i = 0 To ELEMENTS - 1
    Console.WriteLine(evens(i))
  Next

  Console.ReadKey()
End Sub
```

Solution

In this Visual Basic program, there are two counted loop structures, the first of which nests a post-test loop structure. The corresponding flowchart is presented next.

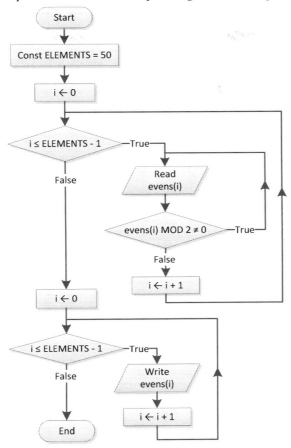

Exercise 36.2-3   *Designing the Flowchart*

Design the flowchart that corresponds to the following Visual Basic program.

```
Const ROWS = 20
Const COLUMNS = 10

Sub Main()
  Dim i, j, max As Integer

  Dim a(ROWS - 1, COLUMNS - 1) As Integer
  For i = 0 To ROWS - 1
    For j = 0 To COLUMNS - 1
      a(i, j) = Console.ReadLine()
    Next
  Next

  max = a(0, 0)
  For i = 0 To ROWS - 1
```

```
      For j = 0 To COLUMNS - 1
        If a(i, j) > max Then
          max = a(i, j)
        End If
      Next
    Next
    Console.Write(max)

    Console.ReadKey()
  End Sub
```

Solution

In this Visual Basic program, there are two nested loop control structures, the second of which nests a single-alternative decision structure. The corresponding flowchart is presented next.

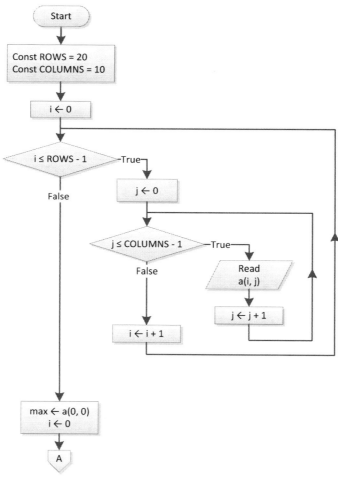

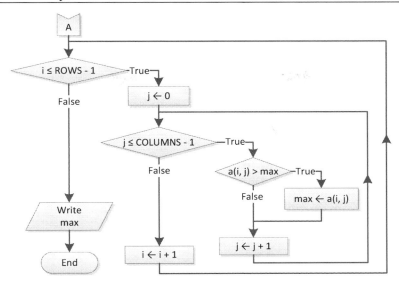

> **Notice**: *Please note that since flowcharts are a loose method to represent an algorithm it would also be correct to write* `a[i, j]` *or even* `a[i][j]`.

36.3   Converting Flowcharts to Visual Basic Programs

As already stated in previous chapters, this conversion is not always an easy one. There are cases in which the flowchart designers follow no particular rules, so the initial flowchart may need some modifications before it can become a Visual Basic program.

Exercise 36.3-1   *Writing the Visual Basic Program*

Write the Visual Basic program that corresponds to the following flowchart fragment.

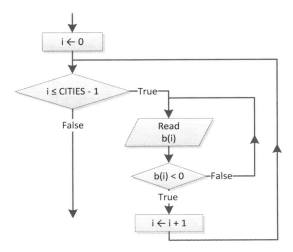

Solution

This exercise is quite simple. A post-test loop structure is nested within a pre-test loop structure (or in a counted loop structure, if you prefer). The only obstacle you must overcome is that the true and false paths of the inner post-test loop structure are not quite in the right positions since the true path, and not the false path, must go upwards. As you have already learned, it is possible to switch the two paths, but you also need to negate the corresponding Boolean expression. The code fragment is as follows.

```
For i = 0 To CITIES - 1
  Do
    b(i) = Console.ReadLine()
  Loop While b(i) >= 0
Next
```

Exercise 36.3-2   *Writing the Visual Basic Program*

Write the Visual Basic program that corresponds to the following flowchart.

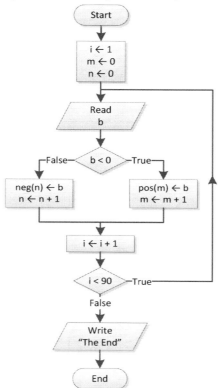

Solution

In this exercise, a dual-alternative decision structure is nested within a post-test loop structure. The worst case scenario is when a user enters only positive values or only negative values. For this reason, the size of both arrays pos and neg must be 90. The corresponding Visual Basic program is as follows.

```
Sub Main()
  Dim i, m, n As Integer
  Dim b As Double
  Dim pos(89) As Double
  Dim neg(89) As Double
```

```
    i = 1
    m = 0
    n = 0
    Do
      b = Console.ReadLine()
      If b < 0 Then
        pos(m) = b
        m += 1
      Else
        neg(n) = b
        n += 1
      End If
      i += 1
    Loop While i < 90
    Console.Write("The End")

    Console.ReadKey()
End Sub
```

Exercise 36.3-3   *Writing the Visual Basic Program*

Write the Visual Basic program that corresponds to the following flowchart fragment.

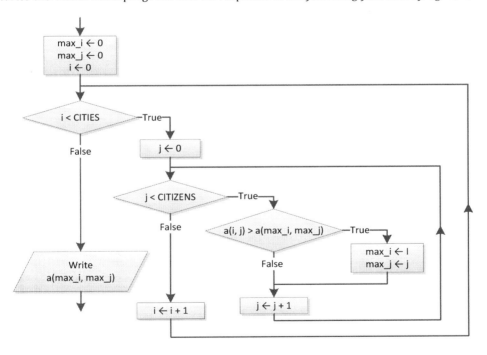

Solution

This flowchart has one single-decision structure nested within a pre-test loop structure, which in turn is nested within another pre-test loop structure.

Since variables `i` and `j` are used as index positions for array `a`, you can assume that they are integers. Therefore, it is permitted to alter the two Boolean expressions to `i <= CITIES - 1` and `j <= CITIZENS - 1`, respectively. This change helps you write the corresponding Visual Basic program using counted loop structures, as follows.

```
max_i = 0
max_j = 0
For i = 0 To CITIES - 1
  For j = 0 To CITIZENS - 1
    If a(i, j) > a(max_i, max_j) Then
      max_i = i
      max_j = j
    End If
  Next
Next


Console.Write(a(max_i, max_j))
```

36.4 Review Exercises

Complete the following exercises.

1. Design the flowchart that corresponds to the following Visual Basic program.

```
Const ELEMENTS = 30

Sub Main()
  Dim i, digit1, digit2 As Integer

  Dim values(ELEMENTS - 1) As Integer
  For i = 0 To ELEMENTS - 1
    Console.Write("Enter a two-digit integer: ")
    values(i) = Console.ReadLine()
  Next

  For i = 0 To ELEMENTS - 1
    digit1 = values(i) \ 10
    digit2 = values(i) Mod 10
    If digit1 < digit2 Then
      Console.WriteLine(values(i))
    End If
  Next

  Console.ReadKey()
End Sub
```

2. Design the flowchart that corresponds to the following Visual Basic program.

```
Const ELEMENTS = 20

Sub Main()
  Dim i, sum, digit3, r, digit2, digit1 As Integer

  Dim values(ELEMENTS - 1) As Integer
  For i = 0 To ELEMENTS - 1
```

```
      Console.Write("Enter a three-digit integer: ")
      values(i) = Console.ReadLine()
   Next

   sum = 0
   For i = 0 To ELEMENTS - 1
      digit3 = values(i) Mod 10
      r = values(i) \ 10

      digit2 = r Mod 10
      digit1 = r \ 10

      If values(i) = digit3 * 100 + digit2 * 10 + digit1 Then
         sum += values(i)
      End If
   Next
   Console.Write(sum)

   Console.ReadKey()
End Sub
```

3. Design the flowchart that corresponds to the following Visual Basic program.

```
Const N = 10

Sub Main()
   Dim i, j, sum, k As Integer

   Dim a(N - 1,  N - 1) As Integer
   For i = 0 To N - 1
      For j = 0 To N - 1
         a(i, j) = Console.ReadLine()
      Next
   Next

   'Calculate Sum
   sum = 0
   For k = 0 To N - 1
      sum += a(k, k)
   Next

   Console.Write("Sum = " & sum)

   Console.ReadKey()
End Sub
```

4. Design the flowchart that corresponds to the following Visual Basic program.

```
Const N = 10

Sub Main()
   Dim i, j As Integer
```

```vb
    Dim a(N - 1, N - 1) As String

    For i = 0 To N - 1
      For j = 0 To N - 1
        If i = j Then
          a(i, j) = "*"
        ElseIf i > j Then
          a(i, j) = "-"
        Else
          a(i, j) = "+"
        End If
      Next
    Next

    For i = 0 To N - 1
      For j = 0 To N - 1
        Console.Write(a(i, j))
      Next
    Next

    Console.ReadKey()
End Sub
```

5. Design the flowchart that corresponds to the following code fragment.

```vb
Dim i, j As Integer

Dim average(ROWS - 1) As Double
For i = 0 To ROWS - 1
  average(i) = 0
  For j = 0 To COLUMNS - 1
    average(i) += values(i, j)
  Next
  average(i) /= COLUMNS
Next

For i = 0 To ROWS - 1
  If average(i) > 89 Then
    Console.WriteLine(average(i))
  End If
Next
```

6. Write the Visual Basic program that corresponds to the following flowchart fragment.

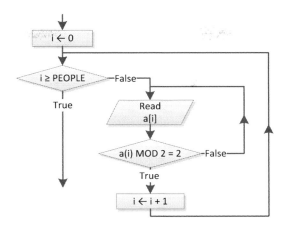

7. Write the Visual Basic program that corresponds to the following flowchart fragment.

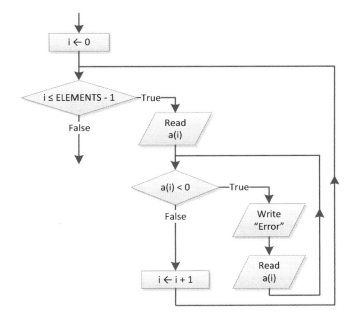

8. Write the Visual Basic program that corresponds to the following flowchart fragment.

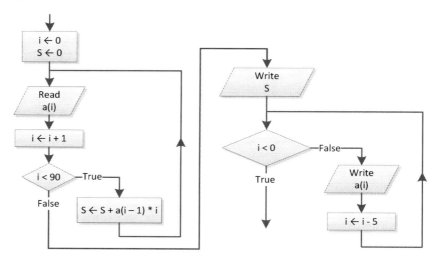

9. Write the Visual Basic program that corresponds to the following flowchart fragment.

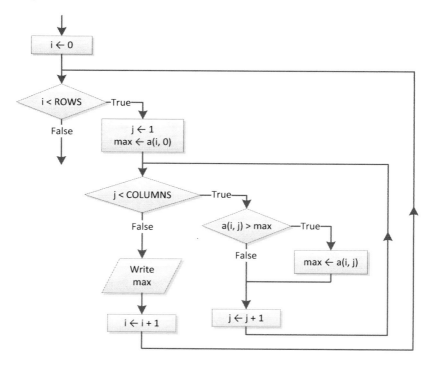

10. Write the Visual Basic program that corresponds to the following flowchart fragment.

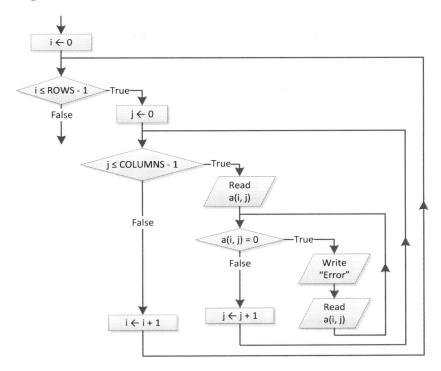

Chapter 37
More Exercises with Arrays

37.1 Simple Exercises with Arrays

Exercise 37.1-1 *Creating an Array that Contains the Average Values of its Neighboring Elements*

Design a flowchart and write the corresponding Visual Basic program that lets the user enter 100 positive numerical values into an array. Then the flowchart, and consequently the program, should create a new array of 98 elements. This new array should contain, in each position the average value of the three elements that exist in the current and the next two positions of the given array.

Solution

Let's try to understand this exercise through an example using 10 elements.

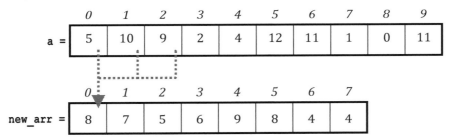

Array new_arr is the new array that is created. In array new_arr, the element at position 0 is the average value of the elements in the current and the next two positions of array a; that is, (5 + 10 + 9) / 3 = 8. The element at position 1 is the average value of the elements in the current and the next two positions of array a; that is, (10 + 9 + 2) / 3 = 7, and so on.

The flowchart is as follows.

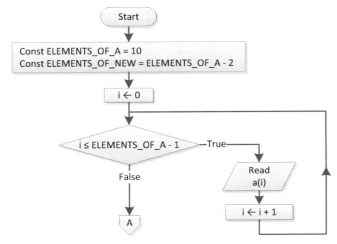

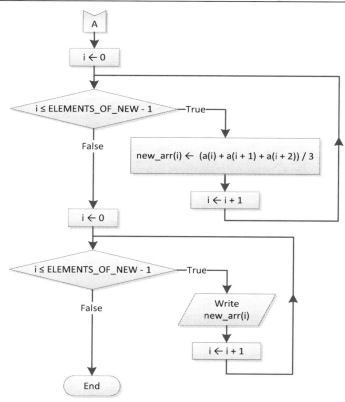

The corresponding Visual Basic program is as follows.

```
project_37_1_1
Const ELEMENTS_OF_A = 10
Const ELEMENTS_OF_NEW = ELEMENTS_OF_A - 2

Sub Main()
  Dim i As Integer

  Dim a(ELEMENTS_OF_A - 1) As Double
  For i = 0 To ELEMENTS_OF_A - 1
    a(i) = Console.ReadLine()
  Next

  Dim new_arr(ELEMENTS_OF_NEW - 1) As Double
  For i = 0 To ELEMENTS_OF_NEW - 1
    new_arr(i) = (a(i) + a(i + 1) + a(i + 2)) / 3
  Next

  For i = 0 To ELEMENTS_OF_NEW - 1
    Console.Write(new_arr(i) & vbTab)
  Next

  Console.ReadKey()
End Sub
```

Exercise 37.1-2   *Creating an Array with the Greatest Values*

Design a flowchart and write the corresponding Visual Basic program that lets the user enter numerical values into arrays a and b of 20 elements each. Then the algorithm, and consequently the program, should create a new array new_arr of 20 elements. The new array should contain in each position the greatest value of arrays a and b of the corresponding position.

Solution

Nothing new here! You need four counted loop structures: two counted loop structures to read the values for arrays a and b, one for creating the array new_arr, and one to display array new_arr on the screen. The flowchart is presented next.

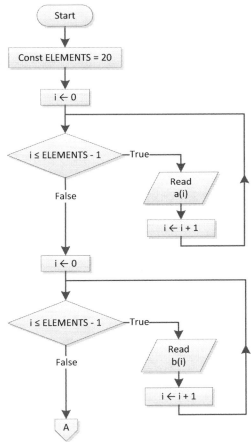

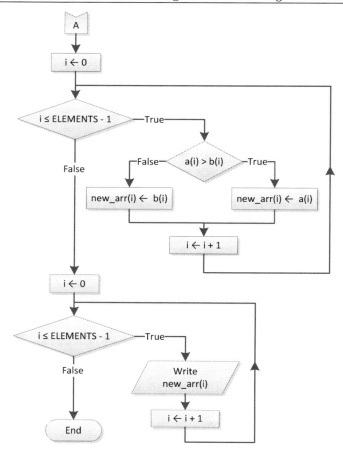

The corresponding Visual Basic program is shown here.

```
project_37_1_2
Const ELEMENTS = 20

Sub Main()
  Dim i As Integer

  'Read arrays a and b
  Dim a(ELEMENTS - 1) As Double
  For i = 0 To ELEMENTS - 1
    a(i) = Console.ReadLine()
  Next
  Dim b(ELEMENTS - 1) As Double
  For i = 0 To ELEMENTS - 1
    b(i) = Console.ReadLine()
  Next

  'Create array new_arr
  Dim new_arr(ELEMENTS - 1) As Double
  For i = 0 To ELEMENTS - 1
    If a(i) > b(i) Then
```

```
        new_arr(i) = a(i)
      Else
        new_arr(i) = b(i)
      End If
    Next

    'Display array new_arr
    For i = 0 To ELEMENTS - 1
      Console.WriteLine(new_arr(i))
    Next

    Console.ReadKey()
End Sub
```

Exercise 37.1-3   *Merging One-Dimensional Arrays*

Write a Visual Basic program that lets the user enter numerical values into arrays a and b of 20 and 30 elements correspondingly. Then, the program should create a new array new_arr of 50 elements. This new array should contain in the first 20 positions the elements of array a, and in the next 30 positions the elements of array b.

Solution

As you can see in the example presented next, there is a one-to-one match between the index positions of the elements of array a and those of array new_arr. The element from position 0 of array a is stored in position 0 of array new_arr, the element from position 1 of array a is stored in position 1 of array new_arr, and so on. However, there is no one-to-one match between the index positions of the elements of array b and those of array new_arr. The element from position 0 of array a should be stored in position 20 of array new_arr, the element from position 1 of array a should be stored in position 21 of array new_arr, and so on.

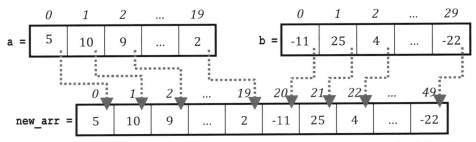

In order to assign the values of array a to array new_arr you can use the following code fragment.

```
For i = 0 To ELEMENTS_OF_A - 1
  new_arr(i) = a(i)
Next
```

However, to assign the values of array b to array new_arr your code fragment should be quite different.

```
For i = 0 To ELEMENTS_OF_B - 1
  new_arr(ELEMENTS_OF_A + i) = a(i)
```

```
Next
```

The final Visual Basic program is as follows.

```
                            project_37_1_3
Const ELEMENTS_OF_A = 20
Const ELEMENTS_OF_B = 30
Const ELEMENTS_OF_NEW = ELEMENTS_OF_A + ELEMENTS_OF_B

Sub Main()
  Dim i As Integer

  'Read arrays a and b
  Dim a(ELEMENTS_OF_A - 1) As Double
  For i = 0 To ELEMENTS_OF_A - 1
    a(i) = Console.ReadLine()
  Next
  Dim b(ELEMENTS_OF_B - 1) As Double
  For i = 0 To ELEMENTS_OF_B - 1
    b(i) = Console.ReadLine()
  Next

  'Create array new_arr
  Dim new_arr(ELEMENTS_OF_NEW - 1) As Double
  For i = 0 To ELEMENTS_OF_A - 1
    new_arr(i) = a(i)
  Next
  For i = 0 To ELEMENTS_OF_B - 1
    new_arr(ELEMENTS_OF_A + i) = b(i)
  Next

  'Display array new_arr
  For i = 0 To ELEMENTS_OF_NEW - 1
    Console.Write(new_arr(i) & vbTab)
  Next

  Console.ReadKey()
End Sub
```

Exercise 37.1-4   *Merging Two-Dimensional Arrays*

Write a Visual Basic program that lets the user enter numerical values into arrays a and b of 10 × 20 and 30 × 20 elements respectively. Then, the program should create a new array new_arr of 40 × 20 elements. In this new array, the first 10 rows should contain the elements of array a and the next 30 rows should contain the elements of array b.

Solution

This exercise can be solved pretty much the same way as the previous one. Below you can find the proposed solution. The approach of iterating through rows has been chosen, but iterating through columns could have been used as well.

```
                            project_37_1_4
Const COLUMNS = 20
Const ROWS_OF_A = 10
Const ROWS_OF_B = 30
Const ROWS_OF_NEW = ROWS_OF_A + ROWS_OF_B

Sub Main()
  Dim i, j As Integer

  'Read array a
  Dim a(ROWS_OF_A - 1,  COLUMNS - 1) As Double
  For i = 0 To ROWS_OF_A - 1
    For j = 0 To COLUMNS - 1
      a(i, j) = Console.ReadLine()
    Next
  Next

  'Read array b
  Dim b(ROWS_OF_B - 1,  COLUMNS - 1) As Double
  For i = 0 To ROWS_OF_B - 1
    For j = 0 To COLUMNS - 1
      b(i, j) = Console.ReadLine()
    Next
  Next

  'Create array new_arr
  Dim new_arr(ROWS_OF_NEW - 1,  COLUMNS - 1) As Double
  For i = 0 To ROWS_OF_A - 1
    For j = 0 To COLUMNS - 1
      new_arr(i, j) = a(i, j)
    Next
  Next
  For i = 0 To ROWS_OF_B - 1
    For j = 0 To COLUMNS - 1
      new_arr(ROWS_OF_A + i, j) = b(i, j)
    Next
  Next

  'Display array new_arr
  For i = 0 To ROWS_OF_NEW - 1
    For j = 0 To COLUMNS - 1
      Console.Write(new_arr(i, j) & vbTab)
    Next
    Console.WriteLine()
  Next

  Console.ReadKey()
End Sub
```

Exercise 37.1-5   *Creating Two Arrays – Separating Positive from Negative*
                        Values

*Write a Visual Basic program that lets the user enter 100 numerical values into an array
and then creates two new arrays, pos and neg. Array pos should contain positive values,
whereas array neg should contain the negative ones. The value 0 (if any) should not be
added to either of the final arrays, pos or neg.*

*Next, design the corresponding flowchart fragment only for that part of your program that
creates the arrays pos and neg.*

Solution

Let's analyze this exercise using the following example.

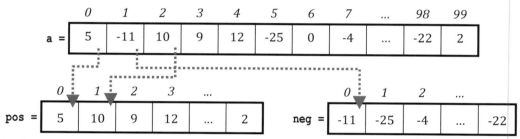

In this exercise, there is no one-to-one match between the index positions of the elements
of array a and the arrays pos and neg. For example, the element from position 1 of array a
is not stored in position 1 of array neg, the element from position 2 of array a is not
stored in position 2 of array pos, and so on. Thus, you **cannot** do the following,

```
For i = 0 To ELEMENTS - 1
  If a(i) > 0 Then
    pos(i) = a(i)
  ElseIf a(i) < 0 Then
    neg(i) = a(i)
  End If
Next
```

because it will result in the following two arrays.

	0	1	2	3	4	5	6	7	...	98	99
pos =	5		10	9	12				...		2

	0	1	2	3	4	5	6	7	...	98	99
neg =		-11				-25		-4	...	-22	

What you need here are two independent index variables: pos_index for the array pos,
and neg_index for the array neg. These index variables must be incremented
independently, and only when an element is added to the corresponding array. The index
variable pos_index must be incremented only when an element is added to the array pos,
and the index variable neg_index must be incremented only when an element is added to
the array neg.

```
pos_index = 0
neg_index = 0
For i = 0 To ELEMENTS - 1
  If a(i) > 0 Then
    pos(pos_index) = a(i)
    pos_index += 1
  ElseIf a(i) < 0 Then
    neg(neg_index) = a(i)
    neg_index += 1
  End If
Next
```

When this loop finishes iterating, the two arrays become as follows.

Notice: *Please note that variables* pos_index *and* neg_index *have dual roles. When the loop iterates, each points to the next position in which a new element should be placed. When the loop finishes iterating, variables* pos_index *and* neg_index *actually contain the total number of elements in each corresponding array!*

The complete solution is presented next.

project_37_1_5

```
Const ELEMENTS = 100

Sub Main()
  Dim i, pos_index, neg_index As Integer

  Dim a(ELEMENTS - 1) As Double
  For i = 0 To ELEMENTS - 1
    a(i) = Console.ReadLine()
  Next

  'Create arrays pos and neg
  Dim pos(ELEMENTS - 1) As Double
  Dim neg(ELEMENTS - 1) As Double
  pos_index = 0
  neg_index = 0
  For i = 0 To ELEMENTS - 1
    If a(i) > 0 Then
      pos(pos_index) = a(i)
      pos_index += 1
    ElseIf a(i) < 0 Then
      neg(neg_index) = a(i)
        neg_index += 1
    End If
  Next

  For i = 0 To pos_index - 1
```

```
      Console.Write(pos(i) & vbTab)
   Next
   Console.WriteLine()
   For i = 0 To neg_index - 1
      Console.Write(neg(i) & vbTab)
   Next

   Console.ReadKey()
End Sub
```

> **Notice**: *Please note that the arrays* pos *and* neg *contain a total number of* pos_index *and* neg_index *elements respectively. This is why the two last loop control structures iterate until variable* i *reaches values* pos_index - 1 *and* neg_index - 1, *respectively, and not until* ELEMENTS - 1, *as you may mistakenly expect. Obviously the sum of* pos_index + neg_index *equals to* ELEMENTS.

Now, let's design the corresponding flowchart fragment only for that part of the program that creates the arrays pos and neg. As you may notice, there is a multiple-alternative decision structure nested within a counted loop structure. The flowchart fragment is as follows.

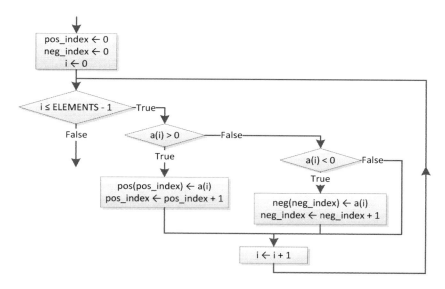

Exercise 37.1-6   *Creating an Array with Those who Contain Digit 5*

Write a Visual Basic program that lets the user enter 100 two-digit integers into an array and then creates a new array of only the integers that contain at least one of the digit 5.

Solution

This exercise requires some knowledge from the past. In Chapter 13 you learned how to use the quotient and the remainder to split an integer into its individual digits. Here, the integer has two digits; therefore, you can use the following flowchart fragment to split any two-digit integer contained in variable x.

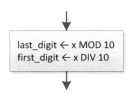

The final flowchart is as follows.

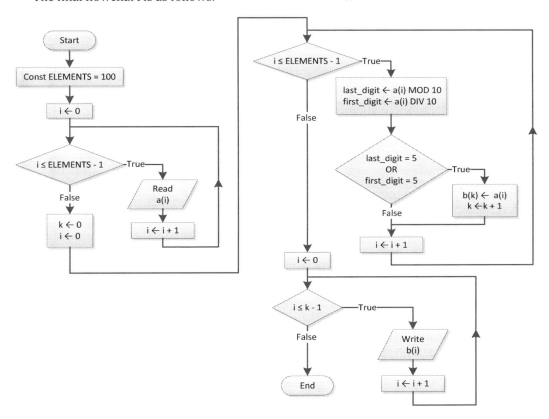

The corresponding Visual Basic program is as follows.

```
                         project_37_1_6
Const ELEMENTS = 100

Sub Main()
  Dim i, k, last_digit, first_digit As Integer

  Dim a(ELEMENTS - 1) As Integer
  For i = 0 To ELEMENTS - 1
    a(i) = Console.ReadLine()
  Next

  Dim b(ELEMENTS - 1) As Integer
  k = 0
  For i = 0 To ELEMENTS - 1
```

```
      last_digit = a(i) Mod 10
      first_digit = a(i) \ 10

      If last_digit = 5 Or first_digit = 5 Then
        b(k) = a(i)
        k += 1
      End If
  Next

  For i = 0 To k - 1
    Console.Write(b(i) & vbTab)
  Next

  Console.ReadKey()
End Sub
```

> **Remember!** When you need to create a new array using values from an old array and there is no one-to-one match between their index positions, you need an extra variable that becomes the index for the new array. Of course, this variable should increase by 1 only when a new element is added into the new array. Moreover, when the loop that creates the new array finishes iterating, the value of this variable matches the total number of elements in the new array!

37.2 Data Validation with Arrays

As you already know, data validation is the process of restricting data input, which forces the user to enter only valid values. As you have already been taught in Chapter 31, there are three approaches that you can use depending on whether or not you wish to display an error message and whether you wish to display individual error messages for each error or just a single error message for any kind of error. Let's see how those three approaches can be adapted and used with arrays.

First Approach – Validating data input without error messages

In Chapter 31 you learned how to validate one single value entered by the user without displaying any error messages. For your convenience, the code fragment given in general form is presented once again.

```
Do
  Console.Write("Prompt message")
  input_data = Console.ReadLine()
Loop While input_data test 1 fails Or input_data test 2 fails Or …
```

Do you remember how this operates? If the user persistently enters an invalid value, the main idea is to prompt him or her repeatedly, until he or she gets bored and finally enters a valid one. Of course, if the user enters a valid value right from the beginning, the flow of execution simply continues to the next part of the program.

You can use the same principle when entering data into arrays. If you use a counted loop structure to iterate for all elements of the array, the code fragment becomes as follows.

```
For i = 0 To ELEMENTS - 1
  Do
    Console.Write("Prompt message")
    input_data = Console.ReadLine()
```

```
  Loop While input_data test 1 fails Or input_data test 2 fails Or …
  input_array(i) = input_data
Next
```

As you can see, when the flow of execution exits the pre-test loop structure, the variable input_data definitely contains a valid value which in turn is assigned to a position of the array input_array. However, the same process can be implemented more simply, without using the extra variable input_data, as follows.

```
For i = 0 To ELEMENTS - 1
  Do
    Console.Write("Prompt message")
    input_array(i) = Console.ReadLine()
  Loop While input_array(i) test 1 fails Or input_array(i) test 2 fails Or …
Next
```

Second Approach – Validating data input with one single error message

As previously, the next code fragment is taken from Chapter 31 and adapted to operate with an array. It validates data input and displays an error message (that is, the same error message for any type of input error).

```
For i = 0 To ELEMENTS - 1
  Console.Write("Prompt message")
  input_array(i) = Console.ReadLine()
  Do While input_array(i) test 1 fails Or input_array(i) test 2 fails Or …
    Console.WriteLine("Error message")
    Console.Write("Prompt message")
    input_array(i) = Console.ReadLine()
  Loop
Next
```

Third Approach – Validating data input with individual error messages

Once again, the next code fragment is taken from Chapter 31 and adapted to operate with an array. It validates data input and displays an error message (that is, individual error messages, one for each type of input error).

```
For i = 0 To ELEMENTS - 1
  Do
    Console.Write("Prompt message")
    input_array(i) = Console.ReadLine()
    failure = False
    If input_array(i) test 1 fails Then
      Console.WriteLine("Error message 1")
      failure = True
    ElseIf input_array(i) test 2 fails Then
      Console.WriteLine("Error message 2")
      failure = True
    ElseIf …

    End If
  Loop While failure = True
Next
```

Exercise 37.2-1   *Displaying Odds in Reverse Order – Validation Without Error Messages*

Write a Visual Basic program that prompts the user to enter 20 odd integers into an array and then displays them in reverse order. The program should also validate data input, allowing the user to enter only odd integers. There is no need to display any error messages.

Solution

As the wording of the exercise implies, not all entered values should be added in the array—only the odd ones. The Visual Basic program is presented next.

```
project_37_2_1

Const ELEMENTS = 20

Sub Main()
  Dim i As Integer                                    Data input and validation

  Dim odds(ELEMENTS - 1) As Integer
  For i = 0 To ELEMENTS - 1
    Do
      Console.Write("Enter an odd integer: ")
      odds(i) = Console.ReadLine()
    Loop While odds(i) Mod 2 = 0
  Next

  'display elements backwards
  For i = ELEMENTS - 1 To 0 Step -1
    Console.Write(odds(i) & vbTab)
  Next

  Console.ReadKey()
End Sub
```

Exercise 37.2-2   *Displaying Odds in Reverse Order – Validation with One Error Message*

Write a Visual Basic program that prompts the user to enter 20 odd integers into an array and then displays them in reverse order. The program should also validate data input and display an error message when the user enters any non-numeric values or any even integers.

Solution

This is the same as you've previously seen, except for data validation. The second approach is used, according to which an error message is displayed when the user enters even integers. The Visual Basic program is presented next.

```
project_37_2_2

Const ELEMENTS = 20

Sub Main()
  Dim i As Integer
```

```
Dim input As String

Dim odds(ELEMENTS - 1) As Integer
For i = 0 To ELEMENTS - 1
  Console.Write("Enter an odd integer: ")
  input = Console.ReadLine()
  Do While Int32.TryParse(input, odds(i)) = False Or odds(i) Mod 2 = 0
    Console.WriteLine("Invalid value!")
    Console.Write("Enter an odd integer: ")
    input = Console.ReadLine()
  Loop
Next

'display elements backwards
For i = ELEMENTS - 1 To 0 Step -1
  Console.WriteLine(odds(i) & vbTab)
Next

Console.ReadKey()
End Sub
```

Data input and validation

Exercise 37.2-3   *Displaying Odds in Reverse Order – Validation with Individual Error Messages*

Write a Visual Basic program that prompts the user to enter 20 odd integers in an array and then displays them in reverse order. The program should also validate data input and display individual error messages when the user enters any non-numeric values, any even integers, or any reals.

Solution

The third approach is used, according to which individual error messages are displayed when the user enters non-numeric values, even integers, or reals. The Visual Basic program is as follows.

```
                        project_37_2_3
Const ELEMENTS = 20

Sub Main()
  Dim i As Integer
  Dim x As Double
  Dim failure As Boolean
  Dim input As String
                                        Data input and validation
  Dim odds(ELEMENTS - 1) As Integer
  For i = 0 To ELEMENTS - 1
    Do
      Console.Write("Enter an odd integer: ")
      input = Console.ReadLine()
      failure = False
      If Double.TryParse(input, x) = False Then
```

```
        Console.WriteLine("Please enter a numeric value!")
        failure = True
      ElseIf x <> Fix(x) Then
        Console.WriteLine("Please enter an integer!")
        failure = True
      ElseIf x Mod 2 = 0 Then
        Console.WriteLine("Please enter an odd!")
        failure = True
      End If
    Loop While failure = True
    odds(i) = x
  Next

  'display elements backwards
  For i = ELEMENTS - 1 To 0 Step -1
    Console.Write(odds(i) & vbTab)
  Next

  Console.ReadKey()
End Sub
```

> **Notice**: *Please note that variable* x *is declared as double. This is correct since you need to let the user enter any number (either a real or an integer) and then act correspondingly, that is: display an error message when a real is entered or assign user's input to array* odds *when an integer is entered.*

37.3   Finding Minimum and Maximum Values in Arrays

This is the third and last time that this subject is raked up in this book. The first time was in Section 4 (Decision Control Structures) and the second time was in Section 5 (Loop Control Structures). So, there is not much left to discuss except that when you want to find the minimum or maximum value of an array that already contains some values, you needn't worry about the initial values of variables min or max because you can just assign to them the value of the first element of the array!

Exercise 37.3-1   *Which Depth is the Greatest?*

Design a flowchart and write the corresponding Visual Basic program that lets the user enter the depths of 20 lakes and then displays the depth of the deepest one.

Solution

After the user enters the depths of the 20 lakes in the array depths, the initial value of variable max can be set as the value of the first element of array depths, that is depths(0). The program can then search for any value greater than this. The final solution is quite simple and is presented next without further explanation.

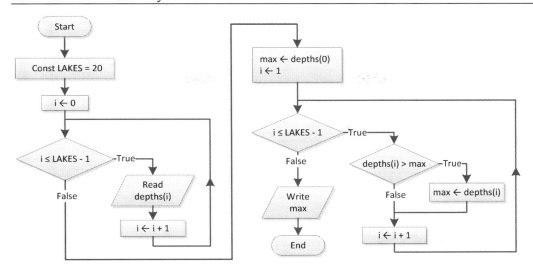

The corresponding Visual Basic program is as follows.

```
                            project_37_3_1
Const LAKES = 20

Sub Main()
  Dim i As Integer
  Dim max As Double

  Dim depths(LAKES - 1) As Double
  For i = 0 To LAKES - 1
    depths(i) = Console.ReadLine()
  Next

  'initial value
  max = depths(0)
  'Search furthermore, starting from position 1
  For i = 1 To LAKES - 1
    If depths(i) > max Then
      max = depths(i)
    End If
  Next

  Console.Write(max)

  Console.ReadKey()
End Sub
```

Notice: *It wouldn't be wrong to start iterating from position 0 instead of 1, though the program would perform one useless iteration.*

> **Notice**: It wouldn't be wrong to assign an "almost arbitrary" initial value to variable `max` but there is no reason to do so. The value of the first element is just fine! If you insist though, you can assign an initial value of 0, since there is no lake on planet Earth with a negative depth.

Exercise 37.3-2   *Which Lake is the Deepest?*

Write a Visual Basic program that lets the user enter the names and the depths of 20 lakes and then displays the name of the deepest one.

Solution

In this exercise, you need two one-dimensional arrays: one to hold the names, and one to hold the depths of the lakes. The solution is presented next.

```
                              project_37_3_2
Const LAKES = 20

Sub Main()
  Dim i As Integer
  Dim max As Double
  Dim m_name As String

  Dim names(LAKES - 1) As String
  Dim depths(LAKES - 1) As Double
  For i = 0 To LAKES - 1
    names(i) = Console.ReadLine()
    depths(i) = Console.ReadLine()
  Next

  max = depths(0)
  m_name = names(0)
  For i = 1 To LAKES - 1
    If depths(i) > max Then
      max = depths(i)
      m_name = names(i)
    End If
  Next

  Console.Write(m_name)

  Console.ReadKey()
End Sub
```

Exercise 37.3-3   *Which Lake, in Which Country, Having Which Average Area, is the Deepest?*

Write a Visual Basic program that lets the user enter the names and the depths of 20 lakes as well as the country in which they belong, and their average area. The program should then display all available information about the deepest lake.

Solution

In this exercise, you need four one-dimensional arrays: one to hold the names, one to hold the depths, one to hold the names of the countries, and one to hold the lakes' average areas. There are two approaches, actually. The first one is pretty much the same as the one used in the previous exercise. The second one is more efficient since it uses fewer variables. Let's study them both!

First Approach – One variable for each

This is pretty much the same as the one used in the previous exercise. The solution is presented next.

```
                         project_37_3_3a
Const LAKES = 20

Sub Main()
  Dim i As Integer
  Dim max, m_area As Double
  Dim m_name, m_country As String

  Dim names(LAKES - 1) As String
  Dim depths(LAKES - 1) As Double
  Dim countries(LAKES - 1) As String
  Dim areas(LAKES - 1) As Double
  For i = 0 To LAKES - 1
    names(i) = Console.ReadLine()
    depths(i) = Console.ReadLine()
    countries(i) = Console.ReadLine()
    areas(i) = Console.ReadLine()
  Next

  max = depths(0)
  m_name = names(0)
  m_country = countries(0)
  m_area = areas(0)
  For i = 1 To LAKES - 1
    If depths(i) > max Then
      max = depths(i)
      m_name = names(i)
      m_country = countries(i)
      m_area = areas(i)
    End If
  Next

  Console.Write(max & " " & m_name & " " & m_country & " " & m_area)

  Console.ReadKey()
End Sub
```

Second Approach – One index for everything

In this approach fewer variables are used. Instead of using all those variables (m_name, m_country, and m_area), you can use just one variable, a variable that holds the index in which the maximum value exists!

Confused? Let's look at the next example of six lakes. The depths are expressed in feet and the average areas in square miles.

	names =		depths =		countries =		areas =	
0	Toba		1660		Indonesia		440	
1	Issyk Kul		2192		Kyrgyzstan		2408	
2	Baikal		5380		Russia		12248	
3	Crater		1950		USA		21	
4	Karakul		750		Tajikistan		150	
5	Quesnel		2000		Canada		103	

Obviously the deepest lake is Lake Baikal at position 2. However, instead of holding the name "Baikal" in variable m_name, the country "Russia" in variable m_country, and the area "12248" in variable m_area as in the previous approach, you can use just one variable to hold the index position in which these values actually exist (in this case, this is value 2). The solution is presented next.

```
project_37_3_3b
Const LAKES = 20

Sub Main()
  Dim i, index_of_max As Integer
  Dim max As Double

  Dim names(LAKES - 1) As String
  Dim depths(LAKES - 1) As Double
  Dim countries(LAKES - 1) As String
  Dim areas(LAKES - 1) As Double
  For i = 0 To LAKES - 1
    names(i) = Console.ReadLine()
    depths(i) = Console.ReadLine()
    countries(i) = Console.ReadLine()
    areas(i) = Console.ReadLine()
  Next

  max = depths(0)
  index_of_max = 0
  For i = 1 To LAKES - 1
    If depths(i) > max Then
      max = depths(i)
      index_of_max = i
```

```
      End If
   Next

   Console.WriteLine(depths(index_of_max) & " " & names(index_of_max))
   Console.Write(countries(index_of_max) & " " & areas(index_of_max))

   Console.ReadKey()
End Sub
```

> **Remember!** Assigning an initial value of 0 to variable index_of_max is necessary since there is always a possibility that the maximum value does exist in position 0.

Exercise 37.3-4   *Which Students are the Tallest?*

Write a Visual Basic program that prompts the user to enter the names and the heights of 100 students and then displays the names of all those who share the one tallest height. Moreover, the program should validate data input and display an error message when the user enters any non-numeric or negative values.

Solution

In this exercise, a loop control structures should search for the greatest value, and afterwards, another loop control structure can search the array for all values that are equal to that greatest value.

The solution in presented next.

```
                          project_37_3_4
Const STUDENTS = 100

Sub Main()
  Dim i, max As Integer
  Dim input As String

  Dim names(STUDENTS - 1) As String
  Dim grades(STUDENTS - 1) As Integer
  For i = 0 To STUDENTS - 1
    Console.Write("Enter name for student No: " & (i + 1))
    names(i) = Console.ReadLine()

    Console.Write("Enter his or her grade: ")
    input = Console.ReadLine()
    Do While Int32.TryParse(input, grades(i)) = False Or grades(i) < 0
      Console.WriteLine("Invalid value!")
      Console.Write("Enter his or her grade: ")
      input = Console.ReadLine()
    Loop
  Next

  max = grades(0)
  For i = 1 To STUDENTS - 1
    If grades(i) > max Then
```

```
      max = grades(i)
    End If
  Next

  Console.WriteLine("The following students have got the greatest grade:")
  For i = 0 To STUDENTS - 1
    If grades(i) = max Then
      Console.WriteLine(names(i))
    End If
  Next

  Console.ReadKey()
End Sub
```

> *Notice*: Please note that this exercise could not have been solved without the use of an array.

Exercise 37.3-5   *Finding the Minimum Value of a Two-Dimensional Array*

Write a Visual Basic program that lets the user enter the temperatures (in degrees Fahrenheit) recorded at 12:00 p.m. on each day in January in 10 different cities. The Visual Basic program should display the lowest temperature.

Next, design the corresponding flowchart fragment for only that part of the program that finds the lowest temperature.

Solution

In this exercise, you need the following array.

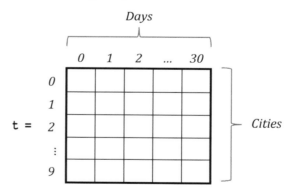

> *Notice*: The array t has 31 columns (0 to 30), as many as there are days in January.

There is nothing new here. The initial value of variable min can be the value of the element t(0, 0). Then, the program can iterate through rows, or even through columns, to search for the minimum value. The solution is presented next.

project_37_3_5

```
Const CITIES = 10
Const DAYS = 31
```

```
Sub Main()
  Dim i, j, min As Integer

  'Read array t
  Dim t(CITIES - 1,  DAYS - 1) As Integer
  For i = 0 To CITIES - 1
    For j = 0 To DAYS - 1
      t(i, j) = Console.ReadLine()
    Next
  Next

  'Find minimum
  min = t(0, 0)
  For i = 0 To CITIES - 1
    For j = 0 To DAYS - 1
      If t(i, j) < min Then
        min = t(i, j)
      End If
    Next
  Next

  Console.Write(min)

  Console.ReadKey()
End Sub
```

Following is the corresponding flowchart fragment for the part of the program that finds the lowest temperature (minimum value of array t).

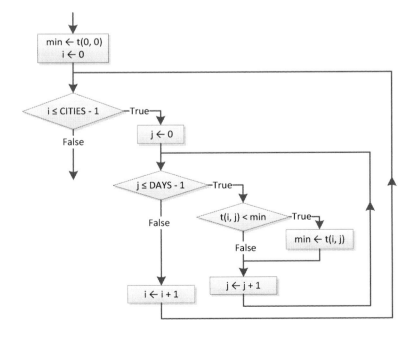

Exercise 37.3-6　　*Finding the City with the Coldest Day*

Write a Visual Basic program that lets the user enter the temperatures (in degrees Fahrenheit) recorded at 12:00 p.m. on each day in January in 10 different cities. The Visual Basic program should display the name of the city that had the lowest temperature and on which day it was recorded.

Solution

In this exercise, the following two arrays are needed.

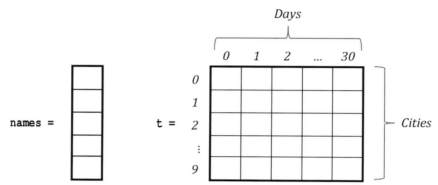

The solution is simple. Every time variable `min` updates its value, two variables, `m_i` and `m_j`, can hold the values of variables `i` and `j` respectively. In the end, these two variables will contain the row index and the column index of the position in which the maximum value exists. The solution is as follows.

```
                          project_37_3_6
Const CITIES = 10
Const DAYS = 31

Sub Main()
  Dim i, j, min, m_i, m_j As Integer

  Dim names(CITIES - 1) As String
  Dim t(CITIES - 1,  DAYS - 1) As Integer
  For i = 0 To CITIES - 1
    names(i) = Console.ReadLine()
    For j = 0 To DAYS - 1
      t(i, j) = Console.ReadLine()
    Next
  Next

  min = t(0, 0)
  m_i = 0
  m_j = 0
  For i = 0 To CITIES - 1
    For j = 0 To DAYS - 1
      If t(i, j) < min Then
        min = t(i, j)
        m_i = i
```

```
            m_j = j
        End If
    Next
  Next

  Console.WriteLine("Minimum temperature: " & min)
  Console.WriteLine("City: " & names(m_i))
  Console.Write("Day: " & (m_j + 1))

  Console.ReadKey()
End Sub
```

> **Remember!** *Assigning an initial value of 0 to variables* `m_i` *and* `m_j` *is necessary since there is always a possibility that the maximum value is the value of the element* `t(0, 0)`.

Exercise 37.3-7   *Finding the Minimum and the Maximum Value of Each Row*

Write a Visual Basic program that lets the user enter values in a 20 × 30 array and then finds and displays the minimum and the maximum values of each row.

Solution

There are two approaches, actually. The first approach creates two auxiliary one-dimensional arrays, min and max, and then displays them. Arrays min and max will contain, in each position, the minimum and the maximum values of each row respectively. On the other hand, the second approach finds and directly displays the minimum and maximum values of each row. Let's study both approaches.

First Approach – Creating auxiliary arrays

To better understand this approach, let's use the "from inner to outer" method. When the following code fragment completes its iterations, the auxiliary one-dimensional arrays min and max contain at position 0 the minimum and the maximum values of the first row (row index 0) of array a respectively. Assume variable i contains value 0.

```
min(i) = a(i, 0)
max(i) = a(i, 0)
For j = 1 To COLUMNS - 1
  If a(i, j) < min(i) Then
    min(i) = a(i, j)
  End If
  If a(i, j) > max(i) Then
    max(i) = a(i, j)
  End If
Next
```

> **Notice:** *Please note that the initial value of variable* j *is 1. It wouldn't be wrong to start iterating from column index 0 instead of 1, though the program would perform one useless iteration.*

Now that everything has been clarified, in order to process the whole array a, you can just nest this code fragment into a counted loop structure which iterates for all rows as shown next.

```
For i = 0 To ROWS - 1
  min(i) = a(i, 0)
  max(i) = a(i, 0)
  For j = 1 To COLUMNS - 1
    If a(i, j) < min(i) Then
      min(i) = a(i, j)
    End If
    If a(i, j) > max(i) Then
      max(i) = a(i, j)
    End If
  Next
Next
```

The final Visual Basic program is as follows.

project_37_3_7a

```
Const ROWS = 30
Const COLUMNS = 20

Sub Main()
  Dim i, j As Integer


  Dim a(ROWS - 1,  COLUMNS - 1) As Double
  For i = 0 To ROWS - 1
    For j = 0 To COLUMNS - 1
      a(i, j) = Console.ReadLine()
    Next
  Next

  Dim min(ROWS - 1) As Double
  Dim max(ROWS - 1) As Double
  For i = 0 To ROWS - 1
    min(i) = a(i, 0)
    max(i) = a(i, 0)
    For j = 1 To COLUMNS - 1
      If a(i, j) < min(i) Then
        min(i) = a(i, j)
      End If
      If a(i, j) > max(i) Then
        max(i) = a(i, j)
      End If
    Next
  Next

  For i = 0 To ROWS - 1
    Console.WriteLine(min(i) & " " & max(i))
  Next

  Console.ReadKey()
End Sub
```

Second Approach – Finding and directly displaying minimum and maximum values

Let's use the "from inner to outer" method once again. The next code fragment finds and directly displays the minimum and the maximum values of the first row (row index 0) of array a. Assume variable i contains the value 0.

```
min = a(i, 0)
max = a(i, 0)
For j = 1 To COLUMNS - 1
  If a(i, j) < min Then
    min = a(i, j)
  End If
  If a(i, j) > max Then
    max = a(i, j)
  End If
Next

Console.WriteLine(min & " " & max)
```

Now that everything has been clarified, in order to process the whole array a, you can just nest this code fragment into a counted loop structure which iterates for all rows, as follows.

```
For i = 0 To ROWS - 1
  min = a(i, 0)
  max = a(i, 0)
  For j = 1 To COLUMNS - 1
    If a(i, j) < min Then
      min = a(i, j)
    End If
    If a(i, j) > max Then
      max = a(i, j)
    End If
  Next

  Console.WriteLine(min & " " & max)
Next
```

The final Visual Basic program is as follows.

```
project_37_3_7b

Const ROWS = 30
Const COLUMNS = 20

Sub Main()
  Dim i, j As Integer
  Dim min, max As Double

  Dim a(ROWS - 1,  COLUMNS - 1) As Double
  For i = 0 To ROWS - 1
    For j = 0 To COLUMNS - 1
      a(i, j) = Console.ReadLine()
    Next
  Next
```

```
    For i = 0 To ROWS - 1
      min = a(i, 0)
      max = a(i, 0)
      For j = 1 To COLUMNS - 1
        If a(i, j) < min Then
          max = a(i, j)
        End If
        If a(i, j) > max Then
          max = a(i, j)
        End If
      Next

      Console.WriteLine(min & " " & max)
    Next

    Console.ReadKey()
  End Sub
```

Exercise 37.3-8   *Finding the Minimum and the Maximum Value of Each Column*

Write a Visual Basic program that lets the user enter values into a 20 × 30 array and then finds and displays the minimum and the maximum values of each column.

Solution

As in the previous exercise, there are two approaches.

First Approach – Creating auxiliary arrays

When the following code fragment completes its iterations, the auxiliary one-dimensional arrays min and max contain at position 0 the minimum and the maximum values of the first column (column index 0) of array a respectively. Assume variable j contains the value 0.

```
min(j) = a(0, j)
max(j) = a(0, j)
For i = 1 To ROWS - 1
  If a(i, j) < min(j) Then
    min(j) = a(i, j)
  End If
  If a(i, j) > max(j) Then
    max(j) = a(i, j)
  End If
Next
```

> ***Notice***: *Please note that the initial value of variable i is 1. It wouldn't be wrong to start iterating from row index 0 instead of 1, though the program would perform one useless iteration.*

To process the whole array a, you can just nest this code fragment into a counted loop structure that iterates for all columns as follows.

```
For j = 0 To COLUMNS - 1
  min(j) = a(0, j)
  max(j) = a(0, j)
  For i = 1 To ROWS - 1
    If a(i, j) < min(j) Then
      min(j) = a(i, j)
    End If
    If a(i, j) > max(j) Then
      max(j) = a(i, j)
    End If
  Next
Next
```

> **Notice**: *Finding the minimum and maximum values of each column is as easy as finding the minimum and the maximum value of each row, as you learned in the previous exercise. Please note that the two counted loop structures of* i *and* j *have switched places.*

The final Visual Basic program is as follows.

```
                           project_37_3_8a
Const ROWS = 30
Const COLUMNS = 20

Sub Main()
  Dim i, j As Integer

  Dim a(ROWS - 1,  COLUMNS - 1) As Double
  For i = 0 To ROWS - 1
    For j = 0 To COLUMNS - 1
      a(i, j) = Console.ReadLine()
    Next
  Next

  Dim min(COLUMNS - 1) As Double
  Dim max(COLUMNS - 1) As Double
  For j = 0 To COLUMNS - 1
    min(j) = a(0, j)
    max(j) = a(0, j)
    For i = 1 To ROWS - 1
      If a(i, j) < min(j) Then
        min(j) = a(i, j)
      End If
      If a(i, j) > max(j) Then
        max(j) = a(i, j)
      End If
    Next
  Next

  For j = 0 To COLUMNS - 1
    Console.WriteLine(min(j) & " " & max(j))
```

```
    Next

    Console.ReadKey()
End Sub
```

Second Approach – Finding and directly displaying minimum and maximum values

Without further clarification, and using the second approach of the previous exercise as a guide, the corresponding solution is as follows.

```
                          project_37_3_8b
Const ROWS = 30
Const COLUMNS = 20

Sub Main()
    Dim i, j As Integer
    Dim min, max As Double

    Dim a(ROWS - 1,  COLUMNS - 1) As Double
    For i = 0 To ROWS - 1
      For j = 0 To COLUMNS - 1
        a(i, j) = Console.ReadLine()
      Next
    Next

    For j = 0 To COLUMNS - 1
      min = a(0, j)
      max = a(0, j)
      For i = 1 To ROWS - 1
        If a(i, j) < min Then
          min = a(i, j)
        End If
        If a(i, j) > max Then
          max = a(i, j)
        End If
      Next
      Console.WriteLine(min & " " & max)
    Next

    Console.ReadKey()
End Sub
```

37.4 Sorting Arrays

Sorting algorithms are an important topic in computer science. A sorting algorithm is an algorithm that puts elements of an array in a certain order. There are many sorting algorithms and each one of them has particular strengths and weaknesses.

Most sorting algorithms work by comparing the elements of the array. They are usually evaluated by their efficiency and their memory requirements.

There are many sorting algorithms. Some of them are:

> ➢   the bubble sort algorithm
> ➢   the modified bubble sort algorithm

> ➤ the selection sort algorithm
> ➤ the insertion sort algorithm
> ➤ the heap sort algorithm
> ➤ the merge sort algorithm
> ➤ the quicksort algorithm

As regards their efficiency, the bubble sort algorithm is considered the least efficient, while each succeeding algorithm in the list performs better than the preceding one. The quicksort algorithm is considered one of the best and fastest sorting algorithms, especially for large scale data operations.

Sorting algorithms can be used for more than just displaying data in ascending or descending order. For example, if an exercise requires you to display the three biggest numbers of an array, the Visual Basic program can sort the array in descending order and then display only the first three elements, that is, those at index positions 0, 1, and 2.

Sorting algorithms can also help you find the minimum and the maximum values from a set of given values. If an array is sorted in ascending order, the minimum value exists at the first index position and the maximum value exists at the last index position. Of course, it is very inefficient to sort an array so as to find minimum and maximum values; you have already learned a more efficient method. But if for some reason an exercise requires that an array be sorted and you need the minimum or the maximum value, you know where you can find them!

Exercise 37.4-1   *The Bubble Sort Algorithm – Sorting One-Dimensional Arrays with Numeric Values*

Write a Visual Basic program that lets the user enter 20 numerical values into an array and then sorts them in ascending order using the bubble sort algorithm.

Solution

The bubble sort algorithm is probably one of the most inefficient sorting algorithms but it is widely used for teaching purposes. The main idea (when asked to sort an array in ascending order) is to repeatedly move the smallest elements of the array to the positions of lowest index. This works as follows: the algorithm iterates through the elements of the array, compares each pair of adjacent elements, and then swaps their contents (if they are in the wrong order). This process is repeated many times until the array is sorted.

For example, let's try to sort the following array in ascending order.

A =		
	17	0
	25	1
	8	2
	5	3
	49	4
	12	5

The lowest value is the value 5. According to the bubble sort algorithm, this value should gradually "bubble" or "rise" to position 0, like bubbles rising in a glass of cola. When the value 5 has been moved into position 0, the next smallest value is the value 8. Now, the value 8 should "bubble" to position 1. Next is the value 12, which should "bubble" to position 2, and so on. This process repeats until all elements are placed in proper position.

But how can this "bubbling" be done using an algorithm? Let's see the whole process in more detail. For the previous array A of six elements, five passes must be performed.

First Pass

1st Compare

Initially, elements at index positions 4 and 5 are compared. Since the value 12 is less than the value 49, these two elements swap their content.

2nd Compare

Elements at index positions 3 and 4 are compared. Since the value 12 is **not** less than the value 5, **no** swapping is done.

3rd Compare

Elements at index positions 2 and 3 are compared. Since the value 5 is less than the value 8, these two elements swap their content.

4th Compare

Elements at index positions 1 and 2 are compared. Since the value 5 is less than the value 25, these two elements swap their content.

5th Compare

Elements at index positions 0 and 1 are compared. Since the value 5 is less than the value 17, these two elements swap their content.

1st Compare		2nd Compare	3rd Compare	4th Compare	5th Compare	
17	0	17	17	17	17	5
25	1	25	25	25	5	17
8	2	8	8	5	25	25
5	3	5	5	8	8	8
49	4	12	12	12	12	12
12	5	49	49	49	49	49

The first pass has been completed but, as you can see, the array has not been sorted yet. The only value that has actually been placed in proper position is the value 5. However, since more passes will follow, there is no need for the value 5 to take part in the subsequent compares. In the pass that follows, one less compare will be performed—that is, four compares.

Second Pass

1st Compare

Elements at index positions 4 and 5 are compared. Since the value 49 is **not** less than the value 12, **no** swapping is done.

2nd Compare

Elements at index positions 3 and 4 are compared. Since the value 12 is **not** less than the value 8, **no** swapping is done.

3rd Compare

Elements at index positions 2 and 3 are compared. Since the value 8 is less than the value 25, these two elements swap their content.

4th Compare

Elements at index positions 1 and 2 are compared. Since the value 8 is less than the value 17, these two elements swap their content.

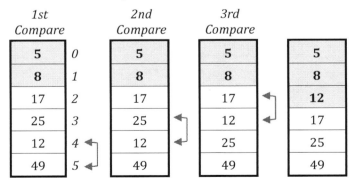

The second pass has been completed and the value of 8 has been placed in proper position. However, since more passes will follow, there is no need for the value 8 (nor 5, of course) to take part in the subsequent compares. In the pass that follows, one less compare will be performed—that is, three compares.

Third Pass

1st Compare

Elements at index positions 4 and 5 are compared. Since the value 49 is **not** less than the value 12, **no** swapping is done.

2nd Compare

Elements at index positions 3 and 4 are compared. Since the value 12 is less than the value 25, these two elements swap their content.

3rd Compare

Elements at index positions 2 and 3 are compared. Since the value 12 is less than the value 17, these two elements swap their content.

The third pass has been completed and the value of 12 has been placed in proper position. As previously, since more passes will follow there is no need for the value 12 (nor the values 5 and 8, of course) to take part in the subsequent compares. In the pass that follows, one compare less will be performed—that is, two compares.

Fourth Pass

1st Compare

Elements at index positions 4 and 5 are compared. Since the value 49 is **not** less than the value 25, **no** swapping is done.

2nd Compare

Elements at index positions 3 and 4 are compared. Since the value 25 is **not** less than the value 17, **no** swapping is done.

	1st Compare			2nd Compare				
	5	0		5				5
	8	1		8				8
	12	2		12				12
	17	3		17				17
	25	4		25				25
	49	5		49				49

The fourth pass has been completed and the value 17 has been placed in proper position. As previously, since one last pass will follow, there is no need for the value 17 (nor the values 5, 8, and 12, of course) to take part in the subsequent compares. In the last pass that follows, one compare less will be performed—that is one compare.

Fifth pass

1st Compare

Elements at index positions 4 and 5 are compared. Since the value 49 is **not** less than the value 12, **no** swapping is done.

	1st Compare			
	5	0		5
	8	1		8
	12	2		12
	17	3		17
	25	4		25
	49	5		49

The fifth pass has been completed and the final two values (25 and 49) have been placed in proper position. The bubble sort algorithm has finished and the array is sorted in ascending order!

Now you need a Visual Basic program that can do the whole previous process. Let's use the "from inner to outer" method. The code fragment that performs the first pass is shown below. Please note that this is the inner (nested) loop control structure. Assume variable m contains the value 1.

```
For n = ELEMENTS - 1 To m Step -1
  If a(n) < a(n - 1) Then
    temp = a(n)
    a(n) = a(n - 1)
    a(n - 1) = temp
  End If
Next
```

> **Notice**: *In the first pass, variable* m *must contain the value 1. This assures that at the last iteration, the elements that are compared are those at positions 1 and 0.*
>
> **Remember**! *Swapping the contents of two elements uses a method you have already learned! Please recall the two glasses of orange juice and lemon juice. If this doesn't ring a bell, you need to refresh your memory and reread the corresponding exercise in Chapter 8.*

The second pass can be performed if you just re-execute the previous code fragment. Variable m, however, needs to contain the value 2. This will ensure that the element at position 0 won't be compared again. Similarly, for the third pass, the previous code fragment can be re-executed but variable m needs to contain the value 3 for the same reason.

Accordingly, the previous code fragment needs to be executed five times (one for each pass), and each time variable m must be incremented by 1. The final code fragment that sorts array a using the bubble sort algorithm is as follows.

```
For m = 1 To ELEMENTS - 1
  For n = ELEMENTS - 1 To m Step -1
    If a(n) < a(n - 1) Then
      temp = a(n)
      a(n) = a(n - 1)
      a(n - 1) = temp
    End If
  Next
Next
```

The complete Visual Basic program is as follows.

```
                        project_37_4_1
Const ELEMENTS = 20

Sub Main()
  Dim i, m, n As Integer
  Dim temp As Double

  Dim a(ELEMENTS - 1) As Double
  For i = 0 To ELEMENTS - 1
    a(i) = Console.ReadLine()
  Next

  For m = 1 To ELEMENTS - 1
```

```
      For n = ELEMENTS - 1 To m Step -1
        If a(n) < a(n - 1) Then
          temp = a(n)
          a(n) = a(n - 1)
          a(n - 1) = temp
        End If
      Next
    Next

    For i = 0 To ELEMENTS - 1
      Console.Write(a(i) & vbTab)
    Next

    Console.ReadKey()
  End Sub
```

> **Notice**: *The bubble sort algorithm is very inefficient. The total number of compares that it performs is $\frac{N(N-1)}{2}$, where N is the total number of array elements.*
>
> **Notice**: *The total number of swaps depends on the given array. The worst case is when you want to sort in ascending order an array that is already sorted in descending order, or vice versa.*

Exercise 37.4-2   *Sorting One-Dimensional Arrays with Alphanumeric Values*

Write a code fragment that sorts the alphanumeric values of an array in descending order using the bubble sort algorithm.

Solution

Comparing this exercise to the previous one, two things are different. First, the bubble sort algorithm needs to sort alphanumeric values, such as names of people or names of cities; and second, it has to sort them in descending order.

In Visual Basic you cannot compare strings using comparison operators such as the less than (<), or the greater than (>) operators. Actually, Visual Basic supports the procedure CompareTo(), that can be used for this purpose. For this procedure the letter "A" is considered "less than" the letter "B", the letter "B" is considered "less than" the letter "C," and so on. Of course, if two strings contain words in which the first letter is identical, Visual Basic moves on and compares their second letters, and perhaps their third letters (if necessary). For example, the name "John" is considered "less than" the name "Jonathan" because the third letter, "h", is "less than" the third letter, "n." In conclusion, if you replace the Boolean expression a(n) < a(n - 1) with the expression a(n).CompareTo(a(n - 1)) < 0, then the bubble sort algorithm becomes able to sort alphanumeric values in ascending order.

> **Notice**: *When you are thinking of alphanumeric sorting, think of your dictionary and how words are sorted there.*

And now let's see what you need to change so that the algorithm can sort in descending order. Do you remember how the bubble sort algorithm actually works? Smaller elements gradually "bubble" to positions of lowest index, like bubbles rise in a glass of cola. What you want in this exercise is to make the bigger (instead of the smaller) elements "bubble" to lower index positions. Therefore, all you need to do is simply reverse the comparison operator of the Boolean expression!

The code fragment that sorts alphanumeric values in descending order is as follows

```
For m = 1 To ELEMENTS - 1
  For n = ELEMENTS - 1 To m Step -1
    If a(n).CompareTo(a(n - 1)) > 0 Then
      temp_str = a(n)
      a(n) = a(n - 1)
      a(n - 1) = temp_str
    End If
  Next
Next
```

> **Notice:** Obviously, if array a is to hold string values, variable `temp_str` must be declared as string.

Exercise 37.4-3   *Sorting One-Dimensional Arrays While Preserving the Relationship with a Second Array*

Write a Visual Basic program that lets the user enter the names of 20 lakes and their corresponding average area. The program should then sort them by average area in ascending order using the bubble sort algorithm.

Solution

In this exercise you need the following two arrays.

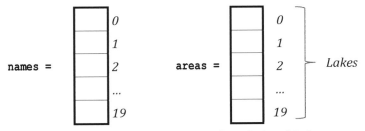

If you want to sort array `areas` while preserving the relationship between the elements of the two arrays, you must rearrange the elements of the array `names` as well. This means that every time two elements of the array `areas` swap contents, the corresponding elements of the array `names` must swap contents as well. The Visual Basic program is as follows.

```
                       project_37_4_3
Const LAKES = 20

Sub Main()
  Dim i, m, n As Integer
  Dim temp As Double
  Dim temp_str As String
```

```
    Dim names(LAKES - 1) As String
    Dim areas(LAKES - 1) As Double
    For i = 0 To LAKES - 1
      names(i) = Console.ReadLine()
      areas(i) = Console.ReadLine()
    Next

    For m = 1 To LAKES - 1
      For n = LAKES - 1 To m Step -1
        If areas(n) < areas(n - 1) Then
          temp = areas(n)
          areas(n) = areas(n - 1)
          areas(n - 1) = temp

          temp_str = names(n)
          names(n) = names(n - 1)
          names(n - 1) = temp_str
        End If
      Next
    Next

    For i = 0 To LAKES - 1
      Console.WriteLine(names(i) & vbTab & areas(i))
    Next

    Console.ReadKey()
End Sub
```

> **Notice**: *Please note that you cannot use the variable* temp *for swapping the contents of two elements of the array* names; *this is because variable* temp *is declared as double while array* names *contains strings. So, you need a second variable (*temp_str*) declared as string for this purpose.*

Exercise 37.4-4   *Sorting Last and First Names*

Write a Visual Basic program that prompts the user to enter the last and first names of 100 people and then displays them with the last names sorted in alphabetical order. Moreover, if two or more people have the same last name, their first names should be displayed in alphabetical order as well.

Solution

In this exercise, you need the following two arrays.

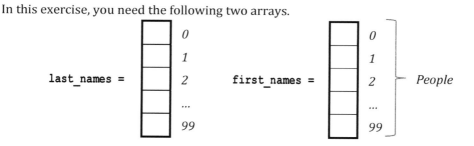

Of course, you already know how to sort the array last_names and at the same time preserve the relationship with the elements of the array first_names. But, what you actually don't know here is how to handle the case when two last names are equal. According to the wording of the exercise, the corresponding first names should be also sorted alphabetically.

For your convenience, the basic version of the bubble sort algorithm is presented once again. Please note that this algorithm preserves the relationship between the elements of arrays last_names and first_names.

```
For m = 1 To PEOPLE - 1
  For n = PEOPLE - 1 To m Step -1
    If last_names(n).CompareTo(last_names(n - 1)) < 0 Then
      temp_str = last_names(n)
      last_names(n) = last_names(n - 1)
      last_names(n - 1) = temp_str

      temp_str = first_names(n)
      first_names(n) = first_names(n - 1)
      first_names(n - 1) = temp_str
    End If
  Next
Next
```

Notice: *Please note that variable* temp_str *is used for swapping the contents of the elements of both arrays* last_names *and* first_names. *This is acceptable since both arrays contain strings.*

To solve this exercise, however, this bubble sort algorithm must be adapted accordingly. According to this basic version of the bubble sort algorithm, when the last name at position n is "less" than the last name at position n - 1, the algorithm swaps the corresponding contents as usual. However, when the last name at position n is equal to the last name at position n - 1, the algorithm then must check if the corresponding first names are in the proper order. If not, they should swap their contents. The adapted bubble sort algorithm is shown in the next code fragment.

```
Dim m, n, temp As Integer

For m = 1 To PEOPLE - 1
  For n = PEOPLE - 1 To m Step -1
    If last_names(n).CompareTo(last_names(n - 1)) < 0 Then
      temp_str = last_names(n)
      last_names(n) = last_names(n - 1)
      last_names(n - 1) = temp_str

      temp_str = first_names(n)
      first_names(n) = first_names(n - 1)
      first_names(n - 1) = temp_str
    ElseIf last_names(n) = last_names(n - 1) Then
      If first_names(n).CompareTo(first_names(n - 1)) < 0 Then
        temp_str = first_names(n)
        first_names(n) = first_names(n - 1)
```

```
              first_names(n - 1) = temp_str
          End If
        End If
    Next
  Next
Next
```

The final Visual Basic program is presented next.

```
                          project_37_4_4
Const PEOPLE = 100

Sub Main()
  Dim i, m, n As Integer
  Dim temp_str As String

  'Read arrays first_names and last_names
  Dim first_names(PEOPLE - 1) As String
  Dim last_names(PEOPLE - 1) As String
  For i = 0 To PEOPLE - 1
    Console.Write("Enter first name for person No. " & (i + 1) & ": ")
    first_names(i) = Console.ReadLine()
    Console.Write("Enter last name for person No. " & (i + 1) & ": ")
    last_names(i) = Console.ReadLine()
  Next

  For m = 1 To PEOPLE - 1
    For n = PEOPLE - 1 To m Step -1
      If last_names(n).CompareTo(last_names(n - 1)) < 0 Then
        temp_str = last_names(n)
        last_names(n) = last_names(n - 1)
        last_names(n - 1) = temp_str

        temp_str = first_names(n)
        first_names(n) = first_names(n - 1)
        first_names(n - 1) = temp_str
      ElseIf last_names(n) = last_names(n - 1) Then
        If first_names(n).CompareTo(first_names(n - 1)) < 0 Then
          temp_str = first_names(n)
          first_names(n) = first_names(n - 1)
          first_names(n - 1) = temp_str
        End If
      End If
    Next
  Next

  'Display arrays last_names and first_names
  For i = 0 To PEOPLE - 1
    Console.WriteLine(last_names(i) & vbTab & first_names(i))
  Next

  Console.ReadKey()
End Sub
```

Exercise 37.4-5   *Sorting a Two-Dimensional Array*

Write a code fragment that sorts each column of a two-dimensional array in ascending order. Assume that the array contains numerical values.

Solution

An example of a two-dimension array is as follows.

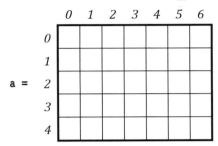

Since this array has seven columns, the bubble sort algorithm needs to be executed seven times, one for each column. Therefore, the whole bubble sort algorithm should be nested within a counted loop structure that iterates seven times.

But let's get things in the right order. Using the "from inner to outer" method, the next code fragment sorts only the first column (column index 0) of the two-dimensional array a. Assume variable j contains the value 0.

```
For m = 1 To ROWS - 1
  For n = ROWS - 1 To m Step -1
    If a(n, j) < a(n - 1, j) Then
      temp = a(n, j)
      a(n, j) = a(n - 1, j)
      a(n - 1, j) = temp
    End If
  Next
Next
```

Now, in order to sort all columns, you can nest this code fragment in a counted loop structure that iterates for all of them, as follows.

```
For j = 0 To COLUMNS - 1
  For m = 1 To ROWS - 1
    For n = ROWS - 1 To m Step -1
      If a(n, j) < a(n - 1, j) Then
        temp = a(n, j)
        a(n, j) = a(n - 1, j)
        a(n - 1, j) = temp
      End If
    Next
  Next
Next
```

That wasn't so difficult, was it?

Exercise 37.4-6 **The Modified Bubble Sort Algorithm – Sorting One-Dimensional Arrays**

Write a Visual Basic program that lets the user enter the weights of 30 people and then displays the three heaviest weights and the three lightest weights. Use the **modified** bubble sort algorithm.

Solution

To solve this exercise, the Visual Basic program can sort the given data in ascending order and then display the elements at index positions 27, 28, and 29 (for the three heaviest weights) and the elements at index positions 0, 1 and 2 (for the three lightest weights).

But how does the modified version of the bubble sort algorithm actually work? Suppose you have the following array containing the weights of six people.

	0	1	2	3	4	5
w =	165	170	180	190	182	200

If you look closer, you can confirm for yourself that the only elements that are not in proper position are those at index positions 3 and 4. If you swap their values, the array w immediately becomes sorted! However, the bubble sort algorithm doesn't operate this way. Unfortunately, for this given array of six elements, it will perform five passes either way, with a total of $\frac{N(N-1)}{2} = 15$ compares, where N is the total number of array elements. For bigger arrays, the total number of compares that the bubble sort algorithm performs increases exponentially!

Of course the modified bubble sort algorithm can overcome this situation as follows: if a complete pass is performed and no swaps have been made, then the array is sorted and there is no need for further passes. To accomplish this, the Visual Basic program can use a flag variable that indicates if any swaps were made. At the beginning of a pass, a value of False can be assigned to the flag variable; when a swap is made, a value of True is assigned. If, at the end of the pass, the flag is still False, this indicates that no swaps have been made, thus iterations should stop. The modified bubble sort is shown next in two versions.

The next approach uses the Exit For statement and a flag variable (swaps).

```
For m = 1 To ELEMENTS - 1
  swaps = False
  For n = ELEMENTS - 1 To m Step -1
    If w(n) < w(n - 1) Then
      temp = w(n)
      w(n) = w(n - 1)
      w(n - 1) = temp

      swaps = True
    End If
  Next
  If swaps = False Then Exit For
Next
```

The next approach, on the other hand, uses a pre-test loop structure and a flag variable.

```
m = 1
swaps = True
Do While m <= ELEMENTS - 1 And swaps = True
  swaps = False
  For n = ELEMENTS - 1 To m Step -1
    If w(n) < w(n - 1) Then
      temp = w(n)
      w(n) = w(n - 1)
      w(n - 1) = temp

      swaps = True
    End If
  Next
  m += 1
Loop
```

So, let's now focus on the given exercise. The final Visual Basic program is shown next. It uses the approach with the Exit For statement, but you can easily rewrite it and make use of the second approach.

```
                         project_37_4_6
Const ELEMENTS = 20

Sub Main()
  Dim i, m, n As Integer
  Dim swaps As Boolean
  Dim temp As Double

  Dim w(ELEMENTS - 1) As Double
  For i = 0 To ELEMENTS - 1
    w(i) = Console.ReadLine()
  Next

  For m = 1 To ELEMENTS - 1
    swaps = False
    For n = ELEMENTS - 1 To m Step -1
      If w(n) < w(n - 1) Then
        temp = w(n)
        w(n) = w(n - 1)
        w(n - 1) = temp

        swaps = True
      End If
    Next
    If swaps = False Then Exit For
  Next

  Console.WriteLine("The three heaviest weights are:")
  Console.WriteLine(w(ELEMENTS - 3))
  Console.WriteLine(w(ELEMENTS - 2))
```

```
Console.WriteLine(w(ELEMENTS - 1))
Console.WriteLine("The three lightest weights are:")
Console.WriteLine(w(0))
Console.WriteLine(w(1))
Console.WriteLine(w(2))

Console.ReadKey()
End Sub
```

Exercise 37.4-7   *The Five Best Scorers*

Write a Visual Basic program that prompts the user to enter the names of the 32 national teams of the FIFA World Cup, the names of the 24 players for each team, and the total number of goals each player scored. The program should then display the name of each team along with its five best scorers. Use the modified bubble sort algorithm.

Solution

In this exercise you need the following three arrays.

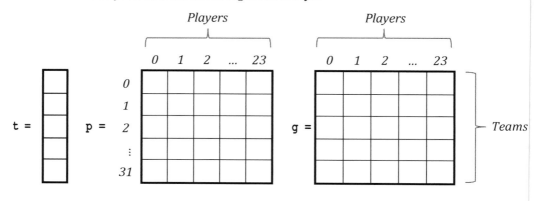

> **Notice**: *To save paper short array names are used, but it is more or less obvious that array t holds the names of the 32 national teams, array p holds the names of the 24 players of each team, and array g holds the total number of goals each player scored.*

Since you need to find the five best scorers for each team, the Visual Basic program must sort each row of array g in descending order but it should also take care to preserve the relationship with the elements of arrays p. This means that, every time the bubble sort algorithm swaps the contents of two elements of array g, the corresponding elements of array p should be swapped as well. When sorting is completed, the five best scorers should appear in the first five columns.

The "from inner to outer" method is used again. The following code fragment sorts the first row (row index 0) of array g in descending order and, at the same time, takes care to preserve the relationship with elements of array p. Assume variable i contains the value 0.

```
m = 1
swaps = True
Do While m <= PLAYERS - 1 And swaps = True
```

```
  swaps = False
  For n = PLAYERS - 1 To m Step -1
    If g(i, n) < g(i, n - 1) Then
      temp = g(i, n)
      g(i, n) = g(i, n - 1)
      g(i, n - 1) = temp

      temp_str = p(i, n)
      p(i, n) = p(i, n - 1)
      p(i, n - 1) = temp_str

      swaps = True
    End If
  Next
  m += 1
Loop
```

Now, in order to sort all rows, you need to nest this code fragment in a counted loop structure that iterates for all of them, as shown next.

```
For i = 0 To TEAMS - 1
  m = 1
  swaps = True
  Do While m <= PLAYERS - 1 And swaps = True
    swaps = False
    For n = PLAYERS - 1 To m Step -1
      If g(i, n) < g(i, n - 1) Then
        temp = g(i, n)
        g(i, n) = g(i, n - 1)
        g(i, n - 1) = temp

        temp_str = p(i, n)
        p(i, n) = p(i, n - 1)
        p(i, n - 1) = temp_str

        swaps = True
      End If
    Next
    m += 1
  Loop
Next
```

The final Visual Basic program is as follows.

```
                        project_37_4_7
Const TEAMS = 32
Const PLAYERS = 24

Sub Main()
  Dim i, j, m, n, temp As Integer
  Dim swaps As Boolean
  Dim temp_str As String
```

```vb
'Read team names, player names and goals all together
Dim t(TEAMS - 1) As String
Dim p(TEAMS - 1,  PLAYERS - 1) As String
Dim g(TEAMS - 1,  PLAYERS - 1) As Integer
For i = 0 To TEAMS - 1
  Console.WriteLine("Enter name for team No. " & (i + 1) & ": ")
  t(i) = Console.ReadLine()
  For j = 0 To PLAYERS - 1
    Console.WriteLine("Enter name of player No. " & (j + 1) & ": ")
    p(i, j) = Console.ReadLine()
    Console.WriteLine("Enter goals of player No. " & (j + 1) & ": ")
    g(i, j) = Console.ReadLine()
  Next
Next

'sort array g
For i = 0 To TEAMS - 1
  m = 1
  swaps = True
  Do While m <= PLAYERS - 1 And swaps = True
    swaps = False
    For n = PLAYERS - 1 To m Step -1
      If g(i, n) > g(i, n - 1) Then
        temp = g(i, n)
        g(i, n) = g(i, n - 1)
        g(i, n - 1) = temp

        temp_str = p(i, n)
        p(i, n) = p(i, n - 1)
        p(i, n - 1) = temp_str

        swaps = True
      End If
    Next
    m += 1
  Loop
Next

'Display 5 best scorers of each team
For i = 0 To TEAMS - 1
  Console.WriteLine("Best scorers of " & t(i))
  Console.WriteLine("---------------------------------")
  For j = 0 To 4
    Console.WriteLine(p(i, j) & " scored " & g(i, j) & " goals")
  Next
Next

Console.ReadKey()
End Sub
```

> **Remember!** *You cannot use the variable* temp *for swapping the contents of two elements of the array* p; *this is because variable* temp *is declared as integer while array* p *contains strings. So, you need a second variable (*temp_str*) declared as string for this purpose.*

Exercise 37.4-8   *The Selection Sort Algorithm – Sorting One-Dimensional Arrays*

Write a code fragment that sorts the elements of an array in ascending order using the selection sort algorithm. Assume that the array contains numerical values.

Solution

The selection sort algorithm is inefficient for large scale data, as is the bubble sort algorithm, but it generally performs better than the latter. It is the simplest of all the sorting algorithms and performs well on computer systems in which limited main memory (RAM) comes into play.

The algorithm finds the smallest (or largest, depending on sorting order) element of the array and swaps its content with that at position 0. Then the process is repeated for the remainder of the array; the next smallest (or largest) element is found and put into the next position, until all elements are examined.

For example, let's try to sort the following array in ascending order.

	0	1	2	3	4	5
A =	18	19	39	36	4	9

The lowest value is the value 4 at position 4. According to the selection sort algorithm, this element swaps its content with that at position 0. The array A becomes

	0	1	2	3	4	5
A =	4	19	41	36	18	9

The lowest value in the remainder of the array is the value 9 at position 5. This element swaps its content with that at position 1. The array A becomes

	0	1	2	3	4	5
A =	4	9	41	36	18	19

The lowest value in the remainder of the array is the value 18 at position 4. This element swaps its content with that at position 2. The array A becomes

	0	1	2	3	4	5
A =	4	9	18	36	41	19

Proceeding the same way, the next lowest value is the value 19 at position 5. The array A becomes

	0	1	2	3	4	5
A =	4	9	18	19	41	36

Finally, the next lowest value is the value 36 at position 5. The array A becomes finally sorted in ascending order!

	0	1	2	3	4	5
A =	4	9	18	19	36	41

Now, let's write the corresponding Visual Basic program. The "from inner to outer" method is used in order to help you better understand the whole process. The next code fragment finds the smallest element and then swaps its content with that at position 0. Please note that this is the inner (nested) loop control structure. Assume variable m contains the value 0.

```
min = a(m)
index_of_min = m
For n = m To ELEMENTS - 1
  If a(n) < min Then
    min = a(n)
    index_of_min = n
  End If
Next

'Minimum found! Now, swap values.
temp = a(m)
a(m) = a(index_of_min)
a(index_of_min) = temp
```

Now, in order to repeat the process for all elements of the array, you can nest this code fragment within a counted loop structure that iterates for all elements.

The final selection sort algorithm that sorts an array in ascending order is as follows.

```
For m = 0 To ELEMENTS - 1
  min = a(m)
  index_of_min = m
  For n = m To ELEMENTS - 1
    If a(n) < min Then
      min = a(n)
      index_of_min = n
    End If
  Next

  'Swap values
  temp = a(m)
  a(m) = a(index_of_min)
  a(index_of_min) = temp
Next
```

Notice: *If you wish to sort an array in descending order, all you need to do is search for maximum instead of minimum values.*

Remember! *As in a bubble sort algorithm, in order to sort alphanumeric data in Visual Basic, you can simply replace the Boolean expression* a(n) < min *with the expression* a(n).CompareTo(min) < 0.

Exercise 37.4-9 *Sorting One-Dimensional Arrays While Preserving the Relationship with a Second Array*

Write a Visual Basic program that prompts the user to enter the electric meter reading recorded at the end of each month for a period of one year. It then displays each reading (in descending order) along with the name of the corresponding month. Use the selection sort algorithm.

Solution

In this exercise you need the following two one-dimensional arrays.

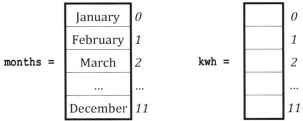

The approach is the same as in the bubble sort algorithm. While the selection sort algorithm sorts the elements of array kwh, the relationship with the elements of array months must also be preserved. This means that every time two elements of array kwh swap contents, the corresponding elements of array months must swap their contents as well. The Visual Basic program is as follows.

```
                          project_37_4_9
Const ELEMENTS = 12

Sub Main()
  Dim i, m, index_of_max, n As Integer
  Dim max, temp As Double
  Dim temp_str As String

  Dim months() As String = {"January", "February", "March", "April",
                   "May", "June", "July", "August",
                   "September", "October", "November", "December"}

  Dim kwh(ELEMENTS - 1) As Double
  For i = 0 To ELEMENTS - 1
    Console.Write("Enter kWh for " & months(i) & ": ")
    kwh(i) = Console.ReadLine()
  Next

  For m = 0 To ELEMENTS - 1
    max = kwh(m)
    index_of_max = m
    For n = m To ELEMENTS - 1
      If kwh(n) > max Then
        max = kwh(n)
        index_of_max = n
      End If
```

```
    Next

    'Swap values of kwh
    temp = kwh(m)
    kwh(m) = kwh(index_of_max)
    kwh(index_of_max) = temp

    'Swap values of months
    temp_str = months(m)
    months(m) = months(index_of_max)
    months(index_of_max) = temp_str
    Next

    For i = 0 To ELEMENTS - 1
      Console.WriteLine(months(i) & ": " & kwh(i))
    Next

    Console.ReadKey()
  End Sub
```

Exercise 37.4-10 *The Insertion Sort Algorithm – Sorting One-Dimensional Arrays*

Write a code fragment that sorts the elements of an array in ascending order using the insertion sort algorithm. Assume that the array contains numerical values.

Solution

The insertion sort algorithm is inefficient for large scale data, as are the selection and the bubble sort algorithms, but it generally performs better than either of them. Moreover, the insertion sort algorithm can prove very fast when sorting very small arrays— even faster than the quicksort algorithm.

The insertion sort algorithm resembles the way you might sort playing cards. You start with all the cards face down on the table. The cards represent the unsorted "array." In the beginning your left hand is empty, but in the end this hand will hold the sorted cards. The process goes as follows: you remove from the table one card at a time and insert it into the correct position in your left hand. To find the correct position for a card, you compare it with each of the cards already in your hand, from right to left. At the end, there should be no cards on the table and your left hand will hold all the cards, sorted.

For example, let's try to sort the following array in ascending order. To better understand this example, the first three elements of the array are already sorted for you.

	0	1	2	3	4	5	6
A =	3	15	24	8	10	18	9

The element at position 3 (which is 8) is removed from the array and all elements on its left with a value greater than 8 are shifted to the right. The array A becomes

	0	1	2	3	4	5	6
A =	3		15	24	10	18	9

Now that a position has been released, the value 8 is inserted in there. The array becomes

	0	1	2	3	4	5	6
A =	3	8	15	24	10	18	9

The element at position 4 (which is 10) is removed from the array and all elements on its left with a value greater than 10 are shifted to the right. The array A becomes

	0	1	2	3	4	5	6
A =	3	8		15	24	18	9

Now that a position has been released, the value of 10 is inserted in there. The array becomes

	0	1	2	3	4	5	6
A =	3	8	10	15	24	18	9

The element at position 5 is removed from the array and all elements on its left with a value greater than 18 are shifted to the right. The array A becomes

	0	1	2	3	4	5	6
A =	3	8	10	15		24	9

Now that a position has been released, the value of 18 is inserted in there. The array becomes

	0	1	2	3	4	5	6
A =	3	8	10	15	18	24	9

The element at position 6 is removed from the array and all elements on its left with a value greater than 9 are shifted to the right. The array A becomes

	0	1	2	3	4	5	6
A =	3	8		10	15	18	24

Now that a position has been released, the value of 9 is inserted in there. This is the last step of the process. The algorithm finishes and the array is now sorted.

	0	1	2	3	4	5	6
A =	3	8	9	10	15	18	24

> **Remember!** What the algorithm actually does is to check the unsorted elements one by one and insert each one in the appropriate position among those considered already sorted.

The code fragment that sorts an array in ascending order using the insertion sort algorithm is as follows.

```
For m = 1 To ELEMENTS - 1
  '"Remove" the element at index position m from the array and
  'keep it in variable element
  element = a(m)

  'Shift appropriate elements to the right
  n = m
  Do While n > 0
    If element > a(n - 1) Then Exit Do
    a(n) = a(n - 1)
    n -= 1
  Loop

  'insert the previously "removed" element at index position n
  a(n) = element
Next
```

> **Notice**: Please note that the element at index position m is not actually removed from the array but is in fact overwritten when shifting to the right is performed. This is why its value is kept in variable element before shifting the elements.
>
> **Notice**: If you wish to sort an array in descending order, all you need to do is alter the Boolean expression of the single-alternative decision structure to element < a(n - 1).
>
> **Remember!** As in previous sort algorithms, in order to sort alphanumeric data in Visual Basic, you can simply replace the Boolean expression element > a(n - 1) with the expression element.CompareTo(a(n - 1)) > 0.

Exercise 37.4-11   *The Three Worst Elapsed Times*

Ten race car drivers run their cars as fast as possible on a racing track. Each car runs 20 laps and for each lap the corresponding elapsed time (in seconds) is recorded. Write a Visual Basic program that prompts the user to enter the name of each driver and their elapsed time for each lap. The program should then display the name of each driver along with his or her three worst elapsed times. Use the insertion sort algorithm.

Solution

In this exercise, you need the following two arrays.

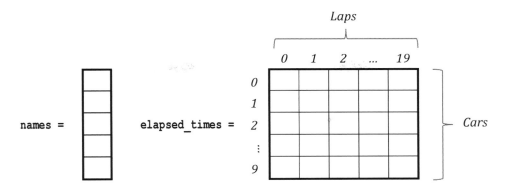

After the user enters all data, the Visual Basic program must sort each row of the array in descending order but, in the end, should display only the first three columns.

Using the "from inner to outer" method, the next code fragment sorts only the first row (row index 0) of the two-dimensional array elapsed_times in descending order using the insertion sort algorithm. Assume variable i contains the value 0.

```
For m = 1 To LAPS - 1
  element = elapsed_times(i, m)
  n = m
  Do While n > 0
    If element < elapsed_times(i, n - 1) Then Exit Do
    elapsed_times(i, n) = elapsed_times(i, n - 1)
    n -= 1
  Loop
  elapsed_times(i, n) = element
Next
```

Now, in order to sort all rows, you need to nest this code fragment in a counted loop structure that iterates for all of them, as follows.

```
For i = 0 To CARS - 1
  For m = 1 To LAPS - 1
    element = elapsed_times(i, m)
    n = m
    Do While n > 0
      If element < elapsed_times(i, n - 1) Then Exit Do
      elapsed_times(i, n) = elapsed_times(i, n - 1)
      n -= 1
    Loop
    elapsed_times(i, n) = element
  Next
Next
```

And now, let's focus on the given exercise. The final Visual Basic program is as follows.

project_37_4_11

```
Const CARS = 10
Const LAPS = 20

Sub Main()
```

```vb
Dim i, j, m, n As Integer
Dim element As Double

'Read names and elapsed times all together
Dim names(CARS - 1) As String
Dim elapsed_times(CARS - 1,  LAPS - 1) As Double
For i = 0 To CARS - 1
  Console.Write("Enter name for driver No. " & (i + 1) & ": ")
  names(i) = Console.ReadLine()
  For j = 0 To LAPS - 1
    Console.Write("Enter elapsed time for lap No. " & (j + 1) & ": ")
    elapsed_times(i, j) = Console.ReadLine()
  Next
Next

'short array elapsed_times
For i = 0 To CARS - 1
  For m = 1 To LAPS - 1
    element = elapsed_times(i, m)
    n = m
    Do While n > 0
      If element < elapsed_times(i, n - 1) Then Exit Do
      elapsed_times(i, n) = elapsed_times(i, n - 1)
      n -= 1
    Loop
    elapsed_times(i, n) = element
  Next
Next

'Display 3 worst elapsed times
For i = 0 To CARS - 1
  Console.WriteLine("Worst elapsed times of " & names(i))
  Console.WriteLine("-------------------------------------")
  For j = 0 To 2
    Console.WriteLine(elapsed_times(i, j))
  Next
Next
Console.ReadKey()
End Sub
```

37.5   Searching Elements in Arrays

In computer science, a search algorithm is an algorithm that searches for an item with specific properties within a set of data. In the case of an array, a search algorithm does exactly the same thing; it searches the array to find the element, or elements, that equal a given value.

There are two cases for searching elements in arrays.

> ➢ You want to search in an array for a given value and find the element (or its corresponding index) that is equal to that given value.

> ➢ You want to search in an array for a given value and find **all** the elements (or their corresponding indexes) that are equal to that given value.

The most commonly used search algorithms are:

> ➢ the linear (or sequential) search algorithm
> ➢ the binary search algorithm

Both linear and binary search algorithms have advantages and disadvantages.

Exercise 37.5-1 *The Linear Search Algorithm – Searching in a One-Dimensional Array that may Contain the Same Value Multiple Times*

Write a code fragment that searches a one-dimensional array for a given value. Assume that the array contains numerical values and may contain the same value multiple times. Use the linear search algorithm.

Solution

The linear (or sequential) search algorithm checks if the first element of the array is equal to a given value, then checks the second element, then the third, and so on until the end of the array. Since this process of checking elements one by one is quite slow, the linear search algorithm is suitable for arrays with few elements.

The code fragment is shown next. It looks for a given value needle in the array haystack!

```
Console.Write("Enter a value to search: ")
needle = Console.ReadLine()

found = False
For i = 0 To ELEMENTS - 1
  If haystack(i) = needle Then
     Console.WriteLine(needle & " found at position: " & i)
     found = True
  End If
Next

If found = False Then
  Console.WriteLine("Nothing found!")
End If
```

Exercise 37.5-2 *Display the Last Names of All Those People Who Have the Same First Name*

Write a Visual Basic program that prompts the user to enter the names of 20 people: their first names in the array first_names, *and their last names in the array* last_names. *The program should then ask the user for a first name, upon which it will search and display the last names of all those whose first name equals the given one.*

Solution

The solution is as follows.

```
                        project_37_5_2
Const PEOPLE = 20
```

```vb
Sub Main()
  Dim i As Integer
  Dim needle As String
  Dim found As Boolean

  Dim first_names(PEOPLE - 1) As String
  Dim last_names(PEOPLE - 1) As String
  For i = 0 To PEOPLE - 1
    Console.Write("Enter first name: ")
    first_names(i) = Console.ReadLine()
    Console.Write("Enter last name: ")
    last_names(i) = Console.ReadLine()
  Next

  Console.Write("Enter a first name to search: ")
  needle = Console.ReadLine()

  found = False
  For i = 0 To PEOPLE - 1
    If first_names(i).ToUpper() = needle.ToUpper() Then
      Console.WriteLine(last_names(i))
      found = True
    End If
  Next

  If found = False Then
    Console.WriteLine("No one found!")
  End If

  Console.ReadKey()
End Sub
```

> **Notice**: Even though it is not very clear in the wording of the exercise, it is true that the array first_names *may contain a value multiple times. How rare is it to meet two people named "John," for example?*
>
> **Notice**: *Since the program works with alphanumeric data, the* ToUpper() *procedure is required so that the program can operate correctly for any given value. For example, if the value "John" exists in the array* first_names *and the user wants to search for the value "JOHN," the* ToUpper() *procedure ensures that the program finds all Johns.*

Exercise 37.5-3   *Searching in a One-Dimensional Array that Contains Unique Values*

Write a code fragment that searches a one-dimensional array for a given value. Assume that the array contains numerical values and each value in the array is unique. Use the linear search algorithm.

Solution

This case is quite different from the previous ones. Since each value in the array is unique, when the given value is found, there is no need to iterate without reason until the end of the array, thus wasting CPU time. There are three approaches, actually! Let's analyze them all!

First Approach – Using the Exit For statement

In this approach, when the given value is found, an Exit For statement is used to break out of the counted loop structure. The solution is as follows.

```
Console.Write("Enter a value to search: ")
needle = Console.ReadLine()

found = False
For i = 0 To ELEMENTS - 1
  If haystack(i) = needle Then
    Console.WriteLine(needle & " found at position: " & i)
    found = True
    Exit For
  End If
Next

If found = False Then
  Console.WriteLine("Nothing found!")
End If
```

Or you can do the same, in a little bit different way.

```
Console.Write("Enter a value to search: ")
needle = Console.ReadLine()

index_position = -1
For i = 0 To ELEMENTS - 1
  If haystack(i) = needle Then
    index_position = i
    Exit For
  End If
Next

If index_position = -1 Then
  Console.WriteLine("Nothing found!")
Else
  Console.WriteLine(needle & " found at position: " & index_position)
End If
```

Second Approach – Using a flag

This book tries to use the Exit For statement as little as possible, and only in certain situations in which it really helps you make your code better. That's because the Exit For statement doesn't actually exist in all computer languages; and since this book's intent is to teach you "Algorithmic Thinking" (and not just special statements that only Visual Basic supports), let's look at an alternate approach.

To break out of a loop using a flag, there is one methodology that you can always follow: the counted loop structure must be converted to a pre-test loop structure, and the Boolean expression of the loop must be modified to evaluate an extra variable. In the next code fragment this extra variable is the variable found which, when the given value is found within array haystack, forces the flow of execution to immediately exit the loop.

```
Console.Write("Enter a value to search: ")
needle = Console.ReadLine()

found = False
i = 0
Do While i <= ELEMENTS - 1 And found = False
  If haystack(i) = needle Then
    found = True
    index_position = i
  End If
  i += 1
Loop

If found = False Then
  Console.WriteLine("Nothing found!")
Else
  Console.WriteLine(needle & " found at position: " & index_position)
End If
```

Third Approach – Using only a pre-test loop structure

This approach is probably the most efficient one. Also, it is so easy to understand the way is works that there is no need to explain anything. The code fragment is as follows.

```
Console.Write("Enter a value to search: ")
needle = Console.ReadLine()

i = 0
Do While i < ELEMENTS - 1 And haystack(i) <> needle
  i += 1
Loop

If haystack(i) <> needle Then
  Console.WriteLine("Nothing found!")
Else
  Console.WriteLine(needle & " found at position: " & i)
End If
```

Exercise 37.5-4   *Searching for a Given Social Security Number*

In the United States, the Social Security Number (SSN) is a nine-digit identity number applied to all U.S. citizens in order to identify them for the purposes of Social Security. Write a Visual Basic program that prompts the user to enter the SSN and the first and last names of 100 people. The program should then ask the user for an SSN, upon which it will search and display the first and last name of the person who holds that SSN.

Solution

According to everything you learned so far, the solution to this exercise is as follows.

```
                              project_37_5_4
Const PEOPLE = 100

Sub Main()
  Dim i As Integer
  Dim needle As String

  Dim SSNs(PEOPLE - 1) As String
  Dim first_names(PEOPLE - 1) As String
  Dim last_names(PEOPLE - 1) As String
  For i = 0 To PEOPLE - 1
    Console.Write("Enter SSN: ")
    SSNs(i) = Console.ReadLine()
    Console.Write("Enter first name: ")
    first_names(i) = Console.ReadLine()
    Console.Write("Enter last name: ")
    last_names(i) = Console.ReadLine()
  Next

  Console.Write("Enter an SSN to search: ")
  needle = Console.ReadLine()

  i = 0
  Do While i < PEOPLE - 1 And SSNs(i) <> needle
    i += 1
  Loop

  If SSNs(i) <> needle Then
    Console.WriteLine("Nothing found!")
  Else
    Console.WriteLine(first_names(i) & " " & last_names(i))
  End If

  Console.ReadKey()
End Sub
```

> **Notice:** In the United States, there is no possibility that two or more people will have the same SSN. Thus, even though it is not very clear in the wording of the exercise, each value in array SSNs is unique!

Exercise 37.5-5   *Searching in a Two-Dimensional Array that may Contain the Same Value Multiple Times*

Twelve teams participate in a football tournament, and each team plays 20 games, one game each week. Write a Visual Basic program that prompts the user to enter the name of each team and the letter "W" for win, "L" for loss, or "T" for tie (draw) for each game. Then the program should prompt the user for a letter (W, L, or T) and display, for each team, the week number(s) in which the team won, lost, or tied respectively. For example, if the user enters "L," the Visual Basic program should search and display, for each team, the week numbers (e.g., week 3, week 14, and so on) in which the team lost the game.

Solution

In this exercise, you need the following two arrays.

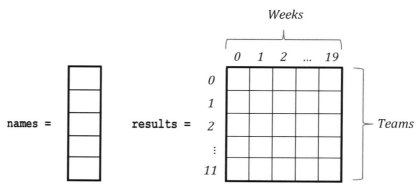

The corresponding Visual Basic program is as follows.

```
                                 project_37_5_5
Const TEAMS = 20
Const WEEKS = 12

Sub Main()

  Dim i, j As Integer
  Dim needle As String
  Dim found As Boolean

  Dim names(TEAMS - 1) As String
  Dim results(TEAMS - 1, WEEKS - 1) As String
  For i = 0 To TEAMS - 1
    Console.Write("Enter name for team No. " & (i + 1) & ": ")
    names(i) = Console.ReadLine()
    For j = 0 To WEEKS - 1
      Console.Write("Enter result for")
      Console.Write(" week No. " & (j + 1) & " for " & names(i) & ": ")
      results(i, j) = Console.ReadLine()
    Next
  Next

  Console.Write("Enter a result to search: ")
  needle = Console.ReadLine()

  For i = 0 To TEAMS - 1
    found = False
    Console.WriteLine("Found results for " & names(i))
    For j = 0 To WEEKS - 1
      If results(i, j).ToUpper() = needle.ToUpper() Then
        Console.WriteLine("Week No " & (j + 1))
        found = True
      End If
    Next
```

```
    If found = False Then
      Console.WriteLine("No results!")
    End If
  Next

  Console.ReadKey()
End Sub
```

Exercise 37.5-6   *Searching in a Two-Dimensional Array that Contains Unique Values*

A public opinion polling company makes phone calls in 10 cities and asks 30 citizens in each city whether or not they exercise. Write a Visual Basic program that prompts the user to enter each citizen's phone number and their answer (Y for Yes, N for No, S for Sometimes). The program should then prompt the user to enter a phone number, and it will search and display the answer that was given at this phone number. The program should also validate data input and accept only the values Y, N, or S as an answer.

Solution

In this exercise, you need the following two arrays.

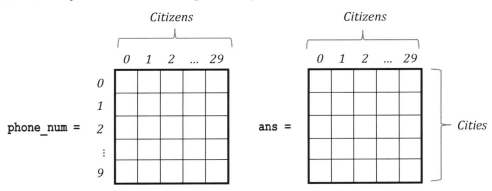

The corresponding Visual Basic program is as follows.

```
                          project_37_5_6
Const CITIES = 10
Const CITIZENS = 30

Sub Main()
  Dim i, j, position_i, position_j As Integer
  Dim found As Boolean
  Dim needle As String

  Dim phone_num(CITIES - 1,  CITIZENS - 1) As String
  Dim ans(CITIES - 1,  CITIZENS - 1) As String

  For i = 0 To CITIES - 1
    Console.WriteLine("City No. " & (i + 1))
```

```vb
    For j = 0 To CITIZENS - 1
      Console.Write("Enter phone number of citizen No. " & (j + 1) & ": ")
      phone_num(i, j) = Console.ReadLine()

      Console.Write("Enter the answer of citizen No. " & (j + 1) & ": ")
      ans(i, j) = Console.ReadLine().ToUpper()
      Do While ans(i, j) <> "Y" And ans(i, j) <> "N" And ans(i, j) <> "S"
        Console.Write("Wrong answer. Please enter a valid answer: ")
        ans(i, j) = Console.ReadLine().ToUpper()
      Loop
    Next
  Next

  Console.Write("Enter a phone number to search: ")
  needle = Console.ReadLine()

  found = False
  position_i = -1
  position_j = -1
  i = 0
  Do While i <= CITIES - 1 And found = False
    j = 0
    Do While j <= CITIZENS - 1 And found = False
      If phone_num(i, j) = needle Then
        found = True
        position_i = i
        position_j = j
      End If
      j += 1
    Loop
    i += 1
  Loop

  If found = False Then
    Console.WriteLine("Phone number not found!")
  Else
    Console.Write("Phone number " & phone_num(position_i, position_j))
    Console.Write(" gave '")

    If ans(position_i, position_j) = "Y" Then
      Console.Write("Yes")
    ElseIf ans(position_i, position_j) = "N" Then
      Console.Write("No")
    Else
      Console.Write("Sometimes")
    End If

    Console.Write("' as an answer")
  End If

  Console.ReadKey()
```

```
End Sub
```

Notice: *Please note how Visual Basic converts the user's answer to uppercase. Procedure chaining is a programming style that most programmers prefer to follow in Visual Basic.*

Exercise 37.5-7 *Checking if a Value Exists in all Columns*

Write a Visual Basic program that lets the user enter numeric values into a 20 × 30 array. After all of the values have been entered, the program then lets the user enter a value. A message should be displayed if the given value exists, at least once, in each column of the array.

Solution

This exercise can be solved using the linear search algorithm and a counter variable count. The Visual Basic program can iterate through the first column and if the given value is found, the variable count should increment by one. Then the program can iterate through the second column and if the given value is found again, the variable count should again increment by one. This process should repeat until all columns have been examined. At the end of the process, if the value of count is equal to the total number of columns, this means that the given value exists, at least once, in each column of the array.

Let's use the "from inner to outer" method. The following code fragment searches in first column (column index 0) of the array and if the given value is found, variable count increments by one. Assume variable j contains the value 0.

```
found = False
i = 0
Do While i <= ROWS - 1 And found = False
  If haystack(i, j) = needle Then
    found = True
  End If
  i += 1
Loop

If found = True Then
  count += 1
End If
```

Now you can nest this code fragment in a counted loop structure that iterates for all columns.

```
For j = 0 To COLUMNS - 1
  found = False
  i = 0
  Do While i <= ROWS - 1 And found = False
    If haystack(i, j) = needle Then
      found = True
    End If
    i += 1
  Loop

  If found = True Then
```

```
      count += 1
   End If
Next
```

You are almost ready—but think about it first! If the inner pre-test loop structure doesn't find the given value in a column, the outer loop control structure should stop iterating. It is pointless to continue because the given value does not exist in at least one column. Thus, a better approach would be to use a post-test loop structure for the outer loop as shown next.

```
j = 0
Do
   found = False
   i = 0
   Do While i <= ROWS - 1 And found = False
      If haystack(i, j) = needle Then
         found = True
      End If
      i += 1
   Loop

   If found = True Then
      count += 1
   End If

   j += 1
Loop While j <= COLUMNS - 1 And found = True
```

The main idea is to break out of the loop when the given value is **not** found in one column.

> **Notice**: You can use a pre-test loop structure as well, but you need to initially assign the value True to the variable found.

The final Visual Basic program is as follows.

```
                      project_37_5_7
Const ROWS = 20
Const COLUMNS = 30

Sub Main()
   Dim i, j, count As Integer
   Dim found As Boolean
   Dim needle As Double

   Dim haystack(ROWS - 1,  COLUMNS - 1) As Double
   For i = 0 To ROWS - 1
      For j = 0 To COLUMNS - 1
         haystack(i, j) = Console.ReadLine()
      Next
   Next

   Console.Write("Enter a value to search: ")
```

```
needle = Console.ReadLine()

count = 0
j = 0
Do
  found = False
  i = 0
  Do While i <= ROWS - 1 And found = False
    If haystack(i, j) = needle Then
      found = True
    End If
    i += 1
  Loop

  If found = True Then
    count += 1
  End If

  j += 1
Loop While j <= COLUMNS - 1 And found = True

If count = COLUMNS Then
  Console.WriteLine(needle & " found in every column!")
End If

Console.ReadKey()
End Sub
```

> **Notice**: *If you need a message to be displayed when a given value exists at least once in each* **row**, *the Visual Basic program can do the same as previously shown; however, instead of iterating through columns, it has to iterate through rows.*

Exercise 37.5-8 *The Binary Search Algorithm – Searching in a Sorted One-Dimensional Array*

Write a code fragment that searches a sorted one-dimensional array for a given value. Use the binary search algorithm.

Solution

The binary search algorithm is considered very fast and can be used with large scale data. Its main disadvantage, though, is that the data need to be sorted.

The main idea of the binary search algorithm is to check the value of the element in the middle (approximately). If it is not the "needle in the haystack" that you are looking for, and what you are looking for is actually smaller than the value of the middle element, it means that the "needle" must be in the first half of the array. On the other hand, if what you are looking for is larger than the value of the middle element, it means that the "needle" must be in the last half of the array.

The binary search algorithm continues by checking the value of the middle element in the remaining half part of the array. If it's still not the "needle," the search narrows to the half of the remaining part of the array that the "needle" could be in. This "splitting" process continues until the "needle" is found or the remaining part of the array consists of only one element. If that element is not the "needle," then the given value is not in the array.

Confused? Let's try to analyze the binary search algorithm through an example. The following array contains numeric values in ascending order. Assume that the "needle" that you are looking for is the value 44.

	0	1	2	3	4	5	6	7	8	9	10	11	12	13
A =	12	15	19	24	28	31	39	41	44	53	57	59	62	64

Three variables are used. Initially, variable start contains the value 0 (this is the index of the first element), variable end contains the value 12 (this is the index of the last element) and variable middle contains the value 6 (this is approximately the index of the middle element).

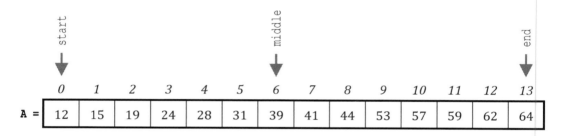

The "needle" (value 44) that you are looking for is larger than the value of 39 in the middle, thus the element that you are looking for must be in the last half of the array. Therefore, variable start is updated to point to index position 7 and variable middle is updated to a point in the middle between start (the new one) and end.

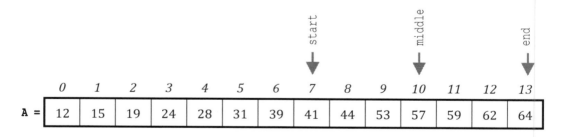

Now, the "needle" (value 44) that you are looking for is smaller than the value of 57 in the middle, thus the element that you are looking for must be in the first half of the remaining part of the array. Therefore, it is the variable end that is now updated to point to index position 9, and variable middle is updated to point to the middle between start and end (the new one).

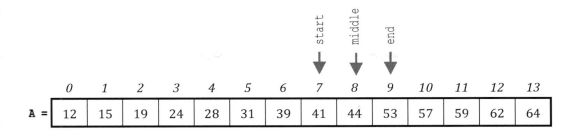

You are done! The "needle" has been found at index position 8 and the whole process can stop!

> **Remember!** *Each unsuccessful comparison reduces the number of elements left to check by half!*

Now, let's see the corresponding code fragment.

```
left = 0
right = ELEMENTS - 1
found = False
Do While left <= right And found = False
  middle = (left + right) \ 2    'This is a DIV 2 operation

  If haystack(middle) > needle Then
    right = middle - 1
  ElseIf haystack(middle) < needle Then
    left = middle + 1
  Else
    found = True
    index_position = middle
  End If
Loop

If found = False Then
  Console.WriteLine("Nothing found!")
Else
  Console.WriteLine(needle & " found at position: " & index_position)
End If
```

> **Notice**: *Using the binary search algorithm on the array of the example, the value of 44 can be found within just three iterations. On the other hand, for the same data, the linear search algorithm would need nine iterations!*
>
> **Notice**: *If the array contains a value multiple times, the binary search algorithm can find only one occurrence.*

Exercise 37.5-9   *Display all the Historical Events for a Country*

Write a Visual Basic program that prompts the user to enter the names of 10 countries and 20 important historical events for each country, including a brief description of each event. The Visual Basic program should then prompt the user to enter a country, and it will search and display all events for that country. Use the binary search algorithm. Assume that the user enters the names of the countries alphabetically.

Solution

In this exercise, the following two arrays are required.

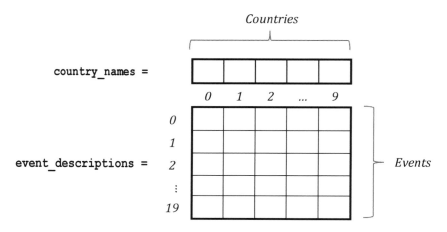

Assume that the user enters a country to search for, and the binary search algorithm finds that country, for example, at index position 2 of array country_names. The program can then use this value of 2 as a column index for the array event_descriptions, and it will display all the event descriptions of column 2.

The Visual Basic program is as follows.

```
                          project_37_5_9
Const EVENTS = 20
Const COUNTRIES = 10

Sub Main()
  Dim j, i, left, right, middle, index_position As Integer
  Dim found As Boolean
  Dim needle As String

  Dim country_names(COUNTRIES - 1) As String
  Dim event_descriptions(EVENTS - 1, COUNTRIES - 1) As String
  For j = 0 To COUNTRIES - 1
    Console.Write("Enter Country No. " & (j + 1) & ": ")
    country_names(j) = Console.ReadLine()
    For i = 0 To EVENTS - 1
      Console.Write("Enter description For event No. " & (i + 1) & ": ")
      event_descriptions(i, j) = Console.ReadLine()
    Next
```

```
    Next

    Console.Write("Enter a country to search: ")
    needle = Console.ReadLine().ToUpper()

    index_position = -1
    left = 0
    right = EVENTS - 1
    found = False
    Do While left <= right And found = False
      middle = (left + right) \ 2

      If country_names(middle).ToUpper().CompareTo(needle) > 0 Then
        right = middle - 1
      ElseIf country_names(middle).ToUpper().CompareTo(needle) < 0 Then
        left = middle + 1
      Else
        found = True
        index_position = middle
      End If
    Loop

    If found = False Then
      Console.WriteLine("No country found!")
    Else
      For i = 0 To EVENTS - 1
        Console.WriteLine(event_descriptions(i, index_position))
      Next
    End If

    Console.ReadKey()
  End Sub
```

Exercise 37.5-10 *Searching in Each Column of a Two-Dimensional Array*

Write a Visual Basic program that prompts the user to enter the names of 10 countries and 20 important historical events for each country, including a brief description and the corresponding year of each event. The Visual Basic program should then prompt the user to enter a year, and it will search and display all events that happened that year for each country. Use the binary search algorithm. Assume that for each country there is only one event in each year and that the user enters the events ordered by year in ascending order.

Solution

In this exercise, the following three arrays are required.

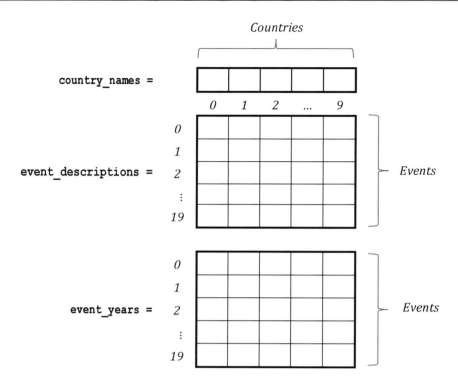

In order to write the code fragment that searches in each column of the array event_years, let's use the "from inner to outer" method. The next binary search algorithm searches in the first column (column index 0) for a given year. Assume that variable j contains the value 0. Since the search is performed vertically, and in order to increase program's readability, variables left and right have been replaced by variables top and bottom correspondingly.

```
top = 0
bottom = EVENTS - 1
found = False
Do While top <= bottom And found = False
  middle = (top + bottom) \ 2

  If event_years(middle, j) > needle Then
    bottom = middle - 1
  ElseIf event_years(middle, j) < needle Then
    top = middle + 1
  Else
    found = True
    row_index = middle
  End If
Loop

If found = False Then
  Console.WriteLine("No event found for country " & country_names(j))
Else
```

```
  Console.WriteLine("Country: " & country_names(j))
  Console.WriteLine("Year: " & event_years(row_index, j))
  Console.WriteLine("Event: " & event_descr(row_index, j))
End If
```

Now, nesting this code fragment in a counted loop structure that iterates for all columns results in the following.

```
For j = 0 To COUNTRIES - 1
  top = 0
  bottom = EVENTS - 1
  found = False
  Do While top <= bottom And found = False
    middle = (top + bottom) \ 2

    If event_years(middle, j) > needle Then
      bottom = middle - 1
    ElseIf event_years(middle, j) < needle Then
      top = middle + 1
    Else
      found = True
      row_index = middle
    End If
  Loop

  If found = False Then
    Console.WriteLine("No event found for country " & country_names(j))
  Else
    Console.WriteLine("Country: " & country_names(j))
    Console.WriteLine("Year: " & event_years(row_index, j))
    Console.WriteLine("Event: " & event_descr(row_index, j))
  End If
Next
```

The final Visual Basic program is as follows.

```
                          project_37_5_10
Const EVENTS = 20
Const COUNTRIES = 10

Sub Main()
  Dim j, i, needle, top, bottom, middle, row_index As Integer
  Dim found As Boolean

  Dim country_names(COUNTRIES - 1) As String
  Dim event_descriptions(EVENTS - 1,  COUNTRIES - 1) As String
  Dim event_years(EVENTS - 1,  COUNTRIES - 1) As Integer
  For j = 0 To COUNTRIES - 1
    Console.Write("Enter Country No. " & (j + 1) & ": ")
    country_names(j) = Console.ReadLine()
    For i = 0 To EVENTS - 1
      Console.Write("Enter description for event No. " & (i + 1) & ": ")
      event_descriptions(i, j) = Console.ReadLine()
```

```
            Console.Write("Enter year for event No. " & (i + 1) & ": ")
            event_years(i, j) = Console.ReadLine()
        Next
    Next

    Console.Write("Enter a year to search: ")
    needle = Console.ReadLine()
    row_index = -1

    For j = 0 To COUNTRIES - 1
        top = 0
        bottom = EVENTS - 1
        found = False
        Do While top <= bottom And found = False
            middle = (top + bottom) \ 2

            If event_years(middle, j) > needle Then
                bottom = middle - 1
            ElseIf event_years(middle, j) < needle Then
                top = middle + 1
            Else
                found = True
                row_index = middle
            End If
        Loop

        If found = False Then
            Console.WriteLine("No event found for country " & country_names(j))
        Else
            Console.WriteLine("Country: " & country_names(j))
            Console.WriteLine("Year: " & event_years(row_index, j))
            Console.WriteLine("Event: " & event_descriptions(row_index, j))
        End If
    Next

    Console.ReadKey()
End Sub
```

37.6 Exercises of a General Nature with Arrays

Exercise 37.6-1 *On Which Days was There a Possibility of Snow?*

Write a Visual Basic program that lets the user enter the temperatures (in degrees Fahrenheit) recorded at 12:00 p.m. each day for the 31 days of January. The Visual Basic program should then display the numbers of those days (1, 2, ..., 31) on which there was a possibility of snow, that is, those on which temperatures were below 36 degrees Fahrenheit (about 2 degrees Celsius).

Solution

The one-dimensional array for this exercise is shown next.

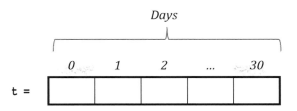

and the Visual Basic program is as follows.

```
                            project_37_6_1
Const DAYS = 31

Sub Main()
  Dim i As Integer

  Dim t(DAYS - 1) As Integer
  For i = 0 To DAYS - 1
    t(i) = Console.ReadLine()
  Next

  For i = 0 To DAYS - 1
    If t(i) < 36 Then
       Console.WriteLine((i + 1) & vbTab)
    End If
  Next

  Console.ReadKey()
End Sub
```

Exercise 37.6-2   *Was There Any Possibility of Snow?*

Write a Visual Basic program that lets the user enter the temperatures (in degrees Fahrenheit) recorded at 12:00 p.m. each day for the 31 days of January. The Visual Basic program should then display a message indicating if there was a possibility of snow, that is, if there were any temperatures below 36 degrees Fahrenheit (about 2 degrees Celsius).

Solution

Of course you **cannot** do what you did in the previous exercise. The next Visual Basic program is **incorrect**.

```
For i = 0 To DAYS - 1
  If t(i) < 36 Then
     Console.WriteLine("There was a possibility of snow in January!")
  End If
Next
```

The program is incorrect because if January had more than one day with a temperature below 36 degrees Fahrenheit, the same message would be displayed multiple times—and obviously you do not want this! You actually want to display a message once, regardless of whether January had one, two, or even more days below 36 degrees Fahrenheit.

There are two approaches, actually. Let's study them both.

First Approach – Counting all temperatures below 36 degrees Fahrenheit

In this approach, you can use a variable in the program to count all the days on which the temperature was below 36 degrees Fahrenheit. After all of the days have been examined, the program can check the value of this variable. If the value is not zero, it means that there was at least one day where there was a possibility of snow.

```
                         project_37_6_2a
Const DAYS = 31

Sub Main()
  Dim i, count As Integer

  Dim t(DAYS - 1) As Integer
  For i = 0 To DAYS - 1
    t(i) = Console.ReadLine()
  Next

  count = 0
  For i = 0 To DAYS - 1
    If t(i) < 36 Then
      count += 1
    End If
  Next

  If count <> 0 Then
    Console.WriteLine("There was a possibility of snow in January!")
  End If

  Console.ReadKey()
End Sub
```

Second Approach – Using a flag

In this approach, instead of counting all those days that had a temperature below 36 degrees Fahrenheit, you can use a Boolean variable (a flag). The solution is presented next.

```
                         project_37_6_2b
Const DAYS = 31

Sub Main()
  Dim i As Integer
  Dim found As Boolean

  Dim t(DAYS - 1) As Integer
  For i = 0 To DAYS - 1
    t(i) = Console.ReadLine()
  Next

  found = False
  For i = 0 To DAYS - 1
```

```
        If t(i) < 36 Then
            found = True
        End If
    Next

    If found = True Then
        Console.WriteLine("There was a possibility of snow in January!")
    End If

    Console.ReadKey()
End Sub
```

Exercise 37.6-3   *In Which Cities was There a Possibility of Snow?*

Write a Visual Basic program that prompts the user to enter the names of ten cities and their temperatures (in degrees Fahrenheit) recorded at 12:00 p.m. each day for the 31 days of January. The Visual Basic program should display the names of the cities in which there was a possibility of snow, that is, those in which temperatures were below 36 degrees Fahrenheit (about 2 degrees Celsius).

Solution

This exercise needs two arrays: one for entering the names of the cities, and one for entering their corresponding temperatures. The third auxiliary array (count), presented next, can be created by the program to count the total number of days on which each city had temperatures lower than 36 degrees Fahrenheit. Of course, you may wonder now why you need this extra array count. Just be patient! You will soon find out why!

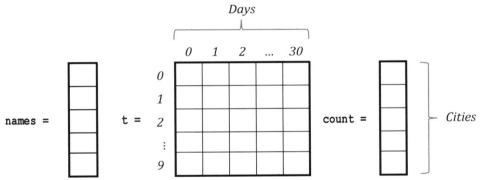

As in the previous exercise, you need to display each city name once, regardless of whether it may had one, two, or even more days below 36 degrees Fahrenheit.

To solve this exercise, there are actually two approaches. The first approach uses the previously mentioned auxiliary array count, whereas the second one uses just one extra Boolean variable (a flag). Obviously the second one is more efficient. But let's study them both.

First Approach – Using an auxiliary array

You were taught in Chapter 35 how to process each row individually. The nested loop control structure that can create the auxiliary array count is as follows.

```
Dim count(CITIES - 1) As Integer
```

```
For i = 0 To CITIES - 1
  count(i) = 0
  For j = 0 To DAYS - 1
    If a(i, j) < 36 Then
      count(i) += 1
    End If
  Next
Next
```

After array count is created you can iterate through it, and when a position contains a value other than zero, it means that the corresponding city had at least one day below 36 degrees Fahrenheit; thus the program must display the name of that city. The final Visual Basic program is presented next

project_37_6_3a

```
Const CITIES = 10
Const DAYS = 31

Sub Main()
  Dim i, j As Integer

  Dim names(CITIES - 1) As String
  Dim t(CITIES - 1,  DAYS - 1) As Integer
  For i = 0 To CITIES - 1
    Console.Write("Enter a name for city No: " & (i + 1) & ": ")
    names(i) = Console.ReadLine()
    For j = 0 To DAYS - 1
      Console.Write("Enter a temperature for day No: " & (j + 1) & ": ")
      t(i, j) = Console.ReadLine()
    Next
  Next

  Dim count(CITIES - 1) As Integer
  For i = 0 To CITIES - 1
    count(i) = 0
    For j = 0 To DAYS - 1
      If t(i, j) < 36 Then
        count(i) += 1
      End If
    Next
  Next

  Console.Write("Cities in which there was")
  Console.WriteLine(" a possibility of snow in January: ")
  For i = 0 To CITIES - 1
    If count(i) <> 0 Then
      Console.WriteLine(names(i))
    End If
  Next

  Console.ReadKey()
End Sub
```

Second Approach – Using a flag

This approach does not use an auxiliary array. It processes array t and directly displays any city name that had a temperature below 36 degrees Fahrenheit. But how can this be done without displaying a city name twice, or even more than twice? This is where you need a flag, that is, an extra Boolean variable.

To better understand this approach, let's use the "from inner to outer" method. The following code fragment checks if the first row of array t (row index 0) contains at least one temperature below 36 degrees Fahrenheit; if so, it displays the corresponding city name that exists at position 0 of the array names. Assume variable i contains the value 0.

```
found = False
For j = 0 To DAYS - 1
  If t(i, j) < 36 Then
     found = True
  End If
Next

If found = True Then
   Console.WriteLine(names(i))
End If
```

Now that everything has been clarified, in order to process the whole array t, you can just nest this code fragment in a counted loop structure that iterates for all cities, as follows.

```
For i = 0 To CITIES - 1
  found = False
  For j = 0 To DAYS - 1
    If t(i, j) < 36 Then
       found = True
    End If
  Next

  If found = True Then
     Console.WriteLine(names(i))
  End If
Next
```

The final Visual Basic program is as follows.

```
                        project_37_6_3b
Const CITIES = 10
Const DAYS = 31

Sub Main()
  Dim i, j As Integer
  Dim found As Boolean

  Dim names(CITIES - 1) As Integer
  Dim t(CITIES - 1,  DAYS - 1) As Integer
  For i = 0 To CITIES - 1
    Console.Write("Enter a name for city No: " & (i + 1) & ": ")
    names(i) = Console.ReadLine()
    For j = 0 To DAYS - 1
```

```
            Console.Write("Enter a temperature for day No: " & (j + 1) & ": ")
            t(i, j) = Console.ReadLine()
        Next
    Next

    Console.Write("Cities in which there was")
    Console.WriteLine(" a possibility of snow in January: ")
    For i = 0 To CITIES - 1
        found = False
        For j = 0 To DAYS - 1
            If t(i, j) < 36 Then
                found = True
            End If
        Next

        If found = True Then
            Console.WriteLine(names(i))
        End If
    Next

    Console.ReadKey()
End Sub
```

Exercise 37.6-4   *Display from Highest to Lowest Grades by Student, and in Alphabetical Order*

There are 10 students and each one of them has received his or her grades for five lessons. Write a Visual Basic program that lets a teacher enter the name of each student and his or her grades for all lessons. The program should then calculate each student's average grade, and display the names of the students sorted by their average grade in descending order. Moreover, if two or more students have the same average grade, their names should be displayed in alphabetical order.

Solution

In this exercise, you need the following three arrays. The values for the arrays names and grades will be entered by the user, whereas the auxiliary array average will be created by the Visual Basic program.

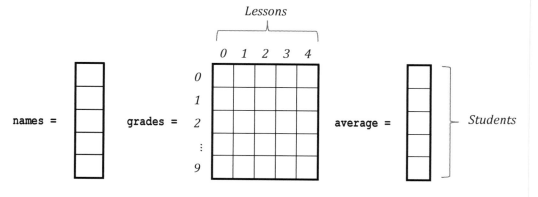

You already know how to do everything in this exercise. You know how to create the auxiliary array average, you know how to sort the array average while preserving the relationship with the elements of the array names, and you know how to handle the case in which, if two average grades are equal, the corresponding student names should be sorted alphabetically. The final Visual Basic program is as follows.

```
                           project_37_6_4
Const STUDENTS = 10
Const LESSONS = 5

Sub Main()
  Dim i, j, m, n As Integer
  Dim temp As Double
  Dim temp_str As String

  'Read array names and grades
  Dim names(STUDENTS - 1) As String
  Dim grades(STUDENTS - 1, LESSONS - 1) As Integer
  For i = 0 To STUDENTS - 1
    Console.Write("Enter name for student No. " & (i + 1) & ": ")
    names(i) = Console.ReadLine()
    For j = 0 To LESSONS - 1
      Console.Write("Enter grade for lesson No. " & (j + 1) & ": ")
      grades(i, j) = Console.ReadLine()
    Next
  Next

  'Create array average
  Dim average(STUDENTS - 1) As Double
  For i = 0 To STUDENTS - 1
    average(i) = 0
    For j = 0 To LESSONS - 1
      average(i) += grades(i, j)
    Next
    average(i) /= LESSONS
  Next

  'Sort arrays average and names
  For m = 1 To STUDENTS - 1
    For n = STUDENTS - 1 To m Step -1
      If average(n) > average(n - 1) Then
        temp = average(n)
        average(n) = average(n - 1)
        average(n - 1) = temp

        temp_str = names(n)
        names(n) = names(n - 1)
        names(n - 1) = temp_str
      ElseIf average(n) = average(n - 1) Then
        If names(n).CompareTo(names(n - 1)) < 0 Then
          temp_str = names(n)
```

```
                names(n) = names(n - 1)
                names(n - 1) = temp_str
            End If
          End If
       Next
     Next

     'Display arrays names and average
     For i = 0 To STUDENTS - 1
        Console.WriteLine(names(i) & vbTab & average(i))
     Next

     Console.ReadKey()
   End Sub
```

Exercise 37.6-5　　*Archery at the Summer Olympics*

In archery at the Summer Olympics, 20 athletes each shoot six arrows. Write a Visual Basic program that prompts the user to enter the name of each athlete, and the points awarded for each shot. The program should then display the names of the three athletes that won the gold, silver, and bronze medals depending on which athlete obtained the highest sum of points. Assume that no two athletes have an equal sum of points.

Solution

In this exercise, you need the following three arrays. The values for the arrays names and points will be entered by the user, whereas the auxiliary array sum will be created by the Visual Basic program.

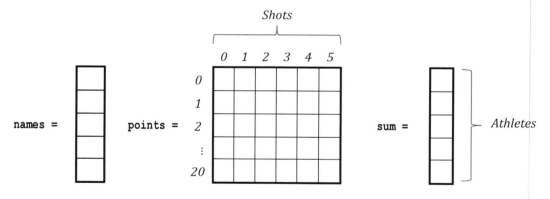

After the auxiliary array sum is created, a sorting algorithm can sort the array sum in descending order (while preserving the relationship with the elements of the array names). The Visual Basic program can then display the names of the three athletes at index positions 0, 1, and 2 (since these are the athletes that should win the gold, the silver, and the bronze medals respectively). The solution is presented next.

```
                          project_37_6_5
Const ATHLETES = 20
Const SHOTS = 6
```

```
Sub Main()
  Dim i, j, m, n, temp As Integer
  Dim temp_str As String

  'Read array names and points
  Dim names(ATHLETES - 1) As String
  Dim points(ATHLETES - 1,  SHOTS - 1) As Integer
  For i = 0 To ATHLETES - 1
    Console.Write("Enter name for athlete No. " & (i + 1) & ": ")
    names(i) = Console.ReadLine()
    For j = 0 To SHOTS - 1
      Console.Write("Enter points for shot No. " & (j + 1) & ": ")
      points(i, j) = Console.ReadLine()
    Next
  Next

  'Create array sum
  Dim sum(ATHLETES - 1) As Integer
  For i = 0 To ATHLETES - 1
    sum(i) = 0
    For j = 0 To SHOTS - 1
      sum(i) += points(i, j)
    Next
  Next

  'Sort arrays names and sum
  For m = 1 To ATHLETES - 1
    For n = ATHLETES - 1 To m Step -1
      If sum(n) > sum(n - 1) Then
        temp = sum(n)
        sum(n) = sum(n - 1)
        sum(n - 1) = temp

        temp_str = names(n)
        names(n) = names(n - 1)
        names(n - 1) = temp_str
      End If
    Next
  Next

  'Display gold, silver and bronze metal
  For i = 0 To 2
    Console.WriteLine(names(i) & vbTab & sum(i))
  Next

  Console.ReadKey()
End Sub
```

37.7   Review Questions: True/False

Choose **true** or **false** for each of the following statements.

1. The main idea of the bubble sort algorithm (when sorting an array in ascending order) is to repeatedly move the smallest elements of the array to the lowest index positions.

2. In an array sorted in ascending order, the first element is the greatest of all.

3. When using the bubble sort algorithm, the total number of swaps depends on the given array.

4. When using the modified bubble sort algorithm, the case in which the algorithm performs the greatest number of swaps is when you want to sort in descending order an array that is already sorted in ascending order.

5. In the bubble sort algorithm, when the decision control structure tests the Boolean expression $A(n) > A(n - 1)$, it means that the elements of array A are being sorted in descending order.

6. Sorting algorithms sort letters in the same way that they sort numbers.

7. If you want to sort an array A but preserve the relationship with the elements of an array B, you must rearrange the elements of array B as well.

8. The bubble sort algorithm sometimes performs better than the modified bubble sort algorithm.

9. According to the bubble sort algorithm, in each pass (except the last one) only one element is placed in proper position.

10. The bubble sort algorithm can be implemented only by using counted loop structures.

11. The quick sort algorithm cannot be used to sort each column of a two-dimensional array.

12. The insertion sort algorithm can sort in either descending or ascending order.

13. One of the fastest sorting algorithms is the modified bubble sort algorithm.

14. The bubble sort algorithm, for a one-dimensional array of N elements, performs $\frac{N-1}{N}$ compares.

15. The bubble sort algorithm, for a one-dimensional array of N elements, performs $\frac{N(N-1)}{2}$ passes.

16. When using the modified bubble sort algorithm, if a complete pass is performed and no swaps have been done, then the algorithm knows the array is sorted and there is no need for further passes.

17. When using the selection sort algorithm, if you wish to sort an array in descending instead of ascending order, you need to search for maximum instead of minimum values.

18. The selection sort algorithm performs very well on computer systems in which the limited main memory comes into play.

19. The selection sort algorithm is suitable for large scale data operations.

20. The selection sort algorithm is a very complex algorithm.

21. The insertion sort algorithm generally performs better than the selection and the bubble sort algorithm.

22. The insertion sort algorithm can sometimes prove even faster than the quicksort algorithm.

23. The quicksort algorithm is considered one of the best and fastest sorting algorithms.

24. A sorted array contains only elements that are different from each other.

25. A search algorithm is an algorithm that searches for an item with specific properties within a set of data.

26. The sequential search algorithm can be used only on arrays that contain arithmetic values.

27. One of the most commonly used search algorithms is the quick search algorithm.

28. One searching algorithm is called the heap algorithm.

29. A linear (or sequential) search algorithm can work as follows: it can check if the last element of the array is equal to a given value, then it can check the last but one element, and so on, until the beginning of the array or until the given value is found.

30. The linear search algorithm can, in certain situations, find an element faster than the binary search algorithm.

31. The linear search algorithm can be used in large scale data operations.

32. The linear search algorithm cannot be used in sorted arrays.

33. The binary search algorithm can be used in large scale data operations.

34. If an array contains a value multiple times, the binary search algorithm can find only the first occurrence of a given value.

35. When using search algorithms, if an array contains unique values and the element that you are looking for is found, there is no need to check any further.

36. The main disadvantage of the binary search algorithm is that data needs to be sorted.

37. The binary search algorithm can be used only in arrays that contain arithmetic values.

38. If the element that you are looking for is in the last position of an array, the linear search algorithm will examine all the elements of the array.

39. The linear search algorithm can be used on two-dimensional arrays.

40. When using the binary search algorithm, if the element that you are looking for is at the first position of an array that contains at least three elements, the algorithm will find it in just one iteration.

37.8   Review Exercises

Complete the following exercises.

1.   Design a flowchart and write the corresponding Visual Basic program that lets the user enter 50 positive numerical values into an array. The algorithm, and consequently the Visual Basic program, should then create a new array of 47 elements. In this new array, each position should contain the average value of four elements: the values that exist in the current and the next three positions of the given array.

2.   Write a Visual Basic program that lets the user enter numerical values into arrays a, b, and c, of 15 elements each. The program should then create a new

array new_arr of 15 elements. In this new array, each position should contain the lowest value of arrays a, b, and c, for the corresponding position.

Next, design the corresponding flowchart fragment for only that part of your program that creates the array new_arr.

3. Write a Visual Basic program that lets the user enter numerical values into arrays a, b, and c, of 10, 5, and 15 elements respectively. The program should then create a new array new_arr of 30 elements. In this new array, the first 15 positions should contain the elements of array c, the next five positions should contain the elements of array b, and the last 10 positions should contains the elements of array a.

Next, design the corresponding flowchart fragment for only that part of your program that creates the array new_arr.

4. Write a Visual Basic program that lets the user enter numerical values into arrays a, b, and c, of 5 × 10, 5 × 15, and 5 × 20 elements respectively. The program should then create a new array new_arr of 5 × 45 elements. In this new array, the first 10 columns should contain the elements of array a, the next 15 columns should contain the elements of array b, and the last 20 rows should contain the elements of array c.

5. Write a Visual Basic program that lets the user enter 50 numerical values into an array and then creates two new arrays, reals and integers. The array reals should contain the real values given, whereas the array integers should contain the integer values. The value 0 (if any) should not be added to any of the final arrays, either reals or integers.

Next, design the corresponding flowchart fragment for only that part of your program that creates the arrays reals and integers.

6. Design a flowchart and write the corresponding Visual Basic program that lets the user enter 50 three-digit integers into an array. The algorithm, and consequently the Visual Basic program, then creates a new array containing only the integers in which the first digit is less than the second digit and the second digit is less than the third digit. For example, the values 357, 456, and 159 are such integers.

7. A public opinion polling company asks 200 citizens to each score 10 consumer products. Write a Visual Basic program that prompts the user to enter the name of each product and the score each citizen gave (A, B, C, or D). The program should then calculate and display the following:

     a. for each product, the name of the product and the number of citizens that gave it an "A"

     b. for each citizen, the number of "B" responses he or she gave

     c. which product or products are considered the best

Moreover, the program should validate data input and display an error message when the user enters any score with a value other than A, B, C, or D.

8. Write a Visual Basic program that prompts the user to enter the names of 20 U.S. cities and the names of 20 Canadian cities and then, for each U.S. city, the distance (in miles) from each Canadian city. Finally, the program should display, for each U.S. city, its closest Canadian city.

9. Design a flowchart and write the corresponding Visual Basic program that lets the user enter the names and the heights of 30 mountains, as well as the country in which each one belongs. The algorithm, and consequently the Visual Basic program, should then display all available information about the highest and the lowest mountain.

10. Design the flowchart fragment of an algorithm that, for a given array A of N × M elements, finds and displays the maximum value as well as the row and the column in which this value was found.

11. Twenty-six teams participate in a football tournament. Each team plays 15 games, one game each week. Write a Visual Basic program that lets the user enter the name of each team and the letter "W" for win, "L" for loss, and "T" for tie (draw) for each game. If a win receives 3 points and a tie 1 point, the Visual Basic program should find and display the name of the team that wins the championship based on which team obtained the greatest sum of points. Assume that no two teams have an equal sum of points.

12. On Earth, a free-falling object has an acceleration of 9.81 m/s² downward. This value is denoted by g. A student wants to calculate that value using an experiment. She allows 10 different objects to fall downward from a known height, and measures the time they need to reach the floor. She does this 20 times for each object. She needs a Visual Basic program that allows her to enter the height (from which objects are left to fall), as well as the measured times that they take to reach the floor. The program should then calculate g and store all calculated values in a 10 × 20 array. However, her chronometer is not so accurate, so she needs the program to find and display the minimum and the maximum calculated values of g for each object, as well as the overall minimum and maximum calculated values of g of all objects.

The required formula is

$$S = u_o + \frac{1}{2}gt^2$$

where

➤ **S** is the distance that the free-falling objects traveled, in meters (m)

➤ **u_o** is the initial velocity (speed) of the free-falling objects in meters per second (m/sec). However, since the free-falling objects start from rest, the value of u_0 should be zero.

➤ **t** is the time that it took the free-falling object to reach the floor, in seconds (sec)

➤ **g** is the acceleration, in meters per second² (m/sec²)

13. Ten measuring stations, one in each city, record the daily CO_2 levels for a period of a year. Write a Visual Basic program that lets the user enter the name of each city and the CO_2 levels recorded at 12:00 p.m. each day. The Visual Basic program then displays the name of the city that has the clearest atmosphere (on average).

14. Design the flowchart fragment of an algorithm that, for a given array A of N × M elements, finds and displays the minimum and the maximum values of each row.

15. Twenty teams participate in a football tournament, and each team plays 10 games, one game each week. Write a Visual Basic program that prompts the user to enter the name of each team and the letter "W" for win, "L" for loss, and "T" for

tie (draw) for each game. If a win receives 3 points and a tie 1 point, the Visual Basic program should find and display the names of the teams that win the gold, the silver, and the bronze medals based on which team obtained the greatest sum of points. Use the modified bubble sort algorithm. Assume that no two teams have an equal sum of points.

Moreover, the program should validate data input and display an error message when the user enters any letter other than W, L, or T.

16. Write a Visual Basic program that prompts the user to enter the names and the heights of 50 people. The program should then display this information, sorted by height, in descending order. Moreover, if two or more people have the same height, their names should be displayed in alphabetical order. Use the bubble sort algorithm, adapted accordingly.

17. In a song contest there are 10 judges, each of whom scores 12 artists for their performance. However, according to the rules of this contest, the total score is calculated after excluding the maximum and the minimum score. Write a Visual Basic program that prompts the user to enter the names of the artists and the score they get from each judge. The program should then display

    a. for each artist, his or her name and total score, after excluding the maximum and the minimum scores.

    b. the final classification, starting with the artist that has the greatest score. However, if two or more artists have the same score, their names should be displayed in alphabetical order. Use the bubble sort algorithm, adapted accordingly.

18. Design the flowchart fragment of an algorithm that, for a given array A of 5 × 10 elements, sorts each column in ascending order using the selection sort algorithm. Assume that the array contains numerical values.

19. In a Sudoku contest, 10 people each try to solve as quickly as possible eight different Sudoku puzzles. Write a Visual Basic program that lets the user enter the name of each contestant and their time to complete each puzzle. The program should then display

    a. for each contestant, his or her name and his or her three best times.

    b. the names of the three contestants that win the gold, the silver, and the bronze medals based on which contestant obtained the lowest average time. Assume that no two contestants have an equal average time.

    Use the selection sort algorithm when necessary.

20. Design the flowchart fragment of an algorithm that, for a given array A of 20 × 8 elements, sorts each row in descending order using the insertion sort algorithm. Assume that the array contains numerical values.

21. Five measuring stations, one in each city, record the daily CO_2 levels on an hourly basis for a period of two days. Write a Visual Basic program that lets the user enter the name of each city and the CO_2 levels recorded every hour (00:00 to 23:00). The Visual Basic program then displays

    a. for each city, its name and its average CO_2 level (per hour)

    b. for each hour, the average CO_2 level (per city)

    c. the hour in which the atmosphere was most polluted (on average)

    d. the hour and the city in which the highest level of CO_2 was recorded

  e. the three cities with the dirtiest atmosphere (on average), using the insertion sort algorithm

22. Design the flowchart fragment of the linear search algorithm that searches array a of N elements for the value `needle` and displays the position(s) at which `needle` is found. If `needle` is not found, the message "Not found" should be displayed. Assume that the array contains numerical values.

23. Design the flowchart fragment of the binary search algorithm that searches array a of N elements for the value `needle` and displays the position at which `needle` is found. If `needle` is not found, the message "Not found" should be displayed. Assume that the array contains numerical values.

24. Ten teams participate in a football tournament, and each team plays 16 games, one game each week. Write a Visual Basic program that prompts the user to enter the name of each team, the number of goals the team scored, and the number of goals the team let in for each match. A win receives 3 points and a tie receives 1 point. The Visual Basic program should prompt the user for a team name and then it finds and displays the total number of points for this team. If the given team name is not found, the message "This team does not exist" should be displayed.

  Assume that no two teams have the same name. Moreover, the program should validate data input and display an error message when the user enters any non-numeric or negative number of goals.

25. In a high school, there are two classes, with 20 and 25 students respectively. Write a Visual Basic program that prompts the user to enter the names of the students in two separate arrays. The program then displays the names of each class independently in ascending order. Afterwards, the program prompts the user to enter a name and it searches for that given name in both arrays. If the student's name is found, the program should display the message "Student found in class No..."; otherwise the message "Student not found in either class" should be displayed. Assume that both arrays contain unique names.

  Hint: Since the arrays are sorted and the names are unique, you can use the binary search algorithm.

26. Suppose there are two arrays, `usernames` and `passwords`, that contain the login information of 100 employees of a company. Design a flowchart fragment and write the corresponding code fragment that prompts the user to enter a username and a password and then displays the message "Login OK!" when the combination of username and password is valid; the message "Login Failed!" should be displayed otherwise. Assume that usernames are unique but passwords are not. Moreover, both usernames and passwords are not case sensitive.

27. Suppose there are two arrays, `names` and `SSNs`, that contain the names and the SSNs (Social Security Numbers) of 1000 U.S. citizens. Write a code fragment that prompts the user to enter a value (it can be either a name or an SSN) and then searches for and displays the names of all the people that have this name or this SSN. If the given value is not found, the message "This value does not exist" should be displayed.

28. There are 12 students and each one of them has received his or her grades for six lessons. Write a Visual Basic program that lets the user enter the grades for all

lessons and then displays a message indicating whether or not there is at least one student that has an average value below 70.

Moreover, the program should validate data input and display individual error messages when the user enters any non-numeric character, negative value, or a value greater than 100.

Review Questions in "Arrays"

Answer the following questions.

1. What limitation do variables have that arrays don't?
2. What is an array?
3. What is each item of an array called?
4. In an array of 100 elements, what is the index of the last element?
5. What does "iterating through rows" mean?
6. What does "iterating through columns" mean?
7. What is the significance to programmers of variables i and j?
8. What is a square array?
9. What is the main diagonal of a square array?
10. What is the antidiagonal of a square array?
11. Write the code fragment in general form that validates data input without displaying any error messages.
12. Write the code fragment in general form that validates data input and displays an error message, regardless of the type of error.
13. Write the code fragment in general form that validates data input and displays an individual error message for each error.
14. What is a sorting algorithm?
15. Name five sorting algorithms.
16. Which sorting algorithm is considered the most inefficient?
17. Can a sorting algorithm be used to find the minimum or the maximum value of an array?
18. Why is a sorting algorithm not the best option to find the minimum or the maximum value of an array?
19. Write the code fragment that sorts array a of N elements in ascending order, using the bubble sort algorithm. Assume that the array contains numerical values.
20. How many compares can the bubble sort algorithm perform?
21. When does the bubble sort algorithm perform the maximum number of swaps?
22. Using the bubble sort algorithm, write the code fragment that sorts array a but preserves the relationship with the elements of array b of N elements in ascending order. Assume that the array a contains numerical values.
23. Using the modified bubble sort algorithm, write the code fragment that sorts array a of N elements in ascending order. Assume that the array contains numerical values.
24. Using the selection sort algorithm, write the code fragment that sorts array a of N elements in ascending order. Assume that the array contains numerical values.
25. Using the insertion sort algorithm, write the code fragment that sorts array a of N elements in ascending order. Assume that the array contains numerical values.
26. What is a searching algorithm?

27. Name the two most commonly used search algorithms.
28. What are the advantages and disadvantages of the linear search algorithm?
29. Using the linear search algorithm, write the code fragment that searches array a for value `needle`. Assume that the array contains numerical values.
30. What are the advantages and disadvantages of the binary search algorithm?
31. Using the binary search algorithm, write the code fragment that searches array a for value `needle`. Assume that the array contains numerical values and is sorted in ascending order.

Section 7
Subprograms

Chapter 38
Introduction to Subprograms (Procedures)

38.1 What is Procedural Programming?

Suppose you were assigned a project to solve the drug abuse problem in your area. One possible approach, which could prove very difficult or even impossible, would be to try to solve this problem by yourself! A better approach would be to subdivide the large problem into smaller subproblems such as prevention, treatment, and rehabilitation. Then, with the help of specialists from a variety of fields, you would build a team to help solve the drug problem. The following diagram shows how each subproblem could be further subdivided into even smaller subproblems.

As the supervisor of this project, you could rent a building and establish within it three departments: the prevention department, with all of its subdepartments; the treatment department, with all of its subdepartments; and the rehabilitation department with all of its subdepartments. Finally, you would hire staff and employ them to do the job for you!

Procedural programming does exactly the same thing. It subdivides an initial problem into smaller subproblems, and each subproblem is further subdivided into smaller subproblems. Finally, for each subproblem a small subprogram (procedure) would be written, and the main program (as does the supervisor), employs (calls) them to do job!

Procedural programming has several advantages:

 ➢ It enables programmers to reuse the same code whenever it is necessary without having to copy it.
 ➢ It is relatively easy to implement.
 ➢ It helps programmers follow the flow of execution more easily.

> *Notice*: A very large program can prove very difficult to debug and maintain when it is all in one piece. For this reason, it is often easier to subdivide it into smaller subprograms, each of which performs a clearly defined process.
>
> *Notice*: Writing large programs without subdividing them into smaller subprograms results in a code referred to as "spaghetti code"!

38.2 What is Modular Programming?

In modular programming, subprograms (procedures) of common functionality are grouped together into separate modules, and each module can have its own set of data. Therefore, a program can consist of more than one part, and each of those smaller parts (modules) can contain one or more subprograms.

If you were to use modular programming in the previous drug problem example, then you could have one building to host the prevention department and all of its subdepartments, a second building to host the treatment department and all of its subdepartments, and a third building to host the rehabilitation department and all of its subdepartments. As shown in the next diagram, the three buildings could be thought as three different modules.

38.3 What Exactly is a Subprogram?

In computer science, a subprogram (Visual Basic calls it procedure) is a block of statements packaged as a unit that performs a specific task. A subprogram can be employed (called) in a program several times, whenever that specific task needs to be performed.

A built-in Visual Basic procedure is an example of such a subprogram. Take the already known Math.Abs() procedure, for example. It consists of a block of statements that are packaged as a unit under the name "Abs," and they perform a specific task—they return the absolute value of a number.

> **Notice**: *If you are wondering what kind of statements might exist inside procedure* Math.Abs(), *here is a possible block of statements.*
>
> ```
> If number < 0 Then
>   Return number * (-1)
> Else
>   Return number
> End If
> ```

In Visual Basic there are two kinds of subprograms: functions and subprocedures. The difference between a function and a subprocedure is that a function returns a result, whereas a subprocedure doesn't. However, in some computer languages, this distinction may not quite be apparent. There are languages in which a function can behave as a subprocedure and return no result, and there are languages in which a subprocedure can return one or even more than one result.

> **Notice**: Depending on the computer language being used, the meaning of the terms "functions" and "subprocedures" may vary. For example, in FORTRAN you can find them as "functions" and "subroutines."

38.4 Review Questions: True/False

Choose **true** or **false** for each of the following statements.

1. Procedural programming helps you write "spaghetti code."

2. Procedural programming subdivides the initial problem into smaller subproblems.

3. An advantage of procedural programming is the ability to reuse the same code whenever it is necessary without having to copy it.

4. Procedural programming helps programmers follow the flow of execution more easily.

5. Modular programming improves a program's execution speed.

6. In modular programming, subprograms of common functionality are grouped together into separate modules.

7. In modular programming, each module can have its own set of data.

8. Modular programming uses different structures than structured programming does.

9. A program can consist of more than one module.

10. A subprogram is a block of statements packaged as a unit that performs a specific task.

11. In Visual Basic, the difference between a function and a subprocedure is that a subprocedure returns a result, whereas a function does not.

12. There are two kinds of subprograms.

13. Visual Basic supports only subprocedures.

Chapter 39
User-Defined Functions

39.1   Writing your Own Functions in Visual Basic

In Visual Basic, and by extension in the majority of computer languages, there are two kinds of functions. There are the built-in functions, such as Fix(), and there are the user-defined functions, those that you can actually write and use in your own programs.

The general form of a Visual Basic function is

```
Function name([arg1 As type1, arg2 As type2, arg3 As type3, …]) As return_type
  Local variables declaration section


  A statement or block of statements
  Return value
End Function
```

where

 ➢ *name* is the name of the function. It follows the same rules as those used for variable names

 ➢ *arg1*, *arg2*, *arg3*, … is a list of arguments (variables) used to pass values from the caller to the function. There can be as many arguments as you want.

 ➢ *type1*, *type2*, *type3*, … is the data type of each argument. Each argument must have a data type.

 ➢ *return_type* is the data type of the value that the function returns.

 ➢ *value* is the arithmetic, alphanumeric, or Boolean value that is returned to the caller. It can be a constant value, a variable, an expression, or even an array. Its data type must match the *return_type* of the function.

> **Notice**: *Please note that arguments are optional; that is, a function may contain no arguments.*

For example, the next function calculates the sum of two numbers and returns the result.

```
Function get_sum(num1 As Double, num2 As Double) As Double
  Dim result As Double


  result = num1 + num2
  Return result
End Function
```

Of course, this can also be written as

```
Function get_sum(num1 As Double, num2 As Double) As Double
  Return num1 + num2
End Sub
```

39.2 How Do You Call a Function?

Every call to a user-defined function is as follows: you write the name of the function followed by a list of arguments (if necessary), either within a statement that assigns function's returned value to a variable or directly within an expression.

Let's see some examples. Suppose there is a function `cube_root()` that accepts an argument (a numeric value) and returns its 3rd root. To calculate the expression

$$y = \sqrt[3]{x} + \frac{1}{x}$$

you can either assign the cube root of x to a variable, as shown here

```
x = Console.ReadLine()
cb = cube_root(x)
y = cb + 1 / x
Console.Write(y)
```

or you can call the function directly in an expression,

```
x = Console.ReadLine()
y = cube_root(x) + 1 / x
Console.Write(y)
```

or you can even call the function directly in an `Console.Write` statement.

```
x = Console.ReadLine()
Console.Write(cube_root(x) + 1 / x)
```

Now let's see a more complete example. The next Visual Basic program creates the function `get_message()` and then the main code calls it. The returned value is assigned to variable a.

project_39_2a

```
Function get_message() As String
    Dim msg As String

    msg = "Hello Zeus"
    Return msg
End Sub
```

This creates the function `get_message()`

This is the main code

```
Sub Main()
    Dim a As String

    Console.WriteLine("Hi there!")
    a = get_message()
    Console.Write(a)

    Console.ReadKey()
End Sub
```

> **Notice:** *Please note that subprograms must be written outside of the* `Main` *subprocedure.*
>
> **Notice:** *Please note that a function does not execute immediately when a program starts running. The first statement that actually executes in this example is the statement* `Console.WriteLine("Hi there!")`*.*

You can also pass (send) values to a function, as long as at least one argument exists within the function's parenthesis. In the next example, the function `display()` is called three times but each time a different value is passed through the argument `color`.

```
project_39_2b
Function display(color As String) As String
  Dim msg As String
  msg = "There is " & color & " in the rainbow"
  Return msg
End Function

Sub Main()
  Console.WriteLine(display("red"))
  Console.WriteLine(display("yellow"))
  Console.WriteLine(display("blue"))

  Console.ReadKey()
End Sub
```

If you run this program, the following messages are displayed.

```
There is red in the rainbow
There is yellow in the rainbow
There is blue in the rainbow
```

In the next example, two values must be passed to function `display()`.

```
project_39_2c
Function display(color As String, exists As Boolean) As String
  Dim neg As String
  neg = ""
  If exists = False Then
    neg = "n't any"
  End If

  Return "There is" & neg & " " & color & " in the rainbow"
End Function

Sub Main()
  Console.WriteLine(display("red", True))
  Console.WriteLine(display("yellow", True))
  Console.Write(display("black", False))

  Console.ReadKey()
End Sub
```

If you run this program the following messages are displayed.

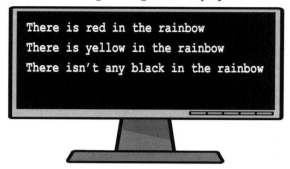

> **Notice**: *You can place your functions either above or below your main code. Most programmers, though, prefer to have them all on the top for better observation.*

39.3   Formal and Actual Arguments

Each function contains an argument list called a "formal argument list." As already stated, arguments in this list are optional; the formal argument list may contain no arguments, one argument, or more than one argument.

When the function is called, an argument list is passed to the function. This list is called an "actual argument list."

In the next example, variables n1, n2, n3, and n4 constitute the formal argument list whereas variables a, b, c, and d constitute the actual argument list.

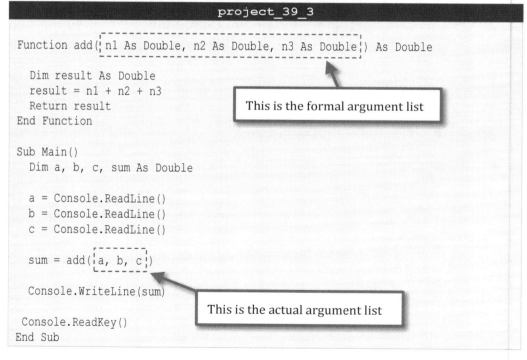

> **Notice:** *Please note that there is a one-to-one match between the formal and the actual arguments. The value of argument* a *is passed to argument* n1, *the value of argument* b *is passed to argument* n2, *and so on. Moreover, the data type of a formal and the data type of an actual argument must match. You cannot, for example, pass a string to an argument of type integer!*

39.4 How Does a Function Execute?

When the main code calls a function the following steps are performed:

> ➤ The execution of the statements of the main code is interrupted.

> ➤ The values of the variables or the result of the expressions that exist in the actual argument list are passed (assigned) to the corresponding arguments (variables) in the formal argument list, and the flow of execution goes to where the function is written.

> ➤ The statements of the function are executed.

> ➤ When the flow of execution reaches the end of the function, a value is returned from the function to the main code and the flow of execution continues from where it was before calling the function.

In the next Visual Basic program, the function maximum() accepts two arguments (numeric values) and returns the greater of the two values.

```
project_39_4
Function maximum(val1 As Double, val2 As Double) As Double
    Dim m As Double

    m = val1
    If val2 > m Then
        m = val2
    End If
    Return m
End Function

Sub Main()
    Dim a, b, max As Double

    a = Console.ReadLine()
    b = Console.ReadLine()
    max = maximum(a, b)
    Console.Write(max)

    Console.ReadKey()
End Sub
```

When the Visual Basic program starts running, the first statement executed is the statement a = Console.ReadLine() (this is considered the first statement of the program). Suppose the user enters the values 3 and 8. Below is a trace table that shows the exact flow of execution, how the values of the variables a and b are passed from the main code to the function, and how the function returns its result.

Step	Statements of Main Code	a	b	max
1	a = Console.ReadLine()	3	?	?

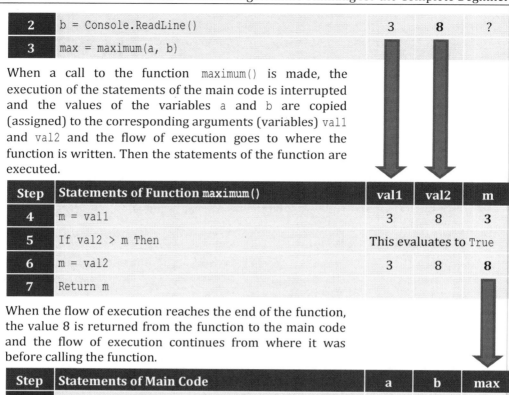

Step		a	b	?
2	`b = Console.ReadLine()`	3	8	?
3	`max = maximum(a, b)`			

When a call to the function `maximum()` is made, the execution of the statements of the main code is interrupted and the values of the variables `a` and `b` are copied (assigned) to the corresponding arguments (variables) `val1` and `val2` and the flow of execution goes to where the function is written. Then the statements of the function are executed.

Step	Statements of Function `maximum()`	val1	val2	m
4	`m = val1`	3	8	3
5	`If val2 > m Then`	This evaluates to True		
6	`m = val2`	3	8	8
7	`Return m`			

When the flow of execution reaches the end of the function, the value 8 is returned from the function to the main code and the flow of execution continues from where it was before calling the function.

Step	Statements of Main Code	a	b	max
8	`Console.Write(max)`	3	8	8

Exercise 39.4-1   *Back to Basics – Calculating the Sum of Two Numbers*

Do the following:

    i.   *Write a function named* sum() *that accepts two numeric values through its formal argument list and then calculates and returns their sum.*

    ii.   *Using the function* sum() *cited above, write a Visual Basic program that lets the user enter two numbers and then displays their sum. Next, create a trace table to determine the values of the variables in each step of the Visual Basic program for two different executions.*

          The input values for the two executions are: (i) 2, 4; and (ii) 10, 20.

Solution

In this exercise you need to write a function that accepts two values from the caller (this is the main code) and then calculates and returns their sum. The solution is shown here.

```
                         project_39_4_1
Function sum(a As Double, b As Double) As Double
   Dim s As Double

   s = a + b
   Return s
End Function
```

```
Sub Main()
  Dim num1, num2, result As Double

  num1 = Console.ReadLine()
  num2 = Console.ReadLine()

  result = sum(num1, num2)
  Console.Write("The sum of " & num1 & " + " & num2 & " is " & result)

  Console.ReadKey()
End Sub
```

Now, let's create the corresponding trace tables. Since you have become more experienced with them, the column "Notes" has been removed.

i. For the input values of 2, 4, the trace table looks like this.

Step	Statement	Main Code			Function sum()		
		num1	num2	result	a	b	s
1	num1 = Console.ReadLine()	2	?	?			
2	num2 = Console.ReadLine()	2	4	?			
3	result = sum(num1, num2)				2	4	?
4	s = a + b				2	4	6
5	Return s	2	4	6			
6	Console.Write("The sum of…	The message "The sum of 2 + 4 is 6" is displayed.					

ii. For the input values of 10, 20, the trace table looks like this.

Step	Statement	Main Code			Function sum()		
		num1	num2	result	a	b	s
1	num1 = Console.ReadLine()	10	?	?			
2	num2 = Console.ReadLine()	10	20	?			
3	result = sum(num1, num2)				10	20	?
4	s = a + b				10	20	30
5	Return s	10	20	30			
6	Console.Write("The sum of…	The message "The sum of 10 + 20 is 30" is displayed.					

Exercise 39.4-2   *Calculating the Sum of Two Numbers Using Fewer Lines of Code!*

Rewrite the Visual Basic program of the previous exercise using fewer lines of code.

Solution

The solution is shown here.

```
project_39_4_2
Function sum(a As Double, b As Double) As Double
  Return a + b
End Function

Sub Main()
  Dim num1, num2 As Double

  num1 = Console.ReadLine()
  num2 = Console.ReadLine()

  Console.Write("The sum of " & num1 & "+" & num2 & " is " & sum(num1, num2))

  Console.ReadKey()
End Sub
```

Contrary to the solution of the previous exercise, in this function `sum()` the sum is not assigned to variable s but it is directly calculated and returned. Furthermore, this main code doesn't assign the returned value to a variable but directly displays it.

Notice: User-defined functions can be called just like the built-in functions of Visual Basic.

39.5   Review Questions: True/False

Choose **true** or **false** for each of the following statements.

1. There are two categories of functions in Visual Basic.
2. The variables that are used to pass values to a function are called arguments.
3. The function `Fix()` is a user-defined function.
4. Every call to a user-defined function is made in the same way as a call to the built-in functions of Visual Basic.
5. There can be as many arguments as you wish in a function's formal argument list.
6. In a function, the formal argument list must contain at least one argument.
7. In a function, the formal argument list is optional.
8. A function cannot return an array.
9. The statement
   ```
   Return x + 1
   ```
   is a valid Visual Basic statement.
10. A formal argument can be an expression.
11. An actual argument can be an expression.
12. A function can have no arguments in the actual argument list.
13. The next statement calls the function `cube_root()` three times.
    ```
    cb = cube_root(x) + cube_root(x) / 2 + cube_root(x) / 3
    ```

14. The following code fragment

```
cb = cube_root(x)
y = cb + 5
Console.Write(y)
```

displays exactly the same value as the statement

```
Console.Write(cube_root(x) + 5)
```

15. A function must always include a Return statement.

16. The name play-the-guitar can be a valid function name.

17. You can place your functions either above or below your main code.

18. When the main code calls a function, the execution of the statements of the main code is interrupted.

19. In general, it is possible for a function to return no values to the caller.

20. The procedure Math.Abs() is a built-in procedure of Visual Basic.

21. The following code fragment

```
Function add(a As Double, b As Double) As Double
   Return a / b
End Function

Sub Main()
   Dim a As Double = 10
   Dim b As Double = 5
   Console.Write(add(b, a))

   Console.ReadKey()
End Sub
```

displays the value 0.5.

22. The following code fragment

```
y = cube_root(x)
y += 5
```

is equivalent to the statement

```
y = 5 + cube_root(x)
```

39.6   Review Exercises

Complete the following exercises.

1. The following function contains two errors. Can you spot them?

```
Function find_max(a As Integer, b As Integer) As Integer
   If a > b Then
      max = a
   Else
      max = b
   End If
End Function
```

2. Create a trace table to determine the values of the variables in each step of the following Visual Basic program.

```vb
Function sum_digits(a As Integer) As Integer
  Dim d1, d2 As Integer

  d1 = a Mod 10
  d2 = a \ 10

  Return d1 + d2
End Function

Sub Main()
  Dim s, i As Integer

  s = 0
  For i = 25 To 27
    s += sum_digits(i)
  Next
  Console.Write(s)

  Console.ReadKey()
End Sub
```

3. Create a trace table to determine the values of the variables in each step of the following Visual Basic program.

```vb
Function sss(a As Integer) As Integer
  Dim k, sum As Integer

  sum = 0
  For k = 1 To a
    sum += k
  Next
  Return sum
End Function

Sub Main()
  Dim i, s As Integer

  i = 1
  s = 0
  Do While i < 6
    If i Mod 2 = 1 Then
      s += 1
    Else
      s += sss(i)
    End If
    i += 1
  Loop
  Console.Write(s)

  Console.ReadKey()
```

```
End Sub
```

4. Create a trace table to determine the values of the variables in each step of the following Visual Basic program when the value 12 is entered.

```
Function custom_div(b As Integer, d As Integer) As Integer
  Return (b + d) \ 2
End Function

Sub Main()
  Dim k, m, a, x As Integer

  k = Console.ReadLine()
  m = 2
  a = 1
  Do While a < 6
    If k Mod m <> 0 Then
      x = custom_div(a, m)
    Else
      x = a + m + custom_div(m, a)
    End If
    Console.WriteLine(m & " " & a & " " & x)
    a += 2
    m += 1
  Loop

  Console.ReadKey()
End Sub
```

5. Write a function named my_round() that accepts a real (a double) through its formal argument list and returns it rounded to two decimal places. Try not to use the Math.Round() procedure of Visual Basic.

6. Do the following:

   i. Write a function named find_min() that accepts two numbers through its formal argument list and returns the lowest one.

   ii. Using the function find_min() cited above, write a Visual Basic program that prompts the user to enter four numbers and then displays the lowest one.

7. Do the following:

   i. Write a function named Kelvin_to_Fahrenheit() that accepts a temperature in degrees Kelvin through its formal argument list and returns its degrees Fahrenheit equivalent.

   ii. Write a function named Kelvin_to_Celsius() that accepts a temperature in degrees Kelvin through its formal argument list and returns its degrees Celsius equivalent.

   iii. Using the functions Kelvin_to_Fahrenheit() and Kelvin_to_Celsius() cited above, write a Visual Basic program that prompts the user to enter a temperature in degrees Kelvin and then displays its degrees Fahrenheit and its degrees Celsius equivalent.

   It is given that

$$Kelvin = \frac{Fahrenheit + 459.67}{1.8}$$

and

$$Kelvin = Celsius + 273.15$$

8. The Body Mass Index (BMI) is often used to determine whether a person is overweight or underweight for his or her height. The formula used to calculate the BMI is

$$BMI = \frac{weight \cdot 703}{height^2}$$

Do the following:

i. Write a function named bmi() that accepts a weight and a height through its formal argument list and then returns an action (a message) according to the following table.

BMI	Action
BMI < 16	You must add weight.
16 ≤ BMI < 18.5	You should add some weight.
18.5 ≤ BMI < 25	Maintain your weight.
25 ≤ BMI < 30	You should lose some weight.
30 ≤ BMI	You must lose weight.

ii. Using the function bmi() cited above, write a Visual Basic program that prompts the user to enter his or her weight (in pounds), age (in years), and height (in inches), and then calculates and displays the corresponding message. Moreover, the program should validate data input and display an error message when the user enters

a. any non-numeric or negative value for weight

b. any non-numeric or negative value for height

c. any non-numeric, or a value less than 18 for age

Chapter 40

User-Defined Subprocedures

40.1 Writing your Own Subprocedures in Visual Basic

The only difference between a subprocedure and a function is that a subprocedure does not directly return a result.

The general form of a Visual Basic subprocedure is

```
Sub name([arg1 As type1, arg2 As type2, arg3 As type3, …])
  Local variables declaration section

  A statement or block of statements
End Sub
```

where

> ➤ *name* is the name of the subprocedure. It follows the same rules as those used for variable names.

> ➤ *arg1, arg2, arg3,* … is a list of arguments (variables) used to pass values from the caller to the subprocedure. There can be as many arguments as you want.

> ➤ *type1, type2, type3,* … is the data type of each argument. Each argument must have a data type.

> **Notice**: *Please note that arguments are optional; that is, a subprocedure may contain no arguments.*
>
> **Remember!** *The difference between a function and a subprocedure is that a function returns a result, whereas a subprocedure doesn't.*

For example, the next subprocedure calculates the sum of two numbers and displays the result.

```
Sub display_sum(num1 As Double, num2 As Double)
  Dim result As Double

  result = num1 + num2
  Console.WriteLine(result)
End Sub
```

> **Notice**: *In C, as well as in other similar computer languages such as C++, a subprogram that returns no result is known as a void function.*

40.2 How Do You Call a Subprocedure?

You can call a subprocedure by just writing its name. The next example creates the subprocedure display_line() and the main code calls the subprocedure whenever it needs to display a horizontal line.

```
                          project_40_2a
Sub display_line()
  Console.WriteLine("----------------------------")
```

```
End Sub

Sub Main()
  Console.WriteLine("Hello there!")
  display_line()
  Console.WriteLine("How Do you do?")
  display_line()
  Console.WriteLine("What is your name?")
  display_line()

  Console.ReadKey()
End Sub
```

You can also pass (send) values to a subprocedure, as long as at least one argument exists in subprocedure's parenthesis. In the next example, the subprocedure display_line() is called three times but each time a different value is passed through the variable length, resulting in three printed lines of different length.

project_40_2b

```
Sub display_line(length As Integer)
  Dim i As Integer

  For i = 1 To length
    Console.Write("-")
  Next
  Console.WriteLine()
End Sub

Sub Main()
  Console.WriteLine("Hello there!")
  display_line(12)
  Console.WriteLine("How Do you do?")
  display_line(14)
  Console.WriteLine("What is your name?")
  display_line(18)

  Console.ReadKey()
End Sub
```

Remember! *Since a subprocedure returns no value, you **cannot** assign the returned value to a variable. The following line of code is **wrong.***

```
y = display line(12)
```

*Also, you **cannot** call a subprocedure within a statement. The following line of code is also **wrong.***

```
Console.WriteLine( "Hello there!" & display_line(12) )
```

40.3 Formal and Actual Arguments

Each subprocedure contains an argument list called a formal argument list. As already stated, arguments in this list are optional. The formal argument list may contain no arguments, one argument, or more than one argument.

When the subprocedure is called, an argument list is passed to the subprocedure. This list is called the actual argument list.

In the next example, the variables n1, n2, n3, and n4 constitute the formal argument list whereas variables a, b, c, and d constitute the actual argument list.

project_40_3

```
Sub add_and_display (n1 As Double, n2 As Double, n3 As Double, n4 As Double)
    Dim result As Double

    result = n1 + n2 + n3 + n4
    Console.WriteLine(result)
End Sub                                    This is the formal argument list


Sub Main()
    Dim a, b, c, d As Double

    a = Console.ReadLine()
    b = Console.ReadLine()
    c = Console.ReadLine()                 This is the actual argument list
    d = Console.ReadLine()

    add_and_display (a, b, c, d)

    Console.ReadKey()
End Sub
```

Remember! There is a one-to-one match between the formal and the actual arguments. The value of argument a is passed to argument number1, the value of argument b is passed to argument number2, and so on. Moreover, the data type of the formal and the data type of the corresponding actual argument must match. You cannot, for example, pass a string to an argument of type integer!

40.4 How Does a Subprocedure Execute?

When the main code calls a subprocedure, the following steps are performed:

➢ The execution of the statements of the main code is interrupted.

➢ The values of the variables or the result of the expressions that exist in the actual argument list are passed (assigned) to the corresponding arguments (variables) in the formal argument list and the flow of execution goes to where the subprocedure is written.

➢ The statements of the subprocedure are executed.

➢ When the flow of execution reaches the end of the subprocedure, the flow of execution continues from where it was before calling the subprocedure.

In the next Visual Basic program, the subprocedure minimum() accepts three arguments (numeric values) through its formal argument list and displays the lowest value.

```
project_40_4
Sub minimum(val1 As Double, val2 As Double, val3 As Double)
    Dim min As Double

    min = val1
    If val2 < min Then
        min = val2
    End If
    If val3 < min Then
        min = val3
    End If
    Console.Write(min)
End Sub

Sub Main()
    Dim a, b, c As Double

    a = Console.ReadLine()
    b = Console.ReadLine()
    c = Console.ReadLine()

    minimum(a, b, c)
    Console.Write("The end")

    Console.ReadKey()
End Sub
```

When the Visual Basic program starts running, the first statement executed is the statement
a = Console.ReadLine() (this is considered the first statement of the program). Suppose the user enters the values 9, 6, and 8.

Step	Statements of Main Code	a	b	c
1	a = Console.ReadLine()	9	?	?
2	b = Console.ReadLine()	9	6	?
3	c = Console.ReadLine()	9	6	8
4	minimum(a, b, c)			

When a call to the subprocedure minimum() is made, the execution of the statements of the main code is interrupted and the values of the variables a, b, and c are copied (assigned) to the corresponding arguments (variables) val1, val2, and val3, and the flow of execution goes to where the subprocedure is written. Then the statements of the subprocedure are executed.

Step	Statements of Subprocedure minimum()	val1	val2	val3	min
5	min = val1	9	6	8	9

6	If val2 < min Then	This evaluates to True			
7	min = val2	9	6	8	6
8	If val3 < min Then	This evaluates to False			
9	Console.Write(min)	Value 6 is displayed			

When the flow of execution reaches the end of the subprocedure the flow of execution simply continues from where it was before calling the subprocedure.

Step	Statements of Main Code	a	b	c
10	Console.Write("The end")	The message "The end" is displayed.		

> *Notice: Please note that at step 10 no values are returned from the subprocedure to the main code.*

Exercise 40.4-1 *Back to Basics – Displaying the Absolute Value of a Number*

Do the following:

i. *Write a subprocedure named* display_abs() *that accepts a numeric value through its formal argument list and then displays its absolute value. Do not use the built-in* Math.Abs() *procedure of Visual Basic.*

ii. *Using the subprocedure* display_abs() *cited above, write a Visual Basic program that lets the user enter a number and then displays its absolute value followed by the initial value given. Next, create a trace table to determine the values of the variables in each step of the Visual Basic program for two different executions.*

The input values for the two executions are: (i) 5, and (ii) -5.

Solution

In this exercise you need to write a subprocedure that accepts a value from the caller (this is the main code) and then calculates and displays its absolute value. The solution is shown here.

```
                        project_40_4_1
Sub display_abs(n As Double)
  If n < 0 Then
    n = (-1) * n
  End If
  Console.WriteLine(n)
End Sub

Sub Main()
  Dim a As Double

  a = Console.ReadLine()
  display_abs(a)          'This displays the absolute value of given number.
  Console.WriteLine(a)    'This displays the initial number given.
```

```
    Console.ReadKey()
End Sub
```

Now, let's create the corresponding trace tables. As already stated, since you have become more experienced with trace tables, the column "Notes" has been removed.

    i.   For the input value of 5, the trace table looks like this.

Step	Statement	Main Code	Subprocedure display_abs()
		a	n
1	a = Console.ReadLine()	5	
2	display_abs(a)		5
3	If n < 0 Then	This evaluates to False	
4	Console.WriteLine(n)	Value 5 is displayed	
5	Console.WriteLine(a)	Value 5 is displayed	

    ii.   For the input value of -5, the trace table looks like this.

Step	Statement	Main Code	Subprocedure display_abs()
		a	n
1	a = Console.ReadLine()	-5	
2	display_abs(a)		-5
3	If n < 0 Then	This evaluates to True	
4	n = (-1) * n		5
5	Console.WriteLine(n)	Value 5 is displayed	
6	Console.WriteLine(a)	Value –5 is displayed	

> **Notice**: Please note that at step 5 the variable n of the subprocedure contains the value 5 but when the flow of execution returns to the main code at step 6, the variable a of the main code contains the value -5. Actually, the value of variable a of the main code had never changed!

Exercise 40.4-2   *A Simple Currency Converter*

Do the following:

    i.   *Write a subprocedure named* display_menu() *that displays the following menu.*

        1. Convert USD to Euro (EUR)

        2. Convert Euro (EUR) to USD

        3. Exit

    ii.   *Using the subprocedure* display_menu() *cited above, write a Visual Basic program that displays the previously mentioned menu and prompts the user to enter a choice (of 1, 2, or 3) and an amount of money. The program should then calculate* *and display the required value. The process should repeat as many times as the user wishes. It is given that $1 = 0.72 EUR (€).*

Solution

The solution is very simple and needs no further explanation.

```
                          project_40_4_2
Sub display_menu()
  Console.WriteLine("1. Convert USD to Euro (EUR)")
  Console.WriteLine("2. Convert Euro (EUR) to USD")
  Console.WriteLine("3. Exit")
  Console.WriteLine("---------------------------")
  Console.Write("Enter a choice: ")
End Sub

Sub Main()
  Dim choice As Integer
  Dim amount As Double

  Do
    display_menu()
    choice = Console.ReadLine()

    If choice = 3 Then
      Console.WriteLine("Bye!")
    Else
      Console.Write("Enter an amount: ")
      amount = Console.ReadLine()
      If choice = 1 Then
        Console.WriteLine(amount & " USD = " & amount * 0.72 & " Euro")
      Else
        Console.WriteLine(amount & " Euro = " & amount / 0.72 & " USD")
      End If
    End If
  Loop While choice <> 3
End Sub
```

40.5   Review Questions: True/False

Choose **true** or **false** for each of the following statements.

1. In Visual Basic, a subprogram that returns no result is known as a subprocedure.
2. In Visual Basic, you can call a subprocedure just by writing its name.
3. In a subprocedure call that is made in main code, within the actual argument list there must be only variables of the main code.
4. In a subprocedure, all formal arguments must have different names.
5. An actual argument can be an expression.
6. A subprocedure must always include at least one argument in its formal argument list.
7. There is a one-to-one match between the formal and the actual arguments.

8. You can call a subprocedure within a statement.

9. When the flow of execution reaches the end of a subprocedure, the flow of execution continues from where it was before calling the subprocedure.

10. A subprocedure returns no values to the caller.

11. It is possible for a subprocedure to accept no values from the caller.

12. A call to a subprocedure is made differently from a call to a function.

13. In the following Visual Basic program

```
Sub message()
  Console.Write("Hello Aphrodite!")
End Sub

Sub Main()
  Console.WriteLine("Hi there!")
  message()

  Console.ReadKey()
End Sub
```

the first statement that executes is the statement `Console.Write("Hello Aphrodite!")`.

40.6 Review Exercises

Complete the following exercises.

1. Create a trace table to determine the values of the variables in each step of the following Visual Basic program when the values 3, 7, 9, 2, and 4 are entered.

```
Sub display(a As Integer)
  If a Mod 2 = 0 Then
     Console.WriteLine(a & " is even")
  Else
     Console.WriteLine(a & " is odd")
  End If
End Sub

Sub Main()
  Dim i, x As Integer

  For i = 1 To 5
    x = Console.ReadLine()
    display(x)
  Next

  Console.ReadKey()
End Sub
```

2. Create a trace table to determine the values of the variables in each step of the following Visual Basic program.

```
Sub division(a As Integer, b As Integer)
  b = b \ a
  Console.WriteLine(a * b)
```

```
End Sub

Sub Main()
  Dim x, y As Integer

  x = 20
  y = 30
  Do While x Mod y < 30
    division(y, x)
    x = 4 * y
    y += 1
  Loop

  Console.ReadKey()
End Sub
```

3. Create a trace table to determine the values of the variables in each step of the following Visual Basic program when the values 2, 3, and 4 are entered.

```
Sub calculate(n As Integer)
  Dim j As Integer
  Dim s As Double

  s = 0
  For j = 2 To 2 * n Step 2
    s = s + j ^ 2
  Next

  Console.WriteLine(s)
End Sub

Sub Main()
  Dim i, m As Integer

  For i = 1 To 3
    m = Console.ReadLine()
    calculate(m)
  Next

  Console.ReadKey()
End Sub
```

4. Write a subprocedure that accepts five values through its formal argument list and then displays the greatest value.

5. Do the following:

   i.   Write a subprocedure named num_of_days() that accepts a year and a month (1 – 12) through its formal argument list and then displays the number of days in that month. Take special care when a year is a leap year; that is, a year in which February has 29 instead of 28 days.

        Hint: A year is a leap year when it is exactly divisible by 4 and not by 100, or when it is exactly divisible by 400.

    ii. Using the subprocedure `num_of_days()` cited above, write a Visual Basic program that prompts the user to enter a year and then displays the number of the days in each month of that year.

6. Do the following:

    i. Write a subprocedure named `display_menu()` that displays the following menu.

       1. Convert meters to miles

       2. Convert miles to meters

       3. Exit

    ii. Write a subprocedure named `meters_to_miles()` that accepts a value in meters through its formal argument list and then displays the message "XX meters equals YY miles" where XX and YY must be replaced by actual values.

    iii. Write a subprocedure named `miles_to_meters()` that accepts a value in miles through its formal argument list and then displays the message "YY miles equals XX meters" where XX and YY must be replaced by actual values.

    iv. Using the subprocedures `meters_to_miles()` and `miles_to_meters()` cited above, write a Visual Basic program that displays the previously mentioned menu and prompts the user to enter a choice (of 1, 2, or 3) and a distance. The program should then calculate and display the required value. The process should repeat as many times as the user wishes. It is given that 1 mile = 1609.344 meters.

7. The LAV Cell Phone Company charges customers a basic rate of $10 per month, and additional rates are charged based on the total number of seconds a customer talks on his or her cell phone within the month. Use the rates shown in the following table.

Number of Seconds a Customer Talks on his or her Cell Phone	Additional Rates (in USD per second)
1 – 600	Free of charge
601 – 1200	$0.01
1201 and above	$0.02

Do the following:

    i. Write a subprocedure named `amount_to_pay()` that accepts a number in seconds through its formal argument list and then displays the total amount to pay. Please note that the rates are progressive. Moreover, federal, state, and local taxes add a total of 11% to each bill

    ii. Using the subprocedure `amount_to_pay()` cited above, write a Visual Basic program that prompts the user to enter the number of seconds he or she talks on the cell phone and then displays the total amount to pay.

Chapter 41
Tips and Tricks with Subprograms

41.1 Can Two Subprograms use Variables of the Same Name?

You should realize something: each subprogram uses its own memory space to hold the values of its variables. Even the main code has its own memory space! This means that you can have a variable named `test` in main code, another variable named `test` in a subprogram, and yet another variable named `test` in another subprogram. Pay attention! Those three variables are three completely different variables, in different memory locations, and they can hold completely different values.

The trace table in the following example can help you understand what really goes on.

```
                          project_41_1a
Function f1() As Boolean
   Dim test As Integer
   test = 22
   Console.WriteLine(test)
   Return True
End Function

Sub f2(test As Integer)
   Console.WriteLine(test)
End Sub

Sub Main()
   Dim test As Integer
   Dim ret As Boolean

   test = 5
   Console.WriteLine(test)
   ret = f1()
   f2(10)
   Console.WriteLine(test)

   Console.ReadKey()
End Sub
```

The trace table is shown here.

Step	Statement	Notes	Main Code		Function f1()	Subprocedure f2()
			test	ret	test	test
1	test = 5		5	?		
2	Console.WriteLine(test)	Value 5 is displayed	5	?		
3	ret = f1()	f1() is called			?	

4	test = 22				22	
5	Console.WriteLine(test)	Value 22 is displayed			22	
6	Return True	It returns to the main code	5	**True**		
7	f2(10)	f2() is called				10
8	Console.WriteLine(test)	Value 10 is displayed				10
9	Console.WriteLine(test)	Value 5 is displayed	5	True		

As you can see in the trace table, there are three variables named test in three different memory locations and each one of them holds a completely different value.

Now, let's see something else. In the next Visual Basic program, the variable test of the main code is passed to function f1() through an argument that also happens to be a variable named test. As already stated, even though both variables have the same name, they are actually two different variables in two different locations in main memory! In reality, this means that although f1() alters the value of its variable test, when the flow of execution returns to the main code, this change does not affect the value of the variable test of the main code.

```
                          project_41_1b
Sub f1(test As Integer)
   test += 1
   Console.WriteLine(test)    'This is the variable of
                              'subprocedure f1(). Value 6 is displayed

End Sub

Sub Main()
   Dim test As Integer

   test = 5
   f1(test)
   Console.WriteLine(test)    'This is the variable of
                              'the main code. Value 5 is displayed

   Console.ReadKey()
End Sub
```

> **Notice**: Please note that variables used in a subprogram "live" as long as the subprogram is being executed. This means that before calling the subprogram, none of its variables (including those in the formal argument list) exists in main memory (RAM). They are all created in the main memory when the subprogram is called, and they are all removed from the main memory when the subprogram finishes and the flow of execution returns to the caller. The only variables that "live" forever, or at least for as long as the Visual Basic program is being executed, are the variables of the main code and the global variables!

41.2 Can a Subprogram Call Another Subprogram?

All the time you've been reading this section, you may have had the impression that only the main code can call a subprogram. Of course, this is not true!

A subprogram can call any other subprogram which in turn can call another subprogram, and so on. You can make whichever combination you wish. For example, you can write a function that calls a subprocedure, a subprocedure that calls a function, a function that calls another function, or even a function that calls one of the built-in procedures of the computer language that you are using to write your programs.

The next example presents exactly this situation. The main code calls the subprocedure display_sum(), which in turn calls the function add().

```
project_41_2
Function add(number1 As Integer, number2 As Integer) As Integer
  Dim result As Integer

  result = number1 + number2
  Return result
End Function

Sub display_sum(num1 As Integer, num2 As Integer)
  Console.WriteLine(add(num1, num2))
End Sub

Sub Main()
  Dim a, b As Integer

  a = Console.ReadLine()
  b = Console.ReadLine()

  display_sum(a, b)

  Console.ReadKey()
End Sub
```

> *Notice: Please note that there is no restriction on the order in which the two subprograms should be written. It would have been exactly the same if the subprocedure* display_sum() *had been written before the function* add()*.*

Exercise 41.2-1   *A Currency Converter – Using Functions with Subprocedures*

Do the following:

i.   *Write a subprogram named* display_menu() *that displays the following menu.*

1.   *Convert USD to Euro (EUR)*

2.   *Convert USD to British Pound Sterling (GBP)*

3.   *Convert USD to Japanese Yen (JPY)*

4.   *Convert USD to Canadian Dollar (CAD)*

5.   *Exit*

    ii.   *Write four different subprograms named* `USD_to_EU()`, `USD_to_GBP()`, `USD_to_JPY()`, *and* `USD_to_CAD()`, *that accept a currency through their formal argument list and then return the corresponding converted value.*

    iii.   *Using the five subprograms cited above, write a Visual Basic program that displays the menu previously mentioned and then prompts the user to enter a choice (of 1, 2, 3, 4, or 5) and an amount in US dollars. The program should then calculate and display the required value. The process should repeat as many times as the user wishes. It is given that*

         ➢   *$1 = 0.72 EUR (€)*
         ➢   *$1 = 0.60 GBP (£)*
         ➢   *$1 = ¥ 102.15 JPY*
         ➢   *$1 = 1.10 CAD ($)*

Solution

This solution combines the use of both functions and subprocedures. The four functions that convert currencies accept a value through an argument and then they return the corresponding value. The solution is shown here.

```
                              project_41_2_1
Sub display_menu()
  Console.WriteLine("1. Convert USD to Euro (EUR)")
  Console.WriteLine("2. Convert USD to British Pound Sterling (GBP)")
  Console.WriteLine("3. Convert USD to Japanese Yen (JPY)")
  Console.WriteLine("4. Convert USD to Canadian Dollar (CAD)")
  Console.WriteLine("5. Exit")
  Console.WriteLine("-----------------------------------------------")
  Console.Write("Enter a choice: ")
End Sub

Function USD_to_EU(value As Double) As Double
  Return value * 0.72
End Function

Function USD_to_GBP(value As Double) As Double
  Return value * 0.6
End Function

Function USD_to_JPY(value As Double) As Double
  Return value * 102.15
End Function

Function USD_to_CAD(value As Double) As Double
  Return value * 1.1
End Function

Sub Main()
  Dim choice As Integer
```

```
Dim amount As Double

Do
  display_menu()
  choice = Console.ReadLine()

  If choice = 5 Then
    Console.WriteLine("Bye!")
  Else
    Console.Write("Enter an amount in US dollars: ")
    amount = Console.ReadLine()
    Select choice
      Case 1
        Console.WriteLine(amount & " USD = " & USD_to_EU(amount) & " Euro")
      Case 2
        Console.WriteLine(amount & " USD = " & USD_to_GBP(amount) & " GBP")
      Case 3
        Console.WriteLine(amount & " USD = " & USD_to_JPY(amount) & " JPY")
      Case 4
        Console.WriteLine(amount & " USD = " & USD_to_CAD(amount) & " CAD")
    End Select
  End If
Loop While choice <> 5
End Sub
```

41.3   Passing Arguments by Value and by Reference

In Visual Basic, variables are passed to subprograms by value. This means that if the value of an argument is changed within the subprogram, it does not get changed outside of it. Take a look at the following example.

```
                        project_41_3a
Sub f1(b As Integer)
  b += 1
  Console.WriteLine(b)      'Value 11 is displayed
End Sub

Sub Main()
  Dim a As Integer

  a = 10
  f1(a)
  Console.WriteLine(a)      'Value 10 is displayed

  Console.ReadKey()
End Sub
```

The value 10 of variable a is passed to subprocedure f1() through argument b. However, although the content of variable b is altered within the subprocedure, when the flow of execution returns to the main code this change does not affect the value of variable a. This is regardless of the fact that the main code and the subprocedure are using two variables with different names. The same would have happened if, for example, both the main code and the subprocedure had used two variables of the same name. The next Visual Basic program operates exactly the same way and displays exactly the same results as previous program did.

```
project_41_3b
Sub f1(a As Integer)
  a += 1
  Console.WriteLine(a)    'Value 11 is displayed
End Sub

Sub Main()
  Dim a As Integer

  a = 10
  f1(a)
  Console.WriteLine(a)    'Value 10 is displayed

  Console.ReadKey()
End Sub
```

Still, if you want a subprogram to change the value of its arguments and also reflect this change outside of the subprogram, you must pass the arguments by reference. To do so, the argument name in the formal argument list must be preceded by the keyword ByRef. Take a look at the following example.

```
project_41_3c
Sub f1(ByRef b As Integer)
  b += 1
  Console.WriteLine(b) 'Value 11 is displayed
End Sub

Sub Main()
  Dim a As Integer

  a = 10
  f1(a)
  Console.WriteLine(a)    'Value 11 is displayed

  Console.ReadKey()
End Sub
```

Be careful about one thing though: in Visual Basic, it is possible to pass by reference a constant value or an expression but, any change within the subprogram is not reflected outside of the subprogram, as shown here.

```
project_41_3d
Sub f1(ByRef b As Integer)
  b += 1
  Console.WriteLine(b)
End Sub

Sub Main()
  Dim x As Integer
```

```
    x = 9
    f1(x)                    'This call displays 10
    Console.WriteLine(x)     'This one displays 10.

    f1(x + 1)                'This call displays 12
    Console.WriteLine(x)     'This one displays 10

    Console.ReadKey()
End Sub
```

> *Notice:* When the flow of execution returns from the subprocedure to the main code, the value of variable b *must be assigned back to an argument in the actual argument list. Obviously, this cannot be done when the argument is either a constant value or an expression.*
>
> *Notice: Keep in mind that in computer languages such as C#, C++, or Java, only variables can be passed by reference. Passing a constant value or an expression by reference is not allowed.*

So, as you have probably realized, passing values by reference can provide an indirect way for a subprogram to "return" values. In the next example, the function div_mod() divides variable a by variable b and finds their integer quotient and their integer remainder. If all goes well, it returns True; otherwise, it returns False. Moreover, through the two arguments int_quotient and int_remainder, the function also indirectly returns the calculated quotient and the calculated remainder.

```
                        project_41_3e
Function div_mod(a As Integer, b As Integer,
                ByRef int_quotient As Integer,
                ByRef int_remainder As Integer) As Boolean

    Dim Return_value As Boolean = True

    If b = 0 Then
        Return_value = False
    Else
        int_quotient = a \ b
        int_remainder = a Mod b
    End If

    Return Return_value
End Function

Sub Main()
    Dim val1, val2 As Integer
    Dim int_q, int_r As Integer
    Dim ret As Boolean

    val1 = Console.ReadLine()
    val2 = Console.ReadLine()
```

```
  ret = div_mod(val1, val2, int_q, int_r)
  If ret = True Then
    Console.WriteLine(int_q & " " & int_r)
  Else
    Console.WriteLine("Sorry, wrong values entered!")
  End If

  Console.ReadKey()
End Sub
```

> *Notice*: A very good tactic regarding the arguments in the formal argument list is to have all of those being passed by value written before those being passed by reference.

Exercise 41.3-1   *Finding the Logic Error*

The following Visual Basic program is supposed to prompt the user to enter an integer and then display the product of that integer multiplied by its number of digits. For example, if the user enters the value 401, the script should display a result of 401 × 3 = 1203. Unfortunately, the Visual Basic program displays 0. Can you find out why?

```
project_41_3_1
Function get_num_of_digits(ByRef x As Integer) As Integer
  Dim count As Integer = 0

  Do While x <> 0
    count += 1
    x = x \ 10
  Loop
  Return count
End Function

Sub Main()
  Dim val As Integer

  val = Console.ReadLine()

  Console.Write(get_num_of_digits(val) * val)

  Console.ReadKey()
End Sub
```

Solution

The function get_num_of_digits() counts the number of digits of the argument x using an already known function proposed in Chapter 31. But before you read the answer below, can you try to find the logic error by yourself?

No? Come on, it isn't that difficult!

Still No? Do you want to give up?

So, let it be!

The problem is that, within the function get_num_of_digits(), variable x eventually becomes 0, and since the variable val is passed to the function by reference, that 0 also reflects back to the main code. So, when the flow of execution returns to the main code, the value of variable val is zeroed!

To resolve this issue, all you have to do is remove the ByRef keyword at the beginning of the argument x. If you do so, the variable val is passed to the function by value, so that no matter what happens to variable x within the function, nothing can affect the value of the variable val of the main code.

41.4   Passing and/or Returning an Array

By default, arrays in Visual Basic are passed by reference. This means that if you pass an array to a subprogram, and that subprogram changes the value of one or more elements of the array, these changes are also reflected outside the subprogram.

Passing an array to a subprogram as an argument is as easy as passing a simple variable. In the next example, the Visual Basic program must find the three lowest values of array t. To do so, the program calls and passes the array to the subprocedure get_array() through its formal argument a, which in turn sorts array a using the insertion sort algorithm. When the flow of execution returns to the main code, array t also gets sorted. This happens because the array is passed by reference. So what the main code finally does is just display the elements of the first three positions of the array.

```
project_41_4a

Const ELEMENTS = 10
                                    By default, arrays in Visual
                                    Basic are passed by reference.
Sub get_array(a() As Integer)
   Dim m, n, element As Integer
   For m = 1 To ELEMENTS - 1
      element = a(m)
      n = m
      Do While n > 0
         If element > a(n - 1) Then Exit Do
         a(n) = a(n - 1)
         n -= 1
      Loop
      a(n) = element
   Next
End Sub

Sub Main()
   Dim i As Integer

   Dim t() As Integer = {75, 73, 78, 70, 71, 74, 72, 69, 79, 77}

   get_array(t)

   Console.WriteLine("Three lowest values are: ")
   Console.WriteLine(t(0) & " " & t(1) & " " & t(2))

   'In this step, array t is now sorted
   For i = 0 To ELEMENTS - 1
```

```
      Console.WriteLine(t(i))
    Next

    Console.ReadKey()
End Sub
```

> **Notice**: *Please note that, since the array* t *of the main code is passed to the subprocedure by reference, when the flow of execution returns to the main code, array* t *also gets sorted.*

However, there are many times when passing an array by reference can be completely disastrous. Suppose you have the following two arrays. Array names contains the names of 10 cities, and array t contains their corresponding temperatures recorded at 12:00 p.m. on a specific day.

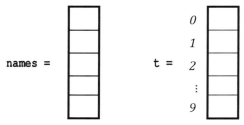

Now, suppose that for array t you wish to display the three lowest temperatures. If you call subprocedure get_array() of the previous Visual Basic program, you have a problem. Although the three lowest temperatures can be displayed as required, the array t becomes sorted; therefore, the relationship between its elements and the elements of array names is lost forever!

One possible solution would be to write a function in which the array is copied to an auxiliary array and the function would return a smaller array that contains only the three lowest values. The proposed solution is shown here.

```
project_41_4b
Const ELEMENTS = 10

Function get_array(a() As Integer) As Integer()
    Dim m, n, element As Integer
    Dim aux_array(ELEMENTS - 1) As Integer

    'copy array a to array aux_array
    For m = 0 To ELEMENTS - 1
      aux_array(m) = a(m)
    Next

    'and sort array aux_array
    For m = 1 To ELEMENTS - 1
      element = aux_array(m)
      n = m
      Do While n > 0
        If aux_array(n - 1) < element Then Exit Do
        aux_array(n) = aux_array(n - 1)
        n -= 1
```

```
      Loop
      aux_array(n) = element
    Next

    Dim ret_array() As Integer = {aux_array(0), aux_array(1), aux_array(2)}
    Return ret_array
  End Function

  Sub Main()
    Dim i As Integer

    Dim names() As String = {"City1", "City2", "City3", "City4", "City5",
                            "City6", "City7", "City8", "City9", "City10"}

    Dim t() As Integer = {75, 73, 78, 70, 71, 74, 72, 69, 79, 77}

    Dim low() As Integer
    low = get_array(t)
    Console.WriteLine("Three lowest values are: ")
    Console.WriteLine(low(0) & " " & low(1) & " " & low(2))

    'In this step, array t is NOT sorted
    For i = 0 To ELEMENTS - 1
      Console.WriteLine(t(i) & vbTab & names(i))
    Next

    Console.ReadKey()
  End Sub
```

41.5   Default Argument Values (Optional Arguments)

If you use the keyword `Optional` and assign a default value to an argument within the formal argument list, it means that if no value is passed for that argument, the default value is used. In the next example, the function `prepend_t()` prepends a title before the name. However, if no value for argument `title` is passed, the function uses the default value "Mr."

```
                              project_41_5a
Function prepend_t(name As String, Optional title As String = "Mr") As String
  Return title & " " & name
End Function

Sub Main()
  'Display Mr John King
  Console.WriteLine(prepend_t("John King"))

  'Display Ms Maria Miller
  Console.WriteLine(prepend_t("Maria Miller", "Ms"))

  Console.ReadKey()
End Sub
```

> **Notice**: *When a default value is assigned to an argument within the formal argument list, this argument is called an optional argument.*
>
> **Notice**: *Within the formal argument list, any optional arguments must be on the right side of any non-optional arguments; to do the opposite of this would be incorrect.*
>
> **Notice**: *The default value must be a constant value, not a variable.*

41.6   The Scope of a Variable

The scope of a variable refers to the range of effect of that variable.

In Visual Basic, a variable can have a local or global scope. A variable declared within a subprogram has a local scope and can be accessed only from within that subprogram. On the other hand, a variable declared outside of a subprogram and outside of the main code has a global scope and can be accessed from within **any** subprogram, as well as from the main code.

Let's see some examples. The next program declares a global variable a as well as a local variable b within the subprocedure. The value of the global variable a, though, is accessed and displayed within the subprocedure.

```
                              project_41_6a
Dim a As Integer            'Global scope

Sub display_values()
    Dim b As Integer        'Local scope

    b = 3

    Console.WriteLine(a & " " & b)   'This displays 10  3
End Sub

Sub Main()
    a = 10
    display_values()

    Console.ReadKey()
End Sub
```

Be careful though! If the value of a global variable is altered within a subprogram, this change is also reflected outside of the subprogram. In the next example, the subprocedure display_values() increases the value of variable a to 11, and when the flow of execution returns to the main code, variable a still contains the value 11.

```
                              project_41_6b
Dim a, b As Integer         'Global scope

Sub display_values()
    a += 1
    Console.WriteLine(a & " " & b)     'This displays 11  20
End Sub

Sub Main()
    a = 10
```

```
    b = 20
    Console.WriteLine(a & " " & b)      'This displays 10   20
    display_values()
    Console.WriteLine(a & " " & b)      'This displays 11   20

    Console.ReadKey()
End Sub
```

The next example declares a global variable a, two local variables a and b within the subprocedure display_values(), and another two local variables a and b within the subprocedure display_other_values(). Keep in mind that the global variable a and the two local variables a are three different variables!

```
                            project_41_6c
Dim a, b As Integer         'Global scope

Sub display_values()
    Dim a, b As Integer     'Local scope

    a = 7
    b = 3
    Console.WriteLine(a & " " & b)  'This displays 7   3
End Sub

Sub display_other_values()
    Dim a, b As Integer     'Local scope

    a = 9
    b = 2
    Console.WriteLine(a & " " & b)  'This displays 9   2
End Sub

Sub Main()
    a = 10
    Console.WriteLine(a)        'This displays 10
    display_values()
    display_other_values()
    Console.WriteLine(a)        'This displays 10

    Console.ReadKey()
End Sub
```

> **Notice**: You can have variables of local scope of the same name within different subprograms, because they are recognized only by the subprogram in which they are declared.

41.7   Converting Parts of Code into Subprograms

As already mentioned, writing large programs without subdividing them into smaller subprograms results in a code called "spaghetti code". Suppose you have a large "spaghetti code" and you wish to subdivide it into smaller subprograms. The next program is an example explaining the steps that must be followed. The parts of the program marked with a dashed rectangle must be converted into subprograms.

```
project_41_7a
Sub Main()
  Dim total_yes, female_no, i As Integer
  Dim temp1, sex, temp2, answer As String

  total_yes = 0
  female_no = 0
  For i = 1 To 100

    Do
      Console.WriteLine("Enter Sex For Citizen No " & i & ": ")
      temp1 = Console.ReadLine()
      sex = temp1.ToLower()
    Loop While sex <> "male" And sex <> "female"

    Do
      Console.WriteLine("Do you go jogging in the afternoon? ")
      temp2 = Console.ReadLine()
      answer = temp2.ToLower()
    Loop While answer <> "yes" And answer <> "no" And answer <> "sometimes"

    If answer = "yes" Then
      total_yes += 1
    End If

    If sex = "female" And answer = "no" Then
      female_no += 1
    End If
  Next

  Console.WriteLine("Total positive answers: " & total_yes)
  Console.WriteLine("Women's negative answers: " & female_no)

  Console.ReadKey()
End Sub
```

To convert parts of this program into subprograms you must:

> ➤ decide, for each part, whether to use a function or a subprocedure. The factor that helps you decide what to use is that a function returns a result, whereas a subprocedure doesn't.

> ➤ determine which variables participate in each part of the program and their roles in that part. The flowchart that follows can help you decide what to do with each variable, whether it should be passed to the subprogram and/or returned from the subprogram, or if it should just be a local variable within the subprogram.

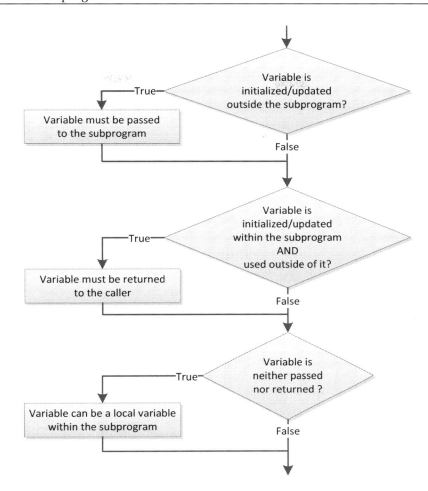

So, with the help of this flowchart, let's discuss each part of the program independently! The parts that are not marked with a dashed rectangle will comprise the main code.

First part

In the first part of the program, there are three variables: i, temp1, and sex. However, not all of them must be included in the formal argument list. Let's find out why!

- ➢ Variable i
  - ➢ is initialized/updated outside the subprogram; thus, it must be passed to the subprogram
  - ➢ is not updated within the subprogram; thus, it should not be returned to the caller
- ➢ Variable temp1
  - ➢ is not initialized/updated outside of the subprogram; thus, it should not be passed to the subprogram
  - ➢ is initialized within the subprogram but its value is not used outside of it; thus, it should not be returned to the caller

According to the flowchart, since variable temp1 should neither be passed nor returned, this variable can just be a local variable within the subprogram.

➢ Variable sex

    ➢ is not initialized/updated outside of the subprogram; thus, it should not be passed to the subprogram

    ➢ is initialized within the subprogram and its value is used outside of it; thus, it must be returned to the caller

Therefore, since only one value must be returned to the main code, a function can be used as shown here.

```
Function part1(i As Integer) As String
  Dim sex, temp1 As String

  Do
    Console.Write("Enter Sex For Citizen No " & i & ": ")
    temp1 = Console.ReadLine()
    sex = temp1.ToLower()
  Loop While sex <> "male" And sex <> "female"

  Return sex
End Sub
```

> **Remember!** *Function's data type must match the data type of the value returned.*

Second part

In the second part of the program there are two variables, temp2 and answer, but they do not both need to be included in the formal argument list. Let's find out why!

➢ Variable temp2

    ➢ is not initialized/updated outside of the subprogram; thus, it should not be passed to the subprogram

    ➢ is initialized/updated within the subprogram but its value is not used outside of it; thus, it should not be returned to the caller

According to the flowchart, since variable temp2 should neither be passed nor returned, this variable can just be a local variable within the subprogram.

➢ Variable answer

    ➢ is not initialized/updated outside of the subprogram; thus, it should not be passed to the subprogram

    ➢ is initialized within the subprogram and its value is used outside of it; thus, it must be returned to the caller

Therefore, since only one value must be returned to the main code, a function can be used, as shown here.

```
Function part2() As String
  Dim temp2, answer As String

  Do
    Console.Write("Do you go jogging in the afternoon? ")
    temp2 = Console.ReadLine()
    answer = temp2.ToLower()
  Loop While answer <> "yes" And answer <> "no" And answer <> "sometimes"
```

```
    Return answer
End Sub
```

Third part

In the third part of the example, there are four variables: answer, total_yes, sex and female_no and all of them must be included in the formal argument list. Let's find out why!

> Both variables answer and sex

> > are initialized/updated outside of the subprogram; thus, they must be passed to the subprogram

> > are not updated within the subprogram; thus, they should not be returned to the caller

> Both variables total_yes and female_no

> > are initialized outside of the subprogram; thus, they must be passed to the subprogram

> > are updated within the subprogram and their value is used outside of it; thus, they must be returned to the caller

Therefore, since two values must be returned to the main code, a subprocedure can be used. The variables total_yes and female_no must be passed by reference so that their values can be returned to the main code (indirectly), as shown here.

```
Sub part3(answer As String, sex As String,
          ByRef total_yes As Integer, ByRef female_no As Integer)

    If answer = "yes" Then
      total_yes += 1
    End If

    If sex = "female" And answer = "no" Then
      female_no += 1
    End If
End Sub
```

> **Remember!** A very good tactic regarding the argument in the formal argument list is to have all of those being passed by value before those being passed by reference.

Fourth part

In the fourth part of the example, there are two variables: total_yes and female_no. Let's see what you should do with them.

> Both variables total_yes and female_no

> > are updated outside of the subprogram; thus, they must be passed to the subprogram

> > are not updated within the subprogram; thus, they should not be returned to the caller

Therefore, since no value should be returned to the main code, a subprocedure can be used, as follows.

```
Sub part4(total_yes As Integer, female_no As Integer)
    Console.WriteLine("Total positive answers: " & total_yes)
```

```
    Console.WriteLine("Women's negative answers: " & female_no)
  End Sub
```

The final program

The final program, including the main code and all the subprograms cited above, is shown here.

```
                              project_41_7b
Function part1(i As Integer) As String
  Dim sex, temp1 As String

  Do
    Console.Write("Enter Sex For Citizen No " & i & ": ")
    temp1 = Console.ReadLine()
    sex = temp1.ToLower()
  Loop While sex <> "male" And sex <> "female"

  Return sex
End Function

Function part2() As String
  Dim temp2, answer As String

  Do
    Console.Write("Do you go jogging in the afternoon? ")
    temp2 = Console.ReadLine()
    answer = temp2.ToLower()
  Loop While answer <> "yes" And answer <> "no" And answer <> "sometimes"

  Return answer
End Function

Sub part3(answer As String, sex As String,
          ByRef total_yes As Integer, ByRef female_no As Integer)

  If answer = "yes" Then
    total_yes += 1
  End If

  If sex = "female" And answer = "no" Then
    female_no += 1
  End If
End Sub

Sub part4(total_yes As Integer, female_no As Integer)
  Console.WriteLine("Total positive answers: " & total_yes)
  Console.WriteLine("Women's negative answers: " & female_no)
End Sub

Sub Main()
  Dim i, total_yes, female_no As Integer
```

```
Dim sex, answer As String

total_yes = 0
female_no = 0
For i = 1 To 100
   sex = part1(i)
   answer = part2()

   part3(answer, sex, total_yes, female_no)
Next

part4(total_yes, female_no)

Console.ReadKey()
End Sub
```

41.8 Recursion

Recursion is a programming technique in which a subprogram calls itself. This might initially seem like an endless loop, but of course this is not true; a subprogram that uses recursion must be written in a way that obviously satisfies the property of finiteness.

Imagine that the next Visual Basic program helps you find your way home. In this program, recursion occurs because the subprocedure find_your_way_home() calls itself within the function.

```
Sub find_your_way_home ()
   If you_are_already_at_home = True Then
      stop_walking()
   Else
      take_one_step_toward_home()
      find_your_way_home()
   End If
End Sub

Sub Main()

   find_your_way_home()

   Console.ReadKey()
End Sub
```

Now, let's try to analyze recursion through a real example. The next Visual Basic program calculates the factorial of 5 using recursion.

```
                          project_41_8
Function factorial(value As Integer) As Integer
   Dim Return_value As Integer
   If value = 1 Then
      Return_value = 1
   Else
      Return_value = value * factorial(value - 1)
   End If
```

```
    Return Return_value
End Function

Sub Main()
    Console.WriteLine(factorial(5)) 'This displays 120
    Console.ReadKey()
End Sub
```

> **Remember!** *In mathematics, the factorial of a non-negative integer N is the product of all positive integers less than or equal to N. It is denoted by N! and the factorial of 0 is, by definition, equal to 1. For example, the factorial of 5 is 1 × 2 × 3 × 4 × 5 = 120.*
>
> **Notice:** *Recursion occurs because the function* `factorial()` *calls itself within the function.*
>
> **Notice**: *Please note that there isn't any loop control structure!*

You are probably confused right now. How on Earth is the product 1 × 2 × 3 × 4 × 5 calculated without using a loop control structure? The next diagram may help you understand. It shows the multiplication operations that are performed as function `factorial()` works its way backwards through the series of calls. When the function `factorial()` returns from the topmost call, you have the final solution. Read this diagram backwards, from bottom to top.

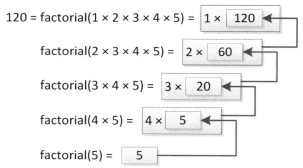

In conclusion, all recursive subprograms must follow three important rules.

1. They must have a base case
2. They must change their state and move toward the base case
3. They must call themselves

where

➢ the base case is the condition that "tells" the subprogram to stop recursions. The base case is usually a very small problem that can be solved directly. It is the solution to the "simplest" possible problem. In the function `factorial()`, the base case is the factorial of 1.   When `factorial(1)` is called, the Boolean expression `(value = 1)` validates to `True` and marks the end of the recursions.

➢ a change of state means that the subprogram alters some of its data. Usually, data are getting smaller and smaller in some way. In the function `factorial()`, since the base case is the factorial of 1, the whole concept relies on the idea of moving toward that base case.

➢ The last rule just states the obvious; the subprogram must call itself.

Exercise 41.8-1 *Calculating the Fibonacci Sequence Recursively*

The Fibonacci sequence is a series of numbers in the following sequence:

$$1, 1, 2, 3, 5, 8, 13, 21, 34, 55, \dots$$

By definition, the first two numbers are 1 and 1 and each subsequent number is the sum of the previous two.

Write a Visual Basic program that lets the user enter a positive integer N and then calculates recursively and finally displays the Nth term of the Fibonacci series.

Solution

In the following Visual Basic program, the function Fib() calculates the Nth term of the Fibonacci series recursively. This is probably not the best algorithm in the world. It is mentioned here, however, just to show you how recursion can sometimes make things worse!

```
project_41_8_1
Function Fib(n As Integer) As Integer
    Dim Return_value As Integer
    If n = 0 Or n = 1 Then
        Return_value = n
    Else
        Return_value = Fib(n - 1) + Fib(n - 2)
    End If

    Return Return_value
End Function

Sub Main()
    Dim num As Integer

    num = Console.ReadLine()
    Console.Write(Fib(num))
    Console.ReadKey()
End Sub
```

To explain how this function works, the best thing to do is use some input values.

For input value 3

If the user enters a value of 3, the following recursive calls are made.

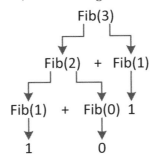

If you calculate the results of these recursive calls, you have

$$(1 + 0) + 1 = 2$$

This is correct! The 3rd term of the Fibonacci series is 2.

For input value 4

If the user enters a value of 4, the following recursive calls are made.

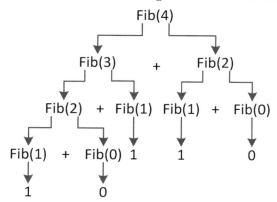

If you calculate the results of these recursive calls, you have

$$((1 + 0) + 1) + (1 + 0) = 3$$

This is also correct! The 4th term of the Fibonacci series is 3.

For input value 5

If the user enters a value of 5, the following recursive calls are made.

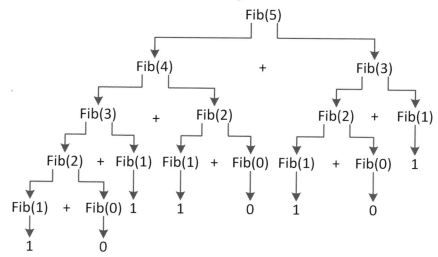

If you calculate the results of these recursive calls, you have

$$(((1 + 0) + 1) + (1 + 0)) + ((1 + 0) + 1) = 5$$

This is correct as well! The 5th term of the Fibonacci series is 5.

Notice: Please note that for each succeeding term of the Fibonacci series, the number of calls increments exponentially. For example, the calculation of the 50th or the 60th term of the Fibonacci series using this function can prove tragically slow!

Recursion helps you write more creative and more elegant programs, but keep in mind that it is not always the best option. The main disadvantage of recursion is that it is hard for a programmer to think through the logic, and therefore it is difficult to debug a code that contains a recursive subprogram. Furthermore, a recursive algorithm may prove worse than a non-recursive algorithm because it may consume too much CPU time or too much main memory (RAM). So, there are times where it would be better to follow the KISS principle and, instead of using a recursion, solve the algorithm using loop control structures.

> *Notice: For you who don't know what the KISS principle is, it is an acronym for "Keep It Simple, Stupid!" It states that most systems work best if they are kept simple, avoiding any unnecessary complexity!*

41.9 Overloading Functions

Function overloading is a feature that allows you to have two or more functions with the same name, as long as their formal argument lists are different. This means that you can perform overloading as long as:

- ➢ the number of arguments in each formal argument list is different; or
- ➢ the data type of the arguments in each formal argument list is different; or
- ➢ the sequence of the data type of the arguments in each formal argument list is different.

To better understand all these concepts, let's try to analyze them using one example for each.

Different number of arguments in each formal argument list

In the following example, there are two functions display(), but they have different numbers of formal arguments. The first function accepts one string through its formal argument list, while the second accepts two strings.

```
                        project_41_9a
Sub display(first_name As String)
  Console.WriteLine("First name: " & first_name)
  Console.WriteLine("-----------------------------")
End Sub

Sub display(first_name As String, last_name As String)
  Console.WriteLine("First name: " & first_name)
  Console.WriteLine("Last name: " & last_name)
  Console.WriteLine("-----------------------------")
End Sub

Sub Main()
  'Call first function
  display("George")
  'Call second function
  display("George", "Washington")

  Console.ReadKey()
End Sub
```

The output result is as follows.

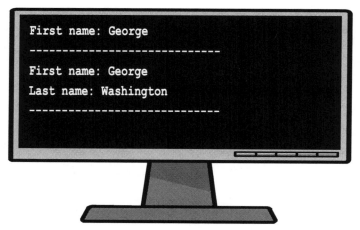

```
First name: George
-------------------------------
First name: George
Last name: Washington
-------------------------------
```

Different data type of arguments in each formal argument list

In the following example, there are two functions my_abs(), but their formal arguments are of different types. The first one function accepts an integer, while the second one accepts a real (a double) through its formal argument list.

```
                          project_41_9b
Function my_abs(a As Integer) As Integer
  If a < 0 Then
    a *= -1
  End If
  Console.WriteLine("1st function is called when an integer is passed to it")
  Return a
End Function

Function my_abs(a As Double) As Double
  If a < 0 Then
    a *= -1
  End If
  Console.WriteLine("2nd function is called when a real is passed to it")
  Return a
End Function

Sub Main()
  'Call first function
  Console.WriteLine(my_abs(-5))
  'Call second function
  Console.Write(my_abs(-5.5))

  Console.ReadKey()
End Sub
```

The output result is shown here.

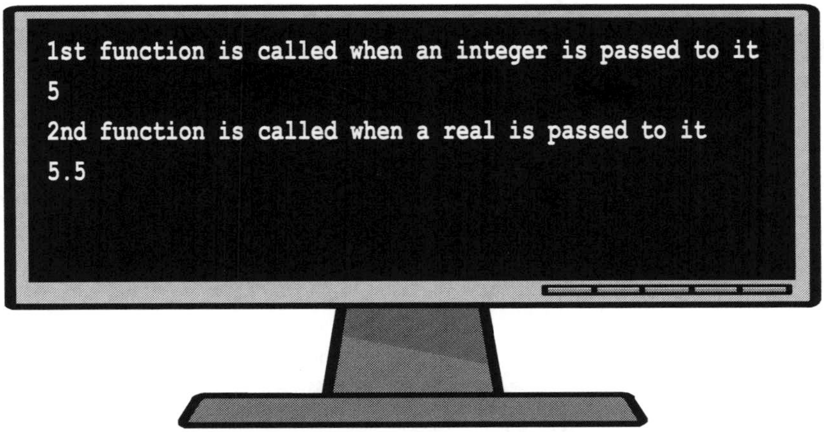

```
1st function is called when an integer is passed to it
5
2nd function is called when a real is passed to it
5.5
```

Different sequence of the data types of arguments in each formal argument list

Last but not least, in the following example, there are two functions display_date(), but the sequence of the data types of the arguments in each formal argument list is different. The first one function accepts three arguments in the order String–Integer–Integer, while the second one accepts three arguments in the order Integer–String–Integer.

```
project_41_9c
Function get_suffix(number As Integer) As String
  Dim ret_value As String = "th"
  If number = 1 Then
    ret_value = "nd"
  ElseIf number = 2 Then
    ret_value = "rd"
  End If
  Return ret_value
End Function

Sub display_date(month As String, day As Integer, year As Integer)
  Console.WriteLine(month & " the " & day & get_suffix(day) & ", " & year)
End Sub

Sub display_date(day As Integer, month As String, year As Integer)
  Console.WriteLine(day & get_suffix(day) & " of " & month & ", " & year)
End Sub

Sub Main()
  display_date(4, "July", 1776)
  display_date("July", 4, 1776)

  Console.ReadKey()
End Sub
```

The output result is as follows.

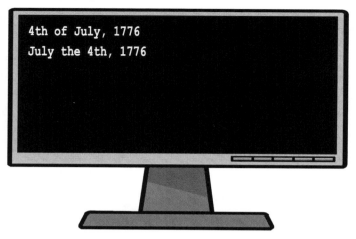

```
4th of July, 1776
July the 4th, 1776
```

41.10 Review Questions: True/False

Choose **true** or **false** for each of the following statements.

1. Each subprogram uses its own memory space to hold the values of its variables.
2. Variables used in a subprogram "live" as long as the subprogram is being executed.
3. The only variables that "live" for as long as the Visual Basic program is being executed are the variables of the main code and the global variables.
4. A subprogram can call the main code.
5. If an argument is passed by value and its value is changed within the subprogram, it does not get changed outside of it.
6. The name of an actual argument and the name of the corresponding formal argument must be the same.
7. The total number of formal and actual arguments must be the same.
8. An expression cannot be passed by value.
9. Arrays in Visual Basic are passed by reference.
10. You can pass an array to a subprocedure but a subprocedure cannot return an array to the caller.
11. A function can accept an array through its formal argument list.
12. In general, a subprocedure can call any function.
13. In general, a function can call any subprocedure.
14. Within a statement, a function can be called only once.
15. A subprocedure can return a value through its formal argument list.
16. A subprogram can be called by another subprogram or by the main code.
17. Overloading is a feature in Visual Basic that allows you to have two or more arguments with the same name.
18. You can perform overloading as long as the number of arguments in the formal argument list is equal.
19. Optional arguments should be on the left side of any non-optional arguments.
20. The default value of an argument can be an expression.

21. The scope of a variable refers to the range of effect of that variable.

22. If the value of a global variable is altered within a subprogram, this change is reflected outside the subprogram as well.

23. You can have two variables of global scope of the same name.

24. Recursion is a programming technique in which a subprogram calls itself.

25. A recursive algorithm must have a base case.

26. Using recursion to solve a specific problem is not always the best option.

27. Overloading is a feature in Visual Basic that allows you to have two or more functions of different names as long as they have exactly the same formal argument list.

28. You cannot perform overloading when the sequence of the data type of the arguments in the formal argument list is different.

41.11 Review Exercises

Complete the following exercises.

1. Without using a trace table, can you find out what the next Visual Basic program displays?

```
Sub f1()
    Dim a As Integer = 22
End Sub

Sub f2()
    Dim a As Integer = 33
End Sub

Sub Main()
    Dim a As Integer

    a = 5
    f1()
    f2()
    Console.Write(a)

    Console.ReadKey()
End Sub
```

2. Without using a trace table, can you find out what the next Visual Basic program displays?

```
Function f1(number1 As Integer) As Integer
    Return 2 * number1
End Function

Function f2(number1 As Integer, number2 As Integer) As Integer
    Return f1(number1) + f1(number2)
End Function

Sub Main()
    Dim a, b As Integer
```

```
        a = 3
        b = 4

        Console.Write(f2(a, b))

        Console.ReadKey()
    End Sub
```

3. Without using a trace table, can you find out what the next Visual Basic program displays?

```
Sub f1(ByRef number1 As Integer) As Integer
    number1 *= 2
End Sub

Function f2(number1 As Integer, number2 As Integer) As Integer
    f1(number1)
    f1(number2)
    Return number1 + number2
End Function

Sub Main()
    Dim a, b As Integer

    a = 2
    b = 5

    Console.Write(f2(a, b))

    Console.ReadKey()
End Sub
```

4. Create a trace table to determine the values of the variables in each step of the following Visual Basic program when the value 12 is entered.

```
Sub swap(ByRef x As Integer, ByRef y As Integer)
    Dim temp As Integer

    temp = x
    x = y
    y = temp
End Sub

Sub Main()
    Dim a, k, m, x As Integer

    k = Console.ReadLine()
    m = 1
    a = 1
    Do While a < 8
        If k Mod m <> 0 Then
            x = a Mod m
            swap(m, a)
```

```
      Else
         x = a + m + Fix(a - m)
      End If

      Console.WriteLine(m & " " & a & " " & x)

      a += 2
      m += 1
      swap(a, m)
   Loop

   Console.ReadKey()
End Sub
```

5. Without using a trace table, can you find out what the next Visual Basic program displays?

```
Sub display(Optional str As String = "hello")
   str = str.Replace("a", "e")
   Console.Write(str)
End Sub

Sub Main()
   display("hello")
   display()
   display("hallo")

   Console.ReadKey()
End Sub
```

6. Without using a trace table, can you find out what the next Visual Basic program displays?

```
Dim a, b As Integer

Sub f1()
   a = a + b
End Sub

Sub Main()
   a = 10
   b = 5
   f1()
   b -= 1

   Console.Write(a)

   Console.ReadKey()
End Sub
```

7. Without using a trace table, can you find out what the next Visual Basic program displays?

```
Dim a, b As Integer
```

```
Sub f2()
  a = a + b
End Sub

Sub f1()
  a = a + b
  f2()
End Sub

Sub Main()
  a = 3
  b = 4
  f1()

  Console.Write(a & " " & b)

  Console.ReadKey()
End Sub
```

8. For the following Visual Basic program, convert the parts marked with a dashed rectangle into subprograms.

```
Const STUDENTS = 10
Const LESSONS = 5

Sub Main()
  Dim i, j, m, n As Integer
  Dim temp As Double
  Dim temp_str As String

  Dim names(STUDENTS - 1) As String
  Dim grades(STUDENTS - 1, LESSONS - 1) As Integer

  For i = 0 To STUDENTS - 1
    Console.Write("Enter name for student No. " & (i + 1) & ": ")
    names(i) = Console.ReadLine()
    For j = 0 To LESSONS - 1
      Console.Write("Enter grade for lesson No. " & (j + 1) & ": ")
      grades(i, j) = Console.ReadLine()
    Next
  Next

  Dim average(STUDENTS - 1) As Double

  For i = 0 To STUDENTS - 1
    average(i) = 0
    For j = 0 To LESSONS - 1
      average(i) += grades(i, j)
    Next
    average(i) /= LESSONS
  Next
```

```
For m = 1 To STUDENTS - 1
  For n = STUDENTS - 1 To m Step -1
    If average(n) > average(n - 1) Then
      temp = average(n)
      average(n) = average(n - 1)
      average(n - 1) = temp

      temp_str = names(n)
      names(n) = names(n - 1)
      names(n - 1) = temp_str
    ElseIf average(n) = average(n - 1) Then
      If names(n).CompareTo(names(n - 1)) < 0 Then
        temp_str = names(n)
        names(n) = names(n - 1)
        names(n - 1) = temp_str
      End If
    End If
  Next
Next

  For i = 0 To STUDENTS - 1
    Console.WriteLine(names(i) & vbTab & average(i))
  Next

  Console.ReadKey()
End Sub
```

9. The next Visual Basic program finds the greatest value among four values given. Rewrite the program without using subprograms.

```
Sub my_max(n As Integer, ByRef m As Integer)
  If n > m Then
    m = n
  End If
End Sub

Sub Main()
  Dim a, b, c, d, max As Integer

  a = Console.ReadLine()
  b = Console.ReadLine()
  c = Console.ReadLine()
  d = Console.ReadLine()

  max = a
  my_max(b, max)
  my_max(c, max)
  my_max(d, max)

  Console.Write(max)

  Console.ReadKey()
```

```
End Sub
```

10. For the following Visual Basic program, convert the parts marked with a dashed rectangle into subprograms.

```
Sub Main()
  Dim last_pos, i, middle_pos, j As Integer
  Dim message, message_clean, letter, left_letter, right_letter As
String
  Dim palindrome As Boolean

  Console.Write("Enter a message: ")
  message = Console.ReadLine()
  message = message.ToLower()

  last_pos = message.Length - 1

  message_clean = ""
  For i = 0 To last_pos
    letter = message(i)
    If letter <> " " And letter <> "," And
        letter <> "." And letter <> "?" Then

      message_clean += letter
    End If
  Next

  middle_pos = (message_clean.Length - 1) \ 2
  j = message_clean.Length - 1
  palindrome = True
  For i = 0 To middle_pos
    left_letter = message_clean(i)
    right_letter = message_clean(j)
    If left_letter <> right_letter Then
      palindrome = False
      Exit For
    End If
    j -= 1
  Next

  If palindrome = True Then
    Console.WriteLine("The message is palindrome")
  End If

  Console.ReadKey()
End Sub
```

11. Write a subprogram that accepts three numbers through its formal argument list and then returns their sum and their average.

12. Write a subprogram named my_round() that accepts a real (a double) and an integer through its formal argument list and then returns the real rounded to as

many decimal places as the integer indicates. Moreover, if no value is passed for the integer, the subprogram should return the real rounded to two decimal places by default. Try not to use the `Math.Round()` procedure of Visual Basic.

13. Do the following:

    i.   Write a subprogram named `get_input()` that prompts the user to enter an answer "yes" or "no" and then returns the value `True` or `False` correspondingly to the caller. Make the subprogram accept the answer in all possible forms such as "yes", "YES", "Yes", "No", "NO", "nO", and so on.

    ii.   Write a subprogram named `find_area()` that accepts the base and the height of a parallelogram through its formal argument list and then returns its area.

    iii. Using the subprograms `get_input()` and `find_area()` cited above, write a Visual Basic program that prompts the user to enter the base and the height of a parallelogram and then calculates and displays its area. The program should iterate as many times as the user wishes. At the end of each calculation, the program should ask the user whether he or she wishes to calculate the area of another parallelogram. If the answer is "yes" the program should repeat.

14. Do the following:

    i.   Write a subprogram named `get_arrays()` that prompts the user to enter the grades and the names of 100 students into the arrays `grades` and `names`, correspondingly. The two arrays must be returned to the caller.

    ii.   Write a subprogram `average()` that accepts the array `grades` through its formal argument list and returns the average grade.

    iii. Write a subprogram named `sort_arrays()` that accepts the arrays `grades` and `names` through its formal argument list and sorts the array `grades` in descending order using the insertion sort algorithm. The subprogram must preserve the relationship between the elements of the two arrays.

    iv. Using the three subprograms cited above, write a Visual Basic program that prompts the user to enter the grades and the names of 100 students and then displays all student names whose grade is less than the average grade, sorted by grade in descending order.

15. In a song contest, there is an artist who is scored by 10 judges. However, according to the rules of this contest, the total score is calculated after excluding the maximum and the minimum score. Do the following:

    i.   Write a subprogram named `get_array()` that prompts the user to enter the scores of the 10 judges into an array and then returns the array to the caller.

    ii.   Write a subprogram named `find_min_max()` that accepts an array through its formal argument list and then returns the maximum and the minimum value.

    iii. Using the subprograms `get_array()` and `find_min_max()` cited above, write a Visual Basic program that lets the user enter the name of the artist and the score he or she gets from each judge. The program should then display the message "Artist NN got XX points" where NN and XX must be replaced by actual values.

16. On a chessboard you must place grains of wheat on each square, such that one grain is placed on the first square, two on the second, four on the third, and so on (doubling the number of grains on each subsequent square). Do the following:

    i.   Write a recursive function named woc() that accepts the index of a square and returns the number of grains of wheat that are on this square. Since a chessboard contains 8 × 8 = 64 squares, assume that the index is an integer between 1 and 64.

    ii. Using the function woc() cited above, write a Visual Basic program that calculates and displays the total number of grains of wheat that are on the chessboard in the end.

17. Do the following:

    i.   Write a recursive function named factorial() that accepts an integer through its formal argument list and then returns its factorial.

    ii. Using the function factorial() cited above, write a recursive function named my_cos() that calculates and returns the cosine of x using the Taylor series, shown next.

$$cosx = 1 - \frac{x^2}{2!} + \frac{x^4}{4!} - \frac{x^6}{6!} + \cdots + \frac{x^{40}}{40!}$$

Hint: Keep in mind that x is in radians and $\frac{x^0}{0!} = 1$.

    iii. Using the function my_cos() cited above, write a Visual Basic program that calculates and displays the cosine of 45°.

Chapter 42
Flowcharts with Subprograms

42.1 Designing and Calling Sub-Algorithms in Flowcharts

First of all, let's clarify something. A sub-algorithm in a flowchart is what a subprogram is in a program—that is, a block of statements packaged as a unit that performs a specific task. Thus, a sub-algorithm can be a function or a subprocedure. In this chapter, you will learn how a sub-algorithm and a call to a sub-algorithm can be represented in flowcharts.

As you already know, a call to a function—whether built-in or user-defined—is made in the same way. You enter the function's name followed by a list of arguments (if necessary), either within a statement that assigns function's returned value to a variable or directly within an expression. Of course, the same applies to calling a function when a flowchart is used. The next example calls the built-in function abs().

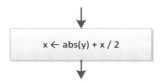

As in Visual Basic, a call to a subprocedure is different from a call to a function. You call a subprocedure by just entering its name within a predefined process symbol. Does this symbol ring a bell to you? Of course it does. This is one of those symbols that you learned about in Chapter 4 but that you haven't used until now. The next example calls a user-defined subprocedure named display_line() and passes two arguments.

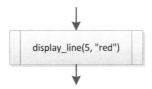

Remember! *The predefined process symbol depicts subprocedures that are formally defined elsewhere, such as in a separate flowchart. The predefined process symbol has one entrance and one exit.*

But how do you represent a sub-algorithm in a flowchart? Below, you can find some examples.

Example 1

In this example the main algorithm calls the function sum(), which calculates and returns the sum of two numbers.

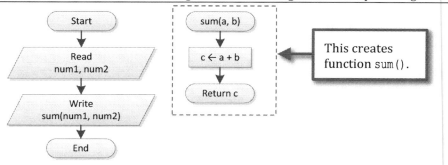

Example 2

In this example the main algorithm calls the function my_abs(), which calculates and returns the absolute value of a number.

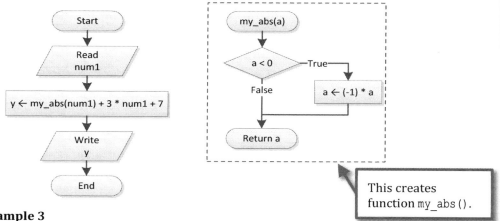

Example 3

In this example the main algorithm calls the subprocedure display_menu(), which displays a currency conversion menu.

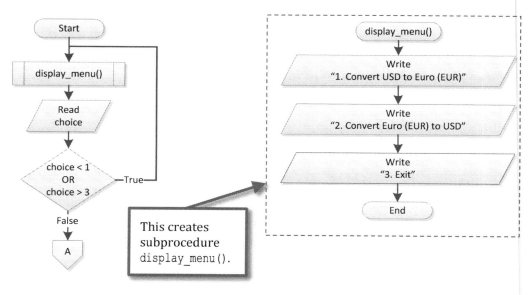

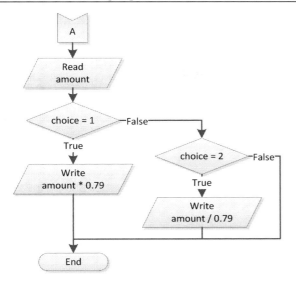

42.2 Converting Visual Basic Programs to Flowcharts

Now, with everything clarified, let's directly start solving some exercises.

Exercise 42.2-1 *Designing the Flowchart*

Design the flowchart that corresponds to the following Visual Basic program.

```
Function find_sum(n As Integer) As Integer
  Dim i As Integer
  Dim s As Integer = 0

  For i = 1 To n
    s = s + i
  Next
  Return s
End Function

Sub Main()
  Dim n As Integer

  Console.Write("Enter a positive integer ")
  n = Console.ReadLine()
  Do While n > 0
    Console.WriteLine(find_sum(n))
    Console.Write("Enter a positive integer ")
    n = Console.ReadLine()
  Loop

  Console.ReadKey()
End Sub
```

Without further explanation, the corresponding flowchart is as follows.

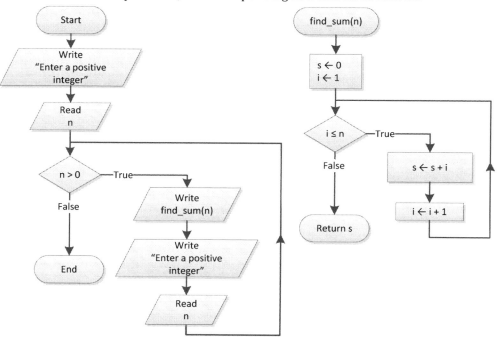

Exercise 42.2-2   *Designing the Flowchart*

Design the flowchart that corresponds to the following Visual Basic program.

```
Function get_num_of_digits(x As Integer) As Integer
  Dim count As Integer = 0
  Do While x <> 0
    count += 1
    x = x \ 10
  Loop
  Return count
End Function

Sub Main()
  Dim val As Integer
  Do
    Console.Write("Enter a four-digit integer ")
    val = Console.ReadLine()
  Loop While get_num_of_digits(val) <> 4

  Console.Write("Congratulations!")

  Console.ReadKey()
End Sub
```

Solution

The solution is as follows

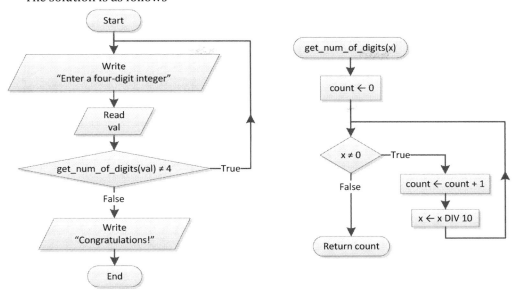

Exercise 42.2-3   *Designing the Flowchart*

Design the flowchart that corresponds to the following code fragment.

```
Sub div_mod(a As Integer, b As Integer,
         ByRef int_quotient As Integer, ByRef int_remainder As Integer,
         ByRef ret_value As Boolean)

  ret_value = True
  If b = 0 Then
    ret_value = False
  Else
    int_quotient = a \ b
    int_remainder = a Mod b
  End If
End Sub

Sub Main()
  Dim val1, val2 As Integer
  Dim int_q, int_r As Integer
  Dim ret As Boolean = False

  val1 = Console.ReadLine()
  val2 = Console.ReadLine()
  div_mod(val1, val2, int_q, int_r, ret)
  If ret = True Then
    Console.WriteLine(int_q & int_r)
  Else
    Console.WriteLine("Sorry, wrong values entered!")
  End If
```

```
        Console.ReadKey()
    End Sub
```

Solution

In this Visual Basic program, the subprocedure div_mod() indirectly returns three values through its arguments int_quotient, int_remainder, and ret_value. This occurs because values to those arguments are passed by reference.

As stated many times in this book, flowcharts are a loose method of representing an algorithm. Thus, you can represent a pass by reference using the byref keyword (as Visual Basic does) which is quite obvious and clearly denotes what it actually does.

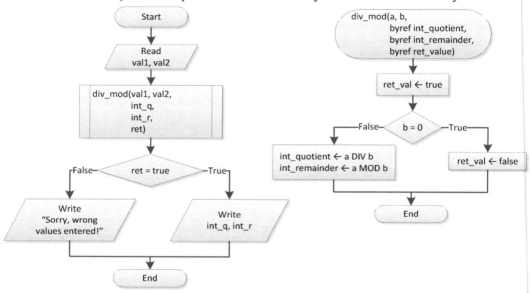

Notice: *Some programmers, instead of using the keyword* byref, *prefer to write the keyword* inout, *which denotes pretty much the same thing— that the variable is both input (it accepts values) and output (it returns values).*

42.3 Converting Flowcharts to Visual Basic Programs

Exercise 42.3-1 *Writing the Visual Basic Program*

Write the Visual Basic program that corresponds to the following flowchart.

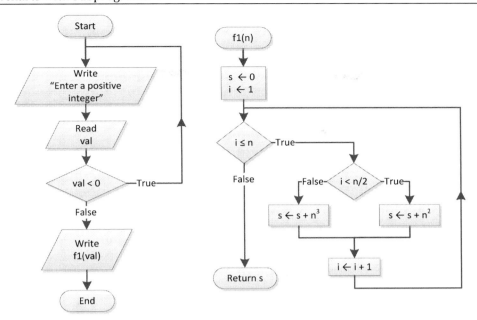

Solution

This exercise is quite simple. Without further explanation, the Visual Basic code is shown here.

```
Function f1(n As Integer) As Double
  Dim s As Double
  Dim i As Integer
  s = 0
  For i = 1 To n
    If i < n / 2 Then
      s += n ^ 2
    Else
      s += n ^ 3
    End If
  Next
  Return s
End Function

Sub Main()
  Dim val As Integer

  Do
    Console.Write("Enter a positive integer ")
    val = Console.ReadLine()
  Loop While val < 0

  Console.Write(f1(val))

  Console.ReadKey()
End Sub
```

Exercise 42.3-2   *Writing the Visual Basic Program*

Write the Visual Basic program that corresponds to the following flowchart fragment.

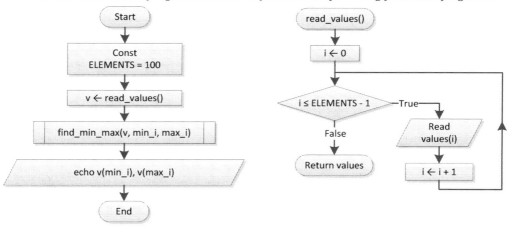

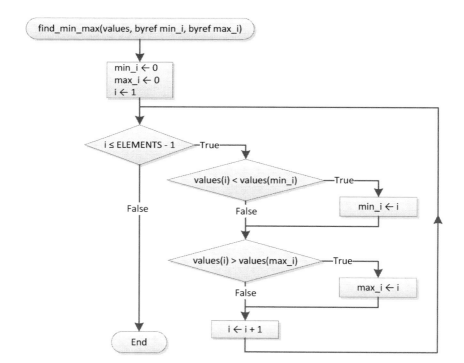

Solution

In this flowchart there is a function named `read_values()` and a subprocedure named `find_min_max()`. As you can see, the former returns the array `values` while the latter returns the values of variables `max_i` and `min_i` indirectly (they are passed by reference). The Visual Basic program is as follows.

```
Const ELEMENTS = 100
```

```
Function read_values() As Double()
  Dim values(ELEMENTS - 1) As Double
  Dim i As Integer

  For i = 0 To ELEMENTS - 1
    values(i) = Console.ReadLine()
  Next
  Return values
End Function

Sub find_min_max(values() As Double,
                 ByRef min_i As Integer, ByRef max_i As Integer)

  Dim i As Integer

  min_i = 0
  max_i = 0
  For i = 1 To ELEMENTS - 1
    If values(i) < values(min_i) Then
      min_i = i
    End If
    If values(i) > values(max_i) Then
      max_i = i
    End If
  Next
End Sub

Sub Main()
  Dim min_i, max_i As Integer

  Dim v() As Double = read_values()
  find_min_max(v, min_i, max_i)

  Console.Write(v(min_i) & ", " & v(max_i))

  Console.ReadKey()
End Sub
```

Notice: *Please study the way the subprocedure* find_min_max() *finds the index positions of the minimum and the maximum values of the array* values. *This method is not the same as the one you learned in Chapter 37; however, it can be used as an alternative.*

42.4 Review Exercises

Complete the following exercises.

1. Design the flowchart that corresponds to the following Visual Basic program.

```
Function test_integer(number As Double) As Boolean
  Dim Return_value As Boolean = False

  If number = Fix(number) Then
```

```
        Return_value = True
      End If
      Return Return_value
End Function

Function test_positive(number As Double) As Boolean
   Dim Return_value As Boolean = False

   If number > 0 Then
      Return_value = True
   End If
   Return Return_value
End Function

Sub Main()
   Dim sum, x As Double
   Dim count As Integer

   sum = 0
   count = 0
   x = Console.ReadLine()
   Do While test_positive(x) = True
     If test_integer(x) = True Then
        sum += x
        count += 1
     End If
     x = Console.ReadLine()
   Loop

   If count > 0 Then
      Console.WriteLine(sum / count)
   End If

   Console.ReadKey()
End Sub
```

2. Design the flowchart that corresponds to the following Visual Basic program.

```
Const PEOPLE = 30

Function get_age() As Integer
   Dim x As Integer
   Do
      x = Console.ReadLine()
   Loop While x <= 0
   Return x
End Function

Function find_max(a() As Integer) As Integer
   Dim max_i As Integer = 0
   Dim i As Integer
   For i = 1 To PEOPLE - 1
```

```
      If a(i) > a(max_i) Then
         max_i = i
      End If
   Next
   Return max_i
End Function

Sub Main()
   Dim i, index_of_max As Integer

   Dim first_names(PEOPLE - 1) As String
   Dim last_names(PEOPLE - 1) As String
   Dim ages(PEOPLE - 1) As Integer
   For i = 0 To PEOPLE - 1
      first_names(i) = Console.ReadLine()
      last_names(i) = Console.ReadLine()
      ages(i) = get_age()
   Next

   index_of_max = find_max(ages)

   Console.WriteLine(first_names(index_of_max))
   Console.WriteLine(last_names(index_of_max))
   Console.Write(ages(index_of_max))

   Console.ReadKey()
End Sub
```

3. Design the flowchart that corresponds to the following Visual Basic program.

```
Const PEOPLE = 40

Sub my_swap(a() As String, index1 As Integer, index2 As Integer)
   Dim temp As String

   temp = a(index1)
   a(index1) = a(index2)
   a(index2) = temp
End Sub

Sub my_sort(a() As String)
   Dim m, n As Integer

   For m = 1 To PEOPLE - 1
      For n = PEOPLE - 1 To m Step -1
         If a(n).CompareTo(a(n - 1)) < 0 Then
            my_swap(a, n, n - 1)
         End If
      Next
   Next
End Sub
```

```
Sub display_array(a() As String, ascending As Boolean)
  Dim i As Integer

  If ascending = True Then
    For i = 0 To PEOPLE - 1
      Console.WriteLine(a(i))
    Next
  Else
    For i = PEOPLE - 1 To 0 Step -1
      Console.WriteLine(a(i))
    Next
  End If
End Sub

Sub Main()
  Dim i As Integer

  Dim names(PEOPLE - 1) As String
  For i = 0 To PEOPLE - 1
    names(i) = Console.ReadLine()
  Next

  my_sort(names)
  display_array(names, True)
  display_array(names, False)

  Console.ReadKey()
End Sub
```

4. Design the flowchart that corresponds to the following Visual Basic program.

```
Function get_consumption() As Integer
  Dim kwh As Integer

  Console.Write("Enter kWh consumed: ")
  kwh = Console.ReadLine()
  Do While kwh < 0
    Console.Write("Error! Enter kWh consumed: ")
    kwh = Console.ReadLine()
  Loop
  Return kwh
End Function

Function find_amount(kwh As Integer) As Double
  Dim amount As Double
  If kwh <= 450 Then
    amount = kwh * 0.07
  ElseIf kwh <= 2200 Then
    amount = 450 * 0.07 + (kwh - 450) * 0.2
  Else
    amount = 450 * 0.07 + 1750 * 0.2 + (kwh - 1750) * 0.33
  End If
```

```
    amount += 0.22 * amount
    Return amount
End Function

Sub Main()
  Dim kwh As Integer
  Dim answer As String

  Do
    kwh = get_consumption()
    Console.WriteLine(find_amount(kwh))

    Console.WriteLine("Repeat?")
    answer = Console.ReadLine()
  Loop While answer.ToUpper() = "YES"
End Sub
```

5. Write the Visual Basic program that corresponds to the following flowchart.

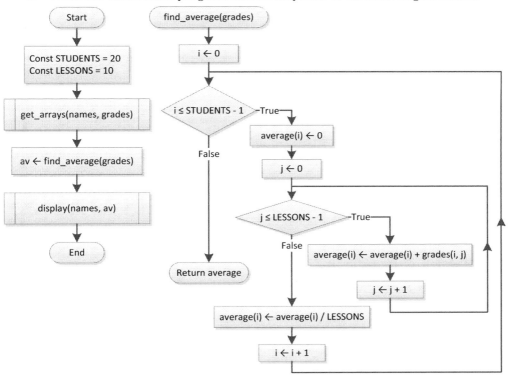

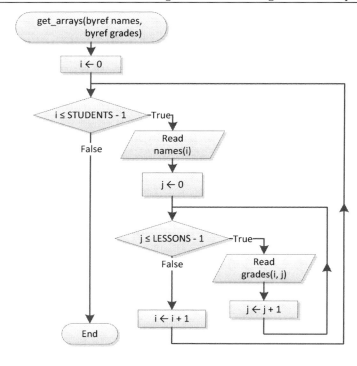

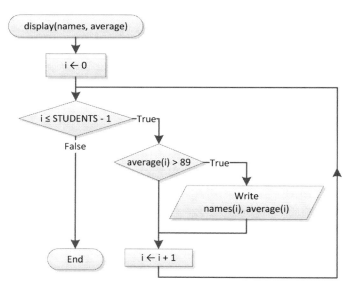

6. Write the Visual Basic program that corresponds to the following flowchart.

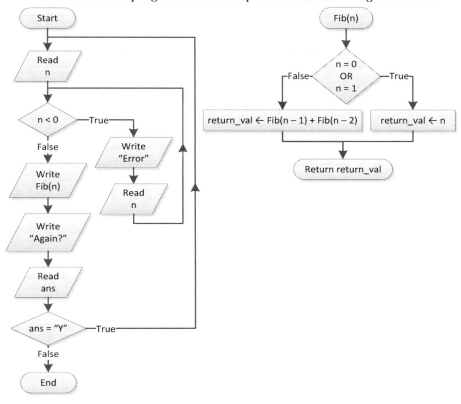

Chapter 43
More Exercises with Subprograms

43.1 Simple Exercises with Subprograms

Exercise 43.1-1   *Finding the Average Values of Positive Integers*

Do the following:

   i.   *Write a subprogram named* test_integer() *that accepts a number through its formal argument list and returns* True *when the passed number is an integer; it must return* False *otherwise.*

   ii.   *Using the subprogram* test_integer() *cited above, write a Visual Basic program that lets the user enter integer values repeatedly until a real one is entered. In the end, the program should display the average value of positive integers entered.*

Solution

Since the subprogram test_integer() returns one value (True or False), it can be written as a function. The solution is presented next.

```
                          project_43_1_1
Function test_integer(number As Double) As Boolean
  Dim Return_value As Boolean = False

  If number = Fix(number) Then
    Return_value = True
  End If
  Return Return_value
End Function

Sub Main()
  Dim sum, count As Integer
  Dim x As Double

  sum = 0
  count = 0
  x = Console.ReadLine()
  Do While test_integer(x) = True
    If x > 0 Then
      sum += x
      count += 1
    End If
    x = Console.ReadLine()
  Loop

  If count > 0 Then
    Console.Write(sum / count)
```

```
  End If

  Console.ReadKey()
End Sub
```

> **Notice**: Please note the last single-alternative decision structure, If count > 0. It is necessary in order for the program to satisfy the property of definiteness. Think about it! If the user enters a real right from the beginning, the variable count, in the end, will contain a value of zero.

Exercise 43.1-2   *Finding the Sum of Odd Positive Integers*

Do the following:

   i.   *Write a subprogram named* test_integer *that accepts a number through its formal argument list and returns* True *when the passed number is an integer; it must return* False *otherwise.*

   ii.   *Write a subprogram named* test_odd *that accepts a number through its formal argument list and returns* True *when the passed number is odd; it must return* False *otherwise.*

   iii.   *Write a subprogram named* test_positive *that accepts a number through its formal argument list and returns* True *when the passed number is positive; it must return* False *otherwise.*

   iv.   *Using the three subprograms cited above, write a Visual Basic program that lets the user enter numeric values repeatedly until a negative one is entered. In the end, the program should display the sum of odd positive integers entered.*

Solution

This exercise is pretty much the same as the previous one. Each subprogram returns one value (which can be True or False) thus, all subprograms can be written as functions. The solution is presented here.

```
                        project_43_1_2
Function test_integer(number As Double) As Boolean
  Dim Return_value As Boolean = False
  If number = Fix(number) Then
    Return_value = True
  End If
  Return Return_value
End Function

Function test_odd(number As Double) As Boolean
  Dim Return_value As Boolean = False

  If number Mod 2 <> 0 Then
    Return_value = True
  End If
  Return Return_value
End Function
```

```
Function test_positive(number As Double) As Boolean
  Dim Return_value As Boolean = False

  If number > 0 Then
     Return_value = True
  End If
  Return Return_value
End Function

Sub Main()
  Dim sum As Integer
  Dim x As Double

  sum = 0
  x = Console.ReadLine()
  Do While test_positive(x) = True
     If test_integer(x) = True And test_odd(x) = True Then
        sum += x
     End If
     x = Console.ReadLine()
  Loop

  Console.Write(sum)

  Console.ReadKey()
End Sub
```

Exercise 43.1-3   *Finding the Values of y*

Write a Visual Basic program that finds and displays the values of y (if possible) in the following formula.

$$y = \begin{cases} \dfrac{3x}{x-5} + \dfrac{7-x}{2x}, & x \geq 1 \\ \dfrac{45-x}{x+2} + 3x, & x < 1 \end{cases}$$

For each part of the formula, write a subprogram that accepts x *through its formal argument list and then calculates and displays the result. An error message should be displayed when the calculation is not possible.*

Solution

Since there are two parts of the formula, two subprograms must be written. Each subprogram should calculate and display the result of the corresponding formula or display an error message when the calculation is not possible. As these two subprograms return no result, they can both be written as subprocedures. The solution is shown here.

project_43_1_3

```
Sub formula1(x As Double)
  Dim y As Double
```

```
   If x = 5 Then
      Console.WriteLine("Error! Division by zero")
   Else
      y = 3 * x / (x - 5) + (7 - x) / (2 * x)
      Console.WriteLine(y)
   End If
End Sub

Sub formula2(x As Double)
   Dim y As Double

   If x = -2 Then
      Console.WriteLine("Error! Division by zero")
   Else
      y = (45 - x) / (x + 2) + 3 * x
      Console.WriteLine(y)
   End If
End Sub

Sub Main()
   Dim x As Double

   Console.WriteLine("Enter a value For x: ")
   x = Console.ReadLine()
   If x >= 1 Then
      formula1(x)
   Else
      formula2(x)
   End If

   Console.ReadKey()
End Sub
```

Exercise 43.1-4   *Roll, Roll, Roll the… Dice!*

Do the following:

i.   *Write a subprogram named* dice() *that returns a random integer between 1 and 6.*

ii. *Write a subprogram named* search_and_count() *that accepts an integer and an array through its formal argument list and returns the number of times the integer exists in the array.*

iii. *Using the subprograms* dice() *and* search_and_count() *cited above, write a Visual Basic program that fills an array with 100 random integers (between 1 and 6) and then lets the user enter an integer. The program should find and display how many times that given integer exists in the array.*

Solution

Both subprograms can be written as functions because they both return one value each. Function dice() returns a random integer between 1 and 6, and function search_and_count() returns a number that indicates the number of times an integer exists in an array. The solution is presented here.

```
                              project_43_1_4
Const ELEMENTS = 100

Dim rnd As New Random()

Function dice() As Integer
  Return rnd.Next(1, 7)
End Function

Function search_and_count(x As Integer, a() As Integer) As Integer
  Dim count As Integer = 0
  Dim i As Integer

  For i = 0 To ELEMENTS - 1
    If a(i) = x Then
      count += 1
    End If
  Next
  Return count
End Function

Sub Main()
  Dim x, i As Integer

  Dim a(ELEMENTS - 1) As Integer
  For i = 0 To ELEMENTS - 1
    a(i) = dice()
  Next

  x = Console.ReadLine()
  Console.WriteLine("Given value exists in the array")
  Console.Write(search_and_count(x, a) & " times")

  Console.ReadKey()
End Sub
```

Exercise 43.1-5   *How Many Times Does Each Number of the Dice Appear?*

Using the functions dice() *and* search_and_count() *cited in the previous exercise, write a Visual Basic program that fills an array with 100 random integers (between 1 and 6) and then displays how many times each of the six numbers appears in the array, as well as which number appears most often.*

Solution

If you were to solve this exercise without using loop control structures, it would be something like the following.

```
'Variable n1 is assigned the number of times that value 1 exists in array a
```

```
n1 = search_and_count(1, a)

'Variable n2 is assigned the number of times that value 2 exists in array a
n2 = search_and_count(2, a)
.

.

.

'Variable n6 is assigned the number of times that value 6 exists in array a
n6 = search_and_count(6, a)

'Display how many times each of the six numbers appears in array a
Console.WriteLine(n1 & " " & n2 & " " & n3)
Console.WriteLine(n4 & " " & n5 & " " & n6)

'Find maximum of n1, n2,… n6
max = n1
max_i = 1

If n2 > max Then
  max = n2
  max_i = 2
End If

If n3 > max Then
  max = n3
  max_i = 2
End If
.

.

.

If n6 > max Then
  max = n6
  max_i = 6
End If

'Display which number appears in the array most often.
Console.WriteLine(max_i)
```

But now that you are reaching the end of the book, of course, you can do something more creative. Instead of assigning each result of the search_and_count() function to individual variables n1, n2, n3, n4, n5, and n6, you can assign those results to the positions 0, 1, 2, 3, 4, and 5 of an array named n, as shown here.

```
Dim n(5) As Integer
For i = 0 To 5
  n(i) = search_and_count(i + 1, a)
Next
```

Next, of course, you can find the maximum of the array n as usual. The complete solution is shown here.

```
                        project_43_1_5
Const ELEMENTS = 100
```

```vbnet
Dim rnd As New Random()

Function dice() As Integer
  Return rnd.Next(1, 7)
End Function

Function search_and_count(x As Integer, a() As Integer) As Integer
  Dim count As Integer = 0
  Dim i As Integer

  For i = 0 To ELEMENTS - 1
    If a(i) = x Then
      count += 1
    End If
  Next
  Return count
End Function

Sub Main()
  Dim i, max, max_i As Integer

  'Create array a of random integers between 1 and 6
  Dim a(ELEMENTS - 1) As Integer
  For i = 0 To ELEMENTS - 1
    a(i) = dice()
  Next

  'Create array n and
  'display how many times each of the six numbers appears in array a
  Dim n(5) As Integer
  For i = 0 To 5
    n(i) = search_and_count(i + 1, a)
    Console.Write("Value " & (i + 1) & " appears ")
    Console.WriteLine(n(i) & " times")
  Next

  'Find maximum of array n
  max = n(0)
  max_i = 0
  For i = 1 To 5
    If n(i) > max Then
      max = n(i)
      max_i = i
    End If
  Next

  'Display which number appears in the array most often.
  Console.Write("Value " & (max_i + 1) & " appears in the array ")
  Console.Write(max & " times.")
```

```
    Console.ReadKey()
End Sub
```

43.2   Exercises of a General Nature with Subprograms

Exercise 43.2-1   *Validating Data Input*

Do the following:

    i.   *Write a subprogram named* get_age() *that prompts the user to enter his or her age and returns it. Moreover, the subprogram should validate data input and display an error message when the user enters any non-numeric or non-positive values.*

    ii.   *Write a subprogram named* find_max() *that accepts an array through its formal argument list and returns the index position of the maximum value of the array.*

    iii.   *Using the subprograms* get_age() *and* find_max() *cited above, write a Visual Basic program that prompts the user to enter the first names, last names, and ages of 50 people into an array and then finds and displays the name of the oldest person.*

Solution

Since the subprogram get_age() returns one value, it can be written as a function. The same applies to subprogram find_max() because it also returns one value. The main code should prompt the user to enter the first names, the last names, and the ages of 50 people into arrays first_names, last_names, and ages respectively. Then, with the help of function find_max(), it can find the index position of the maximum value of array ages. The solution is shown here.

```
project_43_2_1
Const PEOPLE = 50

Function get_age() As Integer
  Dim x As Integer
  Dim input As String

  Console.WriteLine("Enter an age: ")
  input = Console.ReadLine()
  Do While Int32.TryParse(input, x) = False Or x <= 0
    Console.WriteLine("Error: Invalid age!")
    Console.WriteLine("Enter a positive number: ")
    input = Console.ReadLine()
  Loop
  Return x
End Function

Function find_max(a() As Integer) As Integer
  Dim i, max, max_i As Integer

  max = a(0)
  max_i = 0
  For i = 1 To PEOPLE - 1
    If a(i) > max Then
```

```
          max = a(i)
          max_i = i
      End If
  Next
  Return max_i
End Function

Sub Main()
  Dim i, index_of_max As Integer

  Dim first_names(PEOPLE - 1) As String
  Dim last_names(PEOPLE - 1) As String
  Dim ages(PEOPLE - 1) As Integer
  For i = 0 To PEOPLE - 1
    Console.WriteLine("Enter first name of person No " & (i + 1) & ": ")
    first_names(i) = Console.ReadLine()
    Console.WriteLine("Enter last name of person No " & (i + 1) & ": ")
    last_names(i) = Console.ReadLine()
    ages(i) = get_age()
  Next

  index_of_max = find_max(ages)

  Console.WriteLine("The oldest person is:")
  Console.WriteLine(first_names(index_of_max))
  Console.WriteLine(last_names(index_of_max))
  Console.Write("He or she is " & ages(index_of_max) & " years old!")

  Console.ReadKey()
End Sub
```

Exercise 43.2-2   *Sorting an Array*

Do the following:

   i.   *Write a subprogram named* my_swap() *that swaps and returns the values of two arguments.*

   ii. *Using the subprogram* my_swap() *cited above, write a subprogram named* my_sort() *that accepts an array through its formal argument list and then sorts the array using the bubble sort algorithm. It must be able to sort in either ascending or descending order. To do this, include an addition Boolean variable within the formal argument list.*

   iii. *Write a subprogram* display_array() *that accepts an array through its formal argument list and then displays it.*

   iv. *Using the subprograms* my_sort() *and* display_array() *cited above, write a Visual Basic program that prompts the user to enter the names of 20 people and then displays them twice: once sorted in ascending order, and once in descending order.*

Solution

As you can see in the Visual Basic program below, the subprocedure my_sort() uses an adapted version of the bubble sort algorithm. When the value True is passed to the argument ascending, the algorithm sorts array a in ascending order. When the value False is passed, the algorithm sorts array a in descending order.

Moreover, the subprocedure my_sort() calls the subprocedure my_swap() every time a swap is required between the contents of two elements.

project_43_2_2

```
Const PEOPLE = 20

Sub my_swap(ByRef x As String, ByRef y As String)
  Dim temp As String

  temp = x
  x = y
  y = temp
End Sub

Sub my_sort(a() As String, Optional ascending As Boolean = True)
  Dim m, n As Integer

  For m = 1 To PEOPLE - 1
    For n = PEOPLE - 1 To m Step -1
      If ascending = True Then
        If a(n).CompareTo(a(n - 1)) < 0 Then
          my_swap(a(n), a(n - 1))
        End If
      Else
        If a(n).CompareTo(a(n - 1)) > 0 Then
          my_swap(a(n), a(n - 1))
        End If
      End If
    Next
  Next
End Sub

Sub display_array(a() As String)
  Dim i As Integer

  For i = 0 To PEOPLE - 1
    Console.WriteLine(a(i))
  Next
End Sub

Sub Main()
  Dim i As Integer

  Dim names(PEOPLE - 1) As String
  For i = 0 To PEOPLE - 1
    Console.Write("Enter a name: ")
    names(i) = Console.ReadLine()
```

```
    Next

    my_sort(names)              'Sort names in ascending order
    display_array(names)        'and display them


    my_sort(names, False)       'Sort names in descending order
    display_array(names)        'and display them.


    Console.ReadKey()
End Sub
```

> **Notice**: *Please note that the argument* `ascending` *is an optional argument. This means that if no value is passed for that argument, the default value* `True` *is used.*

Exercise 43.2-3 *Progressive Rates and Electricity Consumption*

The LAV Electricity Company charges subscribers for their electricity consumption according to the following table (monthly rates for domestic accounts).

Kilowatt-hours (kWh)	USD per kWh
kWh < 400	$0.08
401 ≤ kWh < 1500	$0.22
1501 ≤ kWh < 3000	$0.35
3001 ≤ kWh	$0.50

Do the following:

i. *Write a subprogram named* `get_consumption()` *that prompts the user to enter the total number of kWh consumed and then returns it. Moreover, the subprogram should validate data input and display an error message when the user enters any non-numeric or negative values.*

ii. *Write a subprogram named* `find_amount()` *that accepts kWh consumed through its formal argument list and then returns the total amount to pay.*

iii. *Using the subprograms* `get_consumption()` *and* `find_amount()` *cited above, write a Visual Basic program that prompts the user to enter the total number of kWh consumed and then calculates and displays the total amount to pay. The program should iterate as many times as the user wishes. At the end of each calculation, the program should ask the user if he or she wishes to calculate the total amount to pay for another consumer. If the answer is "yes" the program should repeat; it should end otherwise. Make your program accept the answer in all possible forms such as "yes", "YES", "Yes", or even "YeS".*

Please note that the rates are progressive and that transmission services and distribution charges, as well as federal, state, and local taxes, add a total of 26% to each bill.

Solution

There is nothing new here. Processing progressive rates is something that you have already learned! If this doesn't ring any bells, you need to refresh your memory and review the corresponding exercises in Chapter 23.

The Visual Basic program is as follows.

```
project_43_2_3
Function get_consumption() As Integer
  Dim kwh As Integer
  Dim input As String

  Console.Write("Enter kWh consumed: ")
  input = Console.ReadLine()
  Do While Int32.TryParse(input, kwh) = False Or kwh < 0
    Console.WriteLine("Error: Invalid number!")
    Console.Write("Enter a non-negative number: ")
    input = Console.ReadLine()
  Loop
  Return kwh
End Function

Function find_amount(kwh As Integer) As Double
  Dim amount As Double

  If kwh <= 400 Then
    amount = kwh * 0.08
  ElseIf kwh <= 2000 Then
    amount = 400 * 0.08 + (kwh - 400) * 0.22
  ElseIf kwh <= 4000 Then
    amount = 400 * 0.08 + 1100 * 0.22 + (kwh - 1500) * 0.35
  Else
    amount = 400 * 0.08 + 1100 * 0.22 + 1500 * 0.35 + (kwh - 3000) * 0.5
  End If

  amount += 0.26 * amount
  Return amount
End Function

Sub Main()
  Dim kwh As Integer
  Dim answer As String

  Do
    kwh = get_consumption()
    Console.WriteLine("You need to pay: " & find_amount(kwh))

    Console.WriteLine("Would you like to repeat?")
    answer = Console.ReadLine()
  Loop While answer.ToUpper() = "YES"
End Sub
```

43.3 Review Exercises

Complete the following exercises.

1. Do the following:

    i. Write a subprogram named `factorial()` that accepts an integer through its formal argument list and returns its factorial.

    ii. Using the subprogram `factorial()` cited above, write a subprogram named `my_sin()` that accepts a value through its formal argument list and returns the sine of x, using the Taylor series (shown next) with an accuracy of 0.0000000001.

$$sinx = x - \frac{x^3}{3!} + \frac{x^5}{5!} - \frac{x^7}{7!} + \cdots$$

Hint: Keep in mind that x is in radians, and $\frac{x^1}{1!} = x$.

    iii. Write a subprogram named `degrees_to_rad()` that accepts an angle in degrees through its formal argument list and returns its radian equivalent. It is given that $2\pi = 360°$.

    iv. Using the subprograms `my_sin()` and `degrees_to_rad()` cited above, write a Visual Basic program that displays the sinus of all integers from 0° to 360°.

2.   Do the following:

    i. Write a subprogram named `is_leap()` that accepts a year through its formal argument list and returns `True` or `False` depending on whether or not that year is a leap year.

    ii. Write a subprogram named `num_of_days()` that accepts a month and a year and returns the number of the days in that month. If that month is February and the year is a leap year, the subprogram must return the value of 29.

Hint: Use the subprogram `is_leap()` cited above.

    iii. Write a subprogram named `check_date()` that accepts a day, a month, and a year and returns `True` or `False` depending on whether or not that date is valid.

    iv. Using the subprograms cited above, write a Visual Basic program that prompts the user to enter a date (a day, a month, and a year) and then calculates and displays the number of days that have passed between the beginning of the given year and the given date. Moreover, the program should validate data input and display an error message when the user enters any non-valid date.

3.   In a computer game, players roll two dice. The player who gets the greatest sum of dice gets one point. After ten rolls, the player that wins is the one with the greatest sum of points. Do the following:

    i. Write a subprogram named `dice()` that returns a random integer between 1 and 6.

    ii. Using the subprogram `dice()` cited above, write a Visual Basic program that prompts two players to enter their names and then each player consecutively "rolls" two dice. This process repeats ten times and the player that wins is the one with the greatest sum of points.

4.   The LAV Car Rental Company has rented 40 cars, which are divided into three categories: hybrid, gas, and diesel. The company charges for a car according to the following table.

Days	Car Type		
	Gas	Diesel	Hybrid
1 – 5	$24 per day	$28 per day	$30 per day
6 – 8	$22 per day	$25 per day	$28 per day
9 and above	$18 per day	$21 per day	$23 per day

Do the following:

i. Write a subprogram named `get_choice()` that displays the following menu.

   1. Gas

   2. Diesel

   3. Hybrid

   The subprogram then prompts the user to enter the type of the car (1, 2, or 3) and returns it to the caller.

ii. Write a subprogram named `get_days()` that prompts the user to enter the total number of rental days and returns it to the caller.

iii. Write a subprogram named `get_charge()` that accepts the type of the car (1, 2, or 3) and the total number of rental days through its formal argument list and then returns the amount of money to pay according to the previous table. Federal, state, and local taxes add a total of 10% to each bill.

iv. Using the subprograms `get_choice()`, `get_days()` and `get_charge()` cited above, write a Visual Basic program that prompts the user to enter all necessary information about the rented cars and then displays the following:

   1.   for each car, the total amount to pay including taxes

   2.   the total number of hybrid cars rented

   3.   the total net profit the company gets after removing taxes

Please note that the rates are progressive.

5. TAM (Television Audience Measurement) is the specialized branch of media research dedicated to quantify and qualify television audience information.

    The LAV Television Audience Measurement Company counts the number of viewers of the main news program on each of 10 different TV channels. The company needs a software application in order to get some useful information. Do the following:

    i. Write a subprogram named `get_data()` that prompts the user to enter into two arrays the names of the channels and the number of viewers of the main news program for each day of the week (Monday to Sunday). It then returns these arrays to the caller.

    ii. Write a subprogram `get_average()` that accepts a one-dimensional array of five numeric elements through its formal argument list and returns their average value.

     iii. Using the subprograms `get_data()` and `get_average()` cited above, write a Visual Basic program that prompts the user to enter the names of the channels and the number of viewers for each day of the week and then displays the following:

         i. the name of the channels whose average viewer numbers on the weekend were at least 20% higher than the average viewer numbers during the rest of the week.

         ii. the name of the channels (if any) that, from day to day, showed constantly increasing viewer numbers. If there is no such channel, a corresponding message must be displayed.

6. A public opinion polling company asks 300 citizens whether they have been hospitalized during the last year. Do the following:

     i. Write a subprogram named `input_data()` that prompts the user to enter the citizen's SSN (Social Security Number) and their answer (Yes, No) into two arrays, SSNs and answers, respectively. The two arrays must be returned to the caller.

     ii. Write a subprogram named `sort_arrays()` that accepts the arrays SSNs and answers through its formal argument list. It then sorts array SSNs in ascending order using the selection sort algorithm. The subprogram must preserve the relationship between the elements of the two arrays.

     iii. Write a subprogram named `search_array()` that accepts array SSNs and an SSN through its formal argument list and then returns the index position of that SSN in the array. If the SSN is not found, a message "SSN not found" should be displayed and the value –1 must be returned. Use the binary search algorithm.

     iv. Write a subprogram named `count_answers()` that accepts the array answers and an answer through its formal argument list. It then returns the number of times this answer exists in the array.

     v. Using the three subprograms cited above, write a Visual Basic program that prompts the user to enter the SSNs and the answers of the citizens. It should then prompt the user to enter an SSN and display the answer that the citizen with this SSN gave, as well as the percentage of citizens that gave the same answer. The program should then ask the user if he or she wishes to search for another SSN. If the answer is "Yes" the process should repeat; it should end otherwise.

7. Eight teams participate in a football tournament, and each team plays 12 games, one game each week. Do the following:

     i. Write a subprogram named `input_data()` that prompts the user to enter into two arrays the name of each team and the letter "W" for win, "L" for loss, or "T" for tie (draw) for each game. It then returns the arrays to the caller.

     ii. Write a subprogram named `display_result()` that prompts the user for a letter (W, L, or T) and then displays, for each team, the week number(s) in which the team won, lost, or tied respectively. For example, if the user enters "L", the subprogram should search and display, for each team, the week numbers (e.g., week 3, week 14, and so on) in which the team lost the game.

    iii. Write a subprogram named `find_team()` that prompts the user to enter the name of a team and returns the index position of that team in the array. If the given team name does not exist, the value –1 must be returned.

    iv. Using the three subprograms cited above, write a Visual Basic program that prompts the user to enter the name of each team and the letter "W" for win, "L" for loss, or "T" for tie (draw) for each game. It should then prompt the user for a letter (W, L, or T) and display, for each team, the week number(s) in which the team won, lost, or tied respectively. Finally, the program should prompt the user to enter the name of a team. If the given team is found, the program should display the total number of points for this team and then prompt the user to enter the name of another team. This process must repeat as long as the user enters an existing team name. If given team name is not found, the message "Team not found" must be displayed and the program should end.

It is given that a win receives 3 points and a tie receives 1 point.

8. During the Cold War, messages were encrypted so that if the enemies intercepted them, they could not decrypt them without the decryption key. A very simple encryption algorithm is alphabetic rotation. The algorithm moves all letters N steps "up" in the alphabet, where N is the encryption key. For example, if the encryption key is 2, you can encrypt a message by replacing the letter A with the letter C, the letter B with the letter D, the letter C with the letter E, and so on. Do the following:

    i. Write a subprogram `my_encrypt()` that accepts a message and an encryption key through its formal argument list and returns the encrypted message.

    ii. Write a subprogram `my_decrypt()` that accepts an encrypted message and the decryption key through its formal argument list and returns the decrypted message.

    iii. Write a subprogram named `display_menu()` that displays the following menu:

        1. Encrypt a message

        2. Decrypt a message

        3. Exit

    iv. Using the three subprograms cited above, write a Visual Basic program that displays the menu previously mentioned and then prompts the user to enter a choice (of 1, 2, or 3). If choice 1 is selected, the program should prompt the user to enter a message and an encryption key and then display the encrypted message. If choice 2 is selected, the program should prompt the user to enter an encrypted message and the decryption key and then display the decrypted message. The process should repeat as many times as the user wishes.

Assume that the user enters only lowercase letters for the message and a value between 1 and 26 for the encryption key.

Review Questions in "Subprograms"

Answer the following questions.

1. What is procedural programming?
2. What are the advantages of procedural programming?
3. What is meant by the term "spaghetti code"?
4. What is modular programming?
5. What is a subprogram? Name an example of a subprogram.
6. What is the general form of a Visual Basic function?
7. How do you make a call to a function?
8. Describe the steps that are performed when the main code makes a call to a function.
9. What is the difference between a function and a subprocedure?
10. What is a subprocedure?
11. What is the general form of a Visual Basic subprocedure?
12. How do you make a call to a subprocedure?
13. Describe the steps that are performed when the main code makes a call to a subprocedure.
14. What is the formal argument list?
15. What is the actual argument list?
16. Can two subprograms use variables of the same name?
17. How long does a subprogram's variable "live" in main memory?
18. How long does a main code's variable "live" in main memory?
19. Can a subprogram call another subprogram? If yes, give some examples.
20. What does it mean to "pass an argument by value"?
21. What does it mean to "pass an argument by reference"?
22. What is an optional argument?
23. What is the scope of a variable?
24. What happens when a variable has a local scope?
25. What happens when a variable has a global scope?
26. What is the difference between a local and a global variable?
27. What is recursion?
28. What are the three rules that all recursive algorithms must follow?
29. What is function overloading?

Index

Made in the USA
Columbia, SC
19 August 2020